FORCIBLE PROTECTION OF CIVILIANS

FORCIBLE PROTECTION OF CIVILIANS

The International Legal Framework for Peace Operations

Hanna Bourgeois

INTERSENTIA
Cambridge – Antwerp – Chicago

Intersentia
Lefebvre Sarrut Belgium SA
Rue Haute, 139/6
1000 Bruxelles
Belgium
contact@larcier-intersentia.com

Distribution for the UK and
Rest of the World (incl. Eastern Europe)
Ingram Publisher Services UK
1 Deltic Avenue, Rooksley
Milton Keynes MK13 8LD
United Kingdom
Tel: +44 1752 202 301 | Fax: +44 1752 202 331
Email: orders@nbninternational.com

Distribution for France and other countries
Interforum Editis
92 avenue de France
75013 Paris
France

Distribution for the USA and Canada
Independent Publishers Group
Order Department
814 North Franklin Street
Chicago, IL 60610
USA
Tel: +1 800 888 4741 (toll free) | Fax: +1 312 337 5985
Email: orders@ipgbook.com

Forcible Protection of Civilians. The International Legal
Framework for Peace Operations

Cover design by Danny Juchtmans / www.dsigngraphics.be
Cover image: Albert Gonzalez Farran / Freelancer via Getty Images

ISBN 978-1-83970-433-8
D/2024/06040/0266
NUR 828

British Library Cataloguing in Publication Data. A catalogue record for this book is available from the British Library.

For Thomas, co-author of my life

CONTENTS

Acknowledgements xv
Table of abbreviations xvii

Introductory Chapter 1

1. Introduction to the problem 1
2. Aim and scope 11
   2.1. UN (mandated) peace operations with a PoC mandate 12
   2.2. International legal framework regulating the use of force 16
3. Sources and methodology 19
4. Structure 25

Part I.
Conceptual Foundations and Introduction to the Political and Legal Framework Governing the Use of Force for PoC 27

1. Introduction to Part I 27
2. Concept of PoC as a mandated task by the UN Security Council 32
   2.1. Institutionalisation of PoC at the UN 33
      2.1.1. The impetus for adopting PoC mandates 33
      2.1.2. The first PoC mandate 37
      2.1.3. Development of the PoC concept in the context of UN peace operations 39
      2.1.4. Current UN understanding of PoC 46
   2.2. Consolidation of PoC at the AU, NATO, and the EU 48
      2.2.1. AU's understanding of PoC 48
      2.2.2. NATO's understanding of PoC 52
      2.2.3. EU's understanding of PoC 59
3. Introduction to policies on the use of force for PoC 67
   3.1. UN policy on the use of force for PoC 67
      3.1.1. Basic Principles of UN Peacekeeping 67
      3.1.2. From self-defence to the (offensive) protection of civilians 68
      3.1.3. UN efforts to develop a policy on the use of force for PoC 71
      3.1.4. From theory to practice: 'I will shoot ... or not' 74

3.2. Other organisational approaches towards the use of force for PoC 79
3.2.1. AU policy on the concept of PoC and the use of force. . . . 79
3.2.2. NATO policy on the concept of PoC and the use of force. . . . 80
3.2.3. EU policy on the concept of PoC and the use of force. . . . 83
4. Introduction to the legal framework governing the use of force for PoC. . . . 85
4.1. Overview of the legal rules that may regulate the use of force for PoC 85
4.1.1. Rules providing a legal basis for UN (mandated) peace operations. . . . 86
4.1.1.1. Legal basis for the establishment of UN (mandated) peace operations. . . . 87
A. Internal laws 88
B. The 'internal' mandate 92
4.1.1.2. Legal basis for the emplacement and functioning of UN (mandated) peace operations 94
A. The UN Charter and customary international law 94
B. The 'external' mandate 100
4.1.2. Rules regulating the conduct of UN (mandated) peace operations. . . . 100
4.1.2.1. Self-defence, defence of others, and defence of the mandate 101
4.1.2.2. Legal regimes 107
A. International law 107
B. National law 110
4.1.2.3. Other relevant rules and practices 112
4.2. The respective roles of the mandate and the legal regimes in regulating the use of force for protective purposes: clearing the fog. . . . 114
4.2.1. Distinction and convergence between the rules providing a legal basis and the rules regulating the conduct 114
4.2.2. From law to practice: levels of authority, command, and control in UN (mandated) peace operations. . . . 114
4.2.2.1. Strategic level 115
4.2.2.2. Operational level 118
4.2.2.3. Tactical level. . . . 120
4.2.3. From practice back to law. . . . 122
5. Summary of Part I 122

Part II.
The PoC Mandate as a Mission-specific Legal Basis Underlying UN (Mandated) Peace Operations Deployed to Protect Civilians 127

1. Introduction to Part II 127
2. Consent of the host State 129
   2.1. Role of consent in UN (mandated) peace operations 130
      2.1.1. Legal value of consent 130
      2.1.2. Political and operational value of consent 134
   2.2. Modalities of consent 136
      2.2.1. Consent *ratione materiae* 136
      2.2.2. Consent *ratione personae* 137
      2.2.3. Consent *ratione temporis* 138
      2.2.4. How should consent be given? 139
3. Mandate of the UN Security Council 140
   3.1. UN Security Council practice of mandating the use of force to protect civilians 140
      3.1.1. The first PoC mandate: UNSC Resolution 1270 (1999) 140
      3.1.2. Standardised PoC language 141
   3.2. Interpretation of UNSC resolutions containing a PoC mandate.... 143
      3.2.1. Rules and methods of interpretation applicable to UNSC resolutions 144
      3.2.2. Interpretation of the term 'protection' 148
         3.2.2.1. Physical protection 149
         3.2.2.2. Rights-based approach 151
         3.2.2.3. Protection by the peacekeeping community... 153
            A. Evolution in PoC language 153
            B. Meaning of 'protection' as a mandated task 158
      3.2.3. Interpretation of the term 'civilians'.................. 160
         3.2.3.1. 'Civilians' within the meaning of IHL........ 162
         3.2.3.2. 'Civilians' in the context of PoC mandates 164
      3.2.4. Interpretation of the terms 'in danger', 'under threat of attack', or 'under threat or imminent threat' of 'physical violence' 166
         3.2.4.1. 'Physical violence' 169
         3.2.4.2. From 'imminent' to temporally undefined 'threats' 170
      3.2.5. Interpretation of terms 'all necessary means, measures, steps, or action' 174
         3.2.5.1. Application of the rules and methods to the expression to use 'all necessary means, measures, steps, or action' 176

A. 'Means, measures, steps, or action' 176
B. 'Necessary' 178
3.2.5.2. What if no explicit authorisation is given to take 'all necessary means'? 180
3.2.6. Interpretation of the terms 'within its capabilities' and 'areas of deployment' 184
3.2.7. Interpretation of the terms 'primary responsibility of host State' 188
3.3. Upper or lower limits to what UN (mandated) peace operations may or must lawfully do to protect civilians 193
3.3.1. Upper limit to what UN (mandated) peace operations may lawfully do to protect civilians 194
3.3.1.1. *Jus cogens* limiting any use of force 194
3.3.1.2. Principles of necessity and proportionality limiting the overall levels of force used 195
3.3.1.3. Legal regimes regulating specific instances of the use of force 200
3.3.2. Emerging lower limit for what UN (mandated) peace operations must lawfully do to protect civilians 201
3.4. Influence of HRL and IHL on the interpretation, implementation, and evaluation of UNSC resolutions that contain a PoC mandate 208
3.4.1. Interpretation and implementation of PoC mandates... 209
3.4.2. Evaluation of the implementation of PoC mandates 211
4. Summary of Part II 212

Part III.
The Legal Regimes Governing the Application of the Use of Force to Protect Civilians by UN (Mandated) Peace Forces 219

1. Introduction to Part III 219
2. Applicability of legal regimes 221
2.1. Applicability of HRL to UN (mandated) peace forces carrying out a PoC mandate 227
2.1.1. Applicability *ratione personae* 227
2.1.1.1. Peace forces as members of UN (mandated) peace operations 231
2.1.1.2. Peace forces as State agents of the States undertaking or taking part in an operation ... 234
2.1.1.3. Peace forces as visitors in the host State 235
2.1.2. Applicability *ratione materiae* 236
2.1.2.1. Obligation 'to respect, protect, and fulfil' HRL 236

2.1.2.2. Specific HRL obligations in the context of the use of force . . . 237
2.1.3. Applicability *ratione loci* . . . 239
2.1.3.1. Models of extraterritorial applicability . . . 240
2.1.3.2. Case law on extraterritorial applicability . . . 241
A. ICJ . . . 241
B. UN HRC . . . 242
C. IACtHR and IAComHR . . . 245
D. ECtHR . . . 246
E. AComHPR . . . 254
2.1.3.3. Distinction between extraterritorial negative and positive HRL obligations . . . 254
2.1.4. Applicability *ratione temporis* . . . 258
2.1.4.1. Derogation in times of public emergency . . . 258
2.1.4.2. Derogation under Chapter VII and Article 103 of the UN Charter . . . 262
2.2. Applicability of IHL to UN (mandated) peace forces carrying out a PoC mandate . . . 262
2.2.1. Applicability *ratione temporis* . . . 263
2.2.1.1. The beginning of IHL application in UN (mandated) peace operations . . . 269
2.2.1.2. The end of IHL application in UN (mandated) peace operations . . . 270
2.2.1.3. Derogation under Chapter VII and Article 103 of the UN Charter . . . 273
2.2.2. Applicability *ratione personae* . . . 273
2.2.2.1. Peace forces as members of UN (mandated) peace operations . . . 275
2.2.2.2. Peace forces as State agents of the States undertaking or taking part in an operation . . . 279
2.2.3. Applicability *ratione materiae* . . . 279
2.2.3.1. Obligation 'to respect and to ensure respect' for IHL . . . 280
2.2.3.2. Specific IHL obligations in the context of the use of force . . . 282
2.2.4. Applicability *ratione loci* . . . 284
3. Use of (lethal) force to protect civilians . . . 286
3.1. Use of (lethal) force to protect civilians that has no clear nexus to an ongoing armed conflict . . . 288
3.1.1. Use of lethal force: identifying the scope of the permissible grounds for deprivation of life . . . 288
3.1.1.1. Principle of legality . . . 290

3.1.1.2. Principle of necessity. 291
3.1.1.3. Principle of proportionality. 296
A. The use of potentially lethal force 296
B. The intentional lethal use of force 298
3.1.1.4. Principle of precautions 299
3.1.1.5. Principle of accountability. 299
3.1.2. Use of less-lethal force: determining the scope of possible actions 300
3.2. Use of (lethal) force to protect civilians that has a clear nexus to an ongoing armed conflict 301
3.2.1. Balancing military necessity and humanity 302
3.2.2. Principle of distinction. 305
3.2.2.1. Distinction between civilians and combatants . . 306
3.2.2.2. Distinction between civilian objects and military objectives. 309
3.2.2.3. Indiscriminate attacks 312
3.2.3. Principle of proportionality. 313
3.2.4. Principles of precautions in attack and against the effects of attacks. 316
3.2.4.1. Principle of precautions in attack. 316
3.2.4.2. Principle of precautions against the effects of attacks. 317
3.2.5. Prohibition of superfluous injury and unnecessary suffering. 318
3.3. Impact of the UNSC mandate on whether or not force can be used in specific instances. 320
3.3.1. Going less far: additional restrictions on the use of force. 321
3.3.1.1. Implementation of the UNSC mandate into military strategic, operational, and tactical instruments 321
3.3.1.2. Limits to the possible impact: case study on military advantage and PoC in the context of UN-mandated peace operations. 322
A. Setting the scene: attacks against objects during Operation Unified Protector 322
B. Drawing from the theoretical approaches to the relationship between *jus ad bellum* and *jus in bello* 324
C. No normative spill-over from the UNSC mandate into IHL 329

3.3.2. Going beyond: overruling or authorising to act contrary to the rules of HRL or IHL 331
3.3.2.1. Possible legal bases for setting aside legally binding rules 331
A. Chapter VII powers 331
B. Article 103 of the UN Charter 331
3.3.2.2. Limits to the possible impact: case study on reconciling threats to civilians, imminence, and the right to life in the context of UN peace operations 338
A. Scrutinising PoC language through the lens of the right to life 339
B. Reconciling law with practice in UN peace operations 343
4. Obligation to (use force to) protect civilians against the threat of physical violence under HRL and IHL 347
4.1. Obligation 'to protect' the human right to life 348
4.2. Obligation 'to ensure respect' for IHL 355
5. Summary of Part III 360

Concluding Chapter 369

Bibliography 387

ACKNOWLEDGEMENTS

This book is the result of several years of research at the Institute for International Law of the KU Leuven, culminating in the defence of a doctoral dissertation in January 2023. I want to express my profound gratitude to a great number of people for their incredible support and guidance throughout this journey.

First and foremost, I am indebted to my supervisor, Professor Jan Wouters, for his guidance, trust, and flexibility, which have allowed me to broaden my outlook and find my own path in developing this research. Over the years, I also greatly benefitted from the support and feedback provided by the members of my doctoral supervisory committee, Professor Terry Gill (University of Amsterdam) and Professor Tom Ruys (Ghent University). Their immense knowledge, insightful comments, and encouragement were invaluable for completing this research project. I am also thankful to Professor Nigel White (University of Nottingham) for introducing me to the fascinating world of peacekeeping. My participation in his LL.M. classes during my Erasmus at the University of Nottingham has largely determined my focus in both my master's dissertation at Ghent University and my doctoral dissertation. In addition to Professor Jan Wouters, Professor Terry Gill, Professor Tom Ruys, and Professor Nigel White, Em. Professor Paul Lemmens (KU Leuven), Professor Gleider Hérnandez (KU Leuven), and Professor Siobhán Wills (Ulster University) have granted me the honour of serving my doctoral jury. I also thank LtCol. Em. Professor Jacques Herbots (KU Leuven) for chairing this jury.

Furthermore, I want to express my appreciation to KU Leuven and the Research Foundation – Flanders (FWO) for funding my research. My FWO scholarship also made it possible to participate in conferences and conduct research stays at the University of Geneva, the University of Amsterdam, and the University of Cambridge. Special thanks are due to the members of the Law of Armed Conflict and Peace Operations (LACPO) network at the University of Amsterdam, the Lauterpacht Centre for International Law at the University of Cambridge, and the International Society for Military Law and the Law of War. They provided me with a rich platform to discuss my research with numerous experts in my field, both in academia and in practice. I also had the pleasure to be part of the wonderful team of researchers at the Leuven Centre for Global Governance Studies and the International Law Institute, KU Leuven. My warm thanks to all of them, not in the least, for the interesting discussions, as well as the necessary distractions during lunch breaks and after-work drinks.

Over the past years, I was also fortunate to receive insightful feedback from researchers and practitioners on publications related to my research topic and on various parts of my doctoral dissertation. These persons include, among others, dr. Hans Boddens Hosang, Professor Stuart Casey-Maslen, Baldwin De Vidts, Professor Yvonne Donders, Professor Gloria Gaggioli, Col. (Ret.) Ben Klappe, dr. Patryk Labuda, dr. Marike Lefevre, dr. Keiichiro Okimoto, Professor Marco Sassòli, dr. Joëlle Trampert, dr. Sâ Benjamin Traoré, Alfons Vanheusden, dr. Anne Verhelst, and Professor Marten Zwanenburg. I would also like to express my gratitude to the following persons for sharing their time and insights: Professor Eyal Benvenisti, Dominique Crêvecoeur, Chris De Cock, Erik De Maeyer, Laurent Gisel, Em. Professor Christine Gray, Jean-Marie Henckaerts, Professor Robert Kolb, Geert Muylle, dr. Frederik Naert, Maureen Patricia O'Brien, Jean-Emmanuel Perrin, Professor Michael Schmitt, and Marleen Steenbrugghe, among others. I also want to express my profound gratitude to Barbara Helms for editing earlier versions of this manuscript with great detail and skill, and this with great patience and despite considerable time constraints, and to Ben Stuit for introducing me to her.

Last but not least, I would like to thank my dear parents, Filip and Vera, and my sister, Eline, as well as their partners, and my parents-in-law, Kris and Katlijn. Their constant encouragement and unfailing support helped me to bring this research project to an end. I would like to extend my sincere thanks to friends and neighbours for their warmth and generosity and providing me with many hours of pleasant distractions. Finally, I would like to express my most loving gratitude to my partner Thomas for standing by me with unfailing love, support, and understanding and to our three children, Louise, Charles, and Henri for making me laugh when I most needed it.

TABLE OF ABBREVIATIONS

ACHPR	African Charter on Human and Peoples' Rights
ACHR	American Convention of Human Rights
ACO	(NATO) Allied Command Operations
AComHPR	African Commission on Human and Peoples' Rights
ACT	(NATO) Allied Command Transformation
ADF	Allied Democratic Forces
AFISMA	International Support Mission to Mali
AJD	(NATO) Allied Joint Doctrine
AMIS I	African Union Mission in Sudan I
AMIS II	African Union Mission in Sudan II
AMISEC	African Union Mission for Support to the Elections in the Comoros
AMISOM	African Union Mission to Somalia
ASIL	American Society of International Law
ASR	(ILC) Articles of State Responsibility (2001)
AU	African Union
AU PSC	African Union Peace and Security Council
C34	UN Special Committee on Peacekeeping Operations
CAR	Central African Republic
CAT	Convention against Torture (1984)
CC	(EU) Component Commander
CIMIC	civil-military co-operation
CONOPS	Concept of Operations
CONTCO	(AU) Contingent Commander
CRC	Convention on the Rights of the Child (1989)
CSDP	(EU) Common Security and Defence Policy
DARIO	(ILC) Draft Articles on the Responsibility of International Organizations (2011)
DRC	Democratic Republic of the Congo
DUF	Directive on the Use of Force
EAPC	Euro-Atlantic Partnership Council
ECHR	European Convention on Human Rights
ECJ	European Court of Justice
ECOFORCE / ECOMINCI	Economic Community of West African States Peacekeeping Force in Côte d'Ivoire

EComHR	European Commission on Human Rights
ECOMOG	Economic Community of West African States Monitoring Group
ECOSOC	United Nations Economic and Social Council
ECOWAS	Economic Community of West African States
ECtHR	European Court of Human Rights
EEAS	(EU) European External Action Service
ESDP	(EU) European Security and Defence Policy
EU	European Union
EU GSC	General Secretariat of the Council of the European Union
EU PSC	European Union Peace and Security Council
EUFOR ALTHEA/BiH	European Union Force in Bosnia and Herzegovina
EUFOR RCA	European Union Force in the Central African Republic
EUFOR RD Congo	European Union Force in the Democratic Republic of Congo
EUFOR Tchad/RCA	European Union Force in Chad and the Central African Republic
EUMC	European Union Military Committee
EUMS	European Union Military Staff
FARDC	Forces armées de la république démocratique du Congo
FC	(EU/UN) Force Commander
FHQ	(EU) Force Headquarters
FRY	Federal Republic of Yugoslavia
HIPPO	High-Level Independent Panel on Peace Operations
HOM	(AU/UN) Head of Mission
HOMC	(UN) Head of Military Component
HRL	human rights law
IAC	international armed conflict
IAComHR	Inter-American Commission on Human Rights
IACtHR	Inter-American Court of Human Rights
ICC	International Criminal Court
ICCPR	International Covenant on Civil and Political Rights
ICESC	International Covenant on Economic, Social and Cultural Rights
ICISS	International Commission on Intervention and State Sovereignty
ICJ	International Court of Justice
ICRC	International Committee of the Red Cross
ICTR	International Criminal Tribunal of Rwanda
ICTY	International Criminal Tribunal of Yugoslavia
IDP	internally displaced people

IEMF	Interim Emergency Multinational Force
IHL	international humanitarian law
IHRL	international human rights law
ILC	International Law Commission
ISAF	International Security Assistance Force
JFC	(NATO) Joint Force Command
JTFHQ	(NATO) Joint Task Force Headquarters
MINUJUSTH	United Nations Mission for Justice Support in Haiti
MINURCAT	United Nations Mission in the Central African Republic and Chad
MINUSCA	United Nations Multidimensional Integrated Stabilization Mission in the Central African Republic
MINUSMA	United Nations Multidimensional Integrated Stabilization Mission in Mali
MINUSTAH	United Nations Stabilization Mission in Haiti
MISCA	International Support Mission to the Central African Republic
MONUC	United Nations Organization Mission in the Democratic Republic of the Congo
MONUSCO	United Nations Organization Stabilization Mission in the Democratic Republic of the Congo
MPCC	(EU) Military Planning and Conduct Capability
NA5CRO	(NATO) Non-Article 5 Crisis Response Operations
NAC	(NATO) North Atlantic Council
NAMC	North Atlantic Military Committee
NATO	North Atlantic Treaty Organization
NCC	(UN) National Contingent Commander
NIAC	non-international armed conflict
OAU	Organization of African Unit
OIOS	Office of Internal Oversight Services
ONUB	United Nations Operation in Burundi
ONUC	United Nations Operation in the Congo
OpCdr	(EU) Operation Commander
OPLAN	Operations (or Operational) Plan
OSCE	Organization for Security and Co-operation in Europe
PAPS	(AU) Political Affairs, Peace and Security
PGM	precision-guided munition
PoC	Protection of Civilians
POW	Prisoners of War
PSD	(AU) Peace and Security Department
PSOD	(AU) Peace and Support Operations Division
ROE	Rules of engagement

RSM	Resolute Support Mission
RtoP	Responsibility to Protect
RwP	Responsibility while Protecting
SACEUR	(NATO) Supreme Allied Commander Europe
SACT	(NATO) Supreme Allied Commander Transformation
SCSL	Special Court for Sierra Leone
SFOR	Stabilization Force
SHAPE	(NATO) Supreme Headquarters Allied Powers Europe
SOFA	Status of Forces Agreement
SRSG	(UN) Special Representative of the Secretary-General
SSC	(NATO) Single Service Command
TCC	Troop Contributing Country
TCC MOU	Memorandum of Understanding with the TCC
TEU	Treaty on European Union (consolidated version 2012)
UDHR	Universal Declaration of Human Rights
UK	United Kingdom
UN	United Nations
UN DFS	United Nations Department of Field Support (replaced by the UN DOS)
UN DOS	United Nations Department of Operational Support (replaced the UN DFS)
UN DPA	United Nations Department of Political Affairs (replaced by the United Nations Department of Political and Peacebuilding Affairs (DPPA))
UN DPKO	United Nations Department of Peacekeeping Operations (replaced by the UN DPO)
UN DPO	United Nations Department of Peace Operations (replaced the UN DPKO)
UN HRC	United Nations Human Rights Committee
UNHRC	United Nations Human Rights Council
UN OCHA	United Nations Office for the Coordination of Humanitarian Affairs
UN OHCHR	United Nations Office of the High Commissioner for Human Rights
UN OLA	United Nations Office of Legal Affairs
UNAMID	United Nations–African Union Hybrid Operation in Darfur
UNAMIR	United Nations Assistance Mission for Rwanda
UNAMSIL	United Nations Mission in Sierra Leone
UNAT	United Nations Administrative Tribunal
UNCRO	United Nations Confidence Restoration Operation in Croatia
UNEF I	United Nations Emergency Force I

UNFICYP	United Nations Peacekeeping Force in Cyprus
UNGA	United Nations General Assembly
UNGA resolution	United Nations General Assembly's resolution
UNIFIL	United Nations Interim Force in Lebanon
UNIO	United Nations Information Organization
UNISFA	United Nations Interim Security Force for Abyei
UNITAF	Unified Task Force
UNMIK	United Nations Mission in Kosovo
UNMIL	United Nations Mission in Liberia
UNMIS	United Nations Mission in Sudan
UNMISS	United Nations Mission in South Sudan
UNMOGIP	United Nations Military Observer Group in India and Pakistan
UNOCI	United Nations Operation in Côte d'Ivoire
UNOSOM I	United Nations Operation in Somalia I
UNOSOM II	United Nations Operation in Somalia II
UNPROFOR	United Nations Protection Force
UNSC	United Nations Security Council
UNSC resolution or mandate	United Nations Security Council's resolution or mandate
UNSG	United Nations Secretary-General
UNTSO	United Nations Truce Supervision Organization
US	United States of America
VCLT	Vienna Convention on the Law of Treaties
WEU	Western European Union

INTRODUCTORY CHAPTER[1]

1. INTRODUCTION TO THE PROBLEM

The diversity of conflicts is considerable, but most have one thing in common: they profoundly affect civilian populations. Civilians suffer disproportionately from targeted attacks, indiscriminate killings, summary executions, sexual slavery, and rape. Civilians are forcibly displaced or forced to join the fighting, causing massive disruption to civilian lives, and leading to loss of livelihood, hunger, and disease.[2]

Aware of this problem, in the 1960s, the United Nations (UN) Security Council began to *implicitly* include the promotion of civilian protection in the mandates issued to military operations, whose overall purpose was to support the maintenance or restoration of international peace and security.[3] In the present study, these types of operations are referred to as 'UN (mandated) peace operations', i.e. operations conceived to support the maintenance or restoration of international peace and security and conducted either by the UN itself

---

1 This Introductory Chapter is partly based on the following publications: Hanna Bourgeois, 'Failure to Protect Civilians in the Context of UN Peace Operations: A Question of Accountability?' (*EJIL: Talk!*, 5 September 2018), www.ejiltalk.org/failure-to-protect-civilians-in-the-context-of-un-peace-operations-a-question-of-accountability/, accessed 5 September 2018; Hanna Bourgeois, '"All Necessary Means" to Protect Civilians: The Interpretation and Implementation of UN Security Council Mandates Authorising the Protection of Civilians' (2020) 24 Journal of International Peacekeeping 53; Hanna Bourgeois and Patryk I Labuda, 'When May UN Peacekeepers Use Lethal Force to Protect Civilians? Reconciling Threats to Civilians, Imminence, and the Right to Life' (2022) Journal of Conflict and Security Law 1; Hanna Bourgeois and Jean-Emmanuel Perrin, 'The Use of Force for Mission Accomplishment: A Pitfall in Contemporary Operations?' (2018) 57 Military Law and Law of War Review 59.

2 AU Assembly, 'Aide Mémoire for the Consideration of Issues Pertaining to the Protection of Civilians in Africa' (2013) para. 2, www.peaceau.org/uploads/01-aide-memoire.pdf, accessed 23 October 2022; UNSG, 'Report of the Secretary-General on the Protection of Civilians in Armed Conflict' (2005) UN Doc. S/2005/740 para. 3.

3 See e.g. 'UNSC Res. 161' (1961) UN Doc. S/RES/161 (1961) para. 1; 'UNSC Res. 794' (1992) UN Doc. S/RES/794 (1992) para. 10; 'UNSC Res. 836' (1993) UN Doc. S/RES/836 (1993) paras 5 and 9; 'UNSC Res. 912' (1994) UN Doc. S/RES/912 (1994) para. 8; 'UNSC Res. 918' (1994) UN Doc. S/RES/918 (1994) paras 3 and 4; 'UNSC Res. 925' (1994) UN Doc. S/RES/925 (1994) paras 4 and 5; 'UNSC Res. 929' (1994) UN Doc. S/RES/929 (1994) paras 2 and 3; 'UNSC Res. 940' (1994) UN Doc. S/RES/940 (1994) paras 4, 9, and 16; 'UNSC Res. 1031' (1995) UN Doc. S/RES/1031 (1995) paras 15 and Annex 1A, Art. VI; 'UNSC Res. 1159' (1998) UN Doc. S/RES/1159 (1998) para. 10; 'UNSC Res. 1244' (1999) UN Doc. S/RES/1244 (1999) para. 9; 'UNSC Res. 1272' (1999) UN Doc. S/RES/1272 (1999) para. 2.

('UN peace operations') or by States or regional or international organisations other than the UN, including the African Union (AU), the North Atlantic Treaty Organization (NATO), and the European Union (EU) ('UN-mandated peace operations'). An example of such an initiative by which the UN Security Council sought to alleviate human suffering can be found in Resolution 836 (1993). In this Resolution, the UN Security Council decided to extend the United Nations Protection Force's (UNPROFOR) mandate 'in order to enable it, in the safe areas [...], to deter attacks against the safe areas [...], in addition to participating in the delivery of humanitarian relief to the population [...]' and authorised UNPROFOR 'to take the necessary measures, including the use of force, in reply to bombardments against the safe areas by any of the parties or to armed incursion into them or in the event of any deliberate obstruction in or around those areas to the freedom of movement of UNPROFOR or of protected humanitarian convoys.'[4] Despite UNPROFOR's mandate to 'deter attacks' on Srebrenica and five other 'safe areas', up to 20,000 people, mainly from the Bosnian Muslim community, were killed in and around those safe areas.[5]

This tragic event led the UN Security Council to rethink how to better protect civilian populations in situations of armed conflict, along with a series of other events highlighting the UN's failure to protect civilians from mass atrocities and genocide. As a result, in 1999, the UN Security Council began adopting mandates in which it *explicitly* authorised UN (mandated) peace operations to 'use all necessary means to protect civilians against the imminent threat of physical violence' (by using exactly these terms or by using similar terms). With these mandates, known as 'Protection of Civilians (PoC) mandates', the UN Security Council sought to signal that it would no longer remain indifferent to attacks on innocent civilians.[6] The first mission to receive such a PoC mandate was the United Nations Mission in Sierra Leone (UNAMSIL). Resolution 1270 (1999) held that UNAMSIL 'may take the necessary action to ensure the security and freedom of movement of its personnel and, within its capabilities and areas of deployment, to afford protection to civilians under imminent threat of physical violence.'[7] From this moment on, most UN (mandated) peace operations have been given a mandate including PoC language, demonstrating an elemental development in respect of the use of force and a shift in the nature of military operations as a new paradigm of international peace and security.[8]

---

4 'UNSC Res. 836' (n. 3) paras 5 and 8.

5 UNSG, 'Report of the Secretary-General Pursuant to General Assembly Resolution 53/35: The Fall of Srebrenica' (1999) UN Doc. A/54/549 para. 3.

6 See e.g. the statement by the Argentinian representative at the time, Mr. Petrella, during the 4054th meeting of the UN Security Council at which the very first UNSC resolution with a PoC mandate was adopted (UNSC, '4054th Meeting (at Which UNSC Res 1270 (1999) Was Adopted)' (1999) UN Doc. S/PV.4054 15–16).

7 'UNSC Res. 1270' (1999) UN Doc. S/RES/1270 (1999) para. 14.

8 Haidi Willmot and Ralph Mamiya, 'Mandated to Protect: Security Council Practice on the Protection of Civilians' in Marc Weller, Alexia Solomou and Jake William Rylatt (eds), *The*

Notwithstanding the growing importance of PoC, actors charged with interpreting and implementing PoC mandates are notably left with unanswered questions on the legal parameters of military interventions for protection purposes. As a result, force is used inconsistently, often with profound consequences for both the UN (mandated) peace forces carrying out the PoC mandates and the civilians that are supposed to be protected by the deployment of the operations. Members of peace forces have been deprived of their freedom, their weapons, their equipment and in some cases even their lives.[9] Civilians have been seriously injured or killed while peace forces did not or could not do enough to protect them. For example, in 2017, the internal oversight body of the UN (the Office of Internal Oversight Services (OIOS)) concluded that in the operations in the Democratic Republic of the Congo (DRC) (the United Nations Organization Stabilization Mission in the Democratic Republic of the Congo (MONUSCO)), Mali (the United Nations Multidimensional Integrated Stabilization Mission in Mali (MINUSMA)), and the Central African Republic (CAR) (the United Nations Multidimensional Integrated Stabilization Mission in the Central African Republic (MINUSCA)), the implementation of mandates was subject to varying individual understandings and preferences.[10] For example, some personnel involved in MINUSCA reported that certain military contingents understood their task of protecting civilians as 'just sitting near a camp.'[11] However, the UN Headquarters expected that, based on its mandate, MINUSCA would effectively deter and confront armed elements in the CAR by using force.[12] According to OIOS, these different approaches have significantly watered down the explicit intent of the UN Security Council.[13]

There are still elementary questions about who is considered a 'civilian' and thus enjoys protection, against which 'threats' civilians must be protected, and what the exact scope of the 'protection' to be provided against these threats is. For example, is 'protection' perceived as the mission's ultimate goal or does the term refer to the acts or risks against which shelter is sought or to the different strategies and methods by which civilians can be safeguarded against the acts or risks?[14] Moreover, who is to enjoy protection? Should a person always

Oxford Handbook of the Use of Force in International Law (1st edn., Oxford University Press 2015) 376.

9 Patryk I Labuda, 'Peacekeeping and Peace Enforcement', *Max Planck Encyclopedia of Public International law* (Oxford Public International Law 2015) para. 39.

10 OIOS, Inspection and Evaluation Division, 'Evaluation of the Effectiveness of United Nations Peacekeeping Operations in Deterring and Confronting Armed Elements in the Democratic Republic of Congo, Mali and the Central African Republic' (2017) IED-17.013 para. 104.

11 *Ibid.* para. 74.

12 *Ibid.* para. 1.

13 *Ibid.* para. 104.

14 See also Julian M Lehmann, 'All Necessary Means to Protect Civilians: What the Intervention in Libya Says about the Relationship between the Jus in Bello and the Jus Ad Bellum' (2012) 17 Journal of Conflict and Security Law 117, 124.

be considered a civilian and thus be protected if they do not appear to pose a threat to another person at first glance? Or should those who can be identified as members of the armed forces or members of an armed opposition group automatically be excluded from protection, even if they pose no direct threat to anyone else at the time? Furthermore, what about individuals who cannot be identified as members of the armed forces or an organised armed group but who have been known to pose a threat to others in the past? Furthermore, what does 'physical violence' mean and how does it relate to the terms 'threat' and 'imminent threat' used in PoC mandates? When must a threat be 'imminent' for UN (mandated) peace forces to react, and when does a simple 'threat' suffice? And if a threat must be 'imminent', what does 'imminent' actually mean? Moreover, if a mandate authorises an operation to use 'all necessary means', which means are considered 'necessary' or 'unnecessary'? Likewise, who may decide what is necessary or not at what material moment in time? Is the use of force ever considered 'necessary', and if so, is there an upper limit to what UN (mandated) peace operations may lawfully do to protect civilians? Which rules determine when and how UN (mandated) armed forces can use force? And can force be used against UN (mandated) armed forces? Also, bearing in mind the UN's repeated failure to protect civilians by force, is there a lower limit for what UN (mandated) peace operations must lawfully do to protect civilians when given a PoC mandate?

Practice shows that questions on the legality of the use of force are often brushed aside or analysed superficially. Instead, legal advisors tend to turn to mission-specific Rules of Engagement (ROE)[15] or policy documents on PoC and the use of force, which are not sources of law *per se*, and, more so, are often not sufficiently aligned with applicable legal rules. For instance, such instruments often do not distinguish between the use of force with a clear nexus to an armed conflict and the use of force with no such nexus. At the same time, the applicable legal rules are substantially different in the two distinct cases. The fact that these instruments do not distinguish between such cases leads to confusion as to which legal provisions apply *de jure* in specific situations. For example, the UN draws on both human rights law (HRL) and international humanitarian law (IHL) in its policy documents on PoC and the use of force: IHL appears to be the relevant framework in its references to 'collateral damage',[16] while the UN's

---

15 As explained below, ROE are for the military and policy components, respectively, which define the degree of force (or other provocative acts) that may be used and how it may be applied (see Part I, Section 4.1.2.3).

16 UN DPKO and UN DFS, 'DPKO/DFS Policy on the Protection of Civilians in United Nations Peacekeeping' (2015) Ref. 2015.07 19 ('Collateral [d]amage: [i]ncidental loss of civilian life, injury to civilians, or damage to civilian property not part of an authorized target'). See also Conor Foley, *UN Peacekeeping Operations and the Protection of Civilians: Saving Succeeding Generations* (Cambridge University Press 2017) 183–184.

adoption of a graduated force continuum for the use of force, where lethal force is a last resort, appears premised on HRL applicability.[17]

By extension, the UN Security Council's Chapter VII powers or broad notions of self-defence have been invoked to justify the use of force on the ground rather than making full use of the relevant legal framework.[18] For example, the UN has coined the concept of using force 'in defence of the mandate'[19] – a concept of self-defence that expressly goes beyond the individual, personal self-defence but is otherwise poorly defined and embedded in the relevant legal framework. Also, NATO has referred to 'defence of the mandate' in its 2014 Allied Joint Doctrine (AJD) for Military Contribution to Peace Support.[20] For one, the necessary link is rarely made between the use of force 'in defence of the mandate' and how this relates to the legal regimes that govern the use of force by UN (mandated) peace forces. Moreover, a tendency exists to justify the use of force based on mission mandates only, grounded on Chapter VII powers, where authorisation from the UN Security Council to use 'all necessary means' is considered a blank cheque for offensive force to protect civilians.[21]

---

17 UN DPKO and UN DFS, 'Guidelines: Use of Force by Military Components in United Nations Peacekeeping Operations' (2017) Ref. 2016.24 paras 11 and 12.

18 As also raised by Siobhán Wills, 'Use of Deadly Force by Peacekeepers Operating Outside of Armed Conflict Situations: What Laws Apply?' (2018) 40 Human Rights Quarterly 663.

19 'Report of the Panel on United Nations Peace Operations (Brahimi Report), Fifty-Fifth Session of the General Assembly, Item 87 of the Provisional Agenda; Fifty-Fifth Year of the Security Council' (2000) UN Doc. A/55/305-S/2000/809 para. 49; UN DPKO and UN DFS, 'United Nations Peacekeeping Operations: Principles and Guidelines (Capstone Doctrine)' (UN 2008) 31. See also UN DPKO and UN DFS, '2017 UN Guidelines on the Use of Force by Military Components in UN Peacekeeping Operations' (n. 17) para. 6 ('"Force" is defined as the use of, or threat to use, physical means to impose one's will. In peacekeeping operations, peacekeepers are authorised to use force in self-defence and to execute their mandated tasks in appropriate situations'). The following UNSC resolutions refer to 'defence of the mandate', e.g. 'UNSC Res. 2098' (2013) UN Doc. S/RES/2098 (2013) pream. para. 3; 'UNSC Res. 2147' (2014) UN Doc. S/RES/2147 (2014) pream. para. 3; 'UNSC Res. 2149' (2014) UN Doc. S/RES/2149 (2014) pream. para. 4; 'UNSC Res. 2164' (2014) UN Doc. S/RES/2164 (2014) pream. para. 4; 'UNSC Res. 2223' (2015) UN Doc. S/RES/2223 (2015) pream. para. 4; 'UNSC Res. 2227' (2015) UN Doc. S/RES/2227 (2015) pream. para. 4; 'UNSC Res. 2228' (2015) UN Doc. S/RES/2228 (2015) pream. para. 5; 'UNSC Res. 2301' (2016) UN Doc. S/RES/2301 (2016) pream. para. 4; 'UNSC Res. 2327' (2016) UN Doc. S/RES/2327 (2016) para. 8; 'UNSC Res. 2363' (2017) UN Doc. S/RES/2363 (2017) pream. para. 5; 'UNSC Res. 2364' (2017) UN Doc. S/RES/2364 (2017) pream. para. 4; 'UNSC Res. 2387' (2017) UN Doc. S/RES/2387 (2017) pream. para. 4; 'UNSC Res. 2406' (2018) UN Doc. S/RES/2406 (2017) para. 8; 'UNSC Res. 2409' (2018) UN Doc. S/RES/2409 (2018) pream. para. 3. There are also a number of thematic resolutions on UN peacekeeping that include a reference to 'defence of the mandate', see e.g. 'UNSC Res. 2167' (2014) UN Doc. S/RES/2167 (2014) pream. para. 7; 'UNSC Res. 2436' (2018) UN Doc. S/RES/2436 (2018) pream. para. 5.

20 NATO, 'Allied Joint Doctrine for the Military Contribution to Peace Support' (NATO Standardization Office (NSO) 2014) NATO Doc. AJP-3.4.1, Edn. A, Version 1 para. 0231.

21 Patryk I Labuda, 'UN Peacekeeping as Intervention by Invitation: Host State Consent and the Use of Force in Security Council-Mandated Stabilisation Operations' (2020) 7 Journal on the Use of Force and International Law 317, 327–328.

Mandates are pivotal in regulating the use of force, but again the dynamics with other legal instruments are sometimes forgotten or trivialised. To illustrate: in June 2016, Wills interviewed a Senior Legal Advisor in the United Nations Office of Legal Affairs (UN OLA) to discuss the role of the mandate in the use of force by UN peace operations. Ostensibly, the UN Senior Legal Advisor said, and subsequently confirmed in writing by email, that under the UN's current approach, the mandate is the key factor determining the circumstances in which their forces can use lethal force.[22] In particular, the staff member confirmed that:[23]

> A person that would not be a military target under traditional IHL may become an authorized military target of a UN peacekeeping operation (and therefore killed) provided that: the peacekeepers' use of force is pursuant to an authorization in a Chapter VII mandate and is provided for in the mission's rule of engagement; that the use of force is proportionate to achieving the authorized objective; that minimum force is used; and that force is used only as a last resort. This framework applies across the board to all UN peacekeeping missions, regardless of whether the situation is one of armed conflict or not.

Another example is an incident dating back to 2017 that involved MINUSCA relying on its PoC mandate to justify a lethal attack by one of its attack helicopters against an armed group that had ignored its warnings not to cross a red line around Bambari, a specially designated 'city without armed groups' under the mission's PoC mandate.[24] Such an incident, however, raises questions about the legality of the use of lethal force under HRL.

Moving on to the relevant legal regimes, the applicability *de jure* of HRL and IHL to UN (mandated) peace operations is not always acknowledged, and there is often disagreement about when and how much force may be used under each legal regime. For example, adopted in 1999, the UN Secretary-General's Bulletin on the Observance by UN Forces of IHL (1999 UN Secretary-General's

---

22 Wills, 'Use of Deadly Force by Peacekeepers Operating Outside of Armed Conflict Situations: What Laws Apply?' (n. 18) 691.

23 As quoted by *ibid.* 691 (Moreover, the UN Senior Legal Advisor stressed that while this summary 'fully captures' their discussion, '[t]he only amplification is that while the authority to use force comes from the Security Council based on the specific mandate and the Chapter VII authority to use "all necessary means" as reflected in the mission-specific ROE – not from IHL except where the mission becomes a party to the conflict or from IHRL [international human rights law] – the customary principles of both IHL and IHRL are nonetheless integral to the conduct of the mission including its military component').

24 Vladimir Monteiro, 'La MINUSCA Intervient Contre Des Éléments Lourdement Armés Au Nord de Bambari' (*MINUSCA*, 26 February 2017), https://minusca.unmissions.org/la-minusca-intervient-contre-des-éléments-lourdement-armés-au-nord-de-bambari, accessed 13 June 2022; Vladimir Monteiro, 'Mise En Garde de La MINUSCA à La Coalition Du FPRC à Propos Des Déplacés de Ippy' (*MINUSCA*, 27 February 2017), https://minusca.unmissions.org/mise-en-garde-de-la-minusca-à-la-coalition-du-fprc-à-propos-des-déplacés-de-ippy, accessed 13 June 2022.

Bulletin on IHL) states that IHL applies to UN peace forces 'when in situations of armed conflict *they are actively engaged therein as combatants, to the extent and for the duration of their engagement.*'[25] However, the UN has never publicly acknowledged that it is bound by IHL when conducting a specific UN peace operation, as this would confirm the loss of protected status for members of UN peace forces.[26] Moreover, the 1999 UN Secretary-General's Bulletin on IHL's premise that UN peace forces are combatants only for the 'duration of their engagement' raises questions about the application threshold for IHL's norms on the conduct of hostilities, including the rules on targeting.

There has also been quite some reluctance among States participating in UN-mandated peace operations to acknowledge that they have become a party to an armed conflict. In 2011, for instance, Jens Stoltenberg, the former Norwegian Prime Minister, stated that Norway was not participating in a war in Libya because it was conducting a UN-mandated peace operation.[27] Hence, soldiers of the Libyan regime could not consider Norwegian soldiers participating in the NATO operation in Libya legitimate targets.[28]

There is also considerable resistance among States and international and regional organisations to accepting the applicability *de jure* of HRL when conducting UN (mandated) peace operations.[29] This reluctance to a critical assessment of their human rights standards is usually motivated by the fear that HRL will be applied *in toto*, without adaptation, and unrealistically to extraterritorial emergencies.[30] Nonetheless, according to most academics, the use of force by UN (mandated) peace forces is governed primarily by HRL.[31]

---

25 Emphasis added. UNSG, 'Secretary-General's Bulletin on the Observance by United Nations Forces of International Humanitarian Law' (1999) UN Doc. ST/SGB/1999/13 para. 1.1.

26 As also confirmed by Magdalena Pacholska, '(Il)Legality of Killing Peacekeepers: The Crime of Attacking Peacekeepers in the Jurisprudence of International Criminal Tribunals' (2015) 13 Journal of International Criminal Justice 43; Stephen Mathias, 'UN Peacekeeping Today: Legal Challenges and Uncertainties' (2017) 18 Melbourne Journal of International Law 138, 142–145; Terry D Gill and others (eds), *Leuven Manual on the International Law Applicable to Peace Operations* (Cambridge University Press 2017) 96–97.

27 Norway, 'Redegjørelse Av Statsministeren Om Situasjonen i Libya Og Norges Deltakelse i Den Internasjonale Koalisjonsstyrken' (2011) Sak nr. 1 [10:02:13], www.stortinget.no/no/Saker-og-publikasjoner/Publikasjoner/Referater/Stortinget/2010-2011/110329/1/, accessed 10 August 2022, as discussed by Kjetil Mujezinović Larsen and others (eds), 'Multinational Peace Operations Forces Involved in Armed Conflict: Who Are the Parties?', *Searching for a 'Principle of Humanity' in International Humanitarian Law* (Cambridge University Press 2012) 259.

28 Norway (n. 27), as referred to by Larsen and others (n. 27) 259.

29 Scott Sheeran, 'Human Rights and Derogation in Peacekeeping' in Evan J Criddle (ed), *Human Rights in Emergencies* (2016) 232.

30 *Ibid.*

31 See e.g. Foley, *UN Peacekeeping Operations and the Protection of Civilians: Saving Succeeding Generations* (n. 16) Chapter 4; Conor Foley, 'The Human Rights Obligations of UN Peacekeepers' (2017) 22 Revista Relações Internacionais no Mundo Atual 1; Wills, 'Use of Deadly Force by Peacekeepers Operating Outside of Armed Conflict Situations: What Laws Apply?' (n. 18) 669; Siobhán Wills, 'The Law Applicable to Peacekeepers Deployed in

In practice, there also seems to be a greater willingness to integrate HRL-based concepts into policy guidelines on the use of force and PoC. Yet, when UN (mandated) peace forces use armed force on the ground to protect civilians, IHL is not infrequently the 'go-to' legal regime, even if the threshold for an international armed conflict (IAC) or a non-international armed conflict (NIAC) has not been reached, simply because UN (mandated) peace operations consist mainly of military contingents trained in IHL for military operations, rather than civilian police familiar with law enforcement tasks.[32]

The reluctance to recognise that IHL or HRL apply *de jure* runs the risk of creating a legal vacuum in which the use of force on the ground is regulated not so much by the applicable legal regimes as by non-binding rules that are set out in policy documents, by legal rules that do not apply *de jure*, or by legal rules that are interpreted in alternative ways and concrete legal responsibility for such action is disregarded.[33] For example, while in the context of HRL, the use of lethal force is linked to strict temporal conditions, UN Security Council's PoC mandates and the UN Secretariat's PoC policies have gone in the opposite direction. They have downplayed the importance of temporal threats to civilians as the legal basis for action by UN peace forces. In particular, while PoC mandates in the past typically referenced protecting civilians under *imminent* threat of violence, the term 'imminent' has increasingly been dropped from United Nations Security Council's resolutions (UNSC resolutions)[34] or, if still present, the UN Secretariat has sought to detach its meaning from questions of temporality.[35] There is a viable risk that such practices could ultimately lead to

Situations Where There Is No Armed Conflict' (*EJIL: Talk!*, 10 April 2013), www.ejiltalk.org/the-law-applicable-to-peacekeepers-deployed-in-situations-where-there-is-no-armed-conflict/, accessed 5 December 2017; Nigel D White, 'Security Council Mandates and the Use of Lethal Force by Peacekeepers: What Place for the Laws of War?' in Caroline Harvey, James Summers and Nigel D White (eds), *Contemporary challenges to the laws of war: essays in honour of Professor Peter Rowe* (Cambridge University Press 2014) 96–97.

32 Oxford Research Group, 'Peacekeeping and Civilian Protection: An Interview with Conor Foley' (20 August 2019), oxfordresearchgroup.org.uk/blog/peacekeeping-and-civilian-protection-an-interview-with-conor-foley, accessed 9 June 2022.

33 Patryk I Labuda, 'UN Peacekeeping as Intervention by Invitation: Host State Consent and the Use of Force in Security Council-Mandated Stabilisation Operations' (2020) 7 Journal on the Use of Force and International Law 317, 327.

34 For instance, MINUSMA's early mandates authorised UN peacekeepers to 'protect civilians against the imminent threat of violence,' whereas current iterations of the same mission's mandate define PoC in relation to generic threats, with no further mention of imminence. Early mandates include 'UNSC Res. 2100' (2013) UN Doc. S/RES/2100 (2013) para. 16(c)(i); 'UNSC Res. 2164' (n. 19) para. 13(a)(ii); 'UNSC Res. 2227' (n. 19) para. 14(d)(i). More recent mandates include: 'UNSC Res. 2295' (2016) UN Doc. S/RES/2295 (2016) para. 19(c)(i); 'UNSC Res. 2364' (n. 19) para. 20(c)(i); 'UNSC Res. 2423' (2018) UN Doc. S/RES/2423 (2018) para. 38(d)(i). For more examples, see the detailed analysis in Part II, Section 3.2.4.

35 E.g. the UN DPO's (or its predecessors, the UN DPKO and DFS) 2015 and 2019 UN Policies on PoC in UN Peacekeeping, the 2017 UN Guidelines on the Use of Force by Military Components in UN Peacekeeping Operations, and the 2020 UN Handbook on PoC in UN Peacekeeping fail to clearly articulate whether and, if so, how 'imminent' a threat must be

the use of force without regard to the strict temporal requirements of HRL and thus violate the right to life. All in all, when force is used to protect civilians, the relevant international legal framework often stands glumly on the side-lines, unable to convey its relevance.

In recent years, several scholars have discussed the political, normative, and legal framework of the concept of PoC and have done so primarily in the context of UN peace operations (and thus less so in the context of UN-mandated peace operations).[36] There is also a plethora of academic writing and analysis of the general legal framework for UN (mandated) peace operations and the use of force.[37] However, little has been published on the relationship between United Nations Security Council's mandates (UNSC mandates) – i.e. strategic-level statements generally concerned with the question of *whether* – and if so, *how much* – force can be used on the territory of a State and serve as a legal basis to that end – and the legal regimes containing the *when* and *how* of the use of force in specific day-to-day situations at the tactical level of the operation.[38] This

---

in order for lethal force to be used (see UN DPKO and UN DFS, '2015 UN Policy on PoC in UN Peacekeeping' (n. 16); UN DPO, 'Policy on the Protection of Civilians in United Nations Peacekeeping' (2019) Ref. 2019.17; UN DPKO and UN DFS, '2017 UN Guidelines on the Use of Force by Military Components in UN Peacekeeping Operations' (n. 17); UN DPO, 'The Protection of Civilians in United Nations Peacekeeping: Handbook' (2020)). This is also discussed in detail in Part I, Section 3.2.4.2.

36 See e.g. Haidi Willmot and others (eds), *Protection of Civilians* (1st edn., Oxford University Press 2016); Benjamin de Carvalho, Ole Jacob Sending and Jan Egeland (eds), *The Protection of Civilians in UN Peacekeeping: Concept, Implementation and Practice* (1st edn., Nomos 2013); Foley, *UN Peacekeeping Operations and the Protection of Civilians: Saving Succeeding Generations* (n. 16) Part I; Willmot and Mamiya (n. 8); Haidi Willmot and Scott Sheeran, 'The Protection of Civilians Mandate in UN Peacekeeping Operations: Reconciling Protection Concepts and Practices' (2013) 95 International Review of the Red Cross 517; Anastasia Shesterinina and Brian L Job, 'Particularized Protection: UNSC Mandates and the Protection of Civilians in Armed Conflict' (2016) 23 International Peacekeeping 240.

37 To name a few: Dieter Fleck, 'The Law Applicable to Peace Operations' in Andrew Clapham and Paola Gaeta (eds), *The Oxford Handbook of International Law in Armed Conflict* (Oxford University Press 2014); Foley, *UN Peacekeeping Operations and the Protection of Civilians: Saving Succeeding Generations* (n. 16) Part II; Gill and others (n. 26); Terry D Gill and Dieter Fleck (eds), *The Handbook of the International Law of Military Operations* (2nd edn., Oxford University Press 2015) Chapters 6, 14, and 24; Brendan Howe, Boris Kondoch and Otto Spijkers, 'Normative and Legal Challenges to UN Peacekeeping Operations' (2015) 19 Journal of International Peacekeeping 1; Ben F Klappe, 'International Peace Operations' in Dieter Fleck (ed), *The Handbook of International Humanitarian Law* (3rd edn., Oxford University Press 2013); Scott Sheeran, 'The Use of Force in United Nations Peacekeeping Operations' in Marc Weller, Alexia Solomou and Jake William Rylatt (eds), *The Oxford Handbook of the Use of Force in International Law* (1st edn., Oxford University Press 2015); Nigel D White, 'Peacekeeping and International Law' in Joachim Alexander Koops and others (eds), *The Oxford Handbook of United Nations Peacekeeping Operations* (1st edn, Oxford University Press 2015); Marten Zwanenburg, 'UN Peace Operations, International Humanitarian Law and International Human Rights Law' in Robert Kolb, Gloria Gaggioli and Pavle Kilibarda (eds), *Research Handbook on Human Rights and Humanitarian Law: Further Reflections and Perspectives* (Edward Elgar Publishing 2022).

38 To the author's knowledge, the following sources are among the few academic contributions that do address this issue: Rob McLaughlin, 'The Legal Regime Applicable to Use of

dearth of research is a lacuna in legal scholarship. Furthermore, there has been little research on how the legal bases and legal regimes should be interpreted and implemented in the context of UN (mandated) peace operations, whose mission is to protect civilians. Specifically, publications on how UNSC resolutions that include a PoC mandate should be interpreted and what role HRL and IHL may play in this regard are scarce;[39] this, too, is a gap in legal scholarship. And while there is much scholarly writing on UN peacekeeping's increasing robustness and expanding PoC mandates,[40] few scholars analyse the extent to which the turn to robust and proactive UN peacekeeping is compatible with applicable legal rules and, in particular, the right to life.[41] The scope of the right to life and the permissible grounds for depriving someone of their life may have been repeatedly analysed and debated. However, these analyses either tend to focus on the 'internal' resort to force by State authorities against their own citizens in law enforcement or on the use of lethal force in armed conflict and the relationship between HRL and IHL in this regard.[42] What is missing is a thorough examination of the role of HRL, and, in particular, the right to life, in regulating the use of force in the context of UN (mandated) peace operations.

Lethal Force When Operating under a United Nations Security Council Chapter VII Mandate Authorising All Necessary Means' (2007) 12 Journal of Conflict and Security Law 389; Kenneth Watkin, *Fighting at the Legal Boundaries: Controlling the Use of Force in Contemporary Conflict* (Oxford University Press 2016), Chapter 11; Gill and others (n. 26), Part II, Chapters 3, 5, and 6, and Part III, Chapter 12.

39 Exceptions include Lehmann (n. 14); McLaughlin (n. 38); Dire Tladi, 'Interpretation of Protection of Civilians Mandates in United Nations Security Resolutions' in Dan Kuwali and Frans Viljoen (eds), *By All Means Necessary: Protecting Civilians and Preventing Mass Atrocities in Africa* (Pretoria University Law Press 2017).

40 See e.g. Charles T Hunt, 'All Necessary Means to What Ends? The Unintended Consequences of the "Robust Turn" in UN Peace Operations' (2017) 24 International Peacekeeping 108; Mona A Khalil, 'Legal Aspects of the Use of Force by United Nations Peacekeepers for the Protection of Civilians' in Haidi Willmot and others (eds), *Protection of Civilians* (1st edn., Oxford University Press 2016); Ray Murphy, 'UN Peacekeeping in the Democratic Republic of the Congo and the Protection of Civilians' (2016) 21 Journal of Conflict and Security Law 209.

41 Exceptions include Nigel D White, 'The Use of Weapons in Peace Operations' in Stuart Casey-Maslen (ed), *Weapons Under International Human Rights Law* (Cambridge University Press 2014); Nigel D White, 'Security Council Mandates and the Use of Lethal Force by Peacekeepers', *Summary of a lecture given to the Australian Centre for Military and Security Law, Australian National University, 2 February 2013*, http://eprints.nottingham.ac.uk/1956/1/White_for_ANU%5B2%5D.pdf, accessed 24 August 2018; Wills, 'Use of Deadly Force by Peacekeepers Operating Outside of Armed Conflict Situations: What Laws Apply?' (n. 18).

42 See e.g. William A Schabas, 'The Right to Life' in Andrew Clapham and Paola Gaeta (eds), *The Oxford Handbook of International Law in Armed Conflict*, vol. 1 (Oxford University Press 2014); Christian Tomuschat, Evelyne Lagrange and Stefan Oeter (eds), *The Right to Life* (Martinus Nijhoff Publishers 2010); Stuart Casey-Maslen and Christof Heyns, *The Right to Life under International Law: An Interpretative Manual* (Cambridge University Press 2021); Louise Doswald-Beck, 'The Right to Life in Armed Conflict: Does International Humanitarian Law Provide All the Answers?' (2006) 88 International Review of the Red Cross 881; Ian Park, *The Right to Life in Armed Conflict*, vol. 1 (Oxford University Press 2018).

In short, there is a gap between military doctrine and practice on the one hand and the doctrine of international law on the other. Where practice often ignores or misuses the applicable international legal framework, academia does pay attention to this framework but neither adequately considers the relationship between legal bases and legal regimes nor thoroughly studies this framework in the context of PoC by UN (mandated) peace operations. Deepening our understanding of the pertinent legal issues at stake is critical to helping actors charged with interpreting and implementing PoC mandates to ensure the effectiveness of protecting civilians from violence and thus contributing to the overall success of UN (mandated) peace operations. After all, the success of UN (mandated) peace operations requires that the domain of academic analysis of the legal parameters of the use of force and the domain of pragmatic application of those rules during the conduct of UN (mandated) peace operations remain connected.

2. AIM AND SCOPE

Based on the observations discussed earlier, the main question that this book seeks to address is what the legal parameters are for the use of force in UN (mandated) peace operations tasked by the UN Security Council to protect civilians. To that end, this book examines the international legal framework on the use of force for the protection of civilians in the context of UN (mandated) peace operations. In doing so, this book explores the diverse legal bases that may underlie UN (mandated) peace operations ordered by the UN Security Council to protect civilians, as well as the legal regimes that govern the use of force by UN (mandated) peace forces carrying out such operations. Additionally, this book investigates the relationship between the mission-specific legal bases (with a particular focus on the UNSC mandate) and the legal regimes (with a particular focus on HRL and IHL). By clearly setting out the international legal framework and indicating how to arrive at answers to the legal questions concerning the use of force to protect civilians, the author ultimately seeks to build a bridge between international legal scholarship on the one hand and military doctrine and practice on the other hand.

The study has two limitations, however. First, it concentrates solely on the use of force by UN (mandated) peace operations with a PoC mandate issued by the UN Security Council. Second, it focuses exclusively on the international legal framework regulating that use of force.

2.1. UN (MANDATED) PEACE OPERATIONS WITH A POC MANDATE

This book focuses on UN (mandated) peace operations, being military operations deployed in the territory of another State in support of the maintenance or restoration of international peace and security, and this with a PoC mandate of the UN Security Council. Whether an operation is labelled as a traditional peacekeeping operation, a robust peacekeeping operation, a multidimensional peace operation, a third-generation peace operation, a peace enforcement operation, or otherwise is irrelevant to whether it is included in this study. Many authors have sought to develop a typology and divide UN peace operations into generations[43] or categorise operations based on the period in which they were active,[44] or the functions and tasks with which they are endowed.[45] This research uses neither the existing typologies nor develops its own typology, as this would be of little value to the research undertaken. What is relevant is that it concerns military operations deployed to protect civilians and find their legal basis in a UNSC resolution, regardless of whether this is complemented by the consent of the host State or not; this has several implications.

First, this book covers operations conducted by the UN itself (UN peace operations) or by States or regional or international organisations other than the UN with the authorisation of the UN Security Council (UN-mandated peace operations). UN peace operations are subsidiary organs of the UN pursuant to Article 29 of the UN Charter.[46] UN peace operations are directed and conducted by the UN and are bound primarily by the international obligations binding

43 See e.g. Kai Michael Kenkel, 'Five Generations of Peace Operations: From the "Thin Blue Line" to "Painting a Country Blue"' (2013) 56 Revista Brasileira de Política Internacional 122; B Kondoch, 'The United Nations Administration of East Timor' (2001) 6 Journal of Conflict and Security Law 245; Ramesh Chandra Thakur and Albrecht Schnabel (eds), *United Nations Peacekeeping Operations: Ad Hoc Missions, Permanent Engagement* (United Nations University Press 2001) 9–14.

44 See e.g. Joachim A Koops and others (eds), *The Oxford Handbook of United Nations Peacekeeping Operations* (1st edn, Oxford University Press 2015); David R Segal, 'Five Phases of United Nations Peacekeeping: An Evolutionary Typology' (1995) 23 Journal of Political and Military Sociology 65; Henry Weisman, 'The United Nations and International Peacekeeping: A Comparative Analysis' in United Nations Institute for Training and Research (ed), *The United Nations and the Maintenance of International Peace and Security* (Martinus Nijhoff Publishers 1987).

45 See e.g. Paul F Diehl, Daniel Druckman and James Wall, 'International Peacekeeping and Conflict Resolution: A Taxonomic Analysis with Implications' (1998) 42 The Journal of Conflict Resolution 33; Alex J Bellamy, Paul D Williams and Stuart Griffin, *Understanding Peacekeeping* (2nd edn., Polity 2010) 153–298.

46 Art. 29 of the UN Charter determines that '[t]he Security Council may establish such subsidiary organs as it deems necessary for the performance of its functions.' Moreover, para. 15 of the 1990 UN Model SOFA for Peacekeeping Operations provides that '[t]he United Nations peace-keeping operation, as a subsidiary organ of the United Nations, enjoys the status, privileges and immunities of the United Nations' (UNGA, 'Model Status-of-Forces Agreement for Peace-Keeping Operations' (1990) UN Doc. A/45/594). Full reference to the

upon the UN. When the UN Security Council authorises Member States or regional or international organisations other than the UN to use military action in the territory of a State to protect civilians, it is up to each one to decide whether to exercise that authorisation. Member States taking part in those UN-mandated peace operations do not necessarily form a single legal entity such as UN peace operations do and are often, first and foremost, bound by their own international obligations. It is worth mentioning at this point to clearly distinguish between these two types of operations when discussing, *inter alia*, the legal bases of such operations or the applicability of HRL and IHL.

Second, this book exclusively focuses on UN (mandated) peace operations with an explicit PoC mandate issued by the UN Security Council. The legal basis for the deployment and functioning of a military operation in the territory of a State can be found in the consent of the host State and/or a UNSC mandate adopted under Chapter VII of the UN Charter. The host State's consent may constitute an independent legal basis for the deployment and operational use of foreign troops on its territory or a secondary legal basis in case the UN Security Council already provides for a mandate under Chapter VII of the UN Charter. This research only scrutinises operations for which the UN Security Council has given an explicit PoC mandate and thus excludes operations that find their sole legal basis in the consent of the host State. However, the fact that PoC mandates are adopted under Chapter VII of the UN Charter does not prevent the operations concerned from also receiving the consent of the host State to operate on its territory.[47] For that reason, although this book focuses on UN (mandated) peace operations with an explicit PoC mandate granted by the UN Security Council, it also addresses consent as a complementary legal basis for UN (mandated) peace operations. Explicit PoC mandates granted by the UN Security Council are mandates in which the UN Security Council authorises UN (mandated) peace operations to 'protect civilians under threat of physical violence' or 'imminent threat of physical violence'. To this language, an authorisation to use 'all necessary means' or to take 'all necessary action', 'the necessary action', 'necessary action', 'the necessary steps', 'all necessary measures', or 'the necessary measures' in the conduct of the mission is usually added. Subsequently, the scope of the authorisation is generally narrowed

---

UN Charter: Charter of the United Nations (adopted on 26 June 1945, entered into force on 24 October 1945) 1 UNTS XVI (UN Charter).

47 See e.g. the comments made by South Sudan when UNSC resolutions concerning MINUSTAH were adopted: UNSC, '6800th Meeting (at Which UNSC Res. 2057 (2012) Was Adopted)' (2012) UN Doc. S/PV.6800 2–3; UNSC, '6998th Meeting (at Which UNSC Res. 2109 (2013) Was Adopted)' (2013) UN Doc. S/PV.6998 32; UNSC, '7182nd Meeting (at Which UNSC Res. 2155 (2014) Was Adopted)' (2014) UN Doc. S/PV.7182 2–3; UNSC, '7322nd Meeting (at Which UNSC Res. 2187 (2014) Was Adopted)' (2014) UN Doc. S/PV.7322 2–3; UNSC, '7840th Meeting (at Which UNSC Res. 2327 (2016) Was Adopted)' (2016) UN Doc. S/PV.7840 8–10; UNSC, '8204th Meeting (at Which UNSC Res. 2406 (2018) Was Adopted)' (2018) UN Doc. S/PV.8204 2–3.

functionally and geographically by adding 'within the capabilities' and the 'areas of deployment' to the task of protecting civilians. Additionally, PoC mandates often stress that the relevant mandate is granted 'without prejudice to the responsibility of the host government,' hereby recognising that the host State (as opposed to the mission) has the primary responsibility to protect civilians. Last but not least, these decisions are typically taken under Chapter VII of the UN Charter. This study conducts a thorough analysis of all explicit PoC mandates issued by the UN Security Council between October 1999 (the month in which the first PoC mandate was adopted, i.e. UNSC Resolution 1270 (1999))[48] and December 2021 (the last PoC mandate adopted in the period in which the present study has been conducted, i.e. UNSC Resolution 2612 (2021)).[49] Since such a comprehensive and detailed analysis of all PoC mandates adopted since 1999 has not yet been conducted, this part of the study represents a new contribution to legal scholarship on PoC. In addition, this study looks into the interpretation of such PoC language and explores whether there are upper and/or lower limits to what UN (mandated) peace operations may or must lawfully do to protect civilians. Because such an extensive study of the meaning of PoC language has yet to be undertaken in legal scholarship, this part of the study is equally a novel, fundamental, and principle-setting contribution to the field.

Third, this book is only concerned with the concept of PoC as a mandated task by the UN Security Council and not with the concepts of 'Responsibility to Protect' (RtoP), 'Responsibility while Protecting' (RwP), or 'unilateral humanitarian intervention'. 'The protected status of civilians under IHL' is discussed, but only as a subset of IHL when discussing the rules regulating the use of force for PoC that has a clear nexus to an armed conflict. Although the history and development of these different concepts are intertwined, they remain distinct concepts with different meaning and rationale.[50] The protected status of civilians under IHL implies, first and foremost, that in the context of an IAC or a NIAC, a distinction must be made between civilians and combatants or civilians directly participating in hostilities. The use of force against a legitimate military target must refrain from harmful acts to civilians and the civilian population, and precautions must be taken to meet these obligations.[51] Now, while the protected status of civilians is an IHL concept that applies

48 'UNSC Res. 1270' (n. 7).

49 'UNSC Res. 2612' (2021) UN Doc. S/RES/2612 (2021).

50 Scott Sheeran and Catherine Kent, 'Protection of Civilians, Responsibility to Protect, and Humanitarian Intervention: Conceptual and Normative Interactions' in Haidi Willmot and others (eds), *Protection of Civilians* (1st edn., Oxford University Press 2016) 29.

51 Khalil, 'Legal Aspects of the Use of Force by United Nations Peacekeepers for the Protection of Civilians' (n. 40) 210; Keiichiro Okimoto, 'Protection of Civilians in International Humanitarian Law and by the Use of Force under Chapter VII of the Charter of the United Nations' (2008) 4 Asia-Pacific Yearbook of International Humanitarian Law 1, 31–32; Jamie A Williamson, 'Protection of Civilians under International Humanitarian Law' in Haidi Willmot and others (eds), *Protection of Civilians* (1st edn., Oxford University Press 2016) 163.

once the threshold for IHL is reached and limits the use of force at the tactical level, a PoC mandate primarily involves the strategic authority to act to protect civilians from harm caused by others. The concepts of unilateral humanitarian intervention, RtoP, and RwP likewise relate to the use of force at the strategic level. However, unilateral humanitarian interventions are understood as military interventions *outside* the UN collective security system (implying action without UNSC authorisation) that are motivated by humanitarian considerations (i.e. the protection of the civilian population against massive human rights violations).[52] In contrast, as for PoC, the UN's collective security agreement is central to RtoP and RwP.[53] The idea behind RtoP is that where a State is 'manifestly failing' to protect its population from mass atrocities, the international community has the responsibility to protect the population, as a last resort, through military intervention. Such collective action is taken through the UN Security Council in accordance with the UN Charter.[54] The concept of RwP, put forward by Brazil to express its unease with the NATO intervention in Libya in 2011, implies that when exercising its responsibility to intervene, the powers of the UN Security Council and the powers of those acting under its authority are constrained.[55] Similar to the concepts of RtoP and RwP, PoC relies on the UN's collective security system and focuses on the responsibilities instead of the rights of the international community.[56] Furthermore, while both RtoP and PoC aim to address instances of physical violence, RtoP has a specific focus on crimes of mass atrocities such as genocide, war crimes, crimes against humanity, and ethnic cleansing.[57] The main difference between RtoP and PoC is, however, the following. While RtoP is a political argument that national governments can use to spur the international community to military action, PoC, in the context of UN (mandated) peace operations, denotes a mandated task contained in resolutions adopted by the UN Security Council after having decided that action is required.[58] As a result, PoC enjoys wide legitimacy, while RtoP must fight for its existence, partly because of its arbitrary and somewhat dubious

---

52 Sheeran and Kent (n. 50) 34; Alan V Lowe, 'Humanitarian Intervention', *Max Planck Encyclopedia of Public International law* (Oxford Public International Law 2011); Tom Ruys, 'International Law on the Use of Force' in Jan Wouters, Philip de Man and Nele Verlinden (eds), *Armed Conflicts and the Law* (Intersentia 2016) 128.

53 Sheeran and Kent (n. 50) 48.

54 'UNGA Res. 60/1, 2005 World Summit Outcome' (2005) UN Doc. A/RES/60/1 para. 139, as reaffirmed in 'UNSC Res. 1674' (2006) UN Doc. S/RES/1674 (2006) para. 4.

55 'Letter Dated 9 November 2011 from the Permanent Representative of Brazil to the United Nations Addressed to the Secretary-General, General Assembly: Sixty-Sixth Session, Agenda Items 14 and 117; Security Council: Sixty-Sixth Year' (2011) UN Doc. A/66/551 and S/2011/701. See also Sheeran and Kent (n. 50) 47–48.

56 Sheeran and Kent (n. 50) 48.

57 UN DPO, '2019 UN Policy on PoC in UN Peacekeeping' (n. 35) 6 and 21.

58 Ralph Mamiya, 'A History and Conceptual Development of the Protection of Civilians' in Haidi Willmot and others (eds), *Protection of Civilians* (1st edn., Oxford University Press 2016) 83.

use.[59] Yet, PoC missions to which the host State has not consented and whose main objective is to protect may come close to RtoP interventions.[60] While PoC remains a mandated task included in the UNSC resolution, PoC language is possibly used to obfuscate an RtoP intervention that would not receive sufficient support in itself.[61] For example, the intervention in Libya is widely regarded as an example of RtoP because the intervention took place in response to the mass atrocities occurring in Libya, against which the Libyan government was unable or unwilling to protect its citizens, and this was without the government's consent. The intervention found support in UNSC Resolution 1973 (2011), which authorised UN Member States to take 'all necessary measures' in order 'to protect civilians and civilian populated areas under threat of attack in the Libyan Arab Jamahiriya, including Benghazi.'[62] While it was already challenging to generate sufficient support for this Resolution,[63] it is quite possible that the Resolution would not have been passed at all had it not included PoC language. The fact that PoC language may have been used to legitimise this RtoP intervention does not warrant exclusion from this study. The UNSC mandate unquestionably includes PoC as a mandated task and should, therefore, be considered a part of this study.

Fourth, this book does not address operations where military forces are not included. Accordingly, the research does not include operations solely consisting of civilian police forces and related personnel. Moreover, UN (mandated) peace operations by the UN Security Council often consist of various components for political affairs, administrative support, military, police, humanitarian aid, the rule of law, civil affairs, reconstruction, and public information, among others. In this book, we focus on the military component of such operations and their use of force to protect civilians.

2.2. INTERNATIONAL LEGAL FRAMEWORK REGULATING THE USE OF FORCE

The legal framework governing the use of force to protect civilians in the context of UN (mandated) peace operations is a complex puzzle, which primarily consists of the UN Charter, customary international law relating to the use of

59 Jon Harald Sande Lie and Benjamin de Carvalho, 'Chapter 3: Conceptual Unclarity and Competition: The Protection of Civilians and the Responsibility to Protect' in Benjamin de Carvalho, Ole Jacob Sending and Jan Egeland (eds), *The Protection of Civilians in UN Peacekeeping: Concept, Implementation and Practice* (1st edn., Nomos 2013) 60–61.

60 See e.g. Victoria K Holt and Tobias C Berkman, *The Impossible Mandate? Military Preparedness, the Responsibility to Protect and Modern Peace Operations* (Stimson Center 2006) 50–51; Sheeran and Kent (n. 50) 52.

61 Sheeran and Kent (n. 50) 59.

62 'UNSC Res. 1973' (2011) UN Doc. S/RES/1973 (2011) para. 4.

63 A number of States abstained in the vote on UNSC Resolution 1973 (2011), including Brazil, China, Germany, India, and Russia (see UNSC, '6498th Meeting (at Which UNSC Res. 1973 (2011) Was Adopted)' (2011) UN Doc. S/PV.6498 3).

force and the maintenance and restoration of international peace and security, the mandate, IHL, HRL, and national law. Where international law is studied in depth, an assessment of national law is beyond this study's scope. First, it would be impossible to do justice to the complexity and depth of national legislation within the scope of this study. Second, while national legislation is particularly relevant to questions concerning the use of lethal force by UN (mandated) peace forces carrying out a PoC mandate, such national legislation must, in principle, comply with relevant international rules and standards, specifically, the right to life. National law can be more protective of life but not less. For these reasons, this book only focuses on international law.

In discussing HRL and IHL, this book focuses on both the question of applicability and normative content. HRL refers to both international and regional HRL. Many questions regarding the applicability of HRL and IHL to UN (mandated) peace operations are thus far unanswered, making a comprehensive discussion on the subject long overdue, but what is notably lacking in legal scholarship is a thorough examination of the role of HRL and, in particular, the right to life, in regulating the use of force in the context of UN (mandated) peace operations. This book includes a thorough examination while offering a novel and fundamental contribution to this field.

The relationship between IHL and HRL is not discussed in detail. While exploring such a relationship is undoubtedly relevant to determining which rules apply and when to UN (mandated) peace operations' activities, it requires a detailed and comprehensive study beyond the scope of this book.[64] The main focus of this book is to uncover the relationship between mission-specific legal

64 For further literature, see e.g. Erika de Wet and Jann Kleffner (eds), *Convergence and Conflicts of Human Rights and International Humanitarian Law in Military Operations* (Pretoria University Law Press 2014); Robert Kolb, 'The Relationship between International Humanitarian Law and Human Rights Law: A Brief History of the 1948 Universal Declaration of Human Rights and the 1949 Geneva Conventions' (1998) 38 International Review of the Red Cross 409; William A Schabas, 'Lex Specialis – Belt and Suspenders – The Parallel Operation of Human Rights Law and the Law of Armed Conflict, and the Conundrum of Jus Ad Bellum Special Issue: Parallel Applicability of International Humanitarian Law and International Human Rights Law' (2007) 40 Israel Law Review 592; Cornelius Wiesener, 'The Application and Interplay of Humanitarian Law and Human Rights Law in Peace Operations, with a Particular Focus on the Use of Force' (DPhil thesis, European University Institute 2015); Nils Melzer and Gloria Gaggioli, 'Conceptual Distinction and Overlaps Between Law Enforcement and the Conduct of Hostilities' in Terry D Gill and Dieter Fleck (eds), *The Handbook of the International Law of Military Operations* (2nd edn., Oxford University Press 2015); Robin Geiß and Heike Krieger (eds), *The 'legal Pluriverse' Surrounding Multinational Military Operations* (1st edn., Oxford University Press 2020), and, in particular, Kenneth Watkin, 'A North American Perspective: The Overlap of the Laws of Armed Conflict and International Human Rights Law' in Robert Geiß and Heike Krieger (eds), *The 'Legal Pluriverse' Surrounding Multinational Military Operations* (Oxford University Press 2019); Gentian Zyberi and Anna Andersson, 'A European Perspective on the International Human Rights and Humanitarian Law Relationship in the Context of Multinational Military Operations' in Robert Geiß and Heike Krieger (eds), *The 'Legal Pluriverse' Surrounding Multinational Military Operations* (Oxford University Press 2019).

bases (in particular, the UN Security Council mandate) and legal regimes (with a particular focus on HRL and IHL) (rather than the relationship between legal regimes themselves). To this end, this book specifically assesses whether – and if so, the extent to which and how – the rules and principles of HRL and IHL affect the interpretation of PoC language. Furthermore, this book explores whether – and if so, how – PoC mandates may regulate the use of force by UN (mandated) peace forces on the ground (a matter primarily governed by legal regimes) and, more specifically, how it impacts whether or not force can be used in specific cases. Since such a comprehensive analysis of the relationship between the mission-specific legal bases and the legal regimes has not been undertaken previously in legal scholarship, this part of the research makes an original and foundational contribution to the field.

Furthermore, not only international law relating to the use of force and the maintenance and restoration of international peace and security, IHL, and HRL, but also other areas of conventional and customary international law are relevant to UN (mandated) peace operations. Think, for example, of international refugee law, international law relative to the status of forces and the exercise of criminal jurisdiction, international law of the sea, international air law, international environmental law, and the law of international organisations.[65] Also, the law of international responsibility of States and international organisations and international criminal law is most relevant to questions concerning the use of force for protective purposes. Unfortunately, while relevant, these areas of international law are not covered in this book. This book focuses primarily on how force can be used to protect civilians in accordance with the relevant international legal framework at the strategic, operational, and tactical levels. However, this book does not explore to what extent a State, an international organisation, or an individual should be held liable for violations of the relevant rules. Addressing such issues thoroughly would necessitate delving into complex matters of accountability and responsibility, which falls outside the intended scope of this book.

Several mission-specific instruments also play a vital role in practice. These include mission-specific agreements between, for example, host States and sending States or international or regional organisations (i.e. so-called Status of Forces Agreement (SOFA)) or arrangements between Troop Contributing Countries (TCC) and international or organisations or leading States (i.e. so-called Memorandums of Understanding with the TCC (TCC MOU)). There are also mission-specific documents, such as ROE. These instruments must not only reflect the terms set out in the legal bases underlying the operations but should also not be more lenient than the legal regime(s) applicable to the

65 Terry D Gill and Dieter Fleck, 'Concept and Sources of the International Law of Military Operations' in Terry D Gill and Dieter Fleck (eds), *The Handbook of the International Law of Military Operations* (2nd edn., Oxford University Press 2015) 8.

operations. Mission-specific documents are not studied in this research as they usually remain confidential and cannot be examined as such (the 2002 Sample ROE serve as a useful albeit imperfect stopgap). Fortunately, regional and international organisations' views on implementing PoC mandates and the use of force are also reflected in their guidelines, policies, and principles on PoC and the use of force. These guidelines, policies, and principles are not sources of law *per se* but play an essential role in complementing binding legal obligations on PoC and the use of force and are thus examined in detail in this study. However, it should be recalled that such non-legally binding instruments should never go beyond what is permitted under the relevant binding legal obligations applicable in each situation.[66]

3. SOURCES AND METHODOLOGY

The research on which this book is based is primarily doctrinal in nature[67] as it seeks to analyse the existing international legal framework regulating the use of force for protection purposes in the context of UN (mandated) peace operations. Accordingly, the book includes a description of how the legal bases and legal regimes regulate the use of force and evaluates the relationship between the mission-specific legal bases and the relevant legal regimes. This analysis is based on extensive desk research into a variety of sources of international law.

In the first place, this research examines the relevant treaties, a primary source of 'positive international law' as enumerated in Article 38(1)(a) of the Statute of the International Court of Justice (ICJ) (ICJ Statute).[68] To this end, it draws from an analysis of relevant HRL treaties (including the International Covenant on Civil and Political (ICCPR),[69] the American Convention of Human Rights (ACHR),[70] the African Charter on Human and Peoples' Rights (ACHPR),[71] and the European Convention on Human Rights (ECHR)),[72] IHL

66 See also *ibid.* 11.

67 Ian Dobinson and Francis Johns, 'Legal Research as Qualitative Research' in Michael McConville and Wing Hong Chui (eds), *Research Methods for Law* (2nd edn., Edinburgh University Press 2017) 20–21.

68 Stephen Hall, 'Researching International Law' in Michael McConville and Wing Hong Chui (eds), *Research Methods for Law* (2nd edn., Edinburgh University Press 2017) 254. Full reference to the ICJ Statute: Statute of the International Court of Justice, Annexed to the UN Charter (adopted 26 June 1945, entered into force 24 October 1945) USTS 993 (ICJ Statute).

69 International Covenant on Civil and Political Rights (adopted 16 December 1966, entered into force 23 March 1976) 999 UNTS 171 (ICCPR).

70 American Convention on Human Rights: 'Pact of San José, Costa Rica' (adopted 22 November 1969, entered into force 18 July 1978) 1144 UNTS 123 (ACHR).

71 African Charter on Human and Peoples' Rights (adopted 27 June 1981, entered into force 21 October 1986) 1520 UNTS 217 (ACHPR).

72 Convention for the Protection of Human Rights and Fundamental Freedoms, as Amended (adopted 4 November 1950, entered into force 3 September 1953) 213 UNTS 221 (ECHR).

treaties (including the 1899 Hague Convention II and its Regulations,[73] the 1907 Hague Convention IV and its Regulations,[74] the Geneva Conventions I–IV,[75] and the Additional Protocols),[76] treaties on (the functioning of) international and regional organisations (including, but not limited to, the UN Charter, the AU Constitutive Act,[77] the North Atlantic Treaty,[78] and the Treaty on European Union (TEU)),[79] and the Vienna Convention on the Law of Treaties (VCLT),[80] among others. This study also looks at general comments from the United Nations Human Rights Committee (UN HRC) and the African Commission on Human and Peoples' Rights (AComHPR) on the ICCPR and the ACHPR, respectively (including the UN HRC's General Comment No. 31 on the Nature of the General Legal Obligation Imposed on States Parties to the Covenant[81] and General Comment No. 36 on the Right to Life,[82] as well as the AComHPR's

---

73 Convention with Respect to the Laws and Customs of War and Land and Its Annex: Regulations concerning the Laws and Customs of War on Land (adopted 29 July 1899, entered into force 4 September 1900) 187 CTS 429 (1899 Hague Convention II and the 1899 Hague Regulations).

74 Convention Respecting the Laws and Customs of War on Land and its Annex: Regulations Concerning the Laws and Customs of War on Land (adopted 18 October 1907, entered into force 26 January 1910) 187 CTS 227 (1907 Hague Convention IV and the 1907 Hague Regulations).

75 Convention for the Amelioration of the Condition of the Wounded and Sick in Armed Forces in the Field (adopted 12 August 1949, entered into force 21 October 1950) 75 UNTS 31 (Geneva Convention I); Convention for the Amelioration of the Condition of Wounded, Sick and Shipwrecked Members of Armed Forces at Sea (adopted 12 August 1949, entered into force 21 October 1950) 75 UNTS 85 (Geneva Convention II); Convention Relative to the Treatment of Prisoners of War (adopted 12 August 1949, entered into force 21 October 1950) 75 UNTS 135 (Geneva Convention III); and Convention Relative to the Protection of Civilian Persons in Time of War (adopted 12 August 1949, entered into force 21 October 1950) 75 UNTS 287 (Geneva Convention IV).

76 Protocol Additional to the Geneva Conventions of 12 August 1949, and Relating to the Protection of Victims of International Armed Conflicts (adopted 8 June 1977, entered into force 7 December 1978) 1125 UNTS 3 (Additional Protocol I); Protocol Additional to the Geneva Conventions of 12 August 1949, and Relating to the Protection of Victims of Non-international Armed Conflicts (adopted 8 June 1977, entered into force 7 December 1978) 1125 UNTS 609 (Additional Protocol II).

77 Constitutive Act of the African Union (adopted 11 July 2000, entered into force 26 May 2001) 2158 UNTS 3 (AU Constitutive Act).

78 North Atlantic Treaty (adopted 4 April 1949, entered into force 24 August 1949) 34 UNTS 243 (North Atlantic Treaty).

79 Consolidated Version of the Treaty on European Union (26 October 2012) OJ C 326/13 (TEU).

80 Vienna Convention on the Law of Treaties (adopted 23 May 1969, entered into force on 27 January 1980) 1155 UNTS 331 (VCLT).

81 UN HRC, 'General Comment No. 31 [80] on The Nature of the General Legal Obligation Imposed on States Parties to the Covenant, Adopted on 29 March 2004' (2004) UN Doc. CCPR/C/21/Rev.1/Add. 13.

82 UN HRC, 'General Comment No. 36 (2019) on Article 6 of the International Covenant on Civil and Political Rights, on the Right to Life' (2019) UN Doc. CCPR/C/GC/36.

General Comment No. 3 on the Right to Life).[83] The research also draws from the International Committee of the Red Cross' (ICRC) commentaries on the Geneva Conventions I–IV and the Additional Protocols (and, in particular, the 1958 ICRC Commentary on Geneva Convention IV,[84] the 1987 ICRC Commentary on Additional Protocols I–II,[85] and the updated 2016 ICRC Commentaries on Geneva Conventions I, II, and III),[86] as well as commentaries by legal scholars on the UN Charter,[87] the VCLT,[88] and the ECHR.[89]

This research also invokes customary international law, a second primary source of 'positive international law' as enumerated in Article 38(1)(b) of the ICJ Statute.[90] To this end, the research draws from well-established rules of customary international law relating to the use of force and the maintenance and restoration of international peace and security, customary IHL, and customary HRL, as identified in case law (e.g. of the ICJ), reports of the ICRC (e.g. the 2005 ICRC Study on Customary IHL),[91] and legal scholarship. In addition, the study is complemented by an assessment of specific soft law instruments, such as the 1990 UN Basic Principles for the Use of Force and Firearms[92] and the 1999 UN Secretary-General's Bulletin on IHL,[93] which are not conventional but whose

83 AComHPR, 'General Comment No. 3 on the African Charter on Human and Peoples' Rights: The Right to Life (Article 4), Adopted during the 57th Ordinary Session of the African Commission on Human and Peoples' Rights Held from 4 to 18 November 2015 in Banjul, The Gambia' (2015).

84 Pictet (ed), *Commentary IV Geneva Convention Relative to the Protection of Civilian Persons in Time of War* (ICRC 1958).

85 Yves Sandoz, Christophe Swinarski and Bruno Zimmermann (eds), *Commentary on the Additional Protocols of 8 June 1977 to the Geneva Conventions of 12 August 1949* (ICRC; Martinus Nijhoff Publishers 1987).

86 ICRC, *Commentary on the First Geneva Convention: Convention (I) for the Amelioration of the Condition of the Wounded and Sick in Armed Forces in the Field* (1st edn, Cambridge University Press 2016); ICRC (ed), *Commentary on the Second Geneva Convention: Convention (II) for the Amelioration of the Condition of Wounded, Sick, and Shipwrecked Members of Armed Forces at Sea* (Cambridge University Press 2017); ICRC (ed), *Commentary on the Third Geneva Convention: Convention (III) Relative to the Treatment of Prisoners of War* (Cambridge University Press 2021).

87 Bruno Simma and others (eds), *The Charter of the United Nations: A Commentary* (3rd edn., Oxford University Press 2012).

88 Oliver Dörr and Kirsten Schmalenbach (eds), *Vienna Convention on the Law of Treaties: A Commentary* (Springer 2012).

89 William A Schabas, *The European Convention on Human Rights: A Commentary* (1st edn., Oxford University Press 2015).

90 Hall (n. 68) 254.

91 Jean-Marie Henckaerts and Louise Doswald-Beck, *ICRC Study on Customary International Humanitarian Law. Volume I: Rules* (Cambridge University Press 2005).

92 UN, 'Basic Principles on the Use of Force and Firearms' (adopted by the Eighth United Nations Congress on the Prevention of Crime and the Treatment of Offenders, Havana, Cuba, 27 August to 7 September 1990), www.ohchr.org/en/professionalinterest/pages/useofforceandfirearms.aspx, accessed 22 November 2018.

93 UNSG, '1999 UN Secretary-General's Bulletin on IHL' (n. 25).

content nevertheless reflects binding international law.[94] Bulletins of the UN Secretary-General are, for example, administrative statements, which the United Nations Administrative Tribunal (UNAT) generally accepts 'as interpreting the Staff Regulations and Staff Rules, or they are recognized as valuable additional regulatory instruments in the application of the Staff Regulations and Rules.'[95] Finally, this study also briefly refers to the 2001 Articles on the Responsibility of States (2001 ASR)[96] and the 2011 Draft Articles on the Responsibility of International Organizations (2011 DARIO),[97] which are also not legally binding but can nevertheless be considered authoritative sources of law.

In accordance with Article 38(1)(d) of the ICJ Statute, the research also considers judicial decisions and authoritative publications to clarify further the existence, scope, and applicability of norms based on the relevant hard law and soft law instruments. Judicial decisions include judgments and decisions from various international courts (including the ICJ, the International Criminal Court (ICC), the European Court of Justice (ECJ), the European Court of Human Rights (ECtHR), and the Inter-American Court of Human Rights (IACtHR)), tribunals (including the International Criminal Tribunal of Yugoslavia (ICTY), the International Criminal Tribunal of Rwanda (ICTR), and the Special Court for Sierra Leone (SCSL)), human rights mechanisms (such as the UN HRC, the former European Commission on Human Rights (EComHR),[98] the Inter-American Commission on Human Rights (IAComHR), and the AComHPR), and, to some extent, national courts.

Furthermore, the practice of the UN, the AU, NATO, and the EU, as embodied in publicly available guidelines, decisions, statements, declarations, policy documents, studies, reports, and other relevant instruments (some of which also make up soft law), is thoroughly examined. For example, this study conducts an extensive analysis of all mission-specific UNSC resolutions including a PoC mandate and the verbatim records of the meetings of the

---

94 Art. 38(1) of the ICJ Statute is recognised as an authoritative but incomplete enumeration of the sources of international law.

95 Wolfgang Stöckl, 'Chapter XV. The Secretariat, Article 101' in Bruno Simma and others (eds), *The Charter of the United Nations: a Commentary*, vol. 2 (3rd. edn., Oxford University Press 2012) 2064, as also referred to by Guglielmo Verdirame, *The UN and Human Rights: Who Guards the Guardians?* (Cambridge University Press 2011) 205.

96 ILC, 'Articles on the Responsibility of States for Internationally Wrongful Acts with Commentaries' (2001) Yearbook of the International Law Commission vol. 2, part two.

97 ILC, 'Draft Articles on the Responsibility of International Organizations with Commentaries' (2011) Yearbook of the International Law Commission vol. 2, part two.

98 The EComHR was a special body of the Council of Europe established in 1954 that decided whether a case brought to it by individuals (who did not have direct access to the ECtHR at that time) was well-founded and warranted bringing a case to the ECtHR on behalf of the individual. The EComHR was dissolved in 1998, the year Protocol 11 of the ECHR came into force, which allowed individuals to take cases directly to the ECtHR (Protocol No. 11 to the Convention for the Protection of Human Rights and Fundamental Freedoms, Restructuring the Control Machinery Established Thereby (adopted 11 May 1994, entered into force 1 November 1998) 2061 UNTS 7 (Protocol No. 11 to the ECHR)).

UN Security Council during which those mandates were adopted. For such an analysis, the research identifies all UNSC resolutions in which the terms 'protect(ion)' and 'civilian' were used in connection with a mandate given to a UN (mandated) peace operation. The first PoC mandate was included in UNSC Resolution 1270 (1999).[99] The last PoC mandate considered by this research was included in UNSC Resolution 2612 (2021).[100] Although PoC mandates are *ad hoc* and operation-specific, the examination of the mission-specific UNSC resolutions adopted by the UN Security Council over the past two decades reveals that the language used is relatively standard. Typically, the following terms are used: 'protect/protection', 'civilians/civilian population', 'in danger/ under threat of attack/under threat or imminent threat of physical violence', 'all necessary means/measures/steps/action', 'within its capabilities' and 'areas of deployment', and 'responsibility/primary responsibility of host State/ host authorities'. This study maps not only the PoC language used in UNSC resolutions but also examines the meaning of such terms by identifying the rules and methods of interpretation applicable to UNSC resolutions. There is no specific treaty on the interpretation of UNSC resolutions; neither case law nor legal scholarship has dealt with it extensively. The study, therefore, invokes the rules of the VCLT to interpret the wording of UNSC resolutions but not without considering the specificities of UNSC resolutions. The study takes this position based on a consideration of relevant ICJ and ICTY case law, UN OLA positions on the matter, and relevant legal scholarship.

This study also considers other documents issued by the UN Security Council, including UN Security Council presidential statements and UNSC resolutions other than the UNSC resolutions containing a PoC mandate (as mentioned above). Furthermore, this study also draws from United Nations General Assembly's resolutions (UNGA resolutions) and policy documents of the UN Secretary-General, the UN General Assembly, the United Nations Department of Peace Operations (UN DPO) (and its predecessors, the United Nations Department of Peacekeeping (UN DPKO) and the United Nations Department of Field Support (UN DFS)),[101] the UN OLA, and the International Law Commission (ILC), among others. The main instruments in this regard are the 2002 UN Sample ROE,[102] the 2015 UN Implementing Guidelines for Military Components of UN Peacekeeping Missions on PoC,[103] the 2017 UN Guidelines on the Use of Force by Military Components in UN Peacekeeping

99 'UNSC Res. 1270' (n. 7).

100 'UNSC Res. 2612' (n. 49).

101 As of 1 January 2019, the UN DPO and the UN DOS have replaced the UN DPKO and the UN DFS. The old acronyms UN DPKO and UN DFS will be used for all activities of the department that took place before 1 January 2019.

102 UN DPKO, 'Guidelines for the Development of Rules of Engagement (ROE) for United Nations Peacekeeping Operations' (2002) UN Doc. MD/FGS/0220.0001.

103 UN DPKO and UN DFS, 'Protection of Civilians: Implementing Guidelines for Military Components of United Nations Peacekeeping Missions' (2015) Ref. 2015.02.

Operations,[104] and the 2019 UN Policy on PoC in UN Peacekeeping.[105] In addition, this study draws from an examination of reports commissioned by the UN Secretary-General, the UN Security Council, the UN General Assembly, the UN DPO (or its predecessors, the UN DPKO and DFS), and the United Nations Office for the Coordination of Humanitarian Affairs (UN OCHA) (including reviews by OIOS,[106] reports of the Special Rapporteur on State Responsibility,[107] the Special Rapporteur on Peremptory Norms of General International Law (*Jus Cogens*),[108] and the Special Rapporteur on Extrajudicial, Summary or Arbitrary Executions,[109] the report of the Independent Inquiry into the Actions of the UN during the 1994 Genocide in Rwanda,[110] the 2000 Brahimi Report,[111] or the 2015 Report of the Independent High-Level Panel on Peace Operations (HIPPO) (2015 HIPPO Report)),[112] as well as reports of other entities, such as the International Commission on Intervention and State Sovereignty's (ICISS) reporting on RtoP,[113] among others.

Furthermore, as for the AU, NATO, and the EU, this study considers publicly available guidelines, statements, decisions, reports, and other relevant instruments that shape their PoC and use of force policies. Guidelines and reports on PoC and the use of force include, for example, the 2012 AU Draft Guidelines for PoC in AU Peace Support Operations,[114] the 2013 AU Aide

---

104 UN DPKO and UN DFS, '2017 UN Guidelines on the Use of Force by Military Components in UN Peacekeeping Operations' (n. 17).

105 UN DPO, '2019 UN Policy on PoC in UN Peacekeeping' (n. 35).

106 E.g. OIOS, 'Evaluation of the Implementation and Results of Protection of Civilians Mandates in United Nations Peacekeeping Operations, Sixty-Eighth Session, Item 142 of the Provisional Agenda' (2014) UN Doc. A/68/787; OIOS, Inspection and Evaluation Division, 'Triennial Review of Implementation of Recommendations Contained in the OIOS Evaluation Report on the Implementation and Results of Protection of Civilians Mandates in United Nations Peacekeeping Operations' (2017) IED-17-010; OIOS, Inspection and Evaluation Division (n. 10).

107 E.g. ILC, 'Second Report on State Responsibility by Mr. James Crawford, Special Rapporteur' (1999) UN Doc. A/CN.4/498 and Add.1–4.

108 E.g. ILC, 'Fourth Report on Peremptory Norms of General International Law (Jus Cogens) by Dire Tladi, Special Rapporteur' (2019) UN Doc. A/CN.4/727.

109 E.g. UNGA, 'Report of the Special Rapporteur on Extrajudicial, Summary or Arbitrary Executions, Christophe Heyns' (2013) UN Doc. A/68/382; UNGA, 'Report of the Special Rapporteur on Extrajudicial, Summary or Arbitrary Executions, Christof Heyns' (2011) UN Doc. A/66/330; UN HRC, 'Report of the Special Rapporteur on Extrajudicial, Summary or Arbitrary Executions, Christof Heyns' (2014) UN Doc. A/HRC/26/36.

110 'Report of the Independent Inquiry into the Actions of the United Nations during the 1994 Genocide in Rwanda' (1999) UN Doc. S/1999/1257.

111 'Report of the Panel on United Nations Peace Operations (Brahimi Report), Fifty-Fifth Session of the General Assembly, Item 87 of the Provisional Agenda; Fifty-Fifth Year of the Security Council' (n. 19).

112 HIPPO, 'Report of the High-Level Independent Panel on Peace Operations on Uniting Our Strengths for Peace: Politics, Partnership and People' (2015) A/70/95 and S/2015/446 9.

113 ICISS, 'The Responsibility to Protect' (International Development Research Centre 2001).

114 AU, 'Draft Guidelines for the Protection of Civilians in African Union Peace Support Operations' (2012), www.peaceau.org/uploads/draft-au-poc-guidelines-english.pdf, accessed 22 October 2022.

Mémoire on PoC,[115] the 2014 NATO AJD for Military Contribution to Peace Support,[116] the 2015 NATO AJD for the Military Contribution to Stabilization and Reconstruction,[117] and the 2016 NATO Policy on PoC.[118] EU instruments include the 2015 EU Concept for the Use of Force in EU-led Military Operations,[119] the 2015 EU Concept on PoC in EU-led Military Operations,[120] and the 2019 EU Concept for Military Command and Control.[121] This study also considers several statements by the African Union Peace and Security Council (AU PSC), decisions of the Council of the EU on EU-led peace operations, as well as statements by the NATO Secretary General and summit declarations by NATO's North Atlantic Council (NAC).

The analysis of relevant documentation was completed in December 2021. The processing of the results and overall analysis of the international legal framework governing the use of force for protection purposes was completed in October 2022.

4. STRUCTURE

This book consists of the present Introductory Chapter, the main body of research, and a Concluding Chapter. The main body of research is divided into three parts.

Part I clarifies and further develops the concept of PoC as a mandated task by the UN Security Council and provides an overview of the political and legal framework governing the use of force for PoC in the context of UN (mandated) peace operations. Whereas Section 1 is an introduction to Part I, Section 2 explores the general concept of PoC. Section 3 discusses different policies on the use of force for PoC, including those of the UN and the AU, NATO, and the EU. Section 4 introduces the legal framework governing the use of force for PoC in the context of UN (mandated) peace operations and thus paves the way for Parts II and III of this book. Section 5 provides a summary of Part I.

---

115 AU Assembly (n. 2).

116 NATO, '2014 NATO AJD for Military Contribution to Peace Support' (n. 20).

117 NATO, 'Allied Joint Doctrine for the Military Contribution to Stabilization and Reconstruction' (2015) NATO Doc. AJP-3.4.5, Edn. A, Version 1.

118 NAC, 'NATO Policy for the Protection of Civilians Endorsed by the Heads of State and Government Participating in the Meeting of the North Atlantic Council in Warsaw 8–9 July 2016' (*NATO*, 9 July 2016), www.nato.int/cps/en/natohq/official_texts_133945.htm, accessed 21 September 2021.

119 EUMC, 'EU Concept for the Use of Force in EU-Led Military Operations' (2015) EU Doc. 17168/2/09 REV 2 EXT 2.

120 EUMC, 'Concept on Protection of Civilians (PoC) in EU-Led Military Operations' (2015) EU Doc. EEAS 00351/6/14 REV 6.

121 EEAS, 'EU Concept for Military Command and Control – Rev 8' (2019) EU Doc. EEAS 02246/8/14 REV 8.

Part II explores the mission-specific legal bases underlying UN (mandated) peace operations deployed to protect civilians, particularly the consent of the host State and mandates granted by the UN Security Council and investigates the possible impact the legal regimes (in particular, HRL and IHL) might have on the interpretation, implementation, and evaluation of PoC mandates granted by the UN Security Council. Section 1 includes an introduction to the issues at stake, followed in Section 2 by a discussion of consent as a legal basis for UN (mandated) peace operations. In Section 3, PoC mandates issued by the UN Security Council, together with the role these instruments play in the use of force to protect civilians, are thoroughly examined. Section 4 concludes Part II with a summary of what has been covered.

Part III examines the legal regimes, and, in particular, HRL and IHL, governing the use of force to protect civilians by UN (mandated) peace forces carrying out PoC mandates and explores the possible impact of the PoC mandate on whether or not force can be used by UN (mandated) peace forces on the ground. Section 1 first introduces Part III, after which Section 2 identifies the applicability *de jure* of HRL and IHL to UN (mandated) peace operations carrying out a PoC mandate. Section 3 discusses under which circumstances and in which manner UN (mandated) peace forces may use force (up to and including lethal force) when carrying out a PoC mandate. Hereby, a distinction is made between the use of force with no clear nexus to an armed conflict and the use of force that does not have such a clear nexus to an armed conflict. Section 4 examines whether there is an obligation to protect civilians (by force) from the threat of physical violence under HRL and IHL. Section 5 contains a summary of what has been discussed in Part III.

Building on the analyses in Parts I to III, the Concluding Chapter critically discusses how the use of force for protection purposes in the context of UN (mandated) peace operations is regulated and what role the different components of the international legal framework play in this regard.

PART I

CONCEPTUAL FOUNDATIONS AND INTRODUCTION TO THE POLITICAL AND LEGAL FRAMEWORK GOVERNING THE USE OF FORCE FOR POC[122]

1. INTRODUCTION TO PART I

PoC has been a core part of UN peace operations for over 20 years. Between 1999 and 2021,[123] the following fifteen UN peace operations have been provided with a PoC mandate: UNAMSIL,[124] the United Nations Organization Mission in the Democratic Republic of the Congo (MONUC)[125] (which was replaced by MONUSCO in 2010[126] and to which, from 2013 onwards, the Intervention Brigade was added),[127] the United Nations Mission in Liberia

---

122 Part I is partly based on the following publications: Bourgeois, 'Failure to Protect Civilians in the Context of UN Peace Operations: A Question of Accountability?' (n. 1); Bourgeois, '"All Necessary Means" to Protect Civilians: The Interpretation and Implementation of UN Security Council Mandates Authorising the Protection of Civilians' (n. 1); Bourgeois and Labuda (n. 1); Bourgeois and Perrin (n. 1).

123 The analysis of relevant UNSC resolutions was completed in December 2021.

124 UNAMSIL's initial PoC mandate was included in 'UNSC Res. 1270' (n. 7). Its PoC mandate was renewed several times, but not every mandate contained an explicit reference to PoC. For the resolutions with an explicit PoC mandate, see: 'UNSC Res. 1289' (2000) UN Doc. S/RES/1289 (2000); 'UNSC Res. 1313' (2000) UN Doc. S/RES/1313 (2000). UNAMSIL was completed on 31 December 2005.

125 MONUC's initial PoC mandate was included in 'UNSC Res. 1291' (2000) UN Doc. S/RES/1291 (2000). Its PoC mandate was renewed and extended several times, but not every mandate contained an explicit reference to PoC. For the resolutions with an explicit PoC mandate, see: 'UNSC Res. 1417' (2002) UN Doc. S/RES/1417 (2002); 'UNSC Res. 1493' (2003) UN Doc. S/RES/1493 (2003); 'UNSC Res. 1565' (2004) UN Doc. S/RES/1565 (2004); 'UNSC Res. 1592' (2005) UN Doc. S/RES/1592 (2005); 'UNSC Res. 1649' (2005) UN Doc. S/RES/1649 (2005); 'UNSC Res. 1756' (2007) UN Doc. S/RES/1756 (2007); 'UNSC Res. 1794' (2007) UN Doc. S/RES/1794 (2007); 'UNSC Res. 1856' (2008) UN Doc. S/RES/1856 (2008); 'UNSC Res. 1906' (2009) UN Doc. S/RES/1906 (2009); 'UNSC Res. 1925' (2010) UN Doc. S/RES/1925 (2010).

126 MONUSCO's first PoC mandates were included in the following resolutions: 'UNSC Res. 1925' (n. 125); 'UNSC Res. 1991' (2011) UN Doc. S/RES/1991 (2011); 'UNSC Res. 2053' (2012) UN Doc. S/RES/2053 (2012).

127 With UNSC Res. 2098 (2013), the Intervention Brigade was added to MONUSCO ('UNSC Res. 2098' (n. 19)). For renewals and extensions of the PoC mandate of MONUSCO and the Intervention Brigade, see: 'UNSC Res. 2147' (n. 19); 'UNSC Res. 2211' (2015) UN Doc. S/RES/2211 (2015); 'UNSC Res. 2277' (2016) UN Doc. S/RES/2277 (2016); 'UNSC Res. 2348'

(UNMIL),[128] the United Nations Operation in Côte d'Ivoire (UNOCI),[129] the United Nations Stabilization Mission in Haiti (MINUSTAH)[130] (which was replaced by the United Nations Mission for Justice Support in Haiti (MINUJUSTH) (i.e. a police mission and thus not included in this study) in 2017),[131] the United Nations Operation in Burundi (ONUB),[132] the United Nations Mission in Sudan (UNMIS)[133] (which was replaced by the United Nations Interim Security Force for Abyei (UNISFA)[134] and the United Nations Mission

(2017) UN Doc. S/RES/2348 (2017); 'UNSC Res. 2409' (n. 19); 'UNSC Res. 2463' (2019) UN Doc. S/RES/2463 (2019); 'UNSC Res. 2502' (2019) UN Doc. S/RES/2502 (2019); 'UNSC Res. 2556' (2020) UN Doc. S/RES/2556 (2020); 'UNSC Res. 2612' (n. 49).

128 UNMIL's initial PoC mandate was included in 'UNSC Res. 1509' (2003) UN Doc. S/RES/1509 (2003). Its PoC mandate was renewed several times, but not every mandate contained an explicit reference to PoC. For the resolutions with an explicit PoC mandate, see 'UNSC Res. 2066' (2012) UN Doc. S/RES/2066 (2012); 'UNSC Res. 2190' (2014) UN Doc. S/RES/2190 (2014); 'UNSC Res. 2239' (2015) UN Doc. S/RES/2239 (2015); 'UNSC Res. 2333' (2016) UN Doc. S/RES/2333 (2016). UNMIL was completed on 30 March 2018.

129 UNOCI's initial PoC mandate was included in 'UNSC Res. 1528' (2004) UN Doc. S/RES/1528 (2004). Its PoC mandate was renewed and extended several times, but not every mandate contained an explicit reference to PoC. For the resolutions with an explicit PoC mandate, see 'UNSC Res. 1609' (2005) UN Doc. S/RES/1609 (2005); 'UNSC Res. 1739' (2007) UN Doc. S/RES/1739 (2007); 'UNSC Res. 1933' (2010) UN Doc. S/RES/1933 (2010); 'UNSC Res. 1962' (2010) UN Doc. S/RES/1962 (2010); 'UNSC Res. 2000' (2011) UN Doc. S/RES/2000 (2011); 'UNSC Res. 2062' (2012) UN Doc. S/RES/2062 (2012); 'UNSC Res. 2112' (2013) UN Doc. S/RES/2112 (2013); 'UNSC Res. 2162' (2014) UN Doc. S/RES/2162 (2014); 'UNSC Res. 2226' (2015) UN Doc. S/RES/2226 (2015); 'UNSC Res. 2284' (2016) UN Doc. S/RES/2284 (2016). UNOCI was completed on 30 June 2017.

130 MINUSTAH's initial PoC mandate was included in 'UNSC Res. 1542' (2004) UN Doc. S/RES/1542 (2004). Its PoC mandate was renewed several times, but none of the resolutions contained an explicit PoC mandate.

131 See 'UNSC Res. 2350' (2017) UN Doc. S/RES/2350 (2017). MINUJUSTH was completed on 15 October 2019.

132 ONUB's initial PoC mandate was included in 'UNSC Res. 1545' (2004) UN Doc. S/RES/1545 (2004). Its PoC mandate was renewed several times, but none of the resolutions contained an explicit PoC mandate. ONUB completed its mandate on 31 December 2006.

133 UNMIS' initial PoC mandate was included in 'UNSC Res. 1590' (2005) UN Doc. S/RES/1590 (2005). With Resolution 1706 (2006), the UN Security Council decided to expand UNMIS' mandate to include its deployment to Darfur, without prejudice to the mission's existing mandate and operations. The UN Security Council also decided that the mandate of UNMIS in Darfur shall also include PoC, see 'UNSC Res. 1706' (2006) UN Doc. S/RES/1706 (2006). However, as UNMIS could not be deployed in Darfur, this due to opposition from the government, the UN Security Council tried to stabilise the region through the phased strengthening of AMIS (as discussed below), before handing over authority to a peace operation jointly conducted by the UN and AU called UNAMID, see 'UNSC Res. 1769' (2007) UN Doc. S/RES/1769 (2007) (as discussed below). UNMIS continued to operate in Sudan and its PoC mandate was renewed and extended several times, but not every mandate contained an explicit reference to PoC. For direct references to UNMIS' PoC mandate, see however 'UNSC Res. 1870' (2009) UN Doc. S/RES/1870 (2009); 'UNSC Res. 1919' (2010) UN Doc. S/RES/1919 (2010). UNMIS was eventually replaced by UNISFA and UNMISS.

134 UNISFA's initial PoC mandate was included in 'UNSC Res. 1990' (2011) UN Doc. S/RES/1990 (2011). Its PoC mandate was renewed and extended several times, but not every mandate contained an explicit reference to PoC. For the resolutions with an explicit PoC mandate, see: 'UNSC Res. 2104' (2013) UN Doc. S/RES/2104 (2013); 'UNSC Res. 2126' (2013) UN Doc. S/RES/2126 (2013); 'UNSC Res. 2156' (2014) UN Doc. S/RES/2156 (2014); 'UNSC Res. 2179'

in South Sudan (UNMISS)),[135] the United Nations Interim Force in Lebanon (UNIFIL),[136] the United Nations—African Union Hybrid Operation in Darfur (UNAMID),[137] the United Nations Mission in the Central African Republic and Chad (MINURCAT),[138] MINUSMA,[139] and MINUSCA.[140]

(2014) UN Doc. S/RES/2179 (2014); 'UNSC Res. 2205' (2015) UN Doc. S/RES/2205 (2015); 'UNSC Res. 2230' (2015) UN Doc. S/RES/2230 (2015); 'UNSC Res. 2251' (2015) UN Doc. S/RES/2251 (2015); 'UNSC Res. 2287' (2016) UN Doc. S/RES/2287 (2016); 'UNSC Res. 2318' (2016) UN Doc. S/RES/2318 (2016); 'UNSC Res. 2352' (2017) UN Doc. S/RES/2352 (2017); 'UNSC Res. 2386' (2017) UN Doc. S/RES/2386 (2017); 'UNSC Res. 2416' (2018) UN Doc. S/RES/2416 (2018); 'UNSC Res. 2445' (2018) UN Doc. S/RES/2445 (2018); 'UNSC Res. 2497' (2019) UN Doc. S/RES/2497 (2019); 'UNSC Res. 2550' (2020) UN Doc. S/RES/2550 (2020).

135 UNMISS' initial PoC mandate was included in 'UNSC Res. 1996' (2011) UN Doc. S/RES/1996 (2011). Its PoC mandate was renewed and extended several times, but not every mandate contained an explicit reference to PoC. For the resolutions with an explicit PoC mandate, see: 'UNSC Res. 2057' (2012) UN Doc. S/RES/2057 (2012); 'UNSC Res. 2109' (2013) UN Doc. S/RES/2109 (2013); 'UNSC Res. 2155' (2014) UN Doc. S/RES/2155 (2014); 'UNSC Res. 2187' (2014) UN Doc. S/RES/2187 (2014); 'UNSC Res. 2223' (n. 19); 'UNSC Res. 2241' (2015) UN Doc. S/RES/2241 (2015); 'UNSC Res. 2252' (2015) UN Doc. S/RES/2252 (2015). From August 2016 until March 2021, the UN Security Council envisaged that UNMISS could be assisted by the Regional Protection Force. For the initial mandate, see 'UNSC Res. 2304' (2016) UN Doc. S/RES/2304 (2016). Also this PoC mandate was renewed and extended several times, but not every mandate contained an explicit reference to PoC. For the resolutions with an explicit PoC mandate, see 'UNSC Res. 2327' (n. 19); 'UNSC Res. 2406' (n. 19); 'UNSC Res. 2459' (2019) UN Doc. S/RES/2459 (2019). 'UNSC Res. 2514' (2020) UN Doc. S/RES/2514 (2020). From 2021 onwards, the following UNSC resolution provided for an explicit PoC mandate for UNMISS without mentioning the Regional Protection Force: 'UNSC Res. 2567' (2021) UN Doc. S/RES/2567 (2021).

136 UNIFIL's initial PoC mandate was included in 'UNSC Res. 1701' (2006) UN Doc. S/RES/1701 (2006). Its PoC mandate was renewed several times, but not every mandate contained an explicit reference to PoC. For the resolutions with an explicit PoC mandate, see 'UNSC Res. 2373' (2017) UN Doc. S/RES/2373 (2017); 'UNSC Res. 2433' (2018) UN Doc. S/RES/2433 (2018); 'UNSC Res. 2485' (2019) UN Doc. S/RES/2485 (2019); 'UNSC Res. 2539' (2020) UN Doc. S/RES/2539 (2020); 'UNSC Res. 2591' (2021) UN Doc. S/RES/2591 (2021).

137 UNAMID's initial PoC mandate was included in 'UNSC Res. 1769' (n. 133). Its PoC mandate was renewed and extended several times, but not every mandate contained an explicit reference to PoC. For the resolutions with an explicit PoC mandate, see: 'UNSC Res. 1881' (2009) UN Doc. S/RES/1881 (2009); 'UNSC Res. 1935' (2010) UN Doc. S/RES/1935 (2010); 'UNSC Res. 2003' (2011) UN Doc. S/RES/2003 (2011); 'UNSC Res. 2063' (2012) UN Doc. S/RES/2063 (2012); 'UNSC Res. 2113' (2013) UN Doc. S/RES/2113 (2013); 'UNSC Res. 2173' (2014) UN Doc. S/RES/2173 (2014); 'UNSC Res. 2228' (n. 19); 'UNSC Res. 2296' (2016) UN Doc. S/RES/2296 (2016); 'UNSC Res. 2363' (n. 19); 'UNSC Res. 2425' (2018) UN Doc. S/RES/2425 (2018); 'UNSC Res. 2429' (2018) UN Doc. S/RES/2429 (2018); 'UNSC Res. 2495' (2019) UN Doc. S/RES/2495 (2019); 'UNSC Res. 2525' (2020) UN Doc. S/RES/2525 (2020). UNAMID completed its mandate on 31 December 2020 (see 'UNSC Res. 2559' (2020) UN Doc. S/RES/2559 (2020)).

138 MINURCAT's initial PoC mandate was included in 'UNSC Res. 1861' (2009) UN Doc. S/RES/1861 (2009). Its PoC mandate was renewed several times, but none of the resolutions contained an explicit PoC mandate. The mission completed its mandate on 31 December 2010.

139 MINUSMA's initial PoC mandate was included in 'UNSC Res. 2100' (n. 34). Its PoC mandate was renewed and extended in the following resolutions: 'UNSC Res. 2164' (n. 19); 'UNSC Res. 2227' (n. 19); 'UNSC Res. 2295' (n. 34); 'UNSC Res. 2364' (n. 19); 'UNSC Res. 2423' (n. 34); 'UNSC Res. 2480' (2019) UN Doc. S/RES/2480 (2019); 'UNSC Res. 2531' (2020) UN Doc. S/RES/2531 (2020); 'UNSC Res. 2584' (2021) UN Doc. S/RES/2584 (2021).

140 MINUSCA's initial PoC mandate was included in 'UNSC Res. 2149' (n. 19). Its PoC mandate was renewed and extended several times, but not every mandate contained an explicit reference to PoC. For the resolutions with an explicit PoC mandate, see 'UNSC Res. 2217' (2015) UN Doc. S/RES/2217 (2015); 'UNSC Res. 2301' (n. 19); 'UNSC Res. 2387' (n. 19);

In the last decades, the UN Security Council has also provided UN Member States and regional or international organisations other than the UN with an explicit mandate to protect civilians in the territory of a third State. In 2001, the UN Security Council initially provided UN Member States with an authorisation to undertake a PoC mandate in Afghanistan.[141] Two years later, the UN Security Council gave France and the Economic Community of West African States (ECOWAS) – i.e. one of the regional economic communities closely integrated with the AU's work – a mandate to protect civilians in Côte d'Ivoire (whereby the French forces launched Operation Licorne, and ECOWAS established the Economic Community of West African States Peacekeeping Force in Côte d'Ivoire (ECOFORCE, also sometimes referred to as ECOMINCI)).[142]

That same year, the EU was provided with its first PoC mandate. With Resolution 1484 (2003), the UN Security Council authorised the EU to deploy the French-led Interim Emergency Multinational Force (IEMF) (Operation Artemis) in Bunia, the DRC, which had to operate in close coordination with MONUC to contribute, *inter alia*, to the safety of the civilian population.[143] In 2006, the UN Security Council adopted UNSC Resolution 1671 (2006), in which it resolved that the European Union Force in the Democratic Republic of Congo (EUFOR RD Congo) was authorised to take all necessary measures to, *inter alia*, contribute to protecting civilians under imminent threat of physical violence for a period of eight months.[144] The EU also received a PoC mandate to be implemented by the European Union Force in Chad and the Central African Republic (EUFOR Tchad/RCA).[145] In 2014, the EU undertook another military operation in the CAR, called the European Union Force in the Central African Republic (EUFOR RCA), for which it indirectly had a PoC mandate.[146]

'UNSC Res. 2448' (2018) UN Doc. S/RES/2448 (2018); 'UNSC Res. 2499' (2019) UN Doc. S/RES/2499 (2019); 'UNSC Res. 2552' (2020) UN Doc. S/RES/2552 (2020); 'UNSC Res. 2605' (2021) UN Doc. S/RES/2605 (2021).

141 'UNSC Res. 1378' (2001) UN Doc. S/RES/1378 (2001).

142 'UNSC Res. 1464' (2003) UN Doc. S/RES/1464 (2003). Their PoC mandate was renewed twice, but only UNSC Res. 1528 (2004) contained an explicit reference to PoC ('UNSC Res. 1528' (n. 129)). While ECOMINCI was eventually replaced by UNOCI (as discussed above), the French forces continued to receive a mandate to support UNOCI to, *inter alia*, help to protect civilians. That said, not every mandate contained an explicit reference to PoC. Only in the following resolutions an explicit PoC mandate was included: 'UNSC Res. 1609' (n. 129); 'UNSC Res. 1739' (n. 129).

143 'UNSC Res. 1484' (2003) UN Doc. S/RES/1484 (2003).

144 'UNSC Res. 1671' (2006) UN Doc. S/RES/1671 (2006).

145 'UNSC Res. 1778' (2007) UN Doc. S/RES/1778 (2007). The mission's mandate was discussed twice in the UN Security Council, but only UNSC Res. 1861 (2009) contained an explicit reference to PoC ('UNSC Res. 1861' (n. 138)).

146 See 'UNSC Res. 2134' (2014) UN Doc. S/RES/2134 (2014), in which a reference was made to a letter that stated that EUFOR RCA would undertake PoC ('Letter Dated 21 January 2014 from Catherine Ashton, the High Representative for Foreign Affairs and Security Policy of the European Union and Vice-President of the European Commission, as Annexed to the Letter Dated 25 February 2014 from the Secretary-General Addressed to the President of the

In 2007, the AU was also provided with a mandate to protect civilians in Darfur in co-operation with the UN, which resulted in the establishment of the earlier-mentioned UN-AU hybrid operation UNAMID.[147] In 2012, the AU, in conjunction with ECOWAS, organised the African-led International Support Mission to Mali (AFISMA) to support the Malian authorities in their primary responsibility to protect the civilian population.[148] Subsequently, French forces received a mandate to intervene in support of MINUSMA (which had by then replaced AFISMA) when under imminent and serious threat.[149] No explicit PoC mandate was, however, given to the French forces.[150] In 2013, the AU established the African-led International Support Mission to the Central African Republic (MISCA) upon a UNSC mandate to protect civilians.[151] French forces were simultaneously authorised to support MISCA in discharging its mandate.[152] While MISCA was eventually replaced by MINUSCA (a UN peace operation, as referred to above),[153] the French forces continued to receive a mandate to support MINUSCA in its tasks (which included PoC), yet again no explicit reference was made to PoC.[154]

Last but not least, in 2011, the UN Security Council adopted Resolution 1973 (2011), authorising Member States, acting nationally or through regional

---

Security Council' (2014) UN Doc. S/2014/45 2). See also Council of the EU, 'Council Decision 2014/73/CFSP of 10 February 2014 on a European Union Military Operation in the Central African Republic (EUFOR RCA)' (2014) OJ L 40/59; Council of the EU, 'Council Decision 2014/183/CFSP of 1 April 2014 on the Launch of a European Union Military Operation in the Central African Republic (EUFOR RCA)' (2014) OJ L 100/12; Council of the EU, 'Council Decision 2014/775/CFSP of 7 November 2014 Extending Decision 2014/73/CFSP on a European Union Military Operation in the Central African Republic (EUFOR RCA)' (2014) OJ L 325/17.

147 UNAMID's initial PoC mandate was included in 'UNSC Res. 1769' (n. 133). As discussed above, its PoC mandate was renewed and extended several times, but not every mandate contained an explicit reference to PoC. For the resolutions with an explicit PoC mandate, see: 'UNSC Res. 1881' (n. 137); 'UNSC Res. 1935' (n. 137); 'UNSC Res. 2003' (n. 137); 'UNSC Res. 2063' (n. 137); 'UNSC Res. 2113' (n. 137); 'UNSC Res. 2173' (n. 137); 'UNSC Res. 2228' (n. 19); 'UNSC Res. 2296' (n. 137); 'UNSC Res. 2363' (n. 19); 'UNSC Res. 2425' (n. 137); 'UNSC Res. 2429' (n. 137); 'UNSC Res. 2479' (2019) UN Doc. S/RES/2479 (2019); 'UNSC Res. 2495' (n. 137); 'UNSC Res. 2525' (n. 137). UNAMID completed its mandate on 31 December 2020 (see 'UNSC Res. 2559' (n. 137)).

148 AFISMA's PoC mandate was included in 'UNSC Res. 2085' (2012) UN Doc. S/RES/2085 (2012). AFISMA was replaced by MINUSMA (see 'UNSC Res. 2100' (n. 34)) (as discussed above).

149 See 'UNSC Res. 2100' (n. 34).

150 See e.g. 'UNSC Res. 2164' (n. 19); 'UNSC Res. 2227' (n. 19); 'UNSC Res. 2295' (n. 34); 'UNSC Res. 2364' (n. 19); 'UNSC Res. 2423' (n. 34); 'UNSC Res. 2480' (n. 139); 'UNSC Res. 2531' (n. 139); 'UNSC Res. 2584' (n. 139).

151 'UNSC Res. 2127' (2013) UN Doc. S/RES/2127 (2013).

152 *Ibid.* para. 50.

153 'UNSC Res. 2149' (n. 19).

154 See e.g. *ibid.*; 'UNSC Res. 2217' (n. 140); 'UNSC Res. 2301' (n. 19); 'UNSC Res. 2387' (n. 19); 'UNSC Res. 2448' (n. 140); 'UNSC Res. 2499' (n. 140).

organisations or arrangements, to carry out a PoC mandate in Libya.[155] Two days after the adoption of the resolution, France was the first Member State to carry out air strikes against the al-Qadhafi forces. The US, the United Kingdom (UK), and Canada soon came to assistance. Under the leadership of the US, an international western coalition was established to end the violence against Libyan civilians. Operation Odyssey Dawn provided support to the rebels from the air by eliminating the air defence of al-Qadhafi to a considerable extent. On 31 March 2011, a NATO coalition consisting of eighteen States was established to enforce the military aspects of UNSC Resolution 1973 (2011).[156] This resulted in Operation Unified Protector, which only ended on 31 October 2011, eleven days after the death of al-Qadhafi.[157]

These different operations have shaped the concept of PoC as a mandated task in the context of UN (mandated) peace operations. To better grasp PoC and particularly to better understand how this concept is approached by the different organisations involved in implementing PoC mandates, Section 2 scrutinises the PoC policies of the UN, the AU, NATO, and the EU. Section 2.1 first looks at the institutionalisation of PoC at the UN and the current UN concept of PoC. Section 2.2 subsequently discusses the policies of the AU, NATO, and the EU, as developed in more recent decades. Hereafter, Section 3 details the different organisational approaches to the use of force for PoC, including those of the UN (Section 3.1), as well as the AU, NATO, and the EU (Section 3.2). Next. Section 4 introduces the legal framework that governs the use of force to protect civilians within the context of UN (mandated) peace operations. Hereto, Section 4.1 distinguishes between the rules that may serve as a legal basis for the establishment, deployment, and functioning of UN (mandated) peace operations and the rules that may govern the conduct of UN (mandated) peace operations. Section 4.2 then introduces how the mission-specific legal bases and legal regimes might relate to each other. In so doing, Section 4.2 lays the foundations for Parts II and III. Finally, Section 5 provides a summary of Part I.

2. CONCEPT OF POC AS A MANDATED TASK BY THE UN SECURITY COUNCIL

Civilian protection, alternatively described as a moral or legal obligation, the pinnacle of humanitarian and development activities, and a mandated task by

155 'UNSC Res. 1973' (n. 62).

156 'NATO Secretary General Statement on NAC Decision to Extend Libya Mission' (*NATO*, 21 September 2011), www.nato.int/cps/en/natohq/news_78355.htm, accessed 14 April 2022. (There seems to be no public statement on the decision of the NAC to launch Operation Unified Protector).

157 NAC, 'North Atlantic Council Statement on Libya' (*NATO*, 21 October 2011), www.nato.int/cps/en/natohq/news_79800.htm?selectedLocale=en, accessed 14 April 2022.

the UN Security Council, has become a major focus of international and regional organisations, governments, and civil society.[158] What 'protection of civilians' means depends on the context in which it is used. For example, the protected status of civilians under IHL includes the obligation not to carry out direct attacks against civilians, as well as to spare civilians in the conduct of hostilities and to take all necessary precautions to meet this obligation. Conversely, when one speaks of the 'protection of civilians' as part of an obligation of the international community to protect (RtoP), this refers to the fact that when a State is unwilling or unable to protect its population from mass atrocities, the international community has a responsibility to do so, as a last resort, through military intervention.

There are various concepts that, in one way or another, have the protection of civilians as their objective. These are undeniably interlinked but remain separate concepts with different meanings and motivations.[159] When discussing the research delimitations, it was explained that this book is only concerned with the concept of PoC in the context of UN (mandated) peace operations and thus with PoC as a mandated task by the UN Security Council and not with, for example, the concepts of RtoP, RwP, or unilateral humanitarian intervention. The protected status of civilians under IHL is discussed in Part III when examining the rules regulating the use of force for protective purposes with a clear nexus to an armed conflict.

The following Section examines the concept of PoC as a mandated task by the UN Security Council and how this concept has been shaped through policy documents issued by the UN, the AU, NATO, and the EU.

2.1. INSTITUTIONALISATION OF POC AT THE UN

2.1.1. The impetus for adopting PoC mandates

For over thirty years, the UN Security Council implicitly included promoting civilian protection in the mandates issued to UN (mandated) peace operations,[160] but until 1999 the UN Security Council never identified 'protection of civilians' as a separate issue.[161] In 1999, the UN Security Council changed course due to a concurrence of circumstances.

158 Haidi Willmot and others, 'Introduction' in Haidi Willmot and others (eds), *Protection of Civilians* (1st edn., Oxford University Press 2016) 1.

159 Sheeran and Kent (n. 50) 29.

160 See e.g. 'UNSC Res. 161' (n. 3) para. 1; 'UNSC Res. 794' (n. 3) para. 10; 'UNSC Res. 836' (n. 3) paras 5 and 9; 'UNSC Res. 912' (n. 3) para. 8; 'UNSC Res. 918' (n. 3) paras 3 and 4; 'UNSC Res. 925' (n. 3) para. 4; 'UNSC Res. 929' (n. 3) paras 2 and 3; 'UNSC Res. 940' (n. 3) paras 4, 9, and 16; 'UNSC Res. 1031' (n. 3) paras 15 and Annex 1A, Art. VI; 'UNSC Res. 1159' (n. 3) para. 10; 'UNSC Res. 1244' (n. 3) para. 9; 'UNSC Res. 1272' (n. 3) para. 2.

161 Shesterinina and Job (n. 36) 242; James Sloan, *The Militarisation of Peacekeeping in the Twenty-First Century* (Hart Publishing 2011) 37.

In the first place, the UN lost much of its credibility after failing to protect civilians from mass atrocities and genocide in Srebrenica and Rwanda. Two ill-prepared UN peace operations, UNPROFOR and UNAMIR (i.e. the United Nations Assistance Mission for Rwanda), failed to protect the very population they were supposed to protect and collapsed, after which conflict reignited, and the consent of the parties to the deployment of the mission was withdrawn.[162] In a critical study on Srebrenica, the UN Secretary-General held the following:[163]

> The cardinal lesson of Srebrenica is that a deliberate and systematic attempt to terrorize, expel or murder an entire people must be met decisively with all necessary means, and with the political will to carry the policy through to its logical conclusion. In the Balkans, in this decade, this lesson has had to be learned not once, but twice. In both instances, in Bosnia and Kosovo, the international community tried to reach a negotiated settlement with an unscrupulous and murderous regime. In both instances it required the use of force to bring a halt to the planned and systematic killing and expulsion of civilians.

One month later, a report of the Independent Inquiry into the actions of the UN during the 1994 genocide in Rwanda was issued.[164] The Inquiry found that while UNAMIR had begun as a traditional peacekeeping operation tasked with overseeing the implementation of an existing peace agreement, the 'onslaught of the genocide' should have led the UN to realise that UNAMIR's original mandate, along with its neutral mediating role, was no longer adequate to protect innocent civilians from massacre.[165] Instead, a more 'assertive response, combined with the means necessary' would have been warranted.[166] After all, the UN should be aware of, and be prepared to respond to, 'the perception and the expectation of protection created by its very presence.'[167]

In January 1997, Kofi Annan was appointed as UN Secretary-General after serving as UN Assistant Secretary-General for Peacekeeping Operations from March 1992 to February 1993 and as UN Under-Secretary-General for Peace Operations from March 1993 to December 1996. He would take on a vision of the UN's obligations and role in UN peace operations far more comprehensive than that of his predecessors.[168] According to Findlay, this was partly driven by

---

162 Victoria Holt and Glyn Taylor, *Protecting Civilians in the Context of UN Peacekeeping Operations Successes, Setbacks and Remaining Challenges, Independent Study Jointly Commissioned by the United Nations Department of Peacekeeping Operations and the United Nations Office for the Coordination of Humanitarian Affairs* (UN 2009) 35.

163 UNSG, 'Report of the Secretary-General Pursuant to General Assembly Resolution 53/35: The Fall of Srebrenica' (n. 5) para. 502.

164 'Report of the Independent Inquiry into the Actions of the United Nations during the 1994 Genocide in Rwanda' (n. 110).

165 *Ibid.* 50–51.

166 *Ibid.* 51.

167 *Ibid.*

168 Kofi Annan's new policy on PoC first became apparent in the following report in which he declared that PoC in situations of armed conflict is a 'humanitarian imperative': UNSG,

the fact that as UN Under-Secretary-General for Peace Operations, Annan bore some responsibility for the inadequate management of the UN peace operations in Srebrenica and Rwanda, which, in Annan's own view, had so affected the UN's credibility and moral standing.[169] This led both the UN Secretary-General and others within the UN to look for alternative ways to achieve the effective protection of civilians.[170]

In January 1999, the then-UN Under-Secretary-General for Humanitarian Affairs gave a crucial briefing on humanitarian assistance in which he stressed that the UN Security Council is charged with ensuring respect for HRL and IHL.[171] In February of the same year, the UN Security Council held its first debates on PoC in armed conflict.[172] The UN Security Council expressed concern about the ongoing targeted attacks against civilians and humanitarian aid workers in flagrant violation of HRL and IHL.[173] As a result, the UN Security Council requested the UN Secretary-General to submit a report with recommendations on how the UN Security Council 'could improve the physical and legal protection of civilians in situations of armed conflict.'[174] Following the open briefing, the UN Security Council issued a presidential statement on the topic, in which it held the following:[175]

> Bearing in mind its primary responsibility for the maintenance of international peace and security, the Council affirms the need for the international community to assist and protect civilian populations affected by armed conflict. [...] The Security Council strongly condemns the deliberate targeting by combatants of civilians in armed conflict and demands that all concerned put an end to such violations of international

---

'The Causes of Conflict and the Promotion of Durable Peace and Sustainable Development in Africa, Report of the Secretary-General, General Assembly: Fifty-Second Session, Agenda Item 10; Security Council: Fifty-Third Year' (1998) UN Doc. A/52/871 and S/1998/318 paras 49–52. See also UNGA, 'In Larger Freedom: Towards Development, Security and Human Rights for All, Report of the Secretary-General, Integrated and Coordinated Implementation of and Follow-up to the Outcomes of the Major United Nations Conferences and Summits in the Economic, Social and Related Fields, Follow-up to the Outcome of the Millennium Summit, Fifty-Ninth Session, Agenda Items 45 and 55' (2005) UN Doc. A/59/2005. For references to other reports demonstrating his vision, see below. See also Trevor Findlay, *The Use of Force in UN Peace Operations* (SIPRI ; Oxford University Press 2002) 326. For an insightful analysis of Annan's Secretary-Generalship, see James Sloan, 'UN Peacekeeping under Kofi Annan: Recourse to Force' (2008) 12 Journal of International Peacekeeping 51.

169 Findlay (n. 168) 326.

170 As discussed hereinafter.

171 UNSC, '3968th Meeting (on Promoting Peace and Security: Humanitarian Activities Relevant to the Security Council)' (1999) UN Doc. S/PV.3968 3.

172 UNSC, '3977th Meeting (on the Protection of Civilians in Armed Conflict)' (1999) UN Doc. S/PV.3977; UNSC, '3978th Meeting (on the Protection of Civilians in Armed Conflict)' (1999) UN Doc. S/PV.3978.

173 UNSC, '3978th Meeting (on the Protection of Civilians in Armed Conflict)' (n. 172) 2.

174 *Ibid.* 3.

175 Emphasis added. UNSC, 'Statement by the President of the Security Council' (1999) UN Doc. S/PRST/1999/6 1–2.

> humanitarian and human rights law. *The Council expresses its willingness to respond*, in accordance with the Charter [...], *to situations in which civilians, as such, have been targeted or humanitarian assistance to civilians has been deliberately obstructed.*

At the end of the month, the UN Security Council held another formal meeting on PoC, whereby it also provided non-members of the UN Security Council with an opportunity to address the issues raised by experts during previous briefings and meetings.[176] More than 20 non-Member States participated in the discussion, demonstrating a growing awareness of the need to place PoC in armed conflict high on the international political agenda and reinvigorate international efforts in this regard.[177]

Even before these words could be translated into action, NATO, however, launched an air campaign in Kosovo in March 1999 to protect the ethnic Albanian minority. The campaign was initiated after the UN Security Council could not agree to undertake strong action to halt the humanitarian catastrophe.[178] Shortly after this NATO intervention – to which the UN Security Council did not give its prior approval – UN Secretary-General Kofi Annan called on the international community to 'find common ground in upholding the principles of the Charter, and acting in defence of our common humanity.'[179] His call was followed up by the Canadian government announcing the establishment of ICISS, which in its turn adopted the influential report on RtoP.[180] The central idea of this report was that 'sovereign states have a responsibility to protect their own citizens from avoidable catastrophe – from mass murder and rape, from starvation – but that when they are unwilling or unable to do so, that responsibility must be borne by the broader community of states.'[181]

While the UN did not want to assume an *obligation* to act to protect civilians, the UN did continue its work on (the less ambitious) PoC with a renewed sense of urgency (for a brief overview of the distinction between RtoP and PoC, see Introductory Chapter, Section 3.1).[182] In September 1999, the UN Secretary-General issued a first report detailing recommendations on how the

176 UNSC, '3980th Meeting (on the Protection of Civilians in Armed Conflict)' (1999) UN Doc. S/PV.3980; UNSC, '3980th Meeting (on the Protection of Civilians in Armed Conflict) (Resumption 1)' (1999) UN Doc. S/PV.3980 (Resumption 1).

177 For a list of participants, see UNSC, '3980th Meeting (on the Protection of Civilians in Armed Conflict)' (n. 176) 2.

178 Sloan (n. 161) 37.

179 UNSG, 'Secretary-General Presents His Annual Report to General Assembly' (1999) UN Doc. SG/SM/7136 and GA/9596, www.un.org/press/en/1999/19990920.sgsm7136.html, accessed 11 February 2021.

180 ICISS (n. 113) 2.

181 *Ibid.* VIII.

182 Haidi Willmot, 'The Evolution of the UN Collective Security System' in Haidi Willmot and others (eds), *Protection of Civilians* (1st edn., Oxford University Press 2016) 128.

UN Security Council could improve PoC.[183] Later that month, the UN Security Council adopted the first in a series of thematic resolutions on the Protection of Civilians in Armed Conflict. In Resolution 1265 (1999), the UN Security Council noted that it was 'gravely concerned by the hardship borne by civilians during armed conflict'[184] and expressed its willingness to consider how mandates should be adapted to better respond to the negative impact of armed conflicts on civilians.[185] In an independent study on PoC in the context of UN peace operations, jointly commissioned by the former UN DPKO and UN OCHA, Holt and Taylor nevertheless referred to an official's suggestion that the UN Security Council 'didn't totally understand' the content of UN Secretary-General's report.[186] A view which was apparently also shared by others.[187]

2.1.2. *The first PoC mandate*

On 22 October 1999, the UN Security Council introduced PoC for the first time as an explicitly mandated task for a peace operation while acting under Chapter VII of the UN Charter. UNSC Resolution 1270 (1999) held that UNAMSIL 'may take the necessary action to ensure the security and freedom of movement of its personnel and, within its capabilities and areas of deployment, to afford protection to civilians under imminent threat of physical violence.'[188] In the debate prior to the adoption, the representative of Sierra Leone Ambassador Ibrahim Kamara emphasised the importance of this paragraph and held that:[189]

> [W]hatever interpretation others may give to this particular paragraph, we regard it as an insurance policy for both international peacekeepers and innocent civilians. We also believe that it sends a clear message to any potential violator of human rights on a gross scale: the international community will not turn a blind eye if and when innocent civilians are under threat of physical violence.

Subsequently, the Members of the UN Security Council debated the implications of the chosen wording in the mandate (being that UNAMSIL 'may take the necessary action to ensure the security and freedom of movement of its personnel and, within its capabilities and areas of deployment, to afford protection to civilians under imminent threat of physical violence').[190] It was undisputed that this formulation constituted an explicit instruction for the

183 UNSG, 'Report of the Secretary-General to the Security Council on the Protection of Civilians in Armed Conflict' (1999) UN Doc. S/1999/957.
184 'UNSC Res. 1265' (1999) UN Doc. S/RES/1265 (1999) pream. para. 5.
185 *Ibid.* para. 11.
186 Holt and Taylor (n. 162) 53.
187 *Ibid.*
188 'UNSC Res. 1270' (n. 7) para. 14.
189 UNSC, '4054th Meeting (at Which UNSC Res 1270 (1999) Was Adopted)' (n. 6) 6.
190 'UNSC Res. 1270' (n. 7) para. 14.

mission not to be indifferent to indiscriminate attacks on the civilian population but instead to take decisive and immediate action if large-scale violence threatened civilians, including through the robust use of force.[191] This paragraph was also not discussed in a vacuum but rather from multiple perspectives whereby the Members observed the ability of the mission to operate effectively, the need for significant levels of military personnel, the adoption of robust ROE, the relationship with the host State, and the consequences of adopting such a PoC mandate for future UN peace operations.[192] Malaysia, France, Gambia, the Netherlands, and Canada, for example, strongly supported deploying a force of credible strength under Chapter VII of the UN Charter, equipped with strong ROE.[193]

In their speeches, the Members of the UN Security Council also reflected on the dire humanitarian situation and the brutal violence suffered by civilians after being briefed by the Special Representative for Children and Armed Conflict Olara Otunnu.[194] In his speech, Otunnu made the Members of the UN Security Council aware of the differences in attitude and response of the international community regarding the situation in Kosovo and Sierra Leone and, in particular, the support and protection granted to children.[195] The UN Security Council did not hesitate to openly discuss the failures of the previous missions, which had not been provided with a robust mandate under Chapter VII of the UN Charter.[196]

UNSC Resolution 1270 (1999) was finally adopted with all fifteen votes in favour, illustrating the broad support for what was, at the time, considered a

191 UNSC, '4054th Meeting (at Which UNSC Res 1270 (1999) Was Adopted)' (n. 6) 16–17.

192 UNSC, '4054th Meeting (at Which UNSC Res 1270 (1999) Was Adopted)' (n. 6) (Malaysia held, e.g., that '[t]he success of UNAMSIL may well have a bearing on future peacekeeping missions that the United Nations is planning in respect of other conflict areas in Africa. For this reason it is important for UNAMSIL to be given the tools to ensure that it has a fair chance of carrying out its mission successfully,' see p. 11). See also discussion by Holt and Taylor (n. 162) 36.

193 UNSC, '4054th Meeting (at Which UNSC Res 1270 (1999) Was Adopted)' (n. 6) 10, 12–13, 17.

194 The delegation of Brazil, e.g. expressed its shock at the figures given by the figures and facts to which Mr. Otunnu had referred on the magnitude of the violence and internal displacement affecting the lives of children in Sierra Leone. They noted that '[t]he expression he used – "diabolical atrocities" – is [a] sad testimony to the levels of irrationality and violence human nature sometimes reaches. Mr. Otunnu has again voiced an eloquent and compelling warning to us. We think that the core of his message is quite simple: The international community has to pay persistent and consistent attention to the plight of children in all parts of the world, without exception or discrimination.' (*ibid.* 15). See also discussion by Holt and Taylor (n. 162) 35.

195 UNSC, '4054th Meeting (at Which UNSC Res 1270 (1999) Was Adopted)' (n. 6) 4.

196 *Ibid.* 16 (Argentina argued, e.g. that they believe that the adoption of this draft resolution 'bears on the credibility of the Security Council and shows that the Council has learned from its own experience and that it will not remain indifferent to indiscriminate attacks against the civilian population'). See also discussion by Holt and Taylor (n. 162) 35–36.

major policy development within the UN.[197] Or, in the words of the Argentinian representative at the time, Ambassador Fernando Petrella:[198]

> We believe that the protection of civilians under Chapter VII is a pertinent development in the context of the mandate of a peacekeeping operation. This draft resolution is significant in that it introduces a new, fundamental political, legal and moral dimension. This bears on the credibility of the Security Council and shows that the Council has learned from its own experience and that it will not remain indifferent to indiscriminate attacks against the civilian population.

As Foley aptly pointed out, while the UN Security Council was aware of the importance of the PoC tasks that it had included in UNAMSIL's mandate, it does not appear to have considered this task within the mission as an important separate task at the operational or tactical level.[199] From the wording of the mission reports to the UN Security Council, it can be inferred that it was believed that civilian protection would be achieved through the success of the overall mission objectives.[200]

2.1.3. Development of the PoC concept in the context of UN peace operations

In 2000, the UN Security Council adopted thematic Resolution 1296 (2000) on PoC, in which it noted that deliberately attacking the civilian population or other protected persons and committing 'systematic, flagrant, and widespread violations' of IHL and HRL in situations of armed conflict may 'constitute a threat to international peace and security.'[201] In this respect, the UN Security Council reaffirmed its willingness to consider such situations and to take appropriate action where necessary, including by giving UN peace operations appropriate mandates and adequate resources to protect civilians under imminent threat of physical violence.[202] This thematic resolution greatly impacted the mandates of UN peace operations. In a later report, the UN Secretary-General referred to UNSC Resolution 1296 (2000) as the basis upon which the mandates of UN peace operations have been expanded to allow

---

197 Conor Foley, 'Defining Protection of Civilians in the Context of Armed Conflict' in Dan Kuwali and Frans Viljoen (eds), *By All Means Necessary: Protecting Civilians and Preventing Mass Atrocities in Africa* (Pretoria University Law Press 2017) 45.

198 UNSC, '4054th Meeting (at Which UNSC Res 1270 (1999) Was Adopted)' (n. 6) 16.

199 Foley, *UN Peacekeeping Operations and the Protection of Civilians: Saving Succeeding Generations* (n. 16) 116.

200 See e.g. UNSG, 'First Report of the Secretary-General on the United Nations Mission in Sierra Leone' (1999) UN Doc. S/1999/ 1223; UNSG, 'Ninth Report of the Secretary-General on the United Nations Mission in Sierra Leone' (2001) UN Doc. S/2001/ 228, as also referred to by Foley, *UN Peacekeeping Operations and the Protection of Civilians: Saving Succeeding Generations* (n. 16) 116.

201 'UNSC Res. 1296' (2000) UN Doc. S/RES/1296 (2000) para. 5.

202 *Ibid.* paras 5 and 13.

UN peace forces to physically protect civilians under imminent threat of violence.[203]

In March 2000, UN Secretary-General Kofi Annan established the Panel on United Nations Peace Operations and tasked it with preparing a report on past UN peace and security activities and recommendations on how the UN could carry out such activities more effectively in the future.[204] The Panel's report, also known as the 2000 Brahimi Report, named after the Chair of the Panel, was issued on 21 August 2000.[205] The Report called for renewed political support from Member States, substantial institutional changes within the UN, and increased financial support.[206] Concerning the role of UN peace forces in PoC, the Panel held that:[207]

> [P]eacekeepers – troops or police – who witness violence against civilians *should be presumed to be authorized* to stop it, within their means, in support of basic United Nations principles and, as stated in the report of the Independent Inquiry on Rwanda, consistent with 'the perception and the expectation of protection created by [an operation's] very presence' (see S/1999/1257, p. 51).

Nevertheless, the Panel also expressed concern about the credibility and achievability of a blanket PoC mandate.[208] UN peace operations cannot protect the hundreds of thousands of civilians that find themselves in areas where the missions are active, even though they are exposed to potential risks of violence.[209] To avoid a mismatch between the desired objective of effectively protecting civilians and the resources available to the peace forces, the Panel suggested that UN peace operations should be provided with adequate resources to carry out their mandates.[210] The 2000 Brahimi Report (in particular, the manner in which it approached the fundamental principles of peacekeeping) was not welcomed by all.[211] Some Members of the UN General Assembly perceived it as an interference in their sovereignty and were hesitant to endorse the report's content.[212]

---

203 UNSG, 'Report of the Secretary-General to the Security Council on the Protection of Civilians in Armed Conflict' (2004) UN Doc. S/2004/431 para. 8. See also Sloan (n. 161) 8.

204 UNSG and UNSC, 'Identical Letters Dated 21 August 2000 from the Secretary-General to the President of the General Assembly and the President of the Security Council, Fifty-Fifth Session of the General Assembly, Item 87 of the Provisional Agenda; Fifty-Fifth Year of the Security Council' (2000) A/55/305-S/2000/809 i.

205 'Report of the Panel on United Nations Peace Operations (Brahimi Report), Fifty-Fifth Session of the General Assembly, Item 87 of the Provisional Agenda; Fifty-Fifth Year of the Security Council' (n. 19).

206 *Ibid.* para. 1.

207 Emphasis added. *Ibid.* para. 62.

208 *Ibid.* para. 63.

209 *Ibid.*

210 *Ibid.*

211 As discussed by Sloan (n. 161) 41–42.

212 *Ibid.* 41.

In the following period, the UN Security Council continued steering the development of the PoC concept, *inter alia*, by supporting three initiatives at the 'thematic level' aimed at moving the debate from 'abstract principles into more practical measures': (i) the development of a 'roadmap' outlining the responsibilities of various organs' bodies;[213] (ii) the drafting of a first UN Aide-Memoire on PoC to assist the UN Security Council in its deliberation of peacekeeping mandates;[214] and (iii) a call for better coordination between the former UN DPKO and UN OCHA.[215]

Nevertheless, the UN Security Council's involvement in PoC declined partly due to the impasse following the US-led invasion of Iraq in 2003.[216] This impasse was further exacerbated by negative media coverage of the UN's failure to act to protect civilians in Somalia, Sudan, Colombia, and northern Uganda, despite the UN's overall commitment to PoC.[217] And even when the UN Security Council adopted ambitious PoC mandates, this resulted in far too little effective protection of civilians. By that time, the UN Security Council had increasingly provided UN (mandated) peace operations with PoC mandates, allowing peace forces to protect civilians against the imminent threat of physical violence. For example, between 1999 and 2005, UN peace operations in the DRC (MONUC), Liberia (UNMIL), Côte d'Ivoire (UNOCI), Haiti (MINUSTAH), Burundi (ONUB), and Sudan (UNMIS), as well as a UN-mandated peace operation in Afghanistan (carried out by UN Member States), Côte d'Ivoire (carried out by ECOWAS and France), and Bunia, the DRC (carried out by the EU), were provided with a PoC mandate.[218] These mandates usually provided a range of mission objectives, including enhancing civilians' security, supporting human rights, maintaining public order and security, and providing a stable environment. Yet, due to a lack of adequate operational guidelines for implementation, PoC mandates were the subject of widely varying interpretations, resulting in civilians not being adequately protected. These failures led to international debates on PoC slipping into discussions of overarching normative dilemmas related to the concept of RtoP.[219]

With Resolution 1674 (2006), the UN Security Council reinforced the normative and operational framework for action concerning PoC. It did so by,

213 UNSG, 'Report of the Secretary-General on the Protection of Civilians in Armed Conflict' (2002) UN Doc. S/2002/1300, Annex: Roadmap for the protection of civilians.

214 UNSC, 'Aide-Memoire on the Protection of Civilians in Armed Conflict, Annexed to the Statement by the President of the Security Council' (2002) UN Doc. S/PRST/2002/6.

215 Security Council Report, 'Cross-Cutting Report 2008 No. 2: Protection of Civilians' (2008) 8, www.securitycouncilreport.org/research-reports/lookup_c_glkwlemtisg_b_7566867.php, accessed 25 February 2019.

216 *Ibid.*

217 *Ibid.*

218 For detailed references to the PoC mandates of those missions, see Part I, Section 1.

219 Haidi Willmot and Scott Sheeran, 'The Protection of Civilians Mandate in UN Peacekeeping Operations: Reconciling Protection Concepts and Practices' (2013) 95 International Review of the Red Cross 517, 522.

inter alia, developing a framework for action that foresees the incorporation in the mandates of UN peace operations, where appropriate and on a case-by-case basis, of provisions for (i) the protection of civilians under imminent threat of physical danger; (ii) the facilitation of the delivery of humanitarian assistance; and (iii) the creation of conditions that facilitate the voluntary and safe return of refugees and internally displaced persons (i.e. persons that have fled their homes and cannot return (IDPs)).[220] The UN Security Council also expressed its commitment to ensuring that: (i) PoC mandates contain clear guidance on what missions can and should do to attain those goals; (ii) PoC is prioritised in decisions about the use of available capacity and resources in implementing the mandates; and (iii) PoC mandates are effectively implemented.[221] Last but not least, the UN Security Council also recognised the critical role that regional organisations and other intergovernmental institutions play with respect to PoC.[222]

The focus on PoC in the context of UN peace operations returned.[223] After MONUC repeatedly failed to protect civilians in the DRC and, in particular, failed to prevent the killings in Kiwanja in November 2008,[224] the UN Security Council made PoC a priority of this mission's mandate and other UN peace operations. In 2009, the UN Security Council also established MINURCAT, providing it with an explicit PoC mandate, yet without making PoC a priority.[225] That same year, the UN Security Council also established an Informal Expert Group on the Protection of Civilians to consider a wide range of issues pertaining to PoC based on briefings from UN OCHA and other UN entities.[226] Furthermore, the UN Security Council adopted an updated UN Aide-Memoire on PoC to reflect emerging trends in that area.[227] The Special Committee on Peacekeeping Operations, known as the C34, also started entering references to PoC as a mandated task into its reports.[228]

---

220 'UNSC Res. 1674' (n. 54) para. 16.

221 *Ibid.*

222 *Ibid.* para. 24.

223 Willmot (n. 182) 131.

224 Human Rights Watch, 'Killings in Kiwanja: The UN's Inability to Protect Civilians' (Human Rights Watch 2008) 22–27.

225 'UNSC Res. 1861' (n. 138).

226 Security Council Report, 'In Hindsight: The Informal Expert Group on the Protection of Civilians' (*Security Council Report*, August 2016), www.securitycouncilreport.org/monthly-forecast/2016-08/in_hindsight_the_informal_expert_group_on_the_protection_of_civilians.php, accessed 11 February 2021.

227 UNSC, 'Aide-Memoire on the Protection of Civilians in Armed Conflict, Annexed to the Statement by the President of the Security Council' (2009) UN Doc. S/PRST/2009/1. In 2018, the UN Security Council adopted the latest version of the Aide Mémoire on PoC, see UNSC, 'Aide-Memoire on the Protection of Civilians in Armed Conflict, Annexed to the Statement by the President of the Security Council' (2018) UN Doc. S/PRST/2018/18.

228 UNGA, 'Report of the Special Committee on Peacekeeping Operations, 2009 Substantive Session (23 February–20 March 2009), Sixty-Third Session, Supplement No. 19' UN Doc. A/63/19 paras 125–128. See also subsequent reports of the C34: UNGA, 'Report of the Special

That same year, the UN Secretary-General emphasised the remaining disconnect between 'mandates, intentions, expectations, interpretations, and real implementation capacity.'[229] He highlighted that PoC mandates in the context of UN peace operations remain 'largely undefined as both a military task and a mission-wide task.'[230] Although those at the strategic military level and operational level must have the freedom to interpret the PoC mandate in light of the given circumstances, such interpretation and implementation should occur within a broader policy framework that offers clear guidance on possible actions, as well as indicative tasks and the capabilities necessary to implement them.[231] Moreover, the UN Secretary-General emphasised the importance of ensuring that the capacity and resources available to operations are not only adequate to fulfil their mandate but also delivered to them in a timely fashion.[232]

With Resolution 1894 (2009), the UN Security Council requested the development of comprehensive operational guidance on UN peace operations' tasks and responsibilities in implementing PoC mandates.[233] The UN Security Council also requested the conduct of mission-wide planning, pre-deployment training, and senior leadership training on PoC, the use of benchmarks and indicators to measure and review progress in the implementation of

---

Committee on Peacekeeping Operations, 2010 Substantive Session (22 February–19 March 2010), Sixty-Fourth Session, Supplement No. 19' UN Doc. A/64/19 paras 143–151; UNGA, 'Report of the Special Committee on Peacekeeping Operations, 2011 Substantive Session (New York, 22 February–18 March and 9 May 2011), Sixty-Fifth Session, Supplement No. 19' UN Doc. A/65/19 paras 172–183; UNGA, 'Report of the Special Committee on Peacekeeping Operations, 2012 Substantive Session (New York, 21 February–16 March and 11 September 2012), Sixty-Sixth Session, Supplement No. 19' UN Doc. A/66/19 paras 191–205; UNGA, 'Report of the Special Committee on Peacekeeping Operations, 2014 Substantive Session (New York, 24 February–21 March 2014), Sixty-Eight Session, Supplement No. 19' UN Doc. A/68/19 paras 212–226; UNGA, 'Report of the Special Committee on Peacekeeping Operations, 2015 Substantive Session (New York, 17 February–13 March 2015), Sixty-Ninth Session, Supplement No. 19' UN Doc. A/69/19 paras 218–233; UNGA, 'Report of the Special Committee on Peacekeeping Operations, 2016 Substantive Session (New York, 16 February–11 March 2016), Seventieth Session, Supplement No. 19' UN Doc. A/70/19 paras 242–262; UNGA, 'Report of the Special Committee on Peacekeeping Operations, 2017 Substantive Session (New York, 21 February–17 March 2017), Seventy-First Session, Supplement No. 19' UN Doc. A/71/19 paras 282–302; UNGA, 'Report of the Special Committee on Peacekeeping Operations, 2018 Substantive Session (New York, 12 February–9 March 2018), Sixty-Second Session, Supplement No. 19' UN Doc. A/72/19 paras 293–321; UNGA, 'Report of the Special Committee on Peacekeeping Operations, 2020 Substantive Session (New York, 17 February–12 March 2020), Seventy-Fourth Session, Supplement No. 19' UN Doc. A/74/19 paras 116–135; UNGA, 'Report of the Special Committee on Peacekeeping Operations, 2021 Substantive Session (New York, 15 February–12 March 2021), Seventy-Fifth Session, Supplement No. 19' UN Doc. A/75/19 paras 128–150.

229 UNSC, 'Report of the Secretary-General on the Protection of Civilians in Armed Conflict' (2009) UN Doc. S/2009/277 para. 51.

230 *Ibid.* para. 52.

231 *Ibid.*

232 *Ibid.* para. 54.

233 'UNSC Res. 1894' (2009) UN Doc. S/RES/1894 (2009) para. 22.

peacekeeping mandates (especially PoC), and country-specific reporting on PoC.[234]

Accordingly, in 2010, the former UN DPKO and DFS developed the 2010 UN Draft Operational Concept on PoC in UN Peacekeeping Operations, in which they proposed a novel, three-tiered approach to PoC in the context of UN peace operations: Tier I – Protection through political process; Tier II – Providing protection from physical violence; and Tier III – Establishing a protective environment.[235] This new approach fundamentally changed how the UN approached PoC in the context of UN peace operations. Whereas PoC was initially considered to be the responsibility of the military component only, implemented through presence and deterrence, PoC was now considered a mission-wide task whereby different actors have distinct roles and responsibilities in providing protection.[236] Following the adoption of UNSC Resolution 1894 (2009) and the issuance of the 2010 Operational Concept on PoC in UN Peacekeeping Operations, PoC mandates of UN peace operations became increasingly broader in scope and detail.

In 2015, the former UN DPKO and DFS revised the 2010 UN Draft Operational Concept on PoC in UN Peacekeeping Operations and replaced it with the 2015 UN Policy on PoC in UN Peacekeeping.[237] This Policy set forth the first definition of PoC in the context of UN peacekeeping:[238]

> [A]ll necessary means, up to and including the use of deadly force, aimed at preventing or responding to threats of physical violence against civilians, within capabilities and areas of operations, and without prejudice to the responsibility of the host government.

Moreover, an important change from the 2010 UN Draft Operational Concept on PoC in UN Peacekeeping Operations was the approach to Tier I. Whereas the 2010 UN Draft Operational Concept referred to 'support to the political process,'[239] the 2015 UN Policy on PoC in UN Peacekeeping spoke of 'protection through dialogue and engagement.'[240] In doing so, the former UN DPKO and DFS went beyond the support of implementing a peace agreement or an existing political process by setting forth the following:[241]

---

234 *Ibid.* paras 23, 27, and 32.

235 UN DPKO and UN DFS, 'Draft DPKO/DFS Operational Concept on the Protection of Civilians in United Nations Peacekeeping Operations' (2010) 1, www.peacekeeping.org.uk/wp-content/uploads/2013/02/100129-DPKO-DFS-POC-Operational-Concept.pdf,accessed 27 February 2018.

236 *Ibid.* 1–2.

237 UN DPKO and UN DFS, '2015 UN Policy on PoC in UN Peacekeeping' (n. 16).

238 *Ibid.* para. 13.

239 UN DPKO and UN DFS, '2010 UN Draft Operational Concept on PoC in UN Peacekeeping Operations' (n. 235) paras 14 and 18.

240 UN DPKO and UN DFS, '2015 UN Policy on PoC in UN Peacekeeping' (n. 16) para. 30.

241 *Ibid.*

> [A]ctivities include dialogue with a perpetrator or potential perpetrator, conflict resolution and mediation between parties to the conflict, persuading the government and other relevant actors to intervene to protect civilians, public information and reporting on POC, and other initiatives that seek to protect civilians through public information, dialogue and direct engagement.

Nonetheless, with the 2015 UN Policy on PoC in UN Peacekeeping, the former UN DPKO and DFS mainly consolidated the existing frameworks, concepts and lessons learned, and related guidelines for military components to implement PoC mandates at the strategic, operational, and tactical levels.[242]

By 2015, ten UN peace operations were actively implementing a PoC mandate, including MONUSCO (to which, from 2013 onwards, the Intervention Brigade had been added), UNMIL, UNOCI, MINUSTAH, UNISFA and UNMISS (which had replaced UNMIS in 2011), UNIFIL, UNAMID (with the caveat that UNAMID was hybrid and was carried out by both the UN and the AU), MINUSMA, and MINUSCA.[243] In addition, eight of them had a whole-of-mission strategy in place that not only identified threats to civilians but also laid out a coordinated approach to address them.[244]

By this time, however, the UN also realised that changes in conflict (think of situations where there is little or no peace to be kept) may have exceeded the ability of UN peace operations to respond as expected.[245] Problems often arose in rapidly rolling out an operation, delivering clear mandates tailored to the situation, and providing sufficient resources. With its 2015 Report on Uniting our Strengths for Peace, the High-level Independent Panel on Peace Operations put forward recommendations for improving PoC in UN peace operations (2015 HIPPO Report).[246] In this regard, the Panel recognised that significant progress had already been made in advancing norms and frameworks for PoC but also stressed that expectations and capacities must be more aligned and that PoC mandates must be linked to a broader political approach.[247] Moreover, it emphasised the need for clarity on the use of force, hereby recognising the importance of the Basic Principles of UN Peacekeeping[248] but simultaneously emphasising the need to interpret these principles 'progressively and with flexibility in the face of new challenges.'[249]

---

242 UN DPKO and UN DFS, '2015 UN Policy on PoC in UN Peacekeeping' (n. 16), as also discussed by OIOS, Inspection and Evaluation Division (n. 106) para. 57.

243 For detailed references to the PoC mandates of those missions, see Part I, Section 1.

244 UNSG, 'Report of the Secretary-General on the Protection of Civilians in Armed Conflict' (2016) UN Doc. S/2016/447 para. 56.

245 As recognised in the following report: HIPPO (n. 112).

246 *Ibid.*

247 *Ibid.* 11 and 25 (para. 38(b)), and 41–42.

248 As discussed below, see Part I, Section 3.1.1.

249 HIPPO (n. 112) 12 and 25 (para. 38(c)), and 42–48.

2.1.4. *Current UN understanding of PoC*

Today, PoC is still a priority for UN peace operations[250] and is present in almost all mandates provided to UN peace operations. As of 31 December 2021, eight operations with a PoC mandate are still active, including MINUSCA, MINUSMA, MONUSCO and its Intervention Brigade, UNIFIL, UNISFA, and UNMISS.[251] Yet, as the nature of conflicts has changed in which UN peace operations have been deployed, so have the PoC mandate and the tasks, activities, roles, and responsibilities required to carry it out.[252] These days, most PoC mandates are very specific and detailed and require UN peace operations to have comprehensive, mission-wide protection strategies (including, but not limited to, early warning and response mechanisms), prioritise civilian protection when making decisions about the use of available resources, and designate PoC as a 'strategic priority' or a 'priority task' of the mission.[253]

The UN's current PoC policy (as presented in the 2019 UN Policy on PoC in UN Peacekeeping, the most recent UN DPO policy document on PoC) equally focuses on a comprehensive and integrated approach to PoC, i.e. an approach that, on the one hand, considers and addresses the multitude of factors that have an impact on, and underlie, threats to civilians, both short and long-term, including political, security, and economic factors, and on the other hand, involves a concerted effort by all components of the mission: civilian, police, and military, and where necessary and appropriate, coordination with other UN actors.[254] On that basis, and building upon previous policy documents, the 2019 UN Policy on PoC in UN Peacekeeping defines PoC in the context of UN peace operations as follows:[255]

> [W]ithout prejudice to the primary responsibility of the host state, integrated and coordinated activities by all civilian and uniformed mission components to prevent, deter or respond to threats of physical violence against civilians within the mission's capabilities and areas of deployment through the use of all necessary means, up to and including deadly force.

In that regard, UN peace operations have an 'active duty to protect,' meaning, *inter alia*, that 'all mission components must constantly work to prevent,

250 As also stressed in recent reports: UNSG, 'Protection of Civilians in Armed Conflict, Report of the Secretary-General' (2019) UN Doc. S/2019/373 para. 16; UNSC, 'Protection of Civilians in Armed Conflict. Report of the Secretary-General' (2020) UN Doc. S/2020/366 para. 46.

251 For detailed references to the PoC mandates of those missions, see Part I, Section 1. The analysis of relevant UNSC resolutions was completed in December 2021.

252 UN DPO, '2020 UN Handbook on PoC in UN Peacekeeping' (n. 35) 3.

253 UN OCHA, 'Building a Culture of Protection: 20 Years of Security Council Engagement on the Protection of Civilians' (UN OCHA 2019) Occasional Policy Paper 41–42.

254 UN DPO, '2019 UN Policy on PoC in UN Peacekeeping' (n. 35) para. 8.

255 *Ibid.* para. 18.

pre-empt and respond to threats to civilians, and not just react to attacks.'[256] Simultaneously, all mission components must observe the 'do not harm' principle in their activities and contacts with individuals and communities,[257] implying that they should not put civilians at risk or cause harm, including by exposing civilians to possible reprisals for their assistance to the mission.[258]

Furthermore, the UN DPO beholds PoC mandates as an expression of the determination of the international community to prevent the most serious violations of IHL, HRL, and international refugee law, as well as related standards.[259] Accordingly, these mandates must be implemented both in the letter and spirit of these legal regimes.[260] Subsequently, the UN DPO has categorised the various approaches and instruments available to UN peace operations when entrusted with a PoC mandate under three tiers, including Tier I – Protection through dialogue and engagement; Tier II – Provision of physical protection; and Tier III – Establishment of a protective environment.[261] The three tiers are aligned and mutually reinforcing and are carried out simultaneously and strategically in accordance with the PoC mandate, the phase in which the mission finds itself, and the conditions on the ground.[262] In other words, there is no hierarchy between the different tiers or any specific sequence.[263] Short-term and long-term actions are necessary to effectively protect civilians on the ground.[264] Such actions must be taken based on an analysis of the situation, the possible conflict phase, if any, the mission's lifecycle, and of course, the nature of the threat.[265]

The three tiers are implemented together with the following four phases:[266]

(i) prevention: where no clear threat to civilians has been identified (longer term),
(ii) pre-emption: where likely threats are identified and attacks against civilians are anticipated (short term),
(iii) response: where threats to civilians are imminent or occurring (short term), and
(iv) consolidation: where violence against civilians is subsiding (longer term).

256 *Ibid.* para. 32.
257 *Ibid.* para. 35.
258 *Ibid.*
259 *Ibid.* para. 27.
260 *Ibid.* On the applicability of HRL and IHL to UN peace operations, see Part III, Section 2.
261 *Ibid.* para. 40.
262 UN DPO, '2020 UN Handbook on PoC in UN Peacekeeping' (n. 35) 12.
263 *Ibid.*
264 *Ibid.*
265 *Ibid.*
266 UN DPO, '2019 UN Policy on PoC in UN Peacekeeping' (n. 35) para. 41.

As with the tiers, these phases are not mutually exclusive and may overlap. The 2020 UN Handbook on PoC in UN Peacekeeping furthermore explains that there may not only be phases for individual threats in specific places and at specific times but also phases for entire conflicts.[267] A mission's action can address several phases at the same time.[268]

The UN continues to tinker with the concept of PoC in an attempt to bring it more in line with contemporary realities. The main areas of work identified by the UN Secretary-General in his latest reports on PoC in armed conflict are: (i) the importance of a renewed focus on the accountability of senior leadership for implementing PoC mandates;[269] (ii) the need for UN Member States to reach consensus on PoC language and the implications of peacekeeping tasks, including clarity regarding the expectations of peace forces and recognition of situations beyond their ability to respond;[270] and (iii) the need for the UN to adopt a more structured approach to protecting civilians during transitions and changes in UN presence.[271]

2.2. CONSOLIDATION OF POC AT THE AU, NATO, AND THE EU

The involvement of UN Member States and regional and international organisations other than the UN in the active protection of civilians in third States has furthered the protection agenda at the regional level, with the various organisations taking tentative steps to develop policies on PoC. These policies are discussed in the following Sections.

2.2.1. AU's understanding of PoC

The Organization of African Unity (OAU), the AU's predecessor, strongly adhered to the principle of non-interference in the internal affairs of its sovereign Member States.[272] Confronted with the atrocities occurring in their region, the failure of the OAU to protect civilian populations, and the development of international legal standards, such as PoC and RtoP, African leaders, however,

---

267 UN DPO, '2020 UN Handbook on PoC in UN Peacekeeping' (n. 35) 13.

268 *Ibid.*

269 UNSG, 'Protection of Civilians in Armed Conflict, Report of the Secretary-General' (2018) UN Doc. S/2018/462 para. 36.

270 *Ibid.* para. 37; UNSG, 'Protection of Civilians in Armed Conflict, Report of the Secretary-General' (n. 250) para. 17.

271 This is particularly true in cases where civilians remain at risk during and after the reconfiguration, withdrawal, and conclusion of UN peace operations, see UNSC, 'Protection of Civilians in Armed Conflict. Report of the Secretary-General' (n. 250) para. 48.

272 Susan J Megy, 'The Protection of Civilians in African Regional and Sub-Regional Peace Operations' in David Curran and others (eds), *Perspectives on Peacekeeping and Atrocity Prevention* (Springer 2015) 130.

recognised a need to develop new policies to address the widening security gap.[273] This need led, at least on paper, to a gradual paradigm shift in African politics from a culture of sovereignty and non-interference to a culture of concern over human security and non-indifference.[274] While the AU still upholds the principles of 'the prohibition of the use of force or threat to use force among Member States of the Union'[275] and 'non-interference by any Member State in the internal affairs of another,'[276] it now also provides for a normative and legal foundation for intervention and PoC in its AU Constitutive Act. This political determination to protect civilians has been further perpetuated in the AU PSC Protocol[277] and the 2002 AU Rules of Procedure of the AU Assembly.[278] For a detailed discussion of these legal instruments, see Part I, Sections 4.1.1.1(A)(ii) and 4.1.1.1(B)(ii).

The AU has taken on an increasingly significant role in protecting civilians in armed conflicts taking place in its region,[279] which is perpetuated by the fact that the UN Security Council has provided two African-led missions and one hybrid mission with an explicit mandate to protect civilians. Specifically, the UN Security Council has authorised AFISMA to support the Malian authorities in their primary responsibility to protect the civilian population and MISCA to carry out a PoC mandate in the CAR.[280] In addition, the UN Security Council provided the AU/UN hybrid mission in Darfur, UNAMID, with a PoC mandate until the mission ended in 2020.[281]

273 International Refugee Rights Initiative, 'From Non-Interference to Non Indifference: The African Union and the Responsibility to Protect' (International Refugee Rights Initiative 2017) 10; Megy (n. 272) 130; Wafula Okumu and Thomas Jaye, 'Introduction' in Benjamin de Carvalho and others (eds), *Peacekeeping in Africa: The Evolving roles of the African Union and Regional Mechanisms* (Norwegian Institute of International Affairs 2010) 12.

274 Ben Kioko, 'The Right of Intervention under the African Union's Constitutive Act: From Non-Interference to Non-Intervention' (2003) 85 International Review of the Red Cross 807, 19; Megy (n. 272) 130; International Refugee Rights Initiative (n. 273) 11.

275 Art. 4(f) of the AU Constitutive Act.

276 Art. 4(g) of the AU Constitutive Act.

277 Protocol Relating to the Establishment of the Peace and Security Council of the African Union (adopted 9 July 2002, entered into force 26 December 2003) available at, https://au.int/sites/default/files/treaties/37293-treaty-0024_-_protocol_relating_to_the_establishment_of_the_peace_and_security_council_of_the_african_union_e.pdf, accessed 18 October 2022 (AU PSC Protocol).

278 Rules of Procedure of the Assembly of the Union, https://archives.au.int/bitstream/handle/123456789/6448/Rules%20of%20Procedure%20of%20the%20Assembly%2C%20Executive%20Council%2C%20PRC%20%26%20Statutes%20of%20the%20Commission%20_E.Pdf?sequence=1&isAllowed=y, accessed 18 October 2022 (2002 AU Rules of Procedure of the AU Assembly).

279 AU, '2012 AU Draft Guidelines for PoC in AU Peace Support Operations' (n. 114) 2; AU Assembly (n. 2) 6. See also Ben Kioko and Lydia Wambugu, 'The African Union and the Protection of Civilians' in Haidi Willmot and others (eds), *Protection of Civilians* (1st edn., Oxford University Press 2016) 275.

280 For detailed references to the PoC mandates of those missions, see Part I, Section 1.

281 For detailed references to the PoC mandates of those missions, see Part I, Section 1, fn. 137.

Furthermore, the AU PSC authorised other peace operations to engage in PoC tasks, even though the UN Security Council has not explicitly mandated them. For example, UNAMID's predecessors – the African Union Mission in Sudan I (AMIS I) and the African Union Mission in Sudan II (AMIS II) – never received an explicit PoC mandate from the UN Security Council but nonetheless received a mandate from the AU PSC to protect civilians.[282] In several resolutions on the situation in Darfur, the UN Security Council endorsed this PoC mandate envisioned by the AU.[283] With UNSC Resolution 1769 (2007), AMIS II was eventually incorporated into UNAMID.[284] In the same year, the AU PSC authorised the deployment of the African Union Mission to Somalia (AMISOM),[285] which the UN Security Council later endorsed.[286] In the first years, AMISOM was given a wide variety of tasks, yet no explicit mandate to protect civilians was provided. In 2013, the UN Security Council encouraged AMISOM to develop an effective approach to PoC, yet again without giving AMISOM an explicit mandate.[287] AMISOM's PoC tasks were eventually introduced through the mission-wide PoC strategy, approved in May 2013 by the AU PSC.[288] Also, the African Union Mission for Support to the Elections in the Comoros (AMISEC) was provided with an AU PSC mandate 'to take all measures necessary to protect its personnel, as well as civilians within the proximity of the polling stations.'[289] Since the scope of this book is limited to UN (mandated) peace operations with a UNSC mandate, these operations are not discussed further. For more information on these missions, see a report on PoC by the AU, edited by Okeke and Williams.[290] Last but not least, African sub-regional organisations, such as ECOWAS, also play a prominent role in deploying UN-mandated peace operations.[291] Yet, a discussion of such sub-regional organisations' policies on PoC goes beyond the scope of this book.

PoC is now marked on the AU's agenda as a central strategic priority.[292] Accordingly, the AU has made considerable effort to develop a normative

---

282 AU PSC, 'AU PSC Communiqué XIII' (2004) AU Doc. PSC/PR/Comm. (XIII) para. 8; AU PSC, 'AU PSC Communiqué XVII' (2004) AU Doc. PSC/PR/Comm. (XVII) para. 6.

283 'UNSC Res. 1556' (2004) UN Doc. S/RES/1556 (2004) para. 2; 'UNSC Res. 1564' (2004) UN Doc. S/RES/1564 (2004) para. 3; 'UNSC Res. 1706' (n. 133) pream. para. 6.

284 'UNSC Res. 1769' (n. 133) para. 2.

285 AU PSC, 'AU PSC Communiqué LXIX' (2007) AU Doc. PSC/PR/Comm. (LXIX) para. 8.

286 'UNSC Res. 1744' (2007) UN Doc. S/RES/1744 (2007) pream. para. 7.

287 'UNSC Res. 2093' (2013) UN Doc. S/RES/2093 (2013) para. 10.

288 AU PSC, 'Report of the Chairperson of the Commission on the Situation in Somalia' (2013) AU Doc. PSC/PR/2.(CCCLXXIX) paras 49–50.

289 AU PSC, 'AU PSC Communiqué XLVII' (2006) AU Doc. PSC/PR/Comm.1(XLVII) para. 9.

290 Jide Martyns Okeke and Paul D Williams, 'Introduction: African Union Peace Support Operations and Civilian Protection' in Jide Martyns Okeke and Paul D Williams (eds), *Protecting Civilians in African Union Support Operations: Key Cases and Lessons Learned* (African Centre for the Constructive Resolution of Disputes 2016) 16–17 and further.

291 Gill and others (n. 26) 71.

292 See e.g. AU PSC, 'The 326th Meeting of the Peace and Security Council of the African Union Was Held on 26 June 2012' (*AU*, 18 February 2013), www.peaceau.org/en/article/the-326th-

framework and operational guidance for PoC. Between 2009 and 2012, the AU developed guidelines for protecting civilians in peace operations carried out by the AU.[293] According to the 2012 AU Draft Guidelines for PoC in AU Peace Support Operations, the concept of PoC includes:[294]

> [A]ctivities undertaken to improve the security of the population and people at risk and to ensure the full respect for the rights of groups and the individual recognised under regional instruments, including the African Charter of Human and Peoples' Rights, the AU Convention for the Protection and Assistance of Internally Displaced Persons, and the Convention Governing the Specific Aspects of Refugee Problems in Africa, and international law, including humanitarian, human rights and refugee law.

In line with the UN approach, the AU has adopted a multi-tiered approach to PoC. In the protection strategy and all other mission documents that spell out protection tasks for the various components of a mission, the following four-tiered approach should be followed: Tier I – Protection as part of the political process (e.g. supporting a peace process that provides for justice and accountability); Tier II – Protection from physical violence (through prevention, pre-emption, response, and consolidation); Tier III – Rights-based protection (e.g. monitoring and reporting HRL violations and assisting in the establishment of transitional justice mechanisms); and Tier IV – Establishment of a protective environment (peace-building through capacity-building measures and broad-based reform measures).[295] The main difference with the 2019 UN Policy on PoC in UN Peacekeeping is that Tier I of the latter is split into Tiers I and III in the AU policy, making it four tiers in total.

The 2012 AU Draft Guidelines for PoC in AU Peace Support Operations informed the development and adoption of the 2013 AU Aide Mémoire on PoC.[296] This Aide Mémoire intended to facilitate the efforts of the relevant organs of the AU working on matters relating to the maintenance of peace and security in Africa to establish appropriate mechanisms to ensure, to the extent possible, the protection of civilians affected by violence.[297] In doing so, the AU has developed its own conceptual understanding of PoC, which, while perhaps

---

meeting-of-the-peace-and-security-council-of-the-african-union-was-held-on-26-june-2012, accessed 21 April 2022 ('Council stressed that, in addition to mainstreaming the Protection of Civilians [PoC] in standard operating procedures of AU peace support operations, PoC must form part of the mandate of future AU missions'). See also Kioko and Wambugu (n. 279) 275; Okeke and Williams (n. 290) 10–11.

293 Kioko and Wambugu (n. 279) 279.

294 AU, '2012 AU Draft Guidelines for PoC in AU Peace Support Operations' (n. 114) 5. See also AU Assembly (n. 2) para. 7.

295 AU, '2012 AU Draft Guidelines for PoC in AU Peace Support Operations' (n. 114) 9.

296 AU Assembly (n. 2).

297 *Ibid.* 7.

not substantially different from broader international normative standards, is tailored to the type of crisis situations the AU faces in its own region.[298] In 2018, the AU PSC dedicated its meeting to 'the Principles on Protection of Civilians in Conflict areas in Africa,' which not only welcomed the initiatives mentioned above but also referred to the newly-developed AU Integrated Protection of Civilians Training Standards.[299]

However, despite all good intentions, the AU has not yet succeeded in effectively translating these normative frameworks and political aspirations into successfully protecting civilians in the field.[300]

2.2.2. NATO's understanding of PoC

In its early days, NATO was predominantly concerned with collective self-defence, whereby an armed attack against one or more of them in Europe or North America was considered an attack against all (see Article 5 of the North Atlantic Treaty). In the 1990s, while maintaining the security of its Members as its fundamental purpose, NATO expanded its scope of action as it became involved in so-called Non-Article 5 Crisis Response Operations (NA5CRO). The post-Cold War era was marked by territorial disputes, ethnic conflicts, extreme nationalism, political strife within States, failed or inadequate political change, and serious economic and social difficulties, and caused a change in the strategic priorities of NATO.[301] Perception grew that conflicts outside NATO's borders could also threaten the security of the territories and populations of allied partners.[302] As a result, NATO added crisis management to its core task of collective defence to tackle such conflicts outside the territory of its Member States. NA5CROs may focus on conflict prevention, peacekeeping, peacemaking, peacebuilding, peace enforcement, and/or humanitarian activities.[303]

In 2001, NATO issued a doctrine for the conduct of NATO and NATO-led peace support operations (2001 NATO AJD on Peace Support Operations) to

---

298 Okeke and Williams (n. 290) 14.

299 AU PSC, 'AU PSC Communiqué DCCLXXV' (2018) AU Doc. PSC/PR/Comm. (DCCLXXV) 2.

300 Megy (n. 272) 131.

301 NAC, 'The Alliance's New Strategic Concept, Agreed by the Heads of State and Government Participating in the Meeting of the North Atlantic Council' (1991) para. 9, www.nato.int/cps/en/natohq/official_texts_23847.htm, accessed 23 March 2022. See also John Kriendler, 'NATO Crisis Management: Cooperation with PfP Partners and Other International Organizations' (2004) 3 Connections 59, 60.

302 NAC, 'The Alliance's New Strategic Concept, Agreed by the Heads of State and Government Participating in the Meeting of the North Atlantic Council' (n. 301) para. 9. See also Stian Kjeksrud and others, 'Protecting Civilians: Comparing Organizational Approaches' in Haidi Willmot and others (eds), *Protection of Civilians* (1st edn., Oxford University Press 2016) 93.

303 NATO, 'Crisis Management' (*NATO*, 8 October 2020), www.nato.int/cps/en/natolive/topics_49192.htm, accessed 19 February 2021.

guide and inform those involved at both the strategic and operational levels.[304] When discussing the application of force, and with the operations in Bosnia in mind, NATO first and foremost recognised that 'collateral damage should be minimised and reasonable measures taken to avoid civilian casualties.'[305] However, it also recognised that the difficulty in the field was whether to act in response to human rights violations directed against civilians 'on the ground.'[306] Although, on the one hand, a narrow and neutral concept of operations, limited to monitoring and reporting, could reduce the risk of casualties for NATO peace operations, in circumstances of widespread violations of fundamental human rights and ethnic cleansing, such a narrow and neutral concept could also seriously undermine the credibility of NATO peace operations.[307] As such, the concept of PoC was shaped by including the 'creation of a secure environment' in the list of subtasks for preventive deployment.[308]

NATO took another step towards developing a separate doctrine on PoC by adopting guidelines for implementing the UN's Women, Peace, and Security agenda, as reflected in UNSC Resolution 1325 (2000) and subsequent resolutions on the matter.[309] In particular, NATO adopted a Policy on Women, Peace, and Security within the Euro-Atlantic Partnership Council (EAPC), in which it recognised the importance of ensuring women's inclusion and participation in dealing with security challenges of the 21st century.[310] Moreover, when UNSC Resolution 1820 (2008) brought attention to conflict-related sexual violence,[311] NATO issued its 2015 Military Guidelines on the Prevention and Response to

---

304 NATO, 'Allied Joint Doctrine for Peace Support Operations' (NATO Military Agency for Standarization (MAS) 2001) NATO Doc. AJP-3.4.1 para. 0002, as also referred to by Joachim A Koops and Christian Patz, 'UN, EU, and NATO Approaches to the Protection of Civilians: Policies, Implementation, and Comparative Advantages' (International Peace Institute 2022) 4.

305 NATO, '2001 NATO AJD on Peace Support Operations' (n. 304) para. 0320. When discussing the applicability of IHL, it was reiterated that '[w]hen military force is used, every effort should be taken to minimise the risk of civilian casualties' (see Annex 4B, para. 4B6).

306 *Ibid.* para. 0322.

307 *Ibid.*

308 *Ibid.* para. 0625(e).

309 'UNSC Res. 1325' (2000) UN Doc. S/RES/1325 (2000); 'UNSC Res. 1820' (2008) UN Doc. S/RES/1820 (2008); 'UNSC Res. 1888' (2009) UN Doc. S/RES/1888 (2009); 'UNSC Res. 1889' (2009) UN Doc. S/RES/1889 (2009); 'UNSC Res. 1960' (2010) UN Doc. S/RES/1960 (2010); 'UNSC Res. 2106' (2013) UN Doc. S/RES/2106 (2013); 'UNSC Res. 2122' (2013) UN Doc. S/RES/2122 (2013); 'UNSC Res. 2242' (2015) UN Doc. S/RES/2242 (2015); 'UNSC Res. 2467' (2019) UN Doc. S/RES/2467 (2019); 'UNSC Res. 2493' (2019) UN Doc. S/RES/2493 (2019).

310 EAPC, 'NATO/EAPC Policy on Implementing UNSCR 1325 on Women, Peace and Security' (2014) NATO Doc. NATO/EAPC(C)D(2007)022. See also EAPC, 'NATO/EAPC Policy for the Implementation of UNSCR 1325 on Women, Peace and Security and Related Resolutions' (2011) NATO Doc. PO(2014)0253; EAPC, 'Revised NATO/EAPC Policy for the Implementation of UNSCR 1325 on Women, Peace and Security and Related Resolutions' (2014) NATO Doc. PO(2014)0253; EAPC, 'NATO/EAPC Women, Peace and Security Policy and Action Plan 2018' (2018).

311 'UNSC Res. 1820' (n. 309).

Conflict-Related Sexual Violence.[312] These Guidelines aim to reduce the risk of conflict-related sexual violence and improve responsive measures, taking into account protection needs.[313]

From August 2003 until December 2014, NATO led the International Security Assistance Force (ISAF), an operation intended to train Afghan security forces and assist in rebuilding government institutions.[314] While ISAF never received a PoC mandate from the UN Security Council, it was, to some extent, PoC-driven. At one point, NATO became concerned with the adverse effects of collateral damage among civilians due to its actions.[315] Broad ambitions and limited means resulted in a high number of civilian casualties.[316] By gradually adopting concrete measures to reduce the number of civilian casualties, NATO eventually succeeded in reducing the harm suffered by the Afghan civilian population.[317] Following the termination of ISAF, NATO launched a new non-combat mission in Afghanistan in January 2015 called the Resolute Support Mission (RSM) to train, advise, and assist the Afghan security forces and institutions.[318] Important to note is that in the training of Afghan security forces and institutions, the focus was not only placed on how to avoid and investigate civilian casualties but also on how to successfully implement both the UNSC Resolution 1325 (2000) on Women, Peace, and Security and UNSC Resolution 1612 (2005) on Children Affected by Armed Conflict and related resolutions (as discussed below).[319]

In 2011, NATO took overall command of Operation Unified Protector in Libya. While the intervention in Libya equally reinforced NATO's focus on harm mitigation following reports of civilian casualties and the destruction of key civilian infrastructure by NATO bombings,[320] NATO also had to actively engage in protecting civilians from violence inflicted by third parties without

---

312 NAMC, 'NATO Military Guidelines on the Prevention of, and Response to, Conflict-Related Sexual and Gender-Based Violence' (2015) NATO Doc. MCM-0009-2015.

313 *Ibid.* para. 8.

314 See further, NATO, 'ISAF's Mission in Afghanistan (2001–2014) (Archived)' (*NATO*, 19 August 2021), www.nato.int/cps/en/natolive/topics_69366.htm, accessed 21 April 2022.

315 Steven Hill and Andreea Manea, 'Protection of Civilians: A NATO Perspective' (2018) 34 Utrecht Journal of International and European Law 146, 147.

316 Sten Rynning, 'As NATO Looks East, Will It Stumble in the South? The Case of Protection of Civilians Policy' in Roberto Belloni, Paul R Viotti and Vincent Della Sala (eds), *Fear and Uncertainty in Europe: the Return to Realism?* (Palgrave Macmillan 2019) 221.

317 Hill and Manea (n. 315) 147–148. See also Joint Analysis Lessons Learned Centre, 'Protection of Civilians, How ISAF Reduced Civilian Casualties' (NATO 2015); Center for Civilians in Conflict, 'Civilian Harm Tracking: Analysis of ISAF Efforts in Afghanistan' (Center for Civilians in Conflict 2014).

318 See further, NATO, 'Resolute Support Mission in Afghanistan (2015–2021) (Archived)' (*NATO*, 8 April 2022), www.nato.int/cps/en/natohq/topics_113694.htm, accessed 21 April 2022.

319 Hill and Manea (n. 315) 153 and 156–157.

320 See e.g. Center for Civilians in Conflict, 'NATO's Time Drawing to a Close, But Protection Work Unfinished' (2011), https://civiliansinconflict.org/press-releases/natos-time-drawing-close-protection-work-unfinished/, accessed 14 April 2022.

having a PoC policy at hand.[321] After all, UNSC Resolution 1973 (2011) provided Operation Unified Protector with an explicit mandate to protect civilians and civilian-populated areas and to enforce a no-fly zone.[322] While Operation Unified Protector would prove a case of trial and error, it would last until 2016, when NATO adopted its own PoC policy (see further below). In both ISAF and Operation Unified Protector, the PoC-driven approach was essentially a means to success, as opposed to a goal in and of itself.[323]

The NATO campaign in Libya was surrounded by criticism from the very beginning. A number of States abstained in the vote on UNSC Resolution 1973 (2011), including Brazil, China, Germany, India, and Russia.[324] During the debate leading up to the adoption of the resolution, Brazil expressed concern that the use of military force could aggravate the situation and possibly cause more harm than good to civilians.[325] Likewise, Germany issued similar concerns about the negative consequences of the use of force.[326] Once deployed, several States continued to sharply criticise the foreign intervention in Libya and how the mandate was implemented.[327] The military intervention equally gave rise to fierce debates among practitioners and academics about the legality and legitimacy of some of the measures taken to carry out the mandate, such as the provision of military support to opposition groups and the forcible regime change.[328]

In 2012, NATO slightly broadened the scope of protection in its doctrine. After initially focusing on the Women, Peace, and Security agenda, NATO extended its protection policy to children in 2012. As the UN Security Council focused on protecting children affected by armed conflict with Resolution 1612

321 Koops and Patz (n. 304) 4–5.

322 'UNSC Res. 1973' (n. 62) paras 4, 6, and 8.

323 Kjeksrud and others (n. 302) 94. See also Koops and Patz (n. 304) 2, 8, and 9.

324 UNSC, '6498th Meeting (at Which UNSC Res. 1973 (2011) Was Adopted)' (n. 63) 3.

325 *Ibid.* para. 6.

326 *Ibid.* para. 5.

327 See e.g. UNSC, '6528th Meeting (on the Situation in Libya)' (2011) UN Doc. S/PV.6528 9–10; UNSC, '6531st Meeting (on the Protection of Civilians in Armed Conflict)' (2011) UN Doc. S/PV.6531 11, 21. See also Nabil Hajjami, 'Que Signifie l'expression "Prendre Toutes Les Mesures Nécessaires" Dans La Pratique Du Conseil de Sécurité Des Nations Unies?' (2013) 1 Revue Belge de Droit International 232, 253.

328 See e.g. AJ Bellamy and PD Williams, 'The New Politics of Protection? Côte d'Ivoire, Libya and the Responsibility to Protect' (2011) 87 International Affairs 825; Olivier Corten and Vaios Koutroulis, 'The Illegality of Military Support to Rebels in the Libyan War: Aspects of Jus Contra Bellum and Jus in Bello' (2013) 18 Journal of Conflict and Security Law 59; Chris De Cock, 'Operation Unified Protector and the Protection of Civilians in Libya' in Michael N Schmitt and Louise Arimatsu (eds), *Yearbook of International Humanitarian Law*, vol. 14 (TMC Asser Press 2012); Geir Ulfstein and Hege Føsund Christiansen, 'The Legality of the NATO Bombing in Libya' (2013) 62 International and Comparative Law Quarterly 159; Natalino Ronzitti, 'NATO's Intervention in Libya: A Genuine Action to Protect a Civilian Population in Mortal Danger or an Intervention Aimed at Regime Change' (2011) 21 The Italian Yearbook of International Law 3.

(2005),[329] NATO heads of State and government addressed this issue at the Chicago Summit in May 2012.[330] NATO committed to taking an active part in preventing, monitoring, and responding to violations against children and decided to develop practical, field-oriented measures to address such violations during armed conflict.[331] Later that year, NATO adopted its first Military Guidelines on Children and Armed Conflict, outlining a broad framework to integrate UNSC Resolution 1612 (2005) and related resolutions into operational activities and education and training.[332] Furthermore, following the Wales Summit in 2014, where NATO heads of State and government decided that NATO, together with the UN, needs to assess how to be sufficiently prepared whenever and wherever children in armed conflict are encountered, NATO adopted the Policy on the Protection of Children in Armed Conflict.[333]

In the 2015 AJD on the Military Contribution to Stabilization and Reconstruction,[334] NATO eventually recognised the more general notion of 'protection of civilians from physical violence' (not just women and children) as a vital aspect of military operations conducted among civilian populations.[335] Also, during the 2016 Warsaw Summit, the participants recognised the imperative of protecting civilians from the effects of armed conflict.[336] For that reason, they endorsed the newly-developed 2016 NATO Policy on PoC, which aims to set forth a 'coherent, consistent and integrated approach to PoC' in NATO and NATO-led operations, missions, and other mandated activities.[337]As mentioned earlier, one of the main lessons NATO had learned from its involvement in the crisis management operation in Afghanistan was the need for a policy on civilian harm mitigation.[338] With the 2016 Policy on PoC, NATO

329 'UNSC Res. 1612' (2015) UN Doc. S/RES/1612 (2005).

330 NAC, 'NATO Chicago Summit Declaration: Issued by the Heads of State and Government Participating in the Meeting of the North Atlantic Council in Chicago on 20 May 2012', www.nato.int/cps/en/natolive/official_texts_87593.htm#unscr1612, accessed 18 February 2021.

331 *Ibid.* para. 17.

332 NATO, 'NATO Military Guidelines on Children and Armed Conflict' (2012).

333 NATO, 'NATO Policy for the Protection of Children in Armed Conflict – the Way Forward' (2015).

334 As also referred to by Koops and Patz (n. 304) 4.

335 NATO, '2015 NATO AJD for the Military Contribution to Stabilization and Reconstruction' (n. 117) para. 0205(c).

336 NAC, 'NATO Warsaw Summit Declaration: Issued by the Heads of State and Government Participating in the Meeting of the North Atlantic Council in Warsaw on 8–9 July 2016' para. 132, www.nato.int/cps/en/natohq/official_texts_133169.htm#civilians, accessed 18 February 2021; NAC, '2016 NATO Policy on PoC' (n. 118).

337 NAC, 'NATO Warsaw Summit Declaration: Issued by the Heads of State and Government Participating in the Meeting of the North Atlantic Council in Warsaw on 8–9 July 2016' (n. 336) para. 132.

338 Hill and Manea (n. 315) 147; Rynning (n. 316) 235. As noted by Koops and Patz, NATO's concept of PoC has its origins in the Bosnian wars, but NATO's approach and vision of PoC has been influenced almost exclusively by the lessons and experiences of ISAF in Afghanistan, see Koops and Patz (n. 304) 4.

aimed to provide an overarching and comprehensive policy that links past crisis management principles and experiences together but also expands the scope of action to protecting civilians from the actions of others and outlines a path forward for NATO.[339]

According to the 2016 Policy on PoC, NATO's approach to PoC is based on 'legal, moral and political imperatives' and is consistent with 'applicable legal frameworks [...] which may include international human rights law and international humanitarian law.'[340] Notably, this is the only, albeit open-ended, reference to applicable law in the policy. NATO has also subjected the exercise of its responsibility under this policy to the legal basis for the specific NATO operation, mission, or activity and to the specific mandate approved by NATO's NAC, without prejudice to force protection and collective defence obligations.[341] Moreover, NATO has left room for discretion by establishing that it must take 'all feasible measures' to avoid, minimise, and mitigate civilian harm.[342] However, it is ultimately up to NATO's NAC to decide which measures are feasible during a given operation.[343]

'Protection of civilians' is defined as follows:[344]

> [A]ll efforts taken to avoid, minimize and mitigate the negative effects that might arise from NATO and NATO-led military operations on the civilian population and, when applicable, to protect civilians from conflict-related physical violence or threats of physical violence by other actors, including through the establishment of a safe and secure environment.

In other words, for NATO, PoC implies, in the first place, that in planning and conducting military operations and missions, it aims to mitigate civilian damage through its own action.[345] Such civil damage mitigation measures must be developed and incorporated into the NATO chain of command and the NATO force structure.[346] Furthermore, and most importantly for this research, NATO expands the scope of action to also include protecting civilians from the actions of others.[347] Understanding the threat to civilians is critical in this context to determine the nature of military force with which to protect the civilian

339 Rynning (n. 316) 221. See also Hill and Manea (n. 315) 147.
340 NAC, '2016 NATO Policy on PoC' (n. 118) paras 4–5.
341 *Ibid.* para. 6.
342 *Ibid.* para. 7.
343 Sten Rynning, 'Rethinking NATO Policy on the Protection of Civilians' (2017) 47 The US Army War College Quarterly: Parameters 39, 45.
344 NAC, '2016 NATO Policy on PoC' (n. 118) para. 9.
345 NATO, 'NATO Policy For The Protection Of Civilians Endorsed by the Heads of State and Government Participating in the Meeting of the North Atlantic Council in Warsaw 8–9 July 2016' (*NATO*) para. 15, www.nato.int/cps/en/natohq/official_texts_133945.htm, accessed 11 December 2017.
346 *Ibid.*
347 *Ibid.* para. 16.

population.[348] In identifying threats to the civilian population, the leadership at the different levels of the chain of command must develop a comprehensive response to effectively protect civilians.[349] NATO also recognises that threats to the physical security of humanitarian workers can negatively impact the delivery of humanitarian aid and, in turn, endanger the civilian population.[350] In line with their mandate, NATO and NATO-led peace operations may play a significant role in establishing a 'safe and secure environment' in which humanitarian actors can do their work and, in exceptional cases, can even go as far as assisting humanitarian actors in delivering humanitarian aid.[351]

Hence, according to commentators, this concept of a 'safe and secure environment' 'can and should' be interpreted broadly and, therefore, can give rise to a wide range of actions, including environmental and capacity building.[352] However, as pointed out by Rynning:[353]

> [T]he ultimate signal from NATO is that it is a political-military actor that can help create secure spaces in conflict areas; that it will be particularly mindful of not causing harm to civilians and protecting them from violence as it does so; but that it does not assume responsibility for wider development and governance issues [e.g. a duty to secure civilians' access to clean water, health care, or education].

After adopting the 2016 Policy on PoC, NATO took additional measures to ensure the implementation of the policy. In February 2017, NATO developed an action plan with clearly defined actions to this effect (i.e. by integrating PoC into trainings, doctrine, education, and exercises, as well as the planning and conduct of operations).[354] Moreover, during the 2018 Brussels Summit, NATO and its partners reiterated once again their commitment to ensuring that all efforts are made to prevent, minimise, and alleviate the negative effects on civilians arising from NATO and NATO-led military operations and missions, as underscored in their new Military Concept for PoC.[355] This Military Concept establishes a framework that seeks to identify and understand threats to civilian populations.[356]

---

348 *Ibid.*
349 *Ibid.*
350 *Ibid.* para. 17.
351 *Ibid.*
352 Hill and Manea (n. 315) 154.
353 Rynning (n. 316) 222.
354 As also referred to in the following summit declaration: NAC, 'NATO Brussels Summit Declaration: Issued by the Heads of State and Government Participating in the Meeting of the North Atlantic Council in Brussels on 11–12 July 2018' para. 11, www.nato.int/cps/en/natohq/official_texts_156624.htm#77, accessed 18 February 2021. See also Koops and Patz (n. 304) 8.
355 NAC, 'NATO Brussels Summit Declaration: Issued by the Heads of State and Government Participating in the Meeting of the North Atlantic Council in Brussels on 11–12 July 2018' (n. 354).
356 See also NATO, 'Human Security' (*NATO*, 11 March 2022), www.nato.int/cps/en/natohq/topics_181779.htm, accessed 21 April 2022; NATO, *Protection of Civilians ACO Handbook* (NATO 2021) 11.

In 2021, NATO Allied Command Operations (ACO) released its PoC Handbook.[357] An innovative aspect of the Handbook is the inclusion of a threat assessment to mitigate actions from third parties based on eight threat scenarios.[358] In the same year as the Handbook's release, the importance of protecting civilians was reaffirmed during the 2021 Brussels Summit.[359] It was done so, however, by subsuming the concept of protection of civilians within the concept of 'Human Security', which focuses on risks and threats to populations in conflict or crisis areas more in general (and thus along with women, peace, and security; cultural property protection; and children and armed conflict).[360] Moreover, while the Communiqué referred to the need to prevent, minimise, and mitigate any adverse effects of NATO missions and activities on civilians, the active role of NATO in the protection from third parties was not mentioned.[361]

Moreover, NATO's increased focus on the threat of inter-state conflict and geopolitical rivalry (think Russia's invasion of Crimea in 2014 and the broader invasion of Ukraine in February 2022) has made PoC a lower priority.[362] On the other hand, as Koops and Patz also rightly pointed out, the US withdrawal from Afghanistan and the resurgence of the Taliban have shown that questions of responsibility for protecting civilians remain relevant to the organisation's credibility even after its missions have formally ended.[363]

2.2.3. EU's understanding of PoC

In 1948, the UK, France, and the Benelux laid the groundwork for the EU's common defence policy by signing the Treaty of Brussels.[364] Article IV of the 1948 Treaty of Brussels contained a mutual defence clause that laid the foundations for forming the Western European Union (WEU), a defensive alliance composed of ten Member States.[365] In 1954, the 1948 Treaty of Brussels was modified to allow Italy and Germany to accede and to organise the

357 NATO, *2021 NATO ACO PoC Handbook* (n. 356).

358 *Ibid.* paras 68–70.

359 NAC, 'NATO Brussels Summit Communiqué: Issued by the Heads of State and Government Participating in the Meeting of the North Atlantic Council in Brussels on 14 June 2021' para. 60, www.nato.int/cps/en/natohq/news_185000.htm, accessed 12 April 2022.

360 *Ibid.*

361 *Ibid.; Koops and Patz (n. 304) 9.*

362 Koops and Patz (n. 304) 5.

363 *Ibid.*

364 EEAS, 'The Shaping of a Common Security and Defence Policy' (*EEAS*, 6 August 2021), www.eeas.europa.eu/eeas/shaping-common-security-and-defence-policy_en, accessed 8 October 2022. Full reference to the 1948 Treaty of Brussels: The Treaty of Economic, Social and Cultural Collaboration and Collective Self-Defence (adopted 17 March 1948, entered into force 25 August 1948), www.nato.int/cps/en/natohq/official_texts_17072.htm., accessed 17 February 2022 (1948 Treaty of Brussels).

365 Art. 51 of the 1948 Treaty of Brussels set forth that 'If any of the High Contracting Parties should be the object of an armed attack in Europe, the other High Contracting Parties will, in accordance with the provisions of Article 51 of the Charter of the United Nations, afford the

establishment of the WEU. Until the end of the 20th century, the WEU, together with NATO, was the main forum for consultation and discussion on European security and defence-related matters.[366]

Throughout the Cold War, the WEU remained in the background and tended to have limited military significance and only little political impact.[367] Yet in 1992, following the end of the Cold War, the WEU's Ministerial Council agreed upon the type of military action that the EU could undertake in crisis management operations, including 'humanitarian and rescue tasks, peacekeeping tasks and tasks of combat forces in crisis management, including peacemaking.'[368] These so-called Petersberg Tasks formed an integral part of the then European Security and Defence Policy (ESDP) (now Common Security and Defence Policy (CSDP)) and were eventually incorporated into the 1997 Treaty of Amsterdam.[369] Although a common defence policy was not yet established at that point, peacekeeping and humanitarian work responsibilities were expanded, including establishing closer ties with the WEU.[370] The 1997 Treaty of Amsterdam also foresaw the possibility of developing a future common defence policy for the EU to enable the EU to take a coherent approach to addressing security challenges.[371]

The UN-EU peacekeeping partnership began to take shape at the turn of the century with the creation of the ESDP.[372] The ESDP aimed to 'Europeanize' the burden of peacekeeping and the Member States' national policies toward Africa.[373] The ESDP became operational through the first ESDP missions and operations in 2003.[374] Between 2003 and 2021, the EU initiated more than thirty overseas civilian and military missions and operations.[375] However, only a handful have been provided with a PoC mandate by the UN Security Council. The first EU-led operation with a PoC mandate was IEMF, codenamed

---

Party so attacked all the military and other aid and assistance in their power.' See also EEAS (n. 364).

366 *Ibid.*

367 Julia Schmidt, *The European Union and the Use of Force* (Koninklijke Brill NV 2021) 36.

368 WEU Council of Ministers, 'Petersberg Declaration' (1992) 6 para. 4.

369 Treaty of Amsterdam Amending the Treaty on European Union, the Treaties Establishing the European Communities and Certain Related Acts (adopted 2 October 1997, entered into force 1 May 1999) OJ C 340/1 (1997 Treaty of Amsterdam).

370 EEAS (n. 364).

371 See Art. 17 of the 1997 Treaty of Amsterdam.

372 Matthias Dembinski and Berenike Schott, 'Converging Around Global Norms? Protection of Civilians in African Union and European Union Peacekeeping in Africa' (2013) 6 African Security 276, 279.

373 *Ibid.*

374 Gustav Lindstrom, 'History and Development of the CSDP' in Jochen Rehrl (ed), *Handbook on CSDP: the Common Security and Defence Policy of the European Union*, vol. 1 (4th edn., Directorate of Security Policy of the Federal Ministry of Defence and Sports of the Republic of Austria 2021) 17.

375 For an overview, see EEAS, 'Missions and Operations' (*EEAS*, 2001), www.eeas.europa.eu/eeas/missions-and-operations_en, accessed 8 October 2022.

Operation Artemis, and was launched in Bunia, the DRC, in the summer of 2003.[376] UNSC Resolution 1484 (2003) authorised IEMF, in close coordination with MONUC, to contribute to the consolidation of the security situation and the enhancement of the humanitarian situation, to assist in the defence of the airport and the protection of IDPs in Bunia's camps and, if required by the situation, to contribute to the security of the civilian population, UN personnel, and the humanitarian presence in Bunia, until no later than 1 September 2003.[377] Operation Artemis has been criticised by observers as 'more a French operation with an EU cover than an EU operation led by the French.'[378] Operation Artemis also faced criticism for the operation's short duration and limited geographical scope, as well as for the fact that some of its troops were not transferred directly to MONUC.[379] Last but not least, there were also accusations of human rights abuses against Congolese civilians by Swedish soldiers.[380]

In November 2003, the Council of the EU sought to further operationalise the PoC concept within its structures by introducing the 2003 EU Draft Guidelines on PoC in EU-led Crisis Management Operations.[381] These Guidelines primarily stated that EU-led crisis management operations must take all necessary steps to help create a safe environment for civilians endangered by the conflict and facilitate safe and unhindered access to civilians by humanitarian personnel.[382] In addition, EU-led crisis management operations must also use all necessary means to facilitate respect for international norms for the protection of civilians.[383] However, as the document was drafted by the body responsible for civilian crisis management operations, rather than the European Union Military Committee (EUMC), in consultation with the UN body primarily responsible for humanitarian affairs, UN OCHA, the Guidelines were grounded in IHL, human rights standards, and themes, such as children and armed conflict, protection of displaced persons, gender and security, and humanitarian action.[384]

---

376 Council of the EU, 'Council Common Position 2003/319/CFSP of 8 May 2003 Concerning European Union Support for the Implementation of the Lusaka Ceasefire Agreement and the Peace Process in the Democratic Republic of Congo (DRC) and Repealing Common Position 2002/203/CFSP' (2003) OJ L 115; Council of the EU, 'Council Joint Action 2003/423/CFSP of 5 June 2003 on the European Union Military Operation in the Democratic Republic of Congo' (2003) OJ L 143; Council of the EU, 'Council Decision 2003/432/CFSP of 12 June 2003 on the Launching of the European Union Military Operation in the Democratic Republic of Congo' (2003) OJ L 147.

377 'UNSC Res. 1484' (n. 143) para. 1.

378 Anand Menon, 'Power, Institutions and the CSDP: The Promise of Institutionalist Theory' (2011) 49 Journal of Common Market Studies 83, 95, as referred to by Schmidt (n. 367) 109.

379 Koops and Patz (n. 304) 13.

380 *Ibid.*

381 Council of the EU, 'Draft Guidelines on Protection of Civilians in EU-Led Crisis Management Operations' (2003) EU Doc. 14805/03.

382 *Ibid.* para. 1.

383 *Ibid.* para. 2.

384 Koops and Patz (n. 304) 3.

A couple of weeks later, the EU presented its 2003 European Security Strategy, further laying the groundwork for action in crisis situations outside the EU.[385] It held, for example, that the EU should 'share in the responsibility for global security.'[386] Most importantly, the EU realised that while the traditional concept of self-defence was based on the threat of a military invasion of one's territory, with new threats, the first line of defence is often outside the EU.[387] Hence, the 2003 European Security Strategy called for a more active approach to pursuing the EU's strategic objectives and making full use of the crisis management and conflict prevention instruments it has at its disposal.[388] To this end, the Strategy set forth that the EU should support the UN in its response to threats to international peace and security and that the EU is committed to strengthening its co-operation with the UN to assist countries emerging from conflicts and to reinforce its support for the UN in short-term crisis management situations.[389]

In the following years, the EU indeed undertook military action in crisis situations. However, the cases in which the UN provided a PoC mandate were limited. On 12 June 2006, following a request from the UN and the provision of a PoC mandate by the UN Security Council, the EU launched its second operation in the DRC. EUFOR RD Congo was established to support MONUC during the election process.[390] Just like the previous operation in the DRC, EUFOR RD Congo was short-term (and was equally criticised for this): five and a half months after being launched, the operation was concluded on 30 November 2006.[391] On 28 January 2008, the EU launched operation EUFOR Tchad/RCA, which sought to provide a safe and secure environment for refugees and IDPs along the border between Chad, Sudan, and the CAR.[392] On 15 March 2009,

---

385 Council of the EU, 'European Security Strategy: A Secure Europe in a Better World' (2003) EU Doc. 15895/03.

386 *Ibid.* 3.

387 *Ibid.* 9.

388 *Ibid.* 13.

389 *Ibid.*

390 'UNSC Res. 1671' (n. 144); Council of the EU, 'Council Decision 2006/412/CFSP of 12 June 2006 on the Launching of the European Union Military Operation in Support of the United Nations Organisation Mission in the Democratic Republic of the Congo (MONUC) during the Election Process' (2006) OJ L 163.

391 Council of the EU, 'Council Joint Action 2007/147/CFSP of 27 February 2007 Repealing Joint Action 2006/319/CFSP on the European Union Military Operation in Support of the United Nations Organisation Mission in the Democratic Republic of the Congo (MONUC) during the Election Process' (2007) OJ L 64, pream. para. 2.

392 'UNSC Res. 1778' (n. 145); Council of the EU, 'Council Joint Action 2007/677/CFSP of 15 October 2007 on the European Union Military Operation in the Republic of Chad and in the Central African Republic' (2007) OJ L 279; Council of the EU, 'Council Decision 2008/101/CFSP of 28 January 2008 on the Launching of the European Union Military Operation in the Republic of Chad and in the Central African Republic (Operation EUFOR Tchad/RCA)' (2008) OJ L 34; Council of the EU, 'Council Joint Action 2008/110/CFSP of 12 February 2008 Amending and Extending the Mandate of the European Union Special Representative for Sudan' (2008) OJ L 143; 'UNSC Res. 1861' (n. 138).

EUFOR Tchad/RCA handed over its authority to MINURCAT.[393] While EUFOR Tchad/RCA succeeded in contributing to the effective protection of civilians in danger, the operation received criticism for not re-hatting its troops directly to MINURCAT.[394]

The EU has also conducted operations that were not provided with an explicit PoC mandate by the UN Security Council but nevertheless contributed to protecting the civilian population. For example, one of the key objectives of the European Union Force in Bosnia and Herzegovina (EUFOR ALTHEA/BiH) is to contribute to a safe and secure environment in Bosnia and Herzegovina. The UN Security Council welcomed the EU's plan to launch an operation with a military component in the country.[395] It authorised the UN Member States, acting through or in co-operation with the EU, to establish EUFOR ALTHEA/BiH as a legal successor to the Stabilization Force (SFOR), under unified command and control to, *inter alia*, support the authorities of Bosnia and Herzegovina in maintaining a safe and secure environment.[396] The EU also established an EU civilian-military action to support the earlier-mentioned AU-led operation in Darfur, AMIS II (AMIS EU Supporting Action). AMIS II equally contributed to the protection of the civilian population and to efforts to improve the security and humanitarian situation but never received an explicit PoC mandate by the UN Security Council.[397] What is striking, however, is that even though several mandates include provisions relating to the protection of civilians, the EU never explicitly included PoC in the internal mandates of the ESDP missions or operations.[398]

Following the entry into force of the Treaty of Lisbon in 2009,[399] the ESDP was renamed the CSDP, and all functions of the WEU were effectively incorporated into the EU.[400] Furthermore, the 2007 Treaty of Lisbon formally endorsed the extension of the Petersberg Tasks, which now include 'joint disarmament operations, humanitarian and rescue tasks, military advice and assistance tasks, conflict prevention and peace-keeping tasks, tasks of

393 Council of the EU, 'Council Joint Action 2009/795/CFSP of 19 October 2009 Repealing Joint Action 2007/677/CFSP on the European Union Military Operation in the Republic of Chad and in the Central African Republic' (2008) OJ L 283 para. 2.

394 Koops and Patz (n. 304) 14.

395 'UNSC Res. 1551' (2004) UN Doc. S/RES/1551 (2004) para. 10.

396 'UNSC Res. 1575' (2004) UN Doc. S/RES/1575 (2004) paras 10, 11, and 14; 'General Framework Agreement for Peace in Bosnia and Herzegovina' (1995) UN Doc. A/50/790-S/1995/999, Annexes 1-A and 2.

397 Council of the EU, 'Council Joint Action 2005/557/CFSP of 18 July 2005 on the European Union Civilian-Military Supporting Action to the African Union Mission in the Darfur Region of Sudan' (2005) OJ L 188, pream. para. 1 and Art. 1 and 9.

398 On the difference between 'internal' and 'external' mandates, see Part I, Section 4.1.1.

399 Treaty of Lisbon amending the Treaty on European Union and the Treaty establishing the European Community (adopted 13 December 2007, entered into force 1 December 2009) 2702 UNTS 3 (2007 Treaty of Lisbon).

400 EEAS (n. 364).

combat forces in crisis management, including peacemaking and post-conflict stabilisation' (Article 43(1) of the TEU). In addition, 'these tasks may contribute to the fight against terrorism, including by supporting third countries in combating terrorism in their territories' (Article 43(1) of the TEU).

In 2010, following the adoption of UNSC Resolution 1894 (2009),[401] the European Union Political and Security Committee (EU PSC) asked the General Secretariat of the Council of the European Union (EU GSC) to review and update, in close co-operation with the EU Commission, the 2003 EU Draft Guidelines on PoC in EU-led Crisis Management Operations.[402] The 2010 EU Draft Revised Guidelines on PoC in CSDP Missions and Operations considered experiences regarding the implementation of the PoC in CSDP missions and operations,[403] yet without thoroughly evaluating the EU operational experiences in this regard. Instead, the EU heavily relied on the UN experience and, to some extent, on the best practices identified by other relevant organisations (such as NATO) to formulate guidelines.[404] Moreover, despite being more detailed than the 2003 EU Draft Guidelines on PoC in EU-led Crisis Management Operations, the 2010 EU Draft Revised Guidelines on PoC in CSDP Missions and Operations were still somewhat vague on how to operationalise PoC. The 2010 EU Draft Revised Guidelines transformed PoC from a concrete mandated task into an overarching vision that was not only difficult to achieve but also not necessarily aligned with EU capabilities and political will.[405]

In February 2014, the Council of the EU established a second military operation in the CAR, called EUFOR RCA, as authorised by the UN Security Council in Resolution 2134 (2014).[406] While UNSC Resolution 2134 (2014) did not contain an explicit reference to a PoC mandate (and instead had a broad and abstract mandate),[407] a letter from the then High Representative of the Union for Foreign Affairs and Security Policy (EU High Representative) Catherine Ashton to which the UN Security Council referred, noted that the EU contribution would take the form of a military operation to contribute to PoC.[408] EUFOR RCA was established on 10 February 2014 and operated in coordination with

401 'UNSC Res. 1894' (n. 233).
402 Council of the EU, 'Draft Revised Guidelines on the Protection of Civilians in CSDP Missions and Operations' (2010) EU Doc. 15091/10 para. 2.
403 *Ibid.*
404 See *ibid.* See also Kjeksrud and others (n. 302) 102; Koops and Patz (n. 304) 7.
405 Kjeksrud and others (n. 302) 97.
406 'UNSC Res. 2134' (n. 146) para. 43.
407 Koops and Patz (n. 304) 14.
408 'Letter Dated 21 January 2014 from Catherine Ashton, the High Representative for Foreign Affairs and Security Policy of the European Union and Vice-President of the European Commission, as Annexed to the Letter Dated 25 February 2014 from the Secretary-General Addressed to the President of the Security Council' (n. 146) 2, as referred to by 'UNSC Res. 2134' (n. 146) para. 43.

the French forces and the AU.[409] After being extended in November 2014, the mandate eventually ended on 15 March 2015.[410]

In 2015, the EUMC developed the EU Concept on PoC in EU-led Military Operations, with more specific instructions to better integrate aspects of PoC in all phases of EU-led military operations (ranging from the education, training, and planning to the implementation and evaluation of operations) and to contribute to the coherence and synergy of action in the field.[411] In doing so, it referred much less to UN practices on PoC. Instead, the EUMC understands PoC as follows:[412]

> [A]ll efforts to reduce the effects of armed conflicts on civilian populations, namely by mitigating negative effects of the conduct of military operations and to actively protect civilians from threat of violence by others.

With this approach, the EU brought together the UN's approach of active protection from third parties and NATO's harm mitigation focus.[413]

Indeed, according to the EUMC, PoC includes both military and non-military aspects and usually involves protecting civilians from physical violence, protecting human rights, contributing to ensuring the right of access to essential services and resources, and contributing to a safe, stable, and equitable environment, as well as contributing in all areas of life.[414] EU-led military operations can assist, together with police services, in creating a so-called 'safe and secure environment' where civilians can be protected from imminent threats of violence.[415] However, until the root causes of the conflict are resolved in the long term, this is only a temporary solution.[416] The EU recognises that achieving comprehensive and long-term PoC often requires a transition of responsibility between the host State, international organisations, and non-governmental organisations.[417] EU armed forces can contribute by taking proactive measures to ensure that civilians are protected during such transitional phases where risks to civilians may increase significantly.[418] Such proactive measures may include

---

409 Council of the EU, 'Council Decision 2014/73/CFSP of 10 February 2014 on a European Union Military Operation in the Central African Republic (EUFOR RCA)' (n. 146) 73; Council of the EU, 'Council Decision 2014/183/CFSP of 1 April 2014 on the Launch of a European Union Military Operation in the Central African Republic (EUFOR RCA)' (n. 146) 183.

410 Council of the EU, 'Council Decision 2014/775/CFSP of 7 November 2014 Extending Decision 2014/73/CFSP on a European Union Military Operation in the Central African Republic (EUFOR RCA)' (n. 146) 775, Art. 1 and 2.

411 EUMC, '2015 EU Concept on PoC in EU-Led Military Operations' (n. 120) paras 7 and 16.

412 *Ibid.* para. 6.

413 Koops and Patz (n. 304) 7.

414 EUMC, '2015 EU Concept on PoC in EU-Led Military Operations' (n. 120) para. 11.

415 *Ibid.* para. 12.

416 *Ibid.*

417 *Ibid.* para. 14.

418 *Ibid.*

the use of all necessary force to prevent, pre-empt, and respond to physical violence.[419] Furthermore, the potential risks to civilians caused by EU forces in the conduct of EU-led military operations are to be mitigated by the principle of 'do no harm', preventing and minimising collateral damages (especially civilian casualties), and using a broad spectrum of non-lethal means.[420] Last but not least, the EU underscored the importance of civil-military co-operation (CIMIC) at all levels of an operation.[421]

Curiously, in its 2014 EU Concept for EU-led Military Operations and Missions, adopted just one year earlier, the EUMC only briefly discussed PoC and, in doing so, took a narrow IHL approach to PoC. When discussing PoC, it explained that IHL 'attempts to provide protection for those involved in or affected by armed conflict or occupation, including combatants and non-combatant members of the population and to regulate the conduct of armed conflict.'[422] It then simply stated that efforts to protect non-combatant members of the population could enhance the protection of EU forces in the field, but in some situations, it can also prove challenging to strike a balance between EU force protection and civilian protection.[423]

Following the entry into force of the 2007 Treaty of Lisbon, some Member States called for an update of the 2003 European Security Strategy.[424] It lasted, however, until 2016, when the EU Global Strategy on Foreign and Security Policy was presented.[425] The 2016 EU Global Strategy identified 'security and defence' as one of five broad priorities and established that Europeans must not only be able to protect Europe but also respond to external crises and assist in developing its partners' security and defence capacities.[426] The protection of 'human lives, notably civilians,' is part of such crisis management.[427] In 2019, EU High Representative Joseph Borrell decided to uphold the 2016 EU Global Strategy on Foreign and Security Policy.[428]

In recent years, despite the existing PoC framework and initial successes, the EU has undertaken fewer PoC activities, and those that have been undertaken

419 *Ibid.* para. 15.
420 *Ibid.* para. 16.
421 *Ibid.* para. 17.
422 EUMC, 'EU Concept for EU-Led Military Operations and Missions' (2014) EU Doc. EEAS 00990/6/14 REV 6 para. 37(a).
423 *Ibid.* para. 37(b).
424 Sven Biscop, 'Analysing the EU Global Strategy on Foreign and Security Policy' in Jochen Rehrl (ed), *Handbook on CSDP: the Common Security and Defence Policy of the European Union*, vol. 1 (4th edn., Directorate of Security Policy of the Federal Ministry of Defence and Sports of the Republic of Austria 2021) 31.
425 EU, 'Shared Vision, Common Action: A Stronger Europe. A Global Strategy for the European Union's Foreign And Security Policy' (2016), www.eeas.europa.eu/sites/default/files/eugs_review_web_0.pdf, accessed 17 February 2021.
426 *Ibid.* 18–19.
427 *Ibid.* 30.
428 Biscop (n. 424) 35.

have been non-executive in nature, focusing on training and capacity building rather than major military CSDP missions.[429]

3. INTRODUCTION TO POLICIES ON THE USE OF FORCE FOR POC

The use of force is inextricably linked to PoC through military initiatives. Not only the UN – the organisation that is the source of PoC as a mandated task – but also the AU, NATO, and the EU have developed policies on the use of force for PoC over the years. These different policies are discussed in the following Sections.

3.1. UN POLICY ON THE USE OF FORCE FOR POC

3.1.1. Basic Principles of UN Peacekeeping

The authority of UN peace forces to use force has a long and convoluted history due to peacekeeping's origins as a consensual form of conflict management grounded on the principle of non-use of force except in self-defence. In 1958, in the aftermath of the establishment of the United Nations Emergency Force I (UNEF I),[430] UN Secretary-General Dag Hammarskjöld spelt out the three basic principles of the operation: (i) the neutrality of the force in the dispute;[431] (ii) the right to fire in self-defence, but the prohibition against any initiative in the use of armed force;[432] and (iii) the consent of the host State.[433] These principles were initially intended to steer the deployment and activities of UN inter-

429 Koops and Patz (n. 304) 16.

430 UNEF I was the earliest armed UN peace operation. The first two UN peace operations were the United Nations Truce Supervision Organization (UNTSO) and the United Nations Military Observer Group in India and Pakistan (UNMOGIP), yet these were unarmed observation missions.

431 UNSG, 'Summary Study of the Experience Derived from the Establishment and Operation of the Force: Report of the Secretary-General, Thirteenth Session, Annexes, Agenda Item 65' (1958) UN Doc A/3943 para. 12 ('[T]here was "no intent […] to influence the military balance in the present conflict and, thereby, the political balance affecting efforts to settle the conflict"'), hereby quoting the following report: UNGA, 'Question Considered by the Security Council at Its 749th and 750th Meetings Held on 30 October 1956, Second and Final Report of the Secretary-General on the Plan for an Emergency International United Nations Force Requested in the Resolution Adopted by the General Assembly on 4 November 1956' (1956) UN Doc. A/3302 para. 8.

432 UNSG, 'Summary Study of the Experience Derived from the Establishment and Operation of the Force: Report of the Secretary-General, Thirteenth Session, Annexes, Agenda Item 65' (n. 431) paras 70 and 179.

433 *Ibid.* paras 15, 155–156.

positional ceasefire monitoring missions and to address the need to maintain the legitimacy of UN peace operations deployed in inter-state conflicts.[434]

Over the past decades, the UN entities further developed and affirmed these principles of consent, impartiality (which replaced neutrality), and defensive use of force (which evolved from personal self-defence to defence of the mission) as the Basic Principles of UN Peacekeeping. Former UN Secretary-General Boutros-Ghali, for example, stated in his 1995 Supplement to an Agenda for Peace that respect for the Basic Principles of UN Peacekeeping is paramount to the success of UN peace operations.[435] Likewise, for their part, the former UN DPKO and DFS have time and again emphasised the importance of the three principles (see e.g. in the 2008 Capstone Doctrine,[436] the 2009 New Horizon Project,[437] and the 2015 HIPPO Report).[438]

3.1.2. From self-defence to the (offensive) protection of civilians

The concept of the use of force in self-defence by UN peace forces has undergone 'a quiet revolution,' especially with the extension to 'in defence of the mandate.'[439] UN peacekeeping's ontology as a form of non-forcible intervention, however, raises the stakes of definitional disputes around self-defence. As Findlay accurately said: '[t]he norm has been stretched and ultimately broken, both inadvertently and deliberately.'[440] While the initial approach to the concept of self-defence was rather strict and in line with the common or legal understanding of the concept (i.e. 'personal self-defence'), the concept quickly evolved into some form of cover for allowing more force without having to acknowledge that the way the UN did peacekeeping had fundamentally changed. Because the non-use of force except in self-defence is still perceived as one of the three core principles of peacekeeping, the UN has an incentive to present its actions as defensive in nature, irrespective of the UN Security Council's increasingly proactive mandates and without regard for factual realities on the ground.

But let's start from the beginning: in 1958, when discussing the Basic Principles of UN Peacekeeping, and, in particular, the 'right to fire in self-

434 Daniel H Levine, 'Peacekeeper Impartiality: Standards, Processes, and Operations' (2011) 15 Journal of International Peacekeeping 422, 423.

435 UNSG, 'Supplement to an Agenda for Peace: Position Paper of the Secretary-General on the Occasion of the Fiftieth Anniversary of the United Nations, General Assembly: Fiftieth Session, Report of the Secretary-General on the Work of the Organization, Security Council: Fiftieth Year' (1995) UN Doc. A/50/60 and S/1995/1 para. 33.

436 UN DPKO and UN DFS, '2008 Capstone Doctrine' (n. 19) 31.

437 UN DPKO and UN DFS, 'A New Partnership Agenda: Charting a New Horizon for UN Peacekeeping' (2009) 2.

438 HIPPO (n. 112) para. 125.

439 Sheeran, 'The Use of Force in United Nations Peacekeeping Operations' (n. 37) 363.

440 Findlay (n. 168) 356.

defence, but the prohibition against any initiative in the use of armed force,'[441] UN Secretary-General Dag Hammarskjöld stressed that 'a wide interpretation of the right of self-defence might well blur the distinction between [UN peace operations] [...] and combat operations which would require a decision under Chapter VII.'[442] Hammarskjöld, nevertheless, went on to clarify that 'the rule is applied that men engaged in the operation may never take the initiative in the use of armed force, but are entitled to respond with force to an attack with arms, including attempts to use force to make them withdraw from [their] positions.'[443]

Except for ONUC (the short-lived but robust United Nations Operation in the Congo[444] that lasted from 1960 until 1964),[445] early UN peace operations generally adhered to the principle of non-use of force except in self-defence, where self-defence was equated with soldiers' personal authority to respond to force at the tactical level. However, the concept of self-defence expanded over time, under the radar, mainly through internal policy guidance rather than top-down UNSC mandates. In 1964, UN Secretary-General U Thant observed that 'self-defence' included '(a) the defence of United Nations posts, premises and vehicles under armed attack; [and] (b) the support of other personnel of UNFICYP [the United Nations Peacekeeping Force in Cyprus] under armed attack.'[446] One of the examples in which the UNFICYP troops were authorised to use force was 'attempts by force to prevent them from carrying out their responsibilities as ordered by their commanders.'[447] By adopting this approach, the UN Secretary-General clearly went beyond the generally accepted approach of the principle of personal self-defence. Nonetheless, both the UN Secretary-General and the UN Security Council reinforced this extensive approach to self-defence at a later stage. For example, in 1973, UN Secretary-General Kurt Waldheim reinforced that '[s]elf-defence would include resistance to attempts by forceful means to prevent it from discharging its duties under the mandate of the Security Council.'[448]

Echoing Waldheim's definition, UNSC Resolution 467 (1980) authorising UNIFIL noted that 'self-defence would include resistance to attempts by forceful means to prevent [the mission] from discharging its duties under the mandate

441 UNSG, 'Summary Study of the Experience Derived from the Establishment and Operation of the Force: Report of the Secretary-General, Thirteenth Session, Annexes, Agenda Item 65' (n. 431) paras 70 and 179.

442 *Ibid.* para. 179.

443 *Ibid.*

444 The DRC has been known in the past as, in chronological order, the Congo Free State, Belgian Congo, the Republic of Congo-Léopoldville (which was the name of the country when ONUC was deployed there), the DRC, and the Republic of Zaire, before returning to its current name, the DRC.

445 Findlay (n. 168) 51–86.

446 UNSG, 'Note by the Secretary-General' (1964) UN Doc. S/5653 para. 16.

447 *Ibid.* para. 18(c).

448 UNSG, 'Report of the Secretary-General on the Implementation of Security Council Resolution 340 (1973)' (1973) UN Doc. S/11052/Rev. 1 para. 4(d).

of the Security Council.'[449] In doing so, the UN Security Council seemed to officially endorse a concept of self-defence that expressly went beyond individual, personal self-defence and extended to defending the mission mandate. Nevertheless, UN peacekeeping remained a defensive and reactive endeavour and prompted limited debate over the legal parameters of peace forces' use of force authority.[450]

This status quo changed rapidly in the 1990s when the UN began deploying peace forces to increasingly hostile environments. Facing armed opposition to its operations in the former Yugoslavia and several African countries (in particular, Somalia, Rwanda, Sierra Leone, Liberia, the DRC, and the CAR), the UN Security Council gradually expanded traditional understandings of self-defence by emphasising UN peace forces' authority to defend mission personnel and mission property and to ensure freedom of movement.[451] Over time, the UN coined the concept of force 'in defence of the mandate'. As the 2000 Brahimi Report noted, 'United Nations military units must be capable of defending themselves, other mission components and the mission's mandate.'[452] Similarly, the 2008 Capstone Doctrine and several mission mandates enshrined in UNSC resolutions emphasised the principle of '[n]on-use of force except in self-defense and defense of the mandate.'[453]

Parallel to the expanding self-defence language, which blurred the line between reactive and proactive force, the UN began invoking language associated with offensive force. In particular, the UN Security Council adopted mandates in which it authorised the use of 'all necessary means', the language traditionally considered code for the use of (offensive) transboundary force.[454]

449 'UNSC Res. 467' (1980) UN Doc. S/RES/467 (1980) pream. para. 6(d).

450 See generally Antonio Cassese (ed), *United Nations Peace-Keeping: Legal Essays* (Sijthoff & Noordhoff (International Publishers) 1978).

451 E.g. as discussed earlier, in Resolution 836 (1993), the UN Security Council decided to extend UNPROFOR's mandate 'in order to enable it, in the safe areas [...], to deter attacks against the safe areas [...], in addition to participating in the delivery of humanitarian relief to the population [...]' and authorised UNPROFOR 'to take the necessary measures, including the use of force, in reply to bombardments against the safe areas by any of the parties or to armed incursion into them or in the event of any deliberate obstruction in or around those areas to the freedom of movement of UNPROFOR or of protected humanitarian convoys' ('UNSC Res. 836' (n. 3) paras 5 and 8); in UNSC Resolution 837 (1993), after an ambush resulted in the death of 24 members of the UN peace forces and left another 57 wounded, the UN Security Council authorised the United Nations Operation in Somalia II (UNOSOM II) to take 'all necessary measures against all those responsible,' including 'their arrest and detention for prosecution, trial and punishment' ('UNSC Res. 837' (1993) UN Doc. S/RES/837 (1993) para. 5).

452 'Report of the Panel on United Nations Peace Operations (Brahimi Report), Fifty-Fifth Session of the General Assembly, Item 87 of the Provisional Agenda; Fifty-Fifth Year of the Security Council' (n. 19) para. 49.

453 UN DPKO and UN DFS, '2008 Capstone Doctrine' (n. 19) 31. For references, see Introductory Chapter, Section 1, fn. 19.

454 Christian Henderson, *The Use of Force and International Law:* (Cambridge University Press 2018) 102–114.

In 1999, phrases such as 'all necessary means' and 'all necessary action' became regularly associated with PoC, as well as other priority tasks (including 'deter[ring] forceful attempts to disrupt the political process' or 'assist[ing] the national authorities in maintaining law and order').[455] Yet, since the adoption of the first PoC mandate in 1999, an often-heard commentary has been that the greatest challenge to the effective protection of civilians is the lack of a common understanding of what the UN can and should be doing to protect civilians when having such a mandate to use 'all necessary means'. While PoC is intimately linked to the use of force, it is not always clear when force can, must or cannot be used. In 2009, the former UN DPKO and UN OCHA commissioned a study on PoC, which emphasised the gap between mandates and UN peace operations' performance and prompted wide-ranging institutional reforms.[456]

3.1.3. UN efforts to develop a policy on the use of force for PoC

In recent years, different UN bodies have made considerable efforts to clarify the strategic, operational, and tactical approaches to protecting civilians by force.

As discussed above, the UN's current PoC policy distinguishes between three protection tiers, whereby protection through dialogue and engagement (Tier I) and the establishment of a protective environment (Tier III) complement classic physical protection (Tier II).[457] The importance of Tier I and Tier III continues to grow in the UN peacekeeping context. Yet, the central function of UN troops providing *physical* security to civilians under Tier II remains a centrepiece of peacekeeping activity.[458] Tier II comprehends activities by all mission components to provide physical protection to civilians, 'whether through protective presence, interpositioning, the threat or use of force, or facilitating safe passage or refuge.'[459] Military components, in particular, may undertake activities, such as 'the show or use of force to prevent, deter, pre-empt and respond to threats to civilians.'[460] When UN peace forces have identified a concrete threat of attack against civilians, they can take proactive and timely

455 UN DPKO and UN DFS, '2008 Capstone Doctrine' (n. 19) 34.

456 Holt and Taylor (n. 162).

457 UN DPO, '2019 UN Policy on PoC in UN Peacekeeping' (n. 35) para. 40. It is worth repeating that the former UN DPKO and DFS already adopted the three-tiered approach in the 2010 Draft Operational Concept, but over time some adjustments were made (as discussed in Part I, Section 2.1.3) (see UN DPKO and UN DFS, '2010 UN Draft Operational Concept on PoC in UN Peacekeeping Operations' (n. 235) paras 14–21; UN DPKO and UN DFS, '2015 UN Implementing Guidelines for Military Components of UN Peacekeeping Missions on PoC' (n. 103) 6–8; UN DPKO and UN DFS, '2015 UN Policy on PoC in UN Peacekeeping' (n. 16) para. 30).

458 UN DPKO and UN DFS, '2015 UN Implementing Guidelines for Military Components of UN Peacekeeping Missions on PoC' (n. 103); UN DPKO and UN DFS, '2017 UN Guidelines on the Use of Force by Military Components in UN Peacekeeping Operations' (n. 17).

459 UN DPO, '2019 UN Policy on PoC in UN Peacekeeping' (n. 35) para. 54.

460 *Ibid.*

measures to remove or mitigate the threat before the violence occurs, including through 'proactive military [...] operations which may extend to pre-empting and neutralising the source of the threat in accordance with the mandate, ROE and DUF [Directive on the Use of Force].'[461]

But what exactly do they mean by all this? According to the 2019 UN Policy on PoC in UN Peacekeeping, 'threats of physical violence' against civilians must be understood to encompass the following:[462]

> [A]ll hostile acts or situations which are likely to lead to death or serious bodily injury of civilians, including sexual violence [...]. 'Threat' includes both violence against civilians which has materialised and is ongoing and violence which has the realistic potential to occur. *The threat need not be imminent, unless the specific Security Council mandate requires this.*

The Policy does not define 'imminent' in this regard. This omission may well be deliberate and indicate that the UN continues to embrace a non-temporal understanding of 'imminence'. For example, in the 2015 UN Implementing Guidelines for Military Components of UN Peacekeeping Missions on PoC, the former UN DPKO and DFS specified that the term 'imminent' does not mean that violence 'is guaranteed to happen in the immediate or near future or is being carried out.'[463] By contrast, a threat is considered 'imminent' 'as soon as the mission reasonably believes that a potential aggressor has the intent and capacity to inflict physical violence.'[464] Once members of UN peace forces reasonably believe that they are in a situation which is intended or is likely to lead to death or serious bodily injury to civilians, they can use lethal force but only as a last resort.[465] The UN DPO considers it irrelevant whether the threat posed to civilians is from elements of the host State's security forces or others.[466] Nevertheless, they also recognise that a robust response to the threats posed by the host State's security forces may exceed the mission's capabilities, may put UN peace forces in precarious situations, and may have an unprecedented effect on the consent of the host State to the deployment of the operation within its territory.[467]

Inherently linked with the notions of 'threat' and 'imminent threat' are the notions of 'hostile act' and 'hostile intent'. In the 2017 UN Guidelines on the Use

461 *Ibid.* para. 56.

462 Emphasis added. *Ibid.* para. 23. See also UN DPKO and UN DFS, '2015 UN Policy on PoC in UN Peacekeeping' (n. 16) 19.

463 UN DPKO and UN DFS, '2015 UN Implementing Guidelines for Military Components of UN Peacekeeping Missions on PoC' (n. 103) 25.

464 *Ibid.*

465 *Ibid.* See also UN DPKO and UN DFS, '2017 UN Guidelines on the Use of Force by Military Components in UN Peacekeeping Operations' (n. 17) 6.

466 UN DPO, '2019 UN Policy on PoC in UN Peacekeeping' (n. 35) para. 61.

467 *Ibid.*

of Force by Military Components in UN Peacekeeping Operations, 'hostile act' is defined as '[a]n action where the intent is to cause death, serious bodily harm or destruction of United Nations designated property,' whereas 'hostile intent' is understood as follows:[468]

> The threat of an impending use of force, which is demonstrated through an action or behavior which appears to be preparatory to a hostile act. Only a reasonable belief in the hostile intent is required before the use of force is authorized. Whether or not hostile intent is being demonstrated must be judged by the on-scene commander, on the basis of one or a combination of the following factors: a. The capability and preparedness of the threat. b. The available evidence which indicates an intention to attack. c. Historical precedent within the Mission's Area of Responsibility.

In the 2002 UN Sample ROE, hostile intent is defined in an almost identical way, with the exception of the first sentence, which reads as follows: '[t]he threat of *imminent* use of force, which is demonstrated through an action which appears to be preparatory to a hostile act.'[469] The term 'impending', as used in the 2017 UN Guidelines on the Use of Force by Military Components in UN Peacekeeping Operations, is nowhere defined in UN policy, yet the concept of hostile intent is deeply intertwined with the use of force in international law (as discussed further in Part II, Section 3.2.4.2).

When members of UN peace forces have identified a threat of physical violence against civilians, they may proceed to use force to provide physical protection to civilians. Force in this regard is understood as 'the use of, or threat to use, physical means to impose one's will.'[470] The 2017 UN Guidelines on the Use of Force by Military Components in UN Peacekeeping Operations set forth that the use of force by UN peace forces finds its legal basis in the mandate of a UN peace operation, as included in a UNSC resolution, and must be exercised in a manner consistent with this mandate.[471] According to the 2015 UN Implementing Guidelines for Military Components of UN Peacekeeping Missions on PoC, a mission that is provided with a mandate to 'use all necessary means to protect civilians' is authorised to use force, up to and including lethal force, to protect civilians, including IDPs and refugees, under threat of physical violence.[472] In certain cases, UN peace forces may also be authorised to counter

---

468 UN DPKO and UN DFS, '2017 UN Guidelines on the Use of Force by Military Components in UN Peacekeeping Operations' (n. 17) 19.

469 UN DPKO (n. 102) Attachment 2: Annex B – 1.

470 UN DPKO and UN DFS, '2017 UN Guidelines on the Use of Force by Military Components in UN Peacekeeping Operations' (n. 17) para. 6.

471 *Ibid.* para. 7.

472 UN DPKO and UN DFS, '2015 UN Implementing Guidelines for Military Components of UN Peacekeeping Missions on PoC' (n. 103) 15. See also UN DPKO and UN DFS, '2017 UN Guidelines on the Use of Force by Military Components in UN Peacekeeping Operations' (n. 17) para. 6.

other threats, such as those from armed spoilers seeking to disturb the peace process.[473]

Any force used 'must be limited in its intensity and duration to what is necessary to achieve the authorized objective and, commensurate with the threat.'[474] This interpretation means that UN peace forces are required to always seek alternatives to the use of force.[475] If force is unavoidable to achieve the mandated objective(s), UN peace forces must adopt a graduated application of increasing levels of force.[476] Such graduated application of force ensures that only the minimum level of force necessary is used, that excessive force is avoided, and that the loss of, or damage to, life and property is minimised as much as possible.[477] To that end, force is categorised into 'three broad levels,' including physical presence of authority, non-lethal force, and lethal force.[478] Authoritative physical presence may include, for example, foot, vehicle, or air patrols.[479] Non-deadly force is understood as force necessary to make aggressors obey or deter and is neither intended nor likely to cause death or serious bodily injury.[480] Lethal force is either intended to cause death or involves a very significant risk of death, regardless of whether death actually results.[481] Authoritative physical presence should precede non-lethal force, which in turn must precede lethal force.[482] This gradual approach may nevertheless be overridden if the nature of the threat warrants it (e.g. when an attack is so unexpected and only the immediate use of lethal force can suffice to save someone's life).[483]

3.1.4. From theory to practice: 'I will shoot ... or not'

Over the years, UN peace forces have provided physical protection to millions of people not only through their mere presence but also by being proactive in combating violence against civilians.[484] Yet, the practice of tasking UN peace operations to use all necessary means to protect civilians has not yielded

473 UN DPKO and UN DFS, '2017 UN Guidelines on the Use of Force by Military Components in UN Peacekeeping Operations' (n. 17) para. 6.
474 *Ibid.* para. 8.
475 *Ibid.* para. 10.
476 *Ibid.* para. 11. See also UN DPO, '2019 UN Policy on PoC in UN Peacekeeping' (n. 35) para. 57.
477 UN DPKO and UN DFS, '2017 UN Guidelines on the Use of Force by Military Components in UN Peacekeeping Operations' (n. 17) para. 11.
478 *Ibid.* para. 12.
479 *Ibid.* para. 12(a).
480 *Ibid.* para. 12(b).
481 See also *ibid.* para. 12(c).
482 *Ibid.* para. 12.
483 *Ibid.*
484 Charles T Hunt and Shannon Zimmerman, 'Twenty Years of the Protection of Civilians in UN Peace Operations' (2020) Journal of International Peacekeeping 1, 6.

consistent and effective results on the ground.[485] As a result, UN peace operations are criticised for using too much force and not using enough force to protect civilians.

For example, one of the critiques is that the use of force by UN peace forces to defend the civilian population or to 'neutralise' offensively armed groups (see MONUSCO's Intervention Brigade's mandate) may lead to harming the very people the military action is supposed to protect.[486] For example, in the case of MINUSCA, there have been instances where members of the peace forces have been accused of killing and injuring civilians.[487] Correspondingly, MINUSTAH (deployed in Haiti between June 2004 and October 2007, during which time there was no armed conflict) was criticised for the extensive use of force by its peace forces that resulted in civilian casualties.[488] According to Wills, MINUSTAH clearly used excessive force to accomplish its mission.[489] Moreover, while the UN has made substantial efforts to promulgate the concept of robust peacekeeping, this move towards more robust use of force by UN peace forces and the broadening of peacekeeping activities to include stabilisation has not been accompanied by the same level of attention to the legal obligations associated with the use of force.[490] Wills, for example, contended that there were strong indications that MINUSTAH was responsible for civilian casualties between 2004 and 2007 and, in that respect, may have violated international legal standards protecting the right to life.[491]

In 2017, a panel led by MINUSTAH's former Force Commander (FC) General Carlos Alberto dos Santos Cruz published a report on the security of peacekeeping personnel, the main conclusion of which was that not less but more force had to be used in practice.[492] The 2017 Cruz Report made bold

485 United Nations Peacekeeping Law Reform Project, School of Law, University of Essex, 'UN Peacekeeping and The Model Status of Forces Agreement: Background Paper Prepared for the Experts' Workshop Hosted by the New Zealand High Commission in London, 26 August 2010' (2010) 25–26.

486 Hunt (n. 40) 115.

487 X, 'Le Regain de Violences à Bangui Fait Au Moins 18 Morts, Dont Un Casque Bleu' *Le Monde Afrique* (11 April 2018), www.lemonde.fr/afrique/article/2018/04/11/regain-de-violences-a-bangui-ou-un-casque-bleu-a-ete-tue_5283837_3212.html, accessed 20 April 2022.

488 Andrew Buncombe, 'Civilians Caught in Crossfire during Port-Au-Prince Raids' *The Independent* (2 February 2007), www.independent.co.uk/news/world/americas/civilians-caught-in-crossfire-during-portauprince-raids-434723.html, accessed 20 April 2022.

489 Wills, 'Use of Deadly Force by Peacekeepers Operating Outside of Armed Conflict Situations: What Laws Apply?' (n. 18) 673; Rosa Freedman, Nicolas Lemay-Hébert and Siobhán Wills, *The Law and Practice of Peacekeeping: Foregrounding Human Rights* (Cambridge University Press 2021) 116–139.

490 Wills, 'Use of Deadly Force by Peacekeepers Operating Outside of Armed Conflict Situations: What Laws Apply?' (n. 18) 673.

491 Wills, 'Use of Deadly Force by Peacekeepers Operating Outside of Armed Conflict Situations: What Laws Apply?' (n. 18).

492 Lieutenant General (Retired) Carlos Alberto dos Santos Cruz, 'Improving Security of United Nations Peacekeepers: We Need to Change the Way We Are Doing Business' (2017), https://

statements on the use of force, arguing, for example, that 'in high-risk areas featuring high-intensity conflicts [...] troops should use *overwhelming* force and be proactive and preemptive.'[493] The 2017 Cruz Report, in its turn, attracted much criticism. Mona Khalil argued, for example, that the 2017 Cruz Report 'threatens to destroy whatever remains of a distinction between peacekeeping and peace enforcement' and that 'it pays insufficient attention to the implications of aggressive peacekeeping from the IHL perspective including the increasing likelihood of UN peacekeepers becoming parties to the conflict.'[494] One of the consequences of becoming a party to the conflict is that members of UN peace forces are considered a legitimate target and can thus be killed (as discussed in more detail in Part III, Section 2.2.2). For instance, it is widely recognised that MONUSCO's Intervention Brigade is a party to an armed conflict with an armed group called the Allied Democratic Forces (ADF) and, hence, makes not only the members of the Intervention Brigade but perhaps also all military members of MONUSCO and supporting UN mission infrastructure, vulnerable to lawful attack under IHL.[495]

Moreover, other missions, such as MINUSMA and MINUSCA, have been provided with a more robust mandate and deployed into places where there is active conflict and 'no peace to keep.'[496] As a result, they blur the distinction between traditional peacekeeping (premised on the non-use of force except in self-defence) and peace operations involving coercive force (also sometimes referred to as peace enforcement operations).[497] Furthermore, their overtly offensive PoC operations may raise questions about the legality of killings by members of UN peace forces. For example, as also mentioned in the Introductory

---

peacekeeping.un.org/sites/default/files/improving_security_of_united_nations_peacekeepers_report.pdf, accessed 11 September 2018.

493 Emphasis added. *Ibid.* 5. For a more detailed analysis, see 9–33.

494 Mona A Khalil, 'Robust Peacekeeping – Not Aggressive Peacekeeping', *Proceedings of the Annual Meeting of the American Society of International Law, 4–7 April 2018, Washington, DC, vol. 112, 114* (Cambridge University Press 2018) 116.

495 Geneva Academy Rule of Law, 'Non-International Armed Conflicts in Democratic Republic of Congo' (*Geneva Academy Rule of Law*, 22 April 2021), www.rulac.org/browse/conflicts/non-international-armed-conflict-in-democratic-republic-of-congo#collapse4accord, accessed 20 April 2022 ('Several non-international armed conflicts are taking place in the DRC involving different non-state and international actors. The Congolese armed forces [FARDC] are party to a number of non-international armed conflicts against, at least, the Allied Democratic Forces [ADF], the Mai-Mai Yakutumba, the Democratic Forces for the Liberation of Rwanda [FDLR], and the Cooperative for Development of the Congo [CODECO]. The UN Organization Stabilization Mission in the Democratic Republic of the Congo [MONUSCO] is supporting the Congolese Armed Forces [FARDC] and is party to the conflicts'). See also Scott Sheeran and Stephanie Case, 'The Intervention Brigade: Legal Issues for the UN in the Democratic Republic of the Congo' (International Peace Institute 2014) 7.

496 Alex J Bellamy and Charles T Hunt, 'Twenty-First Century UN Peace Operations: Protection, Force and the Changing Security Environment' 91 International Affairs 1277, 1281.

497 Patryk I Labuda, 'The UN Goes to War in the Central African Republic: What Are the Limits of Peacekeeping?' (*Just Security*, 23 March 2017), www.justsecurity.org/39151/war-central-african-republic-limits-peacekeeping/, accessed 20 April 2022.

Chapter, in 2017, MINUSCA invoked its PoC mandate to justify a strike by one of its attack helicopters, resulting in at least one death, against an armed group that had ignored its warnings not to cross a red line around Bambari, a specially designated 'city without armed groups' under the mission's PoC mandate.[498] Such operations raise difficult questions about the legality of the use of force (as is discussed further in Part III, Section 3.3.2.2.(B)(i)).

OIOS, in turn, made critical assessments between 2014 and 2017 of those very operations, stating that, for the most part, not enough force was used to effectively protect civilians.[499] An evaluation of 2014 held that '[a]s things stand, peacekeeping missions with protection of civilians mandates focus on prevention and mitigation activities and force is almost never used to protect civilians under attack.'[500] In 2017, OIOS concluded that several instances of refusals to obey orders had occurred in the five largest peacekeeping missions, including MINUSCA, MINUSMA, MONUSCO, UNAMID, and UNMISS, since 2014.[501] For example, OIOS identified at least three occasions on 11 July 2016 when a battalion from UNMISS turned down an order to respond.[502] Despite the presence of UNMISS, which has an explicit and robust mandate to protect civilians,[503] hundreds of civilians were killed and raped in Juba, the capital of South Sudan, between 8 and 11 July 2016. In response to this crisis, the UN Security Council eventually decided on 12 August 2016 that UNMISS shall include a Regional Protection Force with the responsibility of providing a secure environment in and around Juba.[504] UNMISS' Regional Protection Force was authorised to use 'all necessary means, including undertaking robust action where necessary and actively patrolling' to accomplish its mandate.[505] It was under the obligation to carry out this mandate in an impartial manner and in strict compliance with international law, including, as applicable, IHL.[506]

---

498 Monteiro, 'La MINUSCA Intervient Contre Des Éléments Lourdement Armés Au Nord de Bambari' (n. 24); Monteiro, 'Mise En Garde de La MINUSCA à La Coalition Du FPRC à Propos Des Déplacés de Ippy' (n. 24). See also Introductory Chapter, Section 1.

499 OIOS (n. 106); OIOS, Inspection and Evaluation Division (n. 106); OIOS, Inspection and Evaluation Division (n. 10).

500 OIOS (n. 106) para. 79.

501 OIOS, Inspection and Evaluation Division (n. 106), table pp. 11–12.

502 *Ibid.* 11.

503 The original mandate given to UNMISS was included in UNSC Res. 1996 (2011) ('UNSC Res. 1996' (n. 135) para. 3(b)(v) and 4). In 2013, the UN Security Council explicitly prioritised the protection of civilians and in 2014, the UN Security Council adopted more obligatory language, see 'UNSC Res. 2109' (n. 135) para. 3; 'UNSC Res. 2155' (n. 135) paras 3, 4(a), and 5. The UN Security Council explicitly extended this PoC mandate in the following resolutions: 'UNSC Res. 2187' (n. 135) paras 3, 4(a), and 5; 'UNSC Res. 2223' (n. 19) paras 3, 4(a), and 5; 'UNSC Res. 2241' (n. 135) paras 3, 4(a), and 5; 'UNSC Res. 2252' (n. 135) paras 4, 8(a), and 10.

504 'UNSC Res. 2304' (n. 135) para. 8.

505 *Ibid.* para. 10.

506 *Ibid.* para. 8.

Following the unfortunate conduct of the operation, UNMISS was accused of not responding effectively to protect civilians from the intense fighting that contributed to the collapse of the fragile ceasefire that existed at that time. As a result, the UN Secretary-General established an Independent Special Investigation (also known as the Cammaert Investigation, named after the individual who led the investigation) that found, *inter alia*, that 'a lack of leadership on the part of key senior Mission personnel culminated in a chaotic and ineffective response to the violence' and that 'the lack of preparedness, ineffective command and control and a risk-averse or 'inward-looking' posture resulted in a loss of trust and confidence [...] in the will and skill of UNMISS military [...] to be proactive and show a determined posture to protect civilians under threat, including from sexual violence and human rights violations.'[507]

OIOS also issued another critical report on the performances of MONUSCO, MINUSMA, and MINUSCA in 2017.[508] According to OIOS, the missions were not 'adequately robust,' despite having forceful mandates to be proactive in deterring and confronting armed groups and spoilers[509] to peace (including through the use of force).[510] Inconsistencies were reported in military contingents' approach to proactively protecting civilians from threats.[511] As mentioned in the Introductory Chapter, some personnel involved in MINUSCA reported, for example, that certain military contingents understood their task of protecting civilians as 'just sitting near a camp.'[512] A military official deployed in MINUSMA stated, 'the aim is to get them back alive, not to do robust peacekeeping.'[513] According to OIOS, the failure to protect civilians was not only due to varying interpretations and preferences in operationalising robust mandates but also political considerations, instructions by capitals, or unclear national regulations.[514] Moreover, OIOS also concluded that missions were inadequately equipped and often insufficiently trained to operate in these asymmetrical environments.[515]

---

507 UNSC, 'Executive Summary of the Independent Special Investigation into the Violence in Juba in 2016 and the Response by the United Nations Mission in South Sudan. Annex to the Letter Dated 1 November 2016 from the Secretary-General Addressed to the President of the Security Council' (2016) UN Doc. S/2016/924 paras 7 and 18.

508 OIOS, Inspection and Evaluation Division (n. 10).

509 OIOS treats armed elements that harm civilians as spoilers. Once they lay down arms and/or demonstrate willingness to enter the process of disarmament, demobilisation, and reintegration and participate in peace-talks, they are considered stakeholders. See *ibid.* para. 79, *fn. 136*.

510 *Ibid.* paras 84, 100–101.

511 *Ibid.* para. 84.

512 *Ibid.* para. 74. See also Introductory Chapter, Section 1.

513 *Ibid.* para. 54.

514 *Ibid.* paras 85 and 104.

515 *Ibid.* paras 89–93 and 104.

3.2. OTHER ORGANISATIONAL APPROACHES TOWARDS THE USE OF FORCE FOR POC

3.2.1. *AU policy on the concept of PoC and the use of force*

The AU has made concerted efforts to develop a framework for a consolidated protection response. As mentioned above, the AU has structured protection activities into four tiers, including Tier 1 – Protection as part of the political process; Tier 2 – Protection from physical violence; Tier 3 – Rights-based protection; and Tier 4 – Establishment of a protective environment.[516] The protection from physical violence is divided into phases: Phase 1 – Prevention; Phase 2 – Pre-emption; Phase 3 – Response; and Phase 4: Consolidation.[517] These phases may not necessarily be sequential and may co-exist across the mission area but nevertheless offer a framework for thinking about how to include the physical protection of civilians in the design of AU-led peace operations.

When it comes to the use of force on the ground, the AU does not provide much detail in its policy documents. To avert an imminent threat of physical violence or to gain an advantage over a spoiler group before it begins a planned violent activity, troops may take precautionary measures (Phase 2).[518] According to the 2012 AU Draft Guidelines for PoC in AU Peace Support Operations, a threat can be classified as 'imminent' based on an estimate of time (i.e. about to happen) and indication (i.e. factual information).[519] After an actual outbreak of violence, troops may use proportional force to neutralise or defuse a spoiler group (Phase 3). In certain cases, this may require authorisation from a higher authority.[520] That said, according to the 2012 AU Draft Guidelines for PoC in AU Peace Support Operations, '[a]ny action taken by a peace support operation to implement a protection of civilians mandate shall be in conformity with relevant international law, including international humanitarian law, human rights law and refugee law.'[521]

AFISMA's ROE and Soldiers' Pocket Card authorised the use of force for PoC. According to AFISMA's ROE, force may be used *beyond* self-defence to protect civilians under 'imminent threat of force.'[522] Rule 1.7 of the ROE specified that:[523]

---

516 AU, '2012 AU Draft Guidelines for PoC in AU Peace Support Operations' (n. 114) 9.

517 *Ibid.* See also Part I, Section 2.2.1.

518 *Ibid.*

519 *Ibid.*

520 *Ibid.*

521 *Ibid.* 5.

522 'Rules of Engagement for AFISMA Military Component' (2013), Execution of ROE: Principles, para. 7J(1b). The author does not have AFISMA's ROE in its possession, but they were referred to and quoted by Okeke and Williams (n. 290), Appendix A: examples of PoC language in AU PSOs, p. 31.

523 *Ibid.* Annex B.

> Use of force, up to and including deadly force, to protect civilians, including humanitarian workers, under imminent threat of force is authorized. When and where possible, permission to use force should be sought from the immediate superior commander.

Also, AFISMA Soldiers' Pocket Card included the following authorisation:[524]

> You are authorized to use force, up to and including deadly force: [...] b. To protect civilians, including humanitarian workers, under imminent threat of physical violence.

It is not specified when a 'threat of force' can be considered 'imminent'.

3.2.2. NATO policy on the concept of PoC and the use of force

The 2016 NATO Policy on PoC understands 'protection of civilians' as all feasible efforts made to prevent, minimise, and alleviate the adverse effects NATO and NATO-led military operations may have on the civilian population and, where appropriate, to protect the civilian population from conflict-related physical violence or threats of physical violence by other actors, including through the establishment of a safe and secure environment.[525]

NATO's PoC policy thus primarily reflects a commitment to an obligation that military forces have under IHL, namely the obligation to take all feasible precautions to protect civilians from incidental harm. Article 57(1) of Additional Protocol I, which reflects a rule of customary international law, sets forth that '[i]n the conduct of military operations, constant care shall be taken to spare the civilian population, civilians and civilian objects.'[526] Article 57(2) of Additional Protocol I lists the precautions that must be taken in this respect. NATO's determination to uphold the principle of precautions in attack, or even stronger, to maintain a zero-tolerance policy towards civilian casualties, is rooted in the operations in Afghanistan and Libya. As discussed earlier, the high number of civilian casualties during the deployment of ISAF in Afghanistan compelled NATO to take measures to detect and limit the (deadly) effects of the operation on the civilian population.[527] Also, during the NATO campaign in Libya, great weight was put on the importance of avoiding

524 *Ibid.* Annex E.

525 NAC, '2016 NATO Policy on PoC' (n. 118) para. 9.

526 For an analysis of the customary nature of this rule, see Henckaerts and Doswald-Beck (n. 91) Rule 15, pp. 51–52 ('In the conduct of military operations, constant care must be taken to spare the civilian population, civilians and civilian objects. All feasible precautions must be taken to avoid, and in any event to minimise, incidental loss of civilian life, injury to civilians and damage to civilian objects').

527 Hill and Manea (n. 315) 147; Koops and Patz (n. 304) 4 and 17; Rynning (n. 316) 235.

civilian casualties.[528] However, the air operations in Libya have also shown how difficult it can be to conduct a multinational military operation with such strict ROE.[529] For instance, NATO forces faced opposing forces that deliberately ignored their obligations under IHL by using civilian cars to transport troops and equipment to the combat zones. They also used civilian homes as assembly points, planning hubs, and even command and control posts.[530] According to Chris De Cock (then Legal Adviser to the Belgian armed forces participating in Operation Unified Protector), in light of the zero-tolerance policy, pilots have, in many cases, refrained from striking valid military targets, which affected the course of the operation.[531]

As a secondary consideration, NATO also aims to protect civilians from the actions of others, *inter alia*, through establishing a safe and secure environment.[532] To this end, actions up to and including the use of force may be taken, as appropriate, to 'prevent, deter, pre-empt, and respond to situations in which civilians suffer physical violence or are under threat of physical violence.'[533] According to the 2014 NATO AJD for Military Contribution to Peace Support, any use of force must, however, be restricted to self-defence and defence of the mandate, such as the protection of civilians under the imminent threat of physical violence.[534] Moreover, while force should only be pursued as a last resort and, when used, should be necessary and proportionate,[535] a 'peace support force [(i.e. a NATO or NATO-led military force assigned to peace support)] should be prepared to use force to physically separate the major conflicting parties or to stop atrocities.'[536] While this reflects a broader approach to PoC than just a commitment to IHL obligations, NATO nevertheless regards PoC as an operational rather than a strategic necessity.[537] Using force to defeat the enemy remains the primary strategic objective, not to protect the civilian population.

At the tactical level, NATO recognises four different 'use of force' categories: (i) the use of force in response to an attack or imminent attack (i.e. use of force in self-defence or IHL-based defensive force; usually not expressly regulated in the NATO ROE); (ii) the use of force for designated

528 JA Maj. Lutz, 'Operation Unified Protector: Air Campaign' (Canadian Forces College 2015) JCSP 42 – PCEMI 42 6; Jody M Prescott, 'Tactical Implementation of Rules of Engagement in a Multinational Force Reality' in Geoffrey S Corn, Rachel E VanLandingham and Shane R Reeves (eds), *U.S. Military Operations: Law, Policy, and Practice* (Oxford University Press 2015) 267.

529 Prescott (n. 528) 267.

530 De Cock (n. 328) 231.

531 *Ibid.*

532 NATO (n. 345) para. 16.

533 NAC, '2016 NATO Policy on PoC' (n. 118) para. 11.

534 NATO, '2014 NATO AJD for Military Contribution to Peace Support' (n. 20) para. 0231.

535 *Ibid.* paras 0204, 0215, and 0232.

536 *Ibid.* para. 0115.

537 Koops and Patz (n. 304) 8.

operations or activities; (iii) attacks against persons who are considered a threat or to pose a danger but are not involved in an imminent or ongoing attack (i.e. posing a hostile act or hostile intent); and (iv) attacks against forces declared hostile in accordance with IHL.[538] NATO leaves it to the Member States to define the right of self-defence in accordance with their respective national laws. However, as discussed in more detail below, States differ in their approach to self-defence and defence of others under self-defence rules.[539] Moreover, because the NATO rules on hostile acts and hostile intent are defined by what is not self-defence, there will, as NATO itself points out, 'not always be consistency between the nations as to where the right to use force in self-defence ends and the use of force authorised by the ROE begins.'[540] Therefore, in the context of NATO operations, ROE authorisation is needed to provide NATO forces with the same authority to use force to defend others in situations where the threats posed do not amount to a defence of others for all forces involved.[541] In the absence of such ROE authorisation, NATO troops whose TCCs adhere to a narrow definition of self-defence and defence of others would risk not being allowed to use force to protect civilians on certain occasions, to the detriment of the civilians involved and the success of the operation as a whole.[542] Notably, while the ability to use force in personal self-defence can never be limited or denied by ROE or other military orders, as this would violate a soldier's right to life, ROE may impose restrictions on the use of force in the defence of others.[543]

When NATO foresees ROE authorisation to provide NATO forces with the same authority to use force to defend others, only the ability to act is harmonised, not the legal basis to do so.[544] Such a legal basis must be found in the applicable legal regimes, as discussed in more detail below (see Part I, Section 4.1.2.1 and, more generally, Part III).[545] NATO also confirmed this in its 2014 NATO AJD for Military Contribution to Peace Support by holding that any actions for the protection of civilians must be consistent with 'applicable legal frameworks [...] which may include international human rights law and international humanitarian law.'[546] NATO leaves it mainly to its Member States to interpret the relevant rules on the use of force

538 Camilla Guldahl Cooper, *NATO Rules of Engagement: On ROE, Self-Defence and the Use of Force during Armed Conflict* (Brill 2020) 89–90.

539 *Ibid.* 401–402.

540 NAMC, 'MC 362/1, NATO Rules of Engagement ("NATO Unclassified")' (2003) 1, Annex A, as quoted by Guldahl Cooper (n. 538) 111.

541 *Ibid.* 112 and 402.

542 *Ibid.* 112.

543 *Ibid.* 402, see also 353–359 discussing the possibility to impose restrictions on the use of force in defence of others.

544 *Ibid.* 112.

545 *Ibid.*

546 NAC, '2016 NATO Policy on PoC' (n. 118) para. 5.

in these legal regimes. As explained by one of NATO's Legal Advisers Lone Kjelgaard:[547]

> [W]hether or not Allies other participating States agree on the exact legal justification or explanation underlying them, is in principle of little interest to NATO as an organization. Thus, rather than requiring adherence to a single common body of law, the Alliance's expectation is that all States participating in a NATO or NATO-led operation will act lawfully within the legal framework applicable to them.

Member States, therefore, have the responsibility to judge whether the ROE proposed by NATO conflict with their interpretation of the applicable law.[548] If there is a conflict, they may decide to withhold consent to the ROE being authorised, or they may impose additional restrictions on the use of force in the form of caveats to the ROE.[549]

3.2.3. EU policy on the concept of PoC and the use of force

At the strategic level, there is disagreement within the EU over its role in maintaining and restoring international peace and security.[550] Whereas certain EU Member States consider military interventions in crisis situations as vital to national security (e.g. to protect EU citizens and economic interests and/or to prevent terrorism), others are more reluctant to take military action unless there is an irrefutable humanitarian justification for it.[551] For the EU to respond rapidly to a protection crisis by undertaking military action, it must be able to achieve consensus on a military CSDP operation in the Council of the EU and subsequently activate its military structure and secure sufficient troop contributions rapidly. Disagreement over the EU's role in providing international peace and security is not particularly helpful in this regard.[552] This disparity has also been recognised in the 2016 EU Global Strategy on Foreign and Security Policy: 'CSDP must become rapid and effective,' which 'requires [EU] Member States to enhance the deployability and interoperability of their force through

---

547 Lone Kjelgaard, 'The Importance of Law in the Theatre' in Edoardo Greppi (ed), *Proceedings of the 37th Round Table on Current Issues of International Humanitarian Law: Conduct of Hostilities: the Practice, the Law and the Future, Hosted by the International Institute of Humanitarian Law, 4–6 September 2014, San Remo* (2015) 38.

548 Guldahl Cooper (n. 538) 61.

549 *Ibid.*

550 Major General Maurice de Langlois and Andreas Capstack, 'The Role of the Military in the EU's External Action' (Institut de Recherche Stratégique de l'École Militaire 2014) Laboratoire de l'IRSEM No. 23 18.

551 *Ibid.*

552 See e.g. Criseide Novi, 'EU-UN Cooperation in Multifunctional Peace Operations in Africa' in Giovanni Cellamare and Ivan Ingravallo (eds), *Peace Maintenance in Africa: Open Legal Issues* (1st edn., Springer International Publishing 2018) 69; Schmidt (n. 367) 173.

training and exercises.'[553] To this end, the EU must also tackle the procedural, financial, and political obstacles that prevent the deployment of the armed forces, hinder force generation, and reduce the overall effectiveness of CSDP military operations.[554]

Once deployed, the 2015 EU Concept for the Use of Force in EU-Led Military Operations and the 2015 EU Concept on PoC in EU-led Military Operations give some insights into the EU's policy on the use of force on the ground for PoC. Use of force is considered an elementary tool in EU-led military operations.[555] EU forces can contribute to PoC by taking proactive measures, including the use of all necessary force to prevent, avoid, and respond to physical violence.[556] All use of force, whether in self-defence or under the ROE, must always be in accordance with international standards, particularly as defined in applicable conventional and customary international law and relevant decisions by international organisations.[557] Furthermore, the potential risks to civilians posed by EU forces in the conduct of EU-led military operations should be mitigated by the principle of 'do no harm', the prevention and minimisation of collateral damage (in particular civilian casualties), and the use of a broad spectrum of non-lethal means.[558] Apart from that, neither the 2015 EU Concept for the Use of Force in EU-led Military Operations nor the 2015 EU Concept on PoC in EU-led Military Operations tells us much more about the EU policy on the use of force for PoC, partly because the 2015 EU Concept for the Use of Force in EU-led Military Operations is for the majority not declassified.

As in the context of NATO, EU Member States' understanding of self-defence and defence of others may differ. To accommodate existing disparities in national laws and regulations concerning the use of force in self-defence and to enable some level of uniformity of response to threats occurring in multinational operations, the EU has adopted the concept of 'confirmatory ROE'.[559] This concept of confirmatory ROE addresses specific categories of actions, which for some States would constitute self-defence, whilst for other contributing States, such actions would need to be specifically authorised as part of the mandate, i.e. covered by specific ROE.[560] An example of such a situation would be the use of force to protect property since this is one of the points on which

553 EU (n. 425) 47.

554 *Ibid.*

555 EUMC, '2015 EU Concept for the Use of Force in EU-Led Military Operations' (n. 119) para. 1.

556 EUMC, '2015 EU Concept on PoC in EU-Led Military Operations' (n. 120) paras 14–15.

557 EUMC, '2015 EU Concept for the Use of Force in EU-Led Military Operations' (n. 119) para. 2.

558 EUMC, '2015 EU Concept on PoC in EU-Led Military Operations' (n. 120) para. 16.

559 Johan FR Boddens Hosang, *Rules of Engagement and the International Law of Military Operations* (1st edn, Oxford University Press 2020) 47–48.

560 *Ibid.* 48. See also Gill and others (n. 26) 39–40.

national views diverge.[561] Where one contingent in an EU operation would need additional authorisation and implementation of ROE to have a legal and lawful authorisation to use force in the given circumstances, other contingents for which the use of force is already authorised based on their national laws and regulations would not need the ROE in question but would also not be impeded by it.[562] This explains why the EU labelled it as 'confirmatory ROE': they confirm the right to use force in self-defence while leaving the use of force in response to hostile acts and hostile intent outside the frame of self-defence.[563]

4. INTRODUCTION TO THE LEGAL FRAMEWORK GOVERNING THE USE OF FORCE FOR POC

4.1. OVERVIEW OF THE LEGAL RULES THAT MAY REGULATE THE USE OF FORCE FOR POC

In practice, there is a lack of clarity about the precise legal framework for the use of force to protect civilians and how it should be applied. Instead of thoroughly grounding the use of force in legal rules and principles, reference is often made in an almost mechanical manner to the need to protect civilians and the UNSC mandate under Chapter VII authorising such action, the use of force in self-defence and defence of the mandate, as well as to policy documents on the use of force and mission-specific ROE, although neither of those two is a source of law *per se*.[564] This lack of clarity undoubtedly has dire consequences for the UN (mandated) peace forces who implement the PoC mandates and the civilians presumed to be protected by the deployment of the operations in question.

While it is true that the applicable legal framework is a complex web of rules, it is not so that there are no academic works clarifying the general legal framework for UN (mandated) peace operations and the use of force. On the contrary, many publications describe the legal rules relevant to both UN and UN-mandated peace operations.[565] Not all of them, however, succeed in providing a complete list of the relevant legal rules. Moreover, little has been published on the relationship between the PoC mandate and the legal regimes,[566]

---

561 Boddens Hosang, *Rules of Engagement and the International Law of Military Operations* (n. 559) 47–48. On this point, also see Fiona Leverick, *Killing in Self-Defence* (Oxford University Press 2006) 131–142 as well as 177–196.

562 Boddens Hosang, *Rules of Engagement and the International Law of Military Operations* (n. 559) 48.

563 *Ibid.*

564 As already pointed out in the Introductory Chapter, Section 1.

565 Some examples were listed in the Introductory Chapter, Section 1, fn. 37.

566 To the author's knowledge, only few academic contributions address this issue, as referred to in the Introductory Chapter, Section 1, fn. 38.

causing a gap in legal scholarship. Furthermore, there has been only limited research into how the legal bases and legal regimes should be interpreted and applied in the context of UN (mandated) peace operations with the specific task of protecting civilians.[567] This, too, is a lacuna in legal scholarship.

As the present book attempts to fill these gaps, it is crucial first to draw a general overview of which rules may serve as a legal basis for the establishment, deployment, and functioning of UN (mandated) peace operations and which rules may govern the conduct of UN (mandated) peace operations (Section 4.1). Section 4.2 subsequently lays the groundwork for Parts II and III, explaining how the mission-specific legal bases and legal regimes might relate to each other.

4.1.1. Rules providing a legal basis for UN (mandated) peace operations

In the aftermath of the Second World War, the founding Member States of the UN included the following in the preamble of the UN Charter:

> We the peoples of the United Nations determined to save succeeding generations from the scourge of war, which twice in our lifetime has brought untold sorrow to mankind [...] and for these ends [...] to unite our strength to maintain international peace and security [...].

In order 'to save succeeding generations from the scourge of war,' the founding fathers sought to make possible a centralised, and above all independent, UN military enforcement capability. Accordingly, Article 43 was inserted into the UN Charter, allowing for a special agreement or agreements to be concluded between the UN and its Member States to allow for the provision of armed forces, assistance, and facilities as needed.[568] But unfortunately, Article 43 of the UN Charter never materialised due to Cold War tensions and the fact that the Member States could not agree on who would contribute what and where the forces would be stationed.[569]

However, the need for military measures to maintain and restore international peace and security remained present. In response, the UN has developed two alternative mechanisms, both based on the voluntary co-operation of Member States in providing armed forces, assistance, and facilities.[570] First, the UN has advanced a consensual military option to contribute to peace and security. In the late 1940s, small teams of unarmed UN observers provided the UN Security Council with a reliable account of the facts in areas of importance (such as Indonesia, Kashmir, and Palestine). From the 1950s onwards, the UN Security Council (and, on two occasions, the UN General Assembly) adopted

567 For a reference to some of the exceptions, see Introductory Chapter, Section 1, fn. 39.
568 White, 'Peacekeeping and International Law' (n. 37) 44.
569 Ruys (n. 52) 138.
570 See also *ibid.*

a new approach whereby the use of a military, armed component depended on the consent and the co-operation of the State(s) concerned.[571] Such UN peace operations are sub-organs of the UN composed of troops supplied by the Member States voluntarily, yet which operate under the operational command and control of the UN. Second, the UN Security Council has authorised (and thus not required) Member States or regional or international organisations other than the UN to undertake military action, with or without the host State's consent. In doing so, the UN Security Council delegates part of its powers to Member States or regional or other international organisations.[572]

Any such operation, whether carried out by the UN, Member States, or regional or international organisations other than the UN, needs a legal basis for the *emplacement* and *functioning* within the territory of another State and a mission-specific 'external' mandate to that end.[573] In addition, as international and regional organisations or arrangements only have those powers granted to them by their Member States, they should also have the competence to *establish* an operation and to give the operation in question a mission-specific 'internal' mandate to that end.[574] While it is not necessarily a requirement at the international level, at the national level, too, there are often rules that determine which national authority may take the initiative to deploy national troops on another State's territory. The legal basis for the establishment, emplacement, and functioning can be found in international law and the internal laws of the State, organisation, or arrangement that undertakes such operations.[575]

4.1.1.1. Legal basis for the establishment of UN (mandated) peace operations

The following Section first discusses which rules of internal law a State, organisation, or arrangement can use to set up an operation. Then it discusses which body within this State, organisation, or arrangement can adopt an internal mandate.

---

571 Michael Bothe, 'Peacekeeping' in Bruno Simma and others (eds), *The Charter of the United Nations: a Commentary*, vol. 1 (3rd edn., Oxford University Press 2012) 1175.

572 For a detailed analysis of the concept of regional organisations and arrangements (including the features of regional organisations), see Eric PJ Myjer and Nigel D White, 'Peace Operations Conducted by Regional Organizations and Arrangements' in Terry D Gill and Dieter Fleck (eds), *The Handbook of the International Law of Military Operations* (2nd edn., Oxford University Press 2015) 186–192.

573 Gill and others (n. 26) 35, see also Chapter 3 of the Leuven manual (27–33).

574 In the Leuven Manual, this distinction between 'internal' and 'external' mandate is made (see *ibid.* 34–35).

575 *Ibid.* 35.

A. Internal laws

i. UN peace operations

There is no specific provision in the UN Charter for the establishment of UN peace operations. Former UN Secretary-General Dag Hammarskjöld famously said that the legal basis of UN peacekeeping fell somewhere between Chapter VI and VII and put forward the unwritten 'Chapter VI and a half' as their legal basis.[576] The idea is that the functions of UN peacekeeping exceed the peaceful settlement of disputes under Chapter VI of the UN Charter but do not extend to enforcement measures under Chapter VII of the UN Charter.[577]

The concept of UN peacekeeping was developed at a time when Cold War rivalries deadlocked the UN Security Council (see also Part I, Section 4.1.1).[578] In 1956, the UN General Assembly deployed the first UN peace operation, UNEF I, to the borders between Israel and Egypt to secure and supervise the cessation of hostilities and to serve as a buffer between the conflicting parties once the armed forces of France, Israel, and the UK withdrew.[579] In 1960, the UN Security Council established a more belligerent variant, ONUC, after the main Congolese political leaders requested the international community's intervention.[580] UN forces were tasked with assisting the Congolese government in maintaining law and order, ensuring the withdrawal of all Belgian troops, and providing technical assistance.[581]

Both UNEF I and ONUC eventually gave rise to a heated debate both inside and outside the UN about the competences of the UN bodies involved in establishing such operations.[582] Several States refused to pay for the costs of these operations, arguing that these bodies did not have the institutional competence to mandate peacekeeping forces.[583] In 1962, the ICJ eventually acknowledged in its advisory opinion in the *Certain Expenses* case that both the UN General Assembly and the UN Security Council have the competence

576 Ove Bring, 'The Hammarskjöld Approach to International Law' in Henning Melber and Maxi Schoeman (eds), *The United Nations and Regional Challenges in Africa – 50 Years after Dag Hammarskjöld* (The Dag Hammarskjöld Centre 2011) 54.

577 Sloan (n. 161) 107.

578 Howe, Kondoch and Spijkers (n. 37) 9.

579 'UNGA Res. 1000' (1956) UN Doc. A/RES/1000 (1956) para. 1.

580 Request by the Congolese government: UNSC, 'Cable Dated 12 July 1960 from the President of the Republic of The Congo and Supreme Commander of the National Army and the Prime Minister of National Defence Addressed to Secretary-General of the United Nations' (1960) UN Doc. S/4382 1; UNSC mandate: 'UNSC Res. 143' (1960) UN Doc. S/4387 (1960) para. 2. See also UN DPO, 'Republic of the Congo – ONUC: Mandate' (*UN Peacekeeping*, 2001), https://peacekeeping.un.org/en/mission/past/onucM.htm, accessed 16 April 2021.

581 'UNSC Res. 143' (n. 580) para. 2.

582 See also Bothe, 'Peacekeeping' (n. 571) 1177.

583 See also *ibid.* 1177; White, 'Peacekeeping and International Law' (n. 37) 45.

to organise peacekeeping operations when requested or agreed to by the States concerned and thus do not act *ultra vires* in such cases.[584]

It follows that both the UN General Assembly and the UN Security Council have the implied or general powers to take certain measures necessary to exercise of their responsibilities. In the words of the ICJ, 'the rights and duties of [...] [the UN] must depend upon its purposes and functions as specified or implied in its constituent documents and developed in practice.'[585]

Hence, the UN General Assembly has the general power to make recommendations of a non-mandatory character related to international peace and security and may establish subsidiary organs as it considers necessary for the exercise of its functions. Hence, the combination of Articles 10, 11, 14, and 22 of the UN Charter provides the UN General Assembly with the necessary legal basis for organising a consensual peacekeeping operation.[586] That said, since the early 1960s, the UN Security Council has exclusively mandated and controlled UN peace operations.

The UN Security Council has the primary power under Article 24(1) of the UN Charter to take a wide variety of measures relating to maintaining and restoring international peace and security. The specific powers conferred to the UN Security Council to perform these tasks are contained, *inter alia*, in Chapters VI and VII of the UN Charter (see Article 24(2) of the UN Charter). Chapter VI of the UN Charter provides the UN Security Council with the powers to promote the peaceful settlement of disputes, while Chapter VII of the UN Charter allows for the UN Security Council to undertake enforcement action with respect to threats to the peace, breaches of the peace, and acts of aggression. Such enforcement measures do not require the consent or co-operation of the State or entity against which they are directed. Enforcement measures may either be non-forcible in nature or, if such measures have proved inadequate or are deemed insufficient in the circumstances to restore the situation and prevent further deterioration, may involve such action by air, sea, or land forces as may be necessary to maintain or restore international peace and security.

When establishing a UN peace operation, the UN Security Council does not tend to specify the specific article of the UN Charter that constitutes the legal source of the mission.[587] Scholars have examined the possibilities under Articles 39, 40, 41, 42, and 48 of the UN Charter. While this is an interesting

---

584 *Certain Expenses of the United Nations (Article 17, paragraph 2, of the Charter), Advisory opinion* (1962) ICJ Rep 151, 163–172.

585 *Reparation for Injuries Suffered in the Service of the United Nations, Advisory opinion* (1949) ICJ Rep 174, 180.

586 *Certain Expenses of the United Nations (Article 17, paragraph 2, of the Charter), Advisory opinion* (n. 584) 170–172. See also N Tsagourias, 'Consent, Neutrality/Impartiality and the Use of Force in Peacekeeping: Their Constitutional Dimension' (2006) 11 Journal of Conflict and Security Law 465, 469.

587 Labuda, 'Peacekeeping and Peace Enforcement' (n. 9) para. 19.

debate, a detailed discussion is beyond the scope of this book.[588] This book contends that the UN Security Council can base its initiatives on the general powers it possesses under Chapters VI and VII combined with Articles 1(1) and 24 of the UN Charter (see also further below, Part I, Section 4.1.1.2).[589] In addition, if the UN Security Council deems it necessary to perform its functions, it has the power to establish subsidiary powers (see Art. 29 of the UN Charter). Pursuant to Article 98 of the UN Charter, the UN Security Council may also entrust the UN Secretary-General with certain functions, including overseeing UN peace operations.

ii. UN-mandated peace operations

For UN-mandated peace operations, the following internal rules are of relevance:

AU – To establish a UN-mandated peace operation, the AU may rely on Articles 4(h) and 4(j) of the AU Constitutive Act. While Article 4(h) contends that the AU shall have 'the right [...] to intervene in a Member State pursuant to a decision of the Assembly [of Heads of State and Government (AU Assembly)] in respect of grave circumstances, namely: war crimes, genocide and crimes against humanity,' Article 4(j) provides for the possibility for AU Member States requesting the AU to intervene 'in order to restore peace and security.' 'Restoration of peace and security' is interpreted broadly in this regard. The AU does not only intervene militarily when there is a need to restore peace but also when there is a need to support peace. The 2004 Common African Defence and Security Policy states that one of the goals of the AU is to 'enhance AU's capacity for and coordination of, early action for conflict prevention containment, management, resolution and elimination of conflicts, including the deployment and sustenance of peacekeeping missions and thus [to] promote initiatives that will preserve and strengthen peace and development in Africa.'[590] As revealed by the Leuven Manual, this goal is consistent with one of the AU's core objectives, which is to promote peace, security, and stability on the continent (as included in Article 3(f) of the AU Constitutive Act).[591]

---

[588] For further literature on the specific legal basis within the UN Charter, see e.g. Sloan (n. 161) 64–121; Alexander Orakhelashvili, 'The Legal Basis of the United Nations Peace-Keeping Operations' (2002) 43 Virginia Journal of International Law 485, 489–498; Hitoshi Nasu, *International Law on Peacekeeping: A Study of Article 40 of the UN Charter* (Martinus Nijhoff Publishers 2009); Nico Krisch, 'Chapter VII. Action with Respect to Threats to the Peace, Breaches of the Peace, and Acts of Aggression' in Bruno Simma and others (eds), *The Charter of the United Nations: a Commentary*, vol. 2 (3rd edn., Oxford University Press 2012).

[589] See also Tsagourias, 'Consent, Neutrality/Impartiality and the Use of Force in Peacekeeping: Their Constitutional Dimension' (n. 586) 469; Terry D Gill, 'Characterization and Legal Basis for Peace Operations' in Terry D Gill and Dieter Fleck (eds), *The Handbook of the International Law of Military Operations* (2nd edn., Oxford University Press 2015) 156.

[590] AU, 'Solemn Declaration on a Common African Defence and Security Policy' (2004) para. 13(j), www.peaceau.org/uploads/declaration-cadsp-en.pdf, accessed 22 October 2022.

[591] Gill and others (n. 26) 52.

NATO – At the heart of the North Atlantic Treaty is Article 5, which provides that if one or more NATO Member States is the victim of an armed attack, such attack shall be considered an armed attack against all Member States, and they shall all take such actions as they deem necessary to assist the ally under attack and restore and maintain the security in the North Atlantic Area. For over forty years, collective self-defence was the main focus of NATO. Yet, since the 1990s, NATO has also become involved in crisis response operations outside the framework of Article 5 of the North Atlantic Treaty.[592] Such NA5CROs are multifunctional operations encompassing political, military, and civil activities to contribute to conflict prevention, peacekeeping, peacemaking, peacebuilding, peace enforcement, and/or humanitarian activities.[593] These operations are conducted in support of the UN or the Organization for Security and Co-operation in Europe (OSCE) or at the invitation of a sovereign government and shall involve military forces and diplomatic and humanitarian agencies, and shall be aimed at achieving a long-term political settlement or other conditions specified in the mandate.[594] Despite the fact that such crisis response operations do not find an explicit legal basis in the North Atlantic Treaty, they are now well established in NATO practice.

EU – Under Article 42(1) of the TEU, the EU's CSDP (i.e. its common security and defence policy) foresees the possibility of establishing both civilian and military missions outside the EU for peacekeeping, conflict prevention, and strengthening international security. Article 43 of the TEU sets forth that these missions may include, but are not limited to, 'joint disarmament operations, humanitarian and rescue tasks, military advice and assistance tasks, conflict prevention and peace-keeping tasks, tasks of combat forces in crisis management, including peace-making and post-conflict stabilisation.' Furthermore, if, for some reason, the EU cannot or will not carry out an operation, Articles 42(5) and 44 of the TEU also allow the Council of the EU to entrust the execution of a task, within the framework of the EU, to a group of EU Member States that are willing and able (i.e. have the necessary capability for such a task) to protect the EU's values and serve the EU's interests.

States Unlike international and regional organisations or arrangements that have only those powers granted to them by their Member States and, therefore, must always provide for a legal basis in their internal laws to establish a military operation, military initiatives by States are not subject to such conditions.[595] Nevertheless, most States have national rules for establishing military operations.

---

592 This change was marked in NATO's 1991 Strategic Concept: NAC, 'The Alliance's New Strategic Concept, Agreed by the Heads of State and Government Participating in the Meeting of the North Atlantic Council' (n. 301). See also Part I, Section 2.2.2.

593 NATO, *NATO Legal Deskbook* (2nd edn., NATO 2010) 242; NATO, 'Crisis Management' (n. 303).

594 NATO, 'Crisis Management' (n. 303).

595 Gill and others (n. 26) 34–35.

For example, according to Article 20 of the French Constitution, the French government may deploy the armed forces wherever it deems necessary.[596] The French government has already exercised this power on several occasions by establishing military operations in Côte d'Ivoire, Mali, and the CAR, to name a few.

B. The 'internal' mandate

i. UN peace operations

UN peace operations are, in principle, established by the UN Security Council,[597] and as such, they find their mission-specific internal mandate in a resolution of the UN Security Council. That means that for UN peace operations, the UNSC resolution provides simultaneously for the internal and the external mandate.[598] The external mandate is discussed below (see Part I, Section 4.1.1.2(B)).

ii. UN-mandated peace operations

If an organisation or arrangement is conducting a UN-mandated peace operation, a separate internal mandate is required, which is issued by the competent body of that organisation or arrangement.[599] Such an internal mandate must always be consistent with the external mandate under international law.[600]

AU – Article 7(c) of the AU PSC Protocol states that the AU PSC may authorise the mounting and deployment of peace support missions. The AU PSC may also establish general guidelines for conducting such missions, including the mandate thereof, and review those guidelines regularly (Article 7(f) of the 2002 PSC Protocol). Such decisions must preferably be taken by consensus. If such consensus cannot be reached, the AU PSC shall adopt a decision on peace support missions by a two-thirds majority vote of its Members (Article 8(13) of the AU PSC Protocol). In case of interventions in accordance with Article 4(h) of the AU Constitutive Act, not the AU PSC but the AU's highest political body, the AU Assembly,[601] must decide. Pursuant to Article 7(e) of the AU PSC Protocol, the AU PSC may 'recommend to the Assembly, pursuant to Article 4(h) of the [AU] Constitutive Act, intervention, on behalf of the [African] Union, in a Member State in respect of grave circumstances, namely war crimes, genocide and crimes against humanity, as defined in relevant international conventions and

596 French Constitution of 4 October 1958 (as revised on 23 July 2008).
597 Unless the UN General Assembly establishes them. Yet, as mentioned above, this has not occurred since the early 1960s.
598 Gill and others (n. 26) 35.
599 *Ibid.*
600 *Ibid.*
601 The AU Assembly is the supreme organ of the AU, see Art. 6(2) of the 2000 AU Constitutive Act.

instruments.' The AU Assembly must take the final decision on such intervention (see Rule 4(1)(e) of the 2002 AU Rules of Procedure of the AU Assembly).

NATO – NATO's highest political decision-making body, the NAC, decides whether to undertake a crisis response operation on a case-by-case basis.[602] According to Article 9 of the North Atlantic Treaty:

> The Parties hereby establish a Council, on which each of them shall be represented, to consider matters concerning the implementation of this Treaty. The Council shall be so organised as to be able to meet promptly at any time. The Council shall set up such subsidiary bodies as may be necessary; in particular it shall establish immediately a defence committee which shall recommend measures for the implementation of Articles 3 and 5.

The NAC is composed of the representatives of all NATO Member States representing their respective governments.[603] The work of the NAC is supported by various committees, including the North Atlantic Military Committee (NAMC), the highest military authority within NATO.[604] Yet all the key decisions are made by the NAC, not by the military flank.[605] The NAC decides by consensus only, implying that each and every NATO Member State supports the NAC's decisions.[606] Although this practice of decision-making by consensus is not formally recognised in any of NATO's founding documents, it has been consistently applied in NATO since its inception in 1949.[607] As a result, the NAC exercises political control and strategic direction of NATO operations.

EU – Pursuant to Article 30(1) of the TEU, any EU Member State, the EU High Representative, or the EU High Representative with the EU Commission's support, may submit a proposal to undertake a peace operation. The decision of whether or not to launch an operation is taken by the Council of the EU based on Article 43 of the TEU, in conjunction with Article 31 of the TEU. Such decisions must, in principle, be adopted by unanimity (Article 31 of the TEU). Pursuant to Article 43(2) of the TEU, the Council of the EU shall also define its objectives and scope and the general conditions for their implementation. The EU High Representative, acting under the authority of the Council of the EU and in close liaison with the EU PSC, coordinates the civilian and military aspects of such tasks (Article 43(2) of the TEU). It is, however, the EU PSC that, under the responsibility of the Council of the EU and the EU High Representative, exercises the political control and strategic direction of such operations (Article 38(2) of the TEU). As mentioned above, Articles 42(5) and 44 of the TEU also allow

602 NATO, 'North Atlantic Council' (*NATO*, 11 October 2017), www.nato.int/cps/en/natolive/topics_49763.htm, accessed 7 April 2022.

603 *Ibid.*

604 NATO, 'Military Committee' (*NATO*, 25 August 2021), www.nato.int/cps/en/natohq/topics_49633.htm, accessed 11 April 2022.

605 NATO, *NATO Legal Deskbook* (n. 593) 243.

606 *Ibid.*

607 Gill and others (n. 26) 68.

the Council of the EU to entrust a group of EU Member States to establish a peace operation. Pursuant to Article 44(2) of the TEU, those Member States, in consultation with the EU High Representative, agree on the management of the task, but if the execution of the task has far-reaching implications or requires a change in the objective, scope, and conditions of the task, the Council of the EU makes the necessary decisions. EU Member States have not yet made use of this system.[608]

States – When a State decides to establish a military operation upon a PoC mandate, the competent body of the State may equally have to issue some 'national authorisation', be it political, legal or both.[609] For example, as mentioned above, according to Article 20 of the French Constitution, the French government has at its disposal the armed forces and shall be held accountable to Parliament.[610] The French government, therefore, notifies the Parliament of its decision to allow the armed forces to intervene abroad no later than three days after the start of that intervention (Article 35(2) of the French Constitution). Once deployed abroad, the French President is the Commander-in-Chief of the armed forces (Article 15 of the French Constitution).

4.1.1.2. Legal basis for the emplacement and functioning of UN (mandated) peace operations

Besides the question of whether a State, organisation, or arrangement has the competence to establish an operation, the other aspect to be addressed is what may constitute the legal basis for the emplacement and functioning of a UN (mandated) peace operation within a State.[611] The following Section first discusses which provisions of the UN Charter or rules of customary international law relating to the use of force and the maintenance and restoration of international peace and security, a State, organisation, or arrangement can use to set up an operation. Then it discusses which body can provide the mission with an external mandate.

A. The UN Charter and customary international law

As proclaimed in Article 1(1) of the UN Charter, one of the primary purposes of the UN is to maintain international peace and security, and with that purpose in mind, effective collective measures can be taken to prevent and remove

---

608 *Ibid.* 61.

609 The term 'national authorisation' is better suited than 'internal mandate' in this regard, see also be Terry D Gill, JA Mario Léveillée and Dieter Fleck, 'The Rule of Law in Peace Operations, XVIIth Congress of the International Society for Military Law and the Law of War, Scheveningen, 16–19 May 2006' (2006) 17 Recueils de la Société Internationale de Droit Penal Militaire et de Droit de la Guerre 49, 118.

610 Constitution of 4 October 1958 (as revised on 23 July 2008).

611 See also Tsagourias, 'Consent, Neutrality/Impartiality and the Use of Force in Peacekeeping: Their Constitutional Dimension' (n. 586) 469.

threats to the peace and the suppression of breaches of the peace. Such collective measures can be adopted under Chapter VII of the UN Charter and thus concern collective security *sensu stricto*.[612] Article 1(1) of the UN Charter also refers to the adjustment or settlement of international disputes, as well as to the use of peaceful means in situations that might lead to a breach of the peace, which both concern measures that can be taken under Chapter VI of the UN Charter. Such measures belong to collective security *sensu lato*.[613] As such, collective security *sensu lato* may be understood as a system whereby States as a group respond to threats to and breaches of the peace by one or more States that are part of that same group.[614]

In pursuing collective security, the UN and its Member States are expected to adhere to and are legally bound by the core principles outlined in Article 2 of the UN Charter. Under Article 2(4) of the UN Charter, States are prohibited from using or threatening to use force in their international relations. This general prohibition of the threat or use of force is a 'fundamental or cardinal' principle of the international legal order.[615] This principle is not only expressed in Article 2(4) of the UN Charter. It is also recognised as a customary norm and even considered a norm of *jus cogens* (*jus cogens* or peremptory norms of international law being higher rules of public international law that protect those values and interests that are fundamentally important to the international community as a whole (see also Article 53 of the VCLT, as discussed in Part II, Section 2.1.1)).[616] The law of

---

612 Terry D Gill, 'Legal Characterization and Basis for Enforcement Operations and Peace Enforcement Operations Under the Charter' in Terry D Gill and Dieter Fleck (eds), *The Handbook of the International Law of Military Operations* (2nd edn., Oxford University Press 2015) 98; Rüdiger Wolfrum, 'Ch. I Purposes and Principles, Article 1' in Bruno Simma and others (eds), *The Charter of the United Nations: a Commentary*, vol. 1 (3rd edn., Oxford University Press 2012) 112.

613 Gill, 'Legal Characterization and Basis for Enforcement Operations and Peace Enforcement Operations Under the Charter' (n. 612) 98; Wolfrum (n. 612) 112.

614 Wolfrum (n. 612) 112.

615 *Case Concerning Military and Paramilitary Activities in and against Nicaragua (Nicaragua v. United States of America), Judgment (Merits)* (1986) ICJ Rep 14 para. 190.

616 For case law of the ICJ on this point, see *ibid.*; *Case Concerning Armed Activities on the Territory of the Congo (Democratic Republic of the Congo v. Uganda), Judgment* (2005) ICJ Rep 168, paras 161–165. For an overview of state practice confirming the peremptory nature of the prohibition of the (threat or) use of force, see Olivier Corten, *The Law against War: The Prohibition on the Use of Force in Contemporary International Law*, vol. 4 (Hart Publishing 2010) 201–207. For further support, see e.g. the ILC Commentary to draft article 50 of the draft articles on the law of treaties in which it held that 'the law of the Charter concerning the prohibition of the use of force in itself constitutes a conspicuous example of a rule in international law having the character of *jus cogens*' (ILC, 'Reports of the International Law Commission on the Second Part of Its Seventeenth Session and on Its Eighteenth Session' (1996) UN Doc. A/6309/Rev.1, Yearbook of the International Law Commission, vol. 2, Documents of the Second Part of the Seventeenth Session and of the Eighteenth Session including the reports of the Commission to the General Assembly, UN Doc. A/CN.4/SER.A/1966/Add.1 247), as also referred to by the ICJ (*Case Concerning Military and Paramilitary Activities in and against Nicaragua (Nicaragua v. United States of America), Judgment (Merits)* (n. 615) para. 190). See also *Case Concerning Military and Paramilitary*

the UN Charter provides two applicable exceptions from the general prohibition of the threat or use of force. First, States retain their right to individual or collective self-defence (i.e. the right to respond forcibly to an armed attack) as reflected in Article 51 of the UN Charter.[617] Second, the UN Security Council can authorise the use of force under Chapter VII of the UN Charter. In addition to these two major exceptions, Articles 53, 106, and 107 of the UN Charter contain

---

Activities in and against Nicaragua (Nicaragua v. United States of America), Judgment (Merits), Separate opinion of Judge Singh (1986) ICJ Rep 151, 153; *Legal Consequences of the Construction of a Wall in the Occupied Palestinian Territory, Advisory opinion, Separate opinion of Judge Elaraby* (2004) ICJ Rep 246, 254; ILC, 'Second Report on State Responsibility by Mr. James Crawford, Special Rapporteur' (n. 107) para. 242(b); Anthony Aust, *Handbook of International Law* (2nd edn., Cambridge University Press 2010) 10; James Crawford, *Brownlie's Principles of Public International Law* (9th edn., Oxford University Press 2019); Yoram Dinstein, *War, Aggression and Self-Defence* (6th edn., University Printing House 2017); Martin Dixon, *Textbook on International Law* (7th edn., Oxford University Press 2013) 42; Oliver Dörr, 'Prohibition of the Use of Force', *Max Planck Encyclopedia of Public International law* (Oxford Public International Law 2015) para. 32; Jochen A Frowein, 'Ius Cogens', *Max Planck Encyclopedia of Public International law* (Oxford Public International Law 2013) para. 8; Gill and others (n. 26) 30; Lauri Hannikainen, *Peremptory Norms (Jus Cogens) in International Law: Historical Development, Criteria, Present Status* (Finnish Lawyers' Pub Co 1988) 356; Corten 200–213; Vaughan Lowe, *International Law* (Oxford University Press 2007) 59; Alexander Orakhelashvili, 'The Impact of Peremptory Norms on the Interpretation and Application of United Nations Security Council Resolutions' (2015) 16 The European Journal of International Law 59, 63–64; Bruno Simma, 'NATO, the UN and the Use of Force: Legal Aspects' (1999) 10 European Journal of International Law 1, 3. The following sources refer to 'the prohibition of aggression' and 'the prohibition of aggressive or illegal use of force': ILC, 'Report of the International Law Commission on the Work of Its Fifty-Third Session (23 April–1 June and 2 July–10 August 2001)' (2001) UN Doc. A/56/10, Yearbook of the International Law Commission 2001, vol. 2, part two, UN Doc. A/CN.4/SER.A/2001/Add.1 (part 2) 85 and 112 (ILC commentary on Article 26 of the ASR on compliance with peremptory norms); ILC, 'Fragmentation of International Law: Difficulties Arising from the Diversification and Expansion of International Law, Report of the Study Group of the International Law Commission, Finalized by Martti Koskenniemi' (2006) UN Doc. A/CN.4/L.682 189; ILC, 'Fourth Report on Peremptory Norms of General International Law (Jus Cogens) by Dire Tladi, Special Rapporteur' (n. 108) paras 62–68; ILC, 'Report of the International Law Commission on the Work of Its Seventy-First Session (29 April–7 June and 8 July–9 August 2019), UN General Assembly Records, Seventy-First Session, Supplement No. 10' UN Doc. A/74/10 146–147 (Draft conclusion 23 on peremptory norms of general international law (*jus cogens*), adopted by the Commission on first reading), p. 203–204 (Commentary to draft conclusion 23); Laura Visser, 'May the Force Be with You: The Legal Classification of Intervention by Invitation' (2019) 66 Netherlands International Law Review 21, 38. For criticism, see e.g. Green who argues that since a *jus cogens* norm is one from which no derogation is possible, Art. 2(4) of the UN Charter as such cannot be regarded as a peremptory norm. After all, he argues, the law of the UN Charter itself explicitly recognises the possibility of exceptions to the general rule (James A Green, 'Questioning the Peremptory Status of the Prohibition of the Use of Force' (2011) 32 Michigan Journal of International Law 215, 229). However, as discussed above, the author sees a clear distinction between derogations and exceptions, see also Part I, Section 2.1.1, fn. 803.

617 Art. 51 of the UN Charter proclaims, *inter alia*, that '[n]othing in the present Charter shall impair the inherent right of individual or collective self-defence if an armed attack occurs [...].' For case law identifying this right as an 'inherent' right which forms part of customary international law, see *Case Concerning Military and Paramilitary Activities in and against Nicaragua (Nicaragua v. United States of America), Judgment (Merits)* (n. 615) para. 193.

two additional exceptions in favour of the Allies of the Second World War, yet they have no practical significance today and will therefore not be discussed in detail.[618] Furthermore, a State may also consent to the use of armed force within its territory, in which case there is no violation of Article 2(4) of the UN Charter or the customary rule on the prohibition of the use of force.[619]

Another core principle to which both the UN and its Member States must adhere can be found in Article 2(7) of the UN Charter. This provision prohibits the UN from intervening in matters that are essentially within the internal affairs of a State unless the UN Security Council is taking enforcement measures under Chapter VII of the UN Charter. According to the ICJ, this principle of non-intervention is a 'corollary of the principle of sovereign equality of States' (as contained in Article 2(1) of the UN Charter) and is 'part and parcel of customary international law'[620] and thus also governs the international relations among States.[621] However, what constitutes 'matters essentially within the domestic jurisdiction' is construed narrowly in practice. For instance, Article 2(7) of the UN Charter cannot be invoked to oppose conflict prevention measures in the event of tensions within a State that reach the level of a clear violation of human rights or pose a threat to international peace and security.[622]

i. UN peace operations

In view of the above principles of sovereignty (sovereignty meaning the supreme power and authority over a territory)[623] and non-intervention, unless the host State has consented to the emplacement and functioning of a UN peace operation within its territory, such use of force amounts in and of itself to an unlawful use of force in the sense of Article 2(4) of the UN Charter or the customary rule of prohibition of the use of force. That said, the UN Charter foresees for the UN Security Council to exercise its enforcement powers under Chapter VII of the UN Charter, in which case the use of force on the territory of a third State would constitute a lawful exception to the prohibition of the use of force.[624] The

---

618 Robert Kolb, *International Law on the Maintenance of Peace: Jus Contra Bellum* (Edward Elgar Publishing 2018) 349.

619 As discussed in more detail below, see Part II, Section 2.1.1 on the legal value of consent.

620 *Case Concerning Military and Paramilitary Activities in and against Nicaragua (Nicaragua v. United States of America), Judgment (Merits)* (n. 615) para. 202.

621 Jan Wouters and Philip De Man, 'Legal Instruments for the Prevention of Armed Conflicts' in Jan Wouters, Philip de Man and Nele Verlinden (eds), *Armed Conflicts and the Law* (Intersentia 2016) 38.

622 *Ibid.* 40.

623 Samantha Besson, 'Sovereignty', *Max Planck Encyclopedia of Public International law* (Oxford Public International Law 2011) para. 1.

624 The UN General Assembly does not possess such powers and thus always needs the consent of the host State to emplace a peace operation within the territory of a State and to make it operational.

mandate, whether provided by the host State or the UN Security Council, is a source of legal authority to deploy a mission in the territory of a given State and to use force on that State's territory. It should be reminded that to qualify as a 'UN peace operation' for the purposes of this study, there must be a mandate from the UN Security Council. Today it has become commonplace for the UN Security Council to refer to Chapter VII of the UN Charter when undertaking an action, despite often having already obtained the host State's consent. Part II, Section 2 discusses in more detail 'consent' as a legal basis for an operation and how it relates to a Chapter VII mandate.

ii. UN-mandated peace operations

Chapter VIII of the UN Charter explicitly foresees the possibility for regional organisations and arrangements to address regional peace and security matters.[625] Regional organisations are authorised to deploy both consensual and non-consensual peace operations, provided they are consistent with Chapter VIII of the UN Charter (which includes Articles 52, 53, and 54). The UN Security Council has always supported regionally initiated peace operations without considering as a stumbling block whether such organisations technically qualify or even consider themselves 'regional organisations' in the context of Chapter VIII of the UN Charter (see below).[626] For example, in Resolution 2086 (2013), the UN Security Council underlined 'the importance of partnership and cooperation with regional and subregional arrangements and organizations, in accordance with Chapter VIII of the United Nations Charter, in supporting peacekeeping and peacebuilding activities [...].'[627]

As Chapter VIII refers to 'regional arrangements or agencies,' the question has arisen whether NATO can be considered a regional organisation or arrangement in the sense of Chapter VIII of the UN Charter. NATO has been established as a collective defence organisation, not a regional organisation.[628] NATO's founding treaty deliberately referred to 'the primary responsibility of the UN Security Council to maintain international peace and security' and excluded any reference to Chapter VIII of the UN Charter.[629] In so doing, NATO sought to eliminate any doubt that it could not invoke the right to collective self-defence under Article 51 of the UN Charter. However, this does

625 Gill, 'Characterization and Legal Basis for Peace Operations' (n. 589) 157.
626 *Ibid.* 157–158.
627 'UNSC Res. 2086' (2013) UN Doc. S/RES/2086 (2013) para. 18. Also the following UNSC resolutions explicitly refer to Chapter VIII of the UN Charter: 'UNSC Res. 1464' (n. 142) para. 9; 'UNSC Res. 1935' (n. 137) pream. para. 8; 'UNSC Res. 2167' (n. 19) pream. para. 4 and para. 1; 'UNSC Res. 2429' (n. 137) pream. para. 7.
628 Anne Verhelst and Snežana Trifunovska, *North Atlantic Treaty Organization (NATO)* (2nd edn., Kluwer Law International 2020) para. 236.
629 *Ibid.*

not exclude NATO from undertaking UN-mandated peace operations.[630] When NATO takes military action other than in collective self-defence, it is considered to be acting as a regional organisation or arrangement.[631] Moreover, the UN generally does not directly authorise a specific regional organisation or arrangement to carry out a peacekeeping operation. Only in some cases is it clear that a specific call for an operation is addressed only to NATO, as only NATO has the necessary military capabilities to carry out such an operation.[632]

Chapter VIII of the UN Charter foresees two types of activities: (i) peaceful settlement of disputes under Article 52 of the UN Charter, the competence for which flows from Chapter VI of the UN Charter; and (ii) enforcement action as in Article 53 of the UN Charter, the competence for which flows from Chapter VII of the UN Charter.[633] Consensual peace operations do not require UN Security Council authorisation to be deployed in a State. However, they must meet the conditions outlined in Article 52 of the UN Charter (including the fact that any such initiative must be consistent with the purposes and principles of the UN, as set forth in Chapter I of the UN Charter).

With respect to non-consensual peace operations, Article 53(1) of the UN Charter provides that '[t]he Security Council shall, where appropriate, utilize such regional arrangements or agencies for enforcement action under its authority.' Any enforcement action undertaken by such regional arrangements or regional agencies requires the authorisation of the UN Security Council.[634] The need for a UN Security Council authorisation follows from Articles 2(4) and 2(7) of the UN Charter, as well as Chapter VII of the UN Charter. In addition to the prior authorisation of the UN Security Council, the UN Security Council must at all times exercise 'overall authority and control over the use of its delegated powers.'[635] This duty follows from the UN Security Council's primary responsibility for the maintenance of international peace and security and is explicitly recognised by Article 53(1) of the UN Charter when it says that enforcement action shall take place 'under its authority.' Furthermore, Article 54 of the UN Charter adds that the UN Security Council must at all times be kept fully informed of the activities undertaken or planned by these entities to maintain international peace and security.

In contrast to what the UN Charter provides for regional organisations and arrangements, the UN Charter does not contain an explicit provision to

630 Gill and others (n. 26) 66.
631 Myjer and White (n. 572) 191.
632 Gill and others (n. 26) 67.
633 Myjer and White (n. 572) 195.
634 Unless it concerns the exception of measures 'against any enemy State,' being any State that during the Second World War has been an enemy of any signatory of the UN Charter (see Art. 53(2) of the UN Charter).
635 Dan Sarooshi, 'The Security Council's Authorization of Regional Arrangements to Use Force: The Case of NATO' in Alan V Lowe and others (eds), *The United Nations Security Council and War: the Evolution of Thought and Practice Since 1945* (Oxford University Press 2008) 229.

authorise individual Member States to use force on behalf of the UN Security Council. However, as discussed above, that practice has evolved over time and has become a well-accepted aspect of the UN collective security mechanism.[636]

B. The 'external' mandate

Any use of military force on the territory of another State requires an 'external' mandate, which can either be issued by a competent international organisation (in principle, the UN Security Council under Chapter VII of the UN Charter) or by a host State's government inviting or consenting to a peace operation conducted on its territory.[637] After all, as mentioned above, Article 2(4) of the UN Charter prohibits States from using or threatening to use force in their international relations unless they are exercising their right to individual or collective self-defence or when the UN Security Council has authorised such use of force under Chapter VII of the UN Charter. Furthermore, a State may also consent to the use of armed force in its territory, in which case there is no violation of the general prohibition of the use or threat of the use of force. However, as mentioned above, this book does not discuss operations that find their sole legal basis in the host State's consent. Accordingly, only operations for which the UN Security Council has given an explicit mandate are examined.

Part II looks in detail at host State consent and mandates granted by the UN Security Council as mission-specific legal bases for UN (mandated) peace operations deployed to protect civilians. Part II, Section 2 discusses the legal, political, and operational value of consent, as well as the modalities of consent. Part II, Section 3 examines the specific role of UNSC resolutions in regulating the use of force and how they should be interpreted and implemented from that perspective.

4.1.2. Rules regulating the conduct of UN (mandated) peace operations

Once deployed, UN (mandated) peace forces must abide by the rules that regulate their conduct, especially their use of force to protect civilians. First, the concept of 'self-defence' – a complex legal concept that transcends the distinction between the legal basis (as discussed above) and the different legal regimes applicable to the use of force (as discussed afterwards) – is addressed. Hereafter, the different legal regimes that may play a role are mapped out. In this regard, a distinction is made between international law (with a particular focus on IHL and HRL) and national law. To conclude, other relevant rules and practices are discussed, which, while not always being sources of law *per se*, are highly relevant to the conduct of UN (mandated) peace operations.

636 See also Ruys (n. 52) 138.
637 Gill and others (n. 26) 27.

4.1.2.1. Self-defence, defence of others, and defence of the mandate

The authority to use force in self-defence is part of the standard set of rules regulating the conduct of UN (mandated) peace operations. Yet, despite being central to the PoC use of force doctrine, self-defence is an ill-defined concept in international law. Scholars generally agree on the existence of self-defence authority, but little else is clear about the norm. Gaggioli, for example, speaks of 'a "Babel Tower Phenomenon", whereby everyone refers to self-defence in armed conflicts, but each one understands it in a different way.'[638] Self-defence is indeed a multifaceted concept. Different forms of self-defence, from personal self-defence to national (State) self-defence, are governed by different rules and principles. It is beyond the scope of this book to comprehensively examine, let alone resolve, the question of the legal nature of UN (mandated) peace forces' authority to use force in self-defence, defence of others, and defence of the mandate. This book only offers a brief account of which instruments may legitimately serve as a legal source for such purposes.[639] The source of self-defence determines the principles upon which it is based.

First and foremost, force used in personal self-defence and defence of others is a permissive ground for depriving someone of their human right to life – a legal source (and limitation) of self-defence and defence of others that is often forgotten.[640] Individuals have a human right to life, and to protect that right, individuals may resort to lethal force. This is different from saying that individuals have a human right to self-defence. In case individuals use force in personal self-defence or defence of others, and if the conditions governing such use of force are met (including, but not limited to, the requirement that any use of force must be necessary and proportionate), such use of force does not constitute an arbitrary deprivation of life and thus does not violate that person's human right to life.[641] For example, as explicitly foreseen in Article 2(2) of the ECHR, which sets forth that the '[d]eprivation of life shall not be regarded as inflicted in contravention of this article when it results from the use of force which is no more than absolutely necessary [...] in defence of *any* person from unlawful violence.'[642] In the same vein, international criminal law also recognises personal self-defence and defence of others as grounds for excluding

638 Gloria Gaggioli, 'Soldier Self-Defense Symposium: Self-Defense in Armed Conflicts – The Babel Tower Phenomenon' (*Opinio Juris*, 3 May 2019), http://opiniojuris.org/2019/05/03/soldier-self-defense-symposium-self-defense-in-armed-conflicts-the-babel-tower-phenomenon/, accessed 17 May 2019.

639 *Ibid.*

640 See also *ibid.*

641 As discussed in more detail below, see Part III, Section 3.1.1.

642 Emphasis added. See also Principle 9 of the UN Basic Principles for the Use of Force and Firearms which reads as follows: 'Law enforcement officials shall not use firearms against persons except in self-defence or defence of others against the imminent threat of death or serious injury [...].'

international criminal responsibility.[643] To illustrate, Article 31(1)(c) of the 1998 Rome Statute establishing the ICC sets forth that 'a person shall not be criminally responsible if, at the time of that person's conduct [...] [t]he person acts reasonably to defend himself or herself or another person.'[644]

Personal self-defence is also strongly embedded in national law, with national systems commonly identifying self-defence as a justification for otherwise criminal behaviour.[645] Hereby, personal self-defence is usually understood as a form of 'self-help' allowing persons to protect themselves from bodily harm from the attack of an aggressor by using physical force.[646] Given its almost universal recognition in national criminal law, the right to personal self-defence is widely recognised as a general principle of law.[647] However, national interpretations of the scope of this right vary, as do national views on what factors could (if any) weaken this right or even nullify the justification customarily provided in the national criminal system by an invocation of self-defence.[648]

The concept of personal self-defence is also commonly referred to in the ROE.[649] In this context, self-defence is usually identified as an 'inherent right' that can neither be limited nor be negated by a mission-specific ROE.[650] For

---

643 Gloria Gaggioli, 'The Use of Force in Armed Conflicts Conduct of Hostilities, Law Enforcement, and Self-Defense' in Winston S Williams and Christopher M Ford (eds), *Complex Battlespaces: the Law of Armed Conflict and the Dynamics of Modern Warfare*, vol. 1 (Oxford University Press 2019) 76.

644 That said, Art. 31(1)(c) of the 1998 Rome Statute remains enigmatic and highly contentious, see further *ibid.* 77–79.

645 A justification is a circumstance whereby the course of conduct, which would normally have constituted a criminal offence, loses its unlawful character (Boddens Hosang, *Rules of Engagement and the International Law of Military Operations* (n. 559) 89, fn. 55). See also Gaggioli, 'The Use of Force in Armed Conflicts Conduct of Hostilities, Law Enforcement, and Self-Defense' (n. 643) 80; Lindsey Cameron and Vincent Chetail, *Privatizing War: Private Military and Security Companies under Public International Law* (Cambridge University Press 2013) 455–457.

646 Boddens Hosang, *Rules of Engagement and the International Law of Military Operations* (n. 559) 89; 'Self-Defence, n.', www.dictionary.law.com, accessed 4 March 2022.

647 Jan Arno Hessbruegge, *Human Rights and Personal Self-Defense in International Law* (1 edn, Oxford University Press 2017) 21–73; Gloria Gaggioli, 'Review Essay: Human Rights and Personal Self-Defense in International Law by Jan Arno Hessbruegge' (2017) 18 Melbourne Journal of International Law 460, 461; Melzer and Gaggioli (n. 64) 87; Gaggioli, 'The Use of Force in Armed Conflicts Conduct of Hostilities, Law Enforcement, and Self-Defense' (n. 643) 80.

648 Terry D Gill and others, 'General Report for the 19th Congress of the International Society for Military Law and the Law of War' in Stanislas Horvat and Marco Benatar (eds), *Proceedings of the 19th Congress of the International Society for Military Law and the Law of War on Legal Interoperability and Ensuring Observance of the Law Applicable in Multinational Deployments, 1–4 May 2012, Quebec, 231* (2013) 156. See also Leverick (n. 561).

649 Gaggioli, 'The Use of Force in Armed Conflicts Conduct of Hostilities, Law Enforcement, and Self-Defense' (n. 643) 83.

650 Boddens Hosang, *Rules of Engagement and the International Law of Military Operations* (n. 559) 94. For different views on the meaning of 'inherent', see *ibid.* 73–102; Katherine E Cox, 'Beyond Self-Defense: United Nations Peacekeeping Operations & the Use of Force' (1998) 27 Denver Journal of International Law and Policy 239; Findlay (n. 168) 15–16; Gaggioli, 'Soldier

example, the 2002 UN Sample ROE sets forth the principle that '[n]othing in these ROE negates a Commander's right and obligation to take all necessary and appropriate action for self-defence. All personnel may exercise the inherent right of self-defence.'[651]

Most, but not all, national laws also extend the right to use force in self-defence to the defence of others in some form.[652] In Belgian law, for example, Article 416 of the Belgian Criminal Code provides that there is neither a crime nor a misdemeanour when the homicide, injuries, or blows are commanded by the actual necessity of legitimate defence of oneself *or others*.[653] In other words, under Belgian criminal law, self-defence and defence of others serve as a justification whereby the behaviour is no longer contrary to the law and, therefore, does not constitute a criminal offence. Article 70 of the Belgian Criminal Code also provides that no offence is committed in case the act is ordered by law or at the command of higher authority; such command can be given through duly authorised mission-specific ROE. These two provisions of national law, together with the ROE, establish a link between the authorisation to use force under international law and the justification of such use of force under national law.[654] Members of the armed forces who use force in self-defence do not violate the law if they acted within the scope of legally issued ROE, which in turn reflects the mandate for the mission and, as discussed below, is consistent with HRL and usually reflects the right to use force in self-defence (see further below).[655]

Not all national laws contain a provision on the legitimate use of force in defence of others, or the relevant national provision is more limited in scope than what is foreseen under PoC. In that case, to address problems of interoperability, a specific authorisation can also be foreseen in the mandate and subsequently be

Self-Defense Symposium: Self-Defense in Armed Conflicts – The Babel Tower Phenomenon' (n. 638); Bruce Oswald, 'Soldier Self-Defense Symposium: The Evolution of the UN Doctrine of Self-Defence in UN Peacekeeping' (*Opinio Juris*, 1 May 2019), http://opiniojuris.org/2019/05/01/soldier-self-defense-symposium-the-evolution-of-the-un-doctrine-of-self-defence-in-un-peacekeeping/, accessed 17 May 2019.

651 UN DPKO (n. 102), Attachment 2: p. 3, para. 7(b)(1). See also the United States, Joint Chiefs of Staff, Chairman of the Joint Chiefs of Staff, 'Standing Rules of Engagement/Standing Rules for the Use of Force for US Forces' (2005) Document CJCSI 3121.01B Appendix A, Enclosure A, p. A-2, para. 3(a).

652 Boddens Hosang, *Rules of Engagement and the International Law of Military Operations* (n. 559) 91.

653 Belgian Criminal Code of 8 June 1867.

654 For a similar analysis under Dutch law, see Johan FR Boddens Hosang and Terry D Gill, 'Soldier Self-Defense Symposium: Netherlands Views on Self-Defence for Military Personnel' (*Opinio Juris*, 29 April 2019), https://opiniojuris.org/2019/04/29/soldier-self-defense-symposium-netherlands-views-on-self-defence-for-military-personnel%EF%BB%BF/, accessed 17 May 2019.

655 See also *ibid.*

reflected in the mission-specific ROE.[656] For example, Rule 1.8 of the 2002 UN Sample ROE provides for the following rule:[657]

> Use of force, up to, and including deadly force, to defend any civilian person who is in need of protection against a hostile act or hostile intent, when competent local authorities are not in a position to render immediate assistance, is authorised. When and where possible, permission to use force should be sought from the immediate superior commander.

Along the same lines, the authority to use force in defence of the mandate – a form of self-defence which expressly goes beyond personal self-defence and commonly invoked by the UN[658] – may stem from an express authorisation by the UN Security Council.[659] For example, UNIFIL's mandate has consistently foreseen in an authorisation 'to take all necessary action [...] to resist attempts by forceful means to prevent it from discharging its duties under the mandate of the Security Council.'[660] The extent to which a UN peace operation may use force then largely depends on how comprehensive its mandate is.[661] The broader the mandate, the more occasions in which the UN peace operation may have an authorisation to use force.[662]

Regarding UN peace operations, the authority to use force in defence of the mandate may also derive from the implied or inherent powers of UN peace operations to use force which they may invoke in their capacity as subsidiary organs of the UN.[663] As discussed above, the UN has general powers in maintaining international peace and security, powers which are connected

---

656 Gill and others (n. 648) 142. On interoperability, see Marten Zwanenburg, 'International Humanitarian Law Interoperability in Multinational Operations' (2013) 95 International Review of the Red Cross 681.

657 UN DPKO, *Guidelines for the Development of Rules of Engagement (ROE) for United Nations Peacekeeping Operations*, UN Doc. MD/FGS/0220.0001, 15 May 2002, Attachment 1, p. 2.

658 For references, see Introductory Chapter, Section 1, fn. 19.

659 As already referred to above, the following mission-specific UNSC resolutions include, e.g. a reference to 'defence of the mandate': 'UNSC Res. 2098' (n. 19); 'UNSC Res. 2147' (n. 19); 'UNSC Res. 2149' (n. 19); 'UNSC Res. 2223' (n. 19); 'UNSC Res. 2227' (n. 19); 'UNSC Res. 2228' (n. 19); 'UNSC Res. 2304' (n. 135); 'UNSC Res. 2327' (n. 19); 'UNSC Res. 2363' (n. 19); 'UNSC Res. 2364' (n. 19); 'UNSC Res. 2387' (n. 19); 'UNSC Res. 2406' (n. 19).

660 'UNSC Res. 1701' (n. 136) para. 12. See also subsequent mandates: 'UNSC Res. 1773' (2007) UN Doc. S/RES/1773 (2007) pream. para. 13; 'UNSC Res. 1884' (2009) UN Doc. S/RES/1884 (2009) pream. para. 10; 'UNSC Res. 1937' (2010) UN Doc. S/RES/1937 (2010) pream. para. 11; 'UNSC Res. 2004' (2011) UN Doc. S/RES/2004 (2011) pream. para. 11; 'UNSC Res. 2064' (2012) UN Doc. S/RES/2064 (2012) pream. para. 14; 'UNSC Res. 2172' (2014) UN Doc. S/RES/2172 (2014) pream. para. 14; 'UNSC Res. 2236' (2015) UN Doc. S/RES/2236 (2015) pream. para. 16; 'UNSC Res. 2305' (2016) UN Doc. S/RES/2305 (2016) pream. para. 13; 'UNSC Res. 2373' (n. 136) para. 14; 'UNSC Res. 2433' (n. 136) para. 19; 'UNSC Res. 2485' (n. 136) para. 20; 'UNSC Res. 2539' (n. 136) para. 21; 'UNSC Res. 2591' (n. 136) para. 22.

661 Cox (n. 650) 25.

662 *Ibid.*

663 Gill and others (n. 648) 142.

to the UN Charter's purposes and principles. To fulfil such purposes and functions, the UN must be able to resort to the use of force.[664] According to Sheeran, UN membership implies that States have acknowledged and consented to the UN's general authority to use force.[665] He contends that accepting a UN peace operation on its territory also implies 'accepting that it may use force in self-defence including in defence of the mandate, and against parties to the conflict.'[666]

The UN also seeks to explain peace forces' authority to use force in personal self-defence or to defend (protect) civilians as an emanation of self-defence under international law. As such, the UN has emphasised peace forces' 'inherent' right of self-defence, grounded on Article 51 of the UN Charter and customary international law, as a standalone legal basis for the use of force by UN peace forces. As the UN Office of Legal Affairs observed in 1993:[667]

> [I]t is necessary to point out that the right of self-defence is well established in international law, both under customary international law and Article 51 of the Charter of the United Nations. [...] The right of self-defence is not limited to States and applies as an inherent right also to the United Nations. United Nations forces have, accordingly, always been regarded as entitled to the right of self-defence [...]. This right has been consistently provided for in the rules of engagement established for each peacekeeping operation since their inception. [...] [T]he use of force in self-defence is an inherent right of United Nations forces exercised to preserve a collective and individual defence.

This horizontal conceptualisation of *jus ad bellum* self-defence – as a norm that gives not just the UN as an organisation a strategic right to defend itself but also a personal tactical right for members of the peace forces to defend themselves and others, including civilians – is reproduced in the UN's ROE (see above).

The UN's tendency to justify the use of force by UN peace forces primarily based on *jus ad bellum* self-defence, with no further acknowledgement of what applicable legal regimes govern such uses of force, echoes the tendency to justify the use of force solely based on mission mandates, founded on Chapter VII powers. While the use of force beyond personal self-defence may stem from an express authorisation by the UN Security Council, what is problematic is the

664 Sheeran, 'The Use of Force in United Nations Peacekeeping Operations' (n. 37) 362.
665 *Ibid.*
666 *Ibid.*
667 UN OLA, 'The Right of Self-Defence of United Nations Peacekeeping Forces and the Exercise of This Right – Article 51 of the Charter of the United Nations, July 19, 1993' (1993) United Nations Juridical Yearbook 371, 371–372. See also Findlay (n. 168) 15. Yet the application of Art. 51 self-defence, which concerns States' right to use transboundary force, to peacekeeping, where national units operate under the command of an international organisation, is hardly straightforward (as also raised by Sheeran, 'The Use of Force in United Nations Peacekeeping Operations' (n. 37) 362).

propensity to perceive a UNSC mandate as a blank cheque for offensive force to protect civilians.[668] Indeed, the UN has expanded peace forces' authority to use force by relying on the legal basis, as enshrined in UNSC mandates, and then translated into mission-specific ROE, yet refuses to recognise which legal regime – IHL or HRL – governs the use of force in UN peace operations – also echoing the practice of some States.

In particular, due to re-alignments in the wake of the 11 September 2001 attack, the government of the US has increasingly relied on *jus ad bellum* arguments to expand its troops' authority to use force against non-state actors. A revised doctrine of anticipatory (or pre-emptive) self-defence, where a loosened threshold of imminence enables US forces to use lethal force against specific terrorist targets worldwide even in the absence of temporally defined threats to US interests, has been central to the so-called war on terror. Although various aspects of the war on terror raise legal challenges, most important for our purposes is the US' reliance on its *jus ad bellum* right to so-called 'naked' self-defence – without any further analysis of whether strikes comply with IHL or HRL – to legitimise lethal strikes, including in areas far removed from hostilities, against terrorist targets.[669]

Any use of force in self-defence, whether personal self-defence, defence of others, or defence of the mandate, *must* comply with the applicable legal regime(s) – a condition that is too often forgotten or ignored. Indeed, it is primarily the relevant legal regime that determines under which circumstances and in which manner armed forces may use force against a particular objective or a particular person. Thus, what is essential is that when UN (mandated) peace forces use force, whether in self-defence, defence of others or defence of the mandate, they must do so in accordance with the rules and principles of the legal regimes applicable in that case, such as HRL, IHL, and national law (to the extent it is more protective than international law). For example, troops participating in a UN (mandated) peace operation may use lethal force in defence of others based on their national criminal law, but any such national norms must always be consistent with the relevant international rules and standards, especially the right to life under HRL. National laws can be more protective of life but not less.

---

[668] Labuda, 'UN Peacekeeping as Intervention by Invitation: Host State Consent and the Use of Force in Security Council-Mandated Stabilisation Operations' (n. 33) 327–328.

[669] N Ronzitti, 'The Expanding Law of Self-Defence' (2006) 11 Journal of Conflict and Security Law 343; Mary Ellen O'Connell, Christian J Tams and Dire Tladi, *Self-Defence against Non-State Actors*, vol. 1 (Cambridge University Press 2019). On naked self-defence, see Watkin (n. 38) 311–318.

4.1.2.2. Legal regimes

A. International law

i. HRL and IHL

HRL lays down the fundamental rights and freedoms to which all human beings are entitled. As previously noted, when referring to HRL, this book implies both international and regional HRL. HRL is, in principle, applicable at all times, regardless of the character of a situation in which a UN (mandated) peace operation is deployed.[670] Depending on the organisation of an operation, armed forces carrying out the operation must abide by the HRL obligations deriving from the international organisation undertaking the operation, the States contributing troops to the operation (the TCCs), and/or the State on whose territory the operation takes place (the host State).[671] Which HRL obligations apply as a matter of law to a specific situation depends on whose jurisdiction the persons in question fall under at the relevant time.[672] The most pertinent rule of HRL in the context of the use of force by peace forces on the ground is the right to life, a right governed by the principles of legality, necessity, proportionality, precautions, and accountability.[673]

If force is used in a situation which has a clear nexus to an ongoing armed conflict, that use of force is not only governed by HRL but also by IHL.[674] IHL can be defined as follows:[675]

> [A] set of rules that seek to limit the humanitarian consequences of armed conflicts. [...] The primary purpose of IHL is to restrict the means and methods of warfare that parties to a conflict may employ and to ensure the protection and humane treatment of persons who are not, or no longer, taking a direct part in the hostilities. In short, IHL comprises those rules of international law which establish minimum standards of humanity that must be respected in any situation of armed conflict.

IHL rules and principles principally apply to all armed forces as a matter of treaty or customary law when the conditions for applying this body of law are

---

670 Gill and others (n. 26) 76.

671 *Ibid.* 77.

672 *Ibid.* 150.

673 As discussed further in Part III, Section 3.1.1. See also the General Comments Nos. 36 and 3 on the Right to Life of the UN HRC and AComHPR, respectively (UN HRC, 'General Comment No. 36 on the Right to Life' (n. 82) para. 12; AComHPR (n. 83) para. 12.

674 E.g. according to the UN HRC, '[l]ike the rest of the Covenant, article 6 [of the ICCPR] continues to apply also in situations of armed conflict to which the rules of international humanitarian law are applicable, including to the conduct of hostilities,' see UN HRC, 'General Comment No. 36 on the Right to Life' (n. 82) para. 64.

675 Nils Melzer, *International Humanitarian Law: A Comprehensive Introduction* (ICRC 2019) 17.

met.[676] The conditions are set out in IHL itself and are established by practice. Essentially, once the threshold for an 'armed conflict' is reached, all relevant rules of IHL apply equally to all belligerents, without distinction, irrespective of the cause or the justness of the war, unless a rule cannot be applied because of certain intrinsic characteristics.[677] Under IHL, force can be used, provided that, among others, the principles of distinction, precautions in attack, and prohibition of excessive collateral damage are respected.[678]

Unlike IHL, HRL was never developed with the idea of regulating the use of force by armed forces other than for law enforcement. National human rights law came into place to restrict the 'internal' resort to force by State authorities against their own citizens to maintain or restore public security, the rule of law, and internal order (identified as law enforcement tasks).[679] IHL, on the other hand, was initially developed to limit the impact of 'external' inter-state warfare.[680] To this end, States mainly aimed, on the basis of reciprocity, to regulate humanitarian issues in times of armed conflicts and limit the detrimental effects of armed conflict.[681] After the Second World War, Geneva Convention IV (on the protection of civilians) and the codification of Common Article 3 of the Geneva Conventions I–IV applicable to NIACs brought IHL closer to the idea of HRL, especially by focusing on the treatment of a State's nationals.[682] Simultaneously, with the adoption of the Universal Declaration of Human Rights (UDHR)[683] by the UN General Assembly, HRL became one of the youngest bodies of public international law and was placed beside IHL, one of the oldest bodies of public international law.[684] The UDHR was, however, intended for times of peace, not for situations of armed conflict.[685] And although

---

676 Tristan Ferraro, 'The Applicability and Application of International Humanitarian Law to Multinational Forces' (2013) 95 International Review of the Red Cross 561, 582; Gill and others (n. 26) 91.

677 Ferraro, 'The Applicability and Application of International Humanitarian Law to Multinational Forces' (n. 676) 582.

678 For a more detailed discussion, see Part III, Section 3.2.

679 Gloria Gaggioli, 'The Use of Force in Armed Conflict: Interplay between the Conduct of Hostilities and Law Enforcement Paradigms, ICRC Outcome Report' (ICRC 2013) 7; Watkin (n. 38) 450–451.

680 Kolb, 'The Relationship between International Humanitarian Law and Human Rights Law: A Brief History of the 1948 Universal Declaration of Human Rights and the 1949 Geneva Conventions' (n. 64) (no page numbers available in online version); Watkin (n. 38) 451.

681 Cordula Droege, 'The Interplay between International Humanitarian Law and International Human Rights Law in Situations of Armed Conflict Special Issue: Parallel Applicability of International Humanitarian Law and International Human Rights Law' (2007) 40 Israel Law Review 310, 313.

682 *Ibid.*

683 'UNGA Res. 217 A(III), Universal Declaration of Human Rights' (1948) UNGA Res. 217 A(III).

684 Droege (n. 681) 313; Kolb, 'The Relationship between International Humanitarian Law and Human Rights Law: A Brief History of the 1948 Universal Declaration of Human Rights and the 1949 Geneva Conventions' (n. 64) (no page numbers available in online version).

685 Droege (n. 681) 314.

at the UN, States have gradually recognised the relevance of HRL in situations of armed conflict, it is still not evident that this branch of law plays a role in those types of situations, precisely because this branch of law never intended to apply in such situations when it was developed.[686]

UN (mandated) peace operations often operate in a grey zone between conflict and peace. As a result, neither IHL nor HRL seems particularly suited to regulate the use of force. UN (mandated) peace operations consist mainly of military contingents trained in IHL targeting for military operations rather than civilian police familiar with law enforcement tasks. Yet, most of the time, the threshold for an armed conflict is not reached, but even when it is, it is not always acknowledged that a UN (mandated) peace operation is a party to the armed conflict, and hence IHL is deemed applicable *de jure*. Recognition of the applicability of IHL implies acceptance that the members of peace forces have lost their protected status, particularly against attack. The *de jure* applicability of HRL to the conduct of both UN peace operations and UN-mandated peace operations is, however, also often ignored or denied, partly because there is a fear that HRL will be applied *in toto*, without adaptation, and in an unrealistic manner to extraterritorial emergencies.[687] It can also not be ignored that the HRL rules on the use of force are somewhat restrictive.

If the use of force by peace forces is not considered to be legally regulated by either IHL or HRL, there is a risk of a legal vacuum being created.[688] It may also lead to a 'pick and choose' approach, whereby standards are applied not because they are deemed legally binding but as a matter of (internal) policy.[689] Therefore, Part III examines in detail the applicability of the legal regimes of HRL and IHL to the use of force to protect civilians by UN (mandated) peace forces implementing a PoC mandate. As the precise scope of the obligations in the context of the use of force for PoC under these legal regimes remains a matter of controversy, this, too, is addressed in Part III.

ii. Other relevant areas of conventional and customary international law

Other areas of conventional and customary international law are also relevant to the conduct of UN (mandated) peace operations, such as international law relative to the status of forces, the international law of the sea, international air law, international environmental law, and international refugee law.

To illustrate: under international refugee law, the principle of non-refoulement protects a person against expulsion (refoulement) by any means to the borders of territories where their life or freedom would be endangered on

686 *Ibid.*

687 Sheeran, 'Human Rights and Derogation in Peacekeeping' (n. 29) 232.

688 Labuda, 'UN Peacekeeping as Intervention by Invitation: Host State Consent and the Use of Force in Security Council-Mandated Stabilisation Operations' (n. 33) 327.

689 *Ibid.*

the grounds of their race, religion, nationality, membership of a particular social group, or political opinion. This principle is not only included in the Refugee Convention[690] but is also a norm of customary international law and thus binds subjects of international law.[691] Although the principle of non-refoulement forms an integral part of HRL and IHL, which may constitute an important source of legal protection for persons that are *internally* displaced, the inclusion of the principle in international refugee law is also increasingly seen as applying to IDP, even if they have not crossed an international boundary (as opposed to a refugee).[692] In the case of South Sudan, UNMISS has the mandate to 'maintain public safety and security of and within UNMISS protection of civilians sites.'[693] Since UNMISS has *de facto* authority over IDPs in those PoC sites, this implies that UNMISS is responsible for upholding the legal rights of the IDPs residing therein.[694] Therefore, when seeking to relocate IPDs living in the PoC sites to areas outside of the exclusive control and authority of the UN, UNMISS must take into account the principle of non-refoulement.[695] Accordingly, IDPs cannot be forced to leave a PoC site if there is a well-founded fear of prosecution, torture, or cruel, inhuman, or degrading treatment.[696]

Despite being relevant to the conduct of UN (mandated) peace operations, areas of conventional and customary international law other than IHL and HRL are not discussed further in this book.

B. National law

Peace forces deployed in the territory of a third State usually have to respect not only the host State's law but also remain subject to the law of the sending State.[697]

While the principle of territorial sovereignty entitles each and every State to exercise jurisdiction over persons and entities present in its territory, visiting forces are generally exempted from civil and criminal jurisdiction by the host State (see below). At a minimum, however, visiting forces must 'respect' the host State's law. The 1990 UN Model SOFA for Peacekeeping Operations sets forth, for example, that UN peace operations and its members 'shall respect all local laws and regulations' and that the UN Special Representative or

---

690 Convention Relating to the Status of Refugees (adopted 28 July 1951, entered into force 22 April 1954) 189 UNTS 137 (Refugee Convention).

691 The rule is reflected in Art. 33(1) of the Refugee Convention. See also Caelin Briggs, 'Non-Refoulement in the Context of Internal Displacement: The Case of IDPs in South Sudan's Protection of Civilians Sites' (Norwegian Refugee Council 2017) 7–8.

692 *Ibid.* 8.

693 As foreseen in UNMISS' latest PoC mandate: 'UNSC Res. 2567' (n. 135) para. 3(a)(iii) (see also previous PoC mandates provided to UNMISS).

694 Briggs (n. 691) 16.

695 *Ibid.* 18.

696 *Ibid.* 19.

697 See also Gill and others (n. 26) Chapters 9 (130–134) and 10 (135–138).

Commander shall take 'all appropriate measures to ensure the observance of those obligations.'[698]

The duty 'to respect' host State law is generally recognised in current practice, but there remains debate about the degree of subordination to host State law. While one school of thought is convinced that visiting forces are obliged to comply with host State law to the letter, another school of thought is of the opinion that it is sufficient for visiting forces to take due account of host State law and to avoid, or at least limit as much as possible, any action that directly conflicts with it.[699] Nevertheless, subject to certain exceptions established by SOFAs (as explained in the next Section) and customary international law,[700] the duty 'to respect' means, at a minimum, that the peace forces must consider the law of the host State and respect the host State's legal order in a manner consistent with other legal obligations and the mandate.

Besides their duty to respect host State law, peace forces carrying out an operation shall, in principle, take into consideration the relevant national laws of their sending States. Sending States will often require their armed forces to comply with the relevant national legal framework, which includes not only IHL and HRL obligations of the sending State but also the national (military) criminal and disciplinary laws. Sending States may rightfully do so as long as they observe the relevant rules of international law. After all, despite being deployed in the territory of a third State, States retain the power to regulate and control the conduct of their armed forces.[701] Peace forces operating on the territory of a third State enjoy certain privileges and immunities, as also recognised in customary international law and confirmed in general agreements (such as the UN Privileges and Immunities Convention[702] in the context of UN peace operations) and mission-specific agreements (such as SOFAs (as explained in the next Section)).[703] Hence, it is the sending State that may exercise exclusive or complementary *prescriptive* jurisdiction in the territory of a third State over, for example, personnel administration, labour and disciplinary matters, and criminal conduct.[704] On certain occasions, sending States may also exercise *enforcement* jurisdiction over its organs and officials.[705]

698 UNGA, '1990 UN Model SOFA for Peacekeeping Operations' (n. 46) para. 6.

699 Gill and others (n. 26) 132.

700 Michael Bothe, 'Peacekeeping Forces', *Max Planck Encyclopedia of Public International law* (Oxford Public International Law 2016) para. 41.

701 *Ibid.* para. 48; Gill and others (n. 26) 135.

702 Convention on the Privileges and Immunities of the United Nations (adopted 17 September 1946, entered into force 13 February 1946) 1 UNTS 15 and 90 UNTS 327 (corrigendum) (UN Privileges and Immunities Convention).

703 Dieter Fleck, 'The Legal Status of Personnel Involved in United Nations Peace Operations' (2013) 95 International Review of the Red Cross 613, 616; Gill and others (n. 26) 120–124, 130–131.

704 Bothe, 'Peacekeeping Forces' (n. 700) para. 48. This is not the same as saying that national law generally applies extraterritorially (see Gill and others (n. 26) 135).

705 Gill and others (n. 26) 136–138.

4.1.2.3. Other relevant rules and practices

Mission-specific agreements and arrangements also play a key role in regulating the conduct of UN (mandated) peace operations. For example, before a mission is deployed in the territory of a State, a SOFA is usually concluded. SOFAs are legally binding bilateral or multilateral treaties that specify the legal status of military and civil personnel deployed by one or more States or by an international or regional organisation in the territory of another State with the latter's consent.[706] Such instruments usually concern the freedom of movement, entry and departure of foreign personnel, the use of flags, uniforms and weaponry, taxation, the exercise of civil and criminal jurisdiction over members of the visiting forces, and the settlement of claims by the local population.[707] In addition, international organisations or lead States undertaking a UN (mandated) peace operation may also conclude an arrangement with a TCC that is, depending on the will of the parties, legally binding or not.[708] These so-called TCC MOUs are intended to specify the administrative, logistical, and financial conditions for the contribution of personnel, equipment, and services provided by TCCs in support of UN (mandated) peace operations and to outline responsibilities for conduct, discipline, investigation, and accountability.[709]

There are also mission-specific documents, such as military strategic Concepts of Operations (CONOPS), ROE for the military component, and Operations (or Operational) Plans (OPLAN), that are relevant to the conduct of UN (mandated) peace operations. CONOPS set out how the military component supports the strategic objectives using force, where necessary,[710] while OPLANs set out the elements needed to carry out an operation and concern all relevant topics.[711] ROE are usually understood as guidelines for the military and policy components, respectively, which define the degree of force (or other provocative acts) that may be used and how it may be applied.[712] They set forth when, where,

---

706 Aurel Sari, 'Status of Forces and Status of Mission Agreements under the ESDP: The EU's Evolving Practice' (2008) 19 European Journal of International Law 67, 68; White, 'Peacekeeping and International Law' (n. 37) 48.

707 Sari, 'Status of Forces and Status of Mission Agreements under the ESDP: The EU's Evolving Practice' (n. 706) 68; White, 'Peacekeeping and International Law' (n. 37) 48.

708 Gill and others (n. 26) 139.

709 See UNGA, 'Revised Draft Model Memorandum of Understanding between the United Nations and [Participating State] Contributing Resources to [the United Nations Peacekeeping Operation], 3 October 2006, Sixty-First Session, Agenda Item 33' UN Doc. A/61/494, Art. 3.

710 See UN DPKO and UN DFS, '2017 UN Guidelines on the Use of Force by Military Components in UN Peacekeeping Operations' (n. 17) para. 13.

711 Boddens Hosang, *Rules of Engagement and the International Law of Military Operations* (n. 559) 23.

712 One must be aware that there exist several definitions of ROE, with varying degrees of similarities, see e.g. UN DPKO and UN DFS, '2017 UN Guidelines on the Use of Force by

against whom, and how force can be used.[713] They may also include provisions on the permitted use of certain weapons or guidelines on engaging with the local population.[714] ROE are not a source of law *per se*; ROE clarify peace forces' authority to use force, but its sources and boundaries lie elsewhere.[715] ROE are governed by the UN Charter, the mission-specific mandate, HRL, and IHL, among others.[716]

Last but not least, a number of doctrinal and general documents on PoC and the use of force that are also not sources of law *per se* are nevertheless directly or indirectly relevant for the conduct of UN (mandated) peace operations. For one, over the years, regional and international organisations have issued a number of guidelines, policies, and principles on PoC and the use of force. For example, in 2019, the UN DPO issued a revised Policy on PoC in UN Peacekeeping.[717] In 2015, the EU adopted an EU Concept on PoC in EU-led Military Operations,[718] while the AU adopted its Draft Guidelines for PoC in 2012.[719] In addition, NATO issued its Policy on PoC in 2016.[720] These instruments are not legally binding but play an essential role in supplementing legally binding obligations on PoC and the use of force. Other instruments include command and control arrangements, such as the 2019 EU Concept for Military Command and Control.[721] This Concept provides for the arrangements for the delivery of command and control, from the political-strategic level to the military elements conducting an EU-led military operation or mission.[722] Another instrument is the 1999 UN Secretary-General's Bulletin on IHL, in which the UN's position regarding when IHL applies to UN peace operations has been included.

Military Components in UN Peacekeeping Operations' (n. 17) para. 7; NATO, *NATO Legal Deskbook* (n. 593) 254; EUMC, 'EU Concept for EU-Led Military Operations and Missions' (n. 422) para. 34(c). See further Camilla Guldahl Cooper, 'Rules of Engagement Demystified: A Study of the History, Development and Use of ROEs' (2014) 53 Military Law and Law of War Review 189, 189–246.

713 Gill, Léveillée and Fleck (n. 609) 124.

714 *Ibid.*

715 As explained by Boddens Hosang, ROE 'act as a conduit between the law and the conduct of military operations by reflecting the law or interpreting the law into clear and concise rules on the use of force for the military personnel in question' (Boddens Hosang, *Rules of Engagement and the International Law of Military Operations* (n. 559) 316).

716 Khalil, 'Legal Aspects of the Use of Force by United Nations Peacekeepers for the Protection of Civilians' (n. 40) 209.

717 UN DPO, '2019 UN Policy on PoC in UN Peacekeeping' (n. 35).

718 EUMC, '2015 EU Concept on PoC in EU-Led Military Operations' (n. 120).

719 AU, '2012 AU Draft Guidelines for PoC in AU Peace Support Operations' (n. 114).

720 NAC, '2016 NATO Policy on PoC' (n. 118).

721 EEAS (n. 121).

722 *Ibid.* para. 6. As will also be discussed further in Part I, Section 4.2.2.

4.2. THE RESPECTIVE ROLES OF THE MANDATE AND THE LEGAL REGIMES IN REGULATING THE USE OF FORCE FOR PROTECTIVE PURPOSES: CLEARING THE FOG

4.2.1. Distinction and convergence between the rules providing a legal basis and the rules regulating the conduct

When discussing the use of force for protective purposes, it is crucial to distinguish between the legal bases and the legal regimes. Each has its own playing field in which they regulate the use of force.

The legal basis principally governs the *resort* to armed force on another State's territory as well as the *overall* levels of force used to execute the operation. Such legal basis for the emplacement and functioning within the territory of another State can, in the first place, be found in the UN Charter and the rules of customary international law relating to the use of force and the maintenance and restoration of international peace and security. Moreover, any such use of military force on a third State's territory requires a mission-specific mandate, which can be found in the consent of the host State and/or a UNSC mandate. Such a mandate is a strategic-level statement that is generally concerned with whether – and if so, how much – force can be used on the territory of a State and serves as a mission-specific legal basis to that end.

The applicable legal regimes regulate *specific instances* of the use of force by armed forces on the ground. Indeed, it is primarily the relevant legal regime that determines under which circumstances and in which manner armed forces may use force against a particular objective or a particular person. Depending on the circumstances, either IHL and/or HRL and national law determine when and how armed forces may use force.

Although the distinction between the two is crystal clear in theory, consideration of their respective roles in practice suggests that they may intersect in regulating the use of force for protection purposes. To better understand the possible dynamics, both should first be placed in the context of the distinct levels of authority, command, and control in UN (mandated) peace operations. Conceptualising this structure contributes to a better understanding of the respective roles of the legal bases (and, particularly, the UNSC mandate) and the applicable legal regimes (and, particularly, HRL and IHL) in regulating the use of force at the distinct levels, and how they may overlap each other's playing field.

4.2.2. From law to practice: levels of authority, command, and control in UN (mandated) peace operations

The respective roles that the legal bases and the applicable legal regimes play in regulating the use of force become clearer when placed in the context of the different levels of authority, command, and control in UN (mandated) peace operations. Command and control concern the authority conferred on certain individuals or bodies to direct the actions and exercise authority over (elements of) the armed forces.[723] Authority in this regard refers to the legal power to take specific actions and hence signifies both the legal basis for a command relationship as well as the legal basis to take the action in question in terms of the substance of the action.[724] In theory, the number of levels can be unlimited.[725] However, in the interests of clarity, this book only discusses three general levels, including, from top to bottom, the strategic, operational, and tactical levels.

4.2.2.1. Strategic level

The political strategic level is the highest level of authority, command, and control, which provides the 'legal authority, high-level strategic direction, and political guidance' for an operation.[726] In the case of UN peace operations and UN-mandated peace operations, the UN Security Council determines whether an operation should take place and the overall objectives that the operation will achieve.[727] If a State or an organisation (such as the AU, NATO, or the EU) is authorised to carry out a UNSC mandate, its political strategic leadership retains the authority to accept or refuse the invitation. Upon acceptance, the competent body of that State, organisation, or arrangement will generally adopt a separate internal mandate.[728] Such an internal mandate must always conform with the external mandate under international law.[729] The mandate of the UN Security Council will usually precede an internal mandate. In the exceptional case, an operation may already be established by a State, organisation, or arrangement and only then be endorsed by the UN Security Council.[730]

---

723 Boddens Hosang, *Rules of Engagement and the International Law of Military Operations* (n. 559) 66; Terry D Gill, 'Legal Aspects of the Transfer of Authority in UN Peace Operations' in Ige F Dekker and Ellen Hey (eds), *Netherlands Yearbook of International Law 2011*, vol. 42 (TMC Asser Press 2011) 45.

724 Boddens Hosang, *Rules of Engagement and the International Law of Military Operations* (n. 559) 66; Gill, 'Legal Aspects of the Transfer of Authority in UN Peace Operations' (n. 723) 45.

725 After all, as mentioned by Boddens Hosang, 'in describing command relationships, each relationship represents a level in the hierarchical structure,' see Boddens Hosang, *Rules of Engagement and the International Law of Military Operations* (n. 559) 67.

726 Terminology used by Cammaert and Klappe in Patrick C Cammaert and Ben F Klappe, 'Authority, Command, and Control in United Nations-Led Peace Operations' in Terry D Gill and Dieter Fleck (eds), *The Handbook of the International Law of Military Operations* (2nd edn., Oxford University Press 2015) 181.

727 *Ibid.*

728 For a discussion of 'internal mandates', see also Part I, Section 4.1.1.1(B). See also Gill and others (n. 26) 35.

729 *Ibid.* 35.

730 See e.g. Mor Diandame Mbow and Issaka K Souaré, 'Protecting Civilians in Mali and Central African Republic' in Jide Martyns Okeke and Paul D Williams (eds), *Protecting Civilians in African Union Support Operations: Key Cases and Lessons Learned* (African Centre for the Constructive Resolution of Disputes 2016) 73.

Subsequently, the military strategic level in the UN, States, or regional or international organisations other than the UN translates the mandate(s) into policies and operational guidelines addressed to the operational and tactical levels. This process usually involves the development of a CONOPS,[731] which is then subsumed into an OPLAN.[732] The mandate is also translated into the ROE.[733] In the context of UN peace operations, a so-called Mission Concept precedes the CONOPS and translates the political intent of the UNSC mandate into strategy, plans, and guidance for the military, police, and civilian component.[734] These instruments all reflect the terms laid down in the legal basis underlying the operations. At the same time, they must comply with the legal regime(s) applicable to the operation and, therefore, not be more flexible, at least in principle, than the relevant legal regime(s).

The political and military strategic leadership can assess whether an operation is conducted according to the mandate and is therefore responsible for the overall conduct of an operation. This assessment is carried out continuously from the moment the UN Security Council decides to intervene until the final evaluation of a completed operation. In this respect, it is beneficial to make the following distinction: only the UN Security Council or a body empowered for that purpose by the UN Security Council may give an 'authentic interpretation' to a UNSC resolution.[735] However, this does not detract from the fact that a wide range of authorities and individuals constantly translate and apply UNSC resolutions.[736] Yet, even if the UN Security Council has authorised a State, organisation, or arrangement to take military action, it should keep overall control over implementing the mandate it has given. It may do so by, *inter alia*, modifying the mandate or deciding not to renew it.[737]

The strategic level authority is exercised by the following organs:

UN – The UN Security Council exercises the political strategic authority over UN peace operations. In that capacity, it provides UN peace operations with a mandate and specifies the political objectives of the mission.[738] The operationalisation of mission mandates is vested in the UN Secretary-

---

731 As defined above, see Part I, Section 4.1.2.3.

732 As defined above, see Part I, Section 4.1.2.3.

733 As defined above, see Introductory Chapter, Section 1 and Part I, Section 4.1.2.3.

734 UN DPKO and UN DFS, 'An Overview of United Nations Peacekeeping Operations – Lesson 1.5 on Security Council Mandates in Practice' (2017) CPTM Version 14, http://repository.un.org/bitstream/handle/11176/400652/Lesson%201.5%20Security%20Council%20%20Mandates%20in%20Practice.pdf?sequence=5&isAllowed=y, accessed 8 April 2022.

735 Michael C Wood, 'The Interpretation of Security Council Resolutions' (1998) 2 Max Planck Yearbook of United Nations Law 73, 82–83. See also *Accordance with International Law of the Unilateral Declaration of Independence in Respect of Kosovo, Advisory opinion* (2010) ICJ Rep 403 para. 46; Gill, Léveillée and Fleck (n. 609) 112.

736 Wood (n. 735) 82–83. See also Gill, Léveillée and Fleck (n. 609) 112–116.

737 Tladi (n. 39) 82.

738 UN DPKO and UN DFS, 'Policy on Authority, Command and Control in United Nations Peacekeeping Operations' (2019) Ref. 2019.23 para. 8.

General.[739] The UN Secretary-General has delegated this responsibility to the UN Under-Secretary-General for Peace Operations, who provides political and policy guidance and strategic direction to the UN DPO and UN peace operations. The UN Under-Secretary-General for Peace Operations also leads policy developments and approves guidelines for the planning and execution of missions.[740]

AU – The AU's standing decision-making organ is the AU PSC.[741] The Military Staff Committee, composed of senior military officers of the Members of the AU PSC, advises and assists the AU PSC in all matters pertaining to military and security requirements for promoting and maintaining peace and security in Africa.[742] The Chairperson of the AU Commission, under the direction of the AU PSC, exercises the executive political direction and control of AU peace operations. Within the AU Commission, this responsibility is delegated to the Peace and Security Department (PSD), directed by the Commissioner for Political Affairs, Peace and Security (Commissioner for PAPS), which provides support to the efforts aimed at promoting peace and stability, good governance, democracy, and human rights in Africa.[743] PSD comprises a number of divisions, including the Peace and Support Operations Division (PSOD), which focuses on operationalising AU peace operations.[744] The Commissioner for PAPS, together with the staff of the PSOD, manages ongoing peace support operations and, to this end, develops policies, guidelines, procedures, legal instruments, plans, and directives relevant to the planning, deployment, management, monitoring, support, and liquidation of peace operations.[745]

NATO – In NATO, the strategic political level is vested in the NAC, advised by NATO's most senior military authority, the NAMC.[746] In addition to providing the NAC with advice on military policy and strategy, the NAMC is also responsible for translating political decisions and guidance into the military direction to NATO's two Strategic Commanders and, as such, serves as a link between the political leaders of NATO Headquarters and the two Strategic Commanders.[747] The military strategic level consists of two Strategic Commands: ACO under the command of the Supreme Allied Commander

739 *Ibid.*
740 *Ibid.* para. 11.
741 See Art. 2 of the AU PSC Protocol.
742 AU, 'The Peace & Security Council' (*AU,* Date unknown), https://au.int/en/psc, accessed 11 April 2022.
743 AU, 'PAPS – Mandate and Core Functions' (16 June 2021), www.peaceau.org/en/page/77-paps-mandate-and-core-functions, accessed 11 April 2022.
744 AU, 'Peace Support Operations' (*AU,* Date unknown), https://au.int/en/directorates/peace-support-operations, accessed 11 April 2022.
745 AU, 'The Peace Support Operations Division (PSOD)' (Date unknown), www.peaceau.org/uploads/02-au-psod-brochure-23sep16.pdf, accessed 7 April 2022.
746 NATO, 'North Atlantic Council' (n. 602).
747 NATO, 'Military Organisation and Structures' (*NATO,* 20 May 2021), www.nato.int/cps/en/natohq/topics_49608.htm, accessed 11 April 2022; NATO, 'Military Committee' (n. 604).

Europe (SACEUR) and Allied Command Transformation (ACT) under the command of the Supreme Allied Commander Transformation (SACT). While ACT is at the forefront of NATO's military transformation, ACO is responsible for the planning and execution of all NATO military operations.[748] The SACEUR exercises their responsibilities from SHAPE, the strategic headquarters, which assists in preparing, planning, conducting, and executing NATO military operations.[749]

EU – In the context of the EU, strategic political authority is exercised by the EU PSC, under the authority of the Council of the EU and of the EU High Representative.[750] In doing so, the EU PSC takes into account the military advice and recommendations on the planning and conduct of EU-led military CSDP operations formulated by the EUMC.[751] Under the direction of the EUMC, the European Union Military Staff (EUMS) conducts military planning at the political strategic level.[752] If the EU decides to carry out the operation, the military strategic level of command is exercised by the EU Operation Commander (OpCdr) (despite the choice of terminology, not to be confused with the EU Force Commander who represents the operational level), hereby supported by the EU Operation Headquarters (i.e. static headquarters located outside the area of operations).[753] The OpCdr conducts the operational planning over the assigned forces at the strategic level. To that end, they are responsible for developing the CONOPS, the OPLAN, and the ROE, among others and to co-ordinate the deployment, sustainment, re-deployment, and liquidation of EU CSDP operations.[754] The EU has two basic command options: (i) autonomous EU-led military CSDP operations and missions; or (ii) EU-led military CSDP operations with recourse to NATO common assets and capabilities through establishing an EU Operation Headquarters at SHAPE.[755] The EU Military Planning and Conduct Capability (MPCC) is the static command and control structure at the military strategic level.[756]

4.2.2.2. Operational level

While States may transfer some authority to international or regional organisations or arrangements, they always retain complete and exclusive

---

748 'The NATO Command Structure' (2018) Factsheet, www.nato.int/nato_static_fl2014/assets/pdf/pdf_2018_02/1802-Factsheet-NATO-Command-Structure_en.pdf, accessed 11 April 2022.

749 NATO, 'NATO Military Command Structure' (*NATO SHAPE*), https://shape.nato.int/military_command_structure, accessed 27 April 2020.

750 Art. 38(2) of the TEU. See also EEAS (n. 121) para. 7. For a detailed list of tasks, see para. 17(b).

751 *Ibid.* paras 7 and 17(d).

752 *Ibid.* para. 17(e).

753 *Ibid.* paras 8(a) and (b).

754 *Ibid.* para. 8(a). For a detailed list of tasks, see para. 19.

755 For further details, see *ibid.* paras 14–16.

756 *Ibid.* para. 8(c). See also para. 20.

command over their national armed forces and equipment, including the authority to decide whether they will contribute their troops to a UN (mandated) peace operation and withdraw from such participation in accordance with any agreed terms and conditions.[757] Within that context, TCCs can delegate certain elements of command authority, such as operational command and/or control.[758]

The operational level is mainly the mission level but overlaps to a certain extent with the strategic and tactical levels. While the OPLAN outlines in strategic terms the objective of the operation and describes in broad terms how this objective is to be achieved, the lower levels of command must draw up and implement concrete plans defining, *inter alia*, the specific responsibilities, tasks, and operations of the forces actually deployed in the execution of the operation.[759] Hence, at the operational level, UN (mandated) peace operations are planned and executed to achieve the general objectives set out by the strategic level.[760] The operational leadership has the authority to implement the overall mission strategy and operational concepts developed at the strategic level into their operational planning and formal military orders and directives for coordinated military action directed at the tactical level. The operational planning and the formal military orders and directives reflect the limits set out in the UNSC mandate yet should not be confused with the mandate itself as a legal basis for a UN (mandated) peace operation. Simultaneously, the operational instruments should, at least in principle, not be more lenient than the legal regime(s) applicable to the operation.

The operational level authority is exercised by the following organs:

UN – In the context of UN peace operations, the Head of Mission (HOM), often designated as the UN Special Representative of the Secretary-General (SRSG), balances the strategic and operational levels and sets the political and strategic direction within the parameters determined by the UN Under-Secretary-General for Peace Operations.[761] The HOM also exercises authority over all uniformed components through the heads of those components.[762] The Head of Military Component (HOMC), which in missions with a military contingent is the FC, exercises UN operational command and control over the UN military personnel and units in the mission and, to that end, reports to

757 Gill, 'Legal Aspects of the Transfer of Authority in UN Peace Operations' (n. 723) 46.
758 *Ibid.*
759 Boddens Hosang, *Rules of Engagement and the International Law of Military Operations* (n. 559) 24.
760 *Ibid.* 68.
761 UN DPKO and UN DFS, '2019 UN Policy on Authority, Command and Control in UN Peacekeeping Operations' (n. 738) para. 21.
762 *Ibid.* para. 40.

the HOM.[763] The HOMC may issue a Military Operations Plan or 'Operation Order', which directly supports the CONOPS.[764]

AU – In the context of AU peace operations, the Chairperson of the AU Commission appoints a HOM to exercise operational authority over an AU peace operation.[765] The Chairperson of the AU Commission also appoints an FC who exercises operational authority over all military personnel and reports to the HOM.[766] If a mission is carried out by military personnel only, the FC can also be the designated HOM.[767] Joint Mission Headquarters monitor and administer on behalf of the HOM all AU operations within the area of operation.[768]

NATO – The operational level consists of three standing Joint Force Commands (JFC) that work under the direction of the SACEUR: one in Brunssum, the Netherlands, one in Naples, Italy, and one in Norfolk, Virginia, the US.[769] They operate from their static location or from a deployed headquarters when operating directly in an area of operations (in which case the deployed headquarters is called a Joint Task Force Headquarters (JTFHQ)).[770]

EU – The FC is appointed by the Council of the EU or the EU PSC and is tasked to execute a military operation and authorised to command assigned forces within a designated area of operations.[771] The FC acts under the authority of the OpCdr and is supported by the Force Headquarters (FHQ).[772]

4.2.2.3. Tactical level

The tactical level, being the lowest level of authority, command, and control, is, at least in principle, in the hands of the TCCs since neither the UN nor regional or international organisations other than the UN have military contingents of their own. This level carries out the operation in furtherance or realisation of the objectives set out by the operational level.[773] The tactical level includes the actual combat units whose actions are usually limited in time and geographical scope. Tactical leadership determines the unit's positioning, movement, and deployment in relation to each other and the enemy.[774]

---

763 *Ibid.* paras 30, 31, 43–45.
764 UN DPKO and UN DFS, 'An Overview of United Nations Peacekeeping Operations – Lesson 1.5 on Security Council Mandates in Practice' (n. 734) 16.
765 No up-to-date information on the AU chain of command could be found, so the author made use of the Leuven Manual, see Gill and others (n. 26) 47.
766 *Ibid.*
767 *Ibid.*
768 *Ibid.*
769 NATO, 'NATO Military Command Structure' (n. 748).
770 *Ibid.*
771 EEAS (n. 121) para. 8(e). For a full list of tasks, see para. 21.
772 *Ibid.* paras 8(e) and (f). See also para. 21.
773 Boddens Hosang, *Rules of Engagement and the International Law of Military Operations* (n. 559) 68.
774 *Ibid.*

The tactical commanders are responsible for the actions of their units and subunits and especially for compliance with HRL, IHL (if applicable), relevant national laws, the ROE, and the force orders and directives, among others. Therefore, any use of force at the tactical level should, at least in principle, remain within the limits of the legal regime(s) applicable at the time. Moreover, as repeatedly stated, the UNSC mandate is reflected in these orders and guidelines, but the strategic and tactical instruments should not be confused with one another.

The tactical level authority is exercised by the following organs:

UN – Military commanders are appointed at the sector/region level and below (i.e. battalion and company level).[775] These commanders may assign specific tasks to the forces under their command to accomplish the mission and report through their respective chains of command and in accordance with their field command frameworks.[776] TCCs also appoint a National Contingent Commander (NCC) who exercises administrative control over uniformed contingents and units within the mission area.[777] The NCC is responsible for non-operational tasks on behalf of uniformed personnel and units, such as personnel management and supply services, which is not the same as exercising operational control. National contingents that fall under the operational command and control of the UN may not act on national direction or instruction.[778]

AU – Contingent Commanders (CONTCOs) exercise tactical command and control.[779] However, in some instances, the CONTCOs are also involved in operational planning and decision-making, especially where their respective contingents are concerned.[780]

NATO – The tactical level (or component level) consists of the so-called Single Service Commands (SSC), which include land, sea, and air commands. These SSCs provide expertise and support to the JFCs on the operational level in Brunssum or Naples. These SSCs are generally directed by senior military officials provided by the NATO Member States.[781] The SSCs report directly to SHAPE and are under the command of the SACEUR.[782]

EU – The FC or higher authority appoints the EU Component Commanders (CC), who are responsible for the land, air, maritime, and any

775 UN DPKO and UN DFS, '2019 UN Policy on Authority, Command and Control in UN Peacekeeping Operations' (n. 737) paras 37 and 43.
776 *Ibid.* paras 37 and 102.
777 *Ibid.* paras 52–53.
778 *Ibid.* paras 45 (fn. 34) and 53.
779 No up-to-date information on the AU chain of command could be found, so the author made use of the Leuven Manual, see Gill and others (n. 26) 49.
780 *Ibid.*
781 *Ibid.* 377.
782 NATO, 'NATO Military Command Structure' (n. 748).

other components.[783] In addition, the CCs are responsible for formulating recommendations to the FC on the deployment of their troops and resources and for planning, coordinating, and conducting operations.[784]

4.2.3. From practice back to law

Any use of force must have a legal justification, whether at the strategic, operational, or tactical level. The mission-specific mandate provides a legal basis for the use of armed force in the territory of another State, as well as the overall levels of force used to conduct the operation. But that is not all. Any use of force must also conform with the applicable legal regime(s), including but not limited to HRL, IHL, and national law, which govern when and how force may be used in specific day-to-day situations at the tactical level of the operation. Both the mandate and the relevant legal regimes are, in principle, reflected in one way or another in the various military strategic, operational, and tactical instruments.

On the one hand, the mandate is translated into policies and operational guidelines addressed at the operational and tactical levels. As such, the mandate – a strategic document – continues to have an effect at the various levels and thus also indirectly regulates the use of force mandated at the operational and tactical levels. The mandate thus works from top to bottom.

HRL, IHL, and national law, on the other hand, operate from bottom to top. These rules primarily regulate when and how force can be used in specific day-to-day situations at the tactical level of the operation. Therefore, tactical instruments should, at least in principle, be drafted according to the applicable legal regime(s). By extension, operational and strategic documents must also be interpreted in conformity with the applicable legal regime(s), or at least in principle.

5. SUMMARY OF PART I

Part I sought to clarify and further develop the concept of PoC as a mandated task by the UN Security Council and provide an overview of the political and legal framework governing the use of force for PoC in the context of UN (mandated) peace operations.[785] In doing so, Part I addressed the following questions: How is the concept of PoC defined within the UN, the AU, NATO, and the EU? What is their policy regarding the use of force for PoC? And what are the essential components of the international legal framework governing the use of force to protect civilians in the context of UN (mandated) peace operations?

---

783 EEAS (n. 121) para. 8(g).

784 *Ibid.* paras 8(g) and 23.

785 As also set forth in the Introductory Chapter, Section 2.

Concept of PoC as a mandated task by the UN Security Council

Although various concepts aim to achieve the protection of civilians, this book focuses solely on the concept of the PoC as *a mandated task* by the UN Security Council. In 1999, the UN Security Council adopted the first mandate in which it explicitly instructed UN peace forces to take all necessary measures to protect civilians (UNSC Resolution 1270 (1999)). It did so partly in response to the failures of the UN peace operations in Rwanda and the former Yugoslavia in the late 1990s. Since then, the UN Security Council has not only provided UNAMSIL, but also fourteen other UN peace operations with an explicit mandate to protect civilians. As a result, PoC has become a core strategic goal for the UN system and UN peace operations in particular. Time and again, however, the UN has been accused of not being clear about what exactly PoC entails. In response to this criticism, the UN has taken several initiatives to develop a comprehensive protection strategy.

Today, the UN embraces an ambitious definition whereby PoC is understood as a set of integrated and concerted initiatives by all civilian and uniformed mission components to prevent, deter, or respond to threats of physical violence against civilians within the mission's capabilities and areas of deployment using all necessary means, up to and including lethal force. In that regard, UN peace operations have an active duty to continuously work to prevent, anticipate, and respond to threats to civilians by others but also a duty not to endanger civilians themselves or cause harm to civilians through their own actions.

While the UN has undoubtedly taken the lead in developing a PoC policy in the context of UN peace operations, the AU, NATO, and the EU have followed this trend by developing their own PoC policies. The AU, like the UN, considers PoC a critical strategic priority. Therefore, in recent years, the AU has taken several initiatives to develop a framework for a consolidated protection response and to assume a more prominent role in protecting civilians in armed conflicts in its region. In line with UN policy, the AU has also adopted a multi-layered approach to PoC. However, while the AU has the knowledge, experience, and willingness to use force to protect civilians, it remains heavily dependent on external resources to conduct such operations consistently.

Unlike the UN and AU, NATO approaches PoC as an operational rather than a strategic mission objective. Following its experiences in Bosnia and Afghanistan, NATO interprets PoC primarily as a set of efforts undertaken to prevent, minimise, and mitigate the negative consequences that may result from NATO and NATO-led military operations on the civilian population. Where appropriate, it also includes the protection of civilians from conflict-related physical violence or threat of physical violence by other actors, including by establishing a safe and secure environment. Yet while NATO has sought to develop a PoC policy beyond harm mitigation, its increased focus on the threat of inter-state conflict and geopolitical rivalry has made PoC a lower priority in recent years.

The EU, too, has undertaken fewer PoC activities in recent years, despite its efforts to develop a substantial PoC framework (based primarily on UN policy documents and thus largely reflecting the UN approach) and its ability to mount operations to protect civilians. The activities have focused on training and capacity building rather than large military CSDP missions. When the EU did undertake peace operations with a PoC mandate, they were usually of short duration and mainly aimed at assisting UN missions at critical moments. Such operations were often criticised for the short duration of their involvement, their limited geographical scope, and/or for not re-hatting their troops directly to the UN peace operation. Another often-heard criticism has been that the EU fails to deploy rapidly and effectively when needed.

Policies on the use of force for PoC

The UN's current PoC policy identifies three protection tiers, one of which is classic physical protection (Tier II). Tier II remains the centrepiece of peacekeeping activity. And yet, while different UN bodies have made considerable efforts to clarify the strategic, operational, and tactical approaches to the use of force for PoC, the greatest challenge to effective PoC remains finding agreement on when force can, must, or cannot be used to protect civilians. As a result, the UN is often criticised for using too much force in implementing a PoC mandate or not using enough force to effectively protect civilians on the ground.

While use of force is considered an elementary tool in AU, NATO, and EU operations, none of these organisations actually provide much insight into their policy on the use of force for PoC. What can be inferred from the information available is that peace forces can or even should use force to physically protect civilians from certain threats, but it remains rather unclear under what conditions.

Legal framework governing the use of force for PoC

In practice, there is a great deal of uncertainty about the precise legal framework governing the use of force to protect the civilian population and how it should be applied. As this book seeks to fill in a number of gaps regarding the legal parameters applicable to the use of force to protect civilians, it was crucial first to outline a general overview of which rules can serve as a legal basis for the establishment, emplacement, and functioning of UN (mandated) peace operations, and which rules can govern the conduct of UN (mandated) peace operations. Any operation, whether conducted by the UN, its Member States, or a regional or international organisation other than the UN, requires, first and foremost, a legal basis for its emplacement and functioning on the territory of another State. This legal basis can be found in the UN Charter and customary international law relating to the use of force and the maintenance and restoration of international peace and security. In addition, each mission requires a mission-specific 'external' mandate, which can be granted by a competent international organisation (in principle, the UN Security Council) or by the government of a host State that invites or agrees to a peace operation conducted on its territory. Furthermore, since the international and regional organisations or arrangements only have the powers granted to them by their Member States, the competence to establish an operation must be regulated by the internal laws of the organisation or arrangement, and a mission-specific 'internal' mandate must be adopted for that purpose.

In addition to the rules providing a legal basis for UN (mandated) peace operations, the rules governing the conduct of UN (mandated) peace operations are equally relevant to the use of force for protective purposes. One 'right' often invoked in practice to justify the use of force in specific instances is the right to use force in self-defence – a complex, multifaceted, but above all, ambiguous legal concept. Although it is beyond the scope of this book to resolve the question of the legal nature of the authority of UN (mandated) peace forces to use force in some form of self-defence, Part I did provide a brief outline of which instruments may serve as a legal source for the use of force in self-defence, defence of others, and defence of the mandate, including national (criminal) law and international law (as a general principle of law and/or as a permissive ground to deprive someone of their human right to life). The authority to use force in a particular defence may also derive from an explicit authorisation by the UN Security Council under Chapter VII or, in the case of UN peace operations, possibly also from the implied or inherent powers of such operations to use force, which they may invoke in their capacity as subsidiary organs of the UN. Nevertheless, any use of force must always be in accordance with the rules and principles of the legal regimes applicable in the given case, such as HRL, IHL, and national law.

HRL lays down the fundamental rights and freedoms to which all human beings are entitled, whereas IHL comprises a body of rules that seek to limit the humanitarian consequences of armed conflict. While HRL, in principle, applies at all times, regardless of the nature of the situation in which a UN (mandated) peace operation is deployed, IHL only applies once the threshold of an armed conflict has been reached. In the latter case, any use of force with a clear nexus to an ongoing armed conflict does not only fall under HRL but also under IHL. Within the HRL framework, the rules regulating the use of force are restrictive. The most relevant rule in the context of the use of force by armed forces on the ground is the human right to life, a right to which the principles of legality, necessity, proportionality, precautions, and accountability apply. Under IHL, on the other hand, there is much greater leeway for the use of force, provided that, among others, the principles of distinction, precautions in attack, and prohibition of excessive collateral damage are respected. In addition to HRL and IHL, other areas of conventional and customary international law are relevant to the conduct of UN (mandated) peace operations, such as international refugee law, the analysis of which is beyond the scope of this book. Furthermore, peace forces deployed in the territory of a third State must typically continue to respect sending State law and may also become subject to the law of the host State. Last but not least, in addition to the specialist relevant legal regimes, other relevant rules and practices have been discussed, which are not always sources of law *per se* but are nevertheless highly relevant to the conduct of UN (mandated) peace operations, including mission-specific agreements and arrangements, mission-specific documents, and doctrinal and general documents on PoC and the use of force.

Relationship between HRL and IHL and the UNSC mandate

One could readily conclude from this overview that the legal bases and the legal regimes each regulate the use of force in their own distinct way and, therefore, must be kept strictly separate, which is true in many respects. From a theoretical point of view, a strict distinction must be made between the legal bases and the legal regimes. In practice, however, the legal bases and the legal regimes appear to intersect when regulating the use of force for protective purposes. To test this presumption, both Part II (which focuses on the mandate as a mission-specific legal basis) and Part III (which focuses on HRL and IHL) explore the relationship between the UNSC mandate and HRL/IHL. To set the stage, Part I has placed the legal bases and legal regimes in the context of the distinct levels of authority, command, and control in UN (mandated) peace operations. Conceptualisation of this structure contributes to a better understanding of the respective roles of the legal bases and the legal regimes in regulating the use of force at the distinct levels and of the ways in which they could cross into each other's playing field, as further elaborated in Parts II and III.

PART II

THE POC MANDATE AS A MISSION-SPECIFIC LEGAL BASIS UNDERLYING UN (MANDATED) PEACE OPERATIONS DEPLOYED TO PROTECT CIVILIANS[786]

1. INTRODUCTION TO PART II

As Part I made clear, any peace operation constituting a (physical) intervention in a State needs a legal basis in international law.[787] Such legal basis can be found in the UN Charter or in rules of customary international law relating to the use of force and the maintenance and restoration of international peace and security. In addition, every peace operation requires a mission-specific mandate which can either be issued by a competent international organisation (in principle, the UN Security Council under Chapter VII of the UN Charter) or by a host State's government inviting or consenting to a peace operation conducted on its territory.[788] The mandate, in this context, is a source of legal authority to deploy a mission in the territory of a third State and to use force on that State's territory.

UN (mandated) peace operations covered in this book always operate based on a mandate of the UN Security Council, whether or not complemented by the consent of the host State. Since October 1999, the UN Security Council has, on almost all occasions, provided UN (mandated) peace operations with Chapter VII authorisations, which represents a significant change in UN practice. In the preamble of PoC mandates, the UN Security Council generally determines that a particular situation 'constitutes a threat to the international peace and security' and subsequently authorises an entire mandate (including the PoC tasks) under Chapter VII of the UN Charter. Yet, for specific missions, only the

786 Part II is partly based on the following publications: Bourgeois, 'Failure to Protect Civilians in the Context of UN Peace Operations: A Question of Accountability?' (n. 1); Bourgeois, '"All Necessary Means" to Protect Civilians: The Interpretation and Implementation of UN Security Council Mandates Authorising the Protection of Civilians' (n. 1); Bourgeois and Labuda (n. 1); Bourgeois and Perrin (n. 1).

787 Gill and others (n. 26) 34.

788 *Ibid.* 27. As discussed above, this external legal basis for the emplacement and functioning of a mission within the territory of a given State is not to be confused with the internal legal basis for the establishment of a mission (see Part I, Section 4.1.1).

PoC tasks are authorised under Chapter VII of the UN Charter. For example, in Resolutions 1270 (1999) and 1291 (2000), the UN Security Council determined that the situation constituted a 'threat to the international peace and security' in the preamble and subsequently decided, hereby acting under Chapter VII of the UN Charter, that the mission may take the necessary action to protect civilians under imminent threat of physical violence.[789]

These Chapter VII PoC mandates are generally complemented by the consent of the host State. For example, in Resolution 2100 (2013), the UN Security Council included a reference to a letter from the transitional authorities of Mali in which these authorities explicitly requested the deployment of a UN mission to 'stabilize and restore the authority and the sovereignty of the Malian State throughout its national territory.'[790] At the end of the preamble, the UN Security Council determined that the situation in Mali constituted a threat to international peace and security and that it would act under Chapter VII of the UN Charter.[791] Likewise, in several verbatim records from the debates leading up to the adoption of PoC mandates, host States explicitly gave their consent to the deployment and execution of UN (mandated) peace operations.[792]

As set forth in the Introductory Chapter, one of the aims of this book is to explore the legal bases underlying UN (mandated) peace operations deployed to protect civilians and, in particular, the consent of the host State and mandates granted by the UN Security Council.[793] Many questions arise concerning consent given by the host State to deploy a peace operation with the task of protecting civilians within its territory. For example, what is the legal, political, and

789 'UNSC Res. 1270' (n. 7) pream. para. 6 and para. 14; 'UNSC Res. 1291' (n. 125) pream. para. 21 and para. 8.

790 'UNSC Res. 2100' (n. 34) pream. para. 19.

791 *Ibid. pream.* paras 24 and 25.

792 See e.g. UNSC, '6253rd Meeting (at Which UNSC Res. 1906 (2009) Was Adopted)' (2009) UN Doc. S/PV.6253; UNSC, '6399th Meeting (at Which UNSC Res. 1944 (2010) Was Adopted)' (2010) UN Doc. S/PV. 6399; UNSC, '6800th Meeting (at Which UNSC Res. 2057 (2012) Was Adopted)' (n. 47); UNSC, '6817th Meeting (at Which UNSC Res. 2062 (2012) Was Adopted)' (2012) UN Doc. S/PV.6817; UNSC, '6998th Meeting (at Which UNSC Res. 2109 (2013) Was Adopted)' (n. 47); UNSC, '7153rd Meeting (at Which UNSC Res. 2149 (2014) Was Adopted)' (2014) UN Doc. S/PV.7153; UNSC, '7182nd Meeting (at Which UNSC Res. 2155 (2014) Was Adopted)' (n. 47); UNSC, '7210th Meeting (at Which UNSC Res. 2164 (2014) Was Adopted)' (2014) UN Doc. S/PV.7210; UNSC, '7250th Meeting (at Which UNSC Res. 2173 (2014) Was Adopted)' (2014) UN Doc. S/PV.7250; UNSC, '7322nd Meeting (at Which UNSC Res. 2187 (2014) Was Adopted)' (n. 47); UNSC, '7434th Meeting (at Which UNSC Res. 2217 (2015) Was Adopted)' (2015) UN Doc. S/PV.7434; UNSC, '7471st Meeting (at Which UNSC Res. 2226 (2015) Was Adopted)' (2015) UN Doc. S/PV.7471; UNSC, '7659th Meeting (at Which UNSC Res. 2277 (2016) Was Adopted)' (2016) UN Doc. S/PV.7659; UNSC, '7681st Meeting (at Which UNSC Res. 2284 92016) Was Adopted)' (2016) UN Doc. S/PV.7681; UNSC, '7840th Meeting (at Which UNSC Res. 2327 (2016) Was Adopted)' (n. 47); UNSC, '7989th Meeting (at Which UNSC Res. 2363 (2017) Was Adopted)' (2017) UN Doc. S/PV.7989; UNSC, '8204th Meeting (at Which UNSC Res. 2406 (2018) Was Adopted)' (n. 47); UNSC, '8568th Meeting (at Which UNSC Res. 2480 (2019) Was Adopted)' (2019) UN Doc. S/PV.8568; UNSC, '8932nd Meeting (at Which UNSC Res. 2609 (2021) Was Adopted)' (2021) UN Doc. S/PV.8932.

793 See Introductory Chapter, Section 2.

operational value of consent? And what are the modalities of consent, including consent *ratione materiae*, consent *ratione personae*, consent *ratione temporis*, and how consent should be given? These questions are addressed in Section 2.

Section 3 discusses UNSC mandates authorising or mandating UN (mandated) peace operations to protect civilians. Although UNSC resolutions provide the central legal basis for UN (mandated) operations to use force to protect civilians from physical violence, the text of the resolutions often leaves ample discretion concerning the scope of the mandate and the legal constraints to the use of force provided by the PoC mandates.[794] As a result, PoC mandates have been subject to differing interpretations and applications in the field.[795] For instance, as mentioned above, according to OIOS, the operationalisation of a number of robust PoC mandates was subject to varying interpretations, which significantly weakened the explicit intent of the UN Security Council.[796] One of the main problems is a lack of clarity about *how* UNSC mandates should be interpreted and implemented. In this regard, questions arise as to what rules and methods of interpretation apply to UNSC resolutions and how to understand and evaluate the UN Security Council's practice of authorising the use of force to protect civilians, both in terms of the changing formulation, interpretation, and implementation of PoC mandates. The question that also arises is whether there are upper or lower limits to what UN (mandated) peace operations may or must lawfully do to protect civilians when given the mandate to use all necessary means to protect civilians. This study first provides a brief overview of PoC language (Section 3.1). Next, Section 3.2 looks into the interpretation of such PoC language, while Section 3.3 scrutinises whether there are upper and/or lower limits to what UN (mandated) peace operations may or must lawfully do to protect civilians. Section 3.4 eventually examines the possible influence of HRL and IHL on the interpretation, implementation, and evaluation of UNSC resolutions that contain a PoC mandate. Section 4 gives a summary of what has been discussed in Part II.

2. CONSENT OF THE HOST STATE

In the wake of the establishment of UNEF I, UN Secretary-General Dag Hammarskjöld identified consent, alongside neutrality of the force in the dispute, and the right to fire in self-defence (but the prohibition against any initiative

---

794 As also raised by Giulio Bartolini, 'Air Targeting in Operation Unified Protector in Libya. Jus Ad Bellum and IHL Issues: An External Perspective' in Stanislas Horvat and Marco Benatar (eds), *Proceedings of the 19th Congress of the International Society for Military Law and the Law of War on Legal Interoperability and Ensuring Observance of the Law Applicable in Multinational Deployments, 1–4 May 2012, Quebec, 231* (2013) 244–245.

795 Khalil, 'Legal Aspects of the Use of Force by United Nations Peacekeepers for the Protection of Civilians' (n. 40) 210.

796 OIOS, Inspection and Evaluation Division (n. 10) para. 104. As also referred to in the Introductory Chapter, Section 1.

in the use of armed force), as a fundamental principle of UN peacekeeping.[797] Accordingly, true to the principle of consent, the UN immediately withdrew the UN troops from Egyptian territory as soon as Egypt revoked its consent to UNEF I's deployment on its territory.[798] Also, in the case of UNPROFOR, the UN Security Council replaced UNPROFOR with the United Nations Confidence Restoration Operation in Croatia (UNCRO) in 1995 after Croatia demanded UNPROFOR's withdrawal.[799] More recently, MINURCAT completed its mandate on 31 October 2010 after the government had withdrawn its consent.[800]

2.1. ROLE OF CONSENT IN UN (MANDATED) PEACE OPERATIONS

2.1.1. Legal value of consent

The legal basis for the emplacement and functioning of a peace operation in the territory of a State can be found in the consent of the host State and/or a UNSC mandate adopted under Chapter VII of the UN Charter. In this regard, the host State's consent may provide an independent legal basis for the presence of foreign troops on its territory or a secondary legal basis in case the UN Security Council already foresees a mandate under Chapter VII of the UN Charter. If the host State has authorised the use of force contrary to a UN Security Council mandate adopted under Chapter VII of the UN Charter, the mandate under Chapter VII shall prevail.[801] If the host State withdraws its consent, a UNSC mandate adopted under Chapter VII of the UN Charter constitutes the sole legal basis.

Such a legal basis, whether found in a Chapter VII mandate or the consent of the host State, is necessary to justify the use of force on the territory of another State. After all, the use of force against a State under international law is, in principle, prohibited under international law. Moreover, this prohibition

797 UNSG, 'Summary Study of the Experience Derived from the Establishment and Operation of the Force: Report of the Secretary-General, Thirteenth Session, Annexes, Agenda Item 65' (n. 431) paras 12, 70, 15–156, 179. See also Part I, Section 3.1.1.

798 UNGA, 'Report of the Secretary-General on the Withdrawal of the Emergency Force' (1967) UN Doc. A/6730 and Add. 1–3 and A/6730/Add.3/Corr.1, as also discussed by Tsagourias, 'Consent, Neutrality/Impartiality and the Use of Force in Peacekeeping: Their Constitutional Dimension' (n. 586) 467.

799 'UNSC Res. 981' (1995) UN Doc. S/RES/981 (1995) para. 2, as also referred to by Tsagourias, 'Consent, Neutrality/Impartiality and the Use of Force in Peacekeeping: Their Constitutional Dimension' (n. 586) 467.

800 'UNSC Res. 1923' (2010) UN Doc. S/RES/1923 (2010), pream. para. 17, as also referred to by Labuda, 'UN Peacekeeping as Intervention by Invitation: Host State Consent and the Use of Force in Security Council-Mandated Stabilisation Operations' (n. 33) 339. However, for counter-examples, see Sloan (n. 161).

801 Terry D Gill, 'Military Intervention with the Consent or at the Invitation of a Government' in Terry D Gill and Dieter Fleck (eds), *The Handbook of the International Law of Military Operations* (2nd edn., Oxford University Press 2015) 254.

is not only contained in Article 2(4) of the UN Charter but is also universally recognised as a norm of customary international law or even a peremptory norm.[802] If the UN Security Council authorises forcible action under Chapter VII of the UN Charter, this constitutes an 'exception' to Article 2(4) of the UN Charter. It remains contentious, however, whether consent should also be seen as an 'exception' to the prohibition of the use of force, or instead as a 'circumstance precluding wrongfulness', or as a 'constituent part of the primary rule' on the prohibition of the use of force in international relations.

The ILC identified host State consent as a circumstance precluding wrongfulness in its 2001 ASR. Article 20 of the 2001 ASR sets forth that:

> Valid consent by a State to the commission of a given act by another State precludes the wrongfulness of that act in relation to the former State to the extent that the act remains within the limits of that consent.

At the same time, Article 26 of the 2001 ASR stresses that:

> Nothing in this chapter precludes the wrongfulness of any act of a State which is not in conformity with an obligation arising under a peremptory norm of general international law.

In the same vein, Article 20 of the 2011 DARIO provides that consent to a particular act of an international organisation precludes the wrongfulness of that act, while Article 26 of the 2011 DARIO holds that nothing precludes the wrongfulness of an act of an international organisation that is in breach of an obligation arising from a norm of *jus cogens*.

How can one reconcile the articles on consent and compliance with peremptory norms, assuming that the prohibition of the use of force is a peremptory norm? According to Article 53 of the VCLT, a peremptory norm of general international law is:

> [A] norm accepted and recognized by the international community of States as a whole as a norm from which no derogation is permitted and which can be modified only by a subsequent norm of general international law having the same character.

As such, peremptory norms prohibit any form of derogation (but may allow for exceptions, see below).[803] How, then, can one accept that consent qualifies as a circumstance that precludes the wrongfulness of any use of force in international

802 For sources on the *jus cogens* nature of the prohibition of the use of force or the prohibition of aggression/aggressive or illegal use of force, see Part I, Section 4.1.1.2(A), fn. 616.

803 According to Helmersen, derogations are 'specific acts or rules that diverge from and supplant the content of a more general rule' and whose application is 'limited to some of the parties that are bound by the rule in question.' Exceptions, on the other hand, limit the scope of rules and find themselves 'at the same level of generality as the rules that [they] [...] modif[y].'

relations 'to the extent that the act remains within the limits of that consent' (see Article 20 of the 2001 ASR and Article 20 of the 2011 DARIO), if one knows that such use of force may actually violate a peremptory norm which cannot be derogated from? Special Rapporteur on State Responsibility James Crawford also raised this issue. He suggested deleting consent from the list of circumstances precluding wrongfulness.[804] He argued that consent instead is a constituent part of the primary rule[805] on the prohibition of the use of force:[806]

> Some peremptory norms contain an 'intrinsic' consent element. For example, the rule relating to the non-use of force in international relations embodied in Article 2, paragraph 4, of the Charter [...] does not apply in certain cases where one State has consented to the use of force on its territory by another State. But one State cannot by consent *eliminate* the rule relating to the use of force in international relations in its relations with another State. Thus it may be necessary to distinguish between a consent which applies Article 2, paragraph 4, which may be valid, and a purported consent which displaces or excludes it entirely, which, if Article 2, paragraph 4, is peremptory in character, would be invalid; [...].

If consent is considered a constituent part of the primary rule, it logically follows that no wrongfulness can be established when force is used on the State's territory with its consent validly given,[807] and there is, therefore, no need to invoke any circumstance that excludes the wrongfulness.[808] After all, the prohibition of the use of force must be understood as a prohibition of the non-consensual use of force (i.e. whereby no consent is validly given).[809] Despite all good arguments, the ILC could not settle the issue of whether consent had an intrinsic or

---

(Sondre Torp Helmersen, 'The Prohibition of the Use of Force as Jus Cogens: Explaining Apparent Derogations' (2014) 61 Netherlands International Law Review 167, 175–176).

804 ILC, 'Second Report on State Responsibility by Mr. James Crawford, Special Rapporteur' (n. 107) paras 229 and 232–243.

805 On primary and secondary rules in the context of state responsibility, see Eric David, 'Primary and Secondary Rules' in James Crawford and others (eds), *The Law of International Responsibility* (Oxford University Press 2010); Anastasios Gourgourinis, 'General/Particular International Law and Primary/Secondary Rules: Unitary Terminology of a Fragmented System' (2011) 22 European Journal of International Law 993, 1016–1026. Nevertheless, some authors criticise this distinction, see e.g. Ulf Linderfalk, 'State Responsibility and the Primary-Secondary Rules Terminology – The Role of Language for an Understanding of the International Legal System' (2009) 78 Nordic Journal of International Law 53.

806 ILC, 'Second Report on State Responsibility by Mr. James Crawford, Special Rapporteur' (n. 107) para. 242(b).

807 See further below.

808 ILC, 'Second Report on State Responsibility by Mr. James Crawford, Special Rapporteur' (n. 107) para. 243. See also Corten (n. 616) 253.

809 Although this reflects the mainstream view, not everyone agrees. Paddeu, e.g. challenges this approach and instead argues that the prohibition of the use of force must be perceived as a general ban on all forms of force, including consensual, in international relations. Consent, in her view, must consequently not be perceived as part of the definition of the prohibition of the use of force but instead as a defence. See Federica I Paddeu, 'Military Assistance on Request and General Reasons against Force: Consent as a Defence to the Prohibition of Force' (2020) 7 Journal on the Use of Force and International Law 227.

extrinsic character and ultimately decided to retain consent as a circumstance precluding wrongfulness in the draft articles on state responsibility.[810] Indeed, since a number of States preferred to include consent in the draft articles on state responsibility, the ILC eventually 'agreed to disagree' and retained consent as a circumstance precluding wrongfulness.[811] Similarly, the 2011 DARIO included consent as a circumstance precluding wrongfulness. That said, the assertion made by Crawford that consent constitutes an 'intrinsic' element of the primary rule has, according to Corten, not been necessarily contradicted by state practice or doctrine.[812]

Another approach is to regard consent as an exception to the prohibition of the use of force. It is true that although the prohibition of the use of force is a norm of *jus cogens* from which cannot be derogated, also not with the consent of the third State, the norm does foresee exceptions. As discussed earlier, two main exceptions are foreseen in the UN Charter, which finds themselves at the same level of generality as the rule that they modify,[813] namely self-defence under Article 51 and enforcement action by the UN Security Council under Chapter VII of the UN.[814] The UN Charter does not refer to consent-based use of force. One may question whether we should seek to identify consent as a 'third customary exception' to the prohibition of the use of force. The answer is no. Consent-based use of force falls outside the scope of Article 2(4) of the UN Charter. In case the host State validly consents to the use of force on its territory,[815] there is no violation of the prohibition of the use of force, so there is simply no need to seek an exception to the general rule.[816]

In conclusion, host State consent may either constitute an independent legal basis for deploying troops onto its territory or a secondary legal basis in case the UN Security Council already provides for a mandate under Chapter VII

810 *Ibid.* 242.

811 *Ibid.*

812 Corten (n. 616) 253. He refers, e.g., to the fact that the UK stressed that if consent is validly given 'there is no violation of international law, and, therefore, no question of wrongfulness should arise' (ILC, 'State Responsibility (Agenda Item 2): Comments and Observations Received by Governments, 5 March, 30 April, 4 May, 20 July 1998' (1988) UN Doc. A/CN.4/488 and Add. 1–3, Yearbook of the International Law Commission vol. 2, part one 130). For doctrine, see his references to, *inter alia*, Théodore Christakis, 'Les "Circonstances Excluant l'Illicéité": une Illusion Optique?' in Jean JA Salmon (ed), *Droit du Pouvoir, Pouvoir du Droit: Mélanges Offerts à Jean Salmon* (Bruylant 2007) 244–251; and Théodore Christakis and Karine Mollard-Bannelier, 'Volenti Non Fit Injuria ? Les Effets du Consentement à L'intervention Militaire' (2004) 50 Annuaire français de droit international 102, 111.

813 See Part II, Section 2.1.1, fn. 803 on the distinction between derogations and exceptions.

814 As discussed in Part I, Section 4.1.1.2(A).

815 See further below.

816 For support, see also Max Byrne, 'Consent and the Use of Force: An Examination of "Intervention by Invitation" as a Basis for US Drone Strikes in Pakistan, Somalia and Yemen' (2016) 3 Journal on the Use of Force and International Law 97, 99; Dörr (n. 616) para. 22; International Law Association, 'Report of the Committee on the Use of Force' (International Law Association 2018) Sydney Conference 18; Visser (n. 616) 33.

of the UN Charter. Such consent should neither be considered a circumstance precluding wrongfulness nor an exception to the rule. On the contrary, consent is considered an element of the main rule of the prohibition of the use of force. This main rule must be understood as prohibiting the non-consensual use of force. If valid consent to the use of force on its territory is given, there is no use of force in international relations and, therefore, no violation of the rule.

2.1.2. Political and operational value of consent

The fact that PoC mandates are adopted under Chapter VII of the UN Charter does not prevent the operations concerned from also obtaining the consent of the host State to operate on its territory. On the contrary. Although such consent is not required by law if the UN Security Council authorises an entire mandate under Chapter VII of the UN Charter, and although consent, or even acquiescence, from all other parties involved, is never required by law,[817] consent has an important political and operational value. Indeed, as Bowett explained it: it is driven by 'political wisdom' rather than 'legal necessity.'[818]

First, consent may significantly impact the scope of the mandate. As indicated by Labuda, a Chapter VII mandate of the UN Security Council does not always intend to remedy the host State's lack of consent.[819] On the contrary, it is often the embodiment of the government's support for external intervention.[820] For example, in the case of Mali or the CAR, the governments fiercely supported the deployment of a peace operation, resulting in the adoption of ambitious mandates under Chapter VII of the UN Charter.[821] In the case of Sudan in the mid-2000s, on the other hand, the UN Security Council did not adopt a broad mandate under Chapter VII because the host State's government was not in favour of a peace operation on its territory.[822] Instead, the UN Security Council authorised a joint AU-UN operation to carry out a number of limited tasks under Chapter VII of the UN Charter, including PoC.[823] In the DRC, when former President Kabila began putting pressure on MONUC to

---

817 See further below on consent *ratione personae*, Part II, Section 2.2.2.

818 Derek W Bowett, *United Nations Forces: A Legal Study of United Nations Practice* (Stevens 1964) 412.

819 Labuda, 'UN Peacekeeping as Intervention by Invitation: Host State Consent and the Use of Force in Security Council-Mandated Stabilisation Operations' (n. 33) 347.

820 *Ibid.*

821 For MINUSMA, see e.g. 'UNSC Res. 2480' (n. 139); for MINUSCA, see e.g. 'UNSC Res. 2499' (n. 140), as also referred to by Labuda, 'UN Peacekeeping as Intervention by Invitation: Host State Consent and the Use of Force in Security Council-Mandated Stabilisation Operations' (n. 33) 347.

822 Labuda, 'UN Peacekeeping as Intervention by Invitation: Host State Consent and the Use of Force in Security Council-Mandated Stabilisation Operations' (n. 33) 347.

823 'UNSC Res. 1769' (2007) UN Doc. S/RES/1769 (2007) para. 15. See e.g. also subsequent mandates of UNAMID in which the UN Security Council makes an explicit reference to UNAMID's Chapter VII mandate 'UNSC Res. 2003' (2011) UN Doc. S/RES/2003 (2011).

leave the territory following the 2006 elections,[824] the UN Security Council sent another mission to the DRC (being MONUSCO). It made several compromises, including a new name for the operation and the withdrawal of 2,000 UN troops.[825] Hence, although Kabila's request to withdraw all foreign troops from the territory was not fulfilled, the UN Security Council did change course.[826]

Second, consent may significantly influence the mission's success in fulfilling the mandate. Consent implies the promise that nothing will stand in the way of the deployment and functioning of a mission.[827] Today, the tasks of UN (mandated) peace operations often consist of assisting the government in creating a secure and stable environment for civilians, facilitating the political process, and assisting in restoring the rule of law. Permission and co-operation from the host State are crucial to perform such a range of tasks. Moreover, collaboration with the government is also crucial for a successful exit strategy.[828] After all, a lack of co-operation with government authorities makes it rather difficult to hand over certain tasks when leaving the country.[829] This lack of co-operation means that missions not consented to by the host governments are possibly more concerned with extinguishing fires than building toward strategic exits.[830]

Third, consent also contributes to a safer environment for the troops themselves, which may affect force commitments to UN (mandated) peace operations.[831] In the absence of consent, governments may, for example, prevent food, medical care, or essential equipment from reaching the troops, endangering the lives of members of peace forces.[832] Moreover, when armed forces enter the territory of a third State without its consent, they are in an IAC from that moment on; thus, IHL *a priori* applies,[833] entailing a whole set of rules that increases the risk of battlefield fatalities, as is discussed in greater detail in Part III, Section 3.2. By contrast, when the host State consents to the use of force on its territory, only HRL applies (unless, of course, the host State withdraws its consent and/or the mission becomes involved in hostilities whereby the

824 Sofía Sebastián and Aditi Gorur, 'UN Peacekeeping & Host-State Consent: How Missions Navigate Relationships with Governments' (Stimson Center 2018) 24.

825 'UNSC Res. 1925' (n. 125) paras 1 and 3.

826 See also Eliav Lieblich, 'Intervention in Civil Wars: Intervention and Consent' (DPhil thesis, Columbia University 2012) 50.

827 Orakhelashvili, 'The Legal Basis of the United Nations Peace-Keeping Operations' (n. 588) 521.

828 Sebastián and Gorur (n. 824) 5.

829 *Ibid.*

830 *Ibid.*

831 Levin's analyses of UN peace operations between 1990 and 2011 have, e.g. confirmed that peacekeeper fatalities have had a negative effect upon the size of countries' contributions to UN peace operations (see Andrew Levin, 'Peacekeeper Fatalities and Force Commitments to UN Operations' (2021) 38 Conflict Management and Peace Science 292).

832 Sebastián and Gorur (n. 824) 5.

833 Labuda, 'UN Peacekeeping as Intervention by Invitation: Host State Consent and the Use of Force in Security Council-Mandated Stabilisation Operations' (n. 33) 340.

threshold for an armed conflict is reached).[834] If only HRL applies, the lives of members of peace forces are more protected, which usually results in fewer casualties (see also Part III, Section 3.1).

2.2. MODALITIES OF CONSENT

2.2.1. Consent ratione materiae

Although there are differing views about what a State may consent to and what not,[835] it is generally accepted that consent, *while* possibly avoiding the triggering of Article 2(4) of the UN Charter, may not legitimise an otherwise unlawful act.[836] In other words, consent can never justify violations of, say, IHL or HRL.[837]

Consent of the host State may cover not only access to its territory but also the composition of the force and the terms of the mandate (i.e. the tasks, purposes, and/or objectives that the mission can fulfil).[838] If the consent relates only to the presence of the force, the authorised strategic leadership[839] will still determine how to deploy armed forces, under what composition, and what objectives are to be achieved. On the other hand, when the host State has not only consented to access to its territory but also had a say in the composition of the force and the objectives to be fulfilled, this agreement determines the scope of action unless this would be contrary to a UNSC mandate adopted under Chapter VII of the UN Charter. In such a case, the primary legal basis, the Chapter VII mandate, prevails.[840]

834 *Ibid.* 341.

835 It is e.g. disputed whether an intervention by invitation is permissible when the State is engaged in a civil war, see Christine D Gray, *International Law and the Use of Force* (4th edn., Oxford University Press 2018) 85–92; Karine Bannelier and Theodore Christakis, 'Under the UN Security Council's Watchful Eyes: Military Intervention by Invitation in the Malian Conflict' (2013) 26 Leiden Journal of International Law 855, 860; Karine Bannelier-Christakis, 'Military Interventions against ISIL in Iraq, Syria and Libya, and the Legal Basis of Consent' (2016) 29 Leiden Journal of International Law 743, 745; Gregory H Fox, 'Intervention by Invitation' in Marc Weller, Alexia Solomou and Jake William Rylatt (eds), *The Oxford Handbook of the Use of Force in International Law* (1st edn., Oxford University Press 2016) 827; Institut de Droit International, 'Résolution sur le Principe de Non-Intervention dans les Guerres Civiles' (1975) Wiesbaden Session, 8th Commission, Sub-Group D, Art. 2(1), as also referred to by Visser (n. 616) 22. See also Lieblich, 'Intervention in Civil Wars: Intervention and Consent' (n. 826).

836 International Law Association (n. 816) 19.

837 *Ibid.* 20.

838 Christine D Gray, 'Host-State Consent and United Nations Peacekeeping in Yugoslavia' (1996) 7 Duke Journal of Comparative and International Law 241, 241.

839 Which body exercises such strategic leadership and decides on the various matters depends on who is conducting the operation in question (the UN itself or rather States or regional or international organisations other than the UN), see further Part I, Section 4.2.2.1.

840 Gill, 'Military Intervention with the Consent or at the Invitation of a Government' (n. 801) 252; Gill and others (n. 26) 29.

2.2.2. *Consent ratione personae*

Consent to the use of force within a State's territory is a manifestation of sovereignty.[841] For an inter-state UN (mandated) peace operation to be deployed on each side of the border, the respective government of each State must give its consent.[842] This requirement is rooted in the long-held belief that the recognised government of a State constitutes the legitimate representative of the people, which effectively controls the territory and the people.[843] Yet, even when a government is no longer in effective control of the whole territory (e.g. because it is in exile or has lost control over part of the territory), consent from the State is requested because the State remains the *de jure* sovereign over the territory.[844] It is also possible that an entity is not necessarily the constitutional and/or democratically elected government but has effective governmental power over the territory and population.[845] In that case, such an entity may give its consent. After all, how a government acquires or retains power is not necessarily relevant to determine whether a government has the right to consent to an intervention.[846] Yet, there are many cases beyond the paradigm of an effective government consenting to the use of force on its territory, whereby it becomes very difficult to determine whether or not consent may constitute a legal basis for the deployment of a mission. A discussion of the different scenarios falls outside the scope of this book.[847] However, the bottom line we can adhere to in this study is that a Chapter VII mandate is the only viable option if valid consent by the host State cannot be obtained.[848]

---

841 Paddeu (n. 809) 251; Besson (n. 623) para. 1.

842 In the Nicaragua case, the ICJ recognised that an intervention is generally 'allowable [...] at the request of the government of a State' (see *Case Concerning Military and Paramilitary Activities in and against Nicaragua (Nicaragua v. United States of America), Judgment (Merits)* (n. 615)). See also White, 'Peacekeeping and International Law' (n. 37) 48.

843 David Wippman, 'Military Intervention, Regional Organizations, and Host-State Consent' (1996) 7 Duke Journal of Comparative and International Law 209, 211; Orakhelashvili, 'The Legal Basis of the United Nations Peace-Keeping Operations' (n. 588) 520; Tsagourias, 'Consent, Neutrality/Impartiality and the Use of Force in Peacekeeping: Their Constitutional Dimension' (n. 586) 474.

844 E.g. in the case of Somalia, the UN Security Council relied on the consent of the government who was no longer in effective control of the entire territory to establish the United Nations Operation in Somalia I (UNOSOM I): 'UNSC Res. 733' (1992) UN Doc. S/RES/733 (1992) pream. para. 2; 'UNSC Res. 751' (1992) UN Doc. S/RES/751 (1992) pream. para. 2; 'UNSC Res. 767' (1992) UN Doc. S/RES/767 (1992) pream. para. 2; 'UNSC Res. 775' (1992) UN Doc. S/RES/775 (1992) pream. para. 2, as also discussed by Gray (n. 838) 244. See also Orakhelashvili, 'The Legal Basis of the United Nations Peace-Keeping Operations' (n. 588) 520; International Law Association (n. 816) 19.

845 International Law Association (n. 816) 19.

846 Brad R Roth, 'Governmental Illegitimacy Revisited: "Pro-Democratic" Armed Intervention in the Post-Bipolar World' (1993) 3 Transnational Law and Contemporary Problems 481, 482, as referred to by Wippman (n. 843) 215.

847 For further literature, see e.g. Wippman (n. 843).

848 See also Orakhelashvili, 'The Legal Basis of the United Nations Peace-Keeping Operations' (n. 588) 520.

To avoid disrupting the deployment and operation of a UN (mandated) peace operation, the consent of all parties involved may be highly desirable; however, never a legal requirement.[849] The SCSL has endorsed this position by stating that '[i]n non-international conflicts [...] consent is obtained from the warring parties, not out of legal obligation, but rather to ensure the effectiveness of the peacekeeping operation.'[850] Therefore, the mission must work continuously to ensure support for its mission without necessarily giving in to the other two basic principles (impartiality and defensive use of force).

In the past, the UN has attempted to obtain the consent not only of the host government but also of the warring parties before deploying a UN peace operation within the territory of a State.[851] Recently, however, the UN has increasingly limited itself to obtaining consent from the host State because it is very difficult, if not impossible, to obtain consent from all parties concerned in the face of complex internal conflicts.[852] In the case of intra-state conflicts, not only States but also non-state actors, such as rebels or separatists, are parties to the conflict. The fact that the recognised government or even the main parties to the conflict have given their consent does not warrant that support will also be found locally.[853] For example, when the main parties face internal divisions or have weak command and control systems, it will be difficult to secure local support for the operation.[854] Nationwide support becomes even less likely in unstable environments, characterised by the presence of armed groups who are not under the control of one of the parties or by the presence of other parties or individuals who seek to undermine the peace process, prompted by the idea that this process threatens their power and interests.[855]

2.2.3. *Consent ratione temporis*

UN (mandated) peace operations are, in principle, of a temporary nature. It is, therefore, common for UN (mandated) peace operations to have an initial mandate for a limited period of six to twelve months to one year, which is then periodically renewed.[856]

---

849 HIPPO (n. 112) para. 127. See also Gray (n. 838) 244.

850 *The Prosecutor v. Issa Hassan Sesay, Morris Kallon and Augustine Gbao, Judgment* (2009) SCSL Case No. SCSL-04-15-T para. 226.

851 Gray (n. 838) 318; Nigel D White, *Keeping the Peace: The United Nations and the Maintenance of International Peace and Security* (2nd edn., Manchester University Press 1997) 233.

852 Labuda, 'UN Peacekeeping as Intervention by Invitation: Host State Consent and the Use of Force in Security Council-Mandated Stabilisation Operations' (n. 33) 346.

853 UN DPKO and UN DFS, '2008 Capstone Doctrine' (n. 19) 32.

854 *Ibid.*

855 *Ibid.*

856 Orakhelashvili, 'The Legal Basis of the United Nations Peace-Keeping Operations' (n. 588) 523.

This initial mandate does not preclude a State from withdrawing consent at any time in the exercise of its sovereignty.[857] Yet, if consent is given by formal agreement (e.g. by SOFA, see Part II, Section 2.2.4), parties to the agreement will only be able to legally withdraw their consent when this is done in accordance with the relevant rules that apply to that agreement. Besides a *de jure* withdrawal, the host State may also attempt to restrict the mission's freedom of action, culminating in a *de facto* withdrawal of consent.[858] This withdrawal may equally have an unprecedented effect on the mission's success.[859]

2.2.4. *How should consent be given?*

Any consent must be given freely without any coercion of the State by the threat or use of force or by fraud, corruption, or coercion of a representative of the State.[860] The authorised representative of a government is usually the head of State, the head of government, or the minister of foreign affairs. It speaks for itself that any consent given by a representative who is no longer in office or by a member of the government who is not authorised to speak on behalf of the State cannot be invoked.[861]

Consent may also never be presumed.[862] Consent may be given by formal agreement or in a more informal manner by State officials who are authorised under national or international law to do so.[863] While a formal agreement can be a SOFA, a more informal manner in which consent is given is when a representative of the host State sends an open letter to the President of the UN Security Council requesting the deployment of a peace operation within its territory. For example, in the case of MINUSTAH (a UN peace operation which was operative in Haiti between 2004 and 2017), the government, on the one hand, gave its written consent to the initial deployment of the UN forces within its territory and, on the other hand, gave its verbal consent to the renewals of the mandate by attending the UN Security Council meetings at which the relevant

---

857 See also Byrne (n. 816) 104; Dinstein, *War, Aggression and Self-Defence* (n. 616) 128; Eliav Lieblich, 'Intervention and Consent: Consensual Forcible Interventions in Internal Armed Conflicts as International Agreements' (2011) 29 Boston University International Law Journal 337, 365–366.

858 UN DPKO and UN DFS, '2008 Capstone Doctrine' (n. 19) 32.

859 As also discussed above, Part II, Section 2.1.2.

860 See also James Crawford (ed), *The International Law Commission's Articles on State Responsibility: Introduction, Text, and Commentaries* (Cambridge University Press 2002) 164–165; Gill, 'Military Intervention with the Consent or at the Invitation of a Government' (n. 801) 253.

861 International Law Association (n. 816) 19.

862 Gill and others (n. 26) 29.

863 Gill, 'Military Intervention with the Consent or at the Invitation of a Government' (n. 801) 252–253.

resolutions were discussed and adopted.[864] Parties to the conflict may also sign a peace agreement that includes the request or the approval of the deployment of an operation. An example is UNMIL, established in 2003. In the 2003 Accra Comprehensive Peace Agreements, the parties involved requested 'the United Nations [...] to facilitate, constitute, and deploy a United Nations Chapter VII force in the Republic of Liberia to support the transitional government and to assist in the implementation of this Agreement.'[865]

3. MANDATE OF THE UN SECURITY COUNCIL

Since 1999, the UN Security Council has provided dozens of UN (mandated) peace operations with a mandate in which PoC is set forth as a mandated task. In practice, questions arise about what the UN Security Council has authorised and what it has not. The following Section, therefore, thoroughly examines such PoC mandates issued by the UN Security Council, together with the role these instruments play in the use of force to protect civilians.

3.1. UN SECURITY COUNCIL PRACTICE OF MANDATING THE USE OF FORCE TO PROTECT CIVILIANS

3.1.1. The first PoC mandate: UNSC Resolution 1270 (1999)

The UN has always played a role in combating the suffering of the civilian population, but until 1999 the UN Security Council never included PoC as an explicitly mandated task in a resolution.[866] In Resolution 1270 (1999), the UN Security Council eventually decided that:[867]

864 In February 2004, the President of the UN Security Council drew the attention of the Members of the Council to a letter from Haiti's permanent representative authorising UN security forces to enter and operate in the territory of Haiti (see UNSC, '4919th Meeting (at Which UNSC Res. 1529 (2004) Was Adopted)' (2004) UN Doc. S/PV.4919; 'Letter Dated 29 February 2004 from the Permanent Representative of Haiti to the United Nations Addressed to the President of the Security Council and Annex to the Letter Dated 29 February 2004 from the Permanent Representative of Haiti to the United Nations Addressed to the President of the Security Council' (2004) UN Doc. S/2004/163). Subsequently, a permanent representative of Haiti voluntarily endorsed several renewals of the mandate (see e.g. UNSC, '6330th Meeting (at Which UNSC Res. 1927 (2010) Was Adopted)' (2010) UN Doc. S/PV.6330 2–3; UNSC, '6399th Meeting (at Which UNSC Res. 1944 (2010) Was Adopted)' (n. 792) 2).

865 'Peace Agreement between the Government of Liberia, the Liberians United for Reconciliation and Democracy, the Movement for Democracy in Liberia and the Political Parties, Annex to the Letter Dated 27 August 2003 from the Permanent Representative of Ghana to the United Nations Addressed to the President of the Security Council' (2003) UN Doc. S/2003/850, Art. IV; 'UNSC Res. 1509' (n. 128), pream. para. 9.

866 Shesterinina and Job (n. 36) 242. See also Part I, Sections 2.1.1 and 2.1.2.

867 'UNSC Res. 1270' (n. 7) para. 14.

> Acting under Chapter VII of the Charter [...] UNAMSIL may take the necessary action to ensure the security and freedom of movement of its personnel and, within its capabilities and areas of deployment, to afford protection to civilians under imminent threat of physical violence, taking into account the responsibilities of the Government of Sierra Leone and ECOMOG [Economic Community of West African States Monitoring Group]; [...].

Although the UN Security Council Members recognised the limits to the scope of the mandate's mission, they also clearly supported the deployment of a force of credible strength under Chapter VII of the UN Charter, equipped with strong ROE.[868] By choosing the words 'may take the necessary action,' the UN Security Council already came close to the 'all necessary means or measures' language normally reserved for more robust peace operations, which were openly mandated to use or threaten with the use of military force.[869] Furthermore, the UN Security Council limited the scope of the mandate in three ways by adding that it was authorised 'within its capabilities' and 'areas of deployment' to 'afford protection to civilians under imminent threat of physical violence'. Apparently, these caveats were added to 'avoid creating unrealistic expectations both internationally and in Sierra Leone of the extent of the protection UNAMSIL could give, and to avoid mandating the force beyond what it could realistically do.'[870]

3.1.2. *Standardised PoC language*

Since Resolution 1270 (1999), the UN Security Council has provided UNAMSIL as well as fourteen other UN peace operations (including, but not limited to, MONUSCO, UNMIL, UNOCI, MINUSMA, and MINUSCA) with a PoC mandate.[871] Since 1999, the UN Security Council has also adopted a number of explicit PoC mandates, providing certain UN Member States and regional and international organisations other than the UN with an explicit mandate to protect civilians in the territory of a given State (e.g. EUFOR RD Congo, MISCA, and AFISMA).[872]

PoC mandates are, of course, *ad hoc* and operation-specific, yet an analysis of the mission-specific UNSC resolutions adopted by the UN Security Council between October 1990 and December 2021 reveals that the language used is relatively standard. Usually, the UN Security Council authorises missions

868 Malaysia, France, Gambia, the Netherlands, and Canada, e.g. clearly supported this, see UNSC, '4054th Meeting (at Which UNSC Res 1270 (1999) Was Adopted)' (n. 6) 10, 12–13, 17.
869 Holt and Taylor (n. 162) 40.
870 Quote from a P5 member in an internal memo cited by *ibid.*
871 For a complete overview of UN peace operations with a PoC mandate, see Part I, Section 1.
872 For a complete overview of UN-mandated peace operations with a PoC mandate, see Part I, Section 1.

'to protect civilians under threat of physical violence' or 'imminent threat of physical violence'. Variations include protecting civilians under 'imminent threat of violence' or 'threat of imminent physical violence', contributing 'to protecting civilians in danger' or ensuring or contributing 'to the protection of civilians immediately threatened with physical violence'. To this wording an authorisation to use 'all necessary means' in the execution of the mission is usually added. Other variations include: to take 'all necessary action', 'the necessary action', 'necessary action', 'the necessary steps', 'all necessary measures', or 'the necessary measures' to protect civilians. Moreover, while in most PoC mandates, the mission is explicitly tasked to protect 'civilians', some resolutions invoke the term 'civilian population'.

The following terms are usually added to limit the scope of the authorisation functionally and geographically: 'within the capabilities' and the 'areas of deployment' to the task of protecting civilians. In some resolutions, the UN Security Council only refers to one of the two caveats: 'in the deployment areas of their units', 'within its area of operation', 'within its capabilities', or 'within the limits of its capacity and in the areas of deployment'. In other resolutions, the UN Security Council adds a more specific caveat by, for example, referring to 'areas of deployment of its infantry battalions' or areas of deployment of 'its armed units'.

Furthermore, PoC mandates often emphasise that the relevant mandate is given 'without prejudice to the responsibility of the host government', thus acknowledging that the responsibility for protecting civilians lies primarily with the host State and not with the mission. Finally, these decisions are typically taken under Chapter VII of the UN Charter. While for certain missions, only PoC tasks are authorised under Chapter VII of the UN Charter, most resolutions provide that Chapter VII of the UN Charter covers the entire mandate.

To illustrate this with an example, UNSC Resolution 1990 (2011) reflects the standardised PoC language of a Chapter VII mandate granted to a UN peace operation:[873]

> *Acting* under Chapter VII of the Charter [...], authorizes UNISFA within its capabilities and its areas of deployment to take the necessary action to: [...] (d) without prejudice to the responsibilities of the relevant authorities, [...] protect civilians in the Abyei Area under imminent threat of physical violence [...].

The PoC mandates granted to UN-mandated peace operations differ a bit in wording. For example, in 2012, the UN Security Council provided the African-led military operation in Mali, AFISMA, with the following mandate:[874]

---

873 'UNSC Res. 1990' (n. 134) para. 3.

874 'UNSC Res. 2085' (n. 148) pream. para. 17 and para. 9.

Acting under Chapter VII of the Charter [...] [d]ecides to authorize the deployment of [...] AFISMA [...], which shall take all necessary measures, in compliance with applicable international humanitarian law and human rights law and in full respect of the sovereignty, territorial integrity and unity of Mali to carry out the following tasks: [...] (d) To support the Malian authorities in their primary responsibility to protect the population; [...].

3.2. INTERPRETATION OF UNSC RESOLUTIONS CONTAINING A POC MANDATE

This Section explores the rules and methods of interpretation applicable to UNSC resolutions. The rules set forth in the VCLT are used to interpret PoC language, considering the specificities of UNSC resolutions. In doing so, this Section discusses, among other things, the wording of the UNSC resolutions itself, the verbatim records of the meetings in which these resolutions were adopted, and other relevant practices of UN organs and subsidiary organs, including but not limited to the reports of the UN Secretary-General and policy documents of the UN DPO.

Yet before doing so, an important caveat is to be made: PoC language has changed over time, but not every change in wording or omission of certain elements must necessarily be accompanied by major conclusions. The UN Security Council has not agreed upon standard rules or practices for drafting resolutions.[875] In practice, UNSC resolutions are commonly drafted by permanent missions, which are not necessarily staffed with lawyers.[876] The language that eventually is adopted results from political negotiations and reflects a political compromise between the different stakeholders involved. In the search for consensus, the Members of the UN Security Council do not necessarily aim for absolute theoretical coherence but rather for pragmatic ways to avoid disagreement.[877] As a result, legal and terminological precision is often sacrificed.[878]

Hence, when observing the changing formulation and interpretation of PoC mandates, we must not try at all costs to detect nuances, see coherences, or draw conclusions from certain word choices not necessarily meant by the drafters.[879] For example, as discussed below, the absence of an authorisation 'to take all necessary measures' does not necessarily suggest that the UN Security

875 Michael C Wood, 'The Interpretation of Security Council Resolutions, Revisited' (2017) 20 Max Planck Yearbook of United Nations Law 3, 13.
876 *Ibid.* 12.
877 Hajjami (n. 327) 233.
878 *Ibid.*; Wood (n. 875) 12.
879 Hajjami (n. 327) 244.

Council did not mean to authorise the use of force beyond self-defence.[880] On the other hand, some changes in wording might have more serious repercussions in practice. For example, around 2014, many UNSC resolutions dropped 'imminence' from the authorisation to use all necessary means to protect civilians under threat of physical violence.[881] As discussed in more detail in Part III, Section 3.3.2.2(A), it is not, *per se*, legally problematic if the imminence requirement is omitted from the UNSC mandate. However, what would be problematic is if the UN suggests that such mandates provide sufficient legal authority to use lethal force, in *disregard* for the right to life and, specifically, the imminence requirements imposed by HRL.

3.2.1. Rules and methods of interpretation applicable to UNSC resolutions

Rules on the interpretation of UNSC resolutions have neither been codified in a specific treaty nor been extensively dealt with in case law.[882] Also, in comparison with the numerous studies on the principles governing the interpretation of treaties, little has been written on the rules and methods of interpretation applicable to UNSC resolutions.[883] In the past, authors have dealt with whether general rules of interpretation in international law may apply to all forms of international instruments, including UNSC resolutions.[884] According to Wood, there are none, except maybe for the basic principle that legal instruments should be interpreted in good faith.[885] The drafters of the VCLT included the principle of good faith in the opening words of the general rule of treaty interpretation. This principle, together with the other elements of interpretation applicable to treaties, will be a starting point for our quest to identify rules and methods of interpretation applicable to UNSC resolutions.

In 1971, the ICJ included the following paragraph in its advisory opinion in the *Namibia* case, summing up a number of instruments which could be used to interpret UNSC resolutions: 'having regard to the terms of the resolution to be interpreted, the discussions leading to it, the Charter provisions invoked and, in general, all circumstances that might assist in determining the legal consequences.'[886] Although the VCLT was adopted two years before, the ICJ

880 See Part II, Section 3.2.5.2.

881 As discussed in detail in Part II, Section 3.2.4.

882 Wood (n. 735) 74.

883 *Ibid.* 73.

884 See e.g. Robert Kolb, *Interprétation et Création du Droit International: Esquisses d'une Herméneutique Juridique Moderne Pour le Droit International Public* (Bruylant 2006) 63; Serge Sur, *L'interprétation En Droit International Public* (Librairie Générale de Droit et de Jurisprudence 1974), as referred to by Wood (n. 875) 7.

885 Wood (n. 875) 7.

886 *Legal Consequences for States of the Continued Presence of South Africa in Namibia (South West Africa) notwithstanding Security Council Resolution 276 (1970), Advisory opinion* (1971) ICJ Rep 16 para. 114. In the *Al-Jedda* judgment of 7 July 2011, the ECtHR, when evaluating

did not reference any of these rules to interpret UNSC resolutions.[887] Only forty years later, the ICJ explicitly confirmed in its advisory opinion in the *Kosovo* case that Articles 31 and 32 of the VCLT may provide guidance on interpreting UNSC resolutions.[888] Nevertheless, since differences exist between treaties and UNSC resolutions, the ICJ added that 'other factors' should also be considered when interpreting these instruments.[889]

Article 31(1) of the VCLT suggests that a UNSC resolution is to be interpreted (i) in good faith; (ii) in accordance with the ordinary meaning to be given to its terms; (iii) in their context; and (iv) in light of its object and purpose.[890] The requirement of good faith (the first element) is also underscored in Article 2(2) of the UN Charter, according to which '[a]ll Members, in order to ensure to all of them the rights and benefits resulting from membership, shall fulfil in *good faith* the obligations assumed by them in accordance with the present Charter.'[891] Reading a UNSC resolution in good faith may imply, for example, that it is read

---

the meaning of the UNSC resolutions which formed the framework for the security regime in Iraq, took from this ruling that it should not only interpret the relevant resolutions in light of the language used but also the context in which they were adopted, see *Case of Al-Jedda v. the United Kingdom, Judgment* (2011) ECtHR (Grand Chamber) App. No. 27021/08 para. 76.

887 Wood (n. 735) 75.

888 *Accordance with International Law of the Unilateral Declaration of Independence in Respect of Kosovo, Advisory opinion* (n. 735) para. 94. See also the *Tadić* case in which the Appeals Chamber of the ICTY held that '[n]otwithstanding the fact that the ICTY Statute is legally a very different instrument from an international treaty, in the interpretation of the Statute it is nonetheless permissible to be guided by the principle applied by the International Court of Justice with regard to treaty interpretation' (*Prosecutor v. Tadić, Appeals chamber judgment* (1999) ICTY IT-94-1-A para. 282). For doctrine supporting this position, see Jochen A Frowein, 'Unilateral Interpretation of Security Council Resolutions. A Threat to Collective Security?' in Volkmar Götz, Peter Selmer and Rüdiger Wolfrum (eds), *Liber Amicorum Günther Jaenicke – Zum 85. Geburtstag* (Springer 1998) 99; Sean Aughey and Aurel Sari, 'Targeting and Detention in Non-International Armed Conflict: Serdar Mohammed and the Limits of Human Rights Convergence' (2015) 91 International Law Studies 60, 78; Alexander Orakhelashvili, *Collective Security* (Oxford University Press 2011) 40; Alexander Orakhelashvili, 'The Acts of the Security Council: Meaning and Standards of Review' in Armin von Bogdandy and Rüdiger Wolfrum (eds), *Max Planck Yearbook of United Nations Law*, vol. 11 (Koninklijke Brill 2007) 151–161; Wood (n. 735) 85–95; Wood (n. 875) 7–8. Papastavridis, on the other hand, does not consider the VCLT as the appropriate tool to interpret UNSC resolutions, see Efthymios Papastavridis, 'Interpretation of Security Council Resolutions under Chapter VII in the Aftermath of the Iraqi Crisis' (2007) 56 The International and Comparative Law Quarterly 83, 89–94.

889 *Accordance with International Law of the Unilateral Declaration of Independence in Respect of Kosovo, Advisory opinion* (n. 735) para. 94. For literature confirming this position, see Alain Pellet, '688 (1991): Iraq' in Mélanie Albaret and others (eds), *Les Grandes Résolutions du Conseil de Sécurité des Nations Unies* (Dalloz 2012) 140; Orakhelashvili, *Collective Security* (n. 888) 40–41; Krisch (n. 588) 1264; Wood (n. 875) 7–8.

890 From the outset, it is important to note that these rules of interpretation, together with other Articles of the VCLT governing the interpretation of treaties, are to be applied together and not in isolation from one another, see Richard K Gardiner, *Treaty Interpretation* (2nd edn., Oxford University Press 2015) 161.

891 Emphasis added. See also Wood (n. 735) 89.

in conformity with the limits to the powers of the UN Security Council.[892] The ordinary meaning of a term (the second element) may, for example, be found in dictionaries or other sources of definitions.[893] For example, as discussed below, according to the Oxford English Dictionary, the term 'necessary' (as used in numerous PoC mandates) may be understood as 'that is needed', 'indispensable', 'vital', or 'essential.'[894] Yet, when interpreting the term in good faith, we see that acceptable synonyms of the term 'necessary' include 'needed' or 'required' but not 'indispensable' or 'essential'. As for the context (the third element), one may accept that this refers to the entire text of a UNSC resolution, including its preamble and, if any, the annexes (see also Article 31(2) of the VCLT).[895] The preamble may also shed light on the object and purpose of a UNSC resolution (the fourth element).[896] Yet, to develop a more comprehensive picture of the object and purpose, one may also want to look at other background documents. These may include reports of the UN Secretary-General, formal and informal statements made by the UN Security Council or representatives of its Members before or after the adoption of the relevant resolution, or verbatim records of the meetings leading up to the adoption. For example, when evaluating the object and purpose of UNSC Resolution 1270 (1999) (which provided for the first PoC mandate for UNAMSIL), one may observe the prior report of the UN Secretary-General on the situation in Sierra Leone[897] or the verbatim records of the meeting of the UN Security Council leading up to the adoption of the relevant resolution.[898]

Article 31(3) of the VCLT provides that there shall be considered, together with the context, three other elements: (i) subsequent agreements; (ii) subsequent practice; and (iii) any relevant rules of international law. When applying this Article to UNSC resolutions, one could search for: (i) other UNSC resolutions on the same issue; (ii) subsequent practice of relevant UN organs and States affected by those given resolutions; and (iii) any relevant rules of international law.[899] For

892 For literature on the limits to the powers of the UN Security Council, see e.g. Terry D Gill, 'Legal and Some Political Limitations on the Power of the UN Security Council to Exercise Its Enforcement Powers under Chapter VII of the Charter' (1995) 26 Netherlands Yearbook of International Law 33; Erika de Wet, *The Chapter VII Powers of the United Nations Security Council* (Hart Publishing 2004); Krisch (n. 588) 1256–1263; Anne Peters, 'Ch. V The Security Council, Functions and Powers. Article 25' in Bruno Simma and others (eds), *The Charter of the United Nations: a Commentary*, vol. 1 (3rd edn., Oxford University Press 2012).

893 Gardiner (n. 890) 186.

894 'Necessary, Adj. and n.', www.oed.com, accessed 28 August 2018. See also further below, Part I, Section 3.2.5.1(B).

895 Wood (n. 735) 89.

896 Yet, caution is needed since the preamble is sometimes used to include paragraphs which are too controversial to include in the operative paragraph of the Resolution, see also *ibid.* 86–87.

897 UNSG, 'Eight Report of the Secretary-General on the United Nations Observer Mission in Sierra Leone' (1999) UN Doc. S/1999/1003.

898 UNSC, '4054th Meeting (at Which UNSC Res 1270 (1999) Was Adopted)' (n. 6).

899 *Accordance with International Law of the Unilateral Declaration of Independence in Respect of Kosovo, Advisory opinion* (n. 735) para. 94; Wood (n. 735) 91.

example, to further interpret UNSC Resolution 1270 (1999), one may look at the subsequent UNSC resolutions on UNAMSIL providing for a PoC mandate.[900] Subsequent practice may include the efforts made by the UN DPO (and its predecessors, the UN DPKO and DFS), in consultation with the UN OLA, to provide a conceptual framework, guiding principles, and key considerations for implementing PoC mandates.[901] The extent to which any relevant rules of international law should be taken into account depends, however, on the intentions of the UN Security Council.[902] If the UN Security Council intended to build upon existing legal rules or an existing legal situation, one needs to consider those rules when interpreting the relevant resolution.[903] If, conversely, it appears that the UN Security Council did not have any such intention but instead sought to lay down a new rule irrespective of the prior legal obligations, such intention prevails.[904] Relevant rules of international law may include the rules of HRL and IHL.

Article 32 of the VCLT refers to supplementary means of interpretation, including the preparatory work of the treaty and the circumstances of its conclusion. Considering the political nature of UNSC resolutions and how they are drafted, these elements may call for greater consideration than in the case of treaties,[905] though without being definitive.[906] Moreover, the distinction between the general rule and supplementary means of interpretation is of less importance than in the case of treaties.[907] After all, parallel to the elements listed above, evidence of the preparatory work of a UNSC resolution and the circumstances of its adoption can be found in reports of the UN Secretary-General; formal and informal statements made by the UN Security Council or representatives of its Members before or after the adoption of the relevant resolution;[908] verbatim records of the meetings leading up to the adoption; or earlier drafts of the resolutions which are published as an 'S' document.[909] However, one caveat has to be made, the evidence of the drafting process is not

---

900 Including 'UNSC Res. 1289' (n. 124); 'UNSC Res. 1313' (n. 124); 'UNSC Res. 1389' (2002) UN Doc. S/RES/1389 (2002).

901 Including, but not limited to, UN DPKO and UN DFS, '2010 UN Draft Operational Concept on PoC in UN Peacekeeping Operations' (n. 235); UN DPKO and UN DFS, '2015 UN Policy on PoC in UN Peacekeeping' (n. 16). Although these policy documents have been superseded by the following policy document on PoC, they can still be of relevance for the interpretation of PoC mandates: UN DPO, '2019 UN Policy on PoC in UN Peacekeeping' (n. 35).

902 Wood (n. 735) 92.

903 *Ibid.*

904 *Ibid.*

905 *Ibid.* 95.

906 Krisch (n. 588) 1265.

907 Wood (n. 735) 95.

908 *Accordance with International Law of the Unilateral Declaration of Independence in Respect of Kosovo, Advisory opinion* (n. 735) para. 94.

909 Wood (n. 735) 93.

always publicly available.[910] Only occasionally do the records identify some important points made by the Members of the UN Security Council.[911]

Thus, PoC language needs to be interpreted in good faith, considering the plain meaning which is to be given to these terms when they are read in the context of the resolution as a whole and in light of its object and purpose. In addition, one should consider the relevant circumstances of adopting these UNSC resolutions, the subsequent practice of the UN Security Council and other relevant practices of UN organs and subsidiary organs, and any relevant rules of international law (to the extent consistent with the UN Security Council's intention).[912] As mentioned above, only the UN Security Council or a body authorised by it can give an 'authentic interpretation' to a UNSC resolution.[913] However, UNSC resolutions are continuously translated and applied by a wide range of authorities and individuals.[914] For this reason, where relevant, the study also discusses how the AU, NATO, or the EU interprets certain terms.

3.2.2. Interpretation of the term 'protection'

If a UN (mandated) peace operation is given a mandate to 'protect civilians', what does the concept of 'protection' stand for? Can the term 'protection' be understood as the mission's overall purpose, or does it denote the acts or risks against which shelter is sought or the various strategies and methods by which civilians can be shielded from the acts or risks?[915] And what kind of acts, risks, strategies, and methods might those be?

If we look at the etymology of the word 'protection', the term came into the English language through the Latin verb 'protegere', a combination of 'pro-', meaning 'on behalf of, in place of, before, in exchange for, just as,' and 'tegere', meaning 'to cover.'[916] In the same vein, the Oxford English Dictionary defines 'protection' as '[t]he action of protecting someone or something; the fact or condition of being protected; shelter, defence, or preservation from harm,

910 Wood (n. 874) 13.

911 *Ibid.*

912 See also UN OLA, 'Note to the Under-Secretary-General of the Department of Peacekeeping Operations, United Nations' (2003) United Nations Juridical Yearbook 538, 539 (referring to some of these elements as tools for interpreting UNSC resolutions).

913 Wood (n. 735) 82–83. See also *Accordance with International Law of the Unilateral Declaration of Independence in Respect of Kosovo, Advisory opinion* (n. 735) para. 46; Gill, Léveillée and Fleck (n. 609) 112. As also mentioned above, see Part I, Section 4.2.2.1.

914 Wood (n. 735) 82–83. See also Gill, Léveillée and Fleck (n. 609) 112–116.

915 See also Lehmann (n. 14) 124.

916 See 'Protection, n.', www.etymonline.com/search?q=protection, accessed 15 September 2020; 'Pro-', www.etymonline.com/word/pro-?ref=etymonline_crossreference, accessed 15 September 2020; '(S)Teg-', www.etymonline.com/word/*(s)teg-?ref=etymonline_crossreference, accessed 15 September 2020. See also Welmoet Wels, 'The Many Meanings of Protection of Civilians: A Truth Universally Acknowledged?' (*IPI Global Observatory*, 10 October 2019), https://theglobalobservatory.org/2019/10/the-many-meanings-of-protection-of-civilians-truth-universally-acknowledged/, accessed 6 March 2020.

danger, damage, etc.; guardianship, care; patronage.'[917] This term is clearly given a broad and rather vague meaning and can therefore be evoked in a variety of situations. In past decades, the term 'protection' has indeed been used in a variety of contexts by different actors, ranging from the military to peacekeepers and humanitarian actors, who have different understandings of what protection means and what it does not.[918] These different approaches have influenced how 'protection' is understood as a mandated task by the UN Security Council.

Hence, the following Section first discusses how the term 'protection' was initially associated only with 'physical protection' but has subsequently acquired a broader meaning in both the context of humanitarian action and contemporary peacekeeping. An overview of how the term 'protection' is understood in these different contexts helps us to interpret the term 'protection' in good faith, considering the ordinary meaning given to this term in the context of contemporary PoC mandates and in light of their object and purpose. In further applying the rules of interpretation to the term 'protection' in the context of PoC mandates, this analysis also considers other relevant practices.

3.2.2.1. Physical protection

IHL was one of the first to give legal meaning to the concept of 'protection'. While it has neither done so by imposing a general obligation to protect civilians nor defining the term,[919] the protection of civilians is deeply embedded in IHL and depends on overall compliance with the relevant IHL rules by the conflicting parties.[920] Underlying this is the view that protecting civilians is the equivalent of physical security against violence. To this end, first and foremost, a distinction is to be made between civilians and combatants or civilians directly participating in hostilities.[921] The opposing parties must refrain from harmful acts to civilians and the civilian population and take precautionary measures to effect such obligations.[922]

---

917 'Protection, n.', www.oed.com, accessed 9 September 2020.

918 Holt and Berkman (n. 60) 35; Wels (n. 916); Victoria Metcalfe, 'Protecting Civilians? The Interaction between International Military and Humanitarian Actors' (Humanitarian Policy Group 2012) HPG Working Paper 1.

919 Despite the fact that the Geneva Conventions I–IV refer to the term 'protection' a number of times and Geneva Convention IV is even titled 'Geneva Convention relative to the protection of civilian persons in time of war', these IHL instruments omit to define the term 'protection', see Mamiya (n. 58) 66.

920 Lehmann (n. 14) 125; Okimoto, 'Protection of Civilians in International Humanitarian Law and by the Use of Force under Chapter VII of the Charter of the United Nations' (n. 51) 31.

921 See Art. 48 of Additional Protocol I. For an analysis of the customary nature of this rule, see Henckaerts and Doswald-Beck (n. 91) Rule 1, pp. 3–8 ('The parties to the conflict must at all times distinguish between civilians and combatants. Attacks may only be directed against combatants. Attacks must not be directed against civilians').

922 Okimoto, 'Protection of Civilians in International Humanitarian Law and by the Use of Force under Chapter VII of the Charter of the United Nations' (n. 51) 31–32; Williamson (n. 51) 163.

The specific rules in this regard are included in treaty law applicable to IACs and NIACs and are for the most part considered as rules of customary international law.[923] Article 51(1) of Additional Protocol I and Article 13(1) of Additional Protocol II foresee that '[t]he civilian population and individual civilians shall enjoy general protection against dangers arising from military operations.'[924] Article 51(2)–(8) of Additional Protocol I and Article 13(2)–(3) of Additional Protocol II subsequently set forth several rules which shall be observed to give effect to this protection. In this regard, Article 51(4)–(5) of Additional Protocol I, for example, prohibits indiscriminate attacks, whereas Article 51(6) of Additional Protocol I outlaws attacks against the civilian population or civilians by way of retaliation.[925] Indiscriminate attacks include disproportionate attacks, being attacks 'which may be expected to cause incidental loss of civilian life, injury to civilians, damage to civilian objects, or a combination thereof, which would be excessive in relation to the concrete and direct military advantage anticipated' (Article 51(5)(b) of Additional Protocol I). Last but not least, the principle of precautions in attack can be found in Article 57(1) of Additional Protocol I, whereas the principle of precautions against the effects of attacks can be found in Article 58(c) of Additional Protocol I.[926]

Concretely, the protection of civilians under IHL predominantly involves prohibiting direct targeting and causing disproportionate impact or exposure to risks to civilians and civilian objects. To that end, IHL imposes for example negative obligations on combatants not to cause direct harm to civilians or civilian objects, positive obligations not to use methods of war that create an environment of high risk of harm to civilians, positive obligations to take all feasible precautions to protect the civilian population under their control against the effects of attacks, and positive obligations on State organs and commanders

923 See Henckaerts and Doswald-Beck (n. 91). See also Okimoto, 'Protection of Civilians in International Humanitarian Law and by the Use of Force under Chapter VII of the Charter of the United Nations' (n. 51) 31; Emily Crawford, 'Who Is a Civilian? Membership of Opposition Groups and Direct Participation in Hostilities' in Mark Lattimer and Philippe Sands (eds), *The Grey Zone: Civilian Protection between Human Rights and the Laws of War* (Hart Publishing 2018) 19.

924 For an analysis of the customary nature of these rules, see also Henckaerts and Doswald-Beck (n. 91) Rule 1, pp. 3–8 (as quoted above, see Part II, Section 3.2.2.1, fn. 921).

925 For an analysis of the customary nature of these rules as for example contained in the aforementioned articles, see *ibid.* Rule 11, pp. 37–40 ('Indiscriminate attacks are prohibited'); Rule 14, pp. 46–50 ('Launching an attack which may be expected to cause incidental loss of civilian life, injury to civilians, damage to civilian objects, or a combination thereof, which would be excessive in relation to the concrete and direct military advantage anticipated, is prohibited'); and Rule 146, pp. 520–523 ('Belligerent reprisals against persons protected by the Geneva Conventions are prohibited').

926 For an analysis of the customary nature of these rules as e.g. contained in the aforementioned articles, see *ibid.* Rule 15, pp. 51–55 (as quoted above, see Part I, Section 3.2.2, fn. 526); and Rule 22, pp. 68–71 ('The parties to the conflict must take all feasible precautions to protect the civilian population and civilian objects under their control against the effects of attacks').

to make sure that troops are adequately educated and trained to meet their PoC obligations.[927]

3.2.2.2. Rights-based approach

Contrary to what is prevalent in the IHL community, the terminology 'protection of civilians' is less used in the discourse of the HRL community.[928] The HRL framework traditionally crystallises the obligations of State authorities to respect, protect, and fulfil a set of rights to preserve the inherent dignity and worth of the human person.[929] As such, HRL aims to provide a comprehensive framework for the broadest possible protection of civilians without necessarily referring to the notion of 'protection of civilians'.[930]

Today, HRL permeates a host of other domains, thereby calling for a rights-based approach, but this has certainly not always been the case. As discussed earlier, international and national human rights laws came into place to restrict the internal resort to force by State authorities against their own citizens to maintain or restore public security, the rule of law, and internal order.[931] As such, human rights were initially considered an internal affair of a State. Yet, after the end of the Cold War, the focus of human rights actors broadened as they started engaging in (post-)conflict zones.[932] Moreover, significant geopolitical shifts characterised the 1990s, increasing the number of intra-state conflicts and humanitarian crises of a different, more complex nature.[933] In addition, the traditional principles of international relations, including State sovereignty and non-interference in the internal affairs of other States, were significantly challenged by new values and principles of the international community.[934] As a result, human rights, especially the fulfilment of those rights, came to the forefront, setting an unprecedented impact in a number of areas, including humanitarian assistance and the concept of 'protection' in this regard.

---

927 Hugh Breakey, 'The Protection of Civilians in Armed Conflict: Four Concepts' in Angus Francis, Vesselin Popovski and CJG Sampford (eds), *Norms of Protection: Responsibility to Protect, Protection of Civilians and Their Interaction* (United Nations University Press 2012) 45. For a more detailed discussion of the IHL rules and principles regulating the use of force, see Part III. Section 3.2.

928 Willmot and Sheeran (n. 219) 533.

929 See preamble of the UDHR (UNGA Res. 217 A(III), Universal Declaration of Human Rights' (n. 683)).

930 Willmot and Sheeran (n. 219) 533.

931 Gaggioli, 'The Use of Force in Armed Conflicts Conduct of Hostilities, Law Enforcement, and Self-Defense' (n. 643) 7; Watkin (n. 38) 450–451. See also Part I, Section 4.1.2.2(A)(i).

932 Metcalfe (n. 918) 4.

933 Mark Anderson, Kristin Becknell and Joanna Taliano, 'History of Humanitarian Emergencies' in David Townes (ed), *Health in Humanitarian Emergencies* (1st edn., Cambridge University Press 2018) 18–20; Daniela Santos Nascimento, 'The Inclusion of Human Rights in Humanitarian Assistance: The Difficult but Necessary Way between Theory and Practice' (2004) 1 Yearbook on Humanitarian Action and Human Rights 41, 46.

934 Nascimento (n. 933) 42.

Traditionally, humanitarian assistance was grounded on the basic humanitarian principles of neutrality, impartiality, and independence.[935] The ICRC, for example, mainly focused on saving lives and alleviating human suffering of the victims of the conflict.[936] For fear of losing access to those in need, they often turned a blind eye to human rights violations by the warring parties. Moreover, in delivering humanitarian aid, the recipients were seen as passive victims rather than active subjects and rights-holders.[937] With the end of the Cold War, humanitarian action entered the international agenda, marking a shift towards the globalisation of humanitarianism.[938] Between 1996 and 2001, the ICRC organised a series of workshops to develop a consensus view on the protection of civilians among human rights and humanitarian actors.[939] As a result, the following 'right-based definition' was agreed upon:[940]

> The concept of protection encompasses '[...] all activities aimed at ensuring full respect for the rights of the individual in accordance with the letter and the spirit of the relevant bodies of law, i.e. human rights law, international humanitarian law and refugee law. Human rights and humanitarian organizations must conduct these activities in an impartial manner (not on the basis of race, national or ethnic origin, language or gender)'.

This definition was eventually adopted by the Inter-Agency Standing Committee, the highest-level humanitarian coordination forum of the UN system, as part of an effort to improve overall humanitarian coordination and response.[941] Essentially, protection includes the efforts of humanitarian actors 'to ensure that the rights of affected persons and the obligations of duty bearers under international law are understood, respected, protected and fulfilled without discrimination.'[942] In other words, they should approach the recipients of humanitarian assistance as active subjects and rights-holders with entitlements (as opposed to passive victims and recipients).[943] The primary purpose of

935 *Ibid.*

936 David P Forsythe, *The Humanitarians: The International Committee of the Red Cross* (1st edn., Cambridge University Press 2005) 160; Nascimento (n. 933) 42.

937 Huma Haider, 'International Legal Frameworks for Humanitarian Action: Topic Guide' (Governance and Social Development Resource Centre, University of Birmingham 2013) 20.

938 Anderson, Becknell and Taliano (n. 933) 18.

939 Mamiya (n. 58) 74.

940 ICRC, 'Strengthening Protection in War: A Search for Professional Standards' (ICRC 2001) 19, as also referred to by Mamiya (n. 58) 74; Foley, 'Defining Protection of Civilians in the Context of Armed Conflict' (n. 197) 54.

941 Inter-Agency Standing Committee, 'IASC Policy on the Protection of Internally Displaced Persons' (1999) 4; Inter-Agency Standing Committee, 'IASC Policy on Protection in Humanitarian Action' (2016) 2.

942 Inter-Agency Standing Committee, 'IASC Policy on Protection in Humanitarian Action' (n. 941) 2. See also Foley, 'Defining Protection of Civilians in the Context of Armed Conflict' (n. 197) 54.

943 Haider (n. 937) 20.

protection is to strive to respect, protect, and fulfil the rights of these active subjects (including HRL, IHL, and international refugee law) in an impartial (but not necessarily neutral) and non-discriminatory manner.[944]

The Sphere Humanitarian Charter, a document developed by the Sphere movement as a reference tool for humanitarian agencies, further established that all people affected by crisis have a 'right to life with dignity; the right to receive humanitarian assistance; and the right to protection and security.'[945] This right to receive assistance 'is a necessary element of the right to life with dignity.'[946] Furthermore, any such assistance must be provided in accordance with the principles of impartiality and non-discrimination.[947] The Sphere Humanitarian Charter subsequently developed four protection principles that support the right to life with dignity, the right to receive humanitarian assistance, and the right to protection and security, and that should guide humanitarian actors when conducting humanitarian action:[948]

1. Enhance the safety, dignity and rights of people, and avoid exposing them to harm.
2. Ensure people's access to assistance according to need and without discrimination.
3. Assist people to recover from the physical and psychological effects of threatened or actual violence, coercion or deliberate deprivation.
4. Help people claim their rights.

Preventive, responsive, remedial, and environment-building activities must be undertaken to uphold these principles.[949]

3.2.2.3. Protection by the peacekeeping community

A. Evolution in PoC language

Initial PoC mandates focused mainly on the 'physical protection' of civilians, with physical safety from violence undeniably having its roots in IHL. However, today's mandates are generally expansive, using the term 'protection' not only to refer to physical protection but also, for example, many other ways of protecting civilians in the long term. As a result, the number of tasks and the level of detail with which the UN Security Council instructs missions to conduct PoC tasks has increased remarkably in recent years. For example, when comparing the

---

944 Mamiya (n. 58) 74.

945 Sphere Project (ed), *The Sphere Handbook: Humanitarian Charter and Minimum Standards in Humanitarian Response* (4th edn., Sphere Association 2018) 29, para. 5.

946 *Ibid.* 30, para. 6.

947 *Ibid.*

948 *Ibid.* 36.

949 *Ibid.* 37.

first PoC mandate that was given to MONUC in 2000 and a PoC mandate that was granted to MONUSCO and the Intervention Brigade in 2018, we see a clear difference:

In Resolution 1291 (2000), the UN Security Council decided that:[950]

> MONUC may take the necessary action, in the areas of deployment of its infantry battalions and as it deems it within its capabilities, to [...] protect civilians under imminent threat of physical violence.

In Resolution 2409 (2018), the UN Security Council decided that:[951]

> [T]he mandate of MONUSCO shall include the following priority tasks [...]:
> (i) Protection of civilians
> (a) Ensure effective, dynamic and integrated protection of civilians under threat of physical violence through a comprehensive approach, including by preventing, deterring, and stopping all armed groups and local militias from inflicting violence on the populations, and by supporting and undertaking local mediation efforts to prevent escalation of violence, paying particular attention to civilians gathered in displaced persons and refugee camps, peaceful demonstrators, humanitarian personnel and human rights defenders, in line with the basic principles of peacekeeping and with a focus on violence emerging from any of the parties engaged in the conflict, outbreaks of violence between ethnic or religious rival groups or communities in identified territories, as well as in the context of elections, and mitigating the risk to civilians before, during and after any military operation;
> (b) Work with the Government of the DRC to identify threats to civilians and implement existing prevention and response plans and strengthen civil-military cooperation, including joint planning, *to ensure the protection of civilians from abuses and violations of human rights and violations of international humanitarian law*, including all forms of sexual and gender-based violence and violations and abuses committed against children and persons with disabilities, and requests MONUSCO to accelerate the coordinated implementation of monitoring, analysis and reporting arrangements on sexual violence in conflict and to continue to ensure the effectiveness of the monitoring and reporting mechanism on children and armed conflict;
> (c) Enhance its interaction with civilians, including by the troops, to raise awareness and understanding about its mandate and activities, to strengthen its early warning mechanism, and *to increase its efforts to monitor and document violations of international humanitarian law and violations and abuses of human rights*, including in the context of elections; and continue and strengthen local community engagement and empowerment, as well as strengthening protection of civilians through early warning and response,

950 'UNSC Res. 1291' (n. 125) para. 8.
951 Emphasis added. 'UNSC Res. 2409' (n. 19) para. 36(i).

including prevention, as appropriate, and by ensuring mobility of the mission;

(d) *Neutralize armed groups* through the Intervention Brigade under direct command of MONUSCO Force commander: in support of the authorities of the DRC, on the basis of information collection and analysis, and taking full account of the need to protect civilians and mitigate risk before, during and after any military operation, carry out targeted offensive operations in the DRC through the Intervention Brigade with the support of the whole of MONUSCO, either unilaterally or jointly with the FARDC [Forces armées de la république démocratique du Congo], in a robust, highly mobile and versatile manner and in strict compliance with international law, including international humanitarian law, and in accordance with the standing operating procedures applicable to persons who are captured or who surrender, and with the United Nations HRDDP, prevent the expansion of all armed groups, neutralize these groups, and disarm them in order to contribute to the objective of reducing the threat posed by armed groups to state authority and civilian security in the DRC and to make space for stabilization activities, and for the whole of MONUSCO force component to guarantee effective protection of civilians, including in support of operations conducted by the Intervention Brigade to neutralize armed groups and in areas where armed groups have been neutralized;

(e) Provide good offices, advice and assistance to the Government of the DRC to ensure actions against armed groups are supported by civilian and police components as part of consolidated planning which provides a comprehensive response to area-based stabilization efforts;

(f) Work with the authorities of the DRC, leveraging UN Police investigation capacities and expertise, *to arrest and bring to justice all those allegedly responsible for genocide, war crimes and crimes against humanity and violations of international humanitarian law and violations or abuses of human rights in the country*, including through cooperation with States of the region and the ICC;

(g) Provide good offices, advice and support to the Government of the DRC to promote human rights, in particular civil and political rights, and to fight impunity, including through the implementation of *the Government's 'zero tolerance policy' with respect to discipline and human rights and international humanitarian law violations*, committed by elements of the security sector, and to engage and facilitate mediation efforts at local level to advance sustainable peace; [...].

Where Resolution 1291 (2000) seems to limit the scope to the narrower notion of 'physical protection' from imminent violence, the number of tasks and the level of detail with which the UN Security Council instructs MONUSCO to protect civilians in Resolution 2409 (2018) seems to demonstrate a broader, more rights-based, approach to the concept of protection.[952] For example,

[952] See also Willmot and Sheeran (n. 219) 534; Lie and de Carvalho (n. 59) 52.

UNSC Resolution 2409 (2018) includes multiple references to HRL and IHL (see highlights above).

Moreover, as for physical protection, in recent days, a great many UNSC resolutions make an explicit reference to more robust action for protecting civilians or, more generally, in pursuit of the missions' mandates. For example, in 2013, MONUSCO was authorised to 'carry out *targeted offensive operations* through the Intervention Brigade [...] in a *robust, highly mobile and versatile manner* and in strict compliance with international law [...] to prevent the expansion of all armed groups, neutralize these groups, and to disarm them in order to *contribute* to the objective of reducing the threat posed by armed groups on state authority and *civilian security in eastern DRC* and to make space for stabilization activities.'[953] In 2015, MONUSCO itself (so not necessarily through the Intervention Brigade) was authorised to take all necessary measures to 'ensure [...] effective protection of civilians under threat of physical violence, *including by deterring, preventing and stopping armed groups from inflicting violence* on the populations.'[954] This language is clearly more robust than the language used in Resolution 2147 (2014), whereby the UN Security Council authorised MONUSCO to take all necessary measures to 'ensure [...] effective protection of civilians under threat of physical violence, *including through active patrolling*.'[955]

Likewise, robust language was used over time in the PoC mandates granted to MINUSMA. For example, in UNSC Resolution 2227 (2015), MINUSMA was tasked to 'stabilize the key population centres and other areas where civilians are at risk, notably in the North of Mali, including through long-range patrols, and, in this context, *to deter threats and take active steps* to prevent the return of armed elements to those areas.'[956] UNSC Resolution 2295 (2016) added that 'in this regard [...] [MINUSMA shall have the mandate] to enhance early warning, to anticipate, deter and counter threats, including asymmetric threats, and *to*

953 Emphasis added. 'UNSC Res. 2098' (n. 19) para. 12(b). See also 'UNSC Res. 2147' (n. 19) para. 4(b). See also the comments made by Luxembourg and France on the robust mandate of MONUSCO and the Intervention Brigade during the debate leading up to the adoption of UNSC Res. 2098 (2013), UNSC, '6943rd Meeting (at Which UNSC Res. 2098 (2013) Was Adopted)' (2013) UN Doc. S/PV.6943 6 and 9, respectively.

954 Emphasis added. 'UNSC Res. 2217' (n. 140) para. 9(a). See also 'UNSC Res. 2277' (n. 127) para. 35(i)(a); 'UNSC Res. 2348' (n. 127) para. 34(i)(a). See also the debates leading up to the adoption of UNSC Res 2348 (2017) and notably the comments made by the President of the UN Security Council at that time and Sweden: UNSC, '7910th Meeting (at Which UNSC Res. 2348 (2017) Was Adopted)' (2017) UN Doc. S/PV.7910 4 and 10, respectively. In UNSC Res. 2409 (2018), the UN Security Council adds the following: '[e]nsure effective, dynamic and integrated protection of civilians under threat of physical violence, including by preventing, deterring, and stopping all armed groups and local militias from inflicting violence on the populations, and by supporting and undertaking local mediation efforts to prevent escalation of violence [...] in line with the basic principles of peacekeeping,' see 'UNSC Res. 2409' (n. 19) para. 36(i)(a); 'UNSC Res. 2463' (n. 127) para. 29(i)(a); 'UNSC Res. 2502' (n. 127) para. 29(i)(a); 'UNSC Res. 2556' (n. 127) para. 29(i)(a); 'UNSC Res. 2612' (n. 49) para. 29(i)(a).

955 Emphasis added. 'UNSC Res. 2147' (n. 19) para. 4(a)(i).

956 Emphasis added. 'UNSC Res. 2227' (n. 19) para. 14(d)(i).

take robust and active steps to protect civilians, including through active and effective patrolling in areas where civilians are at risk, and to prevent the return of armed elements to those areas, engaging in direct operations pursuant only to serious and credible threats.'[957] Moreover, to counter asymmetric attacks[958] in active defence of MINUSMA's mandate, the UN Security Council decided that the mandate shall include the task to 'anticipate and deter threats and *to take robust* and active steps […], *to ensure prompt and effective responses to threats of violence* against civilians and *to prevent a return of armed elements to those areas*, engaging in direct operations pursuant only to serious and credible threats.'[959] In Resolution 2423 (2018), the UN Security Council 'request[ed]' MINUSMA 'to continue to carry out its mandate with a *proactive* and *robust* posture'[960] and referred to the tasks listed in UNSC Resolution 2295 (2016), yet without explicitly ordering the mission to counter asymmetric attacks in active defence of its mandate.[961]

Other examples whereby the UN Security Council used robust wording to formulate PoC mandates include UNOCI,[962] UNMISS,[963] UNIFIL,[964] and

957 Emphasis added. 'UNSC Res. 2295' (n. 34) para. 19(c)(ii).

958 Asymmetric attacks can be understood as attacks by which a party to the conflict seeks to compensate for its military, economic, or other weaknesses by resorting to the use of methods or means of warfare that are inconsistent with IHL or other rules of public international law, see Wolff Heintschel von Heinegg, 'Asymmetric Warfare', *Max Planck Encyclopedia of Public International law* (Oxford Public International Law 2010) para. 4.

959 Emphasis added. 'UNSC Res. 2295' (n. 34) para. 19(d). See also the comments made by Russia, Senegal, the US, New Zealand, the UK, and France (who held Presidency of the UN Security Council at that time) in the debates leading up to the adoption of UNSC Res 2295 (2016) (UNSC, '7727th Meeting (at Which UNSC Res. 2295 (2016) Was Adopted)' (2016) UN Doc. S/PV.7727 3–7). See also 'UNSC Res. 2364' (n. 19) para. 20(c)(ii) and (d).

960 Emphasis added. 'UNSC Res. 2423' (n. 34) para. 33.

961 *Ibid.* para. 38(d)(ii). For subsequent robust mandates provided to MINUSMA, see 'UNSC Res. 2480' (n. 139) para. 28(c)(ii); 'UNSC Res. 2531' (n. 139) para. 21; 'UNSC Res. 2584' (n. 139) para. 23.

962 In 2014, the UN Security Council decided that the mandate of UNOCI shall be '[t]o protect […] the civilian population from threat of physical violence […] and encourages UNOCI to move to a more preventive and pre-emptive posture in pursuit of its priorities and in active defence of its mandate, building on positive steps taken so far, without prejudice to the agreed basic principles of peacekeeping' ('UNSC Res. 2162' (n. 129) para. 19(a)). See also 'UNSC Res. 2226' (n. 129) para. 19(a). UNOCI was completed on 30 June 2017.

963 Whereas UNMISS was initially authorised to deter violence including through proactive deployment and patrols in areas of high risk of conflict (see e.g. 'UNSC Res. 2252' (n. 135) para. 8(a)(ii), as well as earlier mandates, as discussed above, see Part I, Section 3.1.4, fn. 503), the UN Security Council authorised the Regional Protection Force (attached to UNMISS) in 2016 to 'use all necessary means, including undertaking robust action where necessary and actively patrolling, to accomplish [its] […] mandate, to […] (c) [p]romptly and effectively engage any actor that is credibly found to be preparing attacks, or engages in attacks, against United Nations protection of civilians sites […] or civilians,' see 'UNSC Res. 2304' (n. 135) para. 10(c). See also 'UNSC Res. 2327' (n. 19) para. 9(iii); 'UNSC Res. 2406' (n. 19) para. 9(iii); 'UNSC Res. 2459' (n. 135) para. 10; 'UNSC Res. 2514' (n. 135) para. 10.

964 In 2017, UNIFIL was explicitly authorised to 'take all necessary action […] to ensure that its area of operations is not utilized for hostile activities of any kind, to resist attempts by

MINUSCA.[965] However, no explicit robust language can be found in th2e mandates granted to UN-mandated peace operations.

B. Meaning of 'protection' as a mandated task

In the 2019 UN Policy on PoC in UN Peacekeeping, the UN DPO builds upon the different traditions set out above. Considering PoC mandates as an expression of the determination of the international community to prevent the most serious violations of IHL, HRL, and international refugee law and related standards,[966] the UN DPO approaches PoC in UN peace operations as a set of integrated and coordinated activities by all civilian and uniformed mission components aimed at preventing, deterring or responding to threats of physical violence against civilians within the mission's capabilities and areas of deployment using all necessary means, up to and including lethal force.[967]

Subsequently, the UN DPO has categorised the various approaches and tools available to UN peace operations when entrusted with a PoC mandate into three tiers. These tiers include one that focuses on protecting civilians through dialogue and engagement (Tier I), one that focuses on providing physical protection (Tier II), and one that aims to establish a protective environment (Tier III).[968]

It follows that the term 'protection' relates not only to the acts or risks against which shelter is sought but also to the different strategies and methods by which civilians can be safeguarded against the acts or risks.[969] First, 'protection' aims at safeguarding civilians from the most serious violations of IHL, HRL,

---

forceful means to prevent it from discharging its duties under the mandate of the Security Council' ('UNSC Res. 2373' (n. 136) para. 14). See also the comment made by the US during the debate leading up to the adoption of UNSC Res. 2373 (2017), UNSC, '8037th Meeting (at Which UNSC Res. 2373 (2017) Was Adopted)' (2017) UN Doc. S/PV.8037 2. See also 'UNSC Res. 2433' (n. 136) para. 19; 'UNSC Res. 2485' (n. 136) para. 20; 'UNSC Res. 2539' (n. 136) para. 21; 'UNSC Res. 2591' (n. 136) para. 22.

965 Also in 2017, the UN Security Council decided that the mandate of MINUSCA shall include to 'in support of CAR Authorities, to take active steps to anticipate, deter and effectively respond to serious and credible threats to the civilian population and, in this regard, to enhance early warning, while maintaining a proactive deployment and a mobile, flexible and robust posture, as well as conducting active patrolling, in particular in high risks areas,' 'UNSC Res. 2387' (n. 19) para. 42(a)(ii). See also the comment made by France during the debate leading up to the adoption of UNSC Res 2387 (2017) UNSC, '8102nd Meeting (at Which UNSC Res. 2387 (2017) Was Adopted)' (2017) UN Doc. S/PV.8102 2. See also 'UNSC Res. 2448' (n. 140) para. 39(a)(ii) for similar robust wording. During the debates leading up to the adoption of UNSC Res 2448 (2018), France made a similar comment, see *ibid.* 2. For subsequent robust mandates provided to MINUSCA, see 'UNSC Res. 2499' (n. 140) para. 32(a)(ii); 'UNSC Res. 2552' (n. 140) para. 31(a)(ii); 'UNSC Res. 2605' (n. 140) para. 34(a)(iii).

966 UN DPO, '2019 UN Policy on PoC in UN Peacekeeping' (n. 35) para. 27.

967 *Ibid.* para. 18. See also Part I, Section 2.1.4.

968 As discussed in more detail in Part 1, Section 2.1.4.

969 See also Lehmann (n. 14) 124.

and international refugee law, as well as related standards. To underline this principle, the UN Security Council regularly refers to these three bodies of law (see e.g. paras 36(i)(b)–(d), (f)–(g) of the abovementioned UNSC Resolution 2409 (2018)).[970] Second, the aim of safeguarding civilians is not only achieved by using force to repel on-the-spot physical violence against civilians but also by addressing the underlying causes of the conflict through mediation or reconciliation or by assisting in the reconstruction of a country to create a safe environment for its civilians. For several UN peace operations, actions to repel on-the-spot physical violence against civilians involve robust measures.[971]

The AU's understanding of PoC is similar to that of the UN. The term 'protection' is used to refer to both the activities carried out under this concept ('activities undertaken to improve the security of the population and people at risk and to ensure the full respect for the rights of groups and the individual recognised under regional instruments')[972] and the acts or risks against which shelter is sought ('[p]rotection from physical violence' and '[r]ights-based protection' (i.e. focus on human rights violations).[973] For NATO, 'protection' initially only referred to the mitigation of civilian damage through their own action. These days, however, the provision of protection is understood to include not only all efforts to prevent, minimise, and mitigate adverse consequences for the civilian population which may result from NATO and NATO-led military operations but also, where appropriate, the protection of the civilian population against physical violence associated with the conflict or against threats of physical violence by other actors, including by providing a safe and secure environment.[974] The term 'protection' is thus used to refer to activities carried out under this concept and acts or risks against which shelter is sought. The same applies to the EU. The EU also interprets the notion of PoC broadly to include all efforts to reduce the impact of armed conflict on civilian populations, which implies both harm mitigation and active protection from third parties.[975] More so, PoC encompasses both military and non-military aspects and usually involves protecting civilians from physical violence, safeguarding human rights, contributing to ensuring the right of access to essential services and resources, and contributing to a safe, stable, and just environment as well as contributing in all areas of life.[976] For a more detailed discussion of AU, NATO, and EU's PoC policies, see Part I, Section 2.2.

---

970 'UNSC Res. 2406' (n. 19) para. 36(i)(b)–(d) and (f)–(g). See also 'UNSC Res. 1925' (n. 125) para. 12(h); 'UNSC Res. 2100' (n. 34) para. 24.
971 For examples of robust PoC language, see previous Section 3.2.2.3(A).
972 AU, '2012 AU Draft Guidelines for PoC in AU Peace Support Operations' (n. 114) 5.
973 *Ibid.* 8.
974 NATO (n. 345) para. 9.
975 EUMC, '2015 EU Concept on PoC in EU-Led Military Operations' (n. 120) para. 6.
976 *Ibid.* para. 11.

3.2.3. *Interpretation of the term 'civilians'*

The success of a UN (mandated) peace operation with a mandate to protect civilians partly depends on whether the actors involved can answer the following question: who is a civilian? Traditional peacekeeping operations were generally confronted with easily recognisable opponents, such as paramilitary or militant groups. However, as new forms of conflict have emerged to replace conventional wars, opposition fighters are harder to identify.[977] At one moment, they are civilians; at another moment, they become actively involved in the conflict by being part of an armed group and/or actively participating in the fighting. As a result, peacekeepers are entrusted with the difficult task of distinguishing those they ought to protect from those who pose a threat to them.[978]

The 2020 UN Handbook on PoC in UN Peacekeeping described the following case study to demonstrate the operational challenges in the field to determine who is a 'civilian':[979]

> In December 2013, when violence broke out in Juba, and then quickly spread to other areas of South Sudan, thousands of people fled to UNMISS compounds seeking refuge. They were men, women and children of all ethnicities. In the immediate moment, and the initial days to follow, the mission had no time or capacity to assess who was coming in to the compounds. Two simple rules were established: no uniforms and no weapons. Anyone willing to abide by those rules was determined to merit protection. The reality of this was that many fighters arrived at the gates, laid down their guns, and changed clothes. Piles of weapons and fatigues grew at the gates, with the mission safely storing the former. This approach drew strong criticism from the government, particularly once fighting had died down and it was suspected that many former fighters were in the POC sites. However, UNMISS stood by its policy that these individuals, even if they were former fighters, should be protected once they ceased to directly participate in hostilities by effectively disengaging from their fighting function.

Similarly, during a debate in the UN Security Council on PoC, the representative of India asked the following question:[980]

> We need to ask: who is the civilian and who is the combatant? Are the civilians the tens of thousands of Nuer who last December took refuge in the compounds of the

---

977 Fiona Blyth and Patrick C Cammaert, 'Using Force to Protect Civilians in United Nations Peacekeeping Operations' in Haidi Willmot and others (eds), *Protection of Civilians* (1st edn., Oxford University Press 2016) 315.

978 *Ibid.* 314. See also Hugo Slim, 'Civilians, Distinctions, and the Compassionate View of War' in Haidi Willmot and others (eds), *Protection of Civilians* (1st edn., Oxford University Press 2016) 24.

979 UN DPO, '2020 UN Handbook on PoC in UN Peacekeeping' (n. 35) 11.

980 UNSC, '7109th Meeting (on the Protection of Civilians in Armed Conflict)' (2014) UN Doc. S/PV.7109 34, as also partly referred to by Blyth and Cammaert (n. 977) 315.

> United Nations Mission in South Sudan (UNMISS) in Juba? Or are they the equal number of Dinka who were doing so in United Nations compounds in Jonglei? We need to question whether a robust mandate automatically translates into the protection of civilians?
>
> On 19 December 2012, some 2,000 armed youths attacked the UNMISS base in Akobo that was providing protection to Dinka refugees. The 40 Indian peacekeepers were heavily outnumbered. They had superior fire power and a robust mandate that would have allowed them to use force, not just in self-defence but also in defence of the mandate. Had they opened, fire hundreds of lives would have been lost. Would those lives have been civilians or combatants? And the troops who availed themselves of their superior fire power, would they have been peacekeepers or war-makers?

'Civilians' are the ones to be protected by UN (mandated) peace operations with a PoC mandate. Yet, from a legal, operational, and political perspective, the key question is: who is to be considered a 'civilian' in the context of PoC mandates and who is not? Unfortunately, UNSC resolutions do not bring any clarity in this regard. In most PoC mandates, only a reference is made to the mandated task to protect 'civilians'. However, in a limited number of resolutions, the UN Security Council also uses the term 'civilian population'.[981] Because the UN Security Council usually refers to the term 'civilian population' under the heading 'protection of civilians' or uses both terms in the same paragraph, it is assumed in the context of the present study that the UN Security Council considers them interchangeable. In the same vein, Article 50(2) of Additional Protocol I determines that the 'civilian population compromises all persons who are civilians.'[982]

In Resolution 1973 (2011), the UN Security Council exceptionally included an authorisation to protect 'civilians and civilian populated areas.'[983] While

---

981 UN peace operations: 'UNSC Res. 1870' (n. 133) para. 14; 'UNSC Res. 1906' (n. 125) para. 21(b); 'UNSC Res. 1919' (n. 133) para. 4; 'UNSC Res. 1944' (2010) UN Doc. S/RES/1944 (2010) para. 12; 'UNSC Res. 2000' (n. 129) para. 7(a); 'UNSC Res. 2012' (2011) UN Doc. S/RES/2012 (2011) para. 15; 'UNSC Res. 2070' (2012) UN Doc. S/RES/2070 (2012) para. 6; 'UNSC Res. 2085' (n. 148) para. 9(d); 'UNSC Res. 2112' (n. 129) para. 6(a); 'UNSC Res. 2119' (2013) UN Doc. S/RES/2119 (2013) para. 19; 'UNSC Res. 2149' (n. 19) para. 30(a)(i); 'UNSC Res. 2155' (n. 135) para. 4(a)(ii); 'UNSC Res. 2162' (n. 129) para. 19(a); 'UNSC Res. 2180' (2014) UN Doc. S/RES/2180 (2014) para. 22; 'UNSC Res. 2187' (n. 135) para. 4(a)(ii); 'UNSC Res. 2190' (n. 128) para. 10(a)(i); 'UNSC Res. 2217' (n. 140) para. 32(a)(i) and (iii); 'UNSC Res. 2223' (n. 19) para. 4(a)(ii); 'UNSC Res. 2226' (n. 129) para. 19(a); 'UNSC Res. 2239' (n. 128) para. 10(a)(i); 'UNSC Res. 2243' (2015) UN Doc. S/RES/2243 (2015) para. 27; 'UNSC Res. 2301' (n. 19) para. 33(a)(i); 'UNSC Res. 2313' (2016) UN Doc. S/RES/2313 (2016) para. 30; 'UNSC Res. 2333' (n. 128) para. 11(a)(i); 'UNSC Res. 2387' (n. 19) para. 42(a)(i) and (ii); 'UNSC Res. 2448' (n. 140) para. 39(a)(i) and (ii); 'UNSC Res. 2480' (n. 139) para. 28(c)(ii); 'UNSC Res. 2499' (n. 140) para. 32(a)(i) and (ii); 'UNSC Res. 2531' (n. 139) para. 28(c)(ii); 'UNSC Res. 2552' (n. 140) para. 31(a)(i) and (ii); 'UNSC Res. 2584' (n. 139) para. 30(c)(ii); 'UNSC Res. 2605' (n. 140) para. 34(a)(i) and (iii); UN-mandated peace operations: 'UNSC Res. 1484' (n. 143) para. 1.

982 See also further below, Part III, Section 3.2.2.1.

983 'UNSC Res. 1973' (n. 62) para. 4.

this exceptional reference to 'civilian populated areas' provides an interesting discussion,[984] the present study limits itself to a discussion of the term 'civilians' since this is the term the UN Security Council uses almost exclusively.

3.2.3.1. 'Civilians' within the meaning of IHL

When looking for the ordinary meaning of a term, dictionaries or other sources of definitions can be helpful.[985] For example, the Oxford English Dictionary puts forward several definitions of 'civilian', the most relevant being that a civilian is '[a] person who is not professionally employed in the armed forces; a non-military person.'[986] Defining 'civilians' by distinguishing them from combatants is a feature of IHL.[987]

In the treaty law of IACs, a civilian is any person who is neither a member of the armed forces of a party to the conflict nor a participant in a *levée en masse* (Article 50(1) of Additional Protocol I).[988] One of IHL's primary objectives is to ensure that parties to the conflict respect and protect those who do not or no longer directly participate in hostilities, such as civilians. Therefore, it draws this fundamental distinction between civilians and combatants (Articles 48 and 51(2) of Additional Protocol I).[989] Civilians, however, lose their protection against attack when and for such time as they take a direct part in hostilities (Article 51(3) of Additional Protocol I).[990]

In NIACs, 'combatant status' does not exist as such, and Additional Protocol II applicable to NIACs does not contain a definition of 'civilian' even though the

---

984 For further literature on this, see e.g. Lehmann (n. 14) 135–137.

985 Gardiner (n. 890) 186.

986 'Civilian, n.', www.oed.com, accessed 9 September 2020 Other definitions put forward by the Oxford English Dictionary include: 'A practitioner of Roman civil law, or of any of the various legal systems or codes historically derived from Roman civil law; an expert in or student of this'; 'A person who is concerned with political matters; a politician'; 'Theology. A person who is good or moral as a result of reason or natural inclination rather than the inspiration of Christian belief'; 'More fully Indian civilian. Originally: a member of the civil service of the East India Company. Later: a member of the Indian Civil Service. Now historical'; 'gen. A person who is not a member of a specified profession or group.'

987 UN DPO, '2020 UN Handbook on PoC in UN Peacekeeping' (n. 35) 9.

988 For an analysis of the customary nature of this rule in IACs, see Henckaerts and Doswald-Beck (n. 91) Rule 5, pp. 17–18 ('Civilians are persons who are not members of the armed forces. The civilian population comprises all persons who are civilians'); Rule 9, pp. 32–33 ('Civilian objects are all objects that are not military objectives').

989 For an analysis of the customary nature of this rule in IACs, see *ibid.* Rule 1, pp. 3–5 (as quoted above, see Part II, Section 3.2.2.1, fn. 921); Rule 7, pp. 25–26 ('The parties to the conflict must at all times distinguish between civilian objects and military objectives. Attacks may only be directed against military objectives. Attacks must not be directed against civilian objects').

990 For an analysis of the customary nature of this rule in IACs, see *ibid.* Rule 6, pp. 19–21 ('Civilians are protected against attack unless and for such time as they take a direct part in hostilities').

terms are used in several provisions.[991] According to Articles 13(1) and 13(2) of Additional Protocol II, '[t]he civilian population and individual civilians shall enjoy general protection against the dangers arising from military operations' and '[t]he civilian population as such, as well as individual civilians, shall not be the object of attack.' Moreover, just as in IACs, civilians lose protection when and for such time as they take a direct part in hostilities (Article 13(3) of Additional Protocol II).[992] Now, who could be considered a 'civilian' in NIACs? Common Article 3 of the Geneva Conventions I–IV sets forth that persons who do not actively participate in hostilities, including members of 'armed forces' who have laid down their arms and those placed *hors de combat*, cannot be killed. When discussing the materiel field of application of Additional Protocol II, Article 1 refers more specifically to the 'armed forces [of a State],' 'dissident armed forces,' and 'other organised armed groups.' Therefore, it could be argued that just as in the context of IACs, the term 'civilians' is defined negatively in the context of NIACs, meaning that all persons who are not members of the 'armed forces of a State', 'dissident armed forces', and 'other organised armed groups' are civilians.[993]

However, as IHL treaties omit definitions of these terms, discussions are present both in practice and in case law as to whether members of organised armed groups ever belong to the category of civilians.[994] In other words, it is disputed whether members of armed opposition groups are civilians who lose protection from attack when they take a direct part in hostilities or whether they can be attacked *as such based on their membership* in an armed opposition group.[995] This discussion is partly prompted by the fact that organised armed groups are generally not considered regular armed forces under national law.[996] As a result, one may be inclined to regard these members as civilians participating permanently in the hostilities.[997] The 2009 ICRC Guidelines on Direct Participation in Hostilities eventually suggested that civilians are those who are neither members of organised armed groups nor members of State armed forces of a party to the conflict.[998] Members of organised armed groups are only those persons who hold a position of 'continuous combat function' and, therefore,

991 *Ibid.* 19.
992 For an analysis of the customary nature of this rule in NIACs, see *ibid.* Rule 6, pp. 21–24 (as quoted above, see fn. 990).
993 *Ibid.* 19; Nils Melzer, 'ICRC Interpretative Guidance on the Notion of Direct Participation in Hostilities under International Humanitarian Law' (ICRC 2009) 30.
994 Henckaerts and Doswald-Beck (n. 91) 21; Melzer, 'ICRC Interpretative Guidance on the Notion of Direct Participation in Hostilities under International Humanitarian Law' (n. 993) 27.
995 Henckaerts and Doswald-Beck (n. 91) 19 and 21.
996 Melzer, 'ICRC Interpretative Guidance on the Notion of Direct Participation in Hostilities under International Humanitarian Law' (n. 993) 27.
997 *Ibid.* 27–28.
998 *Ibid.* 27.

not those people who carry out other tasks for the benefit of the organised armed groups (e.g. cooking or driving).[999] The latter group must be treated as civilians and, as such, are entitled to protection against direct attack.[1000]

The ICRC's position on the 'continuous combat function' is not without controversy;[1001] the main counterargument is that it appears to be contrary to the elementary IHL principle of equality of belligerents.[1002] Based on the ICRC approach, only persons who continuously carry out a combat function are considered members of an organised armed group, whereas, in the case of regular armed forces, persons without a combat function are also considered members.

The result of this complex situation, according to Crawford, is that a definition of 'civilian' in the context of NIACs can only be achieved by defining two concepts: (i) the criteria for membership of an armed group; and (ii) the concept of 'direct participation in hostilities', two concepts on which there is no unanimity in current thinking.[1003]

3.2.3.2. 'Civilians' in the context of PoC mandates

The term 'civilians' in the context of PoC mandates is generally interpreted by analogy with the concept of 'civilians' in IHL.[1004] For example, in the 2019 UN Policy on PoC in UN Peacekeeping, the UN DPO defines 'civilians' as follows:[1005]

> For the purposes of this policy and the protection of civilians mandate in peacekeeping, everyone is to be considered a civilian, except persons falling in one of the following categories:
> - members of the armed forces;
> - members of an organized armed group with continuous combat function; and
> - civilians directly participating in hostilities, for such time as they do so.

999 *Ibid.*

1000 *Ibid.*

1001 Michael N Schmitt, *Essays on Law and War at the Fault Lines* (T M C Asser Press 2012) 526–529.

1002 For literature discussing the principle of equality of belligerents, see Vaios Koutroulis, 'And Yet It Exists: In Defence of the "Equality of Belligerents" Principle' (2013) 26 Leiden Journal of International Law 449; Adam Roberts, 'The Equal Application of the Laws of War: A Principle under Pressure' (2008) 90 International Review of the Red Cross 931; Jonathan Somer, 'Jungle Justice: Passing Sentence on the Equality of Belligerents in Non-International Armed Conflict' (2007) 89 International Review of the Red Cross 655.

1003 Crawford, 'Who Is a Civilian? Membership of Opposition Groups and Direct Participation in Hostilities' (n. 923) 25–26.

1004 UN DPO, '2019 UN Policy on PoC in UN Peacekeeping' (n. 35) para. 21. Interestingly, a couple of years before, the former UN DPKO and UN DFS similarly defined 'civilian', yet without including the requirement of 'continuous combat function' (see UN DPKO and UN DFS, '2015 UN Policy on PoC in UN Peacekeeping' (n. 16) 5 and 9; UN DPKO and UN DFS, 'Protection of Civilians: Implementing Guidelines for Military Components of United Nations Peacekeeping Missions' (n. 109) 25).

1005 *Ibid.*

> In case of doubt whether a person is a civilian, that person shall be considered a civilian.

The 2020 UN Handbook on PoC in UN Peacekeeping makes a distinction between non-armed conflict situations and armed conflict situations: when operating in a non-armed conflict situation, 'everyone except members of armed forces are civilians within the scope of the POC mandate'; when operating in an armed conflict situation, *even when*, as the UN DPO adds, *they are not themselves a party to the conflict(s)*, 'everyone is to be considered a civilian, except [...] members of armed forces; members of organized armed groups who have continuous combat functions; and civilians directly participating in hostilities, for such time as they do so.'[1006]

The 2015 NATO AJD for the Military Contribution to Stabilization and Reconstruction sets forth that:[1007]

> For the purposes of protection of civilians, any person not part of security forces or armed groups (including criminal groups who are armed) is regarded as a civilian. In situations of international armed conflict or occupation, a civilian is any person who does not belong to the armed forces of a party to conflict or to (armed) militias and who has not spontaneously taken up arms to resist a force invading a non-occupied territory (see Article 43 of Additional Protocol I to the Geneva Conventions (Ref. J) and Article 4A of Geneva Convention III). In situations of non-international armed conflicts, it may be considered that all persons who are not members of State armed forces or organized armed groups of a party to the conflict are civilians.

It is unclear from NATO's explanation who are considered to be members of an organised armed group.

According to Okimoto, using the IHL concept of 'civilian' as the *lex specialis* in armed conflict situations seems appropriate in the absence of a definition in the UN Charter or UNSC resolutions.[1008] It seems plausible that the UN Security Council intends to build upon existing IHL rules defining 'civilian'. According to the author, there is insufficient evidence that the UN Security Council effectively intends to give the term 'civilians' a meaning that *differs* from its ordinary meaning and, consequently, from the meaning given to it in the IHL context. Nevertheless, when defining the term 'civilian' in the context of PoC mandates, as in IHL, at least two complications arise, which are discussed below in Part II, Section 3.4.1.

1006 UN DPO, '2020 UN Handbook on PoC in UN Peacekeeping' (n. 35) 9.

1007 NATO, '2015 NATO AJD for the Military Contribution to Stabilization and Reconstruction' (n. 117) 2–4, fn. 13.

1008 Okimoto, 'Protection of Civilians in International Humanitarian Law and by the Use of Force under Chapter VII of the Charter of the United Nations' (n. 51) 56.

3.2.4. *Interpretation of the terms 'in danger', 'under threat of attack', or 'under threat or imminent threat' of 'physical violence'*

Approximately half of the PoC mandates granted to UN peace operations between 1999 and 2021 include an explicit mandate to protect civilians under 'imminent threat of violence,'[1009] under 'imminent threat of physical violence,'[1010] or under 'threat of imminent physical violence.'[1011] The other half uses phrases such as 'contribute to protecting civilians in danger'[1012] or to protect civilians under 'threat of physical violence'[1013] without any reference to imminence. Moreover, a number of those PoC mandates have gradually removed the requirement that a

1009 'UNSC Res. 1870' (n. 133) para. 14; 'UNSC Res. 1919' (n. 133) para. 4.

1010 'UNSC Res. 1270' (n. 7) para. 14; 'UNSC Res. 1289' (n. 124) para. 10; 'UNSC Res. 1291' (n. 125) para. 8; 'UNSC Res. 1389' (n. 900) para. 2; 'UNSC Res. 1417' (n. 125) para. 7; 'UNSC Res. 1493' (n. 125) para. 25; 'UNSC Res. 1509' (n. 128) para. 3(j); 'UNSC Res. 1528' (n. 129) para. 6(i); 'UNSC Res. 1542' (n. 130) para. 7(I)(f); 'UNSC Res. 1545' (n. 132) para. 5; 'UNSC Res. 1565' (n. 125) para. 4(b); 'UNSC Res. 1590' (n. 133) para. 16(i); 'UNSC Res. 1592' (n. 125) para. 7; 'UNSC Res. 1609' (n. 129) para. 2(k); 'UNSC Res. 1649' (n. 125) para. 11; 'UNSC Res. 1701' (n. 136) para. 12; 'UNSC Res. 1739' (n. 129) para. 2(f); 'UNSC Res. 1756' (n. 125) para. 2(a); 'UNSC Res. 1794' (n. 125) para. 8; 'UNSC Res. 1856' (n. 125) para. 3(a); 'UNSC Res. 1925' (n. 125) para. 12(a); 'UNSC Res. 1933' (n. 129) para. 16(b); 'UNSC Res. 1990' (n. 134) para. 3(d); 'UNSC Res. 1996' (n. 135) para. 3(b)(v); 'UNSC Res. 2000' (n. 129) para. 7(a); 'UNSC Res. 2098' (n. 19) para. 12(a)(i); 'UNSC Res. 2100' (n. 34) para. 16(c)(i); 'UNSC Res. 2104' (n. 134) para. 4; 'UNSC Res. 2109' (n. 135) para. 4; 'UNSC Res. 2112' (n. 129) para. 6(a); 'UNSC Res. 2126' (n. 134) para. 5; 'UNSC Res. 2156' (n. 134) para. 8; 'UNSC Res. 2164' (n. 19) para. 13(a)(ii); 'UNSC Res. 2179' (n. 134) para. 8; 'UNSC Res. 2205' (n. 134) para. 9; 'UNSC Res. 2227' (n. 19) para. 14(d)(i); 'UNSC Res. 2230' (n. 134) para. 10; 'UNSC Res. 2251' (n. 134) para. 9; 'UNSC Res. 2287' (n. 134) para. 9; 'UNSC Res. 2318' (n. 134) para. 9; 'UNSC Res. 2352' (n. 134) para. 11; 'UNSC Res. 2373' (n. 136) para. 14; 'UNSC Res. 2386' (n. 134) para. 11; 'UNSC Res. 2410' (2018) UN Doc. S/RES/2410 (2018) para. 15; 'UNSC Res. 2416' (n. 134) para. 10; 'UNSC Res. 2466' (2019) UN Doc. S/RES/2466 (2019) para. 10; 'UNSC Res. 2433' (n. 136) para. 19; 'UNSC Res. 2445' (n. 134) para. 11; 'UNSC Res. 2485' (n. 136) para. 20; 'UNSC Res. 2497' (n. 134) para. 13; 'UNSC Res. 2539' (n. 136) para. 21; 'UNSC Res. 2550' (n. 134) para. 12; 'UNSC Res. 2591' (n. 136) para. 22; 'UNSC Res. 2609' (2021) UN Doc. S/RES/2609 (2021) para. 14.

1011 'UNSC Res. 1313' (n. 124) para. 3(c).

1012 'UNSC Res. 1861' (n. 138) para. 7(a)(i).

1013 'UNSC Res. 1706' (n. 133) para. 12(a); 'UNSC Res. 2147' (n. 19) para. 4(a)(i); 'UNSC Res. 2149' (n. 19) para. 30(a)(i); 'UNSC Res. 2155' (n. 135) para. 4(a)(i); 'UNSC Res. 2162' (n. 129) para. 19(a); 'UNSC Res. 2187' (n. 135) para. 4(a)(i); 'UNSC Res. 2190' (n. 128) para. 10(a)(i); 'UNSC Res. 2211' (n. 127) para. 9(a); 'UNSC Res. 2217' (n. 140) para. 32(a)(i); 'UNSC Res. 2223' (n. 19) para. 4(a)(i); 'UNSC Res. 2226' (n. 129) para. 19(a); 'UNSC Res. 2239' (n. 128) para. 10(a)(i); 'UNSC Res. 2241' (n. 135) para. 4(a)(i); 'UNSC Res. 2252' (n. 135) para. 8(a)(i); 'UNSC Res. 2277' (n. 127) para. 35(i)(a); 'UNSC Res. 2295' (n. 34) para. 19(c)(i); 'UNSC Res. 2301' (n. 19) para. 33(a)(i); 'UNSC Res. 2327' (n. 19) para. 7(a)(i); 'UNSC Res. 2333' (n. 128) para. 11(a)(i); 'UNSC Res. 2348' (n. 127) para. 34(i)(a); 'UNSC Res. 2364' (n. 19) para. 20(c)(i); 'UNSC Res. 2387' (n. 19) para. 42(a)(i); 'UNSC Res. 2406' (n. 19) para. 7(a)(i); 'UNSC Res. 2409' (n. 19) para. 36(i)(a); 'UNSC Res. 2423' (n. 34) para. 38(d)(i); 'UNSC Res. 2448' (n. 140) para. 39(a)(i); 'UNSC Res. 2459' (n. 135) para. 7(a)(i); 'UNSC Res. 2463' (n. 127) para. 29(i)(a); 'UNSC Res. 2480' (n. 139) para. 28(c)(i); 'UNSC Res. 2499' (n. 140) para. 32(a)(i); 'UNSC Res. 2502' (n. 127) para. 29(i)(a); 'UNSC Res. 2514' (n. 135) para. 8(a)(i); 'UNSC Res. 2531' (n. 139) para. 28(c)(i); 'UNSC Res. 2552' (n. 140) para. 31(a)(i); 'UNSC Res. 2556' (n. 127) para. 29(i)(a); 'UNSC Res. 2567' (n. 135) para. 3(a)(i); 'UNSC Res. 2584' (n. 139) para. 30(c)(i); 'UNSC Res. 2605' (n. 140) para. 34(a)(i); 'UNSC Res. 2612' (n. 49) para. 29(i)(a).

threat of physical violence be 'imminent' before the mission can act. For example, MONUSCO's PoC mandate initially required threats to be 'imminent',[1014] but the UN Security Council changed course in 2014 and authorised UN peace forces to respond to a 'threat' of physical violence against civilians without further mentioning 'imminent'.[1015] Likewise, the mandates of UNMISS,[1016] UNOCI,[1017] UNMIL,[1018] and

---

1014 'UNSC Res. 1925' (n. 125) para. 12(a); 'UNSC Res. 2098' (n. 19) para. 12(a)(i). (UNSC Resolutions 1991 and 2053 refer to UNSC Resolution 1925 and thus also to the requirement that the threat is 'imminent': 'UNSC Res. 1991' (n. 126) para. 1; 'UNSC Res. 2053' (n. 126) para. 1).

1015 'UNSC Res. 2147' (n. 19) para. 4(a)(i); 'UNSC Res. 2211' (n. 127) para. 9(a); 'UNSC Res. 2277' (n. 127) para. 35(i)(a); 'UNSC Res. 2348' (n. 127) para. 34(i)(a); 'UNSC Res. 2409' (n. 19) para. 36(i)(a); 'UNSC Res. 2463' (n. 127) para. 29(i)(a); 'UNSC Res. 2502' (n. 127) para. 29(i)(a); 'UNSC Res. 2556' (n. 127) para. 29(i)(a); 'UNSC Res. 2612' (n. 49) para. 29(i)(a).

1016 For UNMISS, from 2011 until 2013, threats had to be 'imminent': 'UNSC Res. 1996' (n. 135) para. 3(b)(v); 'UNSC Res. 2109' (n. 135) para. 4. (UNSC Resolution 2057 refers to UNSC Resolution 1996 and thus also to the requirement that the threat is 'imminent': 'UNSC Res. 2057' (n. 135) para. 1). From 2014 onwards, this requirement was dropped: 'UNSC Res. 2155' (n. 135) para. 4(a)(i); 'UNSC Res. 2187' (n. 135) para. 4(a)(i); 'UNSC Res. 2223' (n. 19) para. 4(a)(i); 'UNSC Res. 2241' (n. 135) 4(a)(i); 'UNSC Res. 2252' (n. 135) para. 8(a)(i); 'UNSC Res. 2304' (n. 135) para. 10(c); 'UNSC Res. 2327' (n. 19) para. 7(a)(i); 'UNSC Res. 2406' (n. 19) para. 7(a)(i); 'UNSC Res. 2459' (n. 135) para. 7(a)(i); 'UNSC Res. 2514' (n. 135) para. 8(a)(i); 'UNSC Res. 2567' (n. 135) para. 3(a)(i). (UNSC Resolutions 2302, 2326, and 2392 refer to preceding UNSC resolutions and thus also to the requirement that there is a simple 'threat': 'UNSC Res. 2302' (2016) UN Doc. S/RES/2302 (2016) para. 1; 'UNSC Res. 2326' (2016) UN Doc. S/RES/2326 para. 1; 'UNSC Res. 2392' (2017) UN Doc. S/RES/2392 (2017) para. 1).

1017 For UNOCI, between 2004 and 2013, threats had to be 'imminent': 'UNSC Res. 1528' (n. 129) para. 6(i); 'UNSC Res. 1609' (n. 129) para. 2(k); 'UNSC Res. 1933' (n. 129) para. 16(b); 'UNSC Res. 2000' (n. 129) 7(a); 'UNSC Res. 2112' (n. 129) para. 6(a). (The following UNSC resolutions simply extend the mandate of UNOCI and thus equally require that the threat be 'imminent': 'UNSC Res. 1594' (2005) UN Doc. S/RES/1594 (2005) para. 1; 'UNSC Res. 1600' (2005) UN Doc. S/RES/1600 (2005) para. 5; 'UNSC Res. 1603' (2005) UN Doc. S/RES/1603 (2005) para. 11; 'UNSC Res. 1652' (2006) UN Doc. S/RES/1652 (2006) para. 1; 'UNSC Res. 1726' (2006) UN Doc. S/RES/1726 (2006) para. 1; 'UNSC Res. 1739' (n. 129) para. 1; 'UNSC Res. 1763' (2007) UN Doc. S/RES/1763 (2007) para. 1; 'UNSC Res. 1765' (2007) UN Doc. S/RES/1765 (2007) para. 1; 'UNSC Res. 1795' (2008) UN Doc. S/RES/1795 (2008) para. 5; 'UNSC Res. 1826' (2008) UN Doc. S/RES/1826 (2008) para. 1; 'UNSC Res. 1865' (2009) UN Doc. S/RES/1865 (2009) para. 15; 'UNSC Res. 1911' (2010) UN Doc. S/RES/1911 (2010) para. 14; 'UNSC Res. 1962' (n. 129) para. 3; 'UNSC Res. 1981' (2011) UN Doc. S/RES/1981 (2011) para. 1; 'UNSC Res. 2062' (n. 129) para. 1). From 2014 onwards, the 'imminence' requirement was dropped: 'UNSC Res. 2162' (n. 129) para. 19(a); 'UNSC Res. 2226' (n. 129) para. 19(a); 'UNSC Res. 2284' (n. 129) para. 15(a).

1018 For UNMIL, threats first had to be 'imminent': 'UNSC Res. 1509' (n. 128) para. 3(j). (The following UNSC resolutions simply extend the mandate of UNMIL and thus equally require that the threat be 'imminent': 'UNSC Res. 1561' (2004) UN Doc. S/RES/1561 (2004) para. 1; 'UNSC Res. 1626' (2005) UN Doc. S/RES/1626 (2005) para. 1; 'UNSC Res. 1667' (2006) UN Doc. S/RES/1667 (2006) para. 1; 'UNSC Res. 1712' (2006) UN Doc. S/RES/1712 (2006) para. 1; 'UNSC Res. 1750' (2007) UN Doc. S/RES/1750 (2007) para. 1; 'UNSC Res. 1777' (2007) UN Doc. S/RES/1777 (2007) para. 1; 'UNSC Res. 1836' (2008) UN Doc. S/RES/1836 (2008) para. 1; 'UNSC Res. 1885' (2009) UN Doc. S/RES/1885 (2009) para. 1; 'UNSC Res. 1938' (2010) UN Doc. S/RES/1938 (2010) para. 1; 'UNSC Res. 2008' (2011) UN Doc. S/RES/2008 (2011) para. 1; 'UNSC Res. 2066' (n. 128) para. 1). From 2014 onwards, this requirement was dropped: 'UNSC Res. 2190' (n. 128) para. 10(a)(i); 'UNSC Res. 2239' (n. 128) para. 10(a)(i); 'UNSC Res. 2333' (n. 128) para. 11(a)(i). (UNSC Resolutions 2116, 2176, and 2308 simply extend the mandate of UNMIL and, therefore, only require the existence of a simple 'threat': 'UNSC Res. 2116' (2013) UN Doc. S/RES/2116 (2013) para. 1; 'UNSC Res. 2176' (2015) UN Doc. S/RES/2176 (2014) para. 1; 'UNSC Res. 2308' (2016) UN Doc. S/RES/2308 (2016) para. 1).

MINUSMA[1019] gradually removed the requirement that the threat be 'imminent'. For MINUSCA, the UN Security Council decided from the outset that the threat did not need to be imminent for the mission to act.[1020] The PoC mandates afforded to UNAMID, conversely, do not even include a reference to 'under (imminent) threat of physical violence' but simply authorise the mission to take the necessary action to 'protect civilians.'[1021] However, one of the mandates, included in UNSC Resolution 2228 (2015), did provide for an annexe with several benchmarks whereby an explicit reference was made to the fact that '[c]ivilians facing *imminent threats* of *physical violence* are protected by UNAMID.'[1022]

Most PoC mandates granted to UN-mandated peace operations do not explicitly refer to 'under (imminent) threat of physical violence.' Only UNSC Resolution 1464 (2003) authorised the Member States participating in ECOWAS, together with the French forces, 'to ensure [...] the protection of civilians immediately threatened with physical violence' in Côte d'Ivoire.[1023] In addition, in UNSC Resolution 1671 (2006), the UN Security Council decided that EUFOR RD Congo was authorised to 'contribute to the protection of civilians under imminent threat of physical violence.'[1024] The remaining UNSC resolutions adopted between 1999 and 2021 either included an authorisation to contribute to the protection of civilians 'in danger'[1025] or to protect civilians 'under threat of attack'[1026] or simply did not indicate against which threat the mission had to protect civilians.[1027]

1019 For MINUSMA, from 2011 until 2015, threats had to be 'imminent': 'UNSC Res. 2100' (n. 34) para. 16(c)(i); 'UNSC Res. 2164' (n. 19) para. 13(a)(ii); 'UNSC Res. 2227' (n. 19) para. 14(d)(i). From 2016 onwards, this requirement was dropped: 'UNSC Res. 2295' (n. 34) para. 19(c)(i); 'UNSC Res. 2364' (n. 19) para. 20(c)(i); 'UNSC Res. 2423' (n. 34) para. 38(d)(i); 'UNSC Res. 2480' (n. 139); 'UNSC Res. 2531' (n. 139); 'UNSC Res. 2584' (n. 139).

1020 'UNSC Res. 2149' (n. 19) 30(a)(i); 'UNSC Res. 2217' (n. 140) para. 32(a)(i); 'UNSC Res. 2301' (n. 19) para. 33(a)(i); 'UNSC Res. 2387' (n. 19) para. 42(a)(i); 'UNSC Res. 2448' (n. 140) 39(a)(i); 'UNSC Res. 2499' (n. 140) para. 32(a)(i); 'UNSC Res. 2552' (n. 140) para. 31(a)(i); 'UNSC Res. 2605' (n. 140) para. 34(a)(i). The following UNSC resolutions also extend MINUSCA's mandate and thus equally to the requirement that there is a simple 'threat': 'UNSC Res. 2281' (2016) UN Doc. S/RES/2281 (2016) para. 1; 'UNSC Res. 2446' (2018) UN Doc. S/RES/2446 (2018) para. 1.

1021 'UNSC Res. 1769' (n. 133) 15(a)(ii); 'UNSC Res. 1881' (n. 137) para. 2; 'UNSC Res. 1935' (n. 137) para. 2; 'UNSC Res. 2003' (n. 137) paras 3 and 5; 'UNSC Res. 2063' (n. 137) paras 3 and 4; 'UNSC Res. 2113' (n. 137) paras 4 and 5; 'UNSC Res. 2173' (n. 137) paras 8 and 9; 'UNSC Res. 2228' (n. 19) paras 4 and 5; 'UNSC Res. 2296' (n. 137) paras 4 and 5; 'UNSC Res. 2363' (n. 19) para. 15(a)(i).

1022 Emphasis added. 'UNSC Res. 2228' (n. 19) Annex A, Benchmark 2, 11.

1023 'UNSC Res. 1464' (n. 142) para. 9. UNSC Res. 1528 (2004) and 1609 (2005) renewed this mandate for the French forces, without, however, making an explicit reference to 'civilians immediately threatened with physical violence' ('UNSC Res. 1528' (n. 129); 'UNSC Res. 1609' (n. 129)).

1024 'UNSC Res. 1671' (n. 144) para. 8(b).

1025 'UNSC Res. 1778' (n. 145) para. 6(a)(i); 'UNSC Res. 1861' (n. 138) para. 1.

1026 'UNSC Res. 1973' (n. 62) para. 4.

1027 'UNSC Res. 1378' (n. 141) para. 5; 'UNSC Res. 1484' (n. 143) para. 1; 'UNSC Res. 2085' (n. 148) para. 9(d); 'UNSC Res. 2127' (n. 151) para. 28 and para. 50.

As with the other terms, there is no consensus on the meaning of 'in danger', 'under threat of attack', or 'under threat or imminent threat' of 'physical violence'. Such disagreement appears to have created problems in the field. As noted by the OIOS, the lack of 'unanimity among troop-contributing countries on the definition of what constitutes 'imminent threat of physical violence'' led to differences of interpretation affecting 'implementation in the field [...] [where] [s]ome contingents were reportedly more willing to use force than others.'[1028]

The terms of the UNSC mandate need to be interpreted in good faith to unravel the precise meaning of an authorisation to protect civilians 'in danger', 'under threat of attack', or 'under threat or imminent threat' of 'physical violence'. The interpretation must consider the ordinary meaning of the terms used in the resolution relative to the meanings these terms are given when they are read in the context of the resolution as a whole, in light of the resolution's object and purpose, the relevant circumstances of its adoption, the subsequent practice of the UN Security Council and other relevant practice of UN organs and subsidiary organs, and any relevant rules of international law (to the extent consistent with the UN Security Council's intention). However, AU, NATO, and EU practice concerning the meaning of the terms 'in danger', 'under threat of attack', 'immediately threatened', or 'under imminent threat' of 'physical violence' is limited, given the relatively restricted use of such terms in mandates for UN (mandated) peace operations and the limited number of mandates *per se* (see overview above). For this reason, the present analysis focuses exclusively on UN practice. Moreover, as the UN Security Council only rarely speaks of 'in danger' or 'under threat of attack', and the last time was in 2009 and 2011, respectively, this study limits itself to discussing the terms 'threat', 'imminent threat', and 'physical violence' in the following Sections.

3.2.4.1. 'Physical violence'

The Oxford English Dictionary defines 'violence', *inter alia*, as 'the unlawful exercise of physical force, intimidation by the exhibition of such force,'[1029] whereby 'physical' is most likely understood as 'relating to the body.'[1030]

The UN DPO interprets 'physical violence' in an equivalent manner but nevertheless seems to limit its scope in the context of PoC mandates. According to the UN DPO, 'physical violence' includes both 'violence that is occurring and violence that has the realistic potential to occur,'[1031] which likely leads to '*death or serious bodily injury to civilians*, including sexual violence.'[1032] Such threats of physical violence may be posed by 'non-state armed forces, self-defence groups,

1028 OIOS (n. 106) paras 31–33.
1029 'Violence, n.', www.oed.com, accessed 20 May 2020.
1030 'Physical, Adj.', www.oed.com, accessed 20 May 2020.
1031 UN DPO, '2020 UN Handbook on PoC in UN Peacekeeping' (n. 35) 83.
1032 Emphasis added. UN DPO, '2019 UN Policy on PoC in UN Peacekeeping' (n. 35) para. 23.

domestic and foreign state defence and security forces and other state agents and state-sponsored armed actors, as well as extremist groups and communities.'[1033] Physical violence against civilians includes:[1034]

(i) Direct and indiscriminate attacks (attacks targeting civilians or those which do not distinguish between civilians and combatants);
(ii) Attempts to kill, torture, maim, rape or sexually exploit, forcibly displace, starve, pillage, abduct or arbitrarily detain, kidnap, disappear or traffic persons;
(iii) The recruitment and use of children by armed forces and groups; and
(iv) Harm associated with the presence of explosive ordnance including mines, explosive remnants of war and improvised explosive devices.

To gain a fuller understanding of the terms 'physical violence', these terms should be linked to the terms 'threat' and 'imminent threat' and the changes in PoC language in this regard.

3.2.4.2. From 'imminent' to temporally undefined 'threats'

According to the Oxford English Dictionary, 'imminent' can be understood as '[i]mpending threateningly, hanging over one's head; ready to befall or overtake one; close at hand in its incidence; coming on shortly.'[1035] 'Threat' is defined as follows:[1036]

> A denunciation to a person of ill to befall him; *esp.* a declaration of hostile determination or of loss, pain, punishment, or damage to be inflicted in retribution for or conditionally upon some course; a menace. Also *figurative* an indication of impending evil.

Similarly, under HRL, determining whether a threat is 'imminent' or 'immediate' is, to quote former Special Rapporteur Christof Heyns, 'a matter of *seconds*, not hours.'[1037] Case law from human rights courts and international human rights mechanisms reveals that the justifiability of self-defence or defence of others depends on how temporally proximate the use of force is to an attack or threat of attack.[1038] Any 'time lag' between the threat or action and the response

1033 *Ibid.*
1034 UN DPO, '2020 UN Handbook on PoC in UN Peacekeeping' (n. 35) 83. See also UN DPO, '2019 UN Policy on PoC in UN Peacekeeping' (n. 35) para. 23.
1035 'Imminent, Adj.', www.oed.com, accessed 25 February 2021.
1036 'Threat, n.', www.oed.com, accessed 25 February 2021.
1037 Emphasis added. UN HRC, 'Report of the Special Rapporteur on Extrajudicial, Summary or Arbitrary Executions, Christof Heyns' (n. 109) para. 59.
1038 See e.g. *Case of McCann and Others v. the United Kingdom, Judgment* (1995) ECtHR (Grand Chamber) App. No. 18984/91 paras 195–200; *Case of Huohvanainen v. Finland, Judgment* (2007) ECtHR App. No. 57389/00 para. 97); *Case of Andronicou and Constantinou v. Cyprus, Judgment* (1997) ECtHR App. No. 27021/08 paras 191–192; *AS, DI, OI and GD v. Malta* (2020)

undermines, in principle, the potential to invoke self-defence or the defence of others.[1039] Moreover, there is often not only temporal proximity between the defensive action and the (foiled) attack but also geographical proximity of the attacker to the target, meaning that the attacker no longer needs to take preparatory steps to carry out the threat.[1040]

This understanding of 'imminence' actually seems to contrast with the UN's approach of disassociating imminence from temporality over the years. As mentioned above, the UN Security Council has gradually de-emphasised imminence in peacekeeping resolutions.[1041] However, this evolution in terminology began even earlier in the UN Secretariat.[1042] Notably, in 2008, the UN OLA issued guidance on MONUC's mandate to '[e]nsure the protection of civilians [...] under *imminent* threat of physical violence,' which it interpreted as:[1043]

> [T]o encompass not only the mounting of reactive operations – armed operations to protect civilians against attacks that were ongoing or on the very point of occurring –, but also proactive operations – operations to seek out armed groups that were known from their past actions to engage in attacks against the civilian population and to use armed force to disrupt their military capabilities and prevent them from mounting such attacks in the future.

The 2015 UN Policy on PoC in UN Peacekeeping mainstreamed this understanding of 'imminence'. It defined PoC as 'all necessary means, up to and including the use of deadly force, aimed at preventing or responding to threats of physical violence against civilians.'[1044] The policy also emphasised

---

UN HRC Communication No. 3043/2017, UN Doc. CCPR/C/128/D/3043/2017 para. 9.5. See also UN HRC, 'Report of the International Fact-Finding Mission to Investigate Violations of International Law, Including International Humanitarian and Human Rights Law, Resulting from the Israeli Attacks on the Flotilla of Ships Carrying Humanitarian Assistance' (2010) UN Doc. A/HRC/15/21 paras 165 and 167.

1039 Onder Bakircioglu, 'The Right to Self-Defence in National and International Law: The Role of the Imminence Requirement' (2009) 19 Indiana International and Comparative Law Review 1, 9.

1040 Hessbruegge (n. 647) 140.

1041 For a detailed overview of the changing language in PoC mandates in this regard, see Part II, Section 3.2.4.

1042 As already shortly discussed in Part I, Section 3.1.3.

1043 Miguel de Serpa Soares, '75 Years of International Law-Making at the United Nations' (2020) 23 Max Planck Yearbook of United Nations Law 1, 32.

1044 UN DPKO and UN DFS, '2015 UN Policy on PoC in UN Peacekeeping' (n. 16) para. 13. Notably absent from this definition is any mention of imminence in regard to threats, even though some UNSC resolutions expressly use this terminology. See also UN DPKO and UN DFS, '2017 UN Guidelines on the Use of Force by Military Components in UN Peacekeeping Operations' (n. 17) para. 18 ('[W]ithout prejudice to the primary responsibility of the host state, integrated and coordinated activities by all civilian and uniformed mission components to prevent, deter or respond to threats of physical violence against civilians within the mission's capabilities and areas of deployment through the use of all necessary means, up to and including deadly force').

that 'peacekeepers will act to prevent, deter, pre-empt, or respond to threats of physical violence' and defined threats as encompassing 'all hostile acts or situations that are likely to lead to death or serious bodily injury, including sexual violence.'[1045] Crucially, after noting that UNSC mandates sometimes associate PoC with 'imminent' threats, the UN explained that:[1046]

> A POC threat is considered imminent as soon as the mission has a *reasonable belief that a potential perpetrator displays a hostile intent, capacity, historical record and opportunity to inflict physical violence.* The term 'imminent' *does not therefore imply that violence is guaranteed to happen in the immediate or near future* or is being carried out. A threat of violence against civilians is imminent from the time it is identified until such time that the mission can determine that the threat no longer exists.

At first glance, this definition seems to dispense with any requirement of temporal proximity for threats and emphasises the subjective intentions and capabilities of hostile actors. However, the policy also muddied the conceptual waters in defining hostile intent as '[t]he threat of *an impending use of force*, which is demonstrated through an action or behaviour which appears to be preparatory to a hostile act,' where '[o]nly a reasonable belief in the hostile intent is required before the use of force is authorized.'[1047] This definition of hostile intent in the 2015 UN Policy on PoC in UN Peacekeeping seems to be a carbon copy of the UN's 2002 Sample ROE, with the exception of the word 'imminent', which was replaced by 'impending.'[1048] This definition was then reproduced by the 2017 UN Guidelines on the Use of Force by Military Components in UN Peacekeeping Operations, which remains the main policy document on these

---

1045 UN DPKO and UN DFS, '2015 UN Policy on PoC in UN Peacekeeping' (n. 16) paras 20 and 15; UN DPO, '2019 UN Policy on PoC in UN Peacekeeping' (n. 35) para. 32 ('[W]ork to prevent, pre-empt and respond to threats to civilians, and not just react to attacks').

1046 Emphasis added. UN DPKO and UN DFS, '2015 UN Policy on PoC in UN Peacekeeping' (n. 16) para. 47. In fn. 14, the Policy adds that '"[i]mminent" does not imply that violence is guaranteed to happen in the immediate or near future or is being carried out [...]. At the time of writing, the word "imminent" has been taken out of the language of Security Council resolutions for MONUSCO, MINUSCA and UNMISS.' See also UN DPKO and UN DFS, '2015 UN Implementing Guidelines for Military Components of UN Peacekeeping Missions on PoC' (n. 103) 25. ('The POC mandate generally specifies an "imminent" threat of physical violence. However, the term "imminent" does not imply that violence is guaranteed to happen in the immediate or near future or is being carried out. A threat of physical violence against civilians is considered imminent as soon as the mission has a reasonable belief that a potential aggressor has the intent and capacity to inflict physical violence. A threat of violence against civilians is imminent from the time it is identified until such time that the mission can determine that the threat no longer exists').

1047 Emphasis added. UN DPKO and UN DFS, '2015 UN Policy on PoC in UN Peacekeeping' (n. 16) 19.

1048 The 2002 UN Sample ROE define hostile intent almost identically, with the exception of the first sentence: 'The threat of imminent use of force, which is demonstrated through an action which appears to be preparatory to a hostile act' (UN DPKO (n. 102) Attachment 2: Annex B – 1).

issues.[1049] However, the term 'impending' is not defined in UN policy. If nothing else, the UN's re-definition of 'imminence' and its substitution of 'impending' for 'imminent' suggests a degree of uncertainty and discomfort with the temporal aspects of peace forces' use of force authority.

The uncertainty persists in current policy iterations. For example, after the 2015 UN Policy on PoC in UN Peacekeeping purported to dissociate imminence from questions of temporality, the UN changed course in its revamped 2019 UN Policy on PoC in UN Peacekeeping. Here it defines 'threats of physical violence against civilians' to encompass:[1050]

> [A]ll hostile acts or situations which are likely to lead to death or serious bodily injury of civilians, including sexual violence [...]. 'Threat' includes both violence against civilians which has materialised and is ongoing and violence which has the realistic potential to occur. The threat need not be imminent, *unless the specific Security Council mandate requires this.*

The last sentence injects considerable confusion into the UN's policy framework. It is unclear what relevance should be given to UNSC mandates that still require 'imminence' if this term can be divorced from temporality. Unfortunately, unlike the 2015 UN Policy on PoC in UN Peacekeeping, the 2019 UN Policy on PoC in UN Peacekeeping does not elaborate on the meaning of 'imminent', nor does it define 'hostile intent'.[1051] The 2020 UN Handbook on PoC in UN Peacekeeping compounds the confusion yet further when it suggests that '[t]he language change [from "imminent threat" to "threat"] clarified that a mission can and should take proactive and preventive action to protect civilians under threat and that these actions can include all necessary means (including the use of deadly force).'[1052] It then adds: '[t]hose missions which still have 'imminent' threat within the [PoC] mandate language are still expected to take a proactive and preventive approach to [PoC], *but short of using force when the threat is not imminent.*'[1053]

The UN's evolving PoC vocabulary is hardly a model of clarity. As Mona Khalil observes:[1054]

1049 UN DPKO and UN DFS, '2017 UN Guidelines on the Use of Force by Military Components in UN Peacekeeping Operations' (n. 17) 19.

1050 Emphasis added. UN DPO, '2019 UN Policy on PoC in UN Peacekeeping' (n. 35) para. 23.

1051 This omission appears to be deliberate in that other UN-wide policies continue to embrace a non-temporal understanding of 'imminence'. The same definitions appear in UN DPKO and UN DFS, '2015 UN Implementing Guidelines for Military Components of UN Peacekeeping Missions on PoC' (n. 103) 25; UN DPKO and UN DFS, '2017 UN Guidelines on the Use of Force by Military Components in UN Peacekeeping Operations' (n. 17).

1052 UN DPO, '2020 UN Handbook on PoC in UN Peacekeeping' (n. 35) 8.

1053 Emphasis added. *Ibid.*

1054 Khalil, 'Legal Aspects of the Use of Force by United Nations Peacekeepers for the Protection of Civilians' (n. 40) 211 ('The UN Secretariat never understood the term 'imminent' as requiring actual or guaranteed attacks on civilians to trigger the mandate. Both the

> Distinctions between the long-standing reference to 'imminent threat' and more recent references to 'threat' alone, while apparently intended to remove some of the confusion, may actually create even greater interpretive confusion by creating two separate standards within the mandates and practice of UN peacekeeping operations.

Khalil further notes that '[w]hile UN guidance has consistently maintained that a threat of physical violence against civilians *is imminent from the time it is identified* [...] such guidance is not found in the 2002 UN Sample ROE and the Annexes of those rules do not contain a specific definition of "imminent threat".'[1055]

In summary, as it remains unclear whether the UN Security Council actually intends to give the term 'imminent' a meaning that differs from its ordinary meaning and, consequently, from the meaning given to it in the HRL context, for now, 'imminent' must be understood as 'impending' and 'a matter of seconds' (see also further below, Part II, Section 3.4.1). That said, delinking 'protection threats' from temporally defined 'imminence' and their assimilation with concepts such as 'hostile intent' raises several questions as to the legal frameworks and standards applicable to the use of force by peace forces. These questions are discussed further in detail in Part III, Section 3.3.2.2.

3.2.5. Interpretation of terms 'all necessary means, measures, steps, or action'

Over time, the UN Security Council has used a variety of expressions to instruct UN (mandated) peace operations to protect civilians. The wording has ranged from using 'all necessary means'[1056] to taking 'all necessary

---

comprehensive and mission-specific protection of civilians strategies seek to enhance the protection-of-civilians mandate by clarifying the right and duty of UN forces to prevent, pre-empt, deter, or respond to threats of physical violence against civilians. Under these strategies and in accordance with the ROE, all that is required is a reasonable belief that a potential aggressor has the intent and capacity to inflict physical violence').

1055 Khalil, 'Legal Aspects of the Use of Force by United Nations Peacekeepers for the Protection of Civilians' (n. 40) 211.

1056 UN peace operations' mandates: 'UNSC Res. 1493' (n. 125) para. 26 (in this mandate, MONUC is also authorised to 'take the necessary measures [...] to protect civilians'); 'UNSC Res. 1528' (n. 129) paras 8 and 16; 'UNSC Res. 1545' (n. 132) para. 5; 'UNSC Res. 1565' (n. 125) para. 6; 'UNSC Res. 1592' (n. 125) para. 7; 'UNSC Res. 1609' (n. 129) paras 8 and 12; 'UNSC Res. 1649' (n. 125) para. 11; 'UNSC Res. 1706' (n. 133) para. 12(a); 'UNSC Res. 1739' (n. 129) paras 5 and 8; 'UNSC Res. 1756' (n. 125) para. 4; 'UNSC Res. 1794' (n. 125) paras 5 and 8; 'UNSC Res. 1856' (n. 125) para. 5; 'UNSC Res. 1906' (n. 125) para. 6; 'UNSC Res. 1925' (n. 125) para. 11; 'UNSC Res. 1933' (n. 129) para. 17; 'UNSC Res. 1962' (n. 129) para. 14; 'UNSC Res. 1996' (n. 135) para. 4; 'UNSC Res. 2000' (n. 129) para. 8; 'UNSC Res. 2057' (n. 135) para. 5; 'UNSC Res. 2062' (n. 129) para. 5; 'UNSC Res. 2100' (n. 34) paras 17 and 18; 'UNSC Res. 2109' (n. 135) para. 8 (in this mandate, it is also underscored that UNMISS' PoC mandate includes 'taking the necessary action to protect civilians'); 'UNSC Res. 2112' (n. 129) para. 7; 'UNSC Res. 2149' (n. 19) paras 29 and 47; 'UNSC Res. 2155' (n. 135) para. 4; 'UNSC Res. 2162' (n. 129) para. 20; 'UNSC Res. 2164' (n. 19) paras 12 and 26; 'UNSC Res. 2187' (n. 135) para. 4; 'UNSC Res. 2217' (n. 140) paras 31 and 50; 'UNSC Res. 2223' (n. 19) para. 4; 'UNSC Res. 2226' (n. 129) para. 20; 'UNSC Res. 2227' (n. 19) paras 13 and 27; 'UNSC Res. 2241' (n. 135) para. 4; 'UNSC Res. 2252' (n. 135) para. 8;

action,'[1057] 'the necessary action,'[1058] 'necessary action,'[1059] 'the necessary steps,'[1060] 'all necessary measures,'[1061] and 'the necessary measures'[1062] to protect civilians.

Such expressions do not stand out for their clarity and often lead to discussions among practitioners and academics about what the UN Security

'UNSC Res. 2281' (n. 1020) para. 2; 'UNSC Res. 2284' (n. 129) para. 16; 'UNSC Res. 2295' (n. 34) paras 17 and 35; 'UNSC Res. 2301' (n. 19) paras 32 and 56; 'UNSC Res. 2302' (n. 1016) para. 1; 'UNSC Res. 2304' (n. 135) paras 4, 5, and 9; 'UNSC Res. 2326' (n. 1016) para. 2; 'UNSC Res. 2327' (n. 19) paras 7, 9, and 11; 'UNSC Res. 2364' (n. 19) paras 18 and 37; 'UNSC Res. 2387' (n. 19) para. 41; 'UNSC Res. 2392' (n. 1016) para. 1; 'UNSC Res. 2406' (n. 19) paras 7, 9, and 12; 'UNSC Res. 2410' (n. 1010) para. 14; 'UNSC Res. 2423' (n. 34) paras 32 and 53; 'UNSC Res. 2445' (n. 134) para. 11 (in this mandate, it is also underscored that UNISFA's PoC mandate includes 'taking the necessary actions to protect civilians'); 'UNSC Res. 2448' (n. 140) para. 38; 'UNSC Res. 2459' (n. 135) paras 7 and 14; 'UNSC Res. 2466' (n. 1010) para. 9; 'UNSC Res. 2480' (n. 139) paras 19 and 42; 'UNSC Res. 2497' (n. 134) para. 13 (in this mandate, it is also underscored that UNISFA's PoC mandate includes 'taking the necessary actions to protect civilians'); 'UNSC Res. 2499' (n. 140) para. 31; 'UNSC Res. 2514' (n. 135) paras 8 and 14; 'UNSC Res. 2531' (n. 139) paras 18 and 41; 'UNSC Res. 2550' (n. 134) para. 12 (in this mandate, it is also underscored that UNISFA's PoC mandate includes 'taking the necessary actions to protect civilians'); 'UNSC Res. 2552' (n. 140) para. 30; 'UNSC Res. 2567' (n. 135) para. 3; 'UNSC Res. 2584' (n. 139) paras 20 and 43; 'UNSC Res. 2609' (n. 1010) para. 14 (in this mandate, it is also underscored that UNISFA's PoC mandate includes 'taking the necessary actions to protect civilians').

1057 UN peace operations' mandates: 'UNSC Res. 1701' (n. 136) para. 12; 'UNSC Res. 2373' (n. 136) para. 14; 'UNSC Res. 2433' (n. 136) para. 19; 'UNSC Res. 2485' (n. 136) para. 20; 'UNSC Res. 2539' (n. 136) para. 21; 'UNSC Res. 2591' (n. 136) para. 22.

1058 'UNSC Res. 1270' (n. 7) para. 14; UN peace operations' mandates: 'UNSC Res. 1289' (n. 124) para. 10; 'UNSC Res. 1291' (n. 125) para. 8; 'UNSC Res. 1389' (n. 900) para. 2; 'UNSC Res. 1417' (n. 125) para. 7; 'UNSC Res. 1590' (n. 133) para. 16(i); 'UNSC Res. 1769' (n. 133) para. 15(a); 'UNSC Res. 1990' (n. 134) para. 3; 'UNSC Res. 2104' (n. 134) para. 4; 'UNSC Res. 2109' (n. 135) para. 4 (in this mandate, UNMISS is also authorised to 'use all necessary means [...] to carry out its protection mandate'); 'UNSC Res. 2126' (n. 134) para. 5; 'UNSC Res. 2156' (n. 134) para. 8; 'UNSC Res. 2173' (n. 137) para. 9; 'UNSC Res. 2179' (n. 134) para. 8; 'UNSC Res. 2205' (n. 134) para. 9; 'UNSC Res. 2228' (n. 19) para. 5; 'UNSC Res. 2230' (n. 134) para. 10; 'UNSC Res. 2251' (n. 134) para. 9; 'UNSC Res. 2287' (n. 134) para. 9; 'UNSC Res. 2296' (n. 137) para. 5; 'UNSC Res. 2318' (n. 134) para. 9; 'UNSC Res. 2352' (n. 134) para. 11; 'UNSC Res. 2363' (n. 19) para. 14; 'UNSC Res. 2386' (n. 134) para. 11; 'UNSC Res. 2416' (n. 134) para. 10; 'UNSC Res. 2425' (n. 137) para. 2; 'UNSC Res. 2429' (n. 137) para. 15; 'UNSC Res. 2445' (n. 134) para. 11 (in this mandate, UNISFA's peace forces are also authorised to 'use all necessary means, which includes the use of force when required, in order to protect civilians under threat of physical violence'); 'UNSC Res. 2497' (n. 134) para. 13 (similar to UNSC Res. 2445 (2018), UNISFA's peace forces are also authorised to 'use all necessary means [...]'); 'UNSC Res. 2550' (n. 134) para. 12; 'UNSC Res. 2609' (n. 1010) para. 14 (similar to UNSC Res. 2445 (2018), UNISFA's peace forces are also authorised to 'use all necessary means [...]').

1059 UN peace operation's mandate: 'UNSC Res. 1919' (n. 133) para. 4.

1060 UN-mandated peace operations' mandates: 'UNSC Res. 1464' (n. 142) para. 9.

1061 UN peace operations' mandates: 'UNSC Res. 1861' (n. 138) para. 7(a); 'UNSC Res. 2098' (n. 19) para. 12; 'UNSC Res. 2147' (n. 19) para. 4; 'UNSC Res. 2211' (n. 127) para. 9; 'UNSC Res. 2277' (n. 127) para. 34; 'UNSC Res. 2348' (n. 127) para. 33; 'UNSC Res. 2409' (n. 19) para. 35; 'UNSC Res. 2502' (n. 127) paras 27 and 29(i)(a); 'UNSC Res. 2556' (n. 127) paras 27 and 29(i)(a); 'UNSC Res. 2612' (n. 49) paras 27 and 29(i)(a). UN-mandated peace operations' mandates: 'UNSC Res. 1671' (n. 144) para. 8; 'UNSC Res. 1778' (n. 145) para. 8; *ibid.* para. 6(a); 'UNSC Res. 1973' (n. 62) para. 4; 'UNSC Res. 2085' (n. 148) para. 9; 'UNSC Res. 2127' (n. 151) paras 28 and 50.

1062 'UNSC Res. 1493' (n. 125) para. 25.

Council has authorised and what it has not.[1063] For example, if a mandate allows a mission to use 'all necessary means, measures, steps, or action', which means are, in fact, deemed 'necessary' or 'unnecessary'? And who gets to decide what is or is not necessary at the relevant material time? Furthermore, is an authorisation to employ 'all necessary means, measures, steps, or action' a permit to use at least some armed force in implementing the mandate? And if so, does this mean that UN (mandated) peace operations may essentially resort to any amount of force to ensure the protection of civilians or are there limits to what UN (mandated) peace operations may or must do to protect civilians? And what if the UN Security Council omits to authorise the use of 'all necessary means, measures, steps, or action'? May the relevant PoC mandate still provide legal authority to use force to protect civilians?

Against this background, the following Section first applies the rules and methods of interpretation to the terms 'all necessary means, measures, steps, or action'. Hereafter, the consequences of a lack of authorisation to use 'all necessary means, measures, steps, or action' are discussed.

3.2.5.1. Application of the rules and methods to the expression to use 'all necessary means, measures, steps, or action'

A. 'Means, measures, steps, or action'

The Oxford English Dictionary defines 'to take measures' as 'to take actions or steps in order to achieve some purpose.'[1064] 'To take a step or steps' is understood as 'to perform a move or moves in a course of action; to take action or measures towards attaining an end.'[1065] 'To take the necessary steps' is defined as 'to take the action prescribed by law as necessary to attain some implied object, e.g. the enforcement of a debt.'[1066] 'To take action' is interpreted as 'to take steps in regard to any matter, to act.'[1067] 'Means', on the other hand, is defined as 'resources available for carrying out something, achieving some objective.'[1068] One may wonder whether the UN Security Council's decision to use the term 'means' as opposed to 'measures' or 'action' reflects the Council's political will to refer to the question of the means allocated to the operation.[1069] However, no evidence supporting such an assumption can be found in practice.

1063 Sâ Benjamin Traoré, 'L'Interprétation Des Résolutions Du Conseil de Sécurité Des Nations Unies' (DPhil thesis, University of Neuchatel 2018) 450.
1064 'Measure, n.', www.oed.com, accessed 28 August 2018.
1065 'Step, n., Fig.', www.oed.com, accessed 9 May 2022.
1066 *Ibid.*
1067 'Action, n.', www.oed.com, accessed 28 August 2018.
1068 'Means, n.', www.oed.com, accessed 28 August 2018.
1069 See discussion by Hajjami (n. 327) 244.

Kirgis seeks to explain the alternating use of the terms 'measures' and 'means' differently:[1070]

> An authorization [...] to use 'all necessary means' might be interpreted simply as an authorization to use force. The authorization to use 'all necessary measures' apparently would include not only an authorization to use force if it is necessary to achieve the Council's goals [...], including restoring and maintaining public order, but also to take other measures that would be appropriate to achieve the Council's humanitarian goals.

Yet, also, his explanation seems to find no resonance in the practice of the UN Security Council, which is much more extensive today than when he wrote his piece in 2004. As already mentioned above, when studying PoC language, it is essential to keep in mind that one must not try at all costs to detect nuances, see coherences, or draw conclusions from certain word choices that the drafters did not necessarily intend.[1071] The language ultimately adopted by the UN Security Council results from political negotiations and reflects a political compromise between the various stakeholders involved. In their search for consensus, UN Security Council Members do not necessarily seek absolute theoretical or terminological coherence but rather pragmatic ways of avoiding disagreement.[1072] As a consequence, legal and terminological precision is often sacrificed.[1073]

Hence, when interpreting the terms 'measures', 'means', 'steps', or 'action' in good faith and in accordance with their ordinary meaning, the present study considers these terms to be synonyms which all imply that 'steps can be taken to achieve a certain objective.' After all, to the author's knowledge, nothing in the verbatim records of the meetings of the UN Security Council or any other background documentation suggests that the drafters intended to make a substantive distinction between the terms 'means, measures, steps, or action'.[1074]

1070 Frederic L Kirgis, 'Security Council Resolution on Multinational Interim Force in Haiti' (2004) 8 American Society of International Law Insights para. 6, www.asil.org/insights/volume/8/issue/4/security-council-resolution-multinational-interim-force-haiti, accessed 26 February 2019. As also mentioned in Part II, Section 3.2.

1071 Hajjami (n. 327) 244.

1072 *Ibid.* 233.

1073 *Ibid.*; Wood (n. 874) 12.

1074 See e.g. UNSC, '4918th Meeting (at Which UNSC Res. 1528 (2004) Was Adopted)' (2004) UN Doc. S/PV.4918; UNSC, '5213th Meeting (at Which UNSC Res. 1609 (2005) Was Adopted)' (2005) UN Doc. S/PV.5213; (during which the Israeli representative stresses that the Resolution 'provides for a radically different international force with a mandate and the capability to use all necessary means' while the UNSC Resolution itself eventually refers to 'the necessary action' UNSC, '5511th Meeting (at Which UNSC Res. 1701 (2006) Was Adopted)' (2006) UN Doc. S/PV.5511 + Corr.1 21; UNSC, '5617th Meeting (at Which UNSC Res. 1739 (2007) Was Adopted)' (2007) UN Doc. S/PV.5617; UNSC, '6064th Meeting (at Which UNSC Res. 1861 (2009) Was Adopted)' (2009) UN Doc. S/PV.6064; UNSC, '6898th Meeting (at Which UNSC Res. 2085 (2012) Was Adopted)' (2012) UN Doc. S/PV.6898; UNSC,

This interpretation also corresponds to the wording chosen by the former UN DPKO and DFS when arguing that 'all necessary action' gives the mission the authority 'to take all steps, up to and including the use of deadly force (as a last resort) to protect civilians under threat.'[1075] Since the terms 'means, measures, steps, or action' can be considered synonyms, this study consistently refers to the term 'means' since this is the term most commonly used in PoC language.

B. 'Necessary'

When including PoC language in its resolutions, the UN Security Council also adds the adjective 'necessary'. According to the Oxford English Dictionary, this adjective may be understood as 'that is needed,' 'indispensable,' 'vital,' or 'essential.'[1076] Yet, it has been argued in doctrine that the term 'necessary' should neither be interpreted as a 'blank cheque' (i.e. without any limits)[1077] nor should it be understood as 'essential' or 'the only means possible.'[1078] Therefore, when interpreting the term in good faith, 'necessary means' can be understood as means which are 'not unnecessary' to obtain a given objective. Acceptable synonyms of the term 'necessary' may include 'needed' or 'required' without being 'indispensable' or 'essential'. In light of its object and purpose, 'necessary means' could then be understood as means which are 'needed' to prevent, deter, pre-empt, or respond to (imminent) threats of physical violence against civilians.[1079]

Which means are 'needed' or 'necessary' and which are not is highly contextual.[1080] As is also apparent from the ruling of the ECtHR in the case of *Nada v. Switzerland*, the term 'necessary' as used in UNSC resolutions is to be construed 'on a case-by-case basis.'[1081] In the context of PoC mandates, the vagueness of the formula 'all necessary means' gives rise to a subjective appreciation of the choice of means and the evaluation of their

'6943rd Meeting (at Which UNSC Res. 2098 (2013) Was Adopted)' (n. 953); UNSC, '7072nd Meeting (at Which UNSC Res. 2127 (2013) Was Adopted)' (2013) UN Doc. S/PV.7072; UNSC, '8298th Meeting (at Which UNSC Res. 2423 (2018) Was Adopted)' (2018) UN Doc. S/PV.2423; UNSC, '8422nd Meeting (at Which UNSC Res. 2448 (2018) Was Adopted)' (2018) UN Doc. S/PV.8422; UNSC, '8692nd Meeting (at Which UNSC Res. 2502 (2019) Was Adopted)' (2019) UN Doc. S/PV.8692.

1075 UN DPKO and UN DFS, 'United Nations Comprehensive Protection of Civilians Training Materials for United Nations Peacekeeping Operations. Military Version' (2017) CPOC V3.0 189.

1076 'Necessary, Adj. and n.' (n. 894).

1077 Corten and Koutroulis (n. 328) 71; Hajjami (n. 327) 232.

1078 Dapo Akande, 'What Does UN Security Council Resolution 1973 Permit?' (*EJIL: Talk!*, 23 March 2011), www.ejiltalk.org/what-does-un-security-council-resolution-1973-permit/, accessed 10 July 2018.

1079 See also UN DPO, '2019 UN Policy on PoC in UN Peacekeeping' (n. 35) 12.

1080 Aughey and Sari (n. 888) 76.

1081 *Case of Nada v. Switzerland, Judgment* (2012) ECtHR (Grand Chamber) App. No. 10593/08 para. 177.

'necessity'.[1082] In other words, since these UNSC resolutions clearly 'authorise' UN (mandated) peace operations to use 'all necessary means' to 'protect civilians', those responsible for implementing the mandate seem to retain the competence to decide *at their discretion which means* are 'needed' to ensure the protection of civilians. When the UN Security Council authorises a State, organisation, or arrangement to use 'all necessary means' to protect civilians, the implementation of that authorisation is left to the military strategic level of that State, organisation, or arrangement. There is a possibility that they consider different means to be necessary to implement the PoC mandate. Yet, even in this case, the UN Security Council should keep at least some kind of control over implementing the PoC mandate it has given.[1083]

Necessary means may include the use of force. Although it does not explicitly say so, the UN Security Council's drafting history of resolutions clearly indicates that an authorisation to use 'all necessary means' has become a permit to use at least some force in implementing the mandate.[1084] This language was initially reserved for operations other than UN peace operations, which were openly authorised to use or threaten to use military force.[1085] For example, in 1990, the UN Security Council adopted Resolution 678 (1990) in response to Iraq's invasion of Kuwait. States were authorised to use 'all necessary means' to restore international peace and security in the Gulf area.[1086]

The first draft of this resolution, shared by the US, explicitly allowed the possibility for States to use force.[1087] However, the former Soviet Union made it clear that this language would not receive its approval.[1088] Instead, the Soviet Minister for Foreign Affairs suggested replacing 'use of force' with less threatening wording.[1089] The US Secretary of State subsequently proposed different 'euphemisms', including the phrase 'all necessary means.'[1090] Upon acceptance, it became clear that the terms 'use of all necessary means' and 'use of force' were considered interchangeable. The use of the euphemism 'all necessary

1082 Traoré (n. 1063) 459.

1083 See also Part I, Section 4.2.2.1.

1084 For doctrine confirming this position, see Aughey and Sari (n. 888) 77–78; Christopher Greenwood, 'New World Order or Old? The Invasion of Kuwait and the Rule of Law' (1992) 55 The Modern Law Review 153, 166; Hajjami (n. 327) 234–237; Traoré (n. 1063) 450. According to Findlay and Dinstein, the formula is a 'euphemism' for the use of force, see Findlay (n. 168) 167, 351, and 361; and Dinstein, *War, Aggression and Self-Defence* (n. 616) 352, para. 927.

1085 Holt and Taylor (n. 162) 40. For a history of the use of the formula by the UN Security Council and the UN General Assembly before it appeared in PoC mandates, see Hajjami (n. 327) 235–242.

1086 'UNSC Res. 678' (1990) UN Doc. S/RES/678 (1990) para. 2.

1087 Helmut Freudenschuss, 'Between Unilateralism and Collective Security: Authorizations of the Use of Force by the UN Security Council' (1994) 5 The European Journal of International Law 492, 497.

1088 *Ibid.*

1089 *Ibid.*

1090 *Ibid.*

means' was dictated only by political and diplomatic requirements.[1091] For that reason, UNSC Resolution 678 (1990) is considered a key step in the process of assimilating the formula 'all necessary means' with the use of military force.[1092]

In the initial PoC mandates, the UN Security Council confined itself to authorising the UN (mandated) peace operations in question to take 'the necessary action' to protect civilians.[1093] With Resolution 1493 (2003), the UN Security Council authorised MONUC to use 'all necessary means' to protect civilians.[1094] In that same year, the former UN Legal Counsel, Hans Corell, argued that if the UN Security Council uses such express language as 'to use all necessary means' or 'to take all necessary measures', there is no doubt that the UN Security Council used its powers under Chapter VII of the UN Charter to authorise the use of armed force.[1095] In 2018, when adopting thematic Resolution 2436 (2018) on Developing a Comprehensive and Integrated Performance Policy Framework for UN Peacekeeping Operations, the UN Security Council explicitly confirmed that when it authorises UN peace operations 'to use all necessary means,' this 'includes the use of force when required.'[1096] In extending UNISFA's PoC mandate through Resolution 2445 (2018) and subsequent resolutions, the UN Security Council also confirmed its position.[1097]

3.2.5.2. What if no explicit authorisation is given to take 'all necessary means'?

An authorisation to use 'all necessary means' provides the legal authority to use force to protect civilians. However, in several PoC mandates, the UN Security Council has omitted to include an explicit authorisation to use 'all necessary means' to protect civilians. For example, in Resolution 1542 (2004), the UN Security Council '*[a]cting* under Chapter VII of the Charter [...] *decide[d]* that MINUSTAH shall have the following mandate: [...] to protect civilians under imminent threat of physical violence.'[1098] Strangely enough, the UN Security Council did not provide the operation with an explicit mandate 'to take all

1091 Hajjami (n. 327) 239.
1092 *Ibid.*
1093 'UNSC Res. 1270' (n. 7) para. 14; 'UNSC Res. 1289' (n. 124) para. 10; 'UNSC Res. 1291' (n. 125) para. 8; 'UNSC Res. 1389' (n. 900) para. 2; 'UNSC Res. 1417' (n. 125) para. 7.
1094 'UNSC Res. 1493' (n. 125) para. 26.
1095 UN OLA (n. 912) 539.
1096 'UNSC Res. 2436' (n. 19) para. 6.
1097 'UNSC Res. 2445' (n. 134) para. 11 (indeed, the UN Security Council 'underline[d] that peacekeepers are authorized to use all necessary means, which includes the use of force when required, in order to protect civilians under threat of physical violence, in accordance with mission mandates, the United Nations Charter and other applicable international law'). See also subsequent resolutions concerning UNISFA: 'UNSC Res. 2469' (2019) UN Doc. S/RES/2469 (2019) para. 12; 'UNSC Res. 2497' (n. 134) para. 13; 'UNSC Res. 2550' (n. 134) para. 12; 'UNSC Res. 2609' (n. 1010) para. 14.
1098 'UNSC Res. 1542' (n. 130) para. 7(I)(f).

necessary measures' to carry out this task.[1099] In contrast, MINUJUSTH, the police mission that replaced MINUSTAH in October 2017, received an explicit authorisation 'to use all necessary means' to protect civilians.[1100] UNMIL is another example of an operation that did not have an explicit mandate 'to take all necessary means'. While acting under Chapter VII of the UN Charter, the UN Security Council decided in Resolution 1509 (2003) that UNMIL shall be mandated to 'protect civilians under imminent threat of physical violence' without giving it an explicit authorisation 'to take all necessary means'.[1101] The question arises whether such PoC mandates can still provide the legal authority to use force to protect civilians.

In 2003, UN Under-Secretary-General for Peace Operations Jean-Marie Guéhenno questioned whether the UN Security Council had authorised UNMIL's peace forces to use armed force in situations other than personal self-defence.[1102] In a Note to the UN Under-Secretary-General of the DPO, the former UN Legal Counsel Hans Corell set out his understanding of UNSC Resolution 1509 (2003).[1103] First, he argued that since the mandate was adopted under Chapter VII of the UN Charter, the UN Security Council expressed its intention to exercise its power under this Chapter.[1104] However, he also stressed that other elements need to be considered to know whether the UN Security Council actually intended to authorise the use of force beyond personal self-defence.[1105] Therefore, the UN Legal Counsel held the following:[1106]

> Whether [...] [the UN Security Council] had done so depends upon the interpretation of the resolution, specifically, on the ordinary and natural meaning which is to be given to its terms when they are read in the context of the resolution as a whole and in the light of its object and purpose, and against the background of the discussion leading to, and the circumstances of, the adoption, in particular the report that the Secretary-General submitted pursuant to resolution 1487 (2003).

According to the UN Legal Counsel, based on an analysis of the wording of Resolution 1509 (2003) and given the history and circumstances of its adoption,

---

1099 See also the subsequent UNSC resolutions that provided MINUSTAH with a PoC mandate: 'UNSC Res. 1944' (n. 981); 'UNSC Res. 2012' (n. 981); 'UNSC Res. 2070' (n. 981); 'UNSC Res. 2119' (n. 981); 'UNSC Res. 2180' (n. 981); 'UNSC Res. 2243' (n. 981); 'UNSC Res. 2313' (n. 981).

1100 'UNSC Res. 2350' (n. 131) para. 12.

1101 'UNSC Res. 1509' (n. 128) pream. para. 23 and para. 3(j). See also subsequent UNSC resolutions that provided UNMIL with a PoC mandate: 'UNSC Res. 2066' (n. 128); 'UNSC Res. 2190' (n. 128); 'UNSC Res. 2239' (n. 128); 'UNSC Res. 2333' (n. 128).

1102 The Permanent Representative of an unidentified State had initially asked the UN Under-Secretary-General for Peace Operations to disclose whether UNMIL was able to use force beyond self-defence, see UN OLA (n. 912) 538–539.

1103 UN OLA (n. 912).

1104 *Ibid.* 539.

1105 *Ibid.*

1106 *Ibid.*

it is clear that the UN Security Council intended to allow UNMIL's peace forces to use force other than for personal self-defence.

In particular, referring to the wording of UNSC Resolution 1509 (2003), the UN Legal Counsel observed that UNMIL would not be able to successfully carry out some of the tasks listed in the Resolution without resorting to armed force beyond self-defence. For example, in para. 3(j) of the relevant Resolution, the UN Security Council mandated UNMIL 'to protect United Nations personnel, facilities, installations, and equipment, ensure the security and freedom of movement of its personnel and, without prejudice to the efforts of the government, to protect civilians under imminent threat of violence, within its capabilities.'[1107] Furthermore, the UN Legal Counsel considered the history and circumstances surrounding the adoption of the Resolution. In 2003, pursuant to UNSC Resolution 1497 (2003), the UN Secretary-General submitted a report on the situation in Liberia in which he made a suggestion for a CONOPS for UNMIL.[1108] The proposed CONOPS stipulated that UNMIL should have 'a robust mandate' that would enable the peace forces 'to take a robust approach, to have the capacity to react adequately to changing circumstances and pre-empt potentially destabilizing events.'[1109] For its part, the UN Security Council reaffirmed the content of the UN Secretary-General's report and welcomed its recommendations.[1110]

Furthermore, Article IV(1) of the 2003 Accra Comprehensive Peace Agreement included the request by the various parties to the UN to install 'a United Nations Chapter VII' force in Liberia to 'support the transitional government and to assist in the implementation of this Agreement.'[1111] Hence, UNMIL's deployment was the UN Security Council's response to that request. The UN Legal Counsel, therefore, concluded that with Resolution 1509 (2003), the UN Security Council sought to authorise UNMIL's peace forces to use force for purposes or in situations other than self-defence.[1112]

Noteworthy, in the debates leading up to the adoption of UNSC Resolution 2333 (2016), Russia abstained in the voting while pointing out that it believed that it was 'unacceptable to extend the mandate [of UNMIL] under Chapter VII of the Charter [...] in circumstances where Blue Helmets are anticipating exclusively peacebuilding tasks.'[1113] Also, the UK abstained from the voting

---

1107 *Ibid.*

1108 *Ibid.*

1109 UNSC, 'Report of the Secretary-General to the Security Council on Liberia' (2003) UN Doc. S/2003/875 para. 57.

1110 'UNSC Res. 1509' (n. 128) pream. para. 19.

1111 'Peace Agreement between the Government of Liberia, the Liberians United for Reconciliation and Democracy, the Movement for Democracy in Liberia and the Political Parties, Annex to the Letter Dated 27 August 2003 from the Permanent Representative of Ghana to the United Nations Addressed to the President of the Security Council' (n. 865).

1112 UN OLA (n. 912) 540.

1113 UNSC, '7851st Meeting (at Which UNSC Res. 2333 (2016) Was Adopted)' (2016) UN Doc. S/PV.7851 3.

because it considered it inappropriate to provide UNMIL with a PoC mandate when there was no active conflict in Liberia, and no reformation of armed groups could be expected any time soon.[1114] Nevertheless, they welcomed 'the inclusion of the human rights promotion and protection mandate [as foreseen in para. 11(c) of UNSC Resolution 2333(2016)], with special attention to continuing violations and abuses committed against children and women.'[1115] Although these insights do not necessarily have an impact on the analysis above, it does give us an indication that not all States necessarily agreed with the mandate that was granted to UNMIL.

We may establish the following when applying the UN Legal Counsel's reasoning to the UNSC resolutions that provide MINUSTAH with a PoC mandate. First, the paragraphs providing the operation's mandate to protect civilians were adopted under Chapter VII of the UN Charter. Second, looking into the ordinary meaning of the terms used in the UNSC resolutions, read in the context of the resolution as a whole and in light of its object and purpose, taking into account the history and circumstances of its adoption, we may establish that the UN Security Council did intend to grant MINUSTAH the authority to use force in situations other than personal self-defence. In the resolutions, the operation is explicitly granted a mandate 'to ensure a secure and stable environment within which the constitutional and political process in Haiti can take place' and 'to protect civilians under imminent threat of physical violence.'[1116] To successfully carry out these tasks, it is quite likely that the use of force beyond personal self-defence is required. In addition, before the adoption of UNSC Resolution 1542 (2004), the UN Secretary-General submitted a report to the UN Security Council in which he gave his recommendation for the operation.[1117] He recommended that the mission should have a 'robust [...] military force' which would operate under 'robust rules of engagement.'[1118] In the resolution itself, the UN Security Council confirmed that MINUSTAH would, *inter alia*, consist of a military component in accordance with the report of the UN Secretary-General.[1119] On a final note, according to Wills, the ROE for the military component of MINUSTAH included an authorisation to use force 'up to and including deadly force in order to put a stop to acts of civil unrest.'[1120]

1114 *Ibid.* 4.

1115 *Ibid.*

1116 'UNSC Res. 1542' (n. 130) para. 7(I)(a) and (f). The PoC mandate was also confirmed in subsequent resolutions: 'UNSC Res. 1944' (n. 981); 'UNSC Res. 2012' (n. 981); 'UNSC Res. 2070' (n. 981); 'UNSC Res. 2119' (n. 981); 'UNSC Res. 2180' (n. 981); 'UNSC Res. 2243' (n. 981); 'UNSC Res. 2313' (n. 981).

1117 UNSC, 'Report of the Secretary-General to the Security Council on Haiti' (2004) UN Doc. S/2004/300.

1118 *Ibid.* paras 73 and 105.

1119 'UNSC Res. 1542' (n. 130) para. 4.

1120 Wills, 'Use of Deadly Force by Peacekeepers Operating Outside of Armed Conflict Situations: What Laws Apply?' (n. 18) 670, fn. 33.

Noteworthy, as was the case for the UNSC resolutions regarding UNMIL, some resolutions providing MINUSTAH with a PoC mandate were criticised by Members of the UN Security Council. During the debates leading up to the adoption of UNSC Resolutions 2119 (2013) and 2180 (2014), the UK stressed, for example, that since there was no military conflict in Haiti in recent times, it was time to hand over the responsibility to maintain security to the government of Haiti.[1121] Nevertheless, in the UN Secretary-General's 2013 report on MINUSTAH, references were still made to robust action taken by MINUSTAH.[1122]

3.2.6. *Interpretation of the terms 'within its capabilities' and 'areas of deployment'*

In most PoC mandates, when mandating the protection of civilians, the UN Security Council adds the general proviso 'within its capabilities and areas of deployment' or some variation thereof.

More specifically, in mandates for UN peace operations, the following similar phrases are used in addition to the phrase 'within its capabilities and areas of deployment':[1123] 'in the areas of deployment of its infantry battalions and as it deems it within its capabilities,'[1124] 'within their zones of operation, using the means available to them,'[1125] 'within its capabilities and its areas of deployment,'[1126] 'within its capacity and in the areas where its armed units are

1121 UNSC, '7040th Meeting (at Which UNSC Res. 2119 (2013) Was Adopted)' (2013) UN Doc. S/PV.7040 2; UNSC, '7277th Meeting (at Which UNSC Res. 2180 (2014) Was Adopted)' (2014) UN Doc. S/PV.7277 3.

1122 UNSC, 'Report of the Secretary-General to the Security Council on the United Nations Stabilization Mission in Haiti' (2013) UN Doc. S/2013/493 para. 12.

1123 UN peace operations' mandates that contain the caveat in this specific wording: 'UNSC Res. 1270' (n. 7) para. 14; 'UNSC Res. 1289' (n. 124) para. 10; 'UNSC Res. 1313' (n. 124) para. 3(c); 'UNSC Res. 1389' (n. 900) para. 2; 'UNSC Res. 1542' (n. 130) para. 7(I)(a); 'UNSC Res. 2000' (n. 129) para. 7(a) (see also para. 8 for a variation on this language); 'UNSC Res. 2112' (n. 129) para. 6(a) (see also para. 7 for a variation on this language); 'UNSC Res. 2149' (n. 19) para. 30(a)(i) (see also para. 29 for a variation on this language); 'UNSC Res. 2162' (n. 129) 19(a) (see also para. 20 for a variation on this language); 'UNSC Res. 2190' (n. 128) para. 10(a)(i); 'UNSC Res. 2217' (n. 140) paras 31 and 32(a)(i); 'UNSC Res. 2226' (n. 129) para. 19(a) (see also para. 20 for a variation on this language); 'UNSC Res. 2239' (n. 128) para. 10(a)(i) (see also para. 16 for a variation on this language); 'UNSC Res. 2277' (n. 127) para. 34; 'UNSC Res. 2281' (n. 1020) para. 2; 'UNSC Res. 2301' (n. 19) paras 32 and 33(a)(i); 'UNSC Res. 2333' (n. 128) para. 11(a)(i); 'UNSC Res. 2387' (n. 19) para. 41; 'UNSC Res. 2410' (n. 1010) para. 15; 'UNSC Res. 2448' (n. 140) para. 38; 'UNSC Res. 2466' (n. 1010) para. 10; 'UNSC Res. 2499' (n. 140) para. 31; 'UNSC Res. 2552' (n. 140) para. 30; 'UNSC Res. 2605' (n. 140) para. 33.

1124 'UNSC Res. 1291' (n. 125) para. 8.

1125 'UNSC Res. 1464' (n. 142) para. 9.

1126 'UNSC Res. 1528' (n. 129) para. 8; 'UNSC Res. 1609' (n. 129) para. 2(k) and 8; 'UNSC Res. 1739' (n. 129) para. 2(k) and 5; 'UNSC Res. 1933' (n. 129) para. 16(b) and 17; 'UNSC Res. 1962' (n. 129) para. 14; 'UNSC Res. 2000' (n. 129) para. 8 (see also para. 7(a) for a variation on this language); 'UNSC Res. 2112' (n. 129) para. 7 (see also para. 6(a) for a variation on

deployed,'[1127] 'in the areas of deployment of its forces and as it deems it within its capabilities,'[1128] 'within its capabilities and in the areas where its armed units are deployed,'[1129] 'in areas of deployment of its forces and as it deems within its capabilities,'[1130] 'within the limits of its capabilities and in its areas of deployment,'[1131] 'within the limits of its capacity and in the areas where its units are deployed,'[1132] 'in the areas of deployment of its forces and as it deems within its capabilities,'[1133] 'within its capabilities and its area of deployment,'[1134] 'within its capabilities and in its areas of deployment,'[1135] 'within its capacities and areas of deployment,'[1136] 'within the limits of its capacities and areas of deployment,'[1137] 'within [the mission's] [...] operational area and existing capabilities,'[1138] 'within its capacity and areas of deployment,'[1139] 'taking into

---

this language); 'UNSC Res. 2149' (n. 19) para. 29 (see also para. 30(a)(i) for a variation on this language); 'UNSC Res. 2162' (n. 129) para. 20 (see also para. 19(a) for a variation on this language); 'UNSC Res. 2164' (n. 19) para. 12; 'UNSC Res. 2226' (n. 129) para. 20 (see also para. 19(a) for a variation on this language); 'UNSC Res. 2227' (n. 19) para. 13; 'UNSC Res. 2284' (n. 129) para. 16 (see also para. 15(a) for a variation on this language); 'UNSC Res. 2295' (n. 34) para. 17; 'UNSC Res. 2364' (n. 19) para. 18; 'UNSC Res. 2423' (n. 34) para. 32.

1127 'UNSC Res. 1545' (n. 132) para. 5; 'UNSC Res. 1565' (n. 125) para. 6. Mandates that include the similar caveat 'in the areas of deployment of its armed units and as it deems it within its capabilities': 'UNSC Res. 1417' (n. 125) para. 7; 'UNSC Res. 1493' (n. 125) para. 25. And last but not least, mandates that include the caveat 'within its capabilities and in the areas where its armed units are deployed': 'UNSC Res. 1592' (n. 125) para. 7; 'UNSC Res. 1649' (n. 125) para. 11.

1128 'UNSC Res. 1590' (n. 133) para. 16(i); 'UNSC Res. 1706' (n. 133) para. 12(a).

1129 'UNSC Res. 1592' (n. 125) para. 7; 'UNSC Res. 1649' (n. 125) para. 11.

1130 'UNSC Res. 1701' (n. 136) para. 12; 'UNSC Res. 2373' (n. 136) para. 14; 'UNSC Res. 2433' (n. 136) para. 19; 'UNSC Res. 2485' (n. 136) para. 20; 'UNSC Res. 2539' (n. 136) para. 21; 'UNSC Res. 2591' (n. 136) para. 22.

1131 'UNSC Res. 1739' (n. 129) para. 2.

1132 'UNSC Res. 1756' (n. 125) para. 4; 'UNSC Res. 1794' (n. 125) para. 5; 'UNSC Res. 1856' (n. 125) para. 5; 'UNSC Res. 1906' (n. 125) para. 6; 'UNSC Res. 1925' (n. 125) para. 11; 'UNSC Res. 1996' (n. 135) para. 4 (see also para. 3(b)(v) for a variation on this language); 'UNSC Res. 2057' (n. 135) para. 5; 'UNSC Res. 2109' (n. 135) para. 8.

1133 'UNSC Res. 1769' (n. 133) para. 15(a).

1134 'UNSC Res. 1990' (n. 134) para. 3.

1135 'UNSC Res. 1996' (n. 135) para. 3(b)(v).

1136 'UNSC Res. 2100' (n. 34) para. 16(c)(i) (see also para. 17 for another variation on this language).

1137 *Ibid.* para. 17 (see also para. 16(c)(i) for another variation on this language).

1138 It is to be mentioned that it is not entirely clear whether the notion of 'within UNISFA's operational area and existing capabilities' in the following mandates of UNISFA refers only to the support of the Joint Border Verification and Monitoring Mechanism (JBVMM) (as provided for in para. 1 of UNSC Resolution 2024 (2011)), or also to the protection of civilians (as provided for in para. 3 of UNSC Resolution 1990 (2011)): 'UNSC Res. 2104' (n. 134) para. 1; 'UNSC Res. 2126' (n. 134) para. 1; 'UNSC Res. 2156' (n. 134) para. 1; 'UNSC Res. 2179' (n. 134) para. 1; 'UNSC Res. 2205' (n. 134) para. 1; 'UNSC Res. 2230' (n. 134) para. 1; 'UNSC Res. 2251' (n. 134) para. 1; 'UNSC Res. 2287' (n. 134) para. 1; 'UNSC Res. 2318' (n. 134) para. 1; 'UNSC Res. 2352' (n. 134) para. 1.

1139 'UNSC Res. 2155' (n. 135) para. 4(a)(i); 'UNSC Res. 2187' (n. 135) para. 4(a)(i); 'UNSC Res. 2223' (n. 19) para. 4(a)(i); 'UNSC Res. 2241' (n. 135) para. 4(a)(i); 'UNSC Res. 2252' (n. 135) para. 8(a)(i); (see also para. 11 for a variation on this language) 'UNSC Res. 2327' (n. 19) para.

account [the mission's] [...] reduced capabilities and areas of deployment,'[1140] or 'within [the mission's] [...] capacity and areas of deployment.'[1141]

In some resolutions, the UN Security Council only refers to one of the two caveats: 'within its capabilities,'[1142] 'consistent with its [...] capabilities,'[1143] or 'within its area of operations.'[1144] In some resolutions, the UN Security Council adds a more specific caveat by, for example, referring to a specific region.[1145]

In UN-mandated peace operation mandates, the following language is used: 'within its means and capabilities [and] in the areas of its deployment,'[1146] 'in the deployment areas of their units,'[1147] 'within its capabilities and its area of operations,'[1148] 'within the limits of their deployment and their capabilities,'[1149] 'within the limits of their deployment and capabilities,'[1150] 'within the limits of their capacities and areas of deployment,'[1151] or 'within [...] the limits of their capacities and areas of deployment.'[1152]

The provisions 'within its capabilities' and 'areas of deployment' are intended to stress the limitations of a mission's ability to protect civilians throughout

7(a)(i); 'UNSC Res. 2406' (n. 19) para. 7(a)(i); 'UNSC Res. 2459' (n. 135) para. 7(a)(i) (see also para. 14 for a variation on this language); 'UNSC Res. 2514' (n. 135) para. 8(a)(i) (see also para. 14 for a variation on this language); 'UNSC Res. 2567' (n. 135) para. 3(a)(i).

1140 'UNSC Res. 2239' (n. 128) para. 16 (see also para. 10(a)(i) for a variation on this language); 'UNSC Res. 2284' (n. 129) para. 15(a) (see also para. 16 for a variation on this language).

1141 'UNSC Res. 2304' (n. 135) para. 5; 'UNSC Res. 2327' (n. 19) para. 11 (see also para. 7(a)(i) for a variation on this language); 'UNSC Res. 2459' (n. 135) para. 14 (see also para. 7(a)(i) for a variation on this language); 'UNSC Res. 2514' (n. 135) para. 14 (see also para. 8(a)(i) for a variation on this language).

1142 'UNSC Res. 1509' (n. 128) para. 3(j).

1143 'UNSC Res. 1870' (n. 133) para. 15.

1144 'UNSC Res. 2098' (n. 19) para. 12(a)(i); 'UNSC Res. 2147' (n. 19) para. 4(a)(i); 'UNSC Res. 2211' (n. 127) para. 9(a); 'UNSC Res. 2277' (n. 127) para. 35(i)(a).

1145 In UNSC Res. 1861 (2009), it is decided that 'MINURCAT shall be authorized to take all necessary measures, within its capabilities and its area of operations in eastern Chad to fulfil [a list of functions] [...]', while in para. 6, it is set forth that MINURCAT operates in both eastern Chad and the north-eastern CAR ('UNSC Res. 1861' (n. 138) paras 6 and 7(a)).

1146 'UNSC Res. 1671' (n. 144) para. 8(b).

1147 'UNSC Res. 1739' (n. 129) para. 8(d).

1148 'UNSC Res. 1778' (n. 145) para. 6(a).

1149 'UNSC Res. 1880' (2009) UN Doc. S/RES/1880 (2009) para. 30; 'UNSC Res. 1911' (n. 1017) para. 20; 'UNSC Res. 1933' (n. 129) para. 24; 'UNSC Res. 1962' (n. 129) para. 17; 'UNSC Res. 2000' (n. 129) para. 17; 'UNSC Res. 2062' (n. 129) para. 14; 'UNSC Res. 2112' (n. 129) para. 21; 'UNSC Res. 2162' (n. 129) para. 28; 'UNSC Res. 2226' (n. 129) para. 28; 'UNSC Res. 2284' (n. 129) para. 25.

1150 'UNSC Res. 1924' (2010) UN Doc. S/RES/1924 (2010) para. 2.

1151 'UNSC Res. 2100' (n. 34) para. 18; 'UNSC Res. 2127' (n. 151) para. 50; 'UNSC Res. 2149' (n. 19) para. 47; 'UNSC Res. 2164' (n. 19) para. 26; 'UNSC Res. 2217' (n. 140) para. 50; 'UNSC Res. 2227' (n. 19) para. 27; 'UNSC Res. 2295' (n. 34) para. 35; 'UNSC Res. 2301' (n. 19) para. 56; 'UNSC Res. 2364' (n. 19) para. 37; 'UNSC Res. 2423' (n. 34) para. 53; 'UNSC Res. 2480' (n. 139) para. 42; 'UNSC Res. 2531' (n. 139) para. 41; 'UNSC Res. 2584' (n. 139) para. 43.

1152 'UNSC Res. 2387' (n. 19) para. 65; 'UNSC Res. 2448' (n. 140) para. 69; 'UNSC Res. 2499' (n. 140) para. 52.

the territory of a host State, mainly if there is an ongoing armed conflict.[1153] UN (mandated) peace operations often have a limited capacity and scope and, therefore, cannot protect every civilian in every place and at every moment.[1154]

The Oxford English Dictionary defines 'area' in the context of 'military operations' as 'an area in which military operations are taking place; spec. one designated for a specific military operation or allocated to a particular unit.'[1155] The OPLAN will usually set out such an area of operations, i.e. a geographical area in which the different units of the mission operate, to which the ROE apply.[1156] The 2019 UN Policy on PoC in UN Peacekeeping further explains that 'areas of deployment' include the following:[1157]

> [T]he area of operational responsibility of any particular unit (civilian or uniformed) of the mission even though that unit may not have established a physical presence in the location concerned.

Units within a mission are only *expected* to protect civilians within their area of operational responsibility (on expectations and lower limits, see further below, Part II, Section 3.3.2).[1158]

Yet, even within its area of deployment, missions are not expected to address all protection threats at all times.[1159] As pointed out by Okimoto, available resources, even in large complex missions involving a large number of troops, are often inadequate when the terrain is vast and rough, logistical problems arise, and the lines of communication are disrupted.[1160] For that reason, the second caveat, 'within its capabilities', is often added. The Oxford English Dictionary defines 'capability' as 'power or ability in general, whether physical or mental; capacity.'[1161] UN (mandated) peace operations often have limited resources and capabilities and may, therefore, face situations where they are not in a position to effectively prevent, stop, or even mitigate certain threats.[1162] Missions must be given the discretion to prioritise those threats with greater potential impact on

---

1153 Khalil, 'Legal Aspects of the Use of Force by United Nations Peacekeepers for the Protection of Civilians' (n. 40) 211–212.

1154 See also UN DPO, '2020 UN Handbook on PoC in UN Peacekeeping' (n. 35) 8.

1155 'Area, n.', www.oed.com, accessed 18 May 2022, P2.

1156 Alan Cole and others (eds), *Sanremo Handbook on Rules of Engagement* (International Institute of Humanitarian Law 2009) 7.

1157 UN DPO, '2019 UN Policy on PoC in UN Peacekeeping' (n. 35) para. 25.

1158 *Ibid.*

1159 UN DPKO and UN DFS, '2015 UN Implementing Guidelines for Military Components of UN Peacekeeping Missions on PoC' (n. 103) 25.

1160 UN DPKO and UN DFS, 'United Nations Comprehensive Protection of Civilians Training Materials for United Nations Peacekeeping Operations. Military Version' (n. 1075) 190.

1161 'Capability, n.', www.oed.com, accessed 18 May 2022, 2.

1162 UN DPO, '2019 UN Policy on PoC in UN Peacekeeping' (n. 35) para. 24.

civilians or a greater destabilising effect and allocate resources accordingly.[1163] They must also be given the discretion to assess whether they are appropriately equipped to engage in certain actions.

This discretion does not prevent an emerging lower limit for what UN (mandated) peace operations must do to protect civilians. The caveat 'within its capabilities and areas of deployment' cannot be used as an excuse for inaction.[1164] Even though UN peace operations usually have limited physical presence and resources, the UN nonetheless recognises that 'missions must always prevent and respond, if possible, to threats of physical violence against civilians where they have the capability to do so effectively' and '[a]t the strategic/operational level, missions must be prepared to re-deploy resources within the mission area to prevent or respond to threats to civilians even if the mission does not have presence in the area of concern.'[1165] To this end, missions must use correct threat and vulnerability assessments and coherent operational planning to deploy existing assets to maximise their protective effect on the civilian population at risk.[1166] A discussion of the obligations that may arise from a mandate is presented in Part II, Section 3.3.2.

3.2.7. *Interpretation of the terms 'primary responsibility of host State'*

Most PoC mandates explicitly refer to the 'primary responsibility of the host government or the host authorities' for the protection of civilians.

While the first set of PoC mandates issued to UNAMSIL (the very first operation with a PoC mandate) included the authorisation to take the necessary action to protect civilians, 'taking into account the responsibilities of the Government of Sierra Leone'[1167] or 'to assist the Government of Sierra Leone,'[1168] subsequent PoC mandates issued to UN peace operations usually contain the caveat without prejudice to 'the responsibility of [the host government],'[1169] 'the

1163 UN DPKO and UN DFS, '2015 UN Implementing Guidelines for Military Components of UN Peacekeeping Missions on PoC' (n. 103) 25; UN DPO, '2019 UN Policy on PoC in UN Peacekeeping' (n. 35) para. 24.

1164 UN DPKO and UN DFS, 'United Nations Comprehensive Protection of Civilians Training Materials for United Nations Peacekeeping Operations. Military Version' (n. 1075) 190–191.

1165 UN DPO, '2019 UN Policy on PoC in UN Peacekeeping' (n. 35) para. 25.

1166 UN DPKO and UN DFS, '2015 UN Implementing Guidelines for Military Components of UN Peacekeeping Missions on PoC' (n. 103) 25.

1167 'UNSC Res. 1270' (n. 7) 14; 'UNSC Res. 1289' (n. 124) para. 10; 'UNSC Res. 1389' (n. 900) para. 2; 'UNSC Res. 2591' (n. 136) para. 22.

1168 'UNSC Res. 1313' (n. 124).

1169 'UNSC Res. 1528' (n. 129) para. 6(i); 'UNSC Res. 1545' (n. 132) para. 5; 'UNSC Res. 1590' (n. 133) para. 16(i); 'UNSC Res. 1609' (n. 129) para. 2(k); 'UNSC Res. 1701' (n. 136) para. 12; 'UNSC Res. 1706' (n. 133) para. 12(a); 'UNSC Res. 1739' (n. 129) para. 2(f); 'UNSC Res. 1769' (n. 133) para. 2(f); 'UNSC Res. 2373' (n. 136) para. 14; 'UNSC Res. 2433' (n. 136) para. 19; 'UNSC Res. 2485' (n. 136) para. 20; 'UNSC Res. 2539' (n. 136) para. 21.

primary responsibility of [the host government],'[1170] or 'the primary responsibility of [the relevant authorities].'[1171] A number of PoC mandates use slightly different wording by referring to 'the responsibilities of the [host transitional authorities] [...] and [police authorities],'[1172] 'the responsibilities of [the host authorities],'[1173] 'the responsibility of the [host] transitional authorities,'[1174] 'the responsibility of [the host authorities],'[1175] or 'primary and ultimate responsibility [of the host government].'[1176] In a number of PoC mandates, that responsibility is (also) referred to in the preamble as: 'primary responsibility of [the host government],'[1177] 'all the parties bear responsibility,'[1178] '[the host authorities] have primary responsibility,'[1179] '[the host government] bears primary responsibility,'[1180] or '[the host government] bears the primary responsibility.'[1181]

1170 'UNSC Res. 2003' (n. 137) para. 5; 'UNSC Res. 2063' (n. 137) para. 4; 'UNSC Res. 2113' (n. 137) para. 5; 'UNSC Res. 2173' (n. 137) para. 9; 'UNSC Res. 2228' (n. 19) para. 5; 'UNSC Res. 2525' (n. 137) para. 4.

1171 'UNSC Res. 1933' (n. 129) para. 16(b); 'UNSC Res. 2000' (n. 129) para. 7(a); 'UNSC Res. 2100' (n. 34) para. 24 (see also para. 16(c)(i) of UNSC Res. 2100 (2013) as mentioned above); 'UNSC Res. 2112' (n. 129) para. 6(a); 'UNSC Res. 2149' (n. 19) para. 30(a)(i); 'UNSC Res. 2162' (n. 129) para. 19(a); 'UNSC Res. 2190' (n. 128) para. 10(a)(i); 'UNSC Res. 2217' (n. 140) para. 32(a)(i); 'UNSC Res. 2226' (n. 129) para. 19(a); 'UNSC Res. 2227' (n. 19) para. 14(d)(i); 'UNSC Res. 2239' (n. 128) para. 10(a)(i); 'UNSC Res. 2295' (n. 34) para. 19(c)(i); 'UNSC Res. 2301' (n. 19) para. 33(a)(i); 'UNSC Res. 2333' (n. 128) para. 11(a)(i); 'UNSC Res. 2363' (n. 19) para. 15(a)(i); 'UNSC Res. 2364' (n. 19) para. 20(c)(i); 'UNSC Res. 2387' (n. 19) para. 42(a)(i); 'UNSC Res. 2423' (n. 34) para. 38(d)(i); 'UNSC Res. 2448' (n. 140) para. 39(a)(i); 'UNSC Res. 2480' (n. 139) para. 28(c)(i); 'UNSC Res. 2499' (n. 140) para. 32(a)(i); 'UNSC Res. 2531' (n. 139) para. 28(c)(i); 'UNSC Res. 2552' (n. 140) para. 31(a)(i); 'UNSC Res. 2584' (n. 139) para. 30(c)(i); 'UNSC Res. 2605' (n. 140) para. 34(a)(i).

1172 'UNSC Res. 1542' (n. 130) para. 5.

1173 'UNSC Res. 1990' (n. 134) para. 3(d). UN Security Council Resolution 1996 (2011) is somewhat ambiguous in this regard, but when one reads the resolution in its entirety, it is clear that the purpose of the UN Security Council is also to point out the primary responsibility of the host State to protect its civilians, see 'UNSC Res. 1996' (n. 135) para. 3(b) and 3(b)(v); 'UNSC Res. 2480' (n. 139) para. 16; 'UNSC Res. 2609' (n. 1010) para. 14.

1174 'UNSC Res. 2100' (n. 34) para. 16(c)(i) (see also para. 24 which stresses again that the 'transitional authorities of Mali have primary responsibility to protect civilians').

1175 'UNSC Res. 2164' (n. 19) para. 13(a)(ii).

1176 'UNSC Res. 2066' (n. 128) para. 2.

1177 'UNSC Res. 1756' (n. 125) pream. para. 5; 'UNSC Res. 1794' (n. 125) pream. para. 6; 'UNSC Res. 1856' (n. 125) pream. para. 4; 'UNSC Res. 1861' (n. 138) pream. para. 12; 'UNSC Res. 1906' (n. 125) pream. para. 4; 'UNSC Res. 1925' (n. 125) pream. para. 5; 'UNSC Res. 1991' (n. 126) pream. para. 4; 'UNSC Res. 2053' (n. 126) pream. para. 4; 'UNSC Res. 2062' (n. 129) pream. para. 16; 'UNSC Res. 2147' (n. 19) pream. para. 5; 'UNSC Res. 2327' (n. 19) pream. para. 14.

1178 'UNSC Res. 1565' (n. 125) pream. para. 6.

1179 'UNSC Res. 2531' (n. 139) pream. para. 3; 'UNSC Res. 2584' (n. 139) para. 14.

1180 'UNSC Res. 2000' (n. 129) pream. para. 9 (see also para. 7(a)); 'UNSC Res. 2112' (n. 129) pream. para. 8 (see also para. 6(a)); 'UNSC Res. 2098' (n. 19) pream. para. 25; 'UNSC Res. 2284' (n. 129) pream. para. 6.

1181 'UNSC Res. 2155' (n. 135) pream. para. 6; 'UNSC Res. 2187' (n. 135) pream. para. 6; 'UNSC Res. 2211' (n. 127) pream. para. 5; 'UNSC Res. 2223' (n. 19) pream. para. 7; 'UNSC Res. 2277' (n. 127) pream. para. 5; 'UNSC Res. 2296' (n. 137) pream. para. 9; 'UNSC Res. 2304' (n. 135) pream. para. 9; 'UNSC Res. 2348' (n. 127) pream. para. 5; 'UNSC Res. 2409' (n. 19) pream.

Several PoC mandates do not explicitly refer to the (primary) responsibility of the host State.[1182] In some cases, the relevant UNSC Resolution essentially extends the existing mandate and tries to keep it 'short'. In other cases, the PoC mandate instead refers to the fact that the mission in question is 'to assist,'[1183] or 'to continue assisting,'[1184] or must act '[i]n support of'[1185] the host State's government or the relevant authorities or more specifically the State's armed forces.[1186] Other variations include that the host State must protect civilians 'with the continued support'[1187] of the mission in question or that the mission works 'in close cooperation'[1188] or 'in liaison'[1189] with the host State's government or is

---

para. 5; 'UNSC Res. 2429' (n. 137) pream. para. 17; 'UNSC Res. 2241' (n. 135) pream. para. 11; 'UNSC Res. 2252' (n. 135) pream. para. 16; 'UNSC Res. 2327' (n. 19) pream. para. 14; 'UNSC Res. 2459' (n. 135) pream. para. 20; 'UNSC Res. 2465' (2019) UN Doc. S/RES/2465 (2019) pream. para. 7; 'UNSC Res. 2502' (n. 127) pream. para. 5; 'UNSC Res. 2514' (n. 135) pream. para. 22; 'UNSC Res. 2556' (n. 127) pream. para. 5; 'UNSC Res. 2567' (n. 135) pream. para. 17; 'UNSC Res. 2612' (n. 49) pream. para. 5 (It is noteworthy that whereas the UN Security Council, in Resolutions 2155 (2014), 2187 (2014), 2223 (2015), 2348 (2017), 2429 (2018), 2556 (2020), and 2612 (2021) gives a number of examples of crimes by stating that the host government 'bears the primary responsibility to protect civilians within its territory and subject to its jurisdiction, including from potential crimes against humanity and war crimes' [or small variations thereupon], the UN Security Council in the resolutions 2211 (2015), 2241 (2015), 2252 (2016), 2327 (2016), 2406 (2018), 2409 (2018), 2429 (2018), 2465 (2019), 2502 (2019), 2514 (2020), and 2567 (2021) seems to refer exclusively to such crimes: the host government 'bears the primary responsibility to protect its populations from crimes against humanity, war crimes, ethnic cleansing, and genocide' [or variations thereupon]).

1182 'UNSC Res. 1291' (n. 125); 'UNSC Res. 1417' (n. 125); 'UNSC Res. 1493' (n. 125); 'UNSC Res. 1509' (n. 128); 'UNSC Res. 1565' (n. 125); 'UNSC Res. 1592' (n. 125); 'UNSC Res. 1649' (n. 125); 'UNSC Res. 1856' (n. 125); 'UNSC Res. 1870' (n. 133); 'UNSC Res. 1919' (n. 133); 'UNSC Res. 1935' (n. 137); 'UNSC Res. 1944' (n. 981); 'UNSC Res. 2053' (n. 126); 'UNSC Res. 2057' (n. 135); 'UNSC Res. 2104' (n. 134); 'UNSC Res. 2119' (n. 981); 'UNSC Res. 2126' (n. 134); 'UNSC Res. 2156' (n. 134); 'UNSC Res. 2179' (n. 134); 'UNSC Res. 2180' (n. 981); 'UNSC Res. 2205' (n. 134); 'UNSC Res. 2230' (n. 134); 'UNSC Res. 2243' (n. 981); 'UNSC Res. 2251' (n. 134); 'UNSC Res. 2287' (n. 134); 'UNSC Res. 2313' (n. 981); 'UNSC Res. 2318' (n. 134); 'UNSC Res. 2352' (n. 134); 'UNSC Res. 2386' (n. 134); 'UNSC Res. 2416' (n. 134); 'UNSC Res. 2445' (n. 134); 'UNSC Res. 2495' (n. 137); 'UNSC Res. 2497' (n. 134); 'UNSC Res. 2550' (n. 134); 'UNSC Res. 2575' (2021) UN Doc. S/RES/2575 (2021).

1183 'UNSC Res. 1756' (n. 125) para. 2.

1184 'UNSC Res. 1944' (n. 981) para. 12; 'UNSC Res. 2119' (n. 981) para. 19; 'UNSC Res. 2180' (n. 981) para. 22; 'UNSC Res. 2243' (n. 981) para. 27; 'UNSC Res. 2313' (n. 981) para. 30.

1185 'UNSC Res. 2480' (n. 139) para. 28(c)(ii).

1186 'UNSC Res. 1794' (n. 125) para. 5; 'UNSC Res. 2284' (n. 129) para. 15(a) ('To support the Ivorian security forces to protect civilians').

1187 'UNSC Res. 1962' (n. 129) (see also pream. para. 6 in which a reference is made to the 'primary responsibility' of the Ivorian leaders 'for ensuring peace and protecting the civilian population in Côte d'Ivoire'); 'UNSC Res. 2062' (n. 129) (similar to UNSC Resolution 1962 (2010), this resolution makes a reference to the primary responsibility of the host State in the preamble, see pream. para. 10).

1188 'UNSC Res. 1856' (n. 125) para. 3; 'UNSC Res. 1906' (n. 125) para. 5.

1189 'UNSC Res. 1861' (n. 138) para. 7(a).

'assisting,'[1190] 'supporting,'[1191] or is 'to continue to support'[1192] the host State's government in protecting civilians (as discussed further below). Eventually, however, at some point, every UN peace operation receives a mandate that includes the caveat on the primary responsibility of the host State's government.

In PoC mandates granted to UN-mandated peace operations, similar references are made to the primary responsibility of the host government. These references include: 'without prejudice to the responsibilities of [the host government],'[1193] 'without prejudice to the responsibility of [the host government],'[1194] '[the host governments] bear primary responsibility,'[1195] 'the responsibility of the [host authorities],'[1196] '[the host authorities'] primary responsibility,'[1197] '[host] transitional authorities [...] have primary responsibility,'[1198] or '[host transitional authorities] have the primary responsibility.'[1199] In one PoC mandate, the UN Security Council, while not referring to the primary responsibility of the host government, did authorise it '[to] [c]ontribute to the safety of the civilian population.'[1200]

The reference to the primary responsibility of the government and/or authorities to protect its people invokes the RtoP benchmark (Pillar One of RtoP: 'The protection responsibilities of the State').[1201] It is widely recognised that, by virtue of its sovereignty and as an attribute of statehood, a State has the primary responsibility for the protection of its own population.[1202] Through PoC mandates, the international community can assist States in fulfilling that primary responsibility.[1203] Therefore, some PoC mandates include language on

---

1190 'UNSC Res. 1944' (n. 981) para. 12; 'UNSC Res. 2012' (n. 981) para. 15.

1191 'UNSC Res. 2062' (n. 129) para. 2.

1192 'UNSC Res. 2066' (n. 128) para. 2.

1193 'UNSC Res. 1464' (n. 142) para. 9.

1194 'UNSC Res. 1671' (n. 144) para. 8(b). In the following PoC mandates, the reference to the primary responsibility of the host government is made when discussing the mandate of the UN peace operation that is deployed simultaneously: 'UNSC Res. 1528' (n. 129) para. 6(j); 'UNSC Res. 1609' (n. 129) para. 2(k); 'UNSC Res. 1739' (n. 129) para. 2(f); 'UNSC Res. 1769' (n. 133) para. 2(f).

1195 'UNSC Res. 1778' (n. 145) pream. para. 6; 'UNSC Res. 1861' (n. 138) pream. para. 12.

1196 'UNSC Res. 1973' (n. 62) pream. para. 5.

1197 'UNSC Res. 2085' (n. 148) para. 9(d); 'UNSC Res. 2295' (n. 34) para. 38; 'UNSC Res. 2364' (n. 19) para. 40.

1198 'UNSC Res. 2100' (n. 34) para. 24.

1199 'UNSC Res. 2127' (n. 151) pream. para. 13 (see also para. 21).

1200 'UNSC Res. 1484' (n. 143) para. 1.

1201 On Pillar One, see UNSG, 'Report of the Secretary-General on Implementing the Responsibility to Protect' (2009) UN Doc. A/63/677 10–14. See also Nicholas Tsagourias, 'Self-Defence, Protection of Humanitarian Values, and the Doctrine of Impartiality and Neutrality in Enforcement Mandates' in Marc Weller, Alexia Solomou and Jake William Rylatt (eds), *The Oxford Handbook of the Use of Force in International Law* (1st edn., Oxford University Press 2015) 411–412.

1202 ICISS (n. 113) xi; UNSG, 'Report of the Secretary-General on Implementing the Responsibility to Protect' (n. 1201) para. 14.

1203 Sheeran and Kent (n. 50) 50.

certain tasks being 'in support of' the host State. For example, in Resolution 2480 (2019), the UN Security Council decides that MINUSMA '[i]n support of the Malian authorities, [is] to take active steps to anticipate, deter and effectively respond to threats to the civilian population.'[1204] However, in reaffirming that the government and/or the authorities of the host State bear the primary responsibility for the protection of civilians, the UN Security Council seeks to confirm that a PoC mandate, while intended to assist the government and/or the authorities of the host State, does not relieve the government and/or the authorities of its primary responsibility for the well-being and safety of persons on its territory.[1205]

When the host State is unable or unwilling to protect its population, UN (mandated) peace operations can act independently and even take military action against members of the State's own armed forces if they pose a threat of physical violence against civilians.[1206] One of UNMISS' PoC mandates, for example, explicitly mentions that UNMISS must protect civilians 'in particular when […] [the host government] is not providing such security.'[1207] Moreover, some PoC mandates explicitly state that the PoC mandate applies 'irrespective of the source of such violence', including the use of force against elements of the State's armed forces if and when they pose a threat of physical violence against civilians. The first explicit reference to 'irrespective of the source of such violence' appeared in UNSC Resolution 2104 (2013), underscoring that UNISFA's PoC mandate includes 'taking the necessary actions to protect civilians under imminent threat of physical violence, irrespective of the source of such violence.'[1208] That same year, the UN Security Council also included the notion of 'irrespective of the source of such violence' in UNMISS' mandate.[1209] In addition, a number of MONUC, MONUSCO, and the Intervention Brigade's

---

1204 'UNSC Res. 2480' (n. 139) 28(c)(ii). See also 'UNSC Res. 2531' (n. 139) 28(c)(ii); 'UNSC Res. 2584' (n. 139) para. 30(c)(ii). For variations, see Part II, Section 3.2.7.

1205 Khalil, 'Legal Aspects of the Use of Force by United Nations Peacekeepers for the Protection of Civilians' (n. 40) 212.

1206 UN DPO, '2019 UN Policy on PoC in UN Peacekeeping' (n. 35) para. 29. See also Khalil, 'Legal Aspects of the Use of Force by United Nations Peacekeepers for the Protection of Civilians' (n. 40) 212.

1207 'UNSC Res. 1996' (n. 135) para. 3(b)(v).

1208 'UNSC Res. 2104' (n. 134) para. 4. See also the subsequent mandates containing the words 'irrespective of the source of such violence': 'UNSC Res. 2126' (n. 134) para. 5; 'UNSC Res. 2179' (n. 134) para. 8; 'UNSC Res. 2205' (n. 134) para. 9; 'UNSC Res. 2230' (n. 134) para. 10; 'UNSC Res. 2251' (n. 134) para. 9; 'UNSC Res. 2287' (n. 134) para. 9; 'UNSC Res. 2318' (n. 134) para. 9; 'UNSC Res. 2352' (n. 134) para. 11; 'UNSC Res. 2416' (n. 134) para. 10; 'UNSC Res. 2445' (n. 134) para. 11; 'UNSC Res. 2459' (n. 135) para. 7(a)(i); 'UNSC Res. 2497' (n. 134) para. 13; 'UNSC Res. 2550' (n. 134) para. 12; 'UNSC Res. 2609' (n. 1010) para. 14.

1209 'UNSC Res. 2109' (n. 135) para. 4. See also subsequent mandates: 'UNSC Res. 2155' (n. 135) para. 4(a)(i); 'UNSC Res. 2187' (n. 135) para. 4(a)(i); 'UNSC Res. 2223' (n. 19) para. 4(a)(i); 'UNSC Res. 2241' (n. 135) para. 4(a)(i); 'UNSC Res. 2252' (n. 135) para. 8(a)(i); 'UNSC Res. 2327' (n. 19) para. 7(a)(i); 'UNSC Res. 2406' (n. 19) para. 7(a)(i); 'UNSC Res. 2514' (n. 135) para. 8(a)(i); 'UNSC Res. 2567' (n. 135) para. 3(a)(i).

mandates refer to 'violence emanating from any of the parties engaged in the conflict'[1210] or 'violence emerging from any of the parties engaged in the conflict.'[1211]

3.3. UPPER OR LOWER LIMITS TO WHAT UN (MANDATED) PEACE OPERATIONS MAY OR MUST LAWFULLY DO TO PROTECT CIVILIANS

PoC language is often vague, but this seems inevitable given that the alternative is a mandate to only use specific means (as opposed to general objectives), which may be wholly inappropriate in certain cases. As discussed earlier, the UN Security Council, in principle, determines the general objectives that are to be carried out by armed forces.[1212] Although the strategic leadership has oversight over the general course of the military operation, it is not its task to translate the overall mission strategy and operational concepts into concrete military orders and directives. UN (mandated) peace operations are planned and executed at the operational level to achieve the general objectives set out by the strategic level.[1213] Ultimately, the operation is carried out at the tactical level to promote or achieve the objectives set by the operational level.[1214] Therefore, it is up to the relevant actors at the operational or tactical level to assess what means need to be taken to promote the more general objectives set out in the mandate. Consequently, it is not necessarily problematic that the language used in PoC mandates is vague.

What is problematic is that there is uncertainty and discussion about the limits to the use of force in implementing PoC mandates. After all, the formula 'to use all necessary means to protect civilians against the (imminent) threat of physical violence' cannot be regarded as a blank cheque to use any amount of force or as a mere authorisation to which there are no expectations attached. There are limits to the scope of action of UN (mandated) peace operations. To that end, the next Section first discusses the extent to which there is an upper limit to actions that UN (mandated) peace operations may lawfully undertake to protect civilians (Section 3.3.1). Hereafter, Section 3.3.2 discusses the extent to

1210 'UNSC Res. 1856' (n. 125) para. 3(a); 'UNSC Res. 1925' (n. 125) para. 12(a).

1211 'UNSC Res. 2098' (n. 19) para. 12(a)(i); 'UNSC Res. 2147' (n. 19) para. 4(a)(i); 'UNSC Res. 2211' (n. 127) para. 9(a); 'UNSC Res. 2277' (n. 127) para. 35(i)(a); 'UNSC Res. 2348' (n. 127) para. 34(i)(a); 'UNSC Res. 2409' (n. 19) para. 36(i)(a); 'UNSC Res. 2463' (n. 127) para. 29(i)(a).

1212 See discussion of levels of authority, command, and control in UN (mandated) peace operations, Part I, Section 4.2.2.

1213 Boddens Hosang, *Rules of Engagement and the International Law of Military Operations* (n. 559) 68.

1214 Johan FR Boddens Hosang, 'Rules of Engagement. Rules on the Use of Force as Linchpin for the International Law of Military Operations' (DPhil thesis, University of Amsterdam 2017) 77.

which there is an emerging lower limit for what UN (mandated) peace operations must lawfully do to protect civilians.

3.3.1. *Upper limit to what UN (mandated) peace operations may lawfully do to protect civilians*

3.3.1.1. *Jus cogens* limiting any use of force

As explained above, *jus cogens* or peremptory norms of international law are higher rules of public international law that protect those values and interests that are fundamentally important to the international community as a whole.[1215] These core rules are binding upon all subjects of international law they address, including States, international organisations, their subsidiary organs, and individuals, and can neither be derogated from nor be waived.[1216] Article 24(2) of the UN Charter requires the UN Security Council to comply with the UN's purposes and principles. The ordinary meaning of Article 24(2) of the UN Charter dictates compliance with *jus cogens* as the necessary condition for a valid action by the UN Security Council.[1217] The UN Security Council, in turn, cannot delegate more powers than they themselves possess. Simultaneously, as discussed below, peace forces carrying out an operation must abide by the applicable rules and principles of HRL and IHL as a matter of treaty or customary law, including applicable norms of *jus cogens*. Therefore, an authorisation to use 'all necessary means' must be implemented to be compatible with *jus cogens*. For example, the force used in the execution of a PoC mandate may not constitute a violation of the right to life or a violation of the fundamental principles of IHL.[1218]

1215 See Part I, Section 4.1.1.2(A) and Part II, Section 2.1.1. See also Orakhelashvili, 'The Impact of Peremptory Norms on the Interpretation and Application of United Nations Security Council Resolutions' (n. 616) 62.

1216 The ECJ, e.g. ruled that *jus cogens* is binding on all subjects of international law, see *Yassin Abdullah Kadi v. Council of the European Union and Commission of the European Communities, Judgment* (2005) ECJ Case T-315/01, ECR II-3649 paras 226–230.

1217 ILC, 'Report of the International Law Commission on the Work of Its Fifty-Eight Session (1 May–9 June and 3 July–11 August 2006), UN General Assembly Official Records, Sixty-First Session, Supplement No. 10' UN Doc A/61/10 422, para. 40; Gill, 'Legal and Some Political Limitations on the Power of the UN Security Council to Exercise Its Enforcement Powers under Chapter VII of the Charter' (n. 892) 79 and 89; Gill, 'Legal Aspects of the Transfer of Authority in UN Peace Operations' (n. 723) 59; Orakhelashvili, 'The Impact of Peremptory Norms on the Interpretation and Application of United Nations Security Council Resolutions' (n. 616) 67. On *jus cogens* as a substantive limit to Security Council decisions, see also de Wet (n. 892) 187–191; ILC, 'Fragmentation of International Law: Difficulties Arising from the Diversification and Expansion of International Law, Report of the Study Group of the International Law Commission, Finalized by Martti Koskenniemi' (n. 616) 176–178, paras 346–350; Peters (n. 892) 852–853.

1218 For sources defending the claim that the right to life is a *jus cogens* norm, see Part III, Section 2.1.2.2, fn. 1397, as regards the peremptory nature of the fundamental principles of IHL, see Part III, Section 2.2.3.2.

In the event of a conflict between a UNSC resolution and a norm of *jus cogens*, the peremptory norm will prevail.[1219] This means that Article 103 of the UN Charter – which provides that where there is a conflict between the obligations of the UN Member States under the UN Charter and their obligations under other international agreements, the obligations under the UN Charter shall prevail – cannot be invoked to justify a breach of a peremptory norm of international law.[1220]

3.3.1.2. Principles of necessity and proportionality limiting the overall levels of force used

Some scholars argue that the principles of necessity and proportionality (or at least one of the two) apply to the use of force under Chapter VII of the UN Charter.[1221] In doing so, they do not always make the distinction between

---

1219 See *Case Concerning Application of the Convention on the Prevention and Punishment of the Crime of Genocide (Bosnia and Herzegovina v. Yugoslavia (Serbia and Montenegro), Order, Separate opinion of Judge Sir Lauterpacht* (1993) 1993 ICJ Rep 407 (ICJ) 440, para. 100 (Judge Lauterpacht argued the following: 'The concept of *jus cogens* operates as a concept superior to both customary international law and treaty. The relief which Art. 103 of the Charter may give the Security Council in case of conflict between one of its decisions and an operative treaty obligation cannot – as a matter of simple hierarchy of norms – extend to a conflict between a Security Council resolution and *jus cogens*. Indeed, one only has to state the opposite proposition thus – that a Security Council resolution may even require participation in genocide – for its unacceptability to be apparent'). See also case law as referred to by Johann Ruben Leiæ and Andreas Paulus, 'Chapter XVI. Miscellaneous Provisions, Article 103' in Bruno Simma and others (eds), *The Charter of the United Nations: a Commentary*, vol. II (3rd. edn., Oxford University Press 2012) 2119, fn. 53.

1220 *Case Concerning Application of the Convention on the Prevention and Punishment of the Crime of Genocide (Bosnia and Herzegovina v. Yugoslavia (Serbia and Montenegro)), Order, Separate opinion of Judge Sir Lauterpacht* (n. 1219) para. 100. See also Matthias J Herdegen, 'The Constitutionalization of the UN Security System' (1994) 27 Vanderbilt Journal of Transnational Law 135, 156; Rain Liivoja, 'The Scope of the Supremacy Clause of the United Nations Charter' (2008) 57 International and Comparative Law Quarterly 583, 610; Aurel Sari, 'The Al-Jedda Case Before the House of Lords' (2009) 13 Journal of International Peacekeeping 181, 189–190; Alix Toublanc, 'L'article 103 et La Valeur Juridique de La Charte Des Nations Unies' (2004) 108 Revue générale de droit international public 439, 446–450. For a more detailed discussion of Art. 103 of the UN Charter, see Part III, Section 3.3.2.1(B).

1221 See e.g. Olivier Corten, 'Necessity' in Marc Weller, Alexia Solomou and Jake William Rylatt (eds), *The Oxford Handbook of the Use of Force in International Law* (1st edn., Oxford University Press 2015) 876–877; Judith G Gardam, *Necessity, Proportionality, and the Use of Force by States* (Cambridge University Press 2004) 6–7, 12, 199–212; Judith G Gardam, 'Legal Restraints on Security Council Military Enforcement Action' (1996) 17 Michigan Journal of International Law 285, 305–312; Christopher Greenwood, 'Self-Defence and the Conduct of International Armed Conflict' in Shabtai Rosenne, Yoram Dinstein and Mala Tabory (eds), *International Law at a Time of Perplexity: Essays in Honour of Shabtai Rosenne* (Martinus Nijhoff Publishers 1989) 274, fn. 9; Lehmann (n. 14) 132–133; Krisch (n. 588) 1265 (referring only to the principle of proportionality, though); Keiichiro Okimoto, *The Distinction and Relationship between Jus Ad Bellum and Jus in Bello*, vol. 33 (Hart 2011) 179–180; Papastavridis (n. 888) 110–111; Dan Sarooshi, *The United Nations and the Development of*

the argument that the UN Security Council is restrained in its powers when deciding to act under Chapter VII of the UN Charter and the argument that the strategic leadership must ensure that Chapter VII mandates are implemented in a necessary and proportionate manner. The arguments for applying the principles of necessity and proportionality to Chapter VII actions also differ. For example, some argue that the principles are intrinsic to regulating the use of force in international law.[1222] On the other hand, since the principles apply to the use of force in national self-defence, some suggest that they should also apply to the use of force under Chapter VII of the UN Charter.[1223] Other arguments include the reference in Article 1(1) of the UN Charter to 'principles of justice and international law,' which ought to include the principles of necessity and proportionality;[1224] the inclusion in Articles 40 and 42 of the UN Charter of the words 'as it deems necessary' or 'as may be necessary' referring to the principle of necessity;[1225] or that the principle of proportionality is enshrined in the UN Charter because it favours the pacific settlement of disputes.[1226] Finally, the principles are often interpreted differently. Whereas Corten argues, for example, that necessity is to be interpreted less strictly in the context of the use of force under Chapter VII of the UN Charter,[1227] Traoré defends the opposite.[1228]

A distinction needs to be made between the question of whether the UN Security Council is restrained in its powers when deciding to act under Chapter VII of the UN Charter and the question of whether the principles of necessity and proportionality apply to the overall implementation of mandates adopted by the UN Security Council. Although the first question provides an interesting debate,[1229] this study only addresses the latter question.

As discussed above, there are two exceptions to the general prohibition of the threat or use of force, including self-defence and Chapter VII enforcement action.[1230] Whether the response to an armed attack constitutes a lawful exercise of the right to self-defence depends on whether the measures taken in

Collective Security: The Delegation by the UN Security Council of Its Chapter VII Powers (Repr, Oxford University Press 1999) 159; Traoré (n. 1063) 499–514.

1222 See e.g. Papastavridis (n. 888) 110; Gardam, 'Legal Restraints on Security Council Military Enforcement Action' (n. 1221) 306; Geoffrey R Watson, 'Constitutionalism, Judicial Review, and the World Court' (1993) 34 Harvard International Law Journal 1, 38.

1223 See e.g. Greenwood, 'Self-Defence and the Conduct of International Armed Conflict' (n. 1220) 274, fn. 9.

1224 See e.g. Lehmann (n. 14) 132–133; Gardam, *Necessity, Proportionality, and the Use of Force by States* (n. 1221) 206–207.

1225 See e.g. Lehmann (n. 14) 132–133; Papastavridis (n. 888) 110; Gardam, *Necessity, Proportionality, and the Use of Force by States* (n. 1221) 6–7.

1226 See e.g. Lehmann (n. 14) 132; Papastavridis (n. 888) 110.

1227 Corten (n. 1221) 877.

1228 Traoré (n. 1063) 500–501.

1229 For literature on the limits to the powers of the UN Security Council, see Part II, Section 3.2.1, fn. 892.

1230 See Part I, Section 4.1.1.2(A).

self-defence comply with the principles of necessity and proportionality.[1231] Pursuant to these principles, the inherent right to self-defence is limited to repelling an armed attack and may never lead to retaliatory, repressive, or purely offensive actions.[1232] Now, just as the use of force in self-defence is limited, so is the use of force based on a Chapter VII mandate. The principles of necessity and proportionality are found in different areas of both national and international law and are inherent in any system of use of force. If the UN Security Council adopts a resolution under Chapter VII of the UN Charter, this mandate should be implemented according to the principles of necessity and proportionality.[1233] If force is used beyond the scope of the UNSC mandate, the conduct of the relevant operation in the territory of a State can no longer be considered a legally acceptable exception to the general prohibition of the use of force. Instead, it becomes a wrongful act under international law.

What if the host State consented to the deployment of an operation on its territory to pursue certain objectives? In this case, the overall means used to implement the objectives agreed to by the State must be necessary and proportionate to that end.[1234] In principle, interventions at the invitation of the

---

1231 For case law of the ICJ, see *Case Concerning Military and Paramilitary Activities in and against Nicaragua (Nicaragua v. United States of America), Judgment (Merits)* (n. 615) paras 176, 194 (endorsing the shared view of the parties to the case that 'whether the response to the [armed] attack is lawful depends on observance of the criteria of the necessity and the proportionality of the measures taken in self-defence' which is 'a rule well established in customary international law'); *Legality of the Threat or Use of Nuclear Weapons, Advisory opinion* (1996) ICJ Rep 226 para. 41 (noting that '[t]he submission of the exercise of the right of self-defence to the conditions of necessity and proportionality is a rule of customary international law'); *Case Concerning Oil Platforms (Islamic Republic of Iran v. United States of America), Judgment (Merits)* (2003) ICJ Rep 161 para. 76 (making a reference to both the *Nicaragua* case and the *Nuclear Weapons* case). See also ILC, 'Addendum – Eighth Report on State Responsibility by Mr. Roberto Ago, Special Rapporteur – the Internationally Wrongful Act of the State, Source of International Responsibility (Part 1)' (1980) UN Doc. A/CN.4/318/Add.5-7 69–70, paragraph 120–121; Raphael van Steenberghe, 'Proportionality under Jus Ad Bellum and Jus in Bello: Clarifying Their Relationship' (2012) 45 Israel Law Review 107, 118–119; James A Green and Christopher PM Waters, 'Military Targeting in the Context of Self-Defence Actions' (2015) 84 Nordic Journal of International Law 3, 11–12.

1232 Ruys (n. 52) 125.

1233 This approach has also been affirmed by the Institute of International Law in its resolution on the authorisation to use force by the UN, except that it defines proportionality differently. In Art. 9 of its resolution on the authorisation of the use of force by the UN, they held, e.g., that '[t]he objectives, scope and modes of control of each authorization should be strictly interpreted and implemented. When the use of force is authorized, it shall be conducted proportionately to the gravity of the situation and in full compliance with international humanitarian law.' See also Art. 10 of the same resolution, Institut de Droit International, 'Résolution sur l'Autorisation du Recours à la Force par les Nations Unies' (2011) Rhodes Session, 10th Commission, Sub-Group D.

1234 During a presentation at the 'Silent Leges Inter Arma?' Conference II organised by the Belgian Group under the auspices of the International Society for Military Law and the Law of War in 2018, the present author labelled the principles of necessity and proportionality constraining the use of force authorised by the UN Security Council as '*jus ad bellum* principles' (see Miek Lamaire and others, 'Report of the Second Silent Leges Inter Arma International Conference

host State involving the use of force fall outside the scope of Article 2(4) of the UN Charter. Yet, if forcible means are used beyond the host State's consent, it falls within the ambit of the prohibition of Article 2(4) of the Charter. Only if the use of force can be justified as self-defence or falls back on a Chapter VII mandate from the UN Security Council can it be regarded as a lawful exception to the general prohibition of the use of force.[1235]

Before discussing how to interpret the principles of necessity and proportionality in the context of the overall use of force on the basis of a mandate (either granted by the UN Security Council or the host State), the following should be clarified to avoid immediate confusion. The principles of proportionality and necessity can be found in different areas of both national and international law.[1236] In that respect, the principles of necessity and proportionality play a role not only in limiting the overall levels of force used in implementing UNSC mandates but also in limiting individual military attacks within the framework of these military operations. As discussed above, *specific* instances of the use of force are ordered by military leadership at the operational and tactical levels and conducted by soldiers at the tactical level.[1237] The legality of these specific instances of the use of force must, in principle, be assessed under the applicable legal regime(s), for example, IHL and/or HRL. Each of these legal regimes has its own understanding of the principles of necessity and proportionality, which is discussed in Part III when examining the HRL principles of necessity and proportionality[1238] and the IHL principles of military necessity and proportionality.[1239] This must be distinguished from the scope of these principles in the context of the overall implementation of UNSC mandates at the strategic level, which is discussed in the present Section.

Going forward, the principles of necessity and proportionality as they apply in the context of the use of force in national self-defence should not be defined in the same way in the context of military intervention by invitation or the use of force under Chapter VII. Ultimately, the principles must always be interpreted in light of the type and level of force being used. Consequently, the principles of necessity and proportionality are defined and implemented differently in HRL than, for example, in IHL or the international law on the use of force in national self-defence. Therefore, this study proposes to launch the debate on the meaning

---

Held in Bruges from 19 to 21 September 2018' (2018) 57 Military Law and Law of War Review 189, 209). In doing so, the author did not explicitly acknowledge that (i) the principles also apply when a military operation finds its legal basis in the consent of the host State; and (ii) the principles of necessity and proportionality must be understood differently in the context of military intervention upon invitation or on the basis of a Chapter VII mandate than in the context of the use of force in national self-defence (see below).

1235 See also Part II, Section 2.1.1.

1236 With respect to the principle of proportionality, see e.g. Emily Crawford, 'Proportionality', *Max Planck Encyclopedia of Public International law* (Oxford Public International Law 2011).

1237 See Part I, Sections 4.2.2.2 and 4.2.2.3.

1238 See Part III, Sections 3.1.1.2 and 3.1.1.3.

1239 See Part III, Sections 3.2.1 and 3.2.3.

of necessity and proportionality in the context of PoC mandates by defining these principles as follows.

The principle of necessity requires that the mandate be strictly implemented and that only those authorised objectives are pursued. This principle also implies that the overall levels of force used should be no more than necessary to pursue those objectives. However, contrary to what is required to justify resorting to self-defence, this does not mean all alternatives must be absent. In the context of PoC mandates, the principle of necessity requires that the forcible means used to implement the mandate serve the aim of protecting civilians without going beyond the scope of the mandate *in general*.[1240] To put it another way, although not every single measure has to directly provide for the protection of civilians, the set of forcible means considered as a whole needs to serve the aim of protecting civilians and/or other objectives outlined in the mandate. By explicitly authorising a UN (mandated) peace operation to use 'all *necessary* means' to protect civilians, the UN Security Council seems to restate this principle. Yet, for these reasons, even without an explicit reference to 'all necessary means', the PoC mandate must be implemented according to the principle of necessity.

The principle of proportionality dictates that the set of means adopted to execute the mandate must be rational and reasonable to achieve the objectives set out in the mandate without unduly encroaching on the protected rights of the subjects concerned under international law.[1241] In other words, if the overall levels of force used to carry out a PoC mandate were clearly excessive, this should be considered disproportionate and, hence, unlawful. It is to be stressed that this definition does not refer to the need for the means used to be proportional to the initial situation (for comparison, in the context of self-defence, the extent to which the reaction is proportionate to the initial attack is considered). Instead, the principle of proportionality relies heavily on the principle of necessity. Moreover, as stated above, for necessity, not every measure taken in implementing the mandate must be proportionate. The principle of proportionality must be measured against the military operation as a whole and by the overall levels of force used.

An example of how these principles are used to evaluate the implementation of a PoC mandate can be found in practice following the adoption of UNSC Resolution 1973 (2011). As mentioned above, UNSC Resolution 1973 (2011) authorised UN Member States to use 'all necessary measures' in order 'to protect civilians and civilian populated areas under threat of attack in the Libyan Arab Jamahiriya, including Benghazi.'[1242] Several States, however, sharply criticised the foreign intervention in Libya and some of the measures taken to carry out the mandate, such as the provision of military support to opposition groups

---

1240 See also Art. 11, Institut de Droit International (n. 1233).

1241 See also Crawford, 'Proportionality' (n. 1236) para. 1.

1242 'UNSC Res. 1973' (n. 62) para. 4.

and the forcible regime change.[1243] In their criticism, States often stressed the importance of strict implementation in light of a resolution's object and purpose. Brazil held, for example, that:[1244]

> When the Council does authorize the use of force, such as in the case of Libya, we must hold ourselves to a high standard. The Council has a responsibility to ensure the appropriate implementation of its resolutions. Force must be used carefully, with due regard for the principle of *proportionality* and *in strict accordance with the terms of the authorization*. The use of force to protect civilians does not abrogate international law, but underlines the need for strict adherence to it.

Russia and China also called for strict implementation of the UNSC resolution containing a PoC mandate.[1245] Remarkably, those States that were carrying out the mandate also used the term 'strict' to defend their implementation of UNSC Resolution 1973 (2011).[1246] The UN Secretary-General similarly held that 'Security Council resolution 1973, I believe, was *strictly enforced* within that limit, within the mandate. This military operation done by the NATO forces was strictly within (resolution) 1973.'[1247]

3.3.1.3. Legal regimes regulating specific instances of the use of force

When the UN Security Council has authorised a UN (mandated) peace operation to use 'all necessary means to protect civilians against the (imminent)

1243 See references to relevant sources in Part I, Section 2.2.2, fn. 327.

1244 Emphasis added. UNSC, '6531st Meeting (on the Protection of Civilians in Armed Conflict)' (n. 327) 11.

1245 See e.g. statements made by Russia and China during the 6528th and 6531the meeting of the UN Security Council, UNSC, '6528th Meeting (on the Situation in Libya)' (n. 327) 9–10; UNSC, '6531st Meeting (on the Protection of Civilians in Armed Conflict)' (n. 327) 21, as also discussed by Hajjami (n. 327) 253.

1246 E.g. during a press conference, former NATO Secretary-General Rasmussen argued that 'in the conduct of that operation we do not go beyond the text or the spirit of UN Security Council resolution 1973. On the contrary, we are implementing the Security Council resolution in strict conformity with both the letter and the spirit of that resolution,' see NATO, 'Questions and Answers at the Press Conference by NATO Secretary-General Anders Fogh Rasmussen on the Second Day of the Meeting of NATO Foreign Affairs Ministers, Berlin', www.nato.int/cps/en/natolive/opinions_72785.htm, accessed 26 February 2019. During a meeting of the NATO-Russia Council, he made similar remarks on the 'strict' implementation of the mandate, BBC News, 'Libya: Nato Defends Operation during Russia Talks' (4 July 2011), www.bbc.com/news/world-europe-14010305, accessed 26 February 2019, as also referred to by Niels Blokker, 'Outsourcing the Use of Force: Towards More Security Council Control of Authorized Operations?' in Marc Weller, Alexia Solomou and Jake William Rylatt (eds), *The Oxford Handbook of the Use of Force in International Law* (1st edn., Oxford University Press 2015) 205, fn. 9.

1247 Emphasis added. UNSG, 'Secretary-General's Year-End Press Conference' (14 December 2011), www.un.org/sg/en/content/sg/statement/2011-12-14/secretary-generals-year-end-pres s-conference, accessed 26 February 2019, as also referred to by Blokker (n. 1246) 205, fn. 10.

threat of physical violence', such mandate provides a legal authority to use force to achieve that objective. However, any such use of force must comply with any additional body of law that applies in the circumstances. In other words, the armed forces carrying out this mandate may, in principle, only use force in specific instances as permitted under the applicable legal regime(s), including HRL, IHL (if applicable), and relevant national laws of the host State and the TCC(s).[1248]

Although HRL and IHL are discussed in detail in Part III, the following example can already illustrate the dynamic. Suppose a UN peace operation has a mandate to use all necessary means to protect civilians and that this mandate is carried out without becoming a party to an armed conflict, then under HRL, armed forces may only use lethal force intentionally to protect civilians if there is an imminent threat to life. Conversely, suppose the UN peace operation becomes a party to an armed conflict. Then under IHL, those same forces may use lethal force against any legitimate military target (e.g. combatants or civilians directly participating in hostilities), regardless of whether they pose an imminent threat to anyone's life at the time.

3.3.2. *Emerging lower limit for what UN (mandated) peace operations must lawfully do to protect civilians*

In Part I, Section 3.1.4, it has been discussed that the practice of instructing UN (mandated) peace operations to protect civilians has not necessarily resulted in consistent and effective PoC on the ground.[1249] Evaluations conducted by OIOS revealed, for example, that UN peace operations often omit (or even refuse) to protect civilians *despite having an explicit mandate* to protect these people.[1250]

A question that arises is whether a PoC mandate that authorises using 'all necessary means' to pursue particular objectives imposes a lower limit for what UN (mandated) peace operations *must* lawfully do to protect civilians. In other words, can a PoC mandate *in itself* (i.e. independently of other legal bases, such as HRL or IHL, which may generate certain obligations),[1251] give rise to a legal obligation to protect civilians upon actors involved in UN (mandated) peace operations? In this respect, it is essential to note that this does not concern whether the international community has a 'responsibility to protect'.[1252] Instead, this research only confronts the question of whether an operation that has already been granted an explicit mandate by the UN Security Council to

1248 As also discussed in Part I, Section 4.1.2.2.
1249 United Nations Peacekeeping Law Reform Project, School of Law, University of Essex (n. 485) para. 127.
1250 OIOS (n. 106); OIOS, Inspection and Evaluation Division (n. 106); OIOS, Inspection and Evaluation Division (n. 10).
1251 As discussed in Part III, Section 4.
1252 For a short overview of the distinction between RtoP and PoC, see Part I, Section 3.1.

protect civilians in the territory of a State is bound by any kind lower limit for what they must lawfully do to protect civilians.[1253]

In their 2017 UN Guidelines on the Use of Force by Military Components in UN Peacekeeping Operations, the former UN DPKO and DFS held that forces are under the 'obligation to use force to protect civilians from armed attack [...] [i]f the mission is mandated for PoC [...] [and] all other unarmed tactics, techniques and procedures fail.'[1254] When observing the language of PoC mandates, it is not convincing that PoC mandates would give rise to a *legally binding obligation to use force* independently of other legal bases.[1255] The UN Security Council only 'authorises' operations to use 'all necessary means to protect civilians'. Given that the UN Security Council 'authorises' using all necessary means, those actors responsible for implementing this mandate retain the competence to decide at their discretion which means are necessary to achieve their objective. This authorisation may give rise to an order at the tactical level to use (lethal) force, but the mandate does not seem to impose an obligation to do so automatically. Nor could it do so. Determining whether force may be used in a particular case must be done at a tactical level.

Several PoC mandates may be perceived as imposing some obligation to take all reasonable action to protect civilians. For example, in 2003, the UN Security Council adopted Resolution 1493 (2003), which simply '*authorize[d]*' MONUC 'to take the necessary measures [...] to protect civilians [...] under imminent threat of physical violence.'[1256] However, in successive resolutions, the UN Security Council seemed to signal its intent to impose some type of obligation on MONUC and its successor MONUSCO and the Intervention Brigade. In Resolution 1565 (2004), the UN Security Council adopted the following language: '*[d]ecides* that MONUC will have the following mandate

---

1253 See also Bourgeois, 'Failure to Protect Civilians in the Context of UN Peace Operations: A Question of Accountability?' (n. 1). In this blogpost, the author went as far as to argue that PoC mandates can be legally binding on mission personnel involved in the implementation of PoC mandates at every level in the command structure. Although this claim is perhaps (too) hard to make, it cannot be ignored that there is a shift in the approach of both the UN Security Council and the UN Member States towards an obligation to take the best efforts to protect civilians upon all mission personnel. Hence, as defended below, there should at least be a heightened sense of responsibility at the different levels in the chain of command: when adopting a PoC mandate, when accepting to carry out a PoC mandate, and when implementing a PoC mandate. For further literature on whether or not there is an obligation (to use force) to protect civilians on the basis of the mandate or any other basis, see e.g. Khalil, 'Legal Aspects of the Use of Force by United Nations Peacekeepers for the Protection of Civilians' (n. 40); Sheeran and Kent (n. 50) 55–58; Willmot and Sheeran (n. 219); or Siobhán Wills, 'International Responsibility for Ensuring the Protection of Civilians' in Haidi Willmot and others (eds), *Protection of Civilians* (1st edn., Oxford University Press 2016).

1254 UN DPKO and UN DFS, '2017 UN Guidelines on the Use of Force by Military Components in UN Peacekeeping Operations' (n. 17) 23.

1255 Not that the author assumes this was necessarily the position of the former UN DPKO and DFS.

1256 'UNSC Res. 1493' (n. 125) para. 25.

[…] *to ensure* the protection of civilians […] under imminent threat of physical violence.'[1257] To this end, MONUC was '*authorize[d]* […] to use all necessary means.'[1258] Also, in subsequent resolutions, the UN Security Council decided that MONUC should have the mandate to '*ensure* the protection of civilians'[1259] or even '*[e]nsure* the *effective* protection of civilians'[1260] under imminent threat of physical violence. For MONUSCO and the Intervention Brigade, the UN Security Council similarly decided that the mandate shall include the task to '*[e]nsure*' '*effective* protection of civilians,'[1261] '*effective and dynamic* protection of civilians,'[1262] '*effective, dynamic and integrated* protection of civilians,'[1263] or '*effective, timely, dynamic and integrated* protection of civilians.'[1264] Beginning with Resolution 2348 (2017) onwards, the UN Security Council requested the UN Secretary-General 'to immediately inform the Security Council should MONUSCO Force or Police fail [to take all necessary measures to carry out its mandate].'[1265] In subsequent Resolution 2409 (2017), the UN Security Council also began to include a 'mission effectiveness' section in the mandates of MONUSCO and its Intervention Brigade.[1266] As of Resolution 2502 (2019), the UN Security Council explicitly '*[r]ecognise[d]* that the effective implementation of peacekeeping mandates is the responsibility of all stakeholders and is contingent upon several critical factors, including well-defined, realistic, and achievable mandates, political will, leadership, performance and accountability at all levels, adequate resources, policy, planning, and operational guidelines, and training and equipment.'[1267]

Given that the UN Security Council uses expressions such as 'to ensure the protection of civilians', certain PoC mandates may give rise to an 'obligation of conduct.' An 'obligation of conduct' should not be confused with an 'obligation of result.' An 'obligation of result' is the obligation to attain a predetermined

1257 Emphasis added. 'UNSC Res. 1565' (n. 125) paras 4 and 4(b).

1258 *Ibid.* para. 6.

1259 Emphasis added. 'UNSC Res. 1592' (n. 125) para. 7. See also 'UNSC Res. 1649' (n. 125) para. 11; 'UNSC Res. 1756' (n. 125) paras 2 and 2(a); 'UNSC Res. 1856' (n. 125) paras 3 and 3(a).

1260 Emphasis added. 'UNSC Res. 1906' (n. 125) para. 5(a).

1261 Emphasis added 'UNSC Res. 1925' (n. 125) para. 12(a); See also 'UNSC Res. 2098' (n. 19) para. 12(a)(i); 'UNSC Res. 2147' (n. 19) para. 4(a)(i); 'UNSC Res. 2211' (n. 127) para. 9(a); 'UNSC Res. 2277' (n. 127) para. 35(i)(a).

1262 Emphasis added. 'UNSC Res. 2348' (n. 127) para. 34(i)(a).

1263 Emphasis added. 'UNSC Res. 2409' (n. 19) para. 36(i)(a); 'UNSC Res. 2463' (n. 127) para. 29(i)(a).

1264 Emphasis added. 'UNSC Res. 2502' (n. 127) para. 29(i)(a); 'UNSC Res. 2556' (n. 127) para. 44; 'UNSC Res. 2612' (n. 49) op 43.

1265 'UNSC Res. 2348' (n. 127) para. 33; 'UNSC Res. 2409' (n. 19) para. 35; 'UNSC Res. 2463' (n. 127) para. 28; 'UNSC Res. 2502' (n. 127) para. 27; 'UNSC Res. 2556' (n. 127) para. 27; 'UNSC Res. 2612' (n. 49) para. 27.

1266 'UNSC Res. 2409' (n. 19) paras 47–55; 'UNSC Res. 2463' (n. 127) paras 41–43; 'UNSC Res. 2502' (n. 127) paras 40–45.

1267 'UNSC Res. 2502' (n. 127) para. 40; 'UNSC Res. 2556' (n. 127) para. 40; 'UNSC Res. 2612' (n. 49) para. 40.

result. On the other hand, an 'obligation of conduct' is, in the nature of best-effort obligation, the obligation to take all reasonable action to realise a specific objective.[1268] In the context of PoC mandates, this would imply an obligation to make the best efforts to pre-empt, prevent, deter, or respond to attacks or (imminent) threats of physical violence against civilians, irrespective of which means are required to do so.[1269] This obligation could be considered a lower limit for what UN (mandated) peace operations must lawfully do to protect civilians when their mandate includes more obligatory language. An 'obligation of conduct' should be read in light of the relevant circumstances as well as the capabilities of the operation in question and its areas of deployment.

The debates leading up to the adoption of some UNSC resolutions discussed above give further insights. Although States do not address the issue directly, the wording used by some States reveals support for the imposition of some obligation upon UN peace operations actually to implement their PoC mandate. Some examples include when UNSC Resolution 1856 (2008) was adopted (in which MONUC's PoC mandate was extended), Costa Rica stressed that MONUC '*must* protect the civilians from violence committed by any of the parties engaged in the conflict.'[1270] When adopting UNSC Resolution 2098 (2013), the US held that the duty to protect civilians and neutralise armed groups 'are duties that MONUSCO peacekeepers *must do their utmost to perform*.'[1271] In the debates on UNSC Resolution 2409 (2018), the US even openly stated that '[t]oo many peacekeepers and innocent civilians lost their lives in the past year when the [...] [MONUSCO] forces failed to respond.'[1272] They argued that troops must be held to the highest possible standards, and accountability must be ensured if they underperform.[1273]

As already discussed above, in the PoC mandates granted to MINUSMA, the terminology used also changed over time (see analysis of UNSC Resolutions 2227 (2015), 2295 (2016), 2364 (2017), 2423 (2018), 2480 (2019), 2531 (2020), and 2584 (2021)).[1274] When adopting UNSC Resolution 2295 (2016), the US intended to impose a more binding obligation upon the operation in question. According to the US, UNSC Resolution 2295 (2016) emphasises that 'MINUSMA *must* anticipate, deter and counter threats, including asymmetric threats, to

1268 ILC, 'Second Report on State Responsibility by Mr. James Crawford, Special Rapporteur' (n. 107) para. 57; Jean Combacau, 'Obligations de Rêsultat et Obligations de Comportement. Quelques Questions et Pas de Réponses' in Paul Reuter (ed), *Mélanges offerts à Paul Reuter: Le Droit International, Unité et Diversité* (Pedone 1981) 194–196.

1269 See also Part I, Section 2.1.4, fn. 256 in this regard.

1270 Emphasis added. UNSC, '6055th Meeting (at Which UNSC Res. 1856 (2008) Was Adopted)' (2008) UN Doc. S/PV.6055 5.

1271 Emphasis added. UNSC, '6943rd Meeting (at Which UNSC Res. 2098 (2013) Was Adopted)' (n. 953) 8.

1272 UNSC, '8216th Meeting (at Which UNSC Res. 2409 (2018) Was Adopted)' (2018) UN Doc. S/PV.8216 3.

1273 *Ibid.*

1274 As discussed in Part II, Section 3.2.2.3(A).

protect civilians and United Nations personnel.'[1275] Hence, '[t]his means that MINUSMA *must* take robust and active steps, including direct operations if necessary, against serious and credible threats.'[1276] When UNSC Resolution 2480 (2019) was adopted, China stressed that they 'are keen that MINUSMA should fully implement the Council's mandates and strengthen measures to increase the protection of the safety and security of its peacekeepers.'[1277]

Moreover, not only UN peace operations but also several UN-mandated peace operations, including AFISMA and MISCA, received a PoC mandate with a more obligatory language at one point. For example, UNSC Resolutions 2085 (2012) and 2127 (2013) hold, respectively, that AFISMA and MISCA '*shall* take all necessary measures' to (help to) protect civilians.[1278]

Last but not least, in several mission-specific and thematic resolutions, the UN Security Council stresses that it 'expects full delivery of the mandates it authorizes.'[1279]

Besides the language used in the relevant UNSC resolutions, the circumstances of their adoption, and the subsequent practice of the UN Security Council and other relevant practices of UN organs and subsidiary organs, we should also observe the legal bases which have been invoked in each of these resolutions. All relevant resolutions were provided with a Chapter VII mandate for all tasks or only some tasks, including PoC. Resolutions adopted under Chapter VII are generally considered decisions that: (i) prevail over international agreements pursuant to Article 103 of the UN Charter;[1280] and (ii) should be accepted and carried out by the UN Member States pursuant to Article 25 of the UN Charter. Article 25 of the UN Charter does not oblige States to contribute to a UN (mandated) peace operation. Yet, if a State agrees to contribute to an operation, it becomes bound to execute the mandate in accordance with the UN Charter.[1281] In addition, it becomes bound by the terms set out in the mandate.[1282] Although Article 25 of the UN Charter only refers to the legally

---

1275 Emphasis added. UNSC, '7727th Meeting (at Which UNSC Res. 2295 (2016) Was Adopted)' (n. 959) 5.

1276 Emphasis added. *Ibid.*

1277 UNSC, '8568th Meeting (at Which UNSC Res. 2480 (2019) Was Adopted)' (n. 792) 10.

1278 Emphasis added. PoC mandate for AFISMA: 'UNSC Res. 2085' (n. 148) paras 9 and 9(d); PoC mandate for MISCA: 'UNSC Res. 2127' (n. 151) paras 28 and 28(i).

1279 Regarding mission-specific resolutions, see e.g. 'UNSC Res. 2252' (n. 135) pream. para. 9; 'UNSC Res. 2406' (n. 19) para. 11; 'UNSC Res. 2448' (n. 140) pream. para. 4; 'UNSC Res. 2499' (n. 140) pream. para. 4; 'UNSC Res. 2514' (n. 135) para. 13; 'UNSC Res. 2567' (n. 135) para. 17. Regarding thematic resolutions, see e.g. 'UNSC Res. 2436' (n. 19) pream. para. 5; 'UNSC Res. 2447' (2018) UN Doc. S/RES/2447 (2018) pream. para. 7.

1280 For a more detailed discussion of Art. 103 of the UN Charter, see Part III, Section 3.3.2.1(B).

1281 As also highlighted by Lord Bingham in the *Al-Jedda* case, see *R (on the application of Al-Jedda) v. Secretary of State for Defence, Appeal judgment* (2007) United Kingdom House of Lords 58, 832 Oxford Reports on International Law in Domestic Courts para. 34.

1282 Sari, 'The Al-Jedda Case Before the House of Lords' (n. 1220) 189. Sarooshi even takes it further by arguing that once a State agrees to carry out a UNSC mandate, it is under the

binding nature of these decisions upon UN Member States, it can be argued that these decisions also impose an obligation upon the UN itself and its organs (e.g. the UN Security Council and the UN Secretariat) and subsidiary organs (e.g. the UN peace operations).[1283] This obligation can also be extended to international and regional organisations other than the UN that decide to undertake a PoC mandate. Currently, there are no *specific* legal grounds presented in the UN Charter to underpin this position, let alone to claim accountability for violations of this obligation. But at the same time, it cannot be ignored that the changing formulation of a number of mandates points to a shift in the approach of both the UN Security Council and the UN Member States toward an obligation to make the best efforts to protect civilians. Indeed, in its 2019 UN Policy on PoC in UN Peacekeeping, the UN DPO determined that '[i]n accordance with mission-specific Security Council resolutions, peacekeeping operations with PoC mandates *are required* to protect civilians under threat of physical violence.'[1284] Moreover, it held that:[1285]

> The Secretariat is *institutionally* – and the Secretary-General *individually* – accountable to the political organs of the UN for the *effective* implementation of the Organization's mandates, including those of peacekeeping operations. This accountability *cascades* in the Organization so that senior leaders at UN Headquarters and in mission are responsible for both their own strategic actions and guidance and for ensuring that organizational and individual performance management systems are fully utilized to ensure that all relevant personnel in missions are accountable for their responsibilities for the delivery of POC mandates.

Hence, there should at least be a heightened sense of responsibility at the different levels in the chain of command: when adopting a PoC mandate, when accepting to carry out a PoC mandate, and when implementing a PoC mandate. To that end, the UN Security Council should, in the first place, adopt clear, realistic, and achievable mandates, either to be carried out by the UN itself or by a State, regional, or other international organisation.[1286] If States or

obligation to assist in the achievement of this objective until the UN Security Council has decided that the objective has been attained, see Sarooshi (n. 1221) 151–153.

1283 See Bourgeois, 'Failure to Protect Civilians in the Context of UN Peace Operations: A Question of Accountability?' (n. 1). Yet also see the caveat which is made in fn. 1253.

1284 Emphasis added. UN DPO, '2019 UN Policy on PoC in UN Peacekeeping' (n. 35) para. 16, see also paras 25 and 32.

1285 Emphasis added. *Ibid.* para. 88.

1286 In the Declaration of Shared Commitments on UN Peacekeeping Operations, undersigning UN Member States committed to 'pursue clear, focused, sequenced, prioritized and achievable mandated by the Security Council,' see UNSG, 'Action for Peacekeeping: Declaration of Shared Commitments on UN Peacekeeping Operations, Shared by the UN Secretary-General with the UN Member States on 16 August 2018; Endorsed by 152 UN Member States and 4 Supporting Organisations' para. 5, https://peacekeeping.un.org/sites/default/files/a4p-declaration-en.pdf, accessed 9 March 2020.

regional or international organisations other than the UN decide to exercise that authorisation, they should do so in accordance with the letter of the UNSC mandate. Both UN peace operations and UN-mandated peace operations should subsequently be diligently planned[1287] and provided with adequate resources and training to execute PoC mandates successfully.[1288] Once deployed in the territory, it is the political and military strategic leadership which has the primary responsibility to monitor and evaluate the performances of the mission continuously and to adjust where appropriate.[1289]

The obligation to make the best efforts to protect civilians trickles down to all levels of personnel active at the different levels of the chain of command.[1290] Indeed, the extent to which civilians are protected, as provided for in the PoC mandate, also depends to a large extent on how diligently the various individuals operating at the different levels of the chain of command carry out their respective duties. These individuals are usually bound by a contractual obligation to perform their duties with due care. At the strategic and operational levels, a system of accountability must continue to be put in place for underperformance, mismanagement, and improper decisions by mission leadership.[1291] At the tactical level, failure to protect should give rise to the repatriation of the national commander or even the entire contingent and possibly even to financial penalties if this is deemed necessary by the operational leadership. A failure to act may also be regarded as insubordination under the applicable domestic conduct and

---

1287 See e.g. UN DPO, '2019 UN Policy on PoC in UN Peacekeeping' (n. 35).

1288 See UNSG, 'Action for Peacekeeping: Declaration of Shared Commitments on UN Peacekeeping Operations, Shared by the UN Secretary-General with the UN Member States on 16 August 2018; Endorsed by 152 UN Member States and 4 Supporting Organisations' (n. 1286) paras 5, 14, and 20 in which the undersigning UN Member States commit to do so. Moreover, UN Headquarters should continue to support and engage with TCCs on the necessary capacity, resources, training, and capabilities of deployed troops, see UN DPO, '2019 UN Policy on PoC in UN Peacekeeping' (n. 35) para. 70.

1289 See also Part I, Section 4.2.2.1.

1290 In its 2019 UN Policy on PoC in UN Peacekeeping, the UN DPO held that: 'In missions with a POC mandate, all relevant personnel: civilian and uniformed, and, in particular, senior leadership, including in UN Headquarters, have roles and responsibilities with respect to the implementation of the POC mandate' (para. 87). They have also explicitly recognised that accountability 'cascades' down the organisation to all levels of personnel (see quote above), UN DPO, '2019 UN Policy on PoC in UN Peacekeeping' (n. 35) paras 88 and 93.

1291 In 2010, the UN General Assembly adopted, e.g., a resolution to install an 'accountability system' in the UN Secretariat for, *inter alia*, under-performance, mismanagement, and wrongful or improper decisions ('UNGA Res. 64/259 Adopted by the General Assembly on 29 March 2010: Towards an Accountability System in the United Nations Secretariat' (2010) UN Doc. A/RES/64/259 259). In September 2018, the UN Security Council adopted landmark Resolution 2436 (2018) to stress the need to improve behaviour, leadership, and accountability in peacekeeping ('UNSC Res. 2436' (n. 19)). The UN DPO is also continuously working to enhance performance management in its peace operations. For example, in its 2019 UN Policy on PoC in UN Peacekeeping, it has defined and further clarified the roles and responsibilities of mission personnel with respect to the implementation of PoC mandates, see UN DPO, '2019 UN Policy on PoC in UN Peacekeeping' (n. 35) paras 87–97.

discipline regime. Although States retain the exclusive authority to discipline, they should strongly consider penalising their troops if they believe they have not carried out legitimate orders to protect civilians.[1292]

That said, UN practice certainly merits further scrutiny to see whether or not this emerging trend continues.

3.4. INFLUENCE OF HRL AND IHL ON THE INTERPRETATION, IMPLEMENTATION, AND EVALUATION OF UNSC RESOLUTIONS THAT CONTAIN A POC MANDATE

Legal bases and legal regimes are, at least in theory, fundamentally different. Grounded on host State consent and/or Chapter VII of the UN Charter, the legal basis for UN (mandated) peace operations regulates the legality of peace forces' presence in the territory of a State and is codified in a mission-specific mandate that sets out tasks, purposes, and/or objectives that the mission can perform. Significantly, this authority to deploy and use strategic force on the territory of a State is distinct from the applicable legal regimes regulating under which circumstances peace forces may use force on the ground. Whereas the mandate is a strategic-level legal source that is concerned with the general question of whether – and if so, how much – force can be used on the territory of a State, the legal regimes contain the when and how of the use of force in specific PoC situations at the tactical level of the operation. Yet, despite the theoretical

[1292] In Principle 13 of the Kigali Principles, the undersigning States already took a step in the right direction by expressing their commitment to take appropriate disciplinary action if their personnel fail to act to protect civilians when circumstances warrant, see 'The Kigali Principles on the Protection of Civilians. High-Level International Conference on the Protection of Civilians, 28–29 May 2015, Kigali'. On 31 July 2018, thirty-two States asked the UN Secretary-General António Guterres to go a step further in addressing the failures of UN peace operations to protect civilians. They emphasised the importance of holding those individuals accountable who have failed to protect civilians in line with their mission's mandate. 'Letter to the UN Secretary-General António Guterres Concerning the Kigali Principles' (2018), www.google.com/url?sa=t&rct=j&q=&esrc=s&source=web&cd=1&ved=2ahUKEwjO0P7Lh_HcAhVH2qQKHZU8BHoQFjAAegQIARAC&url=https%3A%2F%2Fwww.permanentrepresentations.nl%2Fbinaries%2Fnlatio%2Fdocuments%2Fpublications%2F2018%2F7%2F31%2Fletter-to-the-sg-concerning-kigali-principles%2F2018-07-30%2BKigali%2BPrinciples%2BLetter.pdf&usg=AOvVaw2OaLHi2cXrr0PCWifSIFaB, accessed 15 August 2018, as also discussed in Bourgeois, 'Failure to Protect Civilians in the Context of UN Peace Operations: A Question of Accountability?' (n. 1). Furthermore, in the Declaration of Shared Commitments on UN Peacekeeping Operations, undersigning UN Member States committed to 'ensuring the highest level of peacekeeping performance, and to hold all civilian and uniformed peacekeepers, particularly leadership, accountable for effective performance under common parameters while addressing performance shortfalls,' see UNSG, 'Action for Peacekeeping: Declaration of Shared Commitments on UN Peacekeeping Operations, Shared by the UN Secretary-General with the UN Member States on 16 August 2018; Endorsed by 152 UN Member States and 4 Supporting Organisations' (n. 1286) para. 13, see also para. 21.

distinction between the two, the mandate and the legal regimes can enter each other's playing field. The next Section discusses the extent to which legal regimes can influence the interpretation, implementation, and evaluation of UNSC resolutions that contain a PoC mandate. To this end, it builds on the earlier analyses made in Part II.

3.4.1. Interpretation and implementation of PoC mandates

Once adopted, PoC mandates are translated into military strategic, operational, and tactical instruments and, as such, govern the use of force ordered or used at the different levels of the chain of command. Indeed, although only the UN Security Council or a body authorised by it can give an 'authentic interpretation' of UNSC resolutions, the mandates contained therein are continuously translated and applied by a wide range of authorities and individuals.[1293]

As discussed above, PoC language should be interpreted in good faith, considering the ordinary meaning to be given to these terms when they are read in the context of the resolution as a whole and in light of its object and purpose. Account should also be taken of the relevant circumstances of the adoption of these UNSC resolutions, the subsequent practice of the UN Security Council and other relevant practices of UN organs and subsidiary organs, and any relevant rules of international law (to the extent that they are consistent with the UN Security Council's intent).[1294]

The ordinary meaning of a term can reflect the meaning given to a term in the context of HRL or IHL. However, the extent to which any relevant rules of international law can be considered to interpret terms used in UNSC resolutions depends on the intentions of the UN Security Council.[1295] Only if the UN Security Council sought to build on the rules and principles of HRL or IHL is one obliged to consider those rules when interpreting the relevant resolution.[1296]

For example, returning to the meaning of the term 'imminent', as was discussed previously:[1297] the ordinary meaning of the term aligns with the meaning given to it in the context of HRL and, more specifically, the right to life. Imminent is understood as 'impending' and 'a matter of seconds'. However, it is not clear whether this meaning also aligns with the intention of the UN Security Council. Since 2014, the UN Security Council has often refrained from including the term 'imminent' in its resolutions containing a PoC mandate. Also, there is considerable practice from the UN OLA, the former UN DPKO and DFS, and the current UN DPO that points out that even if the term 'imminent' is used in

---

1293 Wood (n. 735) 82–83. See also Gill, Léveillée and Fleck (n. 609) 112–116. As also mentioned above, see Part I, Section 4.2.2.1.

1294 See Part II, Section 3.2.1.

1295 Wood (n. 735) 92.

1296 *Ibid.*

1297 See Part II, Section 3.2.4.

UNSC resolutions, it does not necessarily mean that a threat must be guaranteed to happen in the immediate or near future or is being carried out for force to be used. According to the author, although it is certainly suspected that the UN Security Council intends to give the term a meaning that differs from its ordinary meaning and, consequently, from the meaning given to it in the HRL context, there is currently insufficient evidence to conclude that the UN Security Council has a genuine intention to deviate from this ordinary meaning. After all, to the author's knowledge, nothing in the verbatim records of the meetings of the UN Security Council or any other background documentation suggests such intentions. Therefore, as long as this suspicion is not confirmed by clear evidence, the ordinary meaning can be assumed when interpreting the term 'imminent'. Whether and, if so, how this impacts the use of force by UN (mandated) peace forces on the ground is discussed in depth in a case study in Part III, Section 3.3.2.2.

Another example is the meaning of the term 'civilian' in the context of PoC mandates, as discussed above.[1298] When looking for the ordinary meaning of the term, the Oxford English Dictionary defines 'civilians' by distinguishing them from combatants. This definition is consistent with the IHL definition of 'civilians'. Moreover, as far as this author is aware, there is no indication that this interpretation is inconsistent with the intentions of the UN Security Council, and the relevant practice of the UN DPO also confirms the IHL approach. Nevertheless, when defining the term 'civilian' in the context of PoC mandates, as in IHL, at least two complications arise.[1299]

First, IHL cannot always give a conclusive answer to the question of who is a civilian and who is not in the context of a NIAC.[1300] The UN DPO seems to adhere to the ICRC's understanding of 'civilians' in NIACs by excluding 'members of an organized armed group with continuous combat function.'[1301] By adopting the ICRC understanding of 'civilian', the UN not only joins the debate but may also be dependent on how the understanding of the IHL notion of 'civilian' further develops.

Second, IHL only applies to the parties to an armed conflict,[1302] whereas UN (mandated) peace operations are usually not a party to an armed conflict.[1303] From an operational perspective, it makes sense that the IHL concept of 'civilian' is used to determine which persons they ought to protect. After all, HRL does not normally make a distinction between 'civilian' and 'combatant'.[1304] On the other

1298 See Part II, Section 3.2.3.

1299 Lehmann (n. 14) 124.

1300 See Part II, Section 3.2.3.1.

1301 UN DPO, '2019 UN Policy on PoC in UN Peacekeeping' (n. 35) para. 21.

1302 Taking into account that all States (so not only those who are a part to an armed conflict) and the international community as a whole must respect and ensure respect for IHL (see Common Art. 1 of the Geneva Conventions I–IV).

1303 See also Mamiya (n. 58) 66, fn. 9, and p. 79.

1304 Andrew Clapham, 'Protection of Civilians under International Human Rights Law' in Haidi Willmot and others (eds), *Protection of Civilians* (1st edn., Oxford University Press 2016) 142.

hand, the IHL principle of the distinction between civilians and combatants lies at the foundation of the training of almost all armed forces and thus provides a handy tool to make the division. That said, by allowing the IHL concept of 'civilian' to work through in situations where one is not a party to an armed conflict, the strict distinction between participating in hostilities and operating outside such a situation and the related *legal* rules for the use of force threatens to water down. A major problem with UN (mandated) peace operations is that the troops participating in the operations are generally better trained to operate under IHL than under HRL. When participating in UN (mandated) peace operations, the troops are nevertheless expected to accurately identify which legal regime regulates their actions (i.e. is there a clear nexus to an armed conflict or not?). They must be able to quickly switch from one legal regime to the other and respect the relevant legal constraints on the use of force for PoC as the situation requires. Using an IHL concept in situations where IHL does not apply, troops might get confused. To better illustrate the conundrum with which the forces are confronted: when troops are operating in an armed conflict without being part of it and are to judge whether they should protect a particular person under their PoC mandate, they should look at IHL. However, when they must judge whether and in which manner they can use force in such a situation, they should look at HRL, which may lead to confusion among troops and may eventually result in more force being used outside the conduct of hostilities than legally allowed under HRL.

3.4.2. *Evaluation of the implementation of PoC mandates*

The political and military strategic leadership evaluates whether an operation is conducted in accordance with the PoC mandate and is consequently responsible for the overall conduct of an operation.[1305] This assessment takes place continuously from the moment the UN Security Council decides to intervene until the final evaluation of a completed operation. When force has been used in implementing a PoC mandate, one of the issues to be considered is whether the overall levels of force used on the territory of a State have remained within the limits of the given mandate. In particular, the strategic leadership must assess whether the overall levels of force used were necessary and proportionate to achieve the general objective of protecting civilians.

Such evaluation of the overall implementation of the PoC mandate should be distinguished from assessments of individual violations of rules and principles of HRL and IHL. Violations of HRL or IHL may certainly affect the evaluation of the overall implementation of the PoC mandate, but such violations do not automatically result in the entire operation constituting a violation of the mandate. For example, a violation of IHL or HRL principles of necessity and

[1305] See also Part I, Section 4.2.2.1.

proportionality does not automatically mean that the overall levels of force used in implementing a UNSC mandate have been unnecessary or disproportionate. According to Article 50 of Geneva Convention I, Article 51 of Geneva Convention II, and Article 147 of Geneva Convention IV, 'extensive destruction and appropriation of property, not justified by military necessity and carried out unlawfully and wantonly' are grave breaches of IHL. If a UN (mandated) peace operation with a PoC mandate becomes a party to an IAC and violates this IHL rule by destructing certain property without the military necessity to do so, this would not necessarily make the entire operation disproportionate and unnecessary.

Hence, there is a significant difference between the tactical, circumstantial use of 'necessity and proportionality' in the actual conduct of the operation and the strategic, goal-oriented use of 'necessity and proportionality'. The former addresses the soldier whose finger is on the trigger (or the commander who must choose whether to authorise a certain action), while the latter addresses the strategic leadership supervising the overall implementation of the mandate. It is the strategic leadership's responsibility to ensure that the overall levels of force used in implementing the UNSC mandate are necessary and proportionate to achieve the general objective(s) set out in the mandate. As such, the mandate must be strictly implemented and only authorised objectives, such as PoC, can be pursued. The overall levels of force used cannot exceed what is necessary to achieve this. Furthermore, the means used to implement the mandate must be rational and reasonable to protect civilians, without unduly compromising the rights of those protected under international law. If the overall levels of force used are not considered necessary and proportionate to protect civilians, that could amount to unlawful use of force on the territory of a State.

4. SUMMARY OF PART II

Part II sought to examine the mission-specific legal bases underlying UN (mandated) peace operations deployed to protect civilians, including the consent of the host State and mandates issued by the UN Security Council, and investigate the possible impact the legal regimes (in particular, HRL and IHL) might have on the interpretation, implementation, and evaluation of PoC mandates granted by the UN Security Council.[1306] In doing so, Part II addressed the following questions: How do the mission-specific legal bases underlying UN (mandated) peace operations deployed to protect civilians, including consent given by the host State and mandates issued by the UN Security Council, govern

[1306] As also set forth in the Introductory Chapter, Section 2.

the use of force? To that end, what is the legal, political, and operational value of consent and what are the modalities of consent? And concerning mandates issued by the UN Security Council, what rules and methods of interpretation apply to UNSC resolutions and how to understand and evaluate the UN Security Council's practice of authorising the use of force to protect civilians in terms of the changing formulation, interpretation, and implementation of PoC mandates? Do HRL and IHL influence the interpretation, implementation, and evaluation of PoC mandates issued by the UN Security Council and, if so, in what ways? And when being given the mandate to use all necessary means to protect civilians, are there upper or lower limits to what UN (mandated) peace operations may or must lawfully do to protect civilians?

Two types of legal bases

A legal basis must be identified in international law whenever there is a (physical) intervention in a State. First, such a legal basis can be found in the UN Charter or in the rules of customary international law concerning the use of force and the maintenance and restoration of international peace and security. Additionally, a mission-specific 'external' mandate should be granted to the operation in question. Such a mission-specific mandate constitutes a source of legal authority to deploy a mission on the territory of the third State and to use force on the territory of that State. It can be issued by a competent international organisation (in principle, the UN Security Council under Chapter VII of the UN Charter) or by a host State's government inviting or agreeing to a peace operation carried out on its territory.

Consent of the host State

The host State's consent can be an independent legal basis for deploying troops on its territory or a secondary legal basis in cases where the UN Security Council has already issued a mandate under Chapter VII of the UN Charter. Where the host State has consented to the intervention, there is no violation of the prohibition of the use of force in international relations. As such, consent must not be identified as a 'circumstance precluding wrongfulness' or as a 'third customary exception' to the prohibition of the use of force (in addition to self-defence and Chapter VII enforcement action) because there is no wrongfulness or violation of the primary rule. On the contrary, consent is a constituent part of the primary rule of the prohibition of the use of force, which is a rule that must be understood as a prohibition of the non-consensual use of force only.

Although the host States have approved most interventions by UN (mandated) peace operations with a PoC mandate, such operations were typically also given a Chapter VII mandate. In that case, consent is no longer legally required but still has an essential political and operational value. First, consent can significantly impact the scope of the mandate and, in particular, lead to more ambitious mandates or, conversely, to downsizing the mission in the absence of consent. Second, consent can substantially impact the success of the mission in carrying out the mandate as it guarantees co-operation of the host State or at least no opposition to it. Third, consent contributes to a safer environment for the troops themselves, which may also have consequences for the deployment of troops in other UN (mandated) peace operations.

The modalities of consent are the following. First, consent of the host State may not legitimise an otherwise unlawful act. Consent of the host State can cover not only access to its territory but also the composition of the force and the terms of its mandate (i.e. the tasks, purposes, and/or objectives that the mission can fulfil). Second, consent must be given by the government of the State(s) on whose territory the mission is to be deployed, even if that government no longer exercises effective control over the entire territory and even if the entity exercising governmental power is not the constitutionally and/or democratically elected government. Third, consent is often given for a defined certain period only and can be withdrawn at any time, be it *de facto* or *de jure* (yet, in doing so, an agreement might be breached). Fourth, consent should never be presumed and must be given freely without any coercion from the State by threat or use of force or by deceit, corruption, or coercion of a representative of the State.

Mandate of the UN Security Council

In addition to host State consent, Chapter VII mandates whereby PoC is included as a mandated task by the UN Security Council play a crucial role in regulating the use of force and are an important subject of this study. The first mission with an explicit mandate to protect civilians was UNAMSIL (UNSC Resolution 1270 (1999)). Since 1999, most UN (mandated) peace operations have received such a PoC mandate. In practice, however, questions arise regarding what the UN Security Council has authorised and what has not. Therefore, to unravel the precise meaning of a PoC mandate, the terms used need to be interpreted in good faith, taking into account the ordinary meaning when read in the context of the resolution as a whole and in light of its object and purpose, the relevant circumstances of its adoption, the subsequent practice of the UN Security Council and other relevant practices of UN organs and subsidiary organs, and any relevant rules of international law (to the extent consistent with the UN Security Council's intention).

The term 'protection' has been assigned different meanings in different contexts by different actors, ranging from the military to peacekeepers and humanitarian actors. These different approaches have influenced how 'protection' is understood today by the UN Security Council as a mandated task. Whereas protection primarily referred to protection from physical violence, with physical safety from violence undeniably having its roots in IHL, today it is used to refer to a variety of ways in which civilians can be protected in the short, medium, and long-term (ranging for example from the creation of a safe and secure environment to the use of armed force to protect civilians) from a variety of dangers (ranging for example from dangers caused by one's own actions or the actions of third parties, or from as-yet unidentified dangers to clearly identifiable imminent dangers). As such, the term 'protection' refers not only to the acts or risks against which protection is sought but also to the various strategies and methods by which civilians can be protected from the act or risk. However, how exactly this is interpreted by the organisations undertaking UN (mandated) peace operations is different.

When applying the rules of interpretation to the term 'civilians', it becomes clear that this term is usually understood by analogy with the term 'civilians' in IHL. As such, everyone enjoys protection, except members of armed forces, members of organised armed groups engaged in continuous combat duties, and civilians directly participating in hostilities for as long as they do so.

The terms 'in danger', 'under threat of attack', or 'under threat or imminent threat' of 'physical violence', together with the terms 'all necessary means, measures, steps, or action', are the most difficult terms to comprehend in the context of PoC mandates. While 'threat of physical violence' is usually understood as a threat of force that can cause death or serious bodily harm to civilians, including sexual violence, it is the vague indication of time that makes it difficult to fathom what the UN Security Council has or has not authorised. 'Imminent' must ordinarily be understood as 'impending' and 'a matter of seconds'. Such interpretation aligns with the meaning given to the term in the context of HRL and, more specifically, the right to life. However, whereas PoC mandates previously authorised protecting civilians under 'imminent threat', the word 'imminent' is now increasingly dropped, or, if still present, the UN Secretariat seeks to detach the word's meaning from questions of temporality. While it is not clear whether the UN Security Council also intends to give the term 'imminent' a meaning that differs from its ordinary meaning and, consequently, from the meaning given to it in the HRL context, separating 'protection threats' from time-defined 'imminence' and equating them with notions of 'hostile intent' definitely raises a number of questions regarding the legal frameworks and standards applicable to the use of force by peace forces, which is discussed further in detail in Part III, Section 3.3.2.2.

The authorisation to take 'all necessary means, measures, steps, or action' to protect civilians can be understood as an authorisation to take initiatives needed to prevent, deter, pre-empt, or respond to (imminent) threats of physical violence against civilians. This may include the use of force. However, when the UN Security Council does not expressly include in a PoC mandate, an authorisation to use 'all necessary means', this does not necessarily mean that the PoC mandate does not provide for the legal authority to use force to protect civilians. An interpretation of the resolution in question, in particular of the ordinary meaning of the terms used in the UNSC resolutions, read in the context of the resolution as a whole and in light of its object and purpose, taking into account the history and circumstances of its adoption, must reveal whether there is a legal authority to use force to protect civilians.

The terms 'within its capabilities' and 'areas of deployment' are generally included in a PoC mandate to stress the limitations of the mission's ability to protect civilians throughout the territory of a host State. Units within a mission can only be expected to protect civilians within their area of operational responsibility. Yet even within that area, missions must be given the discretion to give priority to those threats that could potentially have greater potential impact on civilians or a more destabilising effect and to allocate resources accordingly. They should also be given the discretion to assess whether they are adequately equipped to carry out certain actions.

Last but not least, PoC mandates usually contain an explicit reference to 'the (primary) responsibility of the host State's government or authorities' for the protection of civilians. Such a caveat is used to emphasise that, although the deployment of a UN (mandated) peace operation is intended to assist the host State's government and/or authorities providing protection to the population, the host State retains the primary responsibility. When the host State is unable or unwilling to protect its population, UN (mandated) peace operations can act independently and even take military action against members of the host State's own armed forces if they constitute a threat of physical violence against civilians.

The proposed interpretation for the standardised PoC language still leaves plenty of leeway for those actors responsible for implementing a mandate to determine at their discretion which means are, for example, 'needed' to ensure PoC or what falls 'within the mission's capabilities' and 'areas of deployment'. Granting these actors such discretionary power is not necessarily problematic. It might even be unavoidable in light of the cascade structure in which the UNSC mandate is placed and whereby the mandate is interpreted and implemented at the various levels of authority, command, and control. Nonetheless, this does not mean that the UN Security Council always permits the full range of possible means of force when adopting this language or that the PoC mandate always constitutes a mere authorisation to which there are no expectations attached. Therefore, this study has identified an upper limit to what UN (mandated) peace operations may lawfully do to protect civilians and an emerging lower limit for what UN (mandated) peace operations must lawfully do to protect civilians.

As for the upper limit, first, any use of force must strictly comply with the norms of *jus cogens*. Second, the overall levels of force used when carrying out a UNSC mandate must be necessary and proportionate to obtain the general objective(s) set out in the mandate. As such, the mandate must be implemented strictly and only those objectives that have been authorised, such as PoC, can be pursued. When force has been used to carry out the mandate, the overall levels of force used should not exceed what was necessary to attain the general objectives. Relatedly, the means used to execute the mandate must prove rational and reasonable to protect civilians without unduly affecting the rights of those protected under international law. Third, specific instances of the use of force need to comply with HRL, IHL (if applicable), and relevant national laws of the host State and the TCC(s).

Besides an upper limit, there is also an emerging lower limit for what UN (mandated) peace operations must lawfully do to protect civilians. Over the years, the UN Security Council changed its tone in a number of PoC mandates (read: terminology with a more obligatory character was used over time). Based on an analysis of the language used in the relevant UNSC resolutions and the legal basis invoked, the circumstances of their adoption, and the subsequent practice of the UN Security Council and other relevant practices of UN organs and subsidiary organs, this study has found that the revised terminology could indicate the emergence of an obligation of conduct upon States, the UN itself, its organs (e.g. the UN Security Council and the UN Secretariat) and subsidiary organs (e.g. the UN peace operations), and international and regional organisations other than the UN that decide to undertake a PoC mandate. Hence, there might be an obligation to make the best efforts (within the operation's capabilities and areas of deployment) to pre-empt, prevent, deter, or respond to attacks or (imminent) threats of physical violence against civilians. Therefore, those involved in interpreting and implementing PoC mandates at the different levels in the chain of command should be aware of their responsibility to contribute to the successful protection of civilians. Indeed, there should not only be a heightened sense of responsibility when adopting a PoC mandate but also when consenting to carry out a PoC mandate and when implementing a PoC mandate.

UN practice needs further monitoring to see whether or not this emerging trend continues. The question of whether there is a lower limit to what UN (mandated) peace operations should lawfully do to protect civilians thus warrants further academic research.

Relationship between HRL and IHL and the UNSC mandate

Legal bases and legal regimes exercise, at least in theory, fundamentally different functions. Nevertheless, HRL and IHL may influence the interpretation, implementation, and evaluation of UNSC resolutions that contain a PoC mandate, but there are limits to this as well. First, when interpreting terms used in PoC mandates, one can look at the meaning of such terms in HRL or IHL. After all, when read in the context of the resolution as a whole and in light of its object and purpose, the ordinary meaning of a term can reflect the meaning given in the HRL or IHL context. Yet, it depends on the intentions of the UN Security Council to what extent any of such rules of international law can be considered. Only if the UN Security Council sought to draw on existing legal rules or an existing legal situation should those rules be taken into account when interpreting the resolution in question. Second, once adopted, PoC mandates are translated into military strategic, operational, and tactical instruments and, as such, govern the use of force ordered or used at the different levels of the chain of command. As a result, the meaning of a term conveyed at the strategic level in a manner consistent with HRL or IHL can also spill over to the other levels and thus create confusion when certain rules regulating the use of force at, say, the tactical level, are influenced by the PoC mandate, and, in turn, by IHL (who to protect?) and other rules are influenced by HRL (e.g. can lethal force be used against a certain person?). Third, violations of HRL or IHL may influence the evaluation of the implementation of a PoC mandate. However, this does not mean that such violations automatically constitute violations of the PoC mandate.

PART III

THE LEGAL REGIMES GOVERNING THE APPLICATION OF THE USE OF FORCE TO PROTECT CIVILIANS BY UN (MANDATED) PEACE FORCES[1307]

1. INTRODUCTION TO PART III

While Part II dealt with the PoC mandate as a mission-specific legal basis underlying UN (mandated) peace operations deployed to protect civilians, Part III deals with the legal regimes governing the application of the use of force to protect civilians by UN (mandated) peace forces on the ground. Practitioners are confronted with complex questions concerning the legal parameters governing the use of force in such specific PoC situations. By way of illustration, may UN (mandated) peace forces use force against rebels who, after entering a village and firing several rounds, start retreating but are likely to return? Is lethal force justified against rebels in retreat, and if so, under what conditions? May UN (mandated) peace forces launch pre-emptive strikes against hostile actors based on a past pattern of similar attacks, or do they need credible information that attacks will happen in the – immediate or more distant – future? Similarly, if a soldier suspects that a suicide bomber is about to detonate a bomb in a crowded camp for IDP, must he fire warning shots first or may he directly target the suspect in the crowd? Is immediate lethal force in such a situation authorised, and if so, under what conditions?

The legal regimes primarily cover the when and how of the use of force in specific PoC situations at the tactical level of the operation.[1308] While the legal regimes involved can be either international or national, this study has a particular focus on international law. From an international legal perspective, the legal regime most relevant to the application of force is always HRL. Nonetheless,

[1307] Part III is partly based on the following publications: Bourgeois, 'Failure to Protect Civilians in the Context of UN Peace Operations: A Question of Accountability?' (n. 1); Bourgeois, '"All Necessary Means" to Protect Civilians: The Interpretation and Implementation of UN Security Council Mandates Authorising the Protection of Civilians' (n. 1); Bourgeois and Labuda (n. 1); Bourgeois and Perrin (n. 1).

[1308] McLaughlin (n. 38) 413.

IHL becomes the main legal framework that governs the application of lethal force to the extent UN (mandated) peace operations are parties to an armed conflict. That said, the applicability *de jure* of HRL and IHL to UN (mandated) peace operations has not always been recognised, and discussions continue to emerge regarding when and how much force may be used under each legal regime. The legal regime which applies *de jure* has a major effect on the legality of the use of (lethal) force to protect civilians in specific situations. For example, while in the context of HRL, the use of lethal force is linked to strict temporal (and often also geographical) conditions, under IHL, lethal force may always be used against legitimate targets, subject to that body of law's legal conditions for targeting. However, what these conditions are is not always entirely clear.

While the legal regimes primarily encompass the when and how of the use of force in specific PoC situations, questions also arise as to whether the PoC mandate can also regulate the use of force by UN (mandated) peace forces on the ground (a matter primarily governed by legal regimes), and, more specifically, whether it can influence whether or not force is used in specific cases, and if so, how? Little has been published on the relationship between the UNSC mandate and the legal regimes in this regard, which is undoubtedly a lacuna in legal scholarship.[1309] Moreover, while much is written in the academic community about the increasing robustness of UN peacekeeping and the expansion of PoC mandates,[1310] few scholars analyse the implications of the turn towards robust and proactive UN peacekeeping in terms of compatibility with applicable legal rules, particularly the right to life.[1311] There seems to be ambiguity as to whether UN (mandated) peace forces may act upon different, more permissive, rules for the use of force simply because they act upon a Chapter VII mandate and use force for a 'higher good', namely PoC. Another example where it is not always clear if – and if so, how – a PoC mandate affects the legality of the use of force under the applicable legal regimes is when IHL applies. Should the notion of 'collateral damage', for example, be interpreted differently – read: more strictly – when force is used by UN (mandated) peace forces that have a mandate to protect civilians?

Last but not least, when UN (mandated) peace operations are deployed in the territory of a State, the question arises whether missions are obligated to take positive measures for the protection of civilians. In Part II, Section 3.3.2, this study discussed in detail whether a PoC mandate in and of itself can give rise to an obligation to take all necessary measures for the protection of civilians. However, the question arises whether HRL and IHL also impose a legal obligation to protect civilians.

1309 To the author's knowledge, there are very few academic contributions that do address this issue. For an overview, see the Introductory Chapter, Section 1, fn. 38.

1310 For examples of contributions, see the Introductory Chapter, Section 1, fn. 40.

1311 Exceptions are mentioned in the Introductory Chapter, Section 1, fn. 41.

To clarify these issues and to grasp how legal regimes, particularly HRL and IHL, govern the use of force to protect civilians by UN (mandated) peace forces carrying out PoC mandates, the next Section first examines the applicability *de jure* of HRL and IHL to UN (mandated) peace operations implementing a PoC mandate (Section 2). Section 2.1 looks into the applicability of HRL to UN (mandated) peace operations, including the applicability *ratione materiae, ratione temporis, ratione personae*, and *ratione loci*. Section 2.2 similarly examines the applicability of IHL to UN (mandated) peace operations, including the applicability *ratione materiae, ratione temporis, ratione personae*, and *ratione loci*.

Section 3 then discusses under which circumstances and in which manner UN (mandated) UN peace forces may use force (up to and including lethal force) in the execution of a PoC mandate. A distinction is made between the use of force that has no clear nexus to an armed conflict (Section 3.1) and the use of force that takes place inside the conduct of hostilities and does have a clear nexus to an armed conflict (Section 3.2). A further distinction is made between less-lethal force and lethal force. The study then continues with an analysis of the possible impact of the UNSC mandate on whether or not force can be used in specific instances (Section 3.3). To that end, this study first discusses how a UNSC mandate can indirectly impose additional restrictions on the use of force in specific instances and then examines to what extent the UN Security Council can depart from the law.

Section 4 examines whether there is an inherent power or obligation to protect civilians (by force) against the threat of physical violence under HRL and IHL. Whereas Section 4.1 analyses the obligation of UN (mandated) peace forces 'to protect' the human right to life, Section 4.2 explores the obligation 'to ensure respect' for IHL. Section 5 provides a summary of what has been covered in Part III.

2. APPLICABILITY OF LEGAL REGIMES

In the past, there has often been opposition to the application of IHL to troops deployed under a UNSC mandate and, in particular, to troops under the command and control of the UN (i.e. UN peace operations). The following statement from the Committee on Study of Legal Problems of the United Nations of the American Society of International Law (ASIL) is a clear illustration of this:[1312]

1312 Emphasis added. William Bivens and others, 'Report of the Committee on the Study of the Legal Problems of the United Nations: Should the Laws of War Apply to United Nations Enforcement Action?', *Proceedings of the American Society of International Law at Its Annual Meeting (1921–1969), 24–26 April 1952, Washington, DC, vol. 46, 216* (Cambridge University

> The assertion that United Nations enforcement action is war arouses strong opposition. Whatever the definition of war may be, this much of it would be generally accepted, that war is conflict between states, between units of equal legal status; whereas the United Nations, acting on behalf of the organized community of nations against an offender, has a *superior legal and moral position* as compared with the other party to the conflict. A war is fought by a state for its own national interest; United Nations enforcement action is on behalf of order and peace among nations.
> [...]
> The Committee agrees that the use of force by the United Nations to restrain aggression is of a *different nature* from war-making by a state. The purposes for which the laws of war were instituted are not entirely the same as the purposes of regulating the use of force by the United Nations. This we may say without deciding whether United Nations enforcement action is war, police enforcement of criminal law, or *sui generis*. In the present circumstances, then, the proper answer would seem to be, for the time being, that the United Nations *should not feel bound by all the laws of war, but should select such of the laws of war as may seem to fit its purposes* (e.g., prisoners of war, belligerent occupation), adding such others as may be needed, and rejecting those which seem incompatible with its purposes. We think it beyond doubt that the United Nations, representing practically all the nations of the earth, has the right to make such decisions.

As a result, UN peace operations are given safe conduct based on their UNSC mandate. It has also been suggested that the UN cannot apply the Geneva Conventions I–IV because they have no territorial jurisdiction or criminal or disciplinary jurisdiction.[1313]

In addition, HRL has not always been considered the most suitable legal regime, as it was initially developed to regulate 'internal' force by State authorities against their citizens in the context of law enforcement, and thus not necessarily the activities of military operations when used for purposes other than maintaining or restoring public safety, the rule of law, and internal order (the so-called traditional law enforcement functions).[1314] At the same time, it has long been doubted whether international organisations are bound by HRL, and if so, only when they have taken over almost all state functions (e.g. when they act as a territorial administration). It is, for example, illustrative that the

Press) 217 and 220, as also discussed by Zwanenburg, 'UN Peace Operations, International Humanitarian Law and International Human Rights Law' (n. 37) 97; Vaios Koutroulis, 'Jus Ad/Contra Bellum' in Raphael van Steenberghe (ed), *Le Droit International Humanitaire: Un Régime Spécial de Droit International?* (Bruylant 2013) 158.

1313 See e.g. ICRC, 'Report on the Work of the Conference of Government Experts on the Reaffirmation and Development of International Humanitarian Law Applicable in Armed Conflicts, 24 May–12 June 1971, Geneva', (ICRC 1971) ICRC Doc. 345.21/28 52, para. 311, as referred to by Zwanenburg, 'UN Peace Operations, International Humanitarian Law and International Human Rights Law' (n. 37) 97.

1314 See also Part I, Section 4.1.2.2(A)(i).

2002 UN Sample ROE did not even mention HRL, whereas the 'Laws of Armed Conflict' (IHL) were expressly mentioned.[1315]

Nowadays, however, the principle that HRL and IHL may apply to UN (mandated) peace operations is no longer controversial.[1316] The 2008 Capstone Doctrine, for example, has set forth that UN peace operations 'should be conducted in full respect of human rights' and that UN forces 'must have a clear understanding of the principles and rules of international humanitarian law and observe them in situations where they apply.'[1317] Moreover, in the 2017 UN Guidelines on the Use of Force by Military Components in UN Peacekeeping Operations, the most recent authoritative restatement of use of force rules for peace forces, the following is set forth:[1318]

> The legal basis for the use of force by peacekeepers resides in the mandate of the peacekeeping mission, as reflected in the relevant resolution(s) adopted by the Security Council [...] [and] must be exercised in a manner consistent with the mandate [...].Mission-specific ROE provide the authority for the use of force [...] The use of force in peacekeeping operations must comply with international laws, including applicable international humanitarian law and human rights norms, principles and standards. At all times, the use of force must be consistent with the principles of gradation, necessity, proportionality, legality, distinction, precaution, humanity and accountability.

Also, in their policies on PoC in UN peace operations, the UN has consistently confirmed that UN peace operations must abide by HRL and IHL, where applicable, and that HRL and IHL must be implemented 'in both the letter and spirit of these legal frameworks.'[1319] In the 2019 UN Policy on PoC in UN Peacekeeping, it is even explicitly stressed that the obligation to comply with IHL 'is independent of the PoC mandate.'[1320]

1315 UN DPKO (n. 102) 1 ('[I]n accordance with the relevant principles of international law, including the laws of armed conflict'). See also Foley, *UN Peacekeeping Operations and the Protection of Civilians: Saving Succeeding Generations* (n. 16) 143–144 and 235.

1316 E.g. the deputy Legal Counsel of the UN wrote the following in a contribution on legal challenges and uncertainties with respect to UN peacekeeping (hereby only expressing his personal views): '[T]he general question of whether IHL is applicable to UN peacekeeping operations could now be considered as a settled matter' (Mathias (n. 26) 142).

1317 UN DPKO and UN DFS, '2008 Capstone Doctrine' (n. 19) 14–15.

1318 UN DPKO and UN DFS, '2017 UN Guidelines on the Use of Force by Military Components in UN Peacekeeping Operations' (n. 17) paras 7–8. See also UN DPKO and UN DFS, '2015 UN Policy on PoC in UN Peacekeeping' (n. 16) para. 17 ('When using force peacekeeping operations must abide by customary international law, including international human rights and humanitarian law, where applicable. They must also abide by the mission-specific military rules of engagement [ROE] and the police Directive on the Use of Force [DUF]').

1319 UN DPKO and UN DFS, '2015 UN Policy on PoC in UN Peacekeeping' (n. 16) para. 17; UN DPO, '2019 UN Policy on PoC in UN Peacekeeping' (n. 35) paras 22 and 27.

1320 UN DPO, '2019 UN Policy on PoC in UN Peacekeeping' (n. 35) para. 22.

The 2016 NATO Policy on PoC equally states that any actions for the protection of civilians must be consistent with 'applicable legal frameworks [...] which may include international human rights law and international humanitarian law,'[1321] yet NATO largely entrusts its Member States with interpreting the relevant rules on the use of force of these legal regimes.[1322] According to the 2015 EU Concept for the Use of Force in EU-led Military Operations, any use of force, whether in self-defence or under the ROE, must likewise comply with international standards, in particular as defined in applicable conventional and customary international law, and with the relevant decisions of international organisations.[1323] Article 4(c) of the AU PSC Protocol holds that the AU PSC – the AU body that may authorise the mounting and deployment of peace support missions – shall be guided by 'respect for the rule of law, fundamental human rights and freedoms, the sanctity of human life and international humanitarian law.' According to the 2012 AU Draft Guidelines for PoC, '[a]ny action taken by a peace support operation to implement a protection of civilians mandate shall be in conformity with relevant international law, including international humanitarian law, human rights law and refugee law.'[1324]

The UN Security Council has also included multiple references to HRL and IHL in the mandates it has adopted in recent years. For example, in Resolution 2098 (2013), the UN Security Council requested MONUSCO, when acting through the Intervention Brigade, to carry out its mandate 'in strict compliance with international law, including international humanitarian law and with the human rights due diligence policy on UN-support to non-UN forces.'[1325] Similarly, when it decided that UNMISS would include the Regional Protection Force to provide a secure environment in and around Juba, it stressed that the Regional Protection Force would have to carry out its mandate 'in strict compliance with international law, including, as applicable, international humanitarian law.'[1326] However, less forceful UN peace operations were also requested to abide by certain bodies of international law. In 2010, the UN Security Council already requested MONUSCO itself to '[s]upport the efforts of the Government of the [DRC] [...] to bring the ongoing military operations against [certain armed groups] [...], to a completion, in compliance with international humanitarian, human rights and refugee law and the need

1321 NAC, '2016 NATO Policy on PoC' (n. 118) para. 5.

1322 As already discussed above, see Part I, Section 3.2.2.

1323 EUMC, '2015 EU Concept for the Use of Force in EU-Led Military Operations' (n. 119) para. 2. See also Part I, Section 3.2.3.

1324 AU, '2012 AU Draft Guidelines for PoC in AU Peace Support Operations' (n. 114) 5. See also Part I, Section 3.2.1.

1325 'UNSC Res. 2098' (n. 19) para. 12(a)(i). See also subsequent mandates granted to MONUSCO and the Intervention Brigade, including 'UNSC Res. 2147' (n. 19) para. 4(b); 'UNSC Res. 2211' (n. 127) para. 9(e); 'UNSC Res. 2277' (n. 127) para. 35(i)(d); 'UNSC Res. 2348' (n. 127) para. 34(i)(d); 'UNSC Res. 2409' (n. 19) para. 36(i)(d).

1326 'UNSC Res. 2304' (n. 135) para. 8.

to protect civilians.'[1327] In UNSC Resolution 2100 (2013), MINUSMA was requested to 'abide by international humanitarian, human rights and refugee law.'[1328] Similarly, UN-mandated peace operations have been requested to respect certain bodies of international law. For example, in 2012, the UN Security Council stressed that AFISMA 'shall take all necessary measures, in compliance with applicable international humanitarian law and human rights law.'[1329]

However, a distinction must be drawn between applying the legal regimes as a matter of policy and as a matter of law. While the international and regional organisations' policies stress that any use of force must comply with HRL and IHL, where applicable, their view on when each framework applies *de jure* in the context of UN (mandated) peace operations largely remains unclear. The UN has never publicly acknowledged that it is bound by IHL when conducting a specific UN peace operation.[1330] States have also been quite reluctant to acknowledge that they have become a party to an armed conflict when participating in a UN-mandated peace operation. For example, in 2008, Bernard Kouchner, the former French Minister of Foreign Affairs, argued that France was not a party to an armed conflict in Afghanistan because its troops only contributed to the NATO operation following a UNSC mandate.[1331] Similarly, as already referred to in the Introductory Chapter, in 2011, Jens Stoltenberg, the former Norwegian Prime Minister, stated that Norway was not participating in a war in Libya since it was executing a UN-mandated peace operation.[1332] Consequently, Norwegian soldiers who took part in the NATO operation in Libya could not be regarded as legitimate targets by soldiers of the Libyan regime.[1333]

1327 'UNSC Res. 1925' (n. 125) para. 12(h).

1328 'UNSC Res. 2100' (n. 34) para. 24. See also subsequent mandates granted to MINUSMA, including 'UNSC Res. 2164' (n. 19); 'UNSC Res. 2227' (n. 19) para. 33; 'UNSC Res. 2295' (n. 34) para. 38; 'UNSC Res. 2364' (n. 19) para. 40.

1329 'UNSC Res. 2085' (n. 148) para. 9.

1330 As also noted by Pacholska (n. 26); Mathias (n. 26) 142–145; Gill and others (n. 26) 96–97.

1331 France, Assemblée Nationale, 'XIIIe Législature, Compte Rendu N° 36, Commission de La Défense Nationale et Des Forces Armées, Mardi 26 Août 2008' ('Monsieur Lecoq, je conteste le mot " guerre ". Nous ne sommes pas en guerre contre un État, contre un peuple. Nous agissons sous mandat des Nations unies, avec trente-neuf pays de la communauté internationale qui luttent conte le terrorisme. Je vous invite d'ailleurs, si vous accompagnez le président Guy Tessier dans le cadre de la mission parlementaire, à vous rendre dans les vallées et pas seulement dans les camps militaires : vous y verrez que la population est heureuse de voir les forces alliées assurer leur sécurité, que les enfants sont aujourd'hui scolarisés, que les familles afghanes peuvent bénéficier de programmes de santé. L'accueil des populations montre que les Afghans aspirent à la paix et à la sécurité. Après quarante ans de drames permanents, les Afghans ont aussi envie de vivre en paix'), as also referred to by Ferraro, 'The Applicability and Application of International Humanitarian Law to Multinational Forces' (n. 676) 563.

1332 Norway (n. 27), as discussed by Larsen and others (n. 27) 259.

1333 Norway (n. 27), as referred to by Larsen and others (n. 27) 259.

The reluctance to accept that a UN (mandated) peace operation has become a party to an armed conflict is understandable for at least two reasons. First, members of the military component deployed as part of a UN (mandated) peace operation that become party to an armed conflict are considered enemy combatants by the opposing party and may thus be legitimately killed.[1334] Second, if a UN (mandated) peace operation becomes a party to an armed conflict, it is difficult to defend that it is upholding its impartial role, while impartiality is one of the three basic principles with which peacekeeping is traditionally associated.[1335]

States and international and regional organisations conducting UN (mandated) peace operations are also reluctant to have their human rights standards critically assessed.[1336] The resistance to accepting the applicability of HRL is usually motivated by the fear that HRL will be applied *in toto*, without adaptation, and in an unrealistic manner to extraterritorial emergencies.[1337] Nevertheless, most scholars argue that the use of force by UN (mandated) peace forces is governed primarily by HRL, and there seems to be greater openness to integrating HRL-based concepts into the use of force and PoC policy guidelines. For instance, the UN's adoption of a graduated force continuum for the use of force, where lethal force is a last resort, appears premised on HRL applicability. The UN also seems to endorse a human rights-grounded principle of proportionality for any use of force – 'the amount of force which is reasonable in intensity, duration and magnitude, based on all facts known [...] at the time, to decisively counter a hostile act or intent or to otherwise achieve an authorized objective specified in the mission specific ROE' – rather than an IHL-based concept of proportionality, which only prohibits attacks against legitimate targets that 'may be expected to cause incidental loss of civilian life, injury to civilians, damage to civilian objects, or a combination thereof, which would be excessive in relation to the concrete and direct military advantage anticipated.'[1338] Nevertheless, when military force is used on the ground to protect civilians, IHL is the 'go-to' legal regime, even if the threshold for an IAC or a NIAC has not been reached. This reaction is not surprising since UN (mandated) peace operations consist primarily of military contingents trained in IHL for military operations rather than civilian police familiar with law enforcement tasks.[1339]

1334 Gill and others (n. 26) 96. As also discussed in Part I, Section 3.1.1.

1335 *Ibid.*

1336 Sheeran, 'Human Rights and Derogation in Peacekeeping' (n. 29) 232.

1337 *Ibid.*

1338 UN DPKO and UN DFS, '2017 UN Guidelines on the Use of Force by Military Components in UN Peacekeeping Operations' (n. 17) para. 8 and p. 20. Gaggioli, 'The Use of Force in Armed Conflicts Conduct of Hostilities, Law Enforcement, and Self-Defense' (n. 643) 69–71. On proportionality in IHL, see also Part III, Section 3.2.3.

1339 Oxford Research Group (n. 32).

The fact that it is so unclear when HRL and IHL apply *de jure* to the conduct of UN (mandated) peace operations creates a great deal of legal uncertainty and is therefore addressed in the next Section.

2.1. APPLICABILITY OF HRL TO UN (MANDATED) PEACE FORCES CARRYING OUT A POC MANDATE

HRL was developed primarily to regulate the 'internal' use of force by State authorities against their own citizens. The question of whether HRL applies to the conduct of peace forces in UN (mandated) peace operations raises several intricate legal questions. For example, States have HRL obligations to those on their territory because they exercise 'jurisdiction' on that territory.[1340] But what if States operate outside their territory? And what about international and regional organisations? Such actors do not have their own territory and nationals. How, then, can one determine when international and regional organisations are exercising 'jurisdiction' and thus have certain HRL obligations when conducting UN (mandated) peace operations? Moreover, if it is accepted that international and regional organisations may exercise jurisdiction, which HRL obligations apply *de jure* to a specific situation given that peace forces are not only members of UN (mandated) peace operations but also State agents of the States undertaking or taking part in an operation, as well as visitors in the host State? The present Section addresses these issues, as well as other pressing questions concerning the applicability of HRL to the actions of UN (mandated) peace operations, by discussing the applicability *ratione personae*, *ratione materiae*, *ratione temporis*, and *ratione loci* of HRL in the context of UN (mandated) peace operations.

2.1.1. Applicability ratione personae

To date, international and regional organisations involved in UN (mandated) peace operations do not have their own armed forces. Instead, they depend on States that make their armed forces available to the organisations. In doing so, States may transfer some authority to international or regional organisations, but they can never transfer full authority.[1341] Hence, members of armed forces taking part in UN peace operations or UN-mandated peace operations carried out by the AU, NATO, or the EU usually have a dual legal status and role: they become members of UN (mandated) peace forces and act 'in an international capacity as part of the institutional structure' of the international or regional organisation conducting the operation but also remain state agents and act 'in a

[1340] Gill and others (n. 26) 79.

[1341] See also Part I, Section 4.2.2.2.

national capacity' as organs of their sending State.[1342] In addition, when troops are deployed in the territory of a host State (with its consent), UN (mandated) peace forces are also visitors of that State.

Accordingly, HRL obligations that apply in the context of a UN (mandated) peace operation may be derived from the international obligations of the following actors: (i) the international or regional organisation undertaking the operation; (ii) the State undertaking or taking part in the operation; and (iii) the State on whose territory the operation takes place (the host State).[1343]

For each UN (mandated) peace operation, which set(s) of HRL obligations appl(ies)(y) *in general* as a matter of law must be identified, as this determines what the UN (mandated) peace forces can legally do.[1344] Whether the HRL obligations of the international or regional organisation conducting the operation apply, or the HRL obligations of the State undertaking or taking part in the operation, or the HRL obligations of both, depends on the status of an operation. The status of an operation refers to how an operation relates to the State and/or the organisation. Relevant questions are: has the international organisation created its own force, or are the troops contributed to the organisation by States? In the case of the latter, is the operation a subsidiary organ of the organisation, or is it somehow part of the organisation and, therefore, bound by the international obligations that bind the organisation? It is not unusual for members of UN (mandated) peace forces to be bound by both the HRL obligations of the organisation involved and their sending State, given that they take part in an operation that becomes part of the organisation in question, yet also remain agents of their sending State.[1345] Consequently, the applicable sets of HRL obligations may vary significantly or even be contradictory and hence give rise to problems of legal interoperability. In practice, this can be solved by planning and conducting the operation in question in a manner consistent with the legal rules that all partners in the operation consider applicable within their legal framework.[1346]

1342 Aurel Sari, 'Jurisdiction and International Responsibility in Peace Support Operations: The Behrami and Saramati Cases' (2008) 8 Human Rights Law Review 151, 160. See also White, 'Security Council Mandates and the Use of Lethal Force by Peacekeepers: What Place for the Laws of War?' (n. 31) 105–106.

1343 Gill and others (n. 26) 77–79; White, 'Security Council Mandates and the Use of Lethal Force by Peacekeepers: What Place for the Laws of War?' (n. 31) 105–106.

1344 Gill and others (n. 26) 77.

1345 When personnel participate in a UN (mandated) peacekeeping operation in their personal capacity and thus not as State agents, HRL obligations for them do not flow from this source (see also *ibid.* 82). See further Part III, Sections 2.1.1.1 and 2.1.1.2.

1346 For further literature on legal interoperability, see e.g. Zwanenburg, 'International Humanitarian Law Interoperability in Multinational Operations' (n. 656); Johan FR Boddens Hosang, 'An Operational Perspective' in Robert Geiß and Heike Krieger (eds), *The 'Legal Pluriverse' Surrounding Multinational Military Operations* (Oxford University Press 2019) 103; Geiß and Krieger (n. 64) (and, in particular, Michael Newton, 'The Legal Interoperability of the Laws of Armed Conflict' in Robert Geiß and Heike Krieger (eds), *The 'Legal Pluriverse'*

Which HRL obligations apply *de jure* in a *specific* situation on the ground depends on the factual circumstances and can only be assessed on a case-by-case basis.[1347] One of the determinants is the exercise of 'jurisdiction' (i.e. power over a territory, an individual or an individual's rights; on the issue of 'jurisdiction' and 'extraterritorial jurisdiction', see Part III, Section 2.1.3).[1348] However, how can it be determined who – the international or regional organisation or the TCC – exercises jurisdiction when members of UN (mandated) peace forces have a dual legal status and role? To determine *ex post* in what capacity a member of a UN (mandated) peace operation has acted and thus under whose jurisdiction the individual fell, one must seek a link between the conduct of a physical person and a holder of international obligations (i.e. the international or regional organisation or the TCC).[1349]

While the question of who exercises jurisdiction must be distinguished from the question of whether certain conduct of armed forces in UN (mandated) peace operations can be attributed to the TCCs and/or to the international or regional organisations conducting the operation, and thus gives rise to accountability for violations of HRL, the same test can be applied. Yet, to avoid all doubt: while the attribution determines the legal framework relevant for assessing the legality of certain conduct, this does not necessarily determine which legal norms apply in general as a matter of law (as discussed earlier).[1350] For example, while UN HRL obligations may apply during a UN peace operation, specific conduct could be ultimately attributed to the TCC. That said, the agency paradigm of attribution can help link the conduct of an individual soldier to one of the holders of HRL obligations and, as such, help to determine whose HRL obligations applied in a specific situation, those of the international or regional organisation or that of the TCC.

To attribute conduct to the State or to the international or regional organisation in question, which entity exercised command and control must be identified. Command and control structures vary between international and regional organisations and even between different UN (mandated) peace operations conducted by the same organisation.[1351] Furthermore, there can

---

Surrounding Multinational Military Operations (Oxford University Press 2019)); Watkin (n. 64); Zyberi and Andersson (n. 64).

1347 Gill and others (n. 26) 77.

1348 *Ibid.* 150.

1349 Marten Zwanenburg, 'International Organisations vs. Troop Contributing Countries: Which Should Be Considered as the Party to an Armed Conflict during Peace Operations?', *Proceedings of the 12th Bruges Colloquium on International Organisations' Involvement in Peace Operations: Applicable Legal Framework and the Issue of Responsibility, 20–21 October 2011, Bruges, vol. 42, 23* (2012) 26.

1350 Kjetil Mujezinović Larsen, *The Human Rights Treaty Obligations of Peacekeepers* (Cambridge University Press 2014) 106.

1351 Gill and others (n. 26) 100. For literature on command and control, see e.g. Cammaert and Klappe (n. 726); Blaise Cathcart, 'Command and Control in Military Operations' in Terry

sometimes be a difference between what is officially communicated about the structure and exercise of control over the operation and what actually happens on the ground. Several tests have been put forward in case law and literature to determine where control lied during an operation, including the test of 'effective control', the test of 'overall control', and the test of 'ultimate authority and control'.[1352] The rules of control and attribution in UN (mandated) peace operations have, however, remained unresolved to date. Different rules and principles have emerged under different legal systems, and opinions differ on how these rules and principles should be interpreted and applied, making it a highly complex and controversial issue. A detailed analysis of whom should exercise what control to determine to whom certain behaviour can be attributed and, by analogy, whose HRL obligations are at stake falls outside the scope of the present study.[1353]

D Gill and Dieter Fleck (eds), *The Handbook of the International Law of Military Operations* (2nd edn., Oxford University Press 2015); Gill and others (n. 26) 267–287.

1352 The rule that is now often invoked can be found in Art. 7 of the 2011 DARIO: 'The conduct of an organ of a State or an organ or agent of an international organisation that is placed at the disposal of another international organisation shall be considered under international law an act of the latter organisation if the organisation exercises effective control over that conduct.' See also ILC, 'Analytical Guide to the Work of the International Law Commission on the Responsibility of International Organisations' (*ILC*), https://legal.un.org/ilc/guide/9_11.shtml, accessed 16 July 2022. For earlier case law invoking the 'effective control' test, see e.g. *Case Concerning Military and Paramilitary Activities in and against Nicaragua (Nicaragua v. United States of America), Judgment (Merits)* (n. 615) para. 115 ('For this conduct to give rise to legal responsibility of the United States, it would in principle have to be proved that that State had effective control of the military or paramilitary operations in the course of which the alleged violations were committed'). The threshold of effective control was deemed too high by the ICTY, which preferred the lower threshold of 'overall control' in the *Tadić* case, see *Prosecutor v. Tadić, Appeals chamber judgment* (n. 888) para. 120 ('[F]or the attribution to a State of acts of these groups it is sufficient to require that the group as a whole be under the overall control of the State'). In the *Behrami and Saramati* case, the ECtHR also adopted a lower threshold in the form of the 'ultimate authority and control' test: *Case of Behrami and Behrami v. France and Saramati v. France, Germany and Norway, Decision as to the admissibility* (2007] ECtHR (Grand Chamber) App. Nos. 71412/01 and 78166/01 para. 133 ('The Court considers that the key question is whether the UNSC retained ultimate authority and control so that operational command only was delegated'). In the *Genocide* case, the ICJ ultimately applied the 'overall control' test, see *Case Concerning Application of the Convention on the Prevention and Punishment of the Crime of Genocide (Bosnia and Herzegovina v. Yugoslavia (Serbia and Montenegro)), Judgment* (2007) ICJ Rep 43 para. 404 ('Insofar as the "overall control" test is employed to determine whether or not an armed conflict is international, which was the sole question which the Appeals Chamber was called upon to decide, it may well be that the test is applicable and suitable'). For relevant literature, see e.g. Aurel Sari, 'UN Peacekeeping Operations and Article 7 ARIO: The Missing Link' (2012) 9 International Organizations Law Review 77; Ray Murphy and Siobhán Wills, 'United Nations Peacekeeping Operations' in André Nollkaemper and Ilias Plakokefalos (eds), *The Practice of Shared Responsibility in International Law* (Cambridge University Press 2017) 598–603.

1353 For further literature, see e.g. Larsen (n. 1350) 107–164; Murphy and Wills (n. 1352); Ademola Abass, 'African Union Operations' in André Nollkaemper and Ilias Plakokefalos (eds), *The Practice of Shared Responsibility in International Law* (Cambridge University Press 2017); Marten Zwanenburg, 'North Atlantic Treaty Organization-Led Operations'

2.1.1.1. Peace forces as members of UN (mandated) peace operations

The first source of HRL obligations may apply to peace forces as members of UN (mandated) peace operations carried out by, for example, the UN, the AU, NATO, or the EU.

UN – The UN is not a party to any human rights treaty, but it is nevertheless accepted that it is bound by customary HRL.[1354] In the *Reparation for Injuries* case, the ICJ stated in its advisory opinion to the UN General Assembly that the UN is endowed with international legal personality.[1355] In its advisory opinion on the *WHO-Egypt Agreement of 1951*, the ICJ has clarified that '[i]nternational organizations are subjects of international law and, as such, are bound by any obligations incumbent upon them under general rules of international law, under their constitutions or under international agreements to which they are parties.'[1356] According to Verdirame, the most evident interpretation of the reference to 'general rules of international law' is that it is shorthand 'for customary international law of universal or quasi-universal applicability and for general principles of law.'[1357]

Thus, by virtue of its international legal personality, the UN is bound by customary international law as far as that law is relevant to the functions it carries out.[1358] Subsidiary organs of the UN, such as UN peace operations, are,

in André Nollkaemper and Ilias Plakokefalos (eds), *The Practice of Shared Responsibility in International Law* (Cambridge University Press 2017); Frederik Naert, 'European Union Common Security and Defence Policy Operations' in André Nollkaemper and Ilias Plakokefalos (eds), *The Practice of Shared Responsibility in International Law* (Cambridge University Press 2017).

1354 Scott Sheeran, 'A Constitutional Moment: United Nations Peacekeeping in the Democratic Republic of Congo' (2011) 8 International Organizations Law Review 55, 112–119. See further Sheeran, 'Human Rights and Derogation in Peacekeeping' (n. 29) 210–211; Verdirame (n. 95) 72 (on HRL obligations of international organisations more generally, see pp. 55–90); White, 'Security Council Mandates and the Use of Lethal Force by Peacekeepers: What Place for the Laws of War?' (n. 31) 106; Willmot and Sheeran (n. 219) 526–527. On the different possible foundations for the applicability of human rights standards to the UN, the possible meanings of 'applicability' of human rights standards to the UN, and the limits of the applicability of human rights to the UN as a non-state actor, see Frédéric Mégret and Florian Hoffmann, 'The UN as a Human Rights Violator? Some Reflections on the United Nations Changing Human Rights Responsibilities' (2003) 25 Human Rights Quarterly 314, 316–325. See also Sylvia Maus, *United Nations Peace Operations and Human Rights: Normativity and Compliance* (Brill 2020) 79–108.

1355 In particular, the ICJ confirmed that the UN is 'an international person' that is a 'subject of international law and capable of possessing international rights and duties' (*Reparation for Injuries Suffered in the Service of the United Nations, Advisory opinion* (n. 585) 179).

1356 *Interpretation of the Agreement of 25 March 1951 between the WHO and Egypt, Advisory opinion* (1980) ICJ Rep 73, para. 37.

1357 Verdirame (n. 95) 71.

1358 Zwanenburg, 'UN Peace Operations, International Humanitarian Law and International Human Rights Law' (n. 37) 93; Jordan Paust, 'The UN Is Bound by Human Rights: Understanding the Full Reach of Human Rights, Remedies, and Nonimmunity' (Social Science Research Network 2010) SSRN Scholarly Paper ID 1710744 2–5, https://papers.ssrn.com/abstract=1710744, accessed 5 December 2017.

in turn, bound by these customary HRL obligations.[1359] In addition, UN peace operations must also comply with other HRL obligations that bind the UN (such as those principles of HRL which amount to general principles of law within Article 38(1)(c) of the ICJ Statute), as well as the HRL obligations imposed by the UN Security Council, including through the mandate.[1360]

AU, NATO, and EU – It is widely recognised that the AU, NATO, and the EU have legal personality. The legal personality of the EU is explicitly acknowledged in Article 47 of the TEU.[1361] The AU Constitutive Act is silent on the AU having legal personality. However, Article 1 of the AU General Convention[1362] explicitly states that the 'Organization of African Unity shall possess juridical personality and shall have the capacity: (a) To enter into contacts including the rights to acquire and dispose of movable and immovable property; (b) To institute legal proceedings.'[1363] While the North Atlantic Treaty and the additional treaties (such as the 1951 Ottawa Agreement[1364] and the 1952 Paris Protocol[1365]) are also silent on the matter, statements by the NATO Secretary-General and his legal advisor have confirmed that the organisation does have international legal personality.[1366]

1359 See Art. 29 of the UN Charter and para. 15 of the 1990 UN Model SOFA, as referred to above, see Introductory Chapter, Section 3.1, fn. 46 (UNGA, '1990 UN Model SOFA for Peacekeeping Operations' (n. 46)). See also Gill and others (n. 26) 77–78, 83; White, 'Security Council Mandates and the Use of Lethal Force by Peacekeepers: What Place for the Laws of War?' (n. 31) 106.

1360 For a detailed discussion of human rights tasks in UN peace operations mandates, see Maus (n. 1353) 125–131.

1361 See also Frederik Naert, 'International Law Aspects of the EU's Security and Defence Policy, with a Particular Focus on the Law of Armed Conflict and Human Rights' (DPhil thesis, KU Leuven 2008) 199–226.

1362 General Convention on the Privileges and Immunities of the Organization of African Unity (adopted 25 October 1965, entered into force 25 October 1965) 1000 UNTS 393 (AU General Convention).

1363 See also Abass (n. 1353) 614–617.

1364 Agreement on the Status of the North Atlantic Treaty Organization, National Representatives and International Staff (adopted 20 September 1951, entered into force 18 May 1954) 200 UNTS 3 (1951 Ottawa Agreement).

1365 Protocol on the Status of International Military Headquarters set up pursuant to the North Atlantic Treaty (adopted 28 August 1952, entered into force 10 April 1954) 200 UNTS 340 (1952 Paris Protocol).

1366 NATO, '"Strategic Airlift Capability (SAC) – Initiative Adoption of the NAMO Charter", Note by the Secretary-General' (*NATO*, 20 June 2007), www.nato.int/cps/en/natohq/official_texts_56625.htm, accessed 11 July 2022; B. de Vidts, 'Aspects Related to the Legal Status of the North Atlantic Treaty Organization', Speaking notes, 22 November 2004, NATO doc. CJ(2004)0910, cited in Joop ED Voetelink, '"Status of Forces": Strafrechtsmacht over Militairen Vanuit Internationaalrechtelijk & Militair-Operationeelrechtelijk Perspectief' (DPhil thesis, University of Amsterdam 2012) 161, as also referred to by Zwanenburg, 'North Atlantic Treaty Organization-Led Operations' (n. 1353) 640–641. See also the overview given by Larsen (n. 1350) 92–99. See also David RD Nauta, *The International Responsibility of NATO and Its Personnel during Military Operations*, vol. 58 (Brill 2018), Chapter 5 on the International Legal Personality of NATO, 86–107.

It is generally accepted that international and regional organisations are subject to the rules of customary international law in the area in which they operate. Hence, when the AU, NATO, or the EU takes action in the field of peace and security, those activities relate to customary HRL and, therefore, are bound by that set of rules. However, a difference with UN peace operations being a subsidiary organ of the UN is that UN-mandated peace operations conducted by the AU, NATO, and the EU are not (yet) recognised as subsidiary organs of the organisations in question.[1367]

Nevertheless, EU-led peace operations are considered to be bound by the EU's obligations under international law, as well as by EU human rights law.[1368] After all, as discussed in Part I, Section 4.1.1.1(A)(ii), pursuant to Article 42(1) of the TEU, the EU has the possibility of establishing both civilian and military missions outside the EU for peacekeeping, conflict prevention, and strengthening international security. According to Naert, such EU-led military operations 'have a status independent of the participating States, most likely as part of the legal personality of the EU.'[1369] In that capacity, they are bound by the same HRL obligations to which the EU is bound.[1370]

In the context of UN-mandated peace operations conducted by NATO, the operations in question might well share in the legal personality of NATO and

---

[1367] Gill and others (n. 26) 77. Yet, see also Nicholas Tsagourias, 'EU Peacekeeping Operations: Legal and Theoretical Issues' in Martin Trybus and Nigel White (eds), *European Security Law* (Oxford University Press 2007) 121–122.

[1368] Gill and others (n. 26) 77.

[1369] Naert, 'International Law Aspects of the EU's Security and Defence Policy, with a Particular Focus on the Law of Armed Conflict and Human Rights' (n. 1361) 424, see also more extensively 222–224. See also Joni Heliskosi, 'Responsibility and Liability for CSDP Operations' in Steven Blockmans and Panos Koutrakos (eds), *Research Handbook on the EU's Common Foreign and Security Policy* (Edward Elgar Publishing 2018) 137.

[1370] The EU's HRL obligations are, e.g., laid down in the following two instruments: (i) Art. 6 of the TEU, which binds the EU to the ECHR and provides that fundamental rights, as guaranteed by the ECHR and as they result from the constitutional traditions common to the EU Member States, shall constitute general principles of EU law (on a side note, while the EU is already bound to the ECHR in substance, Art. 6(2) of the TEU also provides for the EU's accession to the ECHR, yet the implementation of this provision is still under negotiation); and (ii) the EU Charter of Fundamental Rights, which has the same legal value as the EU treaties (as confirmed in Art. 6(1) of the TEU) (full reference: Charter of Fundamental Rights of the European Union (adopted 7 December 2000, entered into force 1 December 2009) OJ C 364/1 (2000) (EU Charter of Fundamental Rights)). Art. 51(1) of the EU Charter of Fundamental Rights, which sets out the scope of the Charter, provides that its provisions 'are addressed to the institutions, bodies, offices and agencies of the Union with due regard for the principle of subsidiarity and to the Member States only when they are implementing [EU] [...] law. They shall therefore respect the rights, observe the principles and promote the application thereof in accordance with their respective powers and respecting the limits of the powers of the [EU] [...] as conferred on it in the Treaties.' Last but not least, the EU is also bound by customary HRL, general principles of international law, and *jus cogens* (see Naert, 'International Law Aspects of the EU's Security and Defence Policy, with a Particular Focus on the Law of Armed Conflict and Human Rights' (n. 1361) 431. On the sources and extent of the EU's HRL obligations more in general, see 424–430).

thus also be a 'part' of NATO.[1371] NATO Legal Deskbook sets forth that not only NATO Members but also NATO itself is bound to respect the human rights first set out in the UDHR and that the wide range of HRL treaties concluded under the auspices of the UN may have similar implications.[1372] Hence, when NATO conducts an operation, it must comply as a matter of law with the HRL obligations that bind NATO.

Likewise, in the context of AU-led operations, it is prudent to say that when the AU conducts an operation authorised by the UN Security Council, it must comply as a matter of law with the HRL obligations that bind the AU.

2.1.1.2. Peace forces as State agents of the States undertaking or taking part in an operation

The second source for peace forces can be as State agents[1373] and is derived from HRL treaties to which the State undertaking or taking part in the mission is a party and/or customary HRL by which the State is bound (and which they have not persistently opposed). Furthermore, States are bound by those principles of HRL, which amount to general principles of law within Article 38(1)(c) of the ICJ Statute, as well as by HRL obligations contained in applicable binding resolutions of intergovernmental organisations.[1374]

States contributing their troops to UN (mandated) peace operations retain full and exclusive command over their national armed forces. Pursuant to the threefold obligation to respect, protect, and fulfil human rights, States must ensure, to the extent possible, that their State agents comply with the legally binding HRL obligations by which they are bound as States.[1375] What kind of obligations must be complied with when acting abroad is discussed in more detail below when examining the extraterritorial applicability of HRL (see Part III, Sections 2.1.3.3 and, specifically, with respect to the right to life, see Part III, Section 4.1).

In its General Comment No. 31, the UN HRC has explicitly stated that the ICCPR applies to 'forces constituting a *national contingent of a State Party*

1371 See e.g. James A Burger, 'Headquarters IFOR/SFOR' in Dieter Fleck (ed), *The Handbook of the Law of Visiting Forces* (1st edn., Oxford University Press 2001) 328, as also referred to by Naert, 'International Law Aspects of the EU's Security and Defence Policy, with a Particular Focus on the Law of Armed Conflict and Human Rights' (n. 1361) 222, fn. 1321.

1372 NATO, *NATO Legal Deskbook* (n. 593) 268.

1373 As mentioned earlier, when personnel participate in a UN (mandated) peacekeeping operation in their personal capacity and thus not as State agents, HRL obligations for them do not flow from this source (see also Gill and others (n. 26) 82).

1374 Jann K Kleffner, 'Human Rights and International Humanitarian Law: General Issues' in Terry D Gill and Dieter Fleck (eds), *The Handbook of the International Law of Military Operations* (2nd edn., Oxford University Press 2015) para. 32.

1375 On the threefold obligation to respect, protect, and fulfil HRL, see Part III, Section 2.1.2.1. See also Gill, 'Legal Aspects of the Transfer of Authority in UN Peace Operations' (n. 723) 46; Gill and others (n. 26) 78, 81–82. See also White, 'Security Council Mandates and the Use of Lethal Force by Peacekeepers: What Place for the Laws of War?' (n. 31) 105.

assigned to an international peace-keeping or peace-enforcement operation.'[1376] As also remarked by the Leuven Manual, other human rights bodies have not articulated this so explicitly, although the ECtHR has on a number of occasions held TCCs accountable for the conduct of their troops in international military operations, demonstrating that the ECHR is considered applicable to peace operations when the criteria for application are met in the particular case.[1377]

States can have contradictory HRL obligations for the simple reason that States can be parties to different treaties. Of course, many HRL rules and principles have attained customary international law status, but even then, there is a risk that States interpret and apply the rules and principles differently. Such problems of legal interoperability may arise, for example, when the views of the States participating in the operation differ as to the criteria and scope of the concept of 'self-defence'. Where one State has a broad interpretation of what falls within the notion of self-defence and allows for the use of force in defence of property or defence of others, another State may uphold a stricter approach.[1378] Such different views may lead to divergence in the use of force by the units of the different TCCs, making unity of effort and unity of command difficult.[1379] In practice, this is usually solved by planning and conducting the operations in question in a manner consistent with the legal rules that all partners in the operation in question consider applicable within their legal framework.[1380]

2.1.1.3. Peace forces as visitors in the host State

The third source for peace forces is as 'visitors' in the host State (with that State's consent), whereby peace forces have an obligation to respect host State law, including HRL obligations applicable to the host State (derived from HRL treaties, customary HRL, and general principles of law). Article 6 of the 1990 UN Model SOFA for Peacekeeping Operations, for example, states that UN peace operations and its members 'shall respect all local laws and regulations.'[1381] The duty of peace forces to respect the HRL obligations of the host State has also been confirmed in national case law. For example, in the case of *Mehida Mustafić-Mujić and others v. the Netherlands*, the Dutch Court of Appeal held that, according to Dutch private international law, Bosnian law applied to the

[1376] Emphasis added. UN HRC, 'General Comment No. 31 on the Nature of the General Legal Obligation Imposed on States Parties to the ICCPR' (n. 81) para. 10.

[1377] See e.g. *Case of Al-Skeini and Others v. the United Kingdom, Judgment* (2011) ECtHR (Grand Chamber) App. No. 55721/07; *Case of Al-Jedda v. the United Kingdom, Judgment* (n. 886); *Case of Jaloud v. the Netherlands, Judgment* (2014) ECtHR (Grand Chamber) App. No. 47708/08, as also referred to by Gill and others (n. 26) 82.

[1378] See also Part I, Section 4.1.2.1.

[1379] Boddens Hosang, 'An Operational Perspective' (n. 1346) 103. See further, e.g. Geiß and Krieger (n. 64); and, in particular, Watkin (n. 64); Zyberi and Andersson (n. 64).

[1380] For further literature on legal interoperability, see a list of sources in Part III, Section 2.1.1, fn. 1346.

[1381] UNGA, '1990 UN Model SOFA for Peacekeeping Operations' (n. 46) Art. 6.

conduct of Dutchbat.[1382] Accordingly, since the ICCPR was in force for Bosnia and Herzegovina in 1995 and since treaty obligations of Bosnia are considered part of Bosnian law, it followed that Bosnia's HRL obligations were applicable to Dutchbat as well.[1383]

That said, while this duty to respect host State law is generally recognised in current treaty practice, there is debate as to the degree of subordination to host State law. While one school of thought is convinced that visiting forces are obliged to comply with host State law to the letter, another school of thought is of the opinion that it is sufficient for visiting forces to take due account of host State law and to avoid, or at least limit as much as possible, any action that directly conflicts with it.[1384]

2.1.2. *Applicability ratione materiae*

HRL is primarily concerned with regulating the exercise of power by a State against individuals. To that end, a wide variety of civil political, economic, social, and cultural rights have been enshrined in national, regional, and international human rights instruments. Civil and political rights include, for example, the right to life, the right to a fair trial, the right to privacy, the right to vote, the right to be elected, and the right to take part in public affairs, whereas the right to adequate food, the right to adequate housing, the right to education, the right to social security, the right to take part in cultural life, the right to water and sanitation, and the right to work are examples of economic, social, and cultural rights. In addition, several individual human rights, such as the prohibition of torture, slavery, racial discrimination, and the human rights of particularly vulnerable groups, such as women, children, persons with disabilities, and minorities, are also covered by specific instruments. More recently, new human rights have developed, such as the right to development, the right to peace, and the right to a clean, healthy, and sustainable environment.[1385]

2.1.2.1. Obligation 'to respect, protect, and fulfil' HRL

In human rights literature, it is common to distinguish between three sets of HRL obligations: the obligation to respect, to protect, and to fulfil.[1386] This tripartite typology was first introduced by the then-UN Special Rapporteur to the UN Sub-Commission on Prevention of Discrimination and Protection of

1382 *Mehida Mustafić-Mujić and Others v. the Netherlands, Judgment* (2011) Dutch Court of Appeal ECLI:NL:GHSGR:2011:BR0132 para. 6.3.

1383 *Ibid.* para. 6.4.

1384 See further Gill and others (n. 26) 130–134.

1385 See also the introduction to HRL applicability *ratione materiae* given by Kleffner (n. 1374) para. 30.

1386 *Ibid.* para. 31; Larsen (n. 1350) 125.

Minorities Asbjørn Eide in 1987.[1387] The obligation to respect implies a negative obligation not to hinder or restrict the enjoyment of human rights.[1388] It is widely accepted that both States and international and regional organisations must – at least – comply with this obligation to respect when conducting a UN (mandated) peace operation.[1389] Examples are the obligation to respect the prohibition of genocide, slavery, or racial discrimination or the obligation to respect the right to life and the right to a fair trial.[1390] The obligation to protect implies a positive obligation to protect individuals and groups against human rights violations by third parties.[1391] There is no consensus as to whether – and if so, to what extent – an obligation to protect applies in the context of UN (mandated) peace operations. Likewise, there is no consensus as to whether – and if so, to what extent – they are under an obligation to fulfil. The obligation to fulfil is also a positive obligation and includes the obligation to take measures to grant, facilitate, and promote human rights by adopting appropriate legislative, administrative, budgetary, judicial, and other measures to ensure their full implementation.[1392] In any event, the positive obligations to protect and fulfil must be seen in the context of the respective competences of the UN (mandated) peace operation.[1393] For a discussion specifically on the obligation to protect the right to life, see Part III, Section 4.1.

2.1.2.2. Specific HRL obligations in the context of the use of force

The exercise of the power to use force by UN (mandated) peace forces may violate a number of basic rights, such as the right to liberty and security of a person, the respect for their inherent dignity, and above all, the right to life. The right to life, originally proclaimed in Article 3 of the UDHR,[1394] has now been incorporated into a number of international and regional treaties. For example, Article 6(1) of the ICCPR, Article 4(1) of the ACHR, and Article 4 of the ACHPR set forth that no one may be 'arbitrarily' deprived of their life. Article 2 of the ECHR also protects the right to life but does so by setting out more detailed grounds for the possible deprivation of life.[1395]

1387 ECOSOC, Commission on Human Rights, 'The New International Economic Order and the Promotion of Human Rights, Report on the Right to Food as a Human Rights Submitted by Mr. Asbjørn Eide, Special Rapporteur to the UN Sub-Commission on Prevention of Discrimination and Protection of Minorities' (1987) UN Doc. E/CN.4/Sub.2/1987/23 para. 66.

1388 Kleffner (n. 1374) para. 31; Larsen (n. 1350) 125.

1389 This presupposes the extraterritorial application of HRL obligations, as discussed below in Part III, Section 2.1.3.

1390 Maus (n. 1354) 132.

1391 Kleffner (n. 1374) para. 31; Larsen (n. 1350) 125.

1392 Kleffner (n. 1374) para. 31; Larsen (n. 1350) 125–126.

1393 Maus (n. 1354) 134.

1394 Art. 3 of the UDHR reads as follows: 'Everyone has the right to life, liberty and security of person' ('UNGA Res. 217 A(III), Universal Declaration of Human Rights' (n. 683)).

1395 The permissible grounds for deprivation of life are discussed in detail in Part III, Section 3.1.1.

It is beyond dispute that the right to life is a rule of customary international law and thus also binds subjects of international law not party to the HRL treaties mentioned above. Accordingly, international and regional organisations are also bound by the right to life. The right to life applies to every human being without distinction as to race, colour, sex, gender, sexual preference, language, religion, political or other opinion, national or social origin, property, birth, disability, or other status.[1396] Moreover, the right to life, or more precisely, the right not to be arbitrarily deprived of one's life, is widely (yet not unanimously) recognised as a peremptory norm which permits no derogation.[1397]

1396 As mentioned by Casey-Maslen and Heyns, '[t]hat the right to life in toto and applicable to every human being is a norm of customary international law is beyond dispute [...]. But behind this simplicity lies a web of complexity, interweaving treaty rules with customary rules and a small number of peremptory rules.' For a list of customary rules of international law pertaining to the right to life, see Casey-Maslen and Heyns (n. 42) 735–737. As regards peremptory rules of international law pertaining to the right to life, see very next footnote (fn. 1397).

1397 There is no universal agreement as to which rules are peremptory in nature (Gill, 'Legal Aspects of the Transfer of Authority in UN Peace Operations' (n. 723) 59). Yet, for sources defending the claim that the right to life is a *jus cogens* norm, see ECOSOC, Commission on Human Rights, 'Report of the Economic and Social Council on the Protection of Human Rights in Chile, Thirty-Seventh Session, Agenda Item 12' (1982) UN Doc. A/37/564 para. 22; UN HRC, 'Report of the Special Rapporteur on Extrajudicial, Summary or Arbitrary Executions, Christof Heyns' (n. 109) para. 20; *Victims of the Tugboat '13 de Marzo' v. Cuba* (1996) IAComHR Report No. 47/96, Case 11.436, OEA/Ser.L/V/II.95 Doc. 7 rev. at 127 (1997) para. 79; Casey-Maslen and Heyns (n. 42) 737 (Casey-Maslen and Heyns list not only the rule that no one shall be arbitrarily deprived of their life but also other rules such as '[a]ny act of genocide is prohibited' or '[a]cts of aggression are prohibited' as peremptory rules of international law pertaining to the right to life. For a full list, see 737–738); Irene Couzigou, 'The United Nations Security Council Sanctions and International Human Rights' (2016) 10 Vienna Journal on International Constitutional Law 277, 304; Gill, 'Legal and Some Political Limitations on the Power of the UN Security Council to Exercise Its Enforcement Powers under Chapter VII of the Charter' (n. 892) 79; Paul W Gormley, 'The Right to Life and the Rule of Non-Derogability: Peremptory Norms of Jus Cogens' in Bertrand G Ramcharan (ed), *The Right to Life in International Law* (Martinus Nijhoff Publishers 1985) 120–159; Hannikainen (n. 616) 514–520; Christof Heyns and Thomas Probert, 'Securing the Right to Life: A Cornerstone of the Human Rights System' (*EJIL: Talk!*, 11 May 2016), www.ejiltalk.org/securing-the-right-to-life-a-cornerstone-of-the-human-rights-system/, accessed 9 September 2019; Eckart Klein, 'Establishing a Hierarchy of Human Rights: Ideal Solution or Fallacy' (2008) 41 Israel Law Review 477, 482; Karen Parker, 'Jus Cogens: Compelling the Law of Human Rights' (1989) 12 Hastings International and Comparative Law Review 411, 431–432; Jordan Paust, 'The Right to Life in Human Rights Law and the Law of War' (2014) 65 Saskatchewan Law Review 411, 412–413; Eva M Kornicker Uhlmann, 'State Community Interests, Jus Cogens and Protection of the Global Environment: Developing Criteria for Peremptory Norms' (1998) 11 Georgetown International Environmental Law Review 101, 129–130; White, 'The Use of Weapons in Peace Operations' (n. 41) 223; Thomas Weatherall, *Jus Cogens: International Law and Social Contract* (Cambridge University Press 2015) (page numbers not available in online version). Although the Special Rapporteur on peremptory norms of general international law has acknowledged that there is some support for the peremptory character of the right to life, or at least the prohibition on the arbitrary deprivation of life, it has not (yet) made it to the (non-exhaustive) list of norms that the ILC refers to as having the status of *jus cogens* (see ILC, 'Fourth Report on Peremptory Norms

This study assumes that the right not to be arbitrarily deprived of one's life is peremptory in nature. Applied to the use of lethal force in the context of UN (mandated) peace operations, this means that even if a mission has a mandate from the UN Security Council to use all necessary means to protect civilians, peace forces may still never use lethal force in a manner that would violate the right of someone not to be arbitrarily deprived of their life.[1398] Unless UN (mandated) peace forces are engaged in armed conflict, where different rules on targeting regulate lethal force, Chapter VII authorisation will not prevail over States' pre-existing, and above all peremptory, right to life obligations under HRL. Accordingly, outside the conduct of hostilities in an armed conflict, a UNSC mandate may, for example, not be invoked to justify the use of intentional lethal use of force under a 'shoot to kill' policy when there is no temporally imminent threat to life.[1399]

The right to life equally gives rise to three types of HRL obligations: to respect the right to life, to protect the right to life, and to fulfil the right to life. Indeed, the right to life imposes not only the negative obligation upon States and regional, and international organisations to not unlawfully deprive someone of their life but also the positive obligation to take appropriate steps to safeguard the lives of those within their jurisdiction, including by providing a regulatory framework and by taking preventive operational measures. The distinction between positive and negative obligations in the context of the extraterritorial application of HRL obligations is discussed in more detail below in Part III, Section 2.1.3.3. The extent to which there can be a positive extraterritorial obligation to protect the right to life is discussed in Part III, Section 4.1.

2.1.3. *Applicability ratione loci*

HRL obligations of a State or an international or regional organisation are applicable *de jure* towards everyone within the jurisdiction of that State or

---

of General International Law (Jus Cogens) by Dire Tladi, Special Rapporteur' (n. 108) paras 128–130; ILC, 'Peremptory Norms of General International Law (Jus Cogens): Text of the Draft Conclusions and Draft Annex Provisionally Adopted by the Drafting Committee on First Reading, Seventy-First Session, Geneva (29 April–7 June and 8 July–9 August 2019)' (2019) UN Doc. A/CN.4/L.936 Draft conclusion 23 para. 24). On the limits to derogation, see Part III, Sections 2.1.4.1 and 2.1.4.2.

1398 On the permissive grounds to deprive someone from their life under HRL, see Part III, Section 3.1.1.

1399 On the legal parameters for intentional lethal force, see Part III, Section 3.1.1.3(B). On shoot to kill, see Watkin (n. 38) 536–550. See also Nils Melzer, *Targeted Killing in International Law* (Oxford University Press 2008) 22–27. For recent examples of civilian authorities endorsing 'shoot to kill' in ways that appear to breach HRL, see Saun Walker, 'Kazakhstan President Says He Gave Order to "Open Fire with Lethal Force"' *The Guardian* (7 January 2022), www.theguardian.com/world/2022/jan/07/kazakhstan-protests-thousands-detained-as-president-says-order-mostly-restored, accessed 4 April 2022.

international or regional organisation.[1400] In the context of HRL treaties, 'jurisdiction'[1401] primarily indicates that States have HRL obligations within their own territory.[1402] Human rights courts and international human rights mechanisms have broadened the scope of applicability by bringing forward the notion of 'extraterritorial jurisdiction'.[1403] This implies that the HRL obligations of the TCC under whose authority an operation is conducted, may apply extraterritorially to acts committed within its jurisdiction.[1404] To the extent that a regional or international organisation exercises functions in a manner that can be assimilated to the exercise of jurisdiction by a State, it is also considered to be exercising jurisdiction.[1405]

Most States now accept the notion of extraterritorial jurisdiction. Nevertheless, the type of control required for HRL obligations to apply extraterritorially and which HRL obligations should be upheld in such situations remains disputed. Answers to these questions differ depending on which case law and doctrine is followed. While a detailed discussion of the extraterritorial application of HRL obligations is beyond the scope of this study, the next Section briefly discusses the different models of extraterritorial application that find varying degrees of support in the case law of courts and human rights mechanisms and in legal doctrine and indicates how they can be applied in the context of UN (mandated) peace operations. Hereafter, this study gives an overview of the relevant case law of the different courts and human rights mechanisms on the extraterritorial applicability of HRL.

2.1.3.1. Models of extraterritorial applicability

Today, there are three main models of extraterritorial application that find varying degrees of support in the case law of courts and human rights mechanisms and in legal doctrine:

First, a State can have extraterritorial jurisdiction over people when it exercises sufficient territorial control over territory abroad where such persons are located (the spatial model: power over a territory). In the conduct of UN (mandated) peace operations, missions may exercise elements of governmental authority over the territory of a State or part of it by, for example, establishing a transitional authority that exercises legislative and executive authority during a period of transition (think of the United Nations Mission in Kosovo (UNMIK)). Missions may also exercise physical control over a certain part of the territory by

---

1400 Gill and others (n. 26) 150.

1401 On the different meanings of the term 'jurisdiction', see Marko Milanović, *Extraterritorial Application of Human Rights Treaties: Law, Principles and Policy* (Oxford University Press 2011) 19–53.

1402 Gill and others (n. 26) 79.

1403 For an overview of the relevant case law, see below.

1404 Gill and others (n. 26) 76.

1405 Kleffner (n. 1374) para. 33.

establishing, for example, a buffer zone (e.g. the UN buffer zone in Cyprus) or a safe area (e.g. the UN safe area in Srebrenica).

Second, extraterritorial jurisdiction may arise when a State exercises authority or control over a person, whether lawfully or unlawfully, even if the act in question is performed outside its territorial control (the personal model: power over an individual). When conducting PoC mandates, UN (mandated) peace forces may not only exercise authority and control over an individual when using physical power over a person, e.g. through arrest and detention, but also when using kinetic force (or at least some types of kinetic force) against individuals. As discussed below, the IAComHR, for example, considers that the use of lethal force against nationals of another State in the context of a military operation on the territory of that State or in international airspace constitutes a case of jurisdiction.[1406] According to the Strasbourg case law, kinetic use of force currently only gives rise to jurisdiction when it concerns 'isolated and specific acts involving an element of proximity' but not 'bombing and artillery shelling' in the context of an IAC.[1407]

Third, there is also an emerging model focusing on power, control, or authority over an individual's rights (the functional model: power over the rights of an individual). Under the functional conception of jurisdiction, a State could be considered to exercise jurisdiction when it affects the enjoyment of someone's rights through its activities. In the context of UN (mandated) peace operations, this could imply the negative obligation not to use lethal force in a manner that infringes upon the right to life of individuals (whether that lethal force is the result of an incidental use of a firearm at a checkpoint, a targeted drone attack, or a large-scale bombardment) and to investigate each use of lethal force to determine whether the right to life has been infringed.

To further explore the extraterritorial application of HRL obligations, we observe the relevant case law from the different courts and human rights mechanisms.

2.1.3.2. Case law on extraterritorial applicability

A. ICJ

In the *Wall* case, the ICJ recognised that HRL instruments, including the ICCPR, the International Covenant on Economic, Social and Cultural Rights

---

1406 *Coard et al. v. United States* (1999) IAComHR Report No. 109/99, Case 10.951 para. 37; *Armando Alejandre Jr and Others v. Cuba* (1999) IAComHR Report No. 86/99, Case 11.589, OEA/Ser.L/V/II.106 Doc. 3 rev. at 586 (1999) para. 25. As discussed below, see Part III, Section 2.1.3.2(C).

1407 *Case of Georgia v. Russia (II), Judgment (Merits)* (2021) ECtHR (Grand Chamber) App. No. 38263/08 paras 132–133, and more generally paras 125–144. For a more detailed analysis, see Part III, Section 2.1.3.2(D).

(ICESC),[1408] and the Convention of the Rights of the Child (CRC),[1409] are applicable in respect of acts done by States in the exercise of their jurisdiction *outside* their own territory.[1410] The ICJ later confirmed its view in the *DRC v. Uganda* case and the *Georgia v. Russian Federation* case.[1411]

B. UN HRC

Under Article 2(1) of the ICCPR, each State Party 'undertakes to respect and to ensure to all individuals *within its territory and subject to its jurisdiction* the rights recognized in the [ICCPR] [...], without distinction of any kind, such as race, colour, sex, language, religion, political or other opinion, national or social origin, property, birth or other status.'[1412]

The ICCPR's competence clause is usually interpreted broadly. In its General Comment No. 31 on the Nature of the General Legal Obligation Imposed on States Parties to the ICCPR, the UN HRC set forth that Article 2(1) of the ICCPR must be interpreted as 'all persons who may be within their territory *and* to all persons subject to their jurisdiction.'[1413] They argued that this means that 'a State party must respect and ensure the rights laid down in the [ICCPR] [...] to *anyone within the power or effective control* of that State Party, even if not situated within the territory of the State Party.'[1414] This principle applies 'regardless of the circumstances in which such power or effective control was obtained, such as *forces constituting a national contingent of a State Party assigned to an international peace-keeping or peace-enforcement operation*.'[1415] This interpretation endorses the personal notion of jurisdiction and is consistent with its jurisprudence in individual cases and with the positions it has taken in final observations on periodic reports of States. For example, in 1981, the UN HRC ruled on the legality of Uruguay's actions in two nearly identical cases of arrests by Uruguayan agents in Brazil and Argentina, respectively (i.e. the cases of *Delia Saldias de Lopez v. Uruguay* and *Lilian Celiberti de Casariego*

1408 International Covenant on Economic, Social and Cultural Rights (adopted 16 December 1966, entered into force 3 January 1976) 993 UNTS 3 (ICESC).

1409 Convention on the Rights of the Child (adopted 20 November 1989, entered into force 2 September 1990) 1577 UNTS 3 (CRC).

1410 *Legal Consequences of the Construction of a Wall in the Occupied Palestinian Territory, Advisory opinion* (2004) ICJ Rep 136, paras 107–113.

1411 *Case Concerning Armed Activities on the Territory of the Congo (Democratic Republic of the Congo v. Uganda), Judgment* (n. 616) paras 216–220; *Application of the International Convention on the Elimination of All Forms of Racial Discrimination (Georgia v. Russian Federation), Request for the Indication of Provisional Measures, Order* (2008) ICJ Rep 353, para. 109.

1412 Emphasis added.

1413 Emphasis added. UN HRC, 'General Comment No. 31 [80] on the Nature of the General Legal Obligation Imposed on States Parties to the ICCPR' (n. 81) para. 10.

1414 Emphasis added. *Ibid.*

1415 Emphasis added. *Ibid.*

v. Uruguay).[1416] The UN HRC observed that 'it would be unconscionable' to interpret the responsibility under Article 2 of the ICCPR as permitting a State party to commit on the territory of another State violations of rights outlined in the ICCPR, which it cannot commit in its own territory.[1417] In a final observation of periodic reports of Belgium in 1998, the UN HRC expressed concern about the behaviour of Belgian soldiers in Somalia under the aegis of the United Nations Operation in Somalia II (UNOSOM II) and acknowledged that Belgium had recognised the extraterritorial application of the ICCPR in this respect.[1418]

In its General Comment No. 36 on the Right to Life, the UN HRC confirmed its interpretation but made a slight adjustment to it by saying that persons are subject to a State's jurisdiction if that State exercises power or effective control *over the enjoyment of the right to life of those persons*.[1419] This includes 'persons located outside any territory effectively controlled by the State *whose right to life is nonetheless affected* by its military or other activities in a direct and reasonably foreseeable manner.'[1420] In doing so, the UN HRC moved away from the personal model towards the functional model. The approach taken by the UN HRC in its General Comment No. 36 is contested by several States. The Netherlands, for example, expressed concern over the broad language used, covering situations, which in their view, do not fall within the scope of the ICCPR. According to the Dutch government, 'the mere fact that a bullet hits an individual, missile, or rocket fired by armed forces does not bring that individual within the power or effective control of the State party.'[1421]

Similarly, Germany, Austria, France, and Norway found that the UN HRC's approach goes beyond the established interpretation of the extraterritorial application of the ICCPR.[1422] The US and Canada do not accept the

1416 *Delia Saldias de Lopez v. Uruguay* (1981) UN HRC Communication No. 52/1979, UN Doc. CCPR/C/OP/1 at 88 (1984) 12.1–12.3; *Lilian Celiberti de Casariego v. Uruguay* (1981) UN HRC Communication No. 56/1979, UN Doc. CCPR/C/OP/1 at 92 (1984) para. 10.3.

1417 *Delia Saldias de Lopez v. Uruguay* (n. 1416) para. 12.3; *Lilian Celiberti de Casariego v. Uruguay* (n. 1416) para. 10.3.

1418 UN HRC, 'Concluding Observations of the Human Rights Committee: Belgium' (1998) UN Doc. CCPR/C/79/Add.99 para. 14.

1419 UN HRC, 'General Comment No. 31 [80] on the Nature of the General Legal Obligation Imposed on States Parties to the ICCPR' (n. 81) para. 10.

1420 Emphasis added. UN HRC, 'General Comment No. 36 on the Right to Life' (n. 82) para. 63.

1421 The Netherlands, 'Submission from the Netherlands on the Draft General Comment on Article 6 of the International Covenant on Civil and Political Rights – Right to Life' (Undated) para. 29, www.ohchr.org/en/hrbodies/ccpr/pages/gc36-article6righttolife.aspx, accessed 25 November 2021.

1422 Germany, 'Submission from Germany on the Draft General Comment on Article 6 of the International Covenant on Civil and Political Rights – Right to Life' (2017) para. 21, www.ohchr.org/en/hrbodies/ccpr/pages/gc36-article6righttolife.aspx, accessed 25 November 2021; Austria, 'Submission from Austria on the Draft General Comment on Article 6 of the International Covenant on Civil and Political Rights – Right to Life' (Undated) 2, www.ohchr.org/en/hrbodies/ccpr/pages/gc36-article6righttolife.aspx, accessed 25 November 2021; France, 'Submission from France on the Draft General Comment on Article 6 of the

extraterritorial application of HRL obligations in its entirety. The ICCPR, in their view, applies only to individuals who are both within the territory of a State Party *and* subject to its jurisdiction.[1423]

Recently, the UN HRC issued a ruling in two parallel proceedings against Italy and Malta concerning their response to a vessel in distress in the Mediterranean in 2013, whereby more than 200 people died.[1424] In these rulings, the UN HRC applied the functional model (albeit not consistently)[1425] to establish the jurisdiction of both Italy and Malta over the right to life of these migrants. First, despite declaring the case inadmissible for failure to exhaust domestic remedies, the UN HRC found that the migrants were subject to the jurisdiction of Malta.[1426] The UN HRC considered that Malta had effectively controlled the rescue operation, potentially resulting in a direct and reasonably foreseeable causal relationship between Malta's acts and omissions and the outcome of the operation.[1427] Second, upon the question of whether 'the alleged victims could be considered to have been within the power or effective control of the State party, even though the incident took place outside its territory,'[1428] the UN HRC affirmed that the 'relationship of dependency' between persons in distress and Italy receiving calls for assistance is sufficient to trigger extraterritorial jurisdiction.[1429] After all,[1430]

> [T]he individuals on the vessel in distress were directly affected by the decisions taken by the Italian authorities in a manner that was reasonably foreseeable in light of the relevant legal obligations of Italy, and that they were thus subject to Italy's jurisdiction for the purposes of the [ECHR] […], notwithstanding the fact that they

---

International Covenant on Civil and Political Rights – Right to Life' (Undated) para. 37, www.ohchr.org/en/hrbodies/ccpr/pages/gc36-article6righttolife.aspx, accessed 25 November 2021; Norway, 'Submission from Norway on the Draft General Comment on Article 6 of the International Covenant on Civil and Political Rights – Right to Life' (Undated) 4–5, www.ohchr.org/en/hrbodies/ccpr/pages/gc36-article6righttolife.aspx, accessed 25 November 2021.

1423 The United States, 'Submission from the United States of America on the Draft General Comment on Article 6 of the International Covenant on Civil and Political Rights – Right to Life' (2017) para. 13, www.ohchr.org/en/hrbodies/ccpr/pages/gc36-article6righttolife.aspx, accessed 25 November 2021; Canada, 'Submission from Canada on the Draft General Comment on Article 6 of the International Covenant on Civil and Political Rights – Right to Life' (Undated) para. 7, www.ohchr.org/en/hrbodies/ccpr/pages/gc36-article6righttolife.aspx, accessed 25 November 2021.

1424 *AS, DI, OI and GD v. Italy* (2020) UN HRC Communication No. 3042/2017, UN Doc. CCPR/C/130/D/3042/2017; *A.S., D.I., O.I. and G.D. v. Malta* (n. 1038).

1425 For a detailed commentary, see Marko Milanović, 'Drowning Migrants, the Human Rights Committee, and Extraterritorial Human Rights Obligations' (*EJIL: Talk!*, 16 March 2021).

1426 *A.S., D.I., O.I. and G.D. v. Malta* (n. 1038) paras 6.7–6.9.

1427 *Ibid.* para. 6.7.

1428 *A.S., D.I., O.I. and G.D. v. Italy* (n. 1424) para. 7.7.

1429 *Ibid.* para. 7.8.

1430 *Ibid.* paras 7.7 and 7.8.

were within the Maltese search and rescue region and thus also subject concurrently to the jurisdiction of Malta.

Although the question is posed as a question of jurisdiction under the personal model rather than the functional model, the jurisdictional approach is undoubtedly functional.[1431] Italy had the capacity to assist the vessel in distress and, therefore, was obliged to do so. The UN HRC eventually found that Italy had failed to protect the right to life of those persons in distress at sea.[1432]

By invoking the 'relationship of dependency', the UN HRC looked for ways to limit the cases in which States have a positive obligation to protect human rights outside their own territory. Indeed, a plain application of the functional model would imply that States are obliged to act when they are in a position to do so. However, since this may lead to outcomes possibly perceived as politically or practically extreme or unfeasible, mechanisms such as the UN HRC seek to limit the scope.[1433]

C. IACtHR and IAComHR

Article 1(1) of the ACHR stipulates that '[t]he States Parties to this Convention undertake to respect the rights and freedoms recognized herein and to ensure to all persons *subject to their jurisdiction* the free and full exercise of those rights and freedoms [...].'[1434]

In their case law, both the IACtHR and the IAComHR have confirmed the extraterritorial application of the ACHR by pointing out that '[u]nder Inter-American human rights law, each American State is obligated [...] to respect the rights of all persons within its territory and of those present in the territory of another state but subject to the control of its agents' (i.e. the personal model).[1435] For example, in the case of *José Isabel Salas and Others v. United States*, which related to the US military intervention in Panama in December 1989, the IAComHR held that 'human rights are inherent in all human beings and are not based on their citizenship or location.'[1436] This decision confirmed its approach to the extraterritoriality of the ACHR, which it had already followed in the case

1431 Milanović, 'Drowning Migrants, the Human Rights Committee, and Extraterritorial Human Rights Obligations' (n. 1425).

1432 *A.S., D.I., O.I. and G.D. v. Italy* (n. 1424) para. 8.5.

1433 Milanović, 'Drowning Migrants, the Human Rights Committee, and Extraterritorial Human Rights Obligations' (n. 1425).

1434 Emphasis added.

1435 Franklin Guillermo *Aisalla Molina v. Ecuador* (2010) IAComHR Report No. 112/10, Case IP-02, OEA/Ser.L/V/II.140 Doc. 10 (2010) para. 91.

1436 *José Isabel Salas and Others v. United States, Merits* (2018) IAComHR Report No. 121/18, Case 10.573 para. 309. See also earlier case law: *Coard et al. v. United States* (n. 1406) para. 37; *Petition Victor Saldaño v. Argentina* (1999) IAComHR Report No. 38/99 paras 15–20.

of *Coard et al. v. United States*.[1437] In the latter case, the IAComHR examined complaints about the applicants' detention and treatment by US troops during the first days of the military intervention in Grenada in October 1983.[1438]

Moreover, the IAComHR does not only consider cases of 'authority and control' to compromise extraterritorial detention and military operations conducted by a State on the territory of another State but also military air operations in international airspace.[1439] In the case of *Armando Alejandre Jr. and Others v. Cuba*, the IAComHR considered the Cuban military intervention in international airspace and confirmed that the use of lethal force against nationals of another State in international airspace could also constitute a case of jurisdiction over persons.[1440] This ruling contradicts the ECtHR's ruling in the case of *Banković and Others v. Belgium and 16 Other Contracting States*, which raised a similar question, namely whether the use of force through aerial bombardments is sufficient to bring persons affected by such bombardments under the 'jurisdiction' of the States conducting the bombardments (see below).

In 2017, the IACtHR, for the very first time, faced the question of whether the ACHR applies extraterritorially. While recognising the spatial and the personal model as bases of extraterritorial jurisdiction, the IACtHR went one step further than the IAComHR. In its advisory opinion on the environment and human rights, as requested by Colombia, it ruled that 'States have the obligation to avoid transboundary environmental damage that can affect the human rights of individuals outside their territory.'[1441] Persons are considered to fall under the jurisdiction of the State under whose jurisdiction or control the activity that caused environmental damage originated if there is 'a causal link between the act that originated in its territory and the infringement of the human rights of the persons outside its territory.'[1442] The exercise of jurisdiction arises when this State has 'effective control' over the activities that caused the damage and the resulting human rights violations.[1443] In doing so, the IACtHR opened the door for the functional model.

D. ECtHR

Article 1 of the ECHR provides that '[t]he High Contracting Parties shall secure to everyone within their jurisdiction the rights and freedoms defined in Section I

1437 *Coard et al. v. United States* (n. 1406) para. 37. See also *Petition Victor Saldaño v. Argentina* (n. 1434) paras 15–20; *Precautionary Measures in Guantanamo Bay, Cuba* (2002) IAComHR 41 ILM 532 (2002) 532.

1438 *Coard et al. v. United States* (n. 1406) para. 37.

1439 Kleffner (n. 1374) para. 41.

1440 *Armando Alejandre Jr. and Others v. Cuba* (n. 1406) para. 25.

1441 *Advisory Opinion OC-23/17 of November 15, 2017 Requested by the Republic of Colombia: The Environment and Human Rights* (2017) IACtHR OC-23/17 para. 101.

1442 *Ibid.* paras 101 and 104(h).

1443 *Ibid.* paras 102 and 104(h).

of this Convention.' In its case law, the ECtHR has held on various occasions that the ECHR may apply extraterritorially during military presence and/or military intervention outside the territory of State Parties.

As mentioned above, the first model of extraterritorial jurisdiction is the spatial model arising from control over a territory. This model has been invoked in the case law of the ECtHR to address the circumstances in Northern Cyprus and was first mentioned by the ECtHR in the case of *Loizidou v. Turkey.*[1444] To determine whether Turkey had jurisdiction in the present case, the ECtHR did not consider it relevant whether Turkey actually exercised detailed control over the policies and actions of the Turkish Republic of Northern Cyprus authorities.[1445] Instead, it held the following:[1446]

> Bearing in mind the object and purpose of the [ECHR] [...], the responsibility of a Contracting Party may also arise when as a consequence of military action – whether lawful or unlawful – it exercises *effective control of an area outside its national territory*. The obligation to secure, in such an area, the rights and freedoms set out in the [ECHR] [...] derives from the fact of such control whether it be exercised directly, through its armed forces, or through a subordinate local administration.

When ruling over the merits, the ECtHR added the word 'overall' to the effective control test (and hence referred to 'effective overall control').[1447] *In casu*, Turkey was considered to exercise 'effective overall control' in the border area by having a large number of troops on active duty who patrol the territory and by having checkpoints on the main lines of communication.[1448] In its subsequent *Cyprus v. Turkey* judgment, the ECtHR added that, since Turkey had effective overall control over Northern Cyprus, its responsibility could not be limited to the actions of its own soldiers or officials in Northern Cyprus but also extended to the actions of the local administration, which survived thanks to the Turkish military and other support.[1449]

Similarly, in the case of *Banković and Others v. Belgium and 16 Other Contracting States* (a case concerning the NATO bombing of the Radio-Television Serbia headquarters in Belgrade in 1999), the ECtHR held that extraterritorial jurisdiction may exist when a State, 'as a consequence of military occupation

1444 *Case of Loizidou v. Turkey, Judgment (Preliminary Objections)* (1995) ECtHR (Grand Chamber) App. No. 15318/89.

1445 *Case of Loizidou v. Turkey, Judgment* (1996) ECtHR (Grand Chamber) App. No. 15318/89 para. 56.

1446 Emphasis added. *Case of Loizidou v. Turkey, Judgment (Preliminary Objections)* (n. 1444) para. 62.

1447 *Case of Loizidou v. Turkey, Judgment* (n. 1445) para. 56.

1448 *Case of Loizidou v. Turkey, Judgment (Preliminary Objections)* (n. 1444) paras 62–64; *ibid.* paras 16, 52–57, as also discussed by Stuart Wallace, *The Application of the European Convention on Human Rights to Military Operations* (Cambridge University Press 2019) 67.

1449 *Case of Cyprus v. Turkey, Judgment* (2001) ECtHR (Grand Chamber) App. No. 25781/94 para. 77.

or through the consent, invitation or acquiescence of the Government of that territory' exercises 'all or some of the public powers normally to be exercised by that Government' by virtue of its effective control over the territory concerned and its inhabitants abroad.[1450] However, the ECtHR eventually opposed the extraterritorial application of the ECHR in the following terms:[1451]

> [T]he [ECHR] [...] is a multi-lateral treaty operating [...] in an essentially regional context and notably in the legal space (*espace juridique*) of the Contracting States. The FRY [i.e. the Federal Republic of Yugoslavia] clearly does not fall within this legal space. The Convention was not designed to be applied throughout the world, even in respect of the conduct of Contracting States.

Whereas Cyprus is an ECHR State Party, former Yugoslavia was not. With this judgment, the ECtHR set forth a narrow extraterritorial conception of jurisdiction, whereby the ECHR can only be applied extraterritorially if a State exercises effective control over a territory belonging to one of the ECHR's State Parties. In subsequent judgments, the ECtHR eventually broadened its approach and accepted that the ECHR did apply outside the so-called *espace juridique*. For example, in the case of *Issa and Others v. Turkey*, the ECtHR indicated that even if a State, as a consequence of a military action, has control only over a certain part of the territory of another State, and even if this control is short-lived and exercised over the territory of a State that is not a party to the ECHR (*in casu* Iraq), it may be considered 'effective overall control' that triggers jurisdiction.[1452] The '*espace juridique*' logic was eventually explicitly rejected in the case of *Pad v. Turkey*.[1453]

In the recent case of *Georgia v. Russia (II)*, the ECtHR found that Russia exercised effective control over South Ossetia, Abkhazia, and the 'buffer zone' during the occupation phase up to the moment of the withdrawal of its troops several months later.[1454] The ECtHR reached this conclusion relatively quickly by recognising, on the one hand, the significant Russian military presence[1455] and, on the other hand, the economic, financial, military, and political support it had provided to the two separatist entities.[1456] However, in the phase preceding the Russian occupation, namely during the active phase of the fighting, the ECtHR

1450 *Case of Banković and Others v. Belgium and 16 Other Contracting States, Decision as to the admissibility* (2001) ECtHR (Grand Chamber) App. No. 52207/99 para. 71.

1451 *Ibid.* para. 80.

1452 *Case of Issa and Others v. Turkey, Judgment* (2004) ECtHR App. No. 31821/96 para. 74.

1453 *Case of Pad and Others v. Turkey, Decision as to admissibility* (2007) ECtHR App. No. 60167/00 para. 53.

1454 *Case of Georgia v. Russia (II), Judgment (Merits)* (n. 1407) para. 174.

1455 *Ibid.* para. 165.

1456 *Ibid.* paras 165–173, as also discussed by Marko Milanović, 'Georgia v. Russia No. 2: The European Court's Resurrection of Bankovic in the Contexts of Chaos' (*EJIL: Talk!*, 25 January 2021), www.ejiltalk.org/georgia-v-russia-no-2-the-european-courts-resurrection-of-bankovic-in-the-contexts-of-chaos/, accessed 22 November 2021.

held that there could be no 'effective control' and, therefore, Russia did not exercise jurisdiction under the spatial model (nor under the personal model, see below) to assess the legality of kinetic uses of force during the active phase of the conflict. According to the ECtHR:[1457]

> [I]t can be considered from the outset that *in the event of military operations* – including, for example, armed attacks, bombing or shelling – *carried out during an international armed conflict one cannot generally speak of 'effective control' over an area.* The *very reality* of armed confrontation and fighting between enemy military forces seeking to establish control over an area in a context of chaos *means that there is no control* over an area. This is also true in the present case, given that the majority of the fighting took place in areas which were previously under Georgian control [...].

Although it is unfortunate that the ECtHR limits itself to IACs in its ruling (leaving it unclear how it would treat the more common situation where there is a NIAC), this is not necessarily problematic reasoning.[1458] It is plausible that intense fighting hinders effective control. As also pointed out by Milanović, it is a pity, however, that the ECtHR excludes any possibility of gradual control, even if there is still fighting.[1459]

The second model of extraterritorial jurisdiction is the personal model. Although the ECtHR did not accept that jurisdiction could also be based upon effective control over an individual in the case of *Banković and Others v. Belgium and 16 Other Contracting States*,[1460] the ECtHR developed case law both before and after *Banković* that recognises the personal model of jurisdiction. For example, in the case of *Öcalan v. Turkey*, the ECtHR held that the applicant was effectively under Turkish authority once being handed over to Turkish agents by Kenyan agents and thus within the jurisdiction of Turkey for the purposes of Article 1 of the ECHR, 'even though in this instance Turkey exercised its authority outside its territory.'[1461] Also, in the case of *Issa and Others v. Turkey*, the ECtHR established that jurisdiction may be exercised when individuals are on the territory of a State but under another State's authority and control through that State's agents operating, whether lawfully or unlawfully, in the former State.[1462] Following some of the rulings of the UN HRC and the IAComHR, the ECtHR held that the State's accountability in such situations arises from the fact

---

1457 Emphasis added. *Case of Georgia v. Russia (II), Judgment (Merits)* (n. 1407) para. 126.

1458 Milanović, 'Georgia v. Russia No. 2: The European Court's Resurrection of Bankovic in the Contexts of Chaos' (n. 1456).

1459 *Ibid.*

1460 *Case of Banković and Others v. Belgium and 16 Other Contracting States, Decision as to the admissibility* (n. 1450) para. 71.

1461 *Case of Öcalan v. Turkey, Judgment* (2004) ECtHR (Grand Chamber) App. No. 46221/99 para. 91.

1462 *Case of Issa and Others v. Turkey, Judgment* (n. 1452) para. 71, as also confirmed in *Case of Solomou and Others v. Turkey, Judgment* (2008) ECtHR App. No. 36832/97 para. 45.

that Article 1 of the ECHR cannot be interpreted as allowing a State to commit, in the territory of another State, violations of the ECHR which it could not commit in its own territory.[1463] Eventually, the ECtHR was unable to determine, on the basis of the evidence available to it, whether the Iraqi shepherds had been killed by gunfire coming from Turkish troops.[1464]

In *Al-Skeini and Others v. the United Kingdom*, the Grand Chamber of the ECtHR summarised its view on extraterritorial jurisdiction.[1465] It confirmed that as an exception to the principle of territoriality, a State's jurisdiction may extend to acts of State agents generating effects outside its own territory.[1466] Such acts may include activities of its diplomatic or consular agents abroad;[1467] the exercise of another State's public powers with its agreement (through the consent, invitation, or acquiescence);[1468] and the use of force by a State's agents operating outside its territory.[1469] The ECtHR then referred to cases of extraterritorial arrest and detention in which this principle had been applied to determine whether there was jurisdiction.[1470]According to Wallace, the reference to 'the use of force' is curious as this term is normally used to describe the resort to armed force by States in the sense of Article 2(4) of the UN Charter, or the use of force by State agents in the human rights context.[1471] In the relevant case, the ECtHR, however, noted that this principle has been applied in the context of the detention of an individual without explaining whether the jurisdictional link arises from the continuous act of detaining an individual or the instantaneous act of arresting an individual.[1472] We know that the ECtHR only intended to refer to the exercise of *physical* power and control over a person and that, in such cases, a State is obliged to guarantee that individual the rights and freedoms

1463 *Case of Issa and Others v. Turkey, Judgment* (n. 1452) para. 71, as also confirmed in *Case of Solomou and Others v. Turkey, Judgment* (n. 1462) para. 45.

1464 *Case of Issa and Others v. Turkey, Judgment* (n. 1452) para. 82.

1465 *Case of Al-Skeini and Others v. the United Kingdom, Judgment* (n. 1377) paras 130–142.

1466 *Ibid.* para. 133 et al. In its judgment, the ECtHR refers, *inter alia*, to the following cases to support its position: *Case of Loizidou v. Turkey, Judgment (Preliminary Objections)* (n. 1444) para. 62; *Case of Loizidou v. Turkey, Judgment* (n. 1445) para. 52; *Case of Banković and Others v. Belgium and 16 Other Contracting States, Decision as to the admissibility* (n. 1450) para. 69.

1467 *Case of Al-Skeini and Others v. the United Kingdom, Judgment* (n. 1377) para. 134. See also *Case of Banković and Others v. Belgium and 16 Other Contracting States, Decision as to the admissibility* (n. 1450) para. 73; *X v. The Federal Republic of Germany, Decision as to the admissibility* (1965) EComHR App. No. 1611/62, 8 Yearbook of the European Convention on Human Rights 158 168.

1468 *Case of Al-Skeini and Others v. the United Kingdom, Judgment* (n. 1377) para. 135. As also recognised in *Case of Banković and Others v. Belgium and 16 Other Contracting States, Decision as to the admissibility* (n. 1450) para. 71.

1469 *Case of Al-Skeini and Others v. the United Kingdom, Judgment* (n. 1377) para. 136.

1470 To that end, the ECtHR refers, *inter alia*, to the following cases: *Case of Öcalan v. Turkey, Judgment* (n. 1461); *Case of Issa and Others v. Turkey, Judgment* (n. 1452).

1471 Wallace (n. 1448) 57.

1472 *Case of Al-Skeini and Others v. the United Kingdom, Judgment* (n. 1377) para. 136. See also Wallace (n. 1448) 57.

relevant to that individual's situation.[1473] This implies that the rights under the ECHR can be 'divided and tailored.'[1474] Ultimately, the ECtHR ruled that, as British soldiers were involved in security operations in Basrah during the period in question, the UK had assumed authority and responsibility for maintaining security in certain parts of Iraq (i.e. public powers normally exercised by the sovereign government itself).[1475] Consequently, it exercised authority and control over persons killed during such security operations. With this judgment, the ECtHR did not entirely move away from its ruling in the case of *Banković and Others v. Belgium and 16 Other Contracting States* in which it had limited the possibility of extraterritorial jurisdiction to the situation in which inhabitants of a territory are under the *effective territorial control* of another State who is also a party to the ECHR. As argued by Ryngaert, in *Al-Skeini and Others v. United Kingdom*, the ECtHR reintroduced Banković 'through the back door' by requiring the exercise of public powers over a given territory before finding jurisdiction.[1476]

In other judgments, the ECtHR has acknowledged that the notion of 'State agent authority and control' is not limited to physical power and control exercised in the context of arrest or detention abroad. It also extends to the extraterritorial kinetic use of force (or at least some forms of kinetic force). In the earlier-mentioned case of *Pad and Others v. Turkey*, Turkey accepted it had exercised jurisdiction when Turkish soldiers opened fire on and killed seven Iranian men suspected of smuggling, even though it was not clear whether those smugglers found themselves in Turkish or Iranian territory.[1477] In two further cases concerning deaths in the UN buffer zone in Cyprus due to kinetic use of force by Turkish or Turkish-Cypriot military personnel (*Solomou and Others v. Turkey* and *Andreou v. Turkey*), the ECtHR accepted that Turkey had jurisdiction.[1478] For example, in the case of *Andreou v. Turkey*, the ECtHR accepted that the opening of fire on a crowd from close range, causing directly and immediately lethal injuries, gave rise to jurisdiction within Article 1 of the ECHR.[1479] In the recent case of *Georgia v. Russia (II)*, when asked to rule again on the lawfulness of kinetic use of force, the ECtHR distinguished between the use of force in military operations during the active phase of hostilities (the

1473 *Case of Al-Skeini and Others v. the United Kingdom, Judgment* (n. 1377) paras 136 and 137.

1474 *Ibid.* para. 137.

1475 *Ibid.* para. 149.

1476 Cedric Ryngaert, 'Clarifying the Extraterritorial Application of the European Convention on Human Rights' (2012) 28 Utrecht Journal of International and European Law 57, 59. See also Noam Lubell, 'Human Rights Obligations in Military Occupation' (2012) 94 International Review of the Red Cross 317, 321.

1477 *Case of Pad and Others v. Turkey, Decision as to admissibility* (n. 1453) para. 54.

1478 *Case of Solomou and Others v. Turkey, Judgment* (n. 1462); *Case of Andreou v. Turkey, Judgment* (2009) ECtHR App. No. 45653/99.

1479 *Case of Andreou v. Turkey, Judgment* (n. 1478) para. 25. See also *Case of Solomou and Others v. Turkey, Judgment* (n. 1462) paras 48–51.

combat phase) and the other events that occurred during the 'occupation phase' after the cessation of the active phase of hostilities.[1480] It found that Russian troops' kinetic use of force during the active phase of the conflict did not involve jurisdiction.[1481] It contended that earlier case law by the ECtHR (including *Pad and Others v. Turkey*, *Solomou and Others v. Turkey*, and *Andreou v. Turkey* as discussed above) concerned 'isolated and specific acts involving an element of proximity.'[1482] However, in the present case, the ECtHR reasoned that these were not 'isolated and specific acts involving an element of proximity' but 'bombing and artillery shelling' in the context of an IAC.[1483] Such intense fighting, the ECtHR contended, hinders not only 'effective control' over an area (as discussed above) but also excludes any form of 'State agent authority and control' over individuals.[1484] Later in the judgment, the ECtHR nevertheless expressly found that regarding the deprivation of liberty (as opposed to taking someone's life), Russia did have jurisdiction over all persons arrested and detained during the active phase of hostilities.[1485] The ECtHR also found that Russia had an obligation to investigate potentially unlawful uses of force, even if they took place during the active phase of the conflict, since it had jurisdiction.[1486] This ruling is arbitrary at best. How can one defend that the victims of extraterritorial, massive, systematic use of lethal force do not enjoy the protection of their right to life, whereas the victims of 'isolated and specific acts involving an element of proximity' do?[1487] And why draw a distinction between using lethal force and depriving someone of their liberty, as well as between using lethal force and investigating potentially unlawful uses of force? Subsequent case law will have to show whether the ECtHR will adjust its approach to make it less arbitrary.

The third method, the functional model, also finds some support in the case law of the ECtHR. For example, in the case of *Carter v. Russia*, the ECtHR reiterated that jurisdiction can extend to cases where State agents endanger the life of a person in the territory of another State, even without having formally exercised powers of arrest or detention over that person.[1488] While in the case of *Georgia v. Russia (II)*, the ECtHR referred to cases involving actions by States at or near their borders to support this view, the ECtHR in the case of *Carter v. Russia* claimed the following:[1489]

1480 *Case of Georgia v. Russia (II), Judgment (Merits)* (n. 1407) para. 83.
1481 *Ibid.* para. 144.
1482 *Ibid.* para. 132.
1483 *Ibid.* paras 132–133.
1484 *Ibid.* paras 136–137.
1485 *Ibid.* para. 239.
1486 *Ibid.* paras 331–332.
1487 For a detailed commentary, see also Milanović, 'Georgia v. Russia No. 2: The European Court's Resurrection of Bankovic in the Contexts of Chaos' (n. 1456).
1488 *Case of Carter v. Russia, Judgment (Merits)* (2021) ECtHR (Grand Chamber) App. No. 20914/07 para. 129.
1489 *Ibid.* para. 130.

> [T]he principle that a State exercises extraterritorial jurisdiction in cases concerning specific acts involving an element of proximity should apply with equal force in cases of extrajudicial targeted killings by State agents acting in the territory of another Contracting State outside of the context of a military operation.

To establish jurisdiction as to the substantive limb of Article 2 of the ECHR, the ECtHR considered the questions of control and attribution together with the merits. To that end, the ECtHR held that to determine whether Russia could be held liable for the violation of Litvinenko's right to life, it was necessary to consider whether Litvinenko's assassination amounted to 'the exercise of physical power and control over his life in a situation of proximate targeting' and whether it was carried out by State agents.[1490] The Court answered both parts of the question in the affirmative and thus held Russia liable for violating Litvinenko's right to life.[1491] With this approach, the ECtHR arguably adopted the functional model but limited its applicability to all acts of extraterritorial killing by State agents carried out outside the context of an IAC. The functional model also resonated in the Concurring Opinion of Judge Bonello in the earlier case of *Al-Skeini and Others v. the United Kingdom*:[1492]

> A 'functional' test would see a State effectively exercising 'jurisdiction' whenever it falls within its power to perform, or not to perform, any of these five functions. Very simply put, *a State has jurisdiction for the purposes of Article 1 [of the ECHR] whenever the observance or the breach of any of these functions is within its authority and control.*
>
> Jurisdiction means no less and no more than 'authority over' and 'control of'. In relation to Convention obligations, jurisdiction is neither territorial nor extraterritorial: it ought to be functional – in the sense that when it is within a State's authority and control whether a breach of human rights is, or is not, committed, whether its perpetrators are, or are not, identified and punished, whether the victims of violations are, or are not, compensated, it would be an imposture to claim that, ah yes, that State had authority and control, but, ah no, it had no jurisdiction.

Last but not least, in his Partly Concurring Opinion in the case of *Georgia v. Russia (II)*, Judge Serghides raised the point that negative obligations to respect human rights should not be subject to any territorial limitation.[1493] He explained, however, that the negative obligation theory must not be based in Article 1 of the ECHR but instead in other substantive provisions (especially

---

1490 *Ibid.* para. 150.

1491 *Ibid.* paras 151–172.

1492 Emphasis added. *Case of Al-Skeini and Others v. the United Kingdom, Judgment* (n. 1377), Concurring Opinion of Judge Bonello, paras 11–12.

1493 *Case of Georgia v. Russia (II), Judgment (Merits)* (n. 1407) Partly Concurring Opinion of Judge Serghides, paras 3–27.

Articles 2 and 3 of the ECHR).[1494] Since the case was pleaded exclusively under Article 1 of the ECHR, Judge Serghides voted with the majority.[1495]

E. AComHPR

The ACHPR does not contain provisions delimiting the scope of application for the obligations contained in the ACHPR. Article 1 of the ACHPR requires State parties to recognise the rights, duties, and freedoms set forth in Chapter 1 of the ACHPR demands that State parties take legislative or other measures to give effect to them. However, no reference is made to any jurisdictional or territorial limitations in this regard.

In its General Comment No. 3 on the Right to Life, the AComHPR accepts that the ACHPR applies extraterritorially when 'the State has jurisdiction or otherwise exercises effective authority, power, or control over either the perpetrator or the victim (or the victim's rights), or exercises effective control over the territory on which the victim's rights are affected, or whether the State engages in conduct which could reasonably be foreseen to result in an unlawful deprivation of life.'[1496] In doing so, it endorses both the spatial, the personal, and the functional models.

Relevant case law on the extraterritorial application of HRL obligations under the ACHPR is limited. A relevant case is the case of the *Democratic Republic of the Congo v. Burundi, Rwanda and Uganda,* in which the AComHPR had to consider the complaint by the DRC about grave and massive violations of human and people's rights during the occupation of its territory by the armed forces of Burundi, Rwanda, and Uganda.[1497] The AComHPR found that the three States had indeed violated a series of human rights guaranteed in the ACHPR during their armed activities in the territory of the DRC.[1498] None of the States objected to the extraterritorial application of the ACHPR in this regard.[1499]

2.1.3.3. Distinction between extraterritorial negative and positive HRL obligations

All three models come with their advantages and disadvantages. The main problem with the spatial model is that it leaves out a great many situations in

1494 *Ibid.* para. 2.
1495 *Ibid.* para. 2.
1496 AComHPR (n. 83) para. 14.
1497 *Democratic Republic of the Congo v. Burundi, Rwanda and Uganda* (2003) AComHPR 33rd Ordinary Session, Communication No. 227/99.
1498 *Ibid.* 14.
1499 As also discussed in Lilian Chenwi and Takele Soboka Bulto, 'Extraterritoriality in the African Regional Human Rights System from a Comparative Perspective' in Lilian Chenwi and Takele Soboka Bulto (eds), *Extraterritorial Human Rights Obligations From an African Perspective* (Intersentia 2018) 39–40.

which jurisdiction can reasonably be said to exist.[1500] Therefore, the personal model usually complements the spatial model and extends the scope of HRL obligations considerably.[1501] Indeed, there are many situations in which the actions of a State affect individuals without the State actually having control over the territory in which it does so.[1502] Consider, for example, the shooting of a fugitive or the arrest and detention of suspected terrorists on the territory of another State without any control over the territory in question. Then again, one of the problems with the personal model is that it runs counter to the language used in some treaties (for example, those where jurisdiction is clearly limited to territorial jurisdiction).[1503] Moreover, this model cannot be restricted on any principled basis.[1504] Without restrictions, jurisdiction arises whenever State agents exercise power over a person without even having to look into the fact of whether the acts or omissions by a State *actually* affect that person. As Milanović observed "authority and control over individuals' as a basis for state jurisdiction simply boils down to the proposition that a state has obligations under human rights treaties towards all individuals whose human rights it is *able* to violate.'[1505] Indeed, if a State can violate someone's rights, it exercises power over that person. Since courts and mechanisms are aware that this is untenable, they seek to limit the effect in some way. This often leads to arbitrary rulings, for example by limiting the scope to the exercise of physical power over an individual or the use of close-range violence.[1506]

The functional model struggles with the same problem, and its pure application does not differ much from the personal model. A distinction between the actual exercise of power over individual rights and the mere potential to do so is meaningless. If a State is able to respect, protect, or fulfil someone's rights, it means it exercises power over that person's enjoyment of rights. When applied strictly and giving rise to a duty to fulfil both negative and positive HRL obligations extraterritorially, the functional model may equally yield undesirable outcomes. For example, the State may have to fulfil positive HRL obligations

1500 Milanović, *Extraterritorial Application of Human Rights Treaties: Law, Principles and Policy* (n. 1401) 119.

1501 *Ibid.* 173.

1502 *Ibid.* 118, 170–172.

1503 E.g. Art. 2(1) of the CAT sets forth that '[e]ach State Party shall take effective legislative, administrative, judicial or other measures to prevent acts of torture in any territory under its jurisdiction' (Convention against Torture and Other Cruel, Inhuman or Degrading Treatment or Punishment (adopted 10 December 1984, entered into force 26 June 1987) 1465 UNTS 85 (CAT)).

1504 Milanović, *Extraterritorial Application of Human Rights Treaties: Law, Principles and Policy* (n. 1401) 119; 173–175.

1505 Emphasis added. *Ibid.* 207. See also Martin Scheinin, 'Extraterritorial Effect of the International Covenant on Civil and Political Rights' in Fons Coomans and Menno T Kamminga (eds), *Extraterritorial Application of Human Rights Treaties* (Intersentia 2004) 76–78.

1506 See case law discussed above, Part III, Section 2.1.3.1.

towards individuals simply because it is in a position to protect the human rights of those individuals and, as such, actually affects the enjoyment of someone's rights. This may equally lead to results that may be considered as politically or practically extreme or unfeasible, prompting the search for artificial ways of limiting the scope of application. This, in turn, may lead to arbitrary boundaries being drawn, for example by limiting the scope to situations where there is a relationship of dependency.[1507]

To address these problems, Milanović proposes a radically different model.[1508] According to Milanović, the notion of jurisdiction should only have a territorial effect and should concern the obligation of the State to *secure* and *ensure* human rights.[1509] To effectively secure and ensure human rights, a State needs a certain degree of *de jure* or *de facto* control over a territory or an area.[1510] Besides the obligations to secure and ensure, there is also an obligation to *respect* human rights.[1511] To comply with the obligation to respect human rights, control over a territory or an area should not be a prerequisite.[1512] In fact, no threshold should artificially be imposed since only control over the actions of its own organs or agents is needed to fulfil the obligation to respect human rights.[1513] This includes the negative obligation not to infringe upon the rights of an individual without adequate justification.[1514] Moreover, he argues, States should fulfil those positive obligations that exist solely to make the State's negative obligations truly effective.[1515]

Despite the merits of the Milanović model, the author himself recognises that it requires a radical change in courts and human rights mechanisms. Therefore, from a pragmatic point of view, Milanović is willing to accept the personal power model as authority and control of the State over individuals, together with the spatial model, as a substitute. If the personal model is deemed necessary, it should be invoked regarding the negative obligation to respect, while the spatial model should be invoked with respect to the positive obligation to secure or ensure human rights. A similar approach is taken by Roxstrom et al.[1516]

1507 See case law discussed above, Part III, Section 2.1.3.2. See also Milanović, 'Drowning Migrants, the Human Rights Committee, and Extraterritorial Human Rights Obligations' (n. 1425).

1508 Milanović, *Extraterritorial Application of Human Rights Treaties: Law, Principles and Policy* (n. 1401) 209–222.

1509 *Ibid.* 210.

1510 *Ibid.*

1511 *Ibid.*

1512 *Ibid.*

1513 *Ibid.*

1514 *Ibid.* 209.

1515 *Ibid.* 216.

1516 Erik Roxstrom, Mark Gibney and Terje Einarsen, 'The NATO Bombing Case (Bankovic et al v. Belgium et al.) and the Limits of Western Human Rights Protection' (2005) 23 Boston University International Law Journal 55, 72–75.

However, as Lubell rightly points out, in the context of certain extraterritorial situations, the approach based on negative obligations may be insufficient to safeguard fundamental rights. The nature and circumstances of power, authority, or control over a person may require *positive* action extraterritorially. This requires a 'contextual approach', i.e. the extent to which power is exercised over individuals influences the extent to which HRL obligations must be protected and fulfilled.[1517] Thus, while States must refrain from violating human rights both within their territory and outside of their territory, it is suggested that States only have positive obligations extraterritorially in limited circumstances. The following control tests are suggested to identify such circumstances: 'control over the effects said to constitute a violation, subject to a foreseeable victim being foreseeably affected by the act,'[1518] the existence of 'a direct and immediate link between the extraterritorial conduct of a state and the alleged violation of an individual's rights,'[1519] or the fact that a State has 'factual control in respect of facts and events that allegedly constitute a *violation* of a human right,'[1520] that the individual 'is directly dependent on the power exercised by the agents,'[1521] or that the State 'has the power to (intentionally, knowingly, or negligently) affect one or several of his/her human rights.'[1522]

Taking a general position on which of the three models of extraterritorial applicability must be used to determine the extraterritorial jurisdiction and which control test must be applied to limit the scope of obligations is beyond the scope of this study. What is relevant for those in practice is which model will be applied in their specific case. As indicated above, this assessment will depend on the court or human rights mechanism, which will rule *ex post* on the possible violation of human rights. Therefore, in Part III, Section 4.1, a pragmatic approach to the question of the extent to which the right to life should

---

1517 Noam Lubell, *Extraterritorial Use of Force against Non-State Actors* (Oxford University Press 2010) 230. Rick Lawson, 'Life after Banković: On the Extraterritorial Application of the European Convention on Human Rights' in Fons Coomans and Menno T Kamminga (eds), *Extraterritorial Application of Human Rights Treaties* (Intersentia 2004) 120. See also Rick Lawson, 'Really Out of Sight? Issues of Jurisdiction and Control in Situations of Armed Conflict under the ECHR' in Antoine Buyse (ed), *Margins of Conflict: The ECHR and Transitions to and from Armed Conflict* (1st edn, Intersentia 2010) 74–75; Scheinin (n. 1505) 76–77.

1518 Francoise J Hampson, 'The Relationship between International Humanitarian Law and Human Rights Law from the Perspective of a Human Rights Treaty Body' (2008) 90 International Review of the Red Cross 549, 570.

1519 Lawson, 'Life after Banković: On the Extraterritorial Application of the European Convention on Human Rights' (n. 1517) 120.

1520 Scheinin (n. 1505) 76. See also Tom Dannenbaum, 'Translating the Standard of Effective Control into a System of Effective Accountability: How Liability Should Be Apportioned for Violations of Human Rights by Member State Troop Contingents Serving as United Nations Peacekeepers' (2010) 51 Harvard International Law Journal 113, 158 et seq.

1521 Lubell (n. 1517) 230–231.

1522 Roxstrom, Gibney and Einarsen (n. 1516) 74.

be respected, protected, and fulfilled within the framework of UN (mandated) peace operations is suggested.

2.1.4. Applicability ratione temporis

HRL is, in principle, applicable at all times, regardless of the character of a situation in which a UN (mandated) peace operation is deployed.[1523] However, this does not preclude States or international or regional organisations from derogating certain rights in times of public emergency threatening the life of the nation. Moreover, pursuant to Chapter VII and Article 103 of the UN Charter, the UN Security Council may authorise conduct which does not comply with HRL obligations of States or international or regional organisations.

2.1.4.1. Derogation in times of public emergency

Derogations allow States (and by extension also regional or international organisations, as discussed below) to suspend or restrict the exercise of certain rights in whole or in part in emergency situations. It is based on striking a balance between human rights and the pursuit of collective goals such as public order and national security.[1524] Human rights can only be derogated from in exceptional circumstances, and these emergency powers are limited in both time and scope.[1525] While peacekeeping almost always takes place in an emergency situation, and HRL obligations are often invoked, this does not mean that emergency powers are triggered '*en bloc*.'[1526] The possibility of derogating from human rights by declaring a state of emergency may be resorted to on a case-by-case basis in UN (mandated) peace operations to the extent that the situation in question reaches the threshold required for derogation.[1527]

Practice reveals that the concept of derogation is actually conspicuously absent in the context of UN (mandated) peace operations.[1528] To date, no State or international or regional organisation has made use of the possibility to derogate from HRL when operating on the territory of a third State.[1529] There is also a reluctance, especially regarding UN peace operations, to recognise derogation in a general sense as falling within the competence of the UN Security Council since there are limited checks and balances against the UN Security Council's exercise of its powers.[1530]

1523 Gill and others (n. 26) 76.
1524 Carina Lamont, *International Law in the Transition to Peace: Protecting Civilians under Jus Post Bellum* (Routledge 2021) 226.
1525 *Ibid.*
1526 *Ibid.*
1527 *Ibid.*
1528 Sheeran, 'Human Rights and Derogation in Peacekeeping' (n. 29) 205.
1529 *Ibid.; Gill and others (n. 26) 86.*
1530 Sheeran, 'Human Rights and Derogation in Peacekeeping' (n. 29) 227.

Yet, as aptly remarked by Larsen,[1531]

> [R]esort to derogations in UN-mandated peace operations would be a clear advantage. It would create a coherent and transparent legal framework for the assessment of human rights obligations in such operations, it would allow troop contributing states to avoid obligations that it would be unrealistic to comply with, and it would in fact lead to an increased level of human rights protection in the area of deployment, since the scope of application of the ECHR would shift from 'nothing' to 'some'.

Of course, this requires first that the applicability *de jure* of HRL to UN (mandated) peace operations is accepted. Furthermore, this also requires States and regional and international organisations to be deemed to have the same inherent capacity to derogate from human rights in exceptional situations.

Both national and international law regulates emergency powers; as such, derogations must be consistent with the applicable rules.[1532] There are differences in national and international law, as a result of which States and regional and international organisations can be subject to different rules.[1533] Yet, while a textual reading of the various HRL treaties at first sight suggests a divergence in the regulation of the state of emergency, a fairly coherent international legal regime for emergency powers can actually be deduced from them. This does not prevent a number of divergent interpretations from emerging in case law, but a study of such divergent interpretations is beyond the scope of this study.[1534] Nevertheless, the following substantive and procedural limitations can serve as a general guideline in the future to derogate from HRL:

First, States and regional and international organisations do not have *carte blanche* to decide from which human rights they want to derogate.[1535] Indeed, they cannot derogate from certain human rights.[1536] Most HRL treaties contain a clear list of human rights that cannot be derogated from. Article 4(2) of the ICCPR and Article 27(2) of the ACHR, for example, explicitly state that no derogation can be made from the right to life, among others. Article 15(2) of the ECHR sets forth that '[n]o derogation [shall be made] from Article 2 [of the ECHR], except in respect of deaths resulting from lawful acts of war, or from Articles 3, 4 (paragraph 1) and 7 [of the ECHR].' However, in its case law, the

1531 Larsen (n. 1350) 313 (unlike the present study, Larsen uses the term 'UN-mandated peace operations' to refer to peace operations under the command and control of the UN). Sheeran also makes a case for the relevance of derogation in the context of UN peace operations: Sheeran, 'Human Rights and Derogation in Peacekeeping' (n. 29) 227–240.

1532 Gill and others (n. 26) 86; Lamont (n. 1524) 231.

1533 Kleffner (n. 1374) para. 35.

1534 For further reading, see e.g. Lamont (n. 1524) 236–242.

1535 Naert, 'International Law Aspects of the EU's Security and Defence Policy, with a Particular Focus on the Law of Armed Conflict and Human Rights' (n. 1361) 372.

1536 Kleffner (n. 1374) para. 35.

ECtHR has recognised that the safeguards under the ECHR continue to apply in the context of armed conflict, albeit interpreted against the background of the provisions of IHL.[1537] The ACHPR does not contain a derogation clause, as a result of which 'limitations on the rights and freedoms enshrined in the Charter cannot be justified by emergencies and special circumstances.'[1538] Customary HRL also does not have such a uniform list of non-derogable rights, but it is beyond dispute that peremptory norms cannot be derogated from.[1539] The right to life, or more precisely, the right not to be arbitrarily deprived of one's life, is an example of a peremptory norm from which cannot be derogated.[1540] The non-derogable nature of the right to life does not imply that no one can be deprived of their life. Permissible grounds for the deprivation of life are built into conventional law and generally accepted principles and practices.[1541]

Second, derogation from HRL obligations is generally only allowed in the event of certain serious emergencies, typically public emergencies that threaten 'the life of the nation.'[1542] Since UN (mandated) peace operations, in principle, operate outside of the territory of the TCC(s), it is usually difficult to consider such a situation as threatening 'the lives of all nations' contributing to the operation in question, or as an existential threat to the UN or other international or regional organisations conducting the operation.[1543] Therefore, international practice is inconclusive as to whether *extraterritorial* obligations may also be derogated from.[1544] However, since the notion of 'jurisdiction' has been expanded to cover certain extraterritorial conduct,[1545] the scope of the derogation regime should be broadened accordingly.[1546] After all, once it is accepted that a human

1537 See e.g. *Case of Hassan v. the United Kingdom, Judgment* (2014) ECtHR (Grand Chamber) App. No. 29750/09 para. 104; *Case of Al-Skeini and Others v. the United Kingdom, Judgment* (n. 1377) para. 164.

1538 *Media Rights Agenda and Others v. Nigeria* (1998) AComHPR Communication Nos. 105/93, 128/94, 130/94, 152/96 para. 67; *Constitutional Rights Project, Civil Liberties Organisation and Media Rights Agenda v. Nigeria* (1999) AComHPR Communication Nos. 140/94, 141/94, 145/95 para. 41.

1539 Maus (n. 1354) 122–123.

1540 For sources substantiating the position that the right to life is a peremptory norm, see Part III, Section 2.1.2.2, fn. 1397.

1541 Watkin (n. 38) 459. As also discussed in more detail below, see Part III, Section 3.1.1.

1542 As required by, e.g. Art. 4 of the ICCPR and Art. 15 of the ECHR. Art. 27 of the ACHR sets forth '[i]n time of war, public danger, or other emergency that threatens the independence or security of a state party.'

1543 Maus (n. 1354) 118; Sheeran, 'Human Rights and Derogation in Peacekeeping' (n. 29) 223.

1544 See e.g. the United Kingdom, Ministry of Defence and The Rt Hon Sir Michael Fallon, 'Government to Protect Armed Forces from Persistent Legal Claims in Future Overseas Operations' (*Gov.uk*, 4 October 2016), www.gov.uk/government/news/government-to-protect-armed-forces-from-persistent-legal-claims-in-future-overseas-operations, accessed 17 February 2022. For a different view, see UN HRC, 'Report of the Special Rapporteur on the Promotion and Protection of Human Rights and Fundamental Freedoms While Countering Terrorism on the Human Rights Challenge of States of Emergency in the Context of Countering Terrorism' (2018) UN Doc. A/HRC/37/52 para. 68.

1545 As discussed in the previous Section, see Part III, Section 2.1.3.

1546 Larsen (n. 1350) 313.

rights treaty is extraterritorially applicable, even in situations that undoubtedly qualify as emergencies, the impossibility of derogation would indeed lead to an unrealistic and unworkable situation where States would be obliged to apply the treaty in full in circumstances where it is factually impossible to do so while also fulfilling their obligations under the mandate.[1547] In literature, suggestions are made to allow derogations in the context of UN (mandated) peace operations if the state of emergency requirement is met in the area where a peace force is deployed or if the situation, as such, constitutes a threat to international peace and security.[1548]

Third, measures derogating from certain rights must be limited to what is strictly necessary in view of the requirements of the situation.[1549] In other words, a derogation may only be applied if it is absolutely impossible for the derogating State or UN (mandated) peace force to comply with the relevant human rights standard in the execution of its mandate.[1550] A derogation should only be considered as a last resort.[1551] While the ICCPR and the ECHR require that measures be taken only 'to the extent strictly required by the exigencies of the situation,' the ACHR adds an explicit time limit by requiring that such derogative measures may only be taken 'to the extent and for the period of time strictly required.' According to Milanović, such temporal limitation is, however, also implicit in the ICCPR and the ECHR.[1552]

Fourth, derogatory measures may not involve discrimination based on race, colour, sex, language, religion, or social origin. This is, for example, explicitly required by the ICCPR and the ACHR.

Fifth, when a State or a UN (mandated) peace force derogates from certain HRL obligations, they must still comply with their other obligations under international law, including IHL in case the threshold for an armed conflict has been reached.[1553]

Sixth, certain procedural safeguards apply, including that a derogation must normally be communicated.[1554] This communication includes, for example, informing the other parties to the relevant human rights treaty when

1547 Gill and others (n. 26) 86. See also Maus (n. 1354) 118–119.

1548 Gill and others (n. 26) 86; Sheeran, 'Human Rights and Derogation in Peacekeeping' (n. 29) 225 and 229.

1549 Kleffner (n. 1374) para. 35.

1550 Gill and others (n. 26) 86.

1551 *Ibid.*

1552 Marko Milanović, 'Extraterritorial Derogations from Human Rights Treaties in Armed Conflict' in Nehal Bhuta (ed), *The Frontiers of Human Rights* (Oxford University Press 2016) 60.

1553 As required by, e.g. Art. 15(1) of the ECHR, Art. 4(1) of the ICCPR, and Art. 27(1) of the ACHR. The applicability of IHL to UN (mandated) peace operations is discussed in Part III, Section 2.2. The fundamental principles of IHL that govern the use of force that has a clear nexus to an armed conflict are discussed in Part III, Section 3.2.

1554 As required by, e.g. Art. 15(3) of the ECHR, Art. 4(3) of the ICCPR, and Art. 27(3) of the ACHR.

the derogation measures start and when they end, what the human rights provision(s) affected are, and what the reasons are for taking those measures.[1555] The ICCPR also adds that the existence of a public emergency must be 'officially proclaimed.' As remarked by the Leuven Manual, it is not yet a settled issue whether the derogation procedures of the relevant HRL treaties must be followed in case of a derogation under a UNSC resolution.[1556] The dominant view seems to be that failure to follow such a derogation procedure need not preclude recourse to that derogation.[1557]

2.1.4.2. Derogation under Chapter VII and Article 103 of the UN Charter

The UN Security Council has the discretionary power to deviate from the law when resorting to enforcement measures under Chapter VII of the UN Charter.[1558] In addition, under Article 103 of the UN Charter, the UN Security Council may authorise conduct inconsistent with the HRL obligations of States. Derogation from the law based on Chapter VII powers and under Article 103 of the UN Charter is discussed in more detail below when discussing the impact of the UNSC mandate on whether or not force can be used in specific instances (see Part III, Section 3.3.2.1). What is already worth mentioning here, however, is that in the event of a conflict between a UNSC resolution and a *jus cogens* norm, the latter will prevail.[1559] *Jus cogens* is a substantive limit to the discretion of the UN Security Council.[1560] As has already been mentioned several times, the right to life, or more precisely, the right not to be arbitrarily deprived of one's life, is such a peremptory norm that permits no derogation.[1561]

2.2. APPLICABILITY OF IHL TO UN (MANDATED) PEACE FORCES CARRYING OUT A POC MANDATE

If force is used in a situation which has a clear nexus to an ongoing armed conflict, that use of force is not only governed by HRL but also by IHL. The

1555 Kleffner (n. 1374) para. 35.

1556 Gill and others (n. 26) 87; Naert, 'International Law Aspects of the EU's Security and Defence Policy, with a Particular Focus on the Law of Armed Conflict and Human Rights' (n. 1361) 380 and 385.

1557 Gill and others (n. 26) 87; Naert, 'International Law Aspects of the EU's Security and Defence Policy, with a Particular Focus on the Law of Armed Conflict and Human Rights' (n. 1361) 380 and 385.

1558 De Wet (n. 892) 184.

1559 For sources substantiating this position, see Part II, Section 3.3.1.1, fn. 1219.

1560 Gill, 'Legal and Some Political Limitations on the Power of the UN Security Council to Exercise Its Enforcement Powers under Chapter VII of the Charter' (n. 892) 79; de Wet (n. 892) 187.

1561 For sources substantiating the position that the right to life is a peremptory norm, see Part III, Section 2.1.2.2, fn. 1397.

principle that IHL may apply to UN (mandated) peace operations is no longer controversial. What is still under discussion, however, and especially in the context of UN peace operations, is when IHL applies, which status the forces enjoy under IHL and the extent to which the different IHL rules and principles apply to their actions. The present Section addresses these issues, as well as other pressing questions concerning the applicability of IHL to the actions of UN (mandated) peace operations, by discussing the applicability *ratione temporis*, *ratione personae*, *ratione materiae*, and *ratione loci* of IHL in the context of UN (mandated) peace operations.

2.2.1. Applicability ratione temporis

The applicability *ratione temporis* of IHL to UN (mandated) peace operations is subject to debate, and, more specifically, whether the 'standard' test for determining the applicability of IHL also applies to UN (mandated) peace operations or whether a different test must be considered.[1562] The standard conditions for becoming a party to an armed conflict are set out in IHL itself and are established by practice.[1563]

IHL instruments distinguish two types of armed conflicts: (i) an IAC under Common Article 2 of the Geneva Conventions I–IV; and (ii) a NIAC under Common Article 3 of the Geneva Conventions I–IV or even, if certain additional conditions are fulfilled, Additional Protocol II. It is essential to discern these two types of conflicts as different rules on the use of force may apply in IACs and NIACs.[1564]

Common Article 2 of the Geneva Conventions I–IV determines that an IAC exists whenever there is a recourse to armed force between two or more States. In its 1958 ICRC Commentary on Geneva Convention IV, Pictet stated that '[a]ny difference arising between two states and leading to the intervention of members of the armed forces is an armed conflict within Article 2.'[1565] The 2016, 2017, and 2021 ICRC Commentaries to Geneva Conventions I, II, and III, confirmed that the classification of an IAC does not depend on the reasons for the recourse to armed force or the intensity of the confrontation.[1566] Instead, it is based on

1562 Zwanenburg, 'UN Peace Operations, International Humanitarian Law and International Human Rights Law' (n. 37) 98.

1563 Gill and others (n. 26) 93.

1564 See also Marko Milanović and Vidan Hadzi-Vidanovic, 'A Taxonomy of Armed Conflict' in Nigel D White and Christian Henderson (eds), *Research Handbook on International Conflict and Security Law: Jus Ad Bellum, Jus In Bello And Jus Post Bellum* (Edward Elgar 2013) 272–273.

1565 Pictet (n. 84) 20.

1566 ICRC, *2016 ICRC Commentary on Geneva Convention I* (n. 86) para. 218. ICRC, *2017 ICRC Commentary on Geneva Convention II* (n. 86) para. 240; ICRC, *2021 ICRC Commentary on Geneva Convention III* (n. 86) para. 251. See also ICRC, 'How Is the Term "Armed Conflict" Defined in International Humanitarian Law?' (ICRC 2008) Opinion Paper 1.

what actually occurs between two parties. The ICTY has equally held that an IAC exists '*whenever* there is a resort to armed force between States.'[1567] These views, also collectively identified as the 'first-shot' theory as they believe an IAC exists from the first moment force is used, are nevertheless controversial.[1568] Others have argued that a *de minimis* level of violence must occur before there is an IAC. While this provides an interesting debate, an analysis falls outside the scope of this book.[1569]

What is relevant for UN (mandated) peace operations is that, based on an emerging rule of customary IHL, the scope *ratione personae* of IACs may be extended to international organisations.[1570] The condition that an IAC involves armed force between two or more States can be interpreted as such that it also encompasses the resort to armed force by entities with an international legal personality, such as international organisations.[1571] Such an interpretation brings military action by the UN, the AU, NATO, and the EU to fall within the scope of IHL. The NATO intervention in Libya in 2011 is an example whereby there was an IAC between Libya and the States that took part in the coalition, and most likely also between Libya and NATO.[1572] This IAC ran parallel with the NIAC between the Libyan government and the rebel groups.[1573]

1567 *Prosecutor v. Tadić, Decision on the defense motion for interlocutory appeal on jurisdiction* (1995) ICTY IT-94-1-A para. 70.

1568 Gill and others (n. 26) 94; Kleffner (n. 1374) para. 6; Zwanenburg, 'UN Peace Operations, International Humanitarian Law and International Human Rights Law' (n. 37) 98.

1569 For contrasting views on the matter, see e.g. Dapo Akande, 'Classification of Armed Conflicts: Relevant Legal Concepts' in Elizabeth Wilmshurst (ed), *International Law and the Classification of Conflicts* (1st edn., Oxford University Press ; The Royal Institute of International Affairs (Chatham House) 2012); International Law Association, 'Final Report on the Meaning of Armed Conflict in International Law' (2010) The Hague Conference; Dino Kritsiotis, 'The Tremors of Tadić' (2010) 43 Israel Law Review 262, 278–282; Lubell (n. 1517) 94–95; Sylvain Vité, 'Typology of Armed Conflicts in International Humanitarian Law: Legal Concepts and Actual Situations' (2009) 91 International Review of the Red Cross 69, 72–73; Noam Zamir, *Classification of Conflicts in International Humanitarian Law: The Legal Impact of Foreign Intervention in Civil Wars* (Edward Elgar Publishing 2017) 51–57.

1570 Ferraro, 'The Applicability and Application of International Humanitarian Law to Multinational Forces' (n. 676) 575; Gill and others (n. 26) 94.

1571 Ferraro, 'The Applicability and Application of International Humanitarian Law to Multinational Forces' (n. 676) 575.

1572 See Louise Arimatsu, 'Beginning of IHL Application: Overview and Challenges', *Proceedings of the 13th Bruges Colloquium on Scope of Application of International Humanitarian Law, 18–19 October 2012, Bruges, vol. 43, 71* (2013) 109; Bartolini (n. 794) 267; Ferraro, 'The Applicability and Application of International Humanitarian Law to Multinational Forces' (n. 676) 593–594; Lehmann (n. 14) 120–122; Nauta (n. 1366) 136. See also UNHRC, 'Report of the International Commission of Inquiry on Libya' (2012) UN Doc. A/HRC/19/68 (while the International Commission of Inquiry on Libya only explicitly recognises the existence of an IAC between Libya and the States participating in NATO military intervention (para. 28), it also recognises that customary IHL applies to NATO's actions, thus implicitly acknowledging that NATO is also a party to the armed conflict (para. 613).

1573 UNHRC (n. 1572) para. 28. See also the letter dated 23 January 2012 from NATO's legal adviser to the Chair of the International Commission of Inquiry on Libya (Annex II to the report), in which NATO accepted that IHL 'was the *lex specialis* applicable to armed conflict'

The concept of NIAC must be analysed based on Common Article 3 of the Geneva Conventions I–IV and Article 1 of Additional Protocol II. Common Article 3 applies in the case of 'armed conflict not of an international character occurring in the territory of one of the High Contracting Parties.' 'An armed conflict not of an international character' can be understood as a conflict in which at least one of the parties involved is not a State.[1574] With the case of *Prosecutor v. Tadić*, the ICTY has provided an important guideline for identifying 'armed conflicts not of an international character' by stipulating the following two conditions: (i) there must be protracted armed violence meaning that hostilities must reach a minimum level of intensity; and (ii) such violence must occur between governmental authorities and armed groups possessing a certain level of organisation or between such groups within a State.[1575] Subsequent ICTY and ICTR case law has confirmed and further interpreted the *Tadić* criteria as important indicators of the required intensity of violence and of what constitutes an organised armed group.[1576] Accordingly, a number of factors have been listed for determining the organisation of the parties to the conflict and the intensity of the armed violence.[1577] When assessing the intensity of a conflict, the following factors have, for example, been taken into account: the amount and seriousness of individual attacks, the distribution of the conflicts over the territory and over a certain period of time, the number of persons and the type of armed forces participating in the fighting, and the mobilisation and distribution of weapons between the two parties to the conflict. As regards the organisation of the parties to the conflict, factors such as the existence of a chain of command and disciplinary rules and mechanisms within the group, the existence of headquarters, designated areas of operations, and the ability to acquire, transport, and distribute arms, and other military equipment have been considered.

---

and, therefore, the legal standard against which its actions would be judged during Operation Unified Protector, which aimed to prevent attacks on civilians (see p. 2 of the letter).

1574 Vité (n. 1569) 75.

1575 *Prosecutor v. Tadić, Decision on the defense motion for interlocutory appeal on jurisdiction* (n. 1567) para. 70.

1576 See e.g. *Prosecutor v. Kunarac, Kovac, and Vokovic, Appeals chamber judgment* (2002) ICTY IT-96-23 and IT-96-23/1-A para. 56; *Prosecutor v. Fatmir Limaj, Haradin Bala, and Isak Musliu, Trial chamber judgment* (2005) ICTY IT-03-66-T para. 84; *Prosecutor v. Ljube Boškoski and Johan Tarčulovski, Trial chamber judgment* (2008) ICTY IT-04-82-T para. 175; *Prosecutor v. Jean-Paul Akayesu, Judgment* (1998) ICTR ICTR-96-4-T para. 619; *Prosecutor v. Georges Anderson Nderubumwe Rutaganda, Judgment* (1999) ICTR ICTR-96-3-T para. 92. See also ICRC, *2016 ICRC Commentary on Geneva Convention I* (n. 86) para. 387.

1577 *Prosecutor v. Tadić, Trial chamber judgment* (1997) ICTY IT-94-1-T paras 561–568; *Prosecutor v. Fatmir Limaj, Haradin Bala, and Isak Musliu, Trial chamber judgment* (n. 1576) paras 94–170; *Prosecutor v. Ramush Haradinaj, Idriz Balaj, and Lahi Brahimaj, Trial chamber judgment* (2008) ICTY IT-04-84-T paras 49–60; *Prosecutor v. Ljube Boškoski and Johan Tarčulovski, Trial chamber judgment* (n. 1576) paras 177–206.

Additional Protocol II adopted a more restrictive definition of NIAC. Article 1(1) of Additional Protocol I determines that this instrument applies to armed conflicts 'which take place in the territory of a High Contracting Party between its armed forces and dissident armed forces or other organized armed groups which, under responsible command, exercise such control over a part of its territory as to enable them to carry out sustained and concerted military operations.' This definition only covers a subset of NIACs – i.e. conflicts whereby the State is always a party to the conflict and the non-state party has territorial control – and, therefore, is only relevant to the application of Additional Protocol II.

Nothing in IHL suggests that the 'standard' test for determining whether a State has become a party to an armed conflict cannot also be used to determine whether UN (mandated) peace operations are involved in an IAC or a NIAC.[1578] Nevertheless, as mentioned earlier, there remains quite some reluctance among States and international and regional organisations to declare that they have become a party to an armed conflict when undertaking or taking part in a UN (mandated) peace operation.[1579] There is also a tendency for national and international courts and tribunals to raise the threshold of armed conflict required by IHL before acknowledging peace forces' involvement. For example, in 1996, a Canadian court ruled that a Canadian soldier suspected of helping to torture a Somali boy to death was under no legal obligation to ensure the safety of his prisoner because IHL did not apply to the Unified Task Force (UNITAF), a US-led UN-sanctioned multinational force in Somalia.[1580] One year later, in 1997, a Belgian Military Court issued a judgment regarding violations of IHL committed by Belgian UN peacekeepers in Somalia. It ruled that UNOSOM II could only have been considered a party to an armed conflict if the forces had been engaged in combat operations of a 'permanent, widespread, and structured character' against one or more opposing armed groups.[1581]

1578 Ferraro, 'The Applicability and Application of International Humanitarian Law to Multinational Forces' (n. 676) 582; Gill and others (n. 26) 93; Zwanenburg, 'UN Peace Operations, International Humanitarian Law and International Human Rights Law' (n. 37) 99. For further references to sources advocating otherwise, see e.g. Ferraro, 'The Applicability and Application of International Humanitarian Law to Multinational Forces' (n. 676) 580–583; Foley, *UN Peacekeeping Operations and the Protection of Civilians: Saving Succeeding Generations* (n. 16) 139–140.

1579 See Part III, Section 2.

1580 *Her Majesty the Queen v. Private DJ Brocklebank* (1996) Court Martial Appeal Court of Canada Court File No. CMAC-383, 5, Part 3, 1995–1997 Court Martial Appeal Rep para. 62, yet see also the dissenting opinion by Judge Weiler, para. 90.

1581 The Court ruled as follows: 'Attendu qu'avant tout, il faut relever qu'il n'y a pas eu de situation de conflit et, a fortiori, pas de situation de conflit armé, qui soit survenue entre la République démocratique de Somalie et les Nations Unies; Que, comme il a été dit plus haut, les troupes des Nations Unies ne sont pas entrées en jeu dans le cadre des articles 43 et suivants de la Charte, mais bien comme une force de paix, dotée de compétences coercitives pour l'exécution de missions bien définies; Que le fait de confier des compétences contraignantes limitées à cette force de paix ne lui confère pas un autre caractère; Que la cour n'a pas connaissance

Such approaches must be rejected. The threshold is the same for all belligerents. The determination of whether or not an IAC or a NIAC exists and who is a party to it is factual and is based exclusively on an assessment of the facts on the ground and not on the individual views of the parties themselves.[1582] While the UN Security Council has wide powers, including the power to set aside certain norms,[1583] it cannot alter the applicability of IHL.

According to the SCSL, to determine whether IHL applies to a UN peace operation, the totality of circumstances must be observed, including, *inter alia*, the following elements:[1584]

> [T]he relevant [...] [UNSC] resolutions for the operation, the specific operational mandates, the role and practices actually adopted by the peacekeeping mission during the particular conflict, their rules of engagement and operational orders, the nature of the arms and equipment used by the peacekeeping force, the interaction between the peacekeeping force and the parties involved in the conflict, any use of force between the peacekeeping force and the parties in the conflict, the nature and frequency of such force and the conduct of the alleged victim(s) and their fellow personnel.

In the context of UN activities in the DRC, the question has, for example, arisen as to whether involvement in the conflict has triggered the applicability of IHL. Over the years, MONUSCO has been engaged in offensive combat actions against armed groups in 2006 and twice in 2012.[1585] Moreover, from 2013 onwards, MONUSCO has been mandated to conduct targeted offensive operations through the Intervention Brigade to neutralise and disarm the Congolese rebel group. On the basis of this mandate, the Intervention Brigade has carried out several combat operations against the armed groups, often in support of military operations conducted by FARDC.[1586] Therefore, it seems that the UN has not denied that the Intervention Brigade is a party to the conflict in the DRC.[1587]

---

d'autres données, d'où il résulterait que les forces de l'O.N.U. se seraient livrées de facto, sur le territoire de la Somalie – en contravention à leur mission légale – à des opérations de combat (1) permanentes, (2) généralisées et (3) structurées contre une ou plusieurs bandes armées rivales' (*Ministère Public et Centre Pour L'égalité des Chances et la Lutte Contre le Racisme c C et B* (1997) Belgian Military Court, 14(5580) Journal des Tribunaux 286 288–289), as also referred to by Ray Murphy, *UN Peacekeeping in Lebanon, Somalia and Kosovo Operational and Legal Issues in Practice* (Cambridge University Press 2007) 275.

1582 *Prosecutor v. Ljube Boškoski and Johan Tarčulovski, Trial chamber judgment* (n. 1576) para. 174; *Prosecutor v. Fatmir Limaj, Haradin Bala, and Isak Musliu, Trial chamber judgment* (n. 1576) para. 90, as also referred to by Foley, *UN Peacekeeping Operations and the Protection of Civilians: Saving Succeeding Generations* (n. 16) 140. See also Kleffner (n. 1374) para. 19.

1583 As discussed below, see Part III, Sections 2.2.1.3 and 3.3.2.1.

1584 *The Prosecutor v. Issa Hassan Sesay, Morris Kallon and Augustine Gbao, Judgment* (n. 850) para. 234.

1585 Sheeran and Case (n. 495) 8.

1586 Mathias (n. 26) 143.

1587 Sheeran and Case (n. 495) 8.

However, there are now also voices saying that the entire operation (not only the Intervention Brigade but also MONUSCO) had become a party to a NIAC.[1588] During a panel discussion at the annual meeting of ASIL in 2014, Mona Khalil, working for UN OLA at the time, seemed to agree that not only the Intervention Brigade but also MONUSCO as a whole was a party to the conflict in the DRC.[1589] She acknowledged that the question of the applicability of IHL cannot be answered on the basis of a mandate but must be answered with reference to 'the nature, intensity, and duration of actual military actions taken by the UN PKO forces in response to actions taken by other armed actors or in support of government forces in light of the situation in the operating environment.'[1590] However, some UN Security Council Members have, nevertheless, tried to distinguish between the Intervention Brigade and other MONUSCO military units.[1591]

Another threshold theory for the applicability of IHL that has been put forward is that UN (mandated) peace operations may not only become party to an armed conflict when their actions reach the threshold of an IAC or a NIAC but may also become a party to a pre-existing armed conflict, even if the threshold has not been reached. For example, MINUSMA has in the past exchanged intelligence and conducted joint patrols with French troops deployed under a UN Security Council mandate, which raises the question of whether certain forms of support from a UN peace operation to a State's armed forces, such as providing intelligence for use in ongoing military operations, can turn the mission into a party to an armed conflict.[1592] Under the so-called 'support-based approach', first promulgated by Tristan Ferraro (Legal Advisor to the ICRC) and subsequently adopted by the ICRC, multinational forces indeed become a party to a NIAC if they provide military support to one of the parties to a pre-existing NIAC that has a direct impact on the opposing part's ability to carry out military operations.[1593] The support-based approach

1588 See e.g. Geneva Academy Rule of Law (n. 495).

1589 Mona A Khalil, 'Peace Forces at War: Implications Under International Humanitarian Law, Remarks by Mona Khalil', *Proceedings of the American Society of International Law at Its Annual Meeting, 7–12 April 2014, Washington, DC, vol. 108, 152* (Cambridge University Press 2014).

1590 *Ibid.* 153–154.

1591 Mathias (n. 26) 143.

1592 *Ibid.*

1593 Ferraro, 'The Applicability and Application of International Humanitarian Law to Multinational Forces' (n. 676) 583–587; Tristan Ferraro, 'The ICRC's Legal Position on the Notion of Armed Conflict Involving Foreign Intervention and on Determining the IHL Applicable to This Type of Conflict' (2015) 97 International Review of the Red Cross 1227. In 2015, the ICRC adopted the support-based approach and set forth the following conditions that have to be cumulatively met for IHL to apply to multinational forces according to the support-based approach: '(1) there is a pre-existing NIAC taking place on the territory in which multinational forces are called on to intervene; (2) actions related to the conduct of hostilities are undertaken by multinational forces in the context of the pre-existing conflict; (3) the military operations of multinational forces are carried out in support (as described

has received all kinds of criticism[1594] and is definitely not yet settled as a matter of law.[1595]

2.2.1.1. The beginning of IHL application in UN (mandated) peace operations

IHL starts to apply as soon as an armed conflict begins. This is a factual inquiry. Article 6 of Geneva Convention IV, for example, states that it applies 'from the outset of any conflict or occupation.' Article 3 of Additional Protocol I sets forth that the Geneva Conventions I–IV and Additional Protocol I apply 'from the beginning of any situation referred to in Article 1 [of Additional Protocol I].' Thus, as regards IACs, IHL begins to apply to a UN (mandated) peace operation from the time the force becomes a party to an IAC, in accordance with the abovementioned criteria[1596] or in the unlikely event that it starts an occupation.[1597]

As regards NIACs, Common Article 3 of the Geneva Conventions I–IV and Additional Protocol II do not state when IHL starts to apply. In principle, however, as with IACs, IHL begins to apply as soon as the UN (mandated) peace operation becomes a party to a NIAC. In the event a UN (mandated) peace operation becomes entangled in a situation that was not previously a NIAC, IHL will only apply to the situation and the peace operation's involvement in it when

---

above) of a party to the pre-existing conflict; and (4) the action in question is undertaken pursuant to an official decision by the troop-contributing country or the relevant organization to support a party involved in the pre-existing conflict' (ICRC, 'Report on International Humanitarian Law and the Challenges of Contemporary Armed Conflicts, Report for the 32nd International Conference of the Red Cross and Red Crescent, 8–10 December 2015, Geneva' (2015) ICRC Doc. 32IC/15/11 21–23). In 2019, the ICRC set forth that the support-based approach should also be applied in situations in which one armed group supports another armed group (ICRC, 'Report on International Humanitarian Law and the Challenges of Contemporary Armed Conflicts, Recommitting to Protection in Armed Conflicts on the 70th Anniversary of the Geneva Conventions' (2019) ICRC Doc. 4427 75–76).

1594 See Khalil, 'Remarks by Mona Khalil'; N. Verlinden, '"Are We at War"? State Support to Parties in Armed Conflict: Consequences under Jus in Bello, Jus Ad Bellum and Neutrality Law' (Dphil thesis, KU Leuven 2019) 137–72; M. Zwanenburg, 'Remarks by Marten Zwanenburg' (2014) 108 *Proceedings of the ASIL Annual Meeting* 151–52; M. Zwanenburg, 'Double Trouble: The 'Cumulative Approach' and the 'Support-Based Approach' in the Relationship Between Non-State Armed Groups' in T. D. Gill, R. Geiß, H. Krieger, C. Paulussen (eds.), Yearbook of International Humanitarian Law, (The Hague: T.M.C. Asser Press, 2019), 43–61; R. van Steenberghe and P. Lesaffre, 'The ICRC's 'support-based approach': A Suitable but Incomplete Theory. In: Question of International Law' (2019) Zoom-in 59 *Question of International Law* 5–23; T. D. Gill, 'Some thoughts on the ICRC Support Based Approach' Zoom-in 59 *Question of International Law* 45–53.

1595 See e.g. van Steenberghe and Lesaffre (n. 1594); Gill, 'Some Thoughts on the ICRC Support Based Approach' (n. 1594) (short commentary written in response to the article by van Steenberghe and Lesaffre).

1596 See Part III, Section 2.2.1.

1597 For further literature, see e.g. Tristan Ferraro, 'Determining the Beginning and End of an Occupation under International Humanitarian Law' (2012) 94 International Review of the Red Cross 133.

the criteria of intensity, prolonged hostilities, and organisation are met.[1598] If a UN (mandated) peace operation becomes entangled in a situation that already constitutes a NIAC, it depends on the doctrine one adheres to when the UN (mandated) peace operation is considered a party to that NIAC. If the 'support-based theory' is followed, then the UN (mandated) peace operation becomes a party to the NIAC, and, therefore, IHL applies to the peace operation's involvement therein as soon as the UN (mandated) peace operation contributes to the collective conduct of hostilities in such a way as to have a direct impact on the opposing party's ability to conduct military operations.[1599]

2.2.1.2. The end of IHL application in UN (mandated) peace operations

IHL, in principle, ceases to apply to UN (mandated) peace operations when they cease to be a party to an armed conflict.[1600] The termination of an IAC or a NIAC is equally a factual inquiry.

As regards IACs, this implies that hostilities between States must have ceased. Pursuant to Article 6 of the Geneva Convention IV, this Convention ceases to apply 'on the general close of military operations' or, in case of occupation, 'one year after the general close of military operation,' except for certain rules which apply for the duration of the occupation and 'to the extent that [an Occupying Power] exercises the functions of government in such territory.' Moreover, protected persons whose release, repatriation, or resettlement takes place after these dates continue to enjoy the protection provided in the Geneva Convention IV. Article 3 of Additional Protocol I sets forth that the application of the Geneva Conventions I–IV and the Protocol ceases 'in the territory of Parties to the conflict, on the general close of military operations' yet, in the case of occupied territories, 'on the termination of the occupation.' However, in either circumstance, 'those persons whose final release, repatriation or re-establishment takes place thereafter' continue to enjoy the protection provided under Additional Protocol I.

In its 1958 ICRC Commentary on Geneva Convention IV, Pictet explained that in the opinion of the Rapporteur of Committee III, 'the general close of military operations was "when the last shot has been fired".'[1601] However, he went on to explain that a number of other factors must be taken into account.[1602]

1598 See Part III, Section 2.2.1. See also Gill and others (n. 26) 102.

1599 *Ibid.* 103.

1600 Or in the words of Milanović, 'unless there is a good reason of text, principle or policy that warrants an exception, the application of IHL will cease once the conditions that triggered its application in the first place no longer exist' (Marko Milanović, 'End of IHL Application', *Proceedings of the 13th Bruges Colloquium on Scope of Application of International Humanitarian Law, 18–19 October 2012, Bruges, vol. 43, 83* (2013) 86–87).

1601 Pictet (n. 84) 62.

1602 *Ibid.*

When the conflict is between two States, according to Pictet, the date of the end of hostilities is relatively easy to determine: it will depend on either an armistice, a capitulation, or simply on *debellatio* (with which he means 'the end of an armed conflict which results in the occupation of the whole of the enemy's territory and the cessation of all hostilities, without a legal instrument of any kind').[1603] On the other hand, if one or both sides have several States, the issue is more difficult to settle.[1604] Pictet argues that it must be agreed that, in most cases, the general cessation of military operations will mean the definitive end to all fighting between all concerned.[1605]

In the case of *Prosecutor v. Tadić*, the ICTY set forth that IHL continues to apply until there is 'a general conclusion of peace.'[1606] In the case of *Prosecutor v. Ante Gotovina*, it added, however, that once IHL is applicable, 'one should not lightly conclude that its applicability ceases.'[1607] Otherwise, there is the risk that parties to an armed conflict will find themselves 'in a revolving door between applicability and non-applicability,' giving rise to legal uncertainty and confusion.[1608] Therefore, the ICTY examined whether the IAC in question had at any time found 'a sufficiently general, definitive and effective termination' to end the applicability of IHL.[1609] To that end, it examined in particular whether there had been 'a general close of military operations and a general conclusion of peace.'[1610] Thus, the hostilities must have ended 'with a degree of stability and permanence' to determine the termination of an IAC.[1611]

Taking into account the customary nature of these rules, when a UN (mandated) peace operation has been involved in an IAC, the conflict would be considered terminated when the armed confrontation between the forces and the State(s) fighting them has ended to such an extent that the situation can reasonably be construed as a general cessation of military operations.[1612] While only the facts matter to determine whether there is such a general and definitive

1603 *Ibid.*

1604 *Ibid.*

1605 *Ibid.*

1606 *Prosecutor v. Tadić, Decision on the defense motion for interlocutory appeal on jurisdiction* (n. 1567) para. 70.

1607 *Prosecutor v. Ante Gotovina, Ivan Čermak, and Mladen Markač, Trial chamber judgment* (2011) ICTY IT-06-90-T para. 1694.

1608 *Ibid.*

1609 *Ibid.*

1610 *Ibid.*

1611 ICRC, 'Report on International Humanitarian Law and the Challenges of Contemporary Armed Conflicts, Report for the 32nd International Conference of the Red Cross and Red Crescent, 8–10 December 2015, Geneva' (n. 1593) 9. See also Milanović, 'End of IHL Application' (n. 1600) 88.

1612 Ferraro, 'The Applicability and Application of International Humanitarian Law to Multinational Forces' (n. 676) 601. For further literature on determining the end of an occupation under IHL, see Ferraro, 'Determining the Beginning and End of an Occupation under International Humanitarian Law' (n. 1597).

end to all fighting between all concerned, UNSC resolutions or unilateral statements by the UN may, for example, serve as evidence.[1613]

With regard to the question of when IHL ceases to apply to NIACs, the relevant treaties give little guidance. Article 2(2) of Additional Protocol II only provides that the Protocol ceases to apply '[a]t the end of the armed conflict,' with a similar exception as in Additional Protocol I for persons deprived of their liberty or whose liberty is restricted for reasons connected with that conflict, as well as for persons deprived of their liberty or whose liberty is restricted after the conflict for the same reasons. They continue to benefit from a limited number of protection measures until the end of this deprivation or restriction of liberty.

According to the ICTY, IHL continues to apply in case of a NIAC until a peaceful settlement is achieved.[1614] However, as the Leuven Manual points out, this criterion offers little guidance in practice.[1615] A 'peaceful settlement' should be understood as a situation in which actual and lasting peace has been attained.[1616] For example, a NIAC would cease when at least one of the parties to the conflict has disappeared or no longer conforms to the level of organisation required by IHL.[1617] A NIAC would also end when hostilities have ceased completely, and there is no real risk of their resumption, resulting in a general cessation of military operations by UN (mandated) peace forces against a given adversary, even if the parties' level of organisation is still met.[1618]

Where, under the 'support-based theory', IHL applies to UN (mandated) peace forces engaged in a pre-existing NIAC, IHL ceases to apply when the forces in question have permanently withdrawn from the collective conduct of hostilities. For example, according to Ferraro, a sustained cessation of support previously provided to one of the belligerents involved in the pre-existing conflict would be sufficient to establish that the UN (mandated) peace forces are no longer a party to that conflict.[1619]

As also mentioned above, the end of an armed conflict does not mean that IHL ceases to apply completely. A number of specific provisions continue to apply after the armed conflict has ended, including those relating to protected

---

1613 See also Milanović, 'End of IHL Application' (n. 1600) 88.

1614 *Prosecutor v. Tadić, Decision on the defense motion for interlocutory appeal on jurisdiction* (n. 1567) 70; *Prosecutor v. Kunarac, Kovac, and Vokovic, Appeals chamber judgment* (n. 1576) para. 57; *Prosecutor v. Jean-Paul Akayesu, Judgment* (n. 1576) para. 57; *The Prosecutor v. Alex Tamba Brima, Brima Bazzy Kamara and Santigie Borbor Kanu (the AFRC Accused), Judgment* (2007) SCSL Case No.SCSL-04-16-T para. 245; *The Prosecutor v. Thomas Lubanga Dyilo, Judgment* (2012) ICC ICC-01/04-01/06 para. 533.

1615 Gill and others (n. 26) 103.

1616 *Ibid.*

1617 *Ibid.* 103–104.

1618 Ferraro, 'The Applicability and Application of International Humanitarian Law to Multinational Forces' (n. 676) 607; Gill and others (n. 26) 103–104.

1619 Ferraro, 'The Applicability and Application of International Humanitarian Law to Multinational Forces' (n. 676) 607.

persons who are only released, repatriated, or resettled after the end of the conflict.

2.2.1.3. Derogation under Chapter VII and Article 103 of the UN Charter

As mentioned earlier, when discussing the applicability of HRL, the UN Security Council has the discretion to derogate from the law (including IHL) when taking enforcement action under Chapter VII of the UN Charter.[1620] Furthermore, under Article 103 of the UN Charter, the UN Security Council may authorise conduct inconsistent with States' obligations under IHL, provided that the norms in question are not peremptory.[1621] IHL principles that are relevant to the use of force in the context of UN (mandated) peace operations and that have conceivably achieved *jus cogens* status are discussed in Part III, Section 2.2.3.2.

While derogation from the law based on Chapter VII powers and under Article 103 of the UN Charter is addressed in more detail below,[1622] it should be recalled that while the UN Security Council has broad powers, which may include the power to set aside certain norms, it can never alter the applicability of IHL.[1623]

2.2.2. Applicability ratione personae

As soon as the threshold for an 'armed conflict' is reached, IHL applies equally to *all* belligerents, without distinction, irrespective of the cause or the justness of the war.[1624] This follows from the distinction between the international

1620 De Wet (n. 892) 184.

1621 For sources substantiating this position, see Part II, Section 3.3.1.1, fn. 1220.

1622 See Part III, Section 3.3.2.1.

1623 As already mentioned earlier, see Part III, Section 2.2.1.

1624 Keiichiro Okimoto, 'The Relationship Between Jus Ad Bellum and Jus in Bello' in Marc Weller, Alexia Solomou and Jake William Rylatt (eds), *The Oxford Handbook of the Use of Force in International Law* (1st edn., Oxford University Press 2015) 1214. See also Meyrowitz who has devoted an entire book on the principle of equal application of *ius in bello* to all parties to the conflict ('L'égalité des belligérants devant le *jus in bello* est un principe qui sous-tend le droit moderne de la guerre, principe qui allait tellement de soi qu'il n'avait pas besoin d'être formulé. Il est certain que ce principe est toujours solidement établi en droit positif') (Henri Meyrowitz, *Le Principe de l'égalité Des Belligérants Devant Le Droit de La Guerre* (Pedone 1970) 400). See also Ian Brownlie, *International Law and the Use of Force by States* (Oxford University Press 1963) 406–407; François Bugnion, 'Guerre Juste, Guerre d'agression et Droit International Humanitaire' (2002) 84 Revue internationale de la Croix-Rouge 523, 544–545; or Hans Kelsen, *Principles of International Law* (2nd edn., Holt, Rinehart and Winston 1966) 89. Only certain experts still argue that IHL does not apply equally to all parties to the conflict, see e.g. Quincy Wright, 'The Outlawry of War and the Law of War' (1953) 47 The American Journal of International Law 365, 374 (Wright argued that 'some of the law of war is applicable to all states engaged in hostilities, whether their action has a legal character of defence, enforcement, or aggression, but that some of the advantages of this law are denied to aggressors'); Georg Schwarzenberger, *International Law as Applied by International Courts and Tribunals*, vol. 2 (Stevens 1968) 105.

law on the use of force and IHL. Accordingly, IHL rules and principles apply to all armed forces carrying out a UN (mandated) peace operation with a PoC mandate as a matter of treaty or customary law when the requisite conditions for the application of this body of law are met, regardless of whether the operation was established or authorised by the UN Security Council.

UN (mandated) peace forces are bound by IHL obligations primarily arising from: (i) customary IHL to which the international or regional organisation conducting the operation is bound; and (ii) IHL treaties to which the State undertaking or taking part in an operation are a party and/or customary IHL by which that State is bound.[1625] To determine which set(s) of IHL obligations appl(ies)(y), one must determine who is a party to the armed conflict, i.e. the international or regional organisation conducting the operation, the State undertaking or taking part in the operation, or both. After all, UN (mandated) peace operations do not have international legal personality of their own and hence cannot be a party to an armed conflict in the juridical sense.[1626] The question of who is to be considered a party to the armed conflict has so far remained unresolved in legal doctrine. As with HRL, it is about 'linking the conduct of physical persons to a holder of international obligations.'[1627]

While there is disagreement as to how this linkage should be made, many again invoke the agency paradigm of attribution (as also discussed above when analysing the applicability *ratione personae* of HRL, see Part III, Section 2.1.1).[1628] A thorough study of who should exercise what control for their IHL obligations to apply is beyond the scope of the present study. However, from a practical point of view, the following can be said briefly: in the case of peace operations under UN command and control or under AU command and control, the TCCs have usually transferred a substantial part of their authority to the UN or the AU, respectively, so that there is a (rebuttable) presumption that the organisation exercises sufficient control over the troops for it to be argued that only the UN or AU mission, and not the TCCs themselves, are parties to the armed conflict.[1629] However, in the case of NATO operations, the TCCs

1625 Gill, 'Characterization and Legal Basis for Peace Operations' (n. 589) 160.

1626 Eric David and Ola Engdahl, 'Debate: How Does the Involvement of a Multinational Peacekeeping Force Affect the Classification of a Situation?' (2013) 95 International Review of the Red Cross 659, 671.

1627 Zwanenburg, 'International Organisations vs. Troop Contributing Countries: Which Should Be Considered as the Party to an Armed Conflict during Peace Operations?' (n. 1349) 26.

1628 Ferraro, 'The Applicability and Application of International Humanitarian Law to Multinational Forces' (n. 676) 588–595; Gill and others (n. 26) 100; Milanović and Hadzi-Vidanovic (n. 1564) 276–279; Zwanenburg, 'International Organisations vs. Troop Contributing Countries: Which Should Be Considered as the Party to an Armed Conflict during Peace Operations?' (n. 1349) 26.

1629 Ferraro, 'The Applicability and Application of International Humanitarian Law to Multinational Forces' (n. 676) 593; Gill and others (n. 26) 100; Richard D Glick, 'Lip Service to the Laws of War: Humanitarian Law and United Nations Armed Forces' (1995) 17 Michigan Journal of International Law 53, 98.

usually continue to exercise substantial day-to-day control over the troops so that not only NATO but also the TCCs, can be considered a party to the armed conflict.[1630]

That said, both States and international and regional organisations are under the obligation to respect and to ensure respect for IHL (assumingly even if they are not a party to an ongoing armed conflict themselves).[1631] The IHL obligations by which individual States and international and regional organisations are bound may vary significantly. In practice, this is usually solved by planning and conducting the operations in question in a manner consistent with the legal rules that all partners in the operation in question consider applicable within their legal framework.[1632]

2.2.2.1. Peace forces as members of UN (mandated) peace operations

The first source of IHL obligations may apply to peace forces as members of a UN (mandated) peace operation carried out by, for example, the UN, the AU, NATO, or the EU.

UN – In line with what was said above, the UN is not a party to any IHL treaty, but it is nevertheless accepted that it is bound by customary IHL by virtue of its international legal personality if it is a party to an armed conflict.[1633] As UN peace operations are considered subsidiary organs of the UN, UN peace forces must comply with those IHL obligations that bind the UN, as well as the IHL obligations imposed by the UN Security Council, including through the mandate. As members of an organised armed force, members of UN peace forces can be targeted by virtue of their membership once the operation in question has become a party to an armed conflict.

This position does not always find resonance in the UN community. Even more so, by taking this position, this study goes against the UN's approach set out in the 1999 UN Secretary-General's Bulletin on IHL. The Bulletin stipulates that the fundamental principles and rules of IHL apply to UN forces when 'in situations of armed conflict *they are actively engaged therein as combatants, to the extent and for the duration of their engagement*.'[1634] Daphna Shraga, a former senior legal advisor at UN OLA who was involved in drafting the Bulletin, has

---

1630 Peter M Olson, 'A NATO Perspective on Applicability and Application of IHL to Multinational Forces' (2013) 95 International Review of the Red Cross 653, 656; Ferraro, 'The Applicability and Application of International Humanitarian Law to Multinational Forces' (n. 676) 593–594.

1631 See also further below, Part III, Sections 2.2.3.1 and 4.2.

1632 For further literature on legal interoperability, see a list of sources in Part III, Section 2.1.1, fn. 1346.

1633 See also Part III, Section 2.1.1.1 (on the applicability of HRL to UN peace operations). See also Sheeran, 'A Constitutional Moment' (n. 1354) 112–119; Verdirame (n. 95) 75, 85–86.

1634 Emphasis added. UNSG, '1999 UN Secretary-General's Bulletin on IHL' (n. 25) para. 1.1.

interpreted this rule on the applicability of IHL to UN forces as introducing what she has called a 'double-key' test.[1635] She stipulated that '[t]wo cumulative conditions [...] must, therefore be met for [IHL] [...] to apply to UN forces in the theatre of war: (i) the existence of an armed conflict in the area and time of their deployment, and (ii) the engagement of members of the Force in the conflict as combatants – whether in a Chapter-VII enforcement action or in Chapter-VI operation in self-defence.'[1636]

The approach taken in the 1999 UN Secretary-General's Bulletin on IHL finds resonance in the jurisprudence of the SCSL and, to some extent, the ICTY. For example, in the case of *Prosecutor v. Hassan Sesay*, the SCSL ruled as follows on attacks against UNAMSIL peacekeepers:[1637]

> In the Chamber's view, common sense dictates that peacekeepers *are considered to be civilians* only insofar as they fall within the definition of civilians laid down for non-combatants in customary international law and under Additional Protocol II as discussed above – namely, *that they do not take a direct part in hostilities*. It is also the Chamber's view that by force of logic, *personnel of peacekeeping missions are entitled to protection as long as they are not taking a direct part in the hostilities – and thus have become combatants* – at the time of the alleged offence. Where peacekeepers become combatants, they can be legitimate targets for the extent of their participation in accordance with international humanitarian law. As with all civilians, their protection would not cease if the personnel use armed force only in exercising their right to individual self-defence. Likewise, *the Chambers opines that the use of force by peacekeepers in self-defence in the discharge of their mandate, provided that it is limited to such use, would not alter or diminish the protection afforded to peacekeepers.*

To substantiate its approach, the SCSL explicitly referred to the 1999 UN Secretary-General's Bulletin on IHL.[1638] The ICTY seems to follow a similar line of reasoning in the case of *Prosecutor v. Radovan Karadžić*, although it is not equally clear or explicit.[1639] The ICTY first argued that the UN and its associated peacekeeping forces were not a party to the conflict. It then added that 'at the time the UN personnel were detained on 25 and 26 May 1995, they were persons taking *no active part in the hostilities and, as such, were afforded the protection of Common Article 3*.'[1640] As such, the ICTY seems to have equated UNPROFOR

1635 Daphna Shraga, 'The Secretary-General's Bulletin on the Observance by United Nations Forces of International Humanitarian Law: A Decade Later' (2009) 39 Israel Yearbook on Human Rights 357, 359.

1636 *Ibid.*

1637 Emphasis added. *The Prosecutor v. Issa Hassan Sesay, Morris Kallon and Augustine Gbao, Judgment* (n. 850) para. 233.

1638 *Ibid.* para. 234, fn. 419.

1639 *Prosecutor v. Radovan Karadžić, Trial chamber judgment* (2016) ICTY IT-95–5/18-T.

1640 Emphasis added. *Ibid.* para. 5943.

becoming a party to the conflict with UN peace forces taking an active part in hostilities.[1641]

These approaches are problematic for several reasons, the most important being that it seems to conflate the notions of civilians directly participating in hostilities and combatants. It is true that as long as a UN peace operation is *not* a party to an armed conflict, the members of the military component enjoy the protection afforded to civilians unless and for the time they take a direct part in hostilities. But, if a UN peace operation has become a party to the conflict, all members of the military component lose the protection afforded to civilians. They can now be targeted by virtue of their membership of an organised armed force, not because they have become civilians directly participating in hostilities. Put differently, the military personnel's loss of protection against direct attack should not be modelled on that applicable to civilians.[1642] Whereas the former is continuous and status-based, the latter is conduct-based.[1643] Only when a UN peace operation of which they are part is no longer considered a party to an armed conflict will the armed forces again enjoy the protection afforded to civilians.

AU, NATO, and EU – The AU, NATO, and the EU are not a party to any IHL treaty, but it is nevertheless accepted that these organisations are bound by customary IHL by virtue of their international legal personality if they are a party to an armed conflict.[1644] And while UN-mandated peace operations conducted by the AU, NATO, and the EU are not considered subsidiary organs of the organisations concerned, they are nevertheless typically considered part of the organisation in question and share in the legal personality.[1645]

Peter Olson, former Legal Adviser and Director of Legal Affairs at NATO Headquarters, wrote the following in a contribution on NATO's perspective on the applicability and application of IHL to multinational forces:[1646]

> The Allies accept as a given that the Alliance must comply with IHL obligations in conducting its operations, and expect the Alliance to set the standard for the lawful conduct of military operations. Faithful compliance with IHL obligations is thus at the core of the conception, planning and conduct of Alliance military operations, and non-NATO troop-contributing states are expected to share that perspective.

[1641] Zwanenburg, 'UN Peace Operations, International Humanitarian Law and International Human Rights Law' (n. 37) 101. For literature discussing the relevant case law, see e.g. Pacholska (n. 26).

[1642] Ferraro, 'The Applicability and Application of International Humanitarian Law to Multinational Forces' (n. 676) 606.

[1643] *Ibid.* 605.

[1644] See also Part III, Section 2.1.1.1 (on the applicability of HRL to UN-mandated peace operations).

[1645] *Ibid.*

[1646] Olson (n. 1630) 654.

Hence, NATO forces must comply with IHL if they take part in hostilities where the threshold for an armed conflict is reached and, as long as an operation takes part in the armed conflict, the members of NATO forces participating in the operation can be identified as combatants and thus targeted on the basis of their membership of an organised armed force. If NATO is considered a party to the armed conflict, the armed forces must comply with the IHL obligations that bind NATO. For example, as regards the 2011 NATO intervention in Libya, the International Commission of Inquiry on Libya recognised that customary IHL applied to NATO's actions.[1647]

As regards the EU, in line with the requirement for the EU to respect international law in its external relations pursuant to Articles 3(5), 21(1), and 2(b)–(c) of the TEU, the EU and its Member States accept that, should EU-led forces become involved in an armed conflict, IHL will be fully applicable to them.[1648] This being said, the EU-led forces have so far not been involved in any hostilities where the threshold for an armed conflict has been reached and the EU and/or the TCCs consequently has become a party to the armed conflict.[1649]

The AU and AU-led forces are also required to comply with IHL.[1650] However, in the case of *The Prosecutor v. Bahar Idriss Abu Garda*, the ICC did conclude that, under the 1998 Rome Statute, personnel involved in an AU-led peace operation enjoy protection from attacks in the context of a NIAC 'unless and for such time as they take a direct part in hostilities or in combat-related activities.'[1651] The ICC confirmed this approach in the case of *The Prosecutor v. Abdallah Banda Abakaer Nourain and Saleh Mohammed Jerbo Jamus.*[1652] As explained above, this approach is problematic for a number of reasons, the most important of which is that it seems to confuse the notions of civilians directly participating in hostilities and combatants. If the AU has become a party to the conflict, all military personnel conducting the operation lose the protection afforded to civilians and can thus be targeted by virtue of their membership of an organised armed group. In their conduct, the armed forces must also abide by the IHL obligations that bind the AU.

1647 UNHRC (n. 1572) para. 613.

1648 Naert, 'European Union Common Security and Defence Policy Operations' (n. 1353) 682. See also the Salamanca Declaration to which the author refers (Frederik Naert, 'Observance of International Humanitarian Law by Forces under the Command of the European Union' (2013) 95 ICRC 637, 639).

1649 Naert, 'European Union Common Security and Defence Policy Operations' (n. 1353) 683; Naert, 'Observance of International Humanitarian Law by Forces under the Command of the European Union' (n. 1648).

1650 For arguments why customary international law governing IHL applies to the AU's peace and security operations, see Abass (n. 1353) 626–629.

1651 *The Prosecutor v. Bahar Idriss Abu Garda, Decision on the confirmation of charges* (2010) ICC ICC-02/05-02/09 paras 77–84 and 128.

1652 *The Prosecutor v. Abdallah Banda Abakaer Nourain and Saleh Mohammed Jerbo Jamus, Corrigendum of the 'decision on the confirmation of charges', Public redacted version* (2011) ICC ICC-02/05-03/09 paras 102–103.

2.2.2.2. Peace forces as State agents of the States undertaking or taking part in an operation

The second source for peace forces may derive from the status of State agents of the States undertaking or taking part in an operation. States are the primary and original subjects of IHL. UN (mandated) peace forces may be bound by IHL obligations arising from IHL treaties to which the State undertaking or taking part in an operation are a party and/or customary IHL by which those States are bound (and which they have not persistently opposed).[1653] Furthermore, States are bound by those principles of IHL that amount to general principles of law within Article 38(1)(c) of the ICJ Statute, as well as by IHL obligations contained in applicable binding resolutions of intergovernmental organisations.[1654] When a State becomes a party to an armed conflict, the members of the armed forces (with the exception of medical and religious personnel) become legitimate targets under IHL for the duration of the conflict.[1655]

As with HRL obligations, the sending States may have different IHL obligations because they are not all parties to the same conventions and/or because certain obligations, even if they have acquired customary law status, are interpreted or applied differently. In practice, an attempt is usually made to adopt a common framework within which the operation can operate to solve such legal interoperability challenges.[1656]

2.2.3. *Applicability ratione materiae*

Once the threshold has been reached, *all* relevant IHL rules and principles apply equally to all parties to the conflict *unless* a rule cannot be applied because of certain intrinsic characteristics.[1657] For example, international organisations do not always have the same juridical, administrative, or operational capacity as States.[1658] Hence, some IHL rules, such as the obligation under the Mines Protocol to the Conventional Weapons Convention to impose penal sanctions against those persons killing or injuring civilians in violation of the Protocol, can only be enforced by States.[1659] Yet, apart from those exceptions, all IHL rules and principles apply equally to all parties to the conflict.

1653 See also Gill, 'Characterization and Legal Basis for Peace Operations' (n. 589) 160.
1654 Kleffner (n. 1374) para. 22.
1655 Zwanenburg, 'UN Peace Operations, International Humanitarian Law and International Human Rights Law' (n. 37) 99.
1656 For further literature on legal interoperability, see a list of sources in Part III, Section 2.1.1, fn. 1346.
1657 Ferraro, 'The Applicability and Application of International Humanitarian Law to Multinational Forces' (n. 676) 582.
1658 *Ibid.*
1659 See Art. 14 of the Protocol on Prohibitions or Restrictions on the Use of Mines, Booby-Traps and Other Devices as amended on 3 May 1996 annexed to the Convention on Prohibitions

2.2.3.1. Obligation 'to respect and to ensure respect' for IHL

Pursuant to Common Article 1 of the Geneva Conventions I–IV, the contracting States have an obligation to respect the Conventions, as well as an obligation to ensure respect for the Conventions. The Article reads as follows: 'The High Contracting Parties undertake to respect and to ensure respect for the present Convention in all circumstances.' Article 1(1) of Additional Protocol I also included the same provision.

In the *Nicaragua* case, the ICJ held that there is an obligation, in terms of Common Article 1 of the Geneva Conventions I–IV, 'to respect' and even 'to ensure respect' for the Conventions in all circumstances, which 'does not derive only from the Conventions themselves but also from the general principles of humanitarian law to which the Conventions merely give specific expression.'[1660] In the case of *Prosecutor v. Tadić*, the ICTY added that '[t]his general principle lays down an obligation that is incumbent, not only on States, but also on other international entities including the United Nations.'[1661] Moreover, Boisson de Chazournes and Condorelli contend that the obligation reflected in Common Article 1 is a foundational principle that has acquired a special status in the international legal order:[1662]

> This provision [...] belongs to a select group of norms and principles held by the international community to be of cardinal importance for the promotion of 'elementary considerations of humanity' [...]. Such norms play what may be termed a 'constitutional role' in a system of collective security where humanitarian values have become a reason for the adoption of a large number of measures.

The obligation to respect and to ensure respect goes beyond the Geneva Conventions I–IV and Additional Protocol I but covers customary IHL more in general.[1663] Hence, while initially, Common Article 1 applied only to IACs

---

or Restrictions on the Use of Certain Conventional Weapons which may be deemed to be Excessively Injurious or to have Indiscriminate Effects (adopted 3 May 1996, entered into force 3 December 1998) 2048 UNTS 93 (Mines Protocol to the Conventional Weapons Convention), as referred to by *ibid.* 583.

1660 *Case Concerning Military and Paramilitary Activities in and against Nicaragua (Nicaragua v. United States of America), Judgment (Merits)* (n. 615) para. 220.

1661 *Prosecutor v. Tadić, Decision on the defense motion for interlocutory appeal on jurisdiction* (n. 1567) para. 93.

1662 Laurence Boisson de Chazournes and Luigi Condorellui, 'Common Article 1 of the Geneva Conventions Revisited: Protecting Collective Interests' (2000) 82 International Review of the Red Cross 67, 85.

1663 For an analysis of the customary nature of this rule, see Henckaerts and Doswald-Beck (n. 91) Rule 139, pp. 495–498 ('Each party to the conflict must respect and ensure respect for international humanitarian law by its armed forces and other persons or groups acting in fact on its instructions, or under its direction or control'); Rule 144, pp. 509–513 ('States may not encourage violations of international humanitarian law by parties to an armed conflict.

and situations of occupation, it is now considered to apply also to NIACs.[1664] Furthermore, the 2016, 2017, and 2021 ICRC Commentaries to the Geneva Conventions I, II, and III, and, in particular, Common Article 1, sets forth that not only the TCCs but also the international or regional organisations that carry out the operations (and thus exercise operational command and/or operational control) are obliged to respect and to ensure respect for the Geneva Conventions I–IV. While those organisations are not parties to the Conventions, they are considered subjects of international law bound by customary IHL. On that basis, they are equally under the obligation to respect and to ensure respect.[1665] Yet, even when such organisations do not exercise operational command and/or operational control, and even when they are not a party to the armed conflict themselves, they remain obligated to ensure respect for IHL by others.[1666] As such, the obligation also continues to apply during peacetime.[1667] Along the same lines, according to the 2016, 2017, and 2021 ICRC Commentaries to the Geneva Conventions I, II, and III, the obligation to respect and to ensure respect continues to apply when States engage in multinational operations conducted by forces of two or more States under the auspices of an international or regional organisation, a permanent alliance, or an *ad hoc* coalition, even if they are not a party to the armed conflict that takes place in the area where they are deployed.[1668] Accordingly, each and every soldier is bound by the obligation to respect and to ensure respect for IHL.

The next question that arises is whether UN (mandated) peace operations must protect civilian lives by virtue of their obligation to ensure respect for IHL. Part III, Section 4.2, discusses this matter.

They must exert their influence, to the degree possible, to stop violations of international humanitarian law').

1664 See ICRC, *2016 ICRC Commentary on Geneva Convention I* (n. 86) paras 125–126; ICRC, *2017 ICRC Commentary on Geneva Convention II* (n. 86) paras 147–148; ICRC, *2021 ICRC Commentary on Geneva Convention III* (n. 86) paras 158–159.

1665 ICRC, *2016 ICRC Commentary on Geneva Convention I* (n. 86) paras 138–139; ICRC, *2017 ICRC Commentary on Geneva Convention II* (n. 86) paras 160–161; ICRC, *2021 ICRC Commentary on Geneva Convention III* (n. 86) paras 171–172.

1666 ICRC, *2016 ICRC Commentary on Geneva Convention I* (n. 86) para. 142; ICRC, *2017 ICRC Commentary on Geneva Convention II* (n. 86) para. 164; ICRC, *2021 ICRC Commentary on Geneva Convention III* (n. 86) para. 175.

1667 ICRC, *2016 ICRC Commentary on Geneva Convention I* (n. 86) paras 127–129, 185; ICRC, *2017 ICRC Commentary on Geneva Convention II* (n. 86) paras 149–151, 207; ICRC, *2021 ICRC Commentary on Geneva Convention III* (n. 86) paras 160–162, 218. See also Siobhán Wills, *Protecting Civilians: The Obligations of Peacekeepers* (Oxford University Press 2009) 102.

1668 ICRC, *2016 ICRC Commentary on Geneva Convention I* (n. 86) para. 133; ICRC, *2017 ICRC Commentary on Geneva Convention II* (n. 86) para. 155; ICRC, *2021 ICRC Commentary on Geneva Convention III* (n. 86) para. 166.

2.2.3.2. Specific IHL obligations in the context of the use of force

When using lethal force to protect civilians, this must be in accordance with, among others, the IHL principles of distinction, proportionality, precautions in attack, and the prohibition to inflict superfluous injury or unnecessary suffering.[1669]

These fundamental principles have not only been recognised as rules of customary IHL, but national and international jurisprudence has also pointed out that certain fundamental principles have achieved *jus cogens* status. For example, in the advisory opinion on the *Legality of the Threat or Use of Nuclear Weapons*, the ICJ held that a number of 'cardinal' principles of IHL, including the principle of distinction between combatants and non-combatants, the prohibition to cause unnecessary suffering to combatants, and the Martens Clause,[1670] are 'intransgressible principles of international customary law,' and are 'so fundamental to the respect of the human person' that they can be derived directly from a general principle of law, namely 'elementary considerations of humanity.'[1671] The *erga omnes* nature of some IHL rules was later promulgated by the ICJ in its advisory opinion in the *Wall* case.[1672]

In the case of *Prosecutor v. Kupreškić et al.*, the ICTY explicitly held that 'most norms of international humanitarian law, in particular those prohibiting war crimes, crimes against humanity and genocide, are [...] peremptory norms of international law or *jus cogens*, i.e. of a non-derogable and overriding character.'[1673] Similarly, in the case of *Prosecutor v. Tadić*, the ICTY held that it is authorised to apply, 'in addition to customary international law, any treaty which: (i) was unquestionably binding on the parties at the time of the alleged offence; and (ii) was not in conflict with or derogating from *peremptory norms of international law, as are most customary rules of international humanitarian law*.'[1674] In different pronouncements, the ICTY has subsequently confirmed the imperative or peremptory nature of certain specific norms of IHL, including the three principles of distinction, precautions, and human treatment, as well as several specific rules that develop them. For example, in the case of *Prosecutor v.*

1669 As discussed in more detail below, see Part III, Section 3.2.

1670 As discussed below, see Part III, Section 3.2.1.

1671 *Legality of the Threat or Use of Nuclear Weapons, Advisory opinion* (n. 1231) paras 78–79. The ICJ referred to the *Corfu Channel* case in this regard. In that case, the ICJ held that Albania violated certain obligations based on 'certain general and well recognized principles, namely: elementary considerations of humanity, even more exacting in peace than in war' (*Corfu Channel (United Kingdom of Great Britain and Northern Ireland v. Albania), Judgment (Merits)* (1949) 1949 ICJ Rep 4).

1672 *Legal Consequences of the Construction of a Wall in the Occupied Palestinian Territory, Advisory opinion* (n. 1410) ('The obligations *erga omnes* violated by Israel are the obligation to respect the right of the Palestinian people to self-determination, and certain of its obligations under international humanitarian law').

1673 *Prosecutor v. Kupreškić et al., Trial chamber judgment* 5 ICTY IT-95-16-T para. 520.

1674 *Prosecutor v. Tadić, Decision on the defense motion for interlocutory appeal on jurisdiction* (n. 1567) para. 143.

Furundìja, the ICTY stated that the prohibition against torture in both HRL and IHL is a peremptory norm and an obligation *erga omnes*.[1675]

Also, in national case law, the peremptory character of certain IHL principles has been confirmed. For example, in 2007, in the Constitutional Case No. C-291/07, the Plenary Chamber of Colombia's Constitutional Court stated:[1676]

> [E]ssential principles of International Humanitarian Law have acquired *jus cogens* status, because a notorious process of double recognition has taken place with respect to them, specifically in relation to the principles of distinction, precautions and humanitarian treatment, and respect for the fundamental guarantees of the individual.

In *Agent Orange Product Liability Litigation*, the US District Court ruled that '[r]ules against torture, war crimes and genocide are, apart from treaties and statutes, arguably *jus cogens*.'[1677] The Supreme Court of Argentina has similarly held that the prohibition of war crimes is a peremptory norm.[1678]

In light of the ICJ's description of the basic rules of IHL applicable in armed conflict as 'intransgressible,' the ILC also deemed it justified to consider these basic rules as part of *jus cogens*, together with the prohibition of aggression, slavery and slave trade, genocide, racial discrimination and apartheid, torture, and the right to self-determination.[1679] What is referred to here as 'basic rules of international humanitarian law' is referred to elsewhere as 'principles of humanitarian law,' 'principles of international humanitarian law,' 'grave breaches,' and the 'prohibition of war crimes.'[1680] The ILC's Draft Conclusions on

---

1675 *Prosecutor v. Furundìja, Trial chamber judgment* (1998) ICTY IT-95-17/1-T paras 151–157.

1676 *Constitutional Case No. C-291/07* (2007) Constitutional Court of Colombia Case No. C-291/07 75 (translation by the author), as also referred to in the following overview of the ICRC's IHL Database: ICRC, 'Practice Relating to Rule 1. The Principle of Distinction between Civilians and Combatants' (*IHL Database*, [date unknown]), https://ihl-databases.icrc.org/customary-ihl/eng/docs/v1_rul_rule1, accessed 22 August 2022. For earlier case law from the same court, see also *Constitutional Case No. C-223/95* (1995) Constitutional Court of Colombia Case No. C-223/95 para. 7, as also referred to by ILC, 'Fourth Report on Peremptory Norms of General International Law (Jus Cogens) by Dire Tladi, Special Rapporteur' (n. 108) para. 119.

1677 *In Re 'Agent Orange Product Liability Litigation', Judgment* (2005) District Court of the United States, Easter District of New York MDL No. 381, No. 04-CV-400 170, as also referred to by ILC, 'Fourth Report on Peremptory Norms of General International Law (Jus Cogens) by Dire Tladi, Special Rapporteur' (n. 108) para. 119.

1678 *Arancibia Clavel, Enrique Lautaro s/ Homicidio Calificado y Asociación Ilícita y Otros, Judgment* (2004) Supreme Court of Argentina Case No. 259 13–14, para. 28, as referred to by ILC, 'Fourth Report on Peremptory Norms of General International Law (Jus Cogens) by Dire Tladi, Special Rapporteur' (n. 108) para. 119.

1679 ILC, 'Report of the International Law Commission on the Work of Its Fifty-Third Session (23 April–1 June and 2 July–10 August 2001)' (n. 616) Commentary on Article 40, paras 4–6, 112–113. See also ILC, 'Fragmentation of International Law: Difficulties Arising from the Diversification and Expansion of International Law, Report of the Study Group of the International Law Commission, Finalized by Martti Koskenniemi' (n. 616) para. 374.

1680 ILC, 'Fourth Report on Peremptory Norms of General International Law (Jus Cogens) by Dire Tladi, Special Rapporteur' (n. 108) para. 116.

Peremptory Norms of General International Law contain a non-exhaustive list of peremptory norms and also refer to 'basic rules of international humanitarian law.'[1681] While it is still debated which rules of IHL can be identified as 'basic', it seems widely accepted that a number of IHL principles relevant to this study, including the principles of military necessity, humanity, distinction, proportionality, precautions in attack and against the effects of an attack, and the prohibition of superfluous injury and unnecessary suffering, have achieved *jus cogens* status.

2.2.4. Applicability ratione loci

The IHL treaties are almost silent as to the geographical scope of IHL. As regards IACs, neither the Geneva Conventions I–IV nor Additional Protocol I clearly determine the geographical scope of application.[1682] Geneva Convention III only provides, for example, that prisoners of war (POWs) remain protected by the Convention even if they are transferred to a third State (Art. 12 of Geneva Convention III). Article 4 of Geneva Convention I and Article 5 of Geneva Convention II provide that neutral powers must apply the respective Conventions by analogy to certain individuals received or interned on their territory (such as the wounded and sick or members of the medical personnel). Additional Protocol I provides more instructions on the applicability *ratione loci* of its rules. Article 49(2) of Additional Protocol I clearly indicates, for example, that the geographical scope of the Protocol must be interpreted broadly and, in particular, that the provisions relating to attacks must apply to all attacks regardless of the territory in which they are committed. Article 9 of Additional Protocol I defines the field of application of the part on the wounded, sick, and shipwrecked (Part II of Additional Protocol I) and, in that regard, sets forth that Part II applies 'to all those affected by a situation referred to in Article 1 [of Additional Protocol I (i.e. provision on general principles and scope of application of the Protocol)].' Interestingly, the drafters of Additional Protocol I found it too restrictive to limit the scope of Part II to the territory of the parties to the conflict, so they decided to delete any reference to the applicability *ratione loci*. According to the 1987 ICRC Commentary on Additional Protocol I, it was considered that 'the application *ratione personae* in itself determined the field of application of the Protocol in a sufficiently clear manner.'[1683]

1681 ILC, 'Peremptory Norms of General International Law (Jus Cogens): Text of the Draft Conclusions and Draft Annex Provisionally Adopted by the Drafting Committee on First Reading, Seventy-First Session, Geneva (29 April–7 June and 8 July–9 August 2019)' (n. 1397) Draft Conclusion 23 para. 24 and Annex.

1682 See also Vaios Koutroulis, 'International Organisations Involved in Armed Conflict: The Material and Geographical Scope of Application of IHL', *Proceedings of the 12th Bruges Colloquium on International Organisations' Involvement in Peace Operations: Applicable Legal Framework and the Issue of Responsibility, 20–21 October 2011, Bruges, vol. 42, 29* (2012) 37.

1683 Sandoz, Swinarski and Zimmermann (n. 85) 138, para. 413.

Regarding NIACs, Common Article 3 of the Geneva Conventions I–IV does also not give away much on the geographical scope of application.[1684] Article 2 of Additional Protocol II sets forth that the Protocol shall apply 'to all persons affected by an armed conflict as defined in Article 1 [of Additional Protocol II].' As explained in the 1987 ICRC Commentary on Additional Protocol II, '[p]ersons affected by the conflict within the meaning of this paragraph are covered by the Protocol *wherever* they are in the territory of the State engaged in conflict.'[1685] Since the situation may concern only a small part of the territory, the drafters of the Protocol did not explicitly prescribe the applicability *ratione loci*. Indeed, the applicability of Additional Protocol II derives from a criterion that refers to persons but not places.

Determining the geographical scope of IHL is an important but daunting task, particularly when armed conflicts involve forces contributed by different States, as is often the case in the context of UN (mandated) peace operations.

In the case of an IAC, IHL applies to the territory of the belligerent States, including all occupied territories, as well as to any territory other than the territory of the belligerent States, such as the high seas (including the airspace above and the seabed), in so far as actual hostilities occur.[1686] In the case of a NIAC, IHL applies to the entire territory of the State concerned.[1687] Thus, as also broadly recognised in case law of the international courts and tribunals, in both IACs and NIACs, the geographical scope of IHL is not limited to the actual theatre of combat operations or its surroundings but extends to the entire territory of the parties to the conflict.[1688] That said, while some rules, for example, those rules relating to the protection of POWs and civilians, apply to the entire territory, whether or not fighting is taking place; other rules, for

1684 See also Koutroulis, 'International Organisations Involved in Armed Conflict: The Material and Geographical Scope of Application of IHL' (n. 1682) 37–38.

1685 Emphasis added. Sandoz, Swinarski and Zimmermann (n. 85) 1359, para. 4490, as also referred to in *Prosecutor v. Jean-Paul Akayesu, Judgment* (n. 1576) para. 635.

1686 *Prosecutor v. Tadić, Decision on the defense motion for interlocutory appeal on jurisdiction* (n. 1567) paras 68 and 70. For further case law supporting this, see fn. 1688 below. See also Kleffner (n. 1374) para. 29; Tristan Ferraro, 'The Geographical Reach of IHL: The Law and Current Challenges', *Proceedings of the 13th Bruges Colloquium on Scope of Application of International Humanitarian Law, 18–19 October 2012, Bruges, vol. 43, 105* (2013) 105–113, 108.

1687 *Prosecutor v. Tadić, Decision on the defense motion for interlocutory appeal on jurisdiction* (n. 1567) paras 68 and 70. For further case law supporting this, see fn. 1688 below. See also Kleffner (n. 1374) para. 29.

1688 For case law supporting this, see e.g. *Prosecutor v. Tadić, Decision on the defense motion for interlocutory appeal on jurisdiction* (n. 1567) paras 68 and 70; *Prosecutor v. Kunarac, Kovac, and Vokovic, Appeals chamber judgment* (n. 1576) para. 57; *Prosecutor v. Jean-Paul Akayesu, Judgment* (n. 1576) paras 635–636; *The Prosecutor v. Alex Tamba Brima, Brima Bazzy Kamara and Santigie Borbor Kanu (the AFRC Accused), Judgment* (n. 1614) para. 245. See also ICRC, 'Report on International Humanitarian Law and the Challenges of Contemporary Armed Conflicts, Report for the 32nd International Conference of the Red Cross and Red Crescent, 8–10 December 2015, Geneva' (n. 1593) 13.

example, those governing the actual conduct of hostilities, are in practice primarily relevant in the areas where fighting is actually taking place.[1689]

A question that also often arises in the context of UN (mandated) peace operations is whether IHL also applies beyond the territory of the State where the operation is deployed, including the territory of States undertaking or taking part in the mission and/or the territory of non-belligerent States from which the belligerents may operate. While an analysis of such issues is pertinent, it is beyond the scope of this study as this study focuses in the first place on the deployment of operations in a third State and the use of force to protect civilians on that State's territory.[1690]

3. USE OF (LETHAL) FORCE TO PROTECT CIVILIANS

Peace forces may resort to both less-lethal and lethal force to protect civilians from threats. 'Less-lethal force' is usually understood as force necessary to make aggressors obey or deter and is *neither intended nor likely* to cause death or serious bodily injury.[1691] By contrast, lethal force is either intended to cause death ('intentional lethal use of force') or involves a very significant risk of death ('potentially lethal force'), regardless of whether death actually results.[1692] In practice, the use of less-lethal force involves the use of physical effort to overpower someone or the use of less-lethal weapons such as tear gas, stun grenades, smoke grenades, or soft kinetic projectiles.[1693] The use of lethal force

1689 *Prosecutor v. Tadić, Decision on the defense motion for interlocutory appeal on jurisdiction* (n. 1567) para. 68. See also Kleffner (n. 1374) para. 29; Ferraro, 'The Geographical Reach of IHL: The Law and Current Challenges' (n. 1686) 105–113, 108.

1690 For relevant literature, see e.g. Ferraro, 'The Applicability and Application of International Humanitarian Law to Multinational Forces' (n. 676) 610–612; Koutroulis, 'International Organisations Involved in Armed Conflict: The Material and Geographical Scope of Application of IHL' (n. 1682) 36–40; Jelena Pejic, 'The Protective Scope of Common Article 3: More than Meets the Eye' (2011) 93 International Review of the Red Cross 189; Michael N Schmitt, 'Charting the Legal Geography of Non- International Armed Conflict' (2014) 90 International Law Studies 1; ICRC, 'Report on International Humanitarian Law and the Challenges of Contemporary Armed Conflicts, Report for the 32nd International Conference of the Red Cross and Red Crescent, 8–10 December 2015, Geneva' (n. 1593) 14–16.

1691 Emphasis added. As defined by the former UN DPKO and DFS, with the difference that the term 'non-deadly force' is used (UN DPKO and UN DFS, '2017 UN Guidelines on the Use of Force by Military Components in UN Peacekeeping Operations' (n. 17) 19). See also UN OHCHR, *Guidance on Less-Lethal Weapons in Law Enforcement* (UN 2020) 45.

1692 See e.g. *Case of Makaratzis v. Greece, Judgment* (2004) ECtHR (Grand Chamber) App. No. 50385/99 para. 49. See also UN DPKO and UN DFS, '2017 UN Guidelines on the Use of Force by Military Components in UN Peacekeeping Operations' (n. 17) 19; Hessbruegge (n. 647) 92 (note that Hessbruegge prefers to use the term 'deliberately lethal force' as opposed to 'intentional lethal use of force').

1693 UN DPKO and UN DFS, '2017 UN Guidelines on the Use of Force by Military Components in UN Peacekeeping Operations' (n. 17) para. 12(b).

for example involves the use of physical effort to kill someone or the use of lethal weapons such as grenades, artillery, mortars, or firearms loaded with lethal ammunition.

The right to life is applicable in relation to all conduct that is (potentially) lethal and thus endangers life.[1694] Although it is a non-derogable right, lethal force can be used as long as someone is not arbitrarily deprived of his life. What constitutes an arbitrary deprivation of the right to life depends on the situation in which lethal force is used. If the use of lethal force has a clear nexus to an armed conflict, the rules of IHL must be used to assess whether someone has been arbitrarily deprived of their right to life.[1695] Any lethal force against a person that violates IHL is to be considered an arbitrary deprivation of life, as well as a war crime in most cases.[1696] Absent a clear nexus to an armed conflict, the legality of the use of lethal force must be tested against the strict rules for taking a person's life under HRL.

The following Sections discuss the legal parameters of the lawful use of (lethal) force to protect civilians. While Section 3.1 discusses the legal rules

---

1694 Daragh Murray and others (eds), *Practitioners' Guide to Human Rights Law in Armed Conflict* (Oxford University Press ; Royal Institute of International Affairs (Chatham House) 2016) para. 5.26.

1695 According to the UN HRC, '[l]ike the rest of the Covenant, article 6 [of the ICCPR] continues to apply also in situations of armed conflict to which the rules of international humanitarian law are applicable, including to the conduct of hostilities,' see UN HRC, 'General Comment No. 36 on the Right to Life' (n. 82) para. 64. Accordingly, also in the conduct of hostilities, no one shall be arbitrarily deprived of his or her life. For the use of force not to be arbitrary, it must find its legal basis in a rule of international law or more protective domestic law provisions. During the conduct of hostilities, the assessment of what constitutes an arbitrary deprivation of the right to life must be determined in the first place by reference to the rules of IHL. In the *Nuclear Weapons* case, the ICJ held that '[t]he test of what is an arbitrary deprivation of life [...] then falls to be determined by the applicable *lex specialis*, namely, the law applicable in armed conflict which is designed to regulate the conduct of hostilities,' see *Legality of the Threat or Use of Nuclear Weapons, Advisory opinion* (n. 1231) para. 25. Likewise, the IAComHR has used IHL to determine whether persons had been arbitrarily deprived of their right to life in situations amounting to an armed conflict, see *Jean Carlos Abella v. Argentina* (1997) IAComHR Report No. 55/97, Case 11.137, OEA/Ser.L/V/II.98 Doc. 7 rev. at 271 (1997) para. 161; *Riofrío Massacre v. Colombia* (2001) IAComHR Report No. 62/01, Case 11.654, OEA/Ser.L/V/II.111 Doc. 20 rev. at 758 (2000) para. 54. The AComHPR has also indicated that the right to life needs to be interpreted with reference to the rules of IHL, see AComHPR (n. 83) paras 13 and 32. For a discussion of the applicability of the right to life during an IAC, see also PJ Rowe, *The Impact of Human Rights Law on Armed Forces* (Cambridge University Press 2006) 134–147. For a more general discussion of how IHL has become a source of HRL, see Gerd Oberleitner, 'Humanitarian Law as a Source of Human Rights Law' in Dinah Shelton (ed), *The Oxford Handbook of International Human Rights Law* (Oxford University Press 2013) 275–294, http://opil.ouplaw.com/view/10.1093/law/9780199640133.001.0001/law-9780199640133-chapter-12, accessed 19 August 2019.

1696 According to the ICRC Study on Customary International Humanitarian Law, state practice has established the rule that murder is prohibited as a norm of customary international law applicable in both international and non-international armed conflicts, see Henckaerts and Doswald-Beck (n. 91) Rule 89, pp. 311–314 ('Murder is prohibited'). This implies, *inter alia*, that '[t]he prohibition of "arbitrary deprivation of the right to life" under human rights law [...] also encompasses unlawful killing in the conduct of hostilities,' see id., p. 313.

relevant to the use of (lethal) force outside the context of hostilities, Section 3.2 zooms in on the legal rules governing the use of (lethal) force with a clear nexus to an armed conflict. Section 3.3 explores to what extent the PoC mandate may impact the use of force on the ground.

3.1. USE OF (LETHAL) FORCE TO PROTECT CIVILIANS THAT HAS NO CLEAR NEXUS TO AN ONGOING ARMED CONFLICT

3.1.1. Use of lethal force: identifying the scope of the permissible grounds for deprivation of life

Article 6(1) of the ICCPR, Article 4(1) of the ACHR, and Article 4 of the ACHPR stipulate that the deprivation of someone's life does not violate their right to life when it results from force which is not 'arbitrary' in nature. Although the relevant treaties do not, in themselves, define when force is used in an 'arbitrary' manner, the General Comments Nos. 36 and 3 on the Right to Life of the UN HRC and the AComHPR, respectively, are illustrative in this regard (in addition to case law discussed below). Interpretation of 'arbitrariness' must consider the elements of legality, justice, predictability, reasonableness, necessity, and proportionality.[1697] The UN HRC also adds the principle of due process of law to the list.[1698]

Article 2(2) of the ECHR and Principle 9 of the 1990 UN Basic Principles for the Use of Force and Firearms provide more detailed grounds for the possible deprivation of someone's life.[1699] Article 2(2) of the ECHR provides that the '[d]eprivation of life shall not be regarded as inflicted in contravention of this Article when it results from the use of force which is no more than absolutely necessary: (a) in defence of any person from unlawful violence; (b) in order to effect a lawful arrest or to prevent the escape of a person lawfully detained; (c) in action lawfully taken for the purpose of quelling a riot or insurrection.' Principle 9 holds that officials are prohibited from using firearms 'except in self-defence or defence of others against the imminent threat of death or serious injury, to prevent the perpetration of a particularly serious crime involving grave threat to life, to arrest a person presenting such a danger and resisting their authority, or to prevent their escape, and only when less extreme means are insufficient to achieve these objectives.' It adds that 'in any event, intentional lethal use of firearms may only be made when strictly unavoidable in order to protect life.'

1697 UN HRC, 'General Comment No. 36 on the Right to Life' (n. 82) para. 12; AComHPR (n. 83) para. 12.

1698 UN HRC, 'General Comment No. 36 on the Right to Life' (n. 82) para. 12.

1699 In a footnote to the 1990 UN Basic Principles for the Use of Force and Firearms, it is specified that the rules also apply to military personnel when such persons 'exercise police powers' (see UN, '1990 UN Basic Principles for the Use of Force and Firearms' (n. 92), fn. 1).

At first sight, these two sets of provisions seem to diverge. Yet, after reviewing the treaty-based jurisprudence and guidance, it becomes clear that the material scope of the right to life under the ECHR and the 1990 UN Basic Principles for the Use of Force and Firearms, on the one hand, and under the ICCPR, the ACHR, and the ACHPR, on the other, is not fundamentally different. Five main HRL principles govern the recourse to force that endangers life outside the conduct of hostilities: (i) legality; (ii) necessity; (iii) proportionality; (iv) precaution; and (v) accountability.[1700]

These five core principles can be derived not only from the major HRL treaties[1701] or soft law instruments, including the 1990 UN Basic Principles for the Use of Force and Firearms,[1702] but also from the jurisprudence[1703] of

1700 See *also* the General Comments Nos. 36 and 3 on the Right to Life of the UN HRC and AComHPR, respectively, as referred to above in fns. 1697 and 1698. Note that these HRL principles should not be confused with IHL principles of humanity, military necessity, proportionality in attack, precautions in attack, precautions against the effects of attacks, or the prohibition of superfluous injury and unnecessary suffering.

1701 Even though TCCs are not necessarily parties to the same HRL treaties, all States and international and regional organisations possessing international legal personality must comply with the right to life, which is also a norm of customary international law and, as discussed above, even a norm of *jus cogens* (for sources defending the claim that the right to life is a *jus cogens* norm, see Part III, Section 2.1.2.2, fn. 1397).

1702 Although the 1990 UN Basic Principles for the Use of Force and Firearms were originally soft law and thus not legally binding in nature, a large number of States was involved in their development and adoption and general agreement exists on the binding nature of their content. As noted by Special Rapporteur Philip Alston, Principle 9 is a strict application of a rule of law that States have otherwise assumed under customary international law and its content reflects binding international law (UNGA, 'Interim Report of the Special Rapporteur, Philip Alston, on Extrajudicial, Summary or Arbitrary Executions' (2006) UN Doc. A/61/311 para. 35). See also UN HRC, 'Report of the Special Rapporteur on Extrajudicial, Summary or Arbitrary Executions, Christof Heyns' (n. 109) paras 43–44. For a detailed overview of the development of the 1990 UN Basic Principles for the Use of Force and Firearms, see also Nigel Rodley and Matt Pollard, *The Treatment of Prisoners under International Law* (Oxford University Press 2011) 495–508. Human rights courts and international human rights mechanisms also rely on the 1990 UN Basic Principles for the Use of Force and Firearms to interpret the right to life, see e.g. *Noah Kazingachire, John Chitsenga, Elias Chemvura and Batanai Hadzisi (represented by Zimbabwe Human Rights NGO Forum v. Zimbabwe* (2013) AComHPR Communication No. 295/04 para. 117; *Case of Nachova and Others v. Bulgaria, Judgment* (2005) ECtHR (Grand Chamber) App. Nos. 43577/98 and 43579/98 paras 71–73 and 96; UN HRC, 'General Comment No. 36 on the Right to Life' (n. 82) paras 12–14; *Case of Montero-Aranguren et al. (Detention Center of Catia) v. Venezuela, Judgment* (2006) IACtHR Series C No. 150 para. 69; *Case of Zambrano Vélez et al. v. Ecuador, Judgment* (2007) IACtHR Series C No. 166 para. 101; *Case of Nadege Sorzema et al. v. Dominican Republic, Judgment* (2012) IACtHR Series C No. 166 para. 85; *Case of the Landaeta Mejías Brothers et al. v. Venezuela, Judgment* (2014) IACtHR Series C No. 281 para. 131; *Alonso Eugénio da Silva v. Brazil* (2000) IAComHR Report No. 9/00, Case 11.598 para. 34; *Marcos Aurelio de Oliveira v. Brazil* (2000) IAComHR Report No. 10/00, Case 11.599, OEA/Ser.L/V/II.106 Doc. 3 rev. at 413 (1999) para. 33.

1703 Although the relevant case law involves alleged violations by States (not international or regional organisations) and is limited to States within the regions covered by the relevant HRL instruments and oversight mechanisms, it adopts similar reasoning and helps to clarify the scope of the right to life vis-à-vis lethal force in the context of UN (mandated) peace

human rights courts (including the IACtHR and the ECtHR) and decisions and guidance from international human rights mechanisms (including the UN HRC, the IAComHR, the AComHPR, and the EComHR). However, it is worth noting at the outset that while these sources reiterate the same norms, the principles of necessity and proportionality, in particular, give rise to divergent interpretations.[1704]

3.1.1.1. Principle of legality

The right to life must be protected by law, meaning that the use of lethal force to deprive someone of their life must always have a sufficient legal basis. Article 2(1) of the ECHR, Article 6(1) of the ICCPR, and Article 4(1) of the ACHR stipulate that the right to life 'shall be *protected by law*.'[1705] Article 4 of the ACHPR does not explicitly refer to the principle of legality. However, the AComHPR, in its General Comment No. 3 on the Right to Life, recognises that States have a responsibility to develop and implement an appropriate domestic legal framework that complies with international standards to respect, protect, promote, and fulfil the right to life.[1706] Case law has also confirmed that to safeguard the right to life, an appropriate legal framework must be established that strictly controls and limits the circumstances in which lethal force may be used, in accordance with the relevant international standards.[1707] Domestic law can protect the right to life more but not less.

In the context of domestic police operations, for example, an order given under a provision of the law on police action, combined with a provision of the domestic criminal code, may provide a legal basis for police officers to use lethal force in defence of others.[1708] In the context of UN (mandated) peace operations, the legal basis for the use of force by peace forces can be found in the mission mandate, enshrined in the relevant UNSC resolutions, and subsequently detailed in mission-specific ROE. However, while a UNSC mandate to use 'all necessary

---

operations. See also Daniel Collinge, 'The Missing Link' (2019) 23 Journal of International Peacekeeping 82, 85.

1704 As discussed in Part III, Sections 3.1.1.2 and 3.1.1.3.

1705 Emphasis added. See also Principles 1 and 11 of the 1990 UN Basic Principles for the Use of Force and Firearms (n. 92); UN HRC, 'General Comment No. 36 on the Right to Life' (n. 82) paras 13, 18–22.

1706 AComHPR (n. 83) paras 7 and 10.

1707 See e.g. *Case of Makaratzis v. Greece, Judgment* (n. 1692) paras 57–59; *Case of Giuliani and Gaggio v. Italy, Judgment* (2011) ECtHR (Grand Chamber) App. No. 23458/02 para. 209; *Husband of Maria Fanny Suarez de Guerrero v. Colombia, Decision as to the admissibility* (1981) UN HRC Communication No. R.11/45, UN Doc. Supp. No. 40 (A/37/40) at 137 (1982) paras 13.1 and 13.3.

1708 In Belgian law, e.g. the conditions for the use of lethal force by police officers for the protection of others are regulated by Art. 37 and 38 of the Law of 5 August 1992 on the Police Service and Art. 416 of the Belgian Criminal Code of 8 June 1867.

means' to protect civilians authorises peace forces to use force,[1709] the legality of lethal force used to protect civilians will, of course, also depend on compliance with the rules applicable in the circumstances, including the HRL principles discussed hereafter (e.g. principles of necessity and proportionality) and the (more restrictive) rules contained in the national laws of the host State and the TCC(s).[1710]

3.1.1.2. Principle of necessity

For lethal force to be necessary, it must be 'strictly necessary'[1711] or 'absolutely necessary'[1712] to achieve a legitimate aim.[1713] To that end, lethal force must always constitute the last resort that can only be used if less drastic means (such as the arrest of a person) are unavailable or manifestly unreasonable.[1714] If force is unavoidable, the amount of force should not exceed that which is objectively necessary to respond to the threat, and force should only be used as long as necessary to achieve the legitimate aim. In other words, if (and only for as long as) force is needed, graduated force must be applied, and the least harmful measures must be considered first.[1715] Nevertheless, there may be circumstances

1709 With thematic Resolution 2436 (2018) on UN peacekeeping efforts, the UN Security Council explicitly confirmed that when it authorises UN peace operations to use 'all necessary means,' this includes the use of force when required ('UNSC Res. 2436' (n. 19) para. 6). When extending the PoC mandate of UNISFA with Resolution 2445 (2018), it also confirmed its position ('UNSC Res. 2445' (n. 134) para. 11). See also subsequent resolutions concerning UNISFA: 'UNSC Res. 2469' (n. 1097) para. 12; 'UNSC Res. 2497' (n. 134) para. 13; 'UNSC Res. 2550' (n. 134) para. 12; 'UNSC Res. 2609' (n. 1010) para. 14.

1710 For a detailed discussion of the meaning of 'all necessary means', see Part II, Section 3.2.5.1.

1711 UN HRC, 'General Comment No. 36 on the Right to Life' (n. 82) para. 12.

1712 As referred to in Art. 2(2) of the ECHR. When interpreting 'absolutely necessary', the ECtHR, however, seems to assume that these words reflect the principle of proportionality. The ECtHR has explained that a stricter and more compelling test of necessity must be employed from that normally applicable when determining whether state action is 'necessary in a democratic society' under Art. 8(2), 9(2), 10(2), and 11(2) of the ECHR. In particular, the force used must be strictly proportionate to the achievement of the aims set out in Art. 2(2)(a), (b), and (c) of the ECHR (see *Case of McCann and Others v. the United Kingdom, Judgment* (n. 1038) paras 148 and 200).

1713 On legitimate aims, see Part III, Section 3.1.1.3.

1714 Support for the principle that force must constitute a method of last resort can be found in case law: *Case of Barrios Family v. Venezuela, Judgment* (2011) IACtHR Series C No. 237 para. 49(a); *Case of Montero-Aranguren et al. (Detention Center of Catia) v. Venezuela, Judgment* (n. 1702) para. 67; *Case of the Landaeta Mejías Brothers et al. v. Venezuela, Judgment* (n. 1702) para. 131; *Armando Alejandre Jr. and Others v. Cuba* (n. 1406) para. 42; *Noah Kazingachire, John Chitsenga, Elias Chemvura and Batanai Hadzisi (represented by Zimbabwe Human Rights NGO Forum v. Zimbabwe* (n. 1702) para. 113; *Case of Nachova and Others v. Bulgaria, Judgment* (n. 1702) para. 108.

1715 For relevant case law on this requirement, see e.g. *Case of Zambrano Vélez et al. v. Ecuador, Judgment* (n. 1702) para. 108; *Case of Barrios Family v. Venezuela, Judgment* (n. 1714) paras 67–68; *Case of Montero-Aranguren et al. (Detention Center of Catia) v. Venezuela, Judgment* (n. 1702) para. 68. *Case of Juozaitienė and Bikulčius v. Lithuania, Judgment* (2008) ECtHR App. Nos. 70659/01 and 74371/01 paras 80–81; *Case of Güleç v. Turkey, Judgment* (1998)

in which the threat is so significant that a graduated application of force may unduly risk death or serious harm to people. In this case, less-lethal options need not be considered, even if they are available, and lethal force may lawfully be used. Put differently, the immediate use of lethal force is considered strictly necessary to prevent the loss of one's life or the life of another person.[1716]

In most situations, the necessity to use lethal force immediately arises from the existence of an 'imminent' or a 'grave' threat. The distinction between 'imminent' and 'grave' is found in Principle 9 of the 1990 UN Basic Principles for the Use of Force and Firearms: law enforcement officers may use firearms in a potentially lethal manner in self-defence or defence of others against the 'imminent threat of death or serious injury.' They may also use potentially lethal force in case there is a 'grave threat to life', and, in particular, to prevent the perpetration of a particularly serious crime involving such a 'grave threat to life', to apprehend a person who poses such a threat and resists authority, or to prevent their escape. Such firearms may also be used in an intentionally lethal manner but only 'when strictly unavoidable [...] to protect life.'[1717]

Jurisprudence from human rights courts and international human rights mechanisms reveals that the justifiability of self-defence or defence of others depends on how temporally proximate the use of force is to an attack or threat of attack.[1718] Any 'time lag' between the threat or action and the response undermines, in principle, the potential to invoke self-defence or defence of others.[1719] Determining whether a threat is 'imminent' or 'immediate' is, to quote former Special Rapporteur Christof Heyns, 'a matter of *seconds*, not

ECtHR App. No. 54/1997/838/1044 paras 71 and 73; *Husband of Maria Fanny Suarez de Guerrero v. Colombia, Decision as to the admissibility* (n. 1707) para. 13.2. See also UN HRC, 'General Comment No. 36 on the Right to Life' (n. 82) para. 12.

1716 ECOSOC, Commission on Human Rights, 'Civil and Political Rights, Including the Questions of Disappearances and Summary Executions, Report of the Special Rapporteur, Philip Alston, on Extrajudicial, Summary or Arbitrary Executions, Sixty-Second Session, Item 11(b) of the Provisional Agenda' (2006) UN Doc. E/CN.4/2006/53 para. 49.

1717 Principle 9 of the 1990 UN Basic Principles for the Use of Force and Firearms (n. 92). See also UN HRC, 'Report of the Special Rapporteur on Extrajudicial, Summary or Arbitrary Executions, Christof Heyns' (n. 109) paras 32–34; Académie de droit international humanitaire et de droits humains à Genève, *Use of Force in Law Enforcement and the Right to Life: The Role of the Human Rights Council* (Geneva Academy of International Humanitarian Law and Human Rights 2016) 11–13; Amnesty International, 'Use of Force: Guidelines for Implementation of the UN Basic Principles on the Use of Force and Firearms by Law Enforcement Officials' (Amnesty International 2015) 55–59.

1718 See e.g. *Case of McCann and Others v. the United Kingdom, Judgment* (n. 1038) paras 195–200; *Case of Huohvanainen v. Finland, Judgment* (n. 1038) para. 97; *Case of Andronicou and Constantinou v. Cyprus, Judgment* (n. 1038) paras 191–192. See also UN HRC, 'Report of the International Fact-Finding Mission to Investigate Violations of International Law, Including International Humanitarian and Human Rights Law, Resulting from the Israeli Attacks on the Flotilla of Ships Carrying Humanitarian Assistance' (n. 1038) paras 165 and 167.

1719 Bakircioglu (n. 1039) 9.

hours.'[1720] Moreover, often there is not only a temporal proximity between the defensive action and the (foiled) attack but also a geographical proximity of the attacker to the target, meaning that the attacker no longer needs to take preparatory steps to carry out the threat.[1721]

Lethal force may also be warranted in certain situations where there is not necessarily an immediate threat, but a person nevertheless poses an 'ongoing threat' to life that may materialise at any time.[1722] According to Special Rapporteur Christof Heyns, '[a]n ongoing threat is posed by suspects in respect of whom there is a high probability of immediate harm to specified or unspecified individuals' (e.g. a fleeing suspect who has just attacked someone and there are concrete indications he will attack again).[1723] A grave threat to life does not allow preventive lethal measures to be taken against any future threat. Instead, it implies that potentially lethal force can be used against a person when the nature of the threat posed by that person may at any time result in the loss of another person's life.[1724] To illustrate 'grave threats to life', the Geneva Academy gives the example of a serial killer who has escaped from a high-security prison or someone driving through a roadblock when a terrorist attack is feared.[1725]

In the context of UN (mandated) peace operations, a situation that gives rise to a grave, though not imminent, threat to life could be rebels approaching a village, firing a few close shots but leaving after peace forces fire warning shots in the air. However, before the rebels disappear from sight, they signal their intent to return. At that point, the threat such rebels pose to civilians in the village is not imminent but arguably ongoing and thus grave. Moreover, a temporally imminent threat to the lives of the villagers may materialise at any moment. In such a situation, peace forces must be able to use potentially lethal force by, for example, shooting at the rebels' legs to prevent their retreat, provided other HRL principles, such as proportionality and precautions, are also met. These situations must be the absolute exception and presuppose the existence of objective facts from which it can be concluded that there is such a continuing threat to the life of others.[1726]

However, this interpretation does not seem to command unanimous support. In its General Comment No. 3 on the Right to Life, the AComHPR established that '[f]orce may be used in law enforcement only in order to stop

[1720] Emphasis added. UN HRC, 'Report of the Special Rapporteur on Extrajudicial, Summary or Arbitrary Executions, Christof Heyns' (n. 109) para. 59.

[1721] Hessbruegge (n. 647) 140–141.

[1722] UN HRC, 'Report of the Special Rapporteur on Extrajudicial, Summary or Arbitrary Executions, Christof Heyns' (n. 109) para. 33 (discussion of international law standards) and para. 60 (discussion of domestic standards).

[1723] *Ibid.* para. 60 (discussion of domestic standards).

[1724] Amnesty International (n. 1717) 58.

[1725] Académie de droit international humanitaire et de droits humains à Genève (n. 1717) 13.

[1726] Amnesty International (n. 1717) 58.

an *imminent* threat.'[1727] Similarly, in its General Comment No. 36 on the Right to Life, the UN HRC established that '[t]he use of potentially lethal force for law enforcement purposes is an extreme measure, which should be resorted to only when strictly necessary in order to protect life or prevent serious injury from an *imminent* threat.'[1728] Neither one refers to grave threats, and yet, curiously, the UN HRC substantiates its claim by referring to Principle 9 of the 1990 UN Basic Principles for the Use of Force and Firearms, which, as explained, does reference grave threats.[1729] Going one step further, the IACtHR in *Zambrano Vélez et al. v. Ecuador* quotes Principle 9 in an idiosyncratic manner to argue that, instead of a 'grave threat' to life, lethal force to effect an arrest requires an 'imminent threat.'[1730] In *Alonso Eugénio da Silva v. Brazil*, the IAComHR also invokes Principle 9 but establishes instead that there must be an 'extreme danger or legitimate defense.'[1731]

Jurisprudence from the ECtHR creates further confusion on the nature of the threat justifying lethal force for law enforcement purposes. In *Nachova and Others v. Bulgaria* and *Kakoulli v. Turkey*, the ECtHR held that 'the legitimate aim of effecting a lawful arrest can only justify putting human life at risk in circumstances of absolute necessity.'[1732] There can be no such 'necessity' if the person to be arrested does not pose a 'threat to life or limb' *and* 'is not suspected of having committed a violent offence,' even if the failure to use lethal force may result in the loss of the opportunity to arrest the fugitive.[1733] *Juozaitienė*

1727 Emphasis added. AComHPR (n. 83) para. 27. See also *Noah Kazingachire, John Chitsenga, Elias Chemvura and Batanai Hadzisi (represented by Zimbabwe Human Rights NGO Forum v. Zimbabwe* (n. 1702) para. 117.

1728 Emphasis added. UN HRC, 'General Comment No. 36 on the Right to Life' (n. 82) para. 12. See also 'UN HRC Res. 22/10' (2013) UN Doc. A/HRC/RES/22/10 para. 8; UN OHCHR, 'Opening Statement by Ms. Navi Pillay United Nations High Commissioner for Human Rights at the Human Rights Council 24th Session' (2013), https://newsarchive.ohchr.org/EN/NewsEvents/Pages/DisplayNews.aspx?NewsID=13687&LangID=E, accessed 15 March 2021.

1729 UN HRC, 'General Comment No. 36 on the Right to Life' (n. 82) para. 12.

1730 *Case of Zambrano Vélez et al. v. Ecuador, Judgment* (n. 1702) para. 101 (the IACtHR quotes Principle 9 as follows: '[The 1990 UN Basic Principles for the Use of Force and Firearms] prohibit the use of firearms, "except when a suspected offender offers armed resistance or otherwise jeopardizes the lives of others and less extreme measures are not sufficient to restrain or apprehend the suspected offender" and "except in self-defence or defence of others [... or] to arrest a person presenting [imminent threat of death or serious injury] and resisting their authority, or to prevent his or her escape, and only when less extreme means are insufficient to achieve these objectives"'). See also *Case of Nadege Sorzema et al. v. Dominican Republic, Judgment* (n. 1702) paras 84–85 and 91; *Case of the Landaeta Mejías Brothers et al. v. Venezuela, Judgment* (n. 1702) paras 131 and 134–141.

1731 *Alonso Eugénio da Silva v. Brazil* (n. 1702) para. 34. See also *Marcos Aurelio de Oliveira v. Brazil* (n. 1702) paras 33–34.

1732 *Case of Nachova and Others v. Bulgaria, Judgment* (n. 1702) para. 95; *Case of Kakoulli v. Turkey, Judgment* (2005) ECtHR App. No. 38595/97 para. 108.

1733 *Case of Nachova and Others v. Bulgaria, Judgment* (n. 1702) paras 95 and 107; *Case of Kakoulli v. Turkey, Judgment* (n. 1732) para. 108. See also *Case of Finogenov and Others v. Russia, Judgment* (2011) ECtHR App. Nos. 18299/03 and 27311/03 para. 220; *Case of Vasil Sashov Petrov v. Bulgaria, Judgment* (2011) ECtHR App. No. 30054/96 para. 48; *Case of Karandja v.*

and Bikulčius v. Lithuania reinforces that these two elements are to be seen cumulatively and allows lethal force in cases of a 'very *clear* and *imminent* danger' posed by the person in 'the event of his being allowed to escape.'[1734]

It is also worth mentioning that the ECtHR acknowledges the difficulty of upholding the 'absolute necessity' test in the context of military operations. In the cases of *Isayeva, Yusupova and Bazayeva v. Russia* and *Isayeva v. Russia*, the ECtHR accepted that exceptional measures on behalf of Russia were necessary to regain control of the Chechen Republic and suppress the illegal armed rebellion.[1735] Such measures could include the deployment of military aircraft equipped with heavy combat weapons, and if such aircraft were attacked by illegal armed groups, the use of lethal force would be justified under Article 2(2) of the ECHR.[1736] Although the ECtHR clearly used terminology that belongs to HRL,[1737] the judgments also contain some indications that the ECtHR recognises the existence of an armed conflict and the military character of the operation (which would justify the room it leaves for the large-scale use of lethal force absent a proven immediate threat to life).[1738] Similarly, in the more recent case of *Tagayeva and Others v. Russia*, the ECtHR seemed to alter the absolute necessity test by holding that the absolute necessity test formulated in Article 2 of the ECHR is bound to be applied 'with different degrees of scrutiny, depending on whether and to what extent the authorities were in control of the situation and other relevant constraints inherent in operative decision-making in this sensitive sphere.'[1739] The ECtHR defended its position by stressing that it is aware of the difficulties States face in protecting their population from the threats of terrorism and the risks of *ex post* analysis.[1740]

Bulgaria, Judgment (2010) ECtHR App. No. 69180/01 para. 59; *Case of Wasilewska v. Russia, Judgment* (2010) ECtHR App. Nos. 28975/04 and 33406/04 para. 43; *Case of Putintseva v. Russia, Judgment* (2012) ECtHR App. No. 33498/04 para. 69.

1734 Emphasis added. *Case of Juozaitienė and Bikulčius v. Lithuania, Judgment* (n. 1715) paras 78–79.

1735 *Case of Isayeva, Yusupova and Bazayeva v. Russia, Judgment* (2005) ECtHR App. Nos. 57947/00, 57948/00, and 57949/00 para. 178; *Case of Isayeva v. Russia, Judgment* (2005) ECtHR App. No. 57950/00 para. 180.

1736 *Case of Isayeva, Yusupova and Bazayeva v. Russia, Judgment* (n. 1735) para. 178.

1737 *Ibid.* para. 171; *Case of Isayeva v. Russia, Judgment* (n. 1735) para. 175. In the latter case, the ECtHR even explicitly stated that it considers 'using this kind of weapon in a populated area, outside wartime and without prior evacuation of the civilians, is impossible to reconcile with the degree of caution expected from a law-enforcement body in a democratic society' (para. 191).

1738 *Case of Isayeva, Yusupova and Bazayeva v. Russia, Judgment* (n. 1735) paras 175, 178, and 181; *Case of Isayeva v. Russia, Judgment* (n. 1735) para. 188. See also Larsen (n. 1350) 275–276.

1739 *Case of Tagayeva and Others v. Russia, Judgment* (2017) ECtHR App. No.26562/07 para. 481. See also *Case of Finogenov and Others v. Russia, Judgment* (n. 1733) paras 212–214.

1740 *Case of Tagayeva and Others v. Russia, Judgment* (n. 1739) para. 481. See also *Case of Finogenov and Others v. Russia, Judgment* (n. 1733) para. 212.

3.1.1.3. Principle of proportionality

Proportionality signifies that the end does not justify all means, a principle that is particularly important in the context of the right to life.[1741] Even if the use of lethal force appears to be necessary, the amount of force used must still be balanced against the legitimate aim(s) pursued. In other words, the nature and degree of force used must be commensurate to the seriousness of the threat and the legitimate aim to be achieved.[1742]

When examining the principle of proportionality, a distinction must be made between the use of potentially lethal force and the intentional lethal use of force,[1743] as well as between the different legitimate aims that may be pursued by these types of force. Whereas the use of potentially lethal force involves a very significant risk of death, the intentional lethal use of force is intended to cause death. While the terminology may suggest otherwise, in both scenarios, the goal is to stop the threat, not to kill the person posing the threat. In other words, the killing of a person is only ever a means to an end.[1744] However, the likelihood that someone will effectively die is much higher with the intentional lethal use of force than with the use of potentially lethal force. In practice, the use of potentially lethal force for example involves shooting at the arms or the legs, whereas the intentional lethal use of force typically involves a shot fired at a person's head or multiple shots fired at a person's central body mass.[1745]

A. The use of potentially lethal force

Potentially lethal force can be used in the following circumstances:

First, and similar to intentional lethal force, if one or more people are under 'imminent threat of death or serious injury', potentially lethal force can be

---

1741 Amnesty International (n. 1717) 18.

1742 Gaggioli, 'The Use of Force in Armed Conflicts Conduct of Hostilities, Law Enforcement, and Self-Defense' (n. 643) 66.

1743 As defined above, see Part III, Section 3. When reading Art. 2 of the ECHR, one might think that the ECHR is only concerned with intentional lethal force, and thus not with potentially lethal force. Art. 2(1) of the ECHR sets forth that '[n]o one shall be deprived of his life intentionally save in the execution of a sentence of a court following his conviction of a crime for which this penalty is provided by law' (emphasis added). In *Stewart v. the United Kingdom*, the EComHR, however, clarified that Art. 2(2) of the ECHR (which sets forth the permissible grounds for depriving someone of his or her life) is not only concerned with intentional killing, but also defines those situations in which it is permitted 'to "use force" which may result, as the unintended outcome of the use of force, in the deprivation of life' (emphasis added), see *Stewart v. the United Kingdom, Decision as to the admissibility* (1984) EComHR App. No. 10044/82 para. 15. This was subsequently confirmed in a number of cases by the ECtHR, see e.g. *Case of McCann and Others v. the United Kingdom, Judgment* (n. 1038) para. 148; *Case of Kelly and Others v. the United Kingdom, Judgment* (2001) ECtHR App. No. 18984/91 para. 93; *Case of Ramsahai and Others v. the Netherlands, Judgment* (2007) ECtHR (Grand Chamber) App. No. 52391/99 paras 286–289; *Case of Benzer and Others v. the United Kingdom, Judgment* (2013) ECtHR App. No. 23502/06 para. 163.

1744 Amnesty International (n. 1717) 52.

1745 See also Hessbruegge (n. 647) 92; Amnesty International (n. 1717) 115.

used in self-defence or defence of others. As discussed above, 'imminence' in this context implies a matter of seconds or even a split second before fatality strikes.[1746] 'Serious injury' must be interpreted as 'a life threatening or life changing injury, e.g. loss of limb, loss of organ functions, etc.'[1747]

Second, potentially lethal force can also be used beyond self-defence and defence of others scenarios to pursue 'other legitimate aims' upon the condition that there is a 'grave threat to life'. As explained, 'grave threat to life' implies that someone poses a continuing threat to life that may materialise at any time.[1748] 'Other legitimate aims' primarily include law enforcement purposes, such as preventing a crime, arresting a person, or preventing a person from escaping. These categories of legitimate aims are also listed in Article 2(2) of the ECHR.

In the context of UN (mandated) peace operations, a fundamental question is whether the UN Security Council may authorise other legitimate aims, such as discouraging attempts at the violent disruption of the political process or assisting national authorities in the maintenance of law and order.[1749] Under the ICCPR, the ACHR, and the ACHPR, deprivations of life need only not be 'arbitrary', leaving the range of legitimate aims rather open-ended. The only precondition for potentially lethal force to pursue such aims would be a 'grave threat to life'. By contrast, Article 2 of the ECHR is harder to reconcile with the practice of UN (mandated) peace operations. On a strict reading of Article 2(2) of the ECHR, its list of permissible grounds would be exhaustive. However, the case law does not necessarily seem to exclude other non-enumerated permissible grounds. Notably, in *Khatsiyeva and Others v. Russia*, a case concerning a military attack on civilians in an area of conflict, the ECtHR stated that it would leave unanswered the question 'whether a State could be justified under Article 2 §2 of the [ECHR] [...] in using lethal force against civilians for mere failure to comply with official safety instructions in an area of an armed conflict.'[1750]

Moreover, even if the ECHR is read narrowly, UNSC powers under Chapter VII and Article 103 of the UN Charter – as discussed below[1751] – could also be invoked to argue that a UNSC mandate prevails over Article 2(2) on the condition that an underlying norm of *jus cogens* is not violated. Although the right to life, or more precisely, the right not to be arbitrarily deprived of

---

1746 UN HRC, 'Report of the Special Rapporteur on Extrajudicial, Summary or Arbitrary Executions, Christof Heyns' (n. 109) para. 59; UN OHCHR (n. 1691) 43.

1747 Amnesty International (n. 1717) 23.

1748 UN HRC, 'Report of the Special Rapporteur on Extrajudicial, Summary or Arbitrary Executions, Christof Heyns' (n. 109) para. 33 (discussion of international law standards) and para. 60 (discussion of domestic standards).

1749 UN DPKO and UN DFS, '2008 Capstone Doctrine' (n. 19) 34.

1750 *Case of Khatsiyeva and Others v. Russia, Judgment* (2008) ECtHR App. No. 5108/02 para. 139, as referred to by Schabas, *The European Convention on Human Rights: A Commentary* (n. 89) 146–147.

1751 See Part III, Section 3.3.2.1.

one's life, is a peremptory norm that permits no derogation,[1752] Article 2(2)'s permissible grounds are not part of the peremptory norm.[1753] Arguably, even in this scenario, the UN Security Council may put forward other legitimate aims.

B. The intentional lethal use of force

Intentional lethal force is permissible only 'to protect life from imminent threat.'[1754] In other words, the primary purpose of killing someone intentionally must be to save the life of someone else.[1755] The threat to that person's life must be so imminent that their life can only be saved by using lethal force that is intended to cause the death of the person posing the threat. Less-lethal or potentially lethal use of force (as discussed above) would, in that case, be insufficient to stop the threat. Unlike the HRL treaties referenced above, Principle 9 of the 1990 UN Basic Principles for the Use of Force and Firearms incorporated this caveat by stating that 'intentional lethal use of firearms may only be made when strictly unavoidable in order to protect life.'[1756] Broad support can also be found in jurisprudence and authoritative reports for the fact that intentional lethal use of force can only be used when absolutely unavoidable to save a life and thus not to protect law and order or other interests.[1757]

In this regard, outside the conduct of hostilities context in armed conflicts, so-called 'shoot to kill' policies seem to be inherently incompatible with HRL

1752 For sources defending the claim that the right to life is a *jus cogens* norm, see Part III, Section 2.1.2.2, fn. 1397. On the limits to derogation from HRL, see Part III, Sections 2.1.4.1 and 2.1.4.2. More in general, see also Part III, Section 3.3.2.1.

1753 See also Larsen (n. 1350) 380.

1754 Former Special Rapporteur Christof Heyns has termed this the 'protect life' principle, according to which 'a life may be taken intentionally only to save another life' (see UN HRC, 'Report of the Special Rapporteur on Extrajudicial, Summary or Arbitrary Executions, Christof Heyns' (n. 109) para. 70).

1755 *Ibid.* para. 72.

1756 Emphasis added. Principle 9 of the 1990 UN Basic Principles for the Use of Force and Firearms (n. 92).

1757 Support can be found in the case law and practice of the AComHPR, see e.g. *Noah Kazingachire, John Chitsenga, Elias Chemvura and Batanai Hadzisi (represented by Zimbabwe Human Rights NGO Forum v. Zimbabwe* (n. 1702) paras 120–122; AComHPR (n. 83) para. 27. The UN HRC also supports this position, see e.g. UN HRC, 'General Comment No. 36 on the Right to Life' (n. 82) para. 12; UNHRC, 'Report of the Detailed Findings of the Commission of Inquiry on Human Rights in the Democratic People's Republic of Korea' (2014) UN Doc. A/HRC/25/CRP.1 para. 403; *Husband of Maria Fanny Suarez de Guerrero v. Colombia, Decision as to the admissibility* (n. 1707) para. 13.2. Last but not least, wide support can also be found in reports of former Special Rapporteurs, see e.g. UNGA, 'Interim Report of the Special Rapporteur, Philip Alston, on Extrajudicial, Summary or Arbitrary Executions' (n. 1702) paras 39–44; UN HRC, 'Report of the Special Rapporteur on Extrajudicial, Summary or Arbitrary Executions, Philip Alston' (2010) UN Doc. A/HRC/14/24/Add.6 paras 32–33; UN HRC, 'Report of the Special Rapporteur on Extrajudicial, Summary or Arbitrary Executions, Christof Heyns' (n. 109) para. 42; UN HRC, 'Report of the Special Rapporteur on Extrajudicial, Summary or Arbitrary Executions, Christof Heyns' (n. 109) paras 70–72.

conditions for non-arbitrary deprivations of the right to life. Whereas IHL allows status-based targeting, meaning individuals are targeted because they belong to a specific (armed) group, the intentional lethal force under HRL can never be permissible outside the narrow context of temporally imminent threats to life. Hence, outside the context of the conduct of hostilities, operations undertaken by peace forces in response to PoC threats can never be based on 'shoot to kill' policies where intentional lethal force would be directed against actors based on their behaviour other than specific and temporally constrained threats to the life of another person.[1758] Examples of permissible intentional lethal force include a peacekeeper who shoots a sniper in the chest who is about to shoot another peacekeeper patrolling the streets or a peacekeeper who fires their rifle at the head of a suspected suicide bomber who is about to detonate a bomb in a crowded IDPs camp likely killing dozens of civilians.

3.1.1.4. Principle of precautions

Lethal force constitutes a violation of a person's right to life if death could have been avoided by taking reasonable precautionary measures. Military, security, and police personnel must be adequately trained and equipped to ensure they act in accordance with the right to life, implying that, for example, they are equipped with various types of weapons and ammunition, including alternative means to firearms, and that they are trained to use such alternatives.[1759] According to the ECtHR, any intervention or operation must also be adequately planned, organised, and controlled 'so as to minimise, to the greatest extent possible, recourse to lethal force and human losses.'[1760] It is essential to distinguish the principle of precautions under HRL from the principle of precautions in attack and the principle of precautions against the effects of attacks under IHL. Part III, Sections 3.2.4.1 and 3.2.4.2, discusses the latter two principles.

3.1.1.5. Principle of accountability

According to the accountability principle, any use-of-force incident in which someone is killed or seriously injured must be reported to superiors immediately.

1758 On shoot to kill, see sources referred to in Part III, Section 2.1.2.2, fn. 1399.

1759 See e.g. *Case of Güleç v. Turkey, Judgment* (n. 1715) paras 71 and 73. See also UN HRC, 'General Comment No. 36 on the Right to Life' (n. 82) paras 13–14.

1760 *Case of Finogenov and Others v. Russia, Judgment* (n. 1733) para. 208. See also earlier case law of the ECtHR on this point: *Case of McCann and Others v. the United Kingdom, Judgment* (n. 1038) paras 146–150, 194; *Case of Ergi v. Turkey, Judgment* (1998) ECtHR App. No. 66/1997/850/1057 para. 79; *Case of Andronicou and Constantinou v. Cyprus, Judgment* (n. 1038) paras 172, 181, 186, and 192–193; *Case of Ahmet Özkan and Others v. Turkey, Judgment* (2004) ECtHR App. No. 21689/93 paras 297, 307–308; *Case of Isayeva, Yusupova and Bazayeva v. Russia, Judgment* (n. 1735) paras 171 and 199; *Case of Isayeva v. Russia, Judgment* (n. 1735) paras 175 and 200; *Case of Tagayeva and Others v. Russia, Judgment* (n. 1739) paras 562 and 573.

In addition, lethal or other life-threatening incidents must give rise to an adequate review and investigation and, if necessary, the criminal prosecution of perpetrators.[1761] Finally, victims must also have access to justice, including but not limited to non-judicial redress mechanisms.[1762]

3.1.2. *Use of less-lethal force: determining the scope of possible actions*

Not all force to protect civilians is lethal in nature. As with lethal force, UN (mandated) peace forces can use less-lethal force to protect civilians in so far as it complies with the following HRL principles: (i) legality; (ii) necessity; (iii) proportionality; (iv) precaution; and (v) accountability:

(i) Principle of legality: the legal basis for the use of less-lethal force by UN (mandated) peace forces can be provided for in the mission mandate, enshrined in the relevant UNSC resolutions, and subsequently detailed in mission-specific ROE.
(ii) Principle of necessity: less-lethal force can only be used when it is necessary to do so for a legitimate aim, e.g. PoC, as determined by the UN Security Council. For force to be necessary, it must be a last resort that can only be used if less drastic means are unavailable or manifestly unreasonable to protect the civilians in question. A graduated response involves, for example, as appropriate, a verbal warning, show of force, and only then less-lethal force (and, in the last instance, lethal force, see above). If force is unavoidable, the amount of force must not exceed the minimum necessary in the circumstances, and force should only be used as long as necessary to achieve the legitimate aim. Harm and injury must always be kept to a minimum.
(iii) Principle of proportionality: the nature and degree of less-lethal force used must be commensurate to the seriousness of the threat and the legitimate aim to be achieved.[1763]
(iv) Principle of precaution: this principle requires that personnel contributing to an operation be adequately trained and equipped and that those operations be carefully planned, organised, and controlled to prevent or at least minimise the use of force.

1761 For relevant case law of the ECtHR, see e.g. *Case of McCann and Others v. the United Kingdom, Judgment* (n. 1038) paras 161–164; *Case of Al-Skeini and Others v. the United Kingdom, Judgment* (n. 1377) paras 163–177. For relevant case law of the IACtHR on this principle, see e.g. *Case of Montero-Aranguren et al. (Detention Center of Catia) v. Venezuela, Judgment* (n. 1702) paras 79–84; *Case of Zambrano Vélez et al. v. Ecuador, Judgment* (n. 1702) paras 108–110.

1762 White, 'The Use of Weapons in Peace Operations' (n. 41) 224.

1763 Gaggioli, 'The Use of Force in Armed Conflicts Conduct of Hostilities, Law Enforcement, and Self-Defense' (n. 643) 66.

(v) Principle of accountability: an appropriate accountability system must be in place for any use of force that does not comply with the above-mentioned principles.

Any such use of less-lethal force must also comply with any additional legal rules and principles (think of the right not to be subjected to inhumane or degrading treatment or the rules concerning the protection of private property) that apply in the circumstances.

3.2. USE OF (LETHAL) FORCE TO PROTECT CIVILIANS THAT HAS A CLEAR NEXUS TO AN ONGOING ARMED CONFLICT

If force is used in a situation which has a clear nexus to an ongoing armed conflict, that use of force is not only governed by HRL but also by IHL. For example, for any use of lethal force with a clear nexus to an armed conflict, the rules of IHL must be used to assess what constitutes an 'arbitrary' deprivation of the right to life.[1764] Accordingly, in the conduct of hostilities, a direct attack against a civilian, an indiscriminate attack which does not distinguish between military objectives and civilians or civilian objects, and an attack against military objectives causing excessive loss of civilian life all constitute violations of the right to life.

IHL is based on a number of principles reflected in the predominant IHL treaties (including the 1907 Hague Convention IV and its Regulations, the Geneva Conventions I–IV, and the Additional Protocols I–II) and are part of customary IHL. In the first place, IHL is underpinned by the need for a balance between the foundational principles of humanity and military necessity. From the foundational principles of military necessity and humanity flow a number of fundamental IHL principles, including the principles of distinction, proportionality, precautions in attack and against the effects of attacks, and the prohibition of superfluous injury and unnecessary suffering.

These general principles are, in turn, translated into more detailed rules of IHL, as included in IHL treaties and customary IHL. These three sources of IHL primarily govern the use of force for PoC by UN (mandated) peace operations. While the fundamental principles of IHL are discussed below, a discussion of the more detailed rules included in IHL treaties and customary IHL is beyond the scope of this book.

1764 For sources substantiating this position, see Part III, Section 3, fn. 1695.

3.2.1. *Balancing military necessity and humanity*

As IHL seeks to limit the effects of armed conflict and minimise human suffering, a careful balance is sought between military necessity and humanitarian concerns. On the one hand, IHL recognises that it may be militarily necessary for belligerents to cause death, injury, and damage to weaken and ultimately defeat an enemy. But on the other hand, belligerents have an obligation to respect and protect people (whether combatants or non-combatants) and their property and, as such, to treat them humanely.

Considerations of humanity impose limits on the means and methods of warfare and protect both those who take part directly in hostilities and those who do not or no longer take an active part. As such, belligerent parties are under the general obligation to protect and respect those under their control and treat them humanely without any adverse distinction, and hence to refrain from acts that are inhumane, even if there is no express rule prohibiting such acts. Pursuant to the Martens Clause, first included in the preambles of the 1899 Hague Convention II and the 1907 Hague Convention IV, and subsequently included in a more modernised version in Article 1(2) of Additional Protocol I:

> In cases not covered by this Protocol or by other international agreements, civilians and combatants remain under the protection and authority of the principles of international law derived from established custom, from the principles of humanity and from the dictates of public conscience.

The Martens Clause illustrates that the mere absence of an explicit rule on the subject does not necessarily mean that certain acts are not forbidden.[1765] In the *Corfu Channel* case, the ICJ has adopted this rationale by holding that Albania violated certain obligations based on 'certain general and well recognized principles, namely: elementary considerations of humanity, even more exacting in peace than in war.'[1766] The *Corfu Channel* dictum was later confirmed in the *Nicaragua* judgment[1767] and the advisory opinion on the *Legality of the Threat or*

1765 Michael N Schmitt, 'Military Necessity and Humanity in International Humanitarian Law: Preserving the Delicate Balance Commemorative Pieces' (2009) 50 Virginia Journal of International Law 795, 800.

1766 *Corfu Channel (United Kingdom of Great Britain and Northern Ireland v. Albania), Judgment (Merits)* (n. 1671) 22 (Particularly, the ICJ noted that '[t]he obligations incumbent upon the Albanian authorities consisted in notifying, for the benefit of shipping in general, the existence of a minefield in Albanian territorial waters and in warning the approaching British warships of the imminent danger to which the minefield exposed them. Such obligations are based, not on the Hague Convention of 1907, No. VTII, which is applicable in time of war, but on certain general and well-recognized principles, namely: elementary considerations of humanity, even more exacting in peace than in war; the principle of the freedom of maritime communication; and every State's obligation not to allow knowingly its territory to be used for acts contrary to the rights of other States').

1767 *Case Concerning Military and Paramilitary Activities in and against Nicaragua (Nicaragua v. United States of America), Judgment (Merits)* (n. 615) paras 215 and 218 (The ICJ added

Use of Nuclear Weapons.[1768] Furthermore, in the case of *Prosecutor v. Kupreškić et al.*, the ICTY confirmed that 'the 'elementary considerations of humanity' rightly emphasised by the [ICJ] in the *Corfu Channel*, *Nicaragua* and *Legality of the Threat or Use of Nuclear* cases should be fully used when interpreting and applying loose international rules, on the basis that they are illustrative of a general principle of international law.'[1769] Accordingly, the mere absence of an explicit IHL rule on the subject does not necessarily justify action based on military necessity.[1770] Humanity must be respected just as much in the conduct of hostilities.[1771]

While the Martens Clause is only applicable when the written law is silent,[1772] the principle of humanity is further reflected in a number of treaty provisions. Article 12 of Geneva Conventions I and II, for example, determines that the wounded and sick in the armed forces in the field, as well as the wounded, sick, and shipwrecked members of the armed forces at sea 'shall be treated humanely and cared for by the Part[y][ies] to the conflict in whose power they may be, without any adverse distinction founded on sex, race, nationality, religion, political opinions, or any other similar criteria.' Article 16 of Geneva Convention III does not explicitly refer to the principle of humanity but does state that POWs 'shall be treated alike by the Detaining Power, without any adverse distinction based on race, nationality, religious belief or political opinions, or any other distinction founded on similar criteria.' Civilian persons protected under Geneva Convention IV[1773] must also 'at all times be humanely treated, and shall be protected especially against all acts of violence or threats thereof and

---

that it considered it justified to judge the conduct of the US according to the fundamental general principles of international humanitarian law, which result, *inter alia*, from 'the laws of humanity and the dictates of the public conscience').

1768 *Legality of the Threat or Use of Nuclear Weapons, Advisory opinion* (n. 1231) para. 78 (According to the ICJ, 'a great many rules of humanitarian law applicable in armed conflict are so fundamental to the respect of the human person and "elementary considerations of humanity" as the Court put it in its Judgment of 9 April 1949 in the *Corfu Channel* case [I.C.J. Reports 1949, p. 22]).'

1769 *Prosecutor v. Kupreškić et al., Trial chamber judgment* (n. 1673) para. 524.

1770 Melzer, *International Humanitarian Law: A Comprehensive Introduction* (n. 675) 25; Schmitt, 'Military Necessity and Humanity in International Humanitarian Law: Preserving the Delicate Balance Commemorative Pieces' (n. 1765) 800.

1771 Schmitt, 'Military Necessity and Humanity in International Humanitarian Law: Preserving the Delicate Balance Commemorative Pieces' (n. 1765) 800.

1772 *Ibid.* 801.

1773 Art. 4 of Geneva Convention IV provides a definition of 'protected persons':
'Persons protected by the Convention are those who, at a given moment and in any manner whatsoever, find themselves, in case of a conflict or occupation, in the hands of a Party to the conflict or Occupying Power of which they are not nationals.
Nationals of a State which is not bound by the Convention are not protected by it. Nationals of a neutral State who find themselves in the territory of a belligerent State, and nationals of a co-belligerent State, shall not be regarded as protected persons while the State of which they are nationals has normal diplomatic representation in the State in whose hands they are.
The provisions of Part II are, however, wider in application, as defined in Art. 13.

against insults and public curiosity.' Victims of IACs who are in the power of a party to the conflict and who do not benefit from more favourable treatment under the Geneva Conventions I–IV or under Additional Protocol I must equally 'be treated humanely in all circumstances and shall enjoy, as a minimum, the protection provided by this Article without any adverse distinction based upon race, colour, sex, language, religion or belief, political or other opinion, national or social origin, wealth, birth or other status, or on any other similar criteria' pursuant to Article 75 of Additional Protocol I. Last but not least, Common Article 3(1) of the Geneva Conventions I–IV sets forth the following:[1774]

> Persons taking no active part in the hostilities, including members of armed forces who have laid down their arms and those placed 'hors de combat' by sickness, wounds, detention, or any other cause, shall in all circumstances be treated *humanely*, without any adverse distinction founded on race, colour, religion or faith, sex, birth or wealth, or any other similar criteria.

The principle of humanity is counterbalanced by the principle of military necessity. The 1863 Lieber Code contains the traditional definition of the principle of military necessity: '[m]ilitary necessity, as understood by modern civilized nations, consists in the necessity of those measures which are indispensable for securing the ends of the war, and which are lawful according to the modern law and usages of war.'[1775] This definition presupposes two cumulative conditions for the permissibility of violence in armed conflict: (i) its legality under modern law of war and usages of war; and (ii) the necessity to achieve the aim of war.[1776] As demonstrated by Melzer, contemporary military manuals, as well as case law and contemporary legal doctrine, have generally confirmed the interpretation of the principle of military necessity given in the 1863 Lieber Code.[1777]

The principle of military necessity is both permissive and restrictive. It is permissive in the sense that it permits measures that cause death and destruction because they are deemed necessary from a military point of view to ensure the 'ends of war' (without justifying violations of IHL).[1778] The principle of military

---

Persons protected by the Geneva Convention for the Amelioration of the Condition of the Wounded and Sick in Armed Forces in the Field of August 12, 1949, or by the Geneva Convention for the Amelioration of the Condition of Wounded, Sick and Shipwrecked Members of Armed Forces at Sea of August 12, 1949, or by the Geneva Convention relative to the Treatment of Prisoners of War of August 12, 1949, shall not be considered as protected persons within the meaning of the present Convention.'

1774 Emphasis added. See also Art. 2(1) and 4(1) of Additional Protocol II.

1775 Art. 14 of the 1863 Lieber Code (the United States, 'Instructions for the Government of Armies of the United States in the Field' (1863), https://ihl-databases.icrc.org/applic/ihl/ihl.nsf/ART/110-20014?OpenDocument, accessed 17 August 2022).

1776 See also Melzer, *Targeted Killing in International Law* (n. 1399) 283.

1777 For an overview, see *Ibid.* 283–285.

1778 Term used in Art. 14 of the 1863 Lieber Code (the United States (n. 1775)).

necessity is also restrictive in that it does not give belligerents *carte blanche* to wage war as they see fit. The principle limits the lawful use of force to that necessary to achieve a military objective and prohibits the use of excessive force to achieve this objective.

The balance between military necessity and humanitarian considerations underpins every IHL standard, whether customary or treaty-based, such that neither principle individually justifies a deviation from its provisions, unless the law expressly provides otherwise.[1779] As such, it is only where an IHL rule expressly provides for the invocation of military necessity as a basis for a departure from the normally applicable norm that such arguments may be invoked, and then only under the conditions set out by the IHL rule in question.[1780] Each norm reflects the balance between military necessity and humanity differently.[1781] The degree of protection afforded to civilians in armed conflict depends on where the balance lies between the permissive function of military necessity on the one hand and considerations of humanity on the other.[1782] For example, Article 54(2) of Additional Protocol I prohibits attacks against objects 'indispensable to the survival of the civilian population.' Article 54(5) of Additional Protocol I then goes on to state: '[i]n recognition of the vital requirements of any Party to the conflict in the defence of its national territory against invasion, derogation from the prohibitions contained in paragraph 2 [to attack, destroy, remove or render useless objects indispensable to the survival of the civilian population] may be made by a Party to the conflict within such territory under its own control where required by imperative *military necessity*.'[1783]

From the foundational principles of military necessity and humanity flow a number of fundamental IHL principles outlined below.

3.2.2. Principle of distinction

A cardinal reflection of the necessary balance between military necessity and humanity is found in the general principle of distinction. It is one of the cornerstones of IHL, according to which a distinction must be upheld at all times between civilians and combatants and between civilian objects and military objectives. Accordingly, attacks cannot be directed against civilians (unless and

---

1779 Yoram Dinstein, 'Military Necessity', *Max Planck Encyclopedia of Public International law* (Oxford Public International Law 2015) para. 7; Schmitt, 'Military Necessity and Humanity in International Humanitarian Law: Preserving the Delicate Balance Commemorative Pieces' (n. 1765) 801.

1780 Dinstein, 'Military Necessity' (n. 1779) para. 8; Lawrence Hill-Cawthorne, 'The Role of Necessity in International Humanitarian and Human Rights Law' (2014) 47 Israel Law Review 225, 231.

1781 Dinstein, 'Military Necessity' (n. 1779) para. 7.

1782 Lamont (n. 1524) 189.

1783 Emphasis added.

for such time as they take a direct part in hostilities) and civilian objects (unless and for such time as they are military objectives).

3.2.2.1. Distinction between civilians and combatants

The principle of distinction between civilians and combatants (in its generic meaning) is codified in Additional Protocols I–II. While Article 48 of Additional Protocol I requires distinguishing between civilians and combatants at all times,[1784] Article 51(1) and (2) of Additional Protocol I sets forth that the 'civilian population and civilians shall enjoy general protection' and 'shall not be the object of attack.'[1785] Not one State has made a reservation to these provisions.[1786] Furthermore, Article 51(3) of Additional Protocol I foresees that '[c]ivilians shall enjoy [...] protection [...], unless and for such time as they take a direct part in hostilities.' Article 13(1) and (2) of Additional Protocol II similarly sets forth that the civilian population and individual civilians in NIACs 'shall enjoy general protection' and, as such, prohibits making the civilian population and individual civilians 'the object of attack.' In addition, the 2005 ICRC Study on Customary IHL has identified the principle of distinction between civilians and combatants as a rule of customary international law that applies equally in IACs and NIACs.[1787]

Under the principle of distinction, force against people who are legitimate targets is allowed by default and limited only by exception.[1788] Therein it differs radically from HRL. For example, under IHL, lethal force can always be used against legitimate targets (e.g. combatants or civilians directly participating in hostilities), subject to the IHL conditions for targeting. This is in contrast with HRL whereby the use of lethal force is always subject to strict temporal (and often

---

[1784] Art. 48 of Additional Protocol I reads as follows: 'In order to ensure respect for and protection of the civilian population and civilian objects, the Parties to the conflict shall at all times distinguish between the civilian population and combatants and between civilian objects and military objectives and accordingly shall direct their operations only against military objectives.'

[1785] According to Art. 51 (1) and (2) of Additional Protocol I: '1. The civilian population and individual civilians shall enjoy general protection against dangers arising from military operations. To give effect to this protection, the following rules, which are additional to other applicable rules of international law, shall be observed in all circumstances; 2. The civilian population as such, as well as individual civilians, shall not be the object of attack. Acts or threats of violence the primary purpose of which is to spread terror among the civilian population are prohibited.'

[1786] Henckaerts and Doswald-Beck (n. 91) 4.

[1787] Henckaerts and Doswald-Beck (n. 91) Rule 1, pp. 3–8 (as quoted above, see Part II, Section 3.2.2.1, fn. 921). However, see also Rule 6, pp. 19–24 (as quoted above, see Part III, Section 3.2.3.1, fn. 990) and Rule 47, pp. 164–170 ('Attacking persons who are recognised as hors de combat is prohibited. A person hors de combat is: (a) anyone who is in the power of an adverse party; (b) anyone who is defenceless because of unconsciousness, shipwreck, wounds or sickness; or (c) anyone who clearly expresses an intention to surrender; provided he or she abstains from any hostile act and does not attempt to escape').

[1788] Lamont (n. 1524) 198.

also geographical) conditions. Furthermore, while HRL never allows individuals to be targeted because they belong to a specific (armed) group), IHL allows combatants to be targeted at any time on the basis of their status as members of the armed forces, even if they do not pose a specific and present threat.

In a generic sense, combatants are members of the fighting forces of belligerent parties, while civilians are persons who are not members of such fighting forces. The legal categorisation of persons in the context of IACs and NIACs is, however, a lot more complex and, therefore, has not only been the subject of endless discussions but has also given rise to a wealth of literature.[1789] A detailed discussion is not required to formulate answers to the research questions underlying this study, so we can limit ourselves to a brief overview.

In the context of IACs, all members of the armed forces of a party to the conflict are combatants, except medical and religious personnel.[1790] According to Article 43(1) of Additional Protocol I, the armed forces of a party to a conflict 'consist of all organized armed forces, groups and units which are under a command responsible to that [p]arty for the conduct of its subordinates.' It is thereby irrelevant whether that party is represented by a government or an authority recognised by an opposing party. Such armed forces must be subject to 'an internal disciplinary system' which, *inter alia*, must enforce compliance with IHL.[1791] Qualifying as a combatant also confers the status of a combatant, which means that the combatant has the right to take part directly in hostilities for which they cannot be criminally prosecuted or brought to court (also known as the combatant's privilege) but loses the protection from direct attack (attached to civilian status). Combatant status is also given to participants in a *levée en masse* if they carry arms openly and respect the laws and customs of armed conflict.[1792] Persons protected from direct attacks include civilians not taking a direct part in hostilities,[1793] medical, religious, and civilian defence personnel of the armed forces (as long as they do not commit acts harmful to the adversary),[1794] as well

---

1789 To name just a few: Yoram Dinstein, *The Conduct of Hostilities under the Law of International Armed Conflict* (3rd edn., Cambridge University Press 2016) 41–71; Anisseh Van Engeland, *Civilian or Combatant?: A Challenge for the 21st Century* (Oxford University Press 2011). See also a number of relevant chapters in the following books: Andrew Clapham and Paola Gaeta (eds), *The Oxford Handbook of International Law in Armed Conflict* (Oxford University Press 2014); Dieter Fleck and Michael Bothe (eds), *The Handbook of International Humanitarian Law* (3rd edn., Oxford University Press 2013).

1790 See Art. 43(2) of Additional Protocol I. See also Henckaerts and Doswald-Beck (n. 91) Rule 3, pp. 11–12 ('All members of the armed forces of a party to the conflict are combatants, except medical and religious personnel').

1791 Art. 43(1) of Additional Protocol I.

1792 See e.g. Art. 4(a)(6) of Geneva Convention III. See also Henckaerts and Doswald-Beck (n. 91) 386–387.

1793 See Art. 51(3) of Additional Protocol I. For an analysis of the customary nature of this rule in IACs, see Henckaerts and Doswald-Beck (n. 91) Rule 6, pp. 19–21 (as quoted above, see Part III, Section 3.2.3.1, fn. 990).

1794 With regard to medical and religious personnel, see Art. 24–26 of the Geneva Convention I, Art. 36 of the Geneva Convention II, and Art. 20 of the Geneva Convention IV. With

as all persons *hors de combat* (as long as they do not commit hostile acts or attempts to escape).[1795]

Although conventional IHL for NIACs contains few provisions on the categorisation of people, it is now recognised that the main rules and principles applicable in IAC situations have acquired the status of customary IHL and apply in NIAC situations. Just like in IACs, the category of persons protected from direct attacks includes civilians not taking a direct part in hostilities,[1796] medical and religious personnel of the armed forces (as long as they do not commit acts harmful to the adversary),[1797] as well as all persons *hors de combat* (as long as they do not commit hostile acts or attempts to escape).[1798] Yet, as already discussed in Part II, Section 3.2.3.1, IHL does not recognise the status of 'combatant' in NIACs, and Additional Protocol II does not contain a definition of 'civilian'.[1799] Therefore, the 2009 ICRC Guidelines on Direct Participation in Hostilities have suggested (albeit not without controversy) that civilians are those who are neither members of organised armed groups nor members of the armed forces of a State party to the conflict.[1800] Members of organised armed groups are only those persons who hold a 'continuous combat function' and thus do not include those persons who perform other tasks on behalf of the organised armed groups (e.g. cooking or driving).[1801] Under this view, the latter group must be considered civilians and, as such, are entitled to protection against direct attack unless and for such time as they take a direct part in hostilities.[1802]

In the context of UN (mandated) peace operations, when IHL applies *de jure*, the principle of distinction must be strictly upheld at all times, and exceptions

---

regard to civil defence personnel, see Art. 67(1) Additional Protocol I. For an analysis of the customary nature of the rules with regard to medical and religious personnel in IACs, see *ibid.* Rule 25, pp. 79–80 ('Medical personnel exclusively assigned to medical duties must be respected and protected in all circumstances. They lose their protection if they commit, outside their humanitarian function, acts harmful to the enemy'); and Rule 27, pp. 88–89 ('Religious personnel exclusively assigned to religious duties must be respected and protected in all circumstances. They lose their protection if they commit, outside their humanitarian function, acts harmful to the enemy').

1795 See Art. 41(1) of Additional Protocol I. For an analysis of the customary nature of this rule in IACs, see *ibid.* Rule 47, pp. 164–165 (as quoted above, see fn. 1787). See also Melzer, Targeted killing in international law, p. 304.

1796 See Art. 13 of Additional Protocol II. For an analysis of the customary nature of this rule in NIACs, see *ibid.* Rule 6, p. 21 (as quoted above, see Part III, Section 3.2.3.1, fn. 990).

1797 See Art. 9(1) of Additional Protocol II. For an analysis of the customary nature of this rule in NIACs, see *ibid.* Rule 25, pp. 80–81 and Rule 27, pp. 89–90 (as quoted above, see fn. 1794).

1798 See Common Art. 3(1) of Geneva Conventions I–IV, Art. 4(1) and 7(1) of Additional Protocol II. For an analysis of the customary nature of this rule in NIACs, see *ibid.* Rule pp. 47, 165–166 (as quoted above, see fn. 1787). See also Melzer, *Targeted Killing in International Law* (n. 1399) 314.

1799 Henckaerts and Doswald-Beck (n. 91) 19.

1800 Melzer, 'ICRC Interpretative Guidance on the Notion of Direct Participation in Hostilities under International Humanitarian Law' (n. 993) 27.

1801 *Ibid.*

1802 *Ibid.*

can only be made as provided for by IHL itself. While peremptory norms prohibit any form of derogation, they may allow for exceptions, as they find themselves at the same level of generality as the rules they alter.[1803] In the Introductory Chapter to this study, it has been discussed that a UN Senior Legal Advisor has maintained that under the UN's current approach, the mandate is the key factor that determines the circumstances in which their forces can use lethal force and, as a consequence, a person who would not be a legitimate target under IHL, may become an authorised military target of a UN peace operation.[1804] This statement is highly problematic if UN peace forces are commanded to use lethal force against certain persons, in *disregard* for the *jus cogens* principle of distinction between combatants and civilians and the *jus cogens* right not to be arbitrarily deprived of one's life.[1805] A UNSC mandate can never be invoked to justify using lethal force in the conduct of hostilities that violates the peremptory norms of HRL or IHL.[1806]

3.2.2.2. Distinction between civilian objects and military objectives

As in the case of persons, force against objects that constitute legitimate targets is allowed by default and limited only by exception. The principle of distinction between civilian objects and military objectives is codified in Articles 48 and 52(1) and (2) of Additional Protocol I. While Article 48 of Additional Protocol I requires to distinguish at all times between civilian objects and military objectives,[1807] Article 52(1) and (2) of Additional Protocol I sets forth that '[c]ivilian objects shall not be the object of attack or of reprisals'; attacks must be strictly limited to military objectives.[1808] In addition, the 2005 ICRC Study on Customary IHL has identified the principle of distinction between civilian

---

1803 As already explained in Part II, Section 2.1.1 when discussing 'consent' as a legal basis for military operations. See also Helmersen (n. 803) 175.

1804 Wills, 'Use of Deadly Force by Peacekeepers Operating Outside of Armed Conflict Situations: What Laws Apply?' (n. 18) 691. As also referred to in the Introductory Chapter, Section 1.

1805 For sources defending the claim that the right to life is a *jus cogens* norm, see Part III, Section 2.1.2.2, fn. 1397. As regards the peremptory nature of the fundamental principles of IHL, see Part III, Section 2.2.3.2.

1806 See Part III, Sections 2.1.4.1, 2.1.4.2, and 2.2.1.3.

1807 Art. 48 of Additional Protocol I has already been quoted above, see Part III, Section 3.2.1, fn. 1784.

1808 According to Art. 52(1) and 52(2) of Additional Protocol I: '1. Civilian objects shall not be the object of attack or of reprisals. Civilian objects are all objects which are not military objectives as defined in paragraph 2; 2. Attacks shall be limited strictly to military objectives. In so far as objects are concerned, military objectives are limited to those objects which by their nature, location, purpose or use make an effective contribution to military action and whose total or partial destruction, capture or neutralization, in the circumstances ruling at the time, offers a definite military advantage.'

objects and military objectives as a rule of customary international law, which applies equally in IACs and NIACs.[1809]

Civilian objects are negatively defined as 'all objects that are not military objectives.'[1810] Article 52(2) of Additional Protocol I defines 'military objectives' as 'objects which by their nature, location, purpose or use make an effective contribution to military action and whose partial or total destruction, capture or neutralisation, in the circumstances ruling at the time, offers a definite military advantage.' Additional Protocol II does not contain a similar definition of military objectives, but the definition outlined in Article 52(2) of Additional Protocol I is now considered to reflect a rule of customary IHL which applies in both IACs and NIACs.[1811] According to the 2005 ICRC Study on Customary IHL, there is no immediate conflict of practice regarding IACs or NIACs, in the sense that no other definition of a military objective has been officially put forward.[1812]

To qualify as a military objective, an object must meet the following two cumulative criteria:[1813]

First, the object must contribute 'effectively' to the adversary's 'military action' by its 'nature' (i.e. the object has an inherent characteristic or attribute which contributes to the military action of the enemy, such as a warship or military barracks), 'location' (i.e. the object is a specific area of land that has special importance to military operations of the enemy, such as a heavily forested area in which troops are hiding), 'purpose' (i.e. the enemy intends to use the object in the future, such as the effective transformation of a car factory into a factory that can make components for military aircraft), or 'use' (i.e. the enemy makes actual use of an object that, on the face of it, is civilian in nature, such as the use of a civilian broadcast facility for military broadcasting).[1814]

1809 Henckaerts and Doswald-Beck (n. 91) Rule 7, pp. 25–29 (as quoted above, see Part II, Section 3.2.3.1, fn. 989). However, see also Rule 10, pp. 34–36 ('Civilian objects are protected against attack, unless and for such time as they are military objectives').

1810 See Art. 52(1) of Additional Protocol I. For an analysis of the customary nature of this rule in both IACs and NIACs, see *ibid.* Rule 9, pp. 32–34 (as quoted above, see Part II, Section 3.2.3.1, fn. 988).

1811 *Ibid.* Rule 8, pp. 29–32 ('In so far as objects are concerned, military objectives are limited to those objects which by their nature, location, purpose or use make an effective contribution to military action and whose partial or total destruction, capture or neutralisation, in the circumstances ruling at the time, offers a definite military advantage').

1812 *Ibid.* 31.

1813 The Spanish authentic version raises some doubts as to whether the criteria are cumulative or alternative, yet this approach is demonstrably incorrect, see Marco Sassòli, 'Military Objectives', *Max Planck Encyclopedia of Public International law* (Oxford Public International Law 2015) para. 5; Agnieszka Jachec-Neale, *The Concept of Military Objectives in International Law and Targeting Practice* (First issued in paperback, Routledge 2016) 113–114.

1814 Sandoz, Swinarski and Zimmermann (n. 85) paras 2020–2022; Harvard School of Public Health (ed), *Commentary to the HPCR Manual on International Law Applicable to Air and Missile Warfare, Elaborated by the Drafting Committee of the Group of Experts under the Supervision of Professor Yoram Dinstein* (Cambridge University Press 2013) 116–119.

Second, the object's destruction, capture, or neutralisation yields a 'definite military advantage' to the attacker. The term 'definite' indicates that the advantage must, as Melzer puts it, be 'concrete and perceptible, and not merely hypothetical or speculative.'[1815] Decisions on targets must be based on the circumstances 'ruling at the time' and hence should not be based on outdated assessments of the past or unsubstantiated projections about future developments.[1816] Any attack contemplated must offer a clear 'military advantage' under the prevailing circumstances.[1817] The term 'military advantage' implies that the advantage cannot be solely political, economic, or moral.[1818] It must impact the enemy's military operational or tactical level.[1819] The 1868 St. Petersberg Declaration set forth '[t]hat the only legitimate object which States should endeavour to accomplish during war is to weaken the military forces of the enemy.'[1820] An attack can be expected to have a 'military advantage' if the enemy forces are weakened by the attack, whether by killing or wounding enemy personnel or destroying or damaging enemy military equipment or if it prevents the enemy from the use of a certain area.[1821] 'Military advantage' may also exist when the attack allows one's own forces to gain ground or superiority in the air or at sea.[1822] Although the term 'attack' is used here in the singular, it is generally understood that one must consider the military advantage expected from the attack as a whole and not just from individual or specific elements of the attack. In that regard, a number of States (including Australia, Belgium, Canada, France, Germany, Italy, the Netherlands, New Zealand, Spain, and the UK) have explicitly declared that the expression 'military advantage' used in Articles 51, 52, and 57[1823] of Additional Protocol I refers to 'the advantage anticipated from the attack considered as a whole and not only from isolated or particular parts of the attack.'[1824] For example, as pointed out in the 2013 Commentary to the

---

1815 Melzer, *International Humanitarian Law: A Comprehensive Introduction* (n. 675) 92. See also Sandoz, Swinarski and Zimmermann (n. 85) para. 2024.

1816 Melzer, *International Humanitarian Law: A Comprehensive Introduction* (n. 675) 92; Marco Sassòli, 'Legitimate Targets of Attacks under International Humanitarian Law', *Background Paper prepared for the Informal High-Level Expert Meeting on the Reaffirmation and Development of International Humanitarian Law, 27–29 January 2003, Cambridge* (Program on Humanitarian Policy and Conflict Research at Harvard University) 3.

1817 Melzer, *International Humanitarian Law: A Comprehensive Introduction* (n. 675) 92.

1818 Harvard School of Public Health (n. 1814) 36.

1819 *Ibid.* 36 and 99.

1820 Declaration Renouncing the Use, in Time of War, of Explosive Projectiles Under 400 Grammes Weight (adopted 29 November 1868, entered into force 11 December 1868) 138 CTS 297 (1986 St. Petersburg Declaration).

1821 Wolff Heintschel von Heinegg, 'Proportionality and Collateral Damage', *Max Planck Encyclopedia of Public International law* (Oxford Public International Law 2015) para. 18.

1822 *Ibid.*

1823 Art. 57 of Additional Protocol I concerns the principle of precautions in attack, as discussed below, see Part III, Section 3.2.4.1.

1824 Julie Gaudreau, 'The Reservations to the Protocols Additional to the Geneva Conventions for the Protection of War Victims' (2003) 849 International Review of the Red Cross 143, 16.

HPCR Manual on International Law Applicable to Air and Missile Warfare, air attacks are often carried out by multiple military aircraft, in which case it would not be appropriate to consider the effect of each individual flight separately.[1825] Rather, it is necessary to consider the attack as a whole. However, this does not mean that the term 'military advantage' should be interpreted too broadly. It should not be confused with the entire armed conflict.[1826]

Whether the term 'military advantage' must be interpreted differently in the context of UN (mandated) peace operations with a PoC mandate is further explored in a case study discussed in Part III, Section 3.3.1.2.

3.2.2.3. Indiscriminate attacks

By virtue of the principle of distinction, indiscriminate attacks are prohibited. This rule is included in Article 51(4) of Additional Protocol I and is equally recognised as a rule of customary IHL in the 2005 ICRC Study on Customary IHL.[1827] Indiscriminate attacks are attacks: (i) that are not directed against a specific military objective; (ii) that use a method or means of combat that cannot be directed against a specific military objective; or (iii) that use a method or means of combat whose effects cannot be mitigated as required by IHL; and which, in either case, are therefore such that military objectives and civilians or civilian objects are hit indiscriminately.[1828] An example of such a non-discriminatory attack is an area-based bombardment in a densely populated area rather than a series of targeted attacks on certain separate military targets situated there.

According to Article 51(5) of Additional Protocol I, the following two types of attacks, among others, are to be considered indiscriminate:

(a) an attack by bombardment by any methods or means which treats as a single military objective a number of clearly separated and distinct military objectives located in a city, town, village or other area containing a similar concentration of civilians or civilian objects; and
(b) an attack which may be expected to cause incidental loss of civilian life, injury to civilians, damage to civilian objects, or a combination thereof, which would be excessive in relation to the concrete and direct military advantage anticipated.

For links to the relevant declarations, see ICRC, 'Treaties, States Parties and Commentaries: Protocol Additional to the Geneva Conventions of 12 August 1949, and Relating to the Protection of Victims of International Armed Conflicts (Protocol I), 8 June 1977' (*ICRC*), https://ihl-databases.icrc.org/applic/ihl/ihl.nsf/States.xsp?xp_viewStates=XPages_NORMStatesParties&xp_treatySelected=470#divArticle90, accessed 24 August 2022.

1825 Harvard School of Public Health (n. 1814) 99.

1826 *Ibid.* 100; Heintschel von Heinegg (n. 1821) para. 20.

1827 Henckaerts and Doswald-Beck (n. 91) Rule 11, pp. 37–40 (as quoted above, see Part II, Section 3.2.2.1, fn. 925).

1828 See also *ibid.* Rule 12, pp. 40–43.

The second type of attack concerns attacks that violate the principle of proportionality, as discussed in the next Section.

3.2.3. *Principle of proportionality*

The infliction of incidental damage to civilians or civilian objects cannot be avoided at all times in armed conflicts. If in planning an attack against a legitimate military target, it becomes clear that there is a risk of *incidental* damage to civilians or civilian objects, an assessment must be made as to whether such damage is in accordance with the principle of proportionality. To avoid doubt, the rule that attacks may not be aimed *directly* at civilians (unless and as long as they are direct participants in hostilities) and civilian objects (unless and as long as they are military objectives) still stands. Those planning or determining to launch an attack against a legitimate military target must, however, also refrain from, or suspend, an attack if such an attack is expected to result in collateral damage that is excessive in relation to the concrete and direct military advantage anticipated.[1829]

The prohibition of excessive collateral damage is set out in Article 51(5)(b) of Additional Protocol I (as quoted in the previous Section) and is reiterated in Article 57(2)(a)(iii) and (b) of the same Protocol (as discussed below, when exploring the principle of precautions in attack, see Part III, Section 3.2.4.1). In addition, the 2005 ICRC Study on Customary IHL has also identified the principle of proportionality as a rule of customary international law, which is equally applicable in both IACs and NIACs.[1830]

Effective application of the principle of proportionality in combat operations, and, more specifically, in UN (mandated) peace operations that are a party to an armed conflict, requires addressing complex issues of interpretation. For example, it is disputed when there may or may not be a 'reasonable expectation' that the attack may cause collateral damage, or what is a 'concrete and direct military advantage', and when the collateral damage is 'excessive' in relation to

---

1829 See also Art. 57(2)(b) of Additional Protocol I as discussed below.

1830 Henckaerts and Doswald-Beck (n. 91) Rule 14, pp. 46–50 (as quoted above, see Part II, Section 3.2.2.1, fn. 925); Rule 18, pp. 58–60 ('Each party to the conflict must do everything feasible to assess whether the attack may be expected to cause incidental loss of civilian life, injury to civilians, damage to civilian objects, or a combination thereof, which would be excessive in relation to the concrete and direct military advantage anticipated'), and Rule 19, pp. 60–62 ('Each party to the conflict must do everything feasible to cancel or suspend an attack if it becomes apparent that the target is not a military objective or that the attack may be expected to cause incidental loss of civilian life, injury to civilians, damage to civilian objects, or a combination thereof, which would be excessive in relation to the concrete and direct military advantage anticipated').

that military advantage. A detailed study of such issues is beyond the scope of this study,[1831] but some aspects can be briefly highlighted here.

An attack is considered disproportional if the collateral damage expected is excessive in relation to the concrete and direct military advantage anticipated. Collateral damage indicates incidental death or injury to civilians or damage or destruction of civilian objects. Discomfort, irritation, stress, fear, or other intangible conditions of the civilian population are not considered.[1832] Whether such collateral damage is 'excessive' depends on the situation. IHL does not provide an objective threshold above which the causing of incidental damage is automatically excessive.[1833] In each individual case, a balance must be struck between the expected collateral damage and the expected military advantage. Indeed, the principle of proportionality aims to limit the damage caused by such attacks by requiring that the consequences of the means and methods of warfare used are not excessive *in relation to* the 'concrete and direct military advantage anticipated.'

According to the 1987 ICRC Commentary on Additional Protocol I, the words 'concrete and direct' impose stricter conditions on the attacker than those implied by the criteria defining military objectives (i.e. a 'definite' military advantage, see Part III, Section 3.2.2.2).[1834] 'Concrete and direct military advantage anticipated' implies that the advantage concerned must be 'substantial and relatively close' while 'advantages which are hardly perceptible and those which would only appear in the long term should be disregarded.'[1835] The term 'military advantage' has already been discussed when defining military objectives.[1836]

Whether collateral damage is 'excessive' relative to the military advantage has nothing to do with comparing the number of civilian casualties or the amount of damage done to civilian objects on one side of the front line compared to the other.[1837] An obvious form of 'excessive' collateral damage would be the destruction of an entire village killing dozens of civilians solely to eliminate one low-ranking enemy officer.[1838] However, it can also be less obvious. For example,

1831 For further literature, see e.g. Heintschel von Heinegg (n. 1821); Amichai Cohen and David Zlotogorski, *Proportionality in International Humanitarian Law: Consequences, Precautions, and Procedures* (Oxford University Press 2020); Yoram Dinstein, 'The Principle of Proportionality' in Kjetil Mujezinovic Larsen, Camilla Guldahl Cooper and Gro Nystuen (eds), *Searching for a 'Principle of Humanity' in International Humanitarian Law* (Cambridge University Press 2013).

1832 Harvard School of Public Health (n. 1814) 20 and 96.

1833 Melzer, *International Humanitarian Law: A Comprehensive Introduction* (n. 675) 101.

1834 Sandoz, Swinarski and Zimmermann (n. 85) para. 2209.

1835 *Ibid.*

1836 See Part III, Section 3.2.2.2.

1837 Dinstein, *The Conduct of Hostilities under the Law of International Armed Conflict* (n. 1789) 154; Heintschel von Heinegg (n. 1821) para. 14.

1838 Sandoz, Swinarski and Zimmermann (n. 85) para. 2213; Dinstein, *The Conduct of Hostilities under the Law of International Armed Conflict* (n. 1789) 156.

a large number of civilian casualties may be considered not 'excessive' if an entire artillery battery can be eliminated. In contrast, one civilian death may be considered 'excessive' because the destruction of a part of the street network around a village that is only occasionally used by the enemy and thus not crucial to the success of a particular campaign provides a negligible direct and concrete military advantage.[1839]

The prohibition of excessive collateral damage only applies if there is a 'reasonable expectation' that the attack may cause excessive collateral damage. The use of the term 'expectation' denotes that there must be a likelihood of collateral damage if the attack is carried out.[1840] Whether that likelihood exists must be assessed from the point of view of the responsible military commander and against the information that is reasonably available at the time. In the case of *Prosecutor v. Galić* case, the ICTY held the following:[1841]

> In determining whether an attack was proportionate it is necessary to examine whether a reasonably well-informed person in the circumstances of the actual perpetrator, making reasonable use of the information available to him or her, could have expected excessive civilian casualties to result from the attack.

Suppose the responsible military commander concludes, in good faith and based on sufficiently reliable information that is reasonably available, that there is no likelihood of excessive collateral damage to civilians, civilian objects, or a combination thereof in relation to the concrete and direct military advantage anticipated. In that case, the attack does not violate the principle of proportionality.[1842] This interpretation does not change even if an *ex post facto* evaluation shows that excessive collateral damage has been caused that could not be reasonably expected.[1843]

Just as there only has to be a 'reasonable expectation' that the attack will cause collateral damage, only the military advantage that is 'anticipated' is taken into account implying that there only has to be a reasonable probability of a military advantage. Similarly, the validity of the use of force cannot be reassessed *ex post*

1839 Dinstein, *The Conduct of Hostilities under the Law of International Armed Conflict* (n. 1789) 150–151 and 156.

1840 Heintschel von Heinegg (n. 1821) para. 13.

1841 *Prosecutor v. Galić, Trial chamber judgment* (2003) ICTY IT-98–29-T para. 58.

1842 The Australian Manual of the Law of Armed Conflict set forth, e.g., that '[t]he commander is required to make a reasonable and honest effort to minimise civilian injuries and damage after they have considered all the available information, and the requirement to complete the mission' (Australia, 'The Manual of the Law of Armed Conflict' (Australian Defence Headquarters 2006) Publication 06.4 para. 13. See also New Zealand, 'Manual of Armed Forces Law' (New Zealand Defence Force 2017) DM 69 (2nd edn.), vol. 4 para. 8.2.2, fn. 3. For additional references to state practice, see e.g. *Prosecutor v. Galić, Trial chamber judgment* (n. 1841) para. 58, fn. 109 and 110. See also Heintschel von Heinegg (n. 1821) para. 13.

1843 Australia (n. 1842) para. 5.39.

facto if it turns out that the concrete and direct military advantage did not occur after all. It is the responsible military commander that must assess, in good faith and on the basis of sufficiently reliable information that is reasonably available, whether there is a concrete and direct military advantage.[1844]

Whether the principle of proportionality must be interpreted differently in the context of UN (mandated) peace operations with a PoC mandate is further explored in a case study discussed in Part III, Section 3.3.1.2.

3.2.4. *Principles of precautions in attack and against the effects of attacks*

Pursuant to Article 57(1) of Additional Protocol I, '[i]n the conduct of military operations, constant care shall be taken to spare the civilian population, civilians and civilian objects.' This obligation rests on both the attacking party and the party being attacked. First, the principle of precautions in attack imposes the obligation upon the attacking party to take all feasible precautions to avoid, and in any event minimise, inflicting incidental death, injury, and destruction on civilians and civilian objects (see Article 57(1) of Additional Protocol I). Second, the principle of precautions against the effects of attacks imposes the obligation upon the party being attacked to take all necessary precautions to protect the civilian population and civilian objects under their control against the effects of attacks conducted by the opponent (see Article 58 of Additional Protocol I). Both principles have been identified as principles with a customary law status, which apply in IACs, as well as in NIACs.[1845]

3.2.4.1. Principle of precautions in attack

The principle of precautions in attack requires that those planning or deciding to launch an attack first make every effort to verify that the attack does not constitute a direct attack on civilians or civilian objects and that the objects to be attacked are not subject to special protection (e.g. drinking water or nuclear power stations).[1846] Pursuant to the principle of distinction, attacks must be limited strictly to legitimate military targets.[1847] In addition, pursuant to the principle of proportionality, an attack must be refrained from if it is expected to cause incidental loss of civilian life, injury to civilians, and/or damage to civilian objects, which would be disproportionate to the concrete and direct military advantage anticipated.[1848] While the principle of precautions in attack

---

1844 Heintschel von Heinegg (n. 1821) para. 16.

1845 For an analysis of the customary nature of these rules in both IACs and NIACs, see Henckaerts and Doswald-Beck (n. 91) Rule 15, pp. 51–55 (as quoted above, see Part I, Section 3.2.2, fn. 526) and Rule 22, pp. 68–71 (as quoted above, see Part II, Section 3.2.2.1, fn. 926).

1846 See Art. 57(2)(a)(i) of Additional Protocol I.

1847 As discussed above, see Part III, Section 3.2.2.

1848 See Art. 57(2)(a)(iii) of Additional Protocol I. As also discussed in Part III, Section 3.2.3.

must be applied in conjunction with the principle of proportionality during all phases of an attack, the principle of precautions in attack must also operate independently.[1849] Indeed, even if the expected incidental loss of civilian life, injury to civilians, or damage to civilian objects is not excessive in relation to the concrete and direct military advantage anticipated, the attacking party must still take all feasible precautions to choose means and methods of warfare that will prevent as much incidental damage to civilians as possible (e.g. by choosing the type of weapon that causes the least collateral damage, such as precision-guided munition (PGM)).[1850] Where there is a choice between various military objectives to achieve a similar military advantage, the target whose attack is expected to pose the least risk to human life and civilian objects should be chosen.[1851]

Once the attack has been planned, the civilian population must be effectively warned in advance if the attacks are likely to affect them unless the circumstances do not allow this.[1852] For example, if it becomes clear that the target is not a military one (e.g. what was thought to be a military tracked vehicle turns out to be a civilian tractor) or is subject to special protection (e.g. the target appears to be part of an archaeological site), the attack must be cancelled or suspended.[1853] Likewise, if the attack is expected to cause incidental loss of civilian life, injury to civilians, and/or damage to civilian objects, which would be disproportionate to the concrete and direct military advantage anticipated, the attack must be cancelled or suspended.[1854]

3.2.4.2. Principle of precautions against the effects of attacks

Pursuant to the principle of precautions against the effects of attack, the belligerents who are affected by attacks from the enemy must also adopt precautionary measures to protect, as much as possible, the civilian population, individual civilians, and civilian objects under their control from the threats arising from military operations.[1855] Parties to the conflict should therefore strive as much as possible to remove civilian populations, individual civilians, and civilian objects under their control from the vicinity of military targets.[1856] In addition, belligerents must avoid placing their military targets in or near densely populated areas.[1857]

1849 Melzer, *International Humanitarian Law: A Comprehensive Introduction* (n. 675) 102.
1850 See Art. 57(2)(a)(ii) of Additional Protocol I.
1851 See Art. 57(3) of Additional Protocol I.
1852 See Art. 57(2)(c) of Additional Protocol I.
1853 See Art. 57(2)(b) of Additional Protocol I.
1854 See Art. 57(2)(b) of Additional Protocol I.
1855 See Art. 58 of Additional Protocol I.
1856 See Art. 58(a) of Additional Protocol I.
1857 See Art. 58(b) of Additional Protocol I.

3.2.5. *Prohibition of superfluous injury and unnecessary suffering*

Not only does IHL contain rules protecting civilians from the effects of hostilities, but it also outlaws or constrains the means and methods of warfare deemed to inflict needless suffering or injury on combatants. The preamble of the 1868 St. Petersberg Declaration stated:

> That the only legitimate object which States should endeavour to accomplish during war is to weaken the military forces of the enemy;
> That for this purpose it is sufficient to disable the greatest possible number of men;
> That this object would be exceeded by the employment of arms which uselessly aggravate the sufferings of disabled men, or render their death inevitable;
> That the employment of such arms would, therefore, be contrary to the laws of humanity; [...].

This rationale entered positive law through Article 23(e) of the 1899 Hague Regulations and Article 23(e) of the 1907 Hague Regulations.[1858] It was subsequently included in Article 35(2) of Additional Protocol I as a 'basic rule' of IHL (and thereby also expands the scope to include methods of warfare).[1859] Article 35(2) of Additional Protocol I states that '[i]t is prohibited to employ weapons, projectiles and material and methods of warfare of a nature to cause superfluous injury or unnecessary suffering.' The 2005 ICRC Study on Customary IHL has also identified this rule of customary IHL, which is equally applicable in IACs and NIACs.[1860]

The prohibition of inflicting superfluous injury or unnecessary suffering functions, first and foremost, as a general principle against which all means and methods of warfare must be measured. Means of warfare are weapons, weapon systems, weapon platforms, and associated equipment, while methods of warfare may refer to the way, mode, or manner in which means of warfare (especially weapons) are used, but also, more broadly, how warfare is conducted (i.e. tactics and operations).[1861] In the absence of clear treaty criteria on what constitutes 'superfluous' injury and what constitutes 'unnecessary' suffering, it

---

1858 Art. 23(e) of the 1899 Hague Regulations and Art. 23(e) of the 1907 Hague Regulations foresee that in addition to the prohibitions provided by special Conventions, it is especially forbidden to use weapons, projectiles, or material designed to cause unnecessary suffering.

1859 Henri Meyrowitz, 'The Principle of Superfluous Injury or Unnecessary Suffering: From the Declaration of St. Petersburg of 1868 to Additional Protocol 1 of 1977' (1994) 299 International Review of the Red Cross 98, 102.

1860 Henckaerts and Doswald-Beck (n. 91) Rule 70, pp. 237–244 ('The use of means and methods of warfare which are of a nature to cause superfluous injury or unnecessary suffering is prohibited').

1861 Rain Liivoja and Luke Chircop, 'Are Enhanced Warfighters Weapons, Means, or Methods of Warfare?' 94 International Law Studies Series 161, 177 and 181–183.

must be determined *in relation to what it is* superfluous or unnecessary.[1862] In the *Nuclear Weapons* case, the ICJ observed the following:[1863]

> [I]t is prohibited to cause unnecessary suffering to combatants: it is accordingly prohibited to use weapons causing them such harm or uselessly aggravating their suffering. In application of that [...] principle, States do not have unlimited freedom of choice of means in the weapons they use.

To determine whether an injury is 'superfluous' and suffering 'unnecessary', the ICJ set forth that 'a harm [must be] greater than that unavoidable to achieve legitimate military objectives.'[1864] Accordingly, the rule requires that a balance be found between considerations of military necessity and humanity.[1865]

The principle of the prohibition of superfluous injury and unnecessary suffering also underlies specific IHL rules restricting or prohibiting certain types of weapons whose effects are considered disproportionately cruel *regardless* of the circumstances, such as anti-personnel land mines, expanding bullets (e.g. dum-dum bullets), or weapons that wound through fragments which in the human body escape detection by X-rays.[1866]

As for methods of warfare, while many States include in their military manuals and legislation the prohibition of methods of warfare that cause superfluous injury or unnecessary suffering,[1867] they do not give examples of methods of warfare that would be prohibited under this rule.[1868] Methods of warfare that are, for example, forbidden are the starvation of civilians (e.g. Article 54 of Additional Protocol I) or the use of civilians as human shields (e.g. Article 51(7) of Additional Protocol I). However, these rules mainly constitute an application of the principle of distinction. There are also methods of warfare that concern the relation between combatants, such as the protection of persons *hors de combat* (e.g. Article 41 of Additional Protocol I) and the prohibitions against the denial of quarter (e.g. Article 40 of Additional Protocol I), perfidy or treachery (e.g. Article 37 of Additional Protocol I), and misuse of emblems,

---

1862 Meyrowitz (n. 1859) 106.

1863 *Legality of the Threat or Use of Nuclear Weapons, Advisory opinion* (n. 1231) para. 78.

1864 *Ibid.*

1865 Henckaerts and Doswald-Beck (n. 91) 240. For further literature on the meaning of 'superfluous injury or unnecessary suffering', see e.g. Rain Liivoja, 'Protecting Warfighters from Superfluous Injury and Unnecessary Suffering' in Matt Killingsworth and Tim McCormack (eds), *Who Do the Laws of War Protect? Civility, Barbarity and the Evolution of International Humanitarian Law* (Cambridge University Press Forthcoming) 9–14, https://papers.ssrn.com/sol3/papers.cfm?abstract_id=3738501, accessed 23 August 2022; Meyrowitz (n. 1859) 104–112.

1866 Melzer, *International Humanitarian Law: A Comprehensive Introduction* (n. 675) 110. For a summary overview, see e.g. Yoram Dinstein, 'Warfare, Methods and Means', *Max Planck Encyclopedia of Public International law* (Oxford Public International Law 2015).

1867 For an overview, see Henckaerts and Doswald-Beck (n. 91) 242, fn. 35.

1868 *Ibid.*

signs, and uniforms (e.g. Articles 38 and 39 of Additional Protocol I), but these are not necessarily methods of warfare that are prohibited because they cause superfluous injury or unnecessary suffering. However, an example of a method of war which is forbidden because it causes superfluous injury or unnecessary suffering could be the use of a weapon, which is not in itself of such a nature as to cause superfluous injury or unnecessary suffering, but which is used in such a way as to cause superfluous injury or unnecessary suffering.[1869] New Zealand's military manual, for example, prohibits defence forces to 'use any weapon or munition in a *method* other than as they have been trained *with the intention of causing superfluous injury or unnecessary suffering*.'[1870]

3.3. IMPACT OF THE UNSC MANDATE ON WHETHER OR NOT FORCE CAN BE USED IN SPECIFIC INSTANCES

When the UN Security Council has authorised a UN (mandated) peace operation to use all necessary means to protect civilians against the (imminent) threat of physical violence, the applicable legal regimes principally determine when and how force can be used in day-to-day situations at the tactical level of the operation. Occasionally the UNSC mandate, which is, as discussed earlier, a strategic-level statement that is generally concerned with the question of whether – and if so, how much – force can be used on the territory of a State and serves as a legal basis to that end, however, also influences in which specific circumstances armed forces may use force. In doing so, the UNSC mandate not only serves as a legal basis for an operation but also impacts the use of force by armed forces.

The UN Security Council may do so in two ways: first, by imposing additional restrictions on the use of force, and second, by overruling or authorising to act contrary to the rules of HRL or IHL. The UN Security Council's powers in this regard are not unlimited. Indeed, there are limits to the potential influence the UNSC mandate may have on the use of force on the ground. To avoid this discussion remaining purely theoretical, two case studies on the limits to the possible impact are presented. The first case examines whether the IHL concept of 'military advantage' must be interpreted differently – read: more strictly – in the context of UN-mandated peace operations carrying out a PoC mandate. The second case examines how the UN possibly uses the mandate in breach of international norms and considers whether the UN can derogate from the law in this regard, and, if not, how UN practice can be brought into conformity with the law.

1869 Liivoja (n. 1865) 19.

1870 Emphasis added. New Zealand (n. 1842) para. 7.3.1(b).

3.3.1. *Going less far: additional restrictions on the use of force*

3.3.1.1. Implementation of the UNSC mandate into military strategic, operational, and tactical instruments

If the UN Security Council authorises a UN (mandated) peace operation to take all necessary means to protect civilians under threat or imminent threat of physical violence, such mandate should be reflected in the various military strategic, operational, and tactical instruments. As explained earlier, once adopted, a mandate is translated, *inter alia*, into ROE, guidelines which define the degree of force that may be used and how it may be applied.[1871] Such mission-specific ROE may, however, not simply provide rules on the use of force to protect civilians but must also reflect either IHL or HRL standards. For example, Rule 1.8 of the UN Sample ROE provides for the following rule:[1872]

> Use of force, up to, and including deadly force, to defend any civilian person who is in need of protection against a hostile act or hostile intent, when competent local authorities are not in a position to render immediate assistance, is authorised. When and where possible, permission to use force should be sought from the immediate superior commander.

When Rule 1.8 is translated into a mission-specific ROE, it can be interpreted through the lens of either IHL or HRL. If there is a clear link to an armed conflict and IHL is the prevailing paradigm to determine whether someone has been arbitrarily deprived of their right to life, intentional lethal force must comply with IHL rules and principles, such as IHL-based rules on proportionality and collateral damage. If Rule 1.8 is incorporated in mission-specific ROE while there is no similar rule permitting attacks on, for example, declared enemy forces within a given area, the UNSC mandate, however, indirectly imposes *additional* restrictions on the use of force by UN (mandated) peace forces in the context of an armed conflict. After all, in the conduct of hostilities, IHL principally allows the use of lethal force against any lawful military target (e.g. combatants or civilians directly participating in hostilities), regardless of whether they undertake a hostile act or express a hostile intent to someone else's life at that given moment.[1873] Indeed, under IHL, the qualification of a person or an object as a legitimate military target, as opposed to the existence of a hostile act or hostile intent, determines the legality of an attack. It is perfectly possible in this situation that the person or object in question only remotely constitutes a threat to military operations.[1874]

1871 See Introductory Chapter, Section 1 and Part I, Section 4.1.2.3.

1872 UN DPKO (n. 102) Attachment 1, 2.

1873 As discussed above, see Part III, Section 3.2.2.1.

1874 Gaggioli, 'The Use of Force in Armed Conflict: Interplay between the Conduct of Hostilities and Law Enforcement Paradigms, ICRC Outcome Report' (n. 679) 12.

Suppose a UNSC mandate imposes additional restrictions on the use of force in specific instances. In this case, any use of force that goes beyond these limits constitutes a violation of the ROE and/or relevant orders and directives but not necessarily a violation of the applicable legal regime(s). In the example given above, this is rather straightforward. While IHL principally allows the use of lethal force against any lawful military target, the UNSC mandate *indirectly* imposes additional restrictions that lethal force can only be used to defend civilian persons that need protection against hostile acts or hostile intents when competent local authorities are unable to provide immediate assistance. In doing so, the UNSC mandate does not influence the interpretation and implementation of the relevant IHL rules and principles on the categories of persons who may and, respectively, may not be directly attacked.

Yet, it is not always that straightforward. For example, are UN (mandated) peace forces prohibited from causing any collateral damage when they have a PoC mandate, for the very reason that the killing (even incidental) of those they are supposed to protect must always be considered 'excessive' relative to the concrete and direct military advantage expected? And, when analysing whether a particular attack provides a 'military advantage', should one adopt the traditional approach (i.e. does the attack contribute to weakening the opponent?) or should one assess this in light of the mandate (i.e. does the attack contribute to fulfilling the strategic objectives set out in the UNSC mandate, such as PoC)? Accordingly, it is not always clear whether the rules and principles of IHL or HRL are to be interpreted differently simply because the forces operate under a UNSC mandate, as a result of which the mandate has a direct bearing on the use of force in day-to-day situations at the tactical level of the operation. This is further explored in a case study on the concept of 'military advantage' in the context of UN-mandated peace operations under a PoC mandate. As a reminder, 'military advantage' is a crucial element of the definition of military objective and is central to the principles of proportionality and precautions in attack.[1875]

3.3.1.2. Limits to the possible impact: case study on military advantage and PoC in the context of UN-mandated peace operations

A. Setting the Scene: Attacks against Objects during Operation Unified Protector

During the execution of Operation Unified Protector, it was a matter of discussion whether certain objects belonging to pro-al-Qadhafi armed forces could be considered military objectives under IHL if those enemy forces

1875 As discussed in Part III, Sections 3.2.2.2, 3.2.3, and 3.2.4.1.

were engaged in fighting against insurgents *without* posing a direct threat to civilians.[1876] Operation Unified Protected was launched with an explicit mandate to protect civilians. UNSC Resolution 1973 (2011) authorised Member States to use 'all necessary measures' in order 'to protect civilians and civilian populated areas under threat of attack in the Libyan Arab Jamahiriya, including Benghazi.'[1877] Accordingly, the mandate determined that one of the main strategic objectives of the operation was to protect civilians.

While there was already an ongoing NIAC between the Libyan government and the rebel groups, the States that responded to this mandate, and most likely also NATO itself, became parties to an IAC with Libya.[1878] As such, the rules and principles of IHL applied *de jure* to those parties involved. One of the fundamental principles of IHL is that only military objectives, and not civilian objects, may be the object of direct attacks.[1879] Only objects that, by their nature, location, purpose, or use, make an effective contribution to military action and whose partial or total destruction, capture, or neutralisation, under the circumstances of the moment, offers a definite military advantage, can be classified as military objectives.[1880]

As discussed above, traditionally, 'military advantage' is understood as a gain that is military in nature (and thus not solely political, economic, or moral) and generates an effect on the enemy's military operational or tactical level.[1881] For example, a 'military advantage' may be gained from an attack if the enemy forces are weakened by the attack, either by the killing or wounding of enemy personnel or by the damage of enemy military equipment, or by denying the enemy the use of a particular area.[1882] In addition, a military advantage may also be gained from an attack that allows one's own forces to gain ground or dominance in the air or at sea.[1883] To determine the military advantage of an attack, the attack as a whole, and not particular parts of the attack, must be considered.[1884]

While one could argue that an attack against objects belonging to pro-al-Qadhafi armed forces contributes to the defeat of the adversary part (IHL objective), it is questionable whether it also contributes to the protection of civilians (strategic objective as set forth by the UNSC mandate) if those pro-al-Qadhafi armed forces do not pose a threat to civilians.[1885] In this regard, it was

1876 See also Lehmann (n. 14) 134–137.
1877 'UNSC Res. 1973' (n. 62) para. 4.
1878 For sources substantiating this position, see Part III, Section 2.2.1, fns. 1572 and 1573.
1879 See Part III, Section 3.2.2.2.
1880 See Art. 52(2) of Additional Protocol I, as quoted above (Part III, Section 3.2.2.2).
1881 Harvard School of Public Health (n. 1814) 36 and 99. See also Part III, Section 3.2.2.2.
1882 Heintschel von Heinegg (n. 1821) para. 18.
1883 *Ibid.*
1884 For sources defending this view, see Part III, Section 3.2.2.2, fn. 1824.
1885 See also Lehmann (n. 14) 134–135.

questioned whether one must interpret the IHL concept in conformity with the strategic objective of protecting civilians, or whether such an approach would constitute a violation of the strict separation between IHL and the international law on the use of force.

The International Commission of Inquiry on Libya, which was established to investigate all alleged violations of HRL in the Libyan Arab Jamahiriya, did not evaluate the implementation of the UNSC mandate.[1886] After all, it did not consider this to fall within its own mandate.[1887] The International Commission of Inquiry did investigate whether NATO aerial strikes were carried out against targets with military significance and whether there were civilian casualties. It was, however, not assessed whether the target in question posed a direct threat to civilians.[1888] In the end, the International Commission of Inquiry concluded that NATO had conducted a 'highly precise campaign with a demonstrable determination to avoid civilian casualties' in which they succeeded for the most part.[1889] Only on limited occasions did the International Commission of Inquiry find that targets showed no evidence of military utility.[1890] It is clear from this report that the International Commission of Inquiry considered questions about compliance with the legal basis and the legal regimes as distinct from one another.

The approach that a legal basis does not impact what is lawful under a legal regime is not unanimously accepted in literature. To elaborate, the next Section discusses some theoretical approaches to the relationship between *jus ad bellum* and *jus in bello*.

B. Drawing from the theoretical approaches to the relationship between *jus ad bellum* and *jus in bello*

Interesting conclusions regarding the relationship between the UNSC mandate and IHL can be drawn from theoretical approaches to the relationship between *jus ad bellum* and *jus in bello*. Yet, before discussing such literature, the following should be clarified. A substantial number of academic contributions refer to the Latin terms '*jus ad bellum*' (which historically can be translated as 'the right to wage war') and '*jus in bello*' (or IHL) when discussing the relationship between bodies of law relevant to the use of force. Some dispute, however, that *jus ad bellum* is part of the applicable legal framework for UN (mandated) peace operations, as this would imply that the UN Security Council would be subject to *jus ad bellum* limits on the use of force when

1886 UNHRC (n. 1572), Annex 1, para. 604, note 899.
1887 *Ibid.* Annex 1, para. 604, note 899.
1888 *Ibid.* Annex 1, paras 603–655.
1889 *Ibid.* para. 122.
1890 *Ibid.*

taking measures to maintain or restore the international peace and security.[1891] In addition, it is also argued by some that, while *jus ad bellum* implies forcible measures which are taken without the consent of the State on whose territory force is used, UN (mandated) peace operations, and definitely UN peace operations, are almost always deployed with the consent of the host State and thus fall outside the scope of *jus ad bellum*.[1892] Therefore, instead of referring to '*jus ad bellum*' when discussing the legal basis for the emplacement and functioning of UN (mandated) peace operations on the territory of another State, this study has limited itself to referring to 'the UN Charter and customary international law relating to the use of force and the maintenance and restoration of international peace and security.'[1893] In this Section, reference is, however, made to literature on the relationship between *jus ad bellum* and *jus in bello*. Without passing judgment on the scope *jus ad bellum* and whether it constitutes the applicable body of law, this study considers the literature relevant for getting a better understanding of the relationship between the legal basis of the use of force on the territory of a State (with or without its consent) and IHL regulating the conduct of hostilities of the armed forces being deployed in the territory of another State.

Some authors believe there is a normative spill-over from *jus ad bellum* into *jus in bello*.[1894] Such a normative spill-over implies that rules and principles of IHL are either interpreted more restrictively or more broadly under the influence of the legal basis. For example, Greenwood, O'Connell, Henderson, and Orakhelashvili argue that *jus ad bellum* impacts what is lawful under *jus in bello*. They do not consider the *jus in bello* principles necessarily free-

1891 When the present author gave presentations in the early stages of her research, these were some of the objections that were made when reference was made to the '*jus ad bellum*' as part of the applicable legal framework for UN (mandated) peace operations. See e.g. Hanna Bourgeois, 'The Relationship between the International Law on the Use of Force and International Humanitarian Law in the Context of Protection of Civilians Mandates' (Specialist Course International Order and Justice, Seminar with Prof. dr. Georg Nolte, Ghent University, Ghent, Belgium, 19 March 2018); Hanna Bourgeois, 'The Relationship between the International Law on the Use of Force and International Humanitarian Law in the Context of Protection of Civilians Mandates' (7th PhD Day, International Humanitarian and Criminal Law Platform, TMC Asser Instituut, The Hague, the Netherlands, 25 May 2018).

1892 *Ibid.*

1893 See Part I, Section 4.1.1.2(A).

1894 In a recent contribution, Lieblich uses the term 'normative spillover' when discussing the concurrent application of *jus ad bellum* and *jus in bello* and whether there is, or should be, a normative spillover between violations of proportionality *in bello* and proportionality *ad bellum*. See Eliav Lieblich, 'On the Continuous and Concurrent Application of Ad Bellum and In Bello Proportionality' in Claus Kreß and Robert Lawless (eds), *Necessity and Proportionality in International Peace and Security Law* (Oxford University Press 2020) 73–75.

standing concepts but rather an emanation of the strict causes of war under *jus ad bellum*.[1895] Henderson held, for example, the following:[1896]

> [W]here the *jus ad bellum* is provided by a Chapter VII UN Security Council resolution [...] the scope of the [...] [UNSC] mandate will affect what is a military advantage that may lawfully be sought from any particular attack. Accordingly, the *jus ad bellum* will have some impact on what is lawful under the *jus in bello* [...].

Also, in the Final Report to the Prosecutor by the Committee Established to Review the NATO Bombing Campaign Against the Federal Republic of Yugoslavia, it was held that: '[t]he application of the definition [of military objective] to particular objects may [...] differ depending on the scope and objectives of the conflict.'[1897]

This point of view was also reflected in the discussions of the Expert Meeting on 'Targeting Military Objectives', organised by the University Centre for International Humanitarian Law in Geneva.[1898] For example, in one of the discussions, it was questioned whether NATO could consider State institutions that allowed the enemy government to identify people and determine to which ethnic group they belonged to be military objectives as envisaged in Article 52(2) of Additional Protocol I during its Kosovo campaign.[1899] Some experts doubted whether these institutions actually made an effective contribution to the military

1895 Christopher Greenwood, 'Historical Development and Legal Basis' in Dieter Fleck and Michael Bothe (eds), *The Handbook of International Humanitarian Law* (2nd edn., Oxford University Press 2008) 37 (arguing that under *jus in bello*, military necessity must take into account *jus ad bellum* limitations); Mary Ellen O'Connell, 'Historical Development and Legal Basis' in Dieter Fleck (ed), *The Handbook of International Humanitarian Law* (3rd edn., Oxford University Press 2013) 36 (O'Connell was the author of the article on 'Historical Development and Legal Basis' in the 3rd edn. of the Handbook on International Humanitarian Law, whereas Greenwood was the author of this article in the 2nd edn. O'Connell did not make any changes to his position); Christian Henderson, 'International Measures for the Protection of Civilians in Libya and Cote d'Ivoire Current Developments: Public International Law' (2011) 60 International and Comparative Law Quarterly 767, 775; Alexander Orakhelashvili, 'Overlap and Convergence: The Interaction between Jus Ad Bellum and Jus in Bello' (2007) 12 Journal of Conflict and Security Law 157, 161–165.

1896 Ian Henderson, 'Civilian Intelligence Agencies and the Use of Armed Drones', *Yearbook of International Humanitarian Law*, vol. 13 (TMC Asser Press 2011) 139, fn. 36.

1897 Committee Established to Review the NATO Bombing Campaign Against the Federal Republic of Yugoslavia, 'Final Report to the Prosecutor' (2000) para. 37, www.icty.org/en/press/final-report-prosecutor-committee-established-review-nato-bombing-campaign-against-federal, accessed 3 January 2018, as referred to by Marco Sassòli, 'Ius Ad Bellum and Ius in Bello – The Separation between the Legality of the Use of Force and Humanitarian Rules to Be Respected in Warfare: Crucial or Outdated?' in Michael N Schmitt and Jelena Pejic (eds), *International Law and Armed Conflict: Exploring the Faultlines. Essays in Honour of Yoram Dinstein* (Koninklijke Brill 2007) 250.

1898 University Centre for International Humanitarian Law Geneva, 'Targeting Military Objectives, Report of an Expert Meeting Organized by the University Centre for International Humanitarian Law Geneva and Convened at the Centre de Conférences de Varembé in Geneva, Switzerland, 12 May 2005' (2005) 11–12.

1899 *Ibid.* 11.

action of the enemy and whether their destruction could truly be regarded as conferring a definite military advantage.[1900] Other experts, however, referred to the fact that the politically stated objective of the NATO campaign in Kosovo was to stop the ethnic cleansing and put an end to the appalling humanitarian situation.[1901] Accordingly, an attack on such State institutions could be justified with a 'defence of others' argument.[1902] To substantiate this argument, some experts discussed the fact that in the Second World War, the Alliance had carried out strikes against the concentration camps set up by Germany and their infrastructures to stop the atrocities from happening, even though these targets did not constitute military objectives.[1903] Most experts were, however, critical of the argument that the 'defence of others' was one of the elements that could be taken into account when assessing the military character of a specific objective as envisaged under Article 52(2) of Additional Protocol I.[1904]

Bothe, Bring, and Hoffman take it even further by arguing that new rules for interventional armed conflict need to be adopted which accommodate the specificities of interventional armed conflict.[1905] Hoffman considers, for example, that:[1906]

> As with other, less destructive human activities, the characteristics of armed conflict are susceptible to change in their specifics. That such operations may have distinctive legal, political or operational characteristics setting them apart from other military operations is not extraordinary. It should no longer keep us from moving to develop and implement clear, usable standards of international humanitarian law. [...] Peace enforcers are interveners. Their operations are intervention operations. We need not lose further time in developing rules for them simply because we cannot place them within existing legal constructs for war. Armed conflict that involves peace enforcers is interventional conflict. Along with internal and international armed conflict, interventional armed conflict is also a reality of modern war.

1900 *Ibid.*

1901 *Ibid.*

1902 *Ibid.*

1903 *Ibid.* 11–12.

1904 *Ibid.* 12.

1905 Michael Bothe, 'The Protection of the Civilian Population and NATO Bombing on Yugoslavia: Comments on a Report to the Prosecutor of the ICTY' (2001) 12 The European Journal of International Law 531, 535 (arguing that it should deserve further consideration whether the concept of military objective is to be more restricted during a humanitarian intervention than in any other armed conflict). See also Michael Bothe, 'The Responsibility to Protect and International Humanitarian Law' in Gian Luca Beruto (ed), *Proceedings of the 31st Roundtable on Current Problems of International Humanitarian Law: International Humanitarian Law Human Rights and Peace Operations, Hosted by the International Institute of Humanitarian Law, 4–6 September 2008, San Remo, 224* (2008); Ove Bring, 'International Humanitarian Law after Kosovo: Is Lex Lata Sufficient' (2002) 71 Nordic Journal of International Law 39, 50–54; Michael H Hoffman, 'Peace-Enforcement Actions and Humanitarian Law: Emerging Rules for "Interventional Armed Conflict"' (2000) 82 International Review of the Red Cross 193 (page number unknown).

1906 Hoffman (n. 1905) (page number unknown).

Bring advocates for developing a new additional protocol for intervention types of conflict which should include, *inter alia*, a stricter definition of military objectives.[1907]

Many authors, including Bartolini, Bilder, Lehmann, Lieblich, Kolb, Sloan, and van Steenberghe strongly oppose such a spill-over and bring forward a strong separation between *jus ad bellum* and *jus in bello*.[1908] Also to Sassòli, Bouvier, and Quintin 'aucun argument de *jus ad bellum* ne puisse être utilisé pour interpréter le [*jus in bello*].'[1909] Koutroulis similarly holds that 'la

1907 Bring (n. 1905) 50–54.

1908 Bartolini (n. 794) 270 (stating that an approach whereby the notion of military objective would be extended beyond the limits set out by Art. 52(2) of Additional Protocol I must be avoided as '*jus ad bellum* should not interfere with the interpretation of humanitarian norms') (see also 271); Richard B Bilder, 'Kosovo and the New Interventionism: Promise or Peril' (1999) 9 Journal of Transnational Law and Policy 153, 174 ('Somehow, it is hard to accept the idea that 'bombing for peace and human rights' makes moral or legal sense!') (see also 173); Lehmann (n. 14) 137 ('[T]he proportionality assessment of IHL does not allow for the inclusion of *jus ad bellum* considerations, such as by weighting incidental loss of civilian life or damage to civilian objects against the aim to halt or repel the conflict'). Nevertheless, when discussing the concept of definite military advantage, he does argue that this concept can 'accommodate' the goal of protecting civilians when such is the aim of the military operation. He holds that this 'requires simply a change of perspective while building on established concepts of IHL' and that such a flexible approach 'is not equivalent to reading *jus ad bellum* into the *jus in bello*' since that would 'indeed run counter to the dualist approach by opening *jus in bello* up to *ad bellum* considerations on the legality of the use of force' (134–135); Lieblich, 'On the Continuous and Concurrent Application of Ad Bellum and In Bello Proportionality' (n. 1894) 75 ('It seems that we cannot apply the spillover theory without breaking down the campaign to a multitude of *ad bellum* assessments, pertaining to each specific attack. But that would run counter to the idea that *ad bellum* proportionality is assessed in toto') (see also 73–75); Robert Kolb, 'La Nécessité Militaire Dans Le Droit Des Conflits Armés: Essai de Clarification Conceptuelle', *Proceedings of the 40th Colloquium of the Société Française pour le Droit International on La nécessité en Droit International, 8–10 June 2006, Grenoble* (Pendone 2007) 183 ('Pour ce qui est en revanche des décisions opérationnelles, dans le cadre d'une opération militaire concrète et située, la nécessité militaire doit se mesurer uniquement à une utilité militaire qui soit abstraite des considérations du *jus ad bellum*. Il faut se demander quel est l'avantage militaire du point de vue technique dans cette opération-là, et non si cet avantage est licite. En un mot comme en mille, des critères de nécessité du *jus ad bellum* doivent intervenir dans la planification générale des opérations, et les considérations du *jus in bello* prévaloir dans le domaine de l'exécution d'opérations militaires concrètes sur le terrain'); Robert D Sloane, 'The Cost of Conflation: Preserving the Dualism of Jus Ad Bellum and Jus in Bello in the Contemporary Law of War' (2009) 34 Yale Journal of International Law 47, 74 ('In law, even if not in the deep morality of war, it is therefore incorrect to regard *ad bellum* judgments as necessarily determinative of *in bello* proportionality judgments') (see also 69); van Steenberghe (n. 1231) 107 ('[A]lthough sharing common features and being somewhat interconnected, the notions of proportionality provided under these two separate branches of international law remain independent of each other, mainly because of what is referred to in this article as the "general versus particular" dichotomy, which characterises their relations').

1909 Marco Sassòli, Antoine Bouvier and Anne Quintin, *Un Droit Dans La Guerre*, vol. 1 (2nd edn., ICRC) pt I, Chapter 2, p. 18. See also I, Chapter 2, 17 (translation from French: 'no argument of *jus ad bellum* can be invoked to interpret *jus in bello*'). See also Antoine Bouvier, 'Assessing the Relationship Between Jus in Bello and Jus Ad Bellum: An "Orthodox" View', *Proceedings of the American Society of International Law, 29 March–1 April 2006, Washington DC, vol. 100, 109* (2006); Sassòli, 'Ius Ad Bellum and Ius in Bello – The Separation between

caractéristique principale qui régit les relations entre ces deux branches du droit international est l'indépendance. Cette indépendance est absolue en ce qui concerne l'influence du *jus contra bellum*.'[1910]

C. No normative spill-over from the UNSC mandate into IHL

This study does not support a normative spill-over from the international law on the use of force into IHL. On some occasions, it may indeed be tempting to argue that the mandate should inform the IHL analysis. For example, when force is used to defend broadly shared international values, such as the protection of civilians from human rights atrocities, it is tempting to allow for a changed approach towards the interpretation and application of IHL rules and principles.[1911] Let us return to the initial example to further explain this. In the Libya example, it was questioned whether NATO and the intervening States could carry out an attack against certain assets that belonged to pro-al-Qadhafi armed forces if these forces were engaged in fighting against insurgents *without* posing a direct threat to civilians. It is appealing to argue that the answer to the question of whether or not a certain attack would offer a definite military advantage can be found in the UNSC mandate, which sets forth the strategic objective of the mission (*in casu* the protection of civilians and civilian populated areas under threat of attack in the Libyan Arab Jamahiriya, including Benghazi). After all, some questioned why NATO and the intervening States would be allowed to carry out attacks which do not directly contribute to the very reason they are there. Though, there are at least two reasons for rejecting such an approach.

First, an approach that allows for a direct influence of a mandate on the interpretation and implementation of the IHL rules and principles runs counter to the dualistic approach that must be taken with respect to the international law on the use of force and IHL.[1912] The strict separation between these bodies of law implies that the assessment of whether the use of force complies with each of these bodies of law must be done separately. The international law on the use of force and IHL address different legal matters, and decisions concerning these different legal matters must be made at different levels in the chain of command. The IHL rules and principles focus on the specific use of force ordered at the

---

the Legality of the Use of Force and Humanitarian Rules to Be Respected in Warfare: Crucial or Outdated?' (n. 1897) 249 (arguing that '*jus ad bellum* not only has no impact upon the applicability of IHL, but it also may not be used to interpret a provision of IHL') (see also 250–252).

1910 Koutroulis, 'Jus Ad/Contra Bellum' (n. 1312) 162 (translation from French: 'the main characteristic that governs the relationship between these two bodies of international law is independence. This independence is absolute with respect to the influence of *jus contra bellum*').

1911 For other examples, see Bouvier (n. 1909) 111.

1912 Sloane (n. 1908) 55.

operational and tactical levels by military leadership and used by soldiers at the tactical level. In contrast, the international law on the use of force regulates the resort to armed force by States, international organisations, or other non-state actors, as well as their overall use of force. The assessment of compliance with the mandate is done at the strategic level. A soldier operating at the tactical level is not (and should not be) required to assess each instance of the use of force against the more politicised mandate but instead to the very facts on the ground. For example, the IHL principle of proportionality refers to a 'concrete and direct military advantage' that can outweigh collateral damage, not to a 'broader political or strategic objective'. In other words, this concerns the direct link between the advantage and the concrete and direct objective of the attack (rather than the overall conflict).[1913] If the concrete and direct military advantage of one single attack is to be understood as contributing directly to the broader political or strategic objective of the entire operation, this would inflate the advantage of one single attack and hence could justify considerable collateral damage that would otherwise not be allowed.[1914] Or, turning back to the initial Libya example, it could artificially limit the scope of action by interveners with a UNSC mandate as opposed to what their adversary part(y)ies can do. After all, if one would argue that the military assets belonging to pro-al-Qadhafi armed forces do not constitute a military objective because their destruction would not contribute to the defensive cause, those deciding to actually attack these assets would commit a violation of IHL, even if it the tactical harm to the adversary party was significant. We should not only refuse such an approach because it violates the principle of strict separation between the international law on the use of force and IHL but also because it gives rise to a different treatment of parties involved in one and the same conflict.[1915]

Hence, a second reason to reject a normative spill-over from the legal basis into IHL is that the principle of equal application opposes different understandings of the IHL rules and principles to the just and unjust parties. Most authors favouring the normative spill-over from the international law on the use of force into IHL, look at the issue from the perspective of the defending party or the party acting upon a UNSC mandate. With respect to the IHL concept of definite military advantage, this would imply that if one had to decide whether a certain attack carried out by the *unjust* party generated a definite military advantage, one would have to assess whether it contributed to its *overall* unjust cause. After all, it would not be justified to enhance the value of the

1913 See also Lehmann (n. 14) 135.

1914 Lieblich, 'On the Continuous and Concurrent Application of Ad Bellum and In Bello Proportionality' (n. 1894) 66.

1915 See also Bartolini (n. 794) 269; Sassòli, 'Ius Ad Bellum and Ius in Bello – The Separation between the Legality of the Use of Force and Humanitarian Rules to Be Respected in Warfare: Crucial or Outdated?' (n. 1897) 249–250.

definite military advantage of the just party and diminish its value of the unjust party.[1916] For all good reasons, this approach does not seem desirable.

In summary, the UNSC mandate cannot impact what is lawful under IHL. The rules and principles of IHL must not be interpreted differently simply because the forces operate under a UNSC mandate. Of course, this strict approach does not rule out that IHL rules and principles may *de facto* accommodate the broader political or strategic objective. This is not the equivalent of reading international law on the use of force into IHL. Moreover, while the mandate cannot impact what is lawful under IHL, it may impose additional limits on the use of force in specific instances. Any use of force beyond such limits will constitute a violation of the ROE but not necessarily a violation of IHL.

3.3.2. Going beyond: overruling or authorising to act contrary to the rules of HRL or IHL

3.3.2.1. Possible legal bases for setting aside legally binding rules

A. Chapter VII powers

The UN Security Council has the discretionary power to deviate from the law when resorting to enforcement measures.[1917] After all, for the UN Security Council to exercise its enforcement powers under Chapter VII[1918] and thus to be able to act swiftly and effectively to maintain international peace and security, it is sometimes necessary to set aside generally binding legal rules.[1919] This may not only have an impact upon the legal rights and obligations of those States or entities against which the measures are directed but also other States involved (e.g. TTCs taking part in a UN (mandated) peace operation). In addition, this does not only extend to rules of customary international law but also treaty law.[1920]

B. Article 103 of the UN Charter

According to Article 103 of the UN Charter, in the event of a conflict between an obligation under the UN Charter and a UN Member State's obligation under another international agreement, the former prevails. Although this

1916 Lieblich, 'On the Continuous and Concurrent Application of Ad Bellum and In Bello Proportionality' (n. 1894) 66–67.

1917 De Wet (n. 892) 184.

1918 On Chapter VII powers of the UN Security Council, see Part I, Sections 4.1.1.1(A)(i) and 4.1.1.2(A).

1919 Gill, 'Legal and Some Political Limitations on the Power of the UN Security Council to Exercise Its Enforcement Powers under Chapter VII of the Charter' (n. 892) 62–63; de Wet (n. 892) 182.

1920 De Wet (n. 892) 183.

provision has gained prominence since the end of the Cold War – in light of the UN Security Council's increased use of Chapter VII in decision-making and the often-contentious relationship between its decisions and States' other obligations, including HRL obligations[1921] – the precise scope of Article 103 and its effects are marked by uncertainties.[1922]

First, as is clear from the wording of Article 103 of the UN Charter, a 'conflict' between 'obligations under the UN Charter' and 'obligations under other international agreements' triggers the relevant provision. It remains, however, unclear whether an 'authorisation' falls within the scope of 'obligations under the UN Charter'. In other words, there is still disagreement over the question of whether Article 103 of the UN Charter only applies to UNSC resolutions which directly create obligations upon States or also to UNSC resolutions which include recommendations or authorisations that take the form of Chapter VII 'decisions'. Some authors believe that an 'authorisation' does not fall within the scope of Article 103 of the UN Charter as it does not concern an 'obligation under the UN Charter' in the narrow sense.[1923] They argue that the term 'obligation' has a clear and unambiguous meaning and requires States to do or omit something.[1924] If the UN Security Council authorises the use of 'all necessary means', States are not necessarily required to act. Hence, under the strict approach, an 'authorisation' may not trump obligations under other international agreements that do require States to do or omit something. The majority view, to which the present author fully subscribes, disagrees with this strict approach, instead arguing that Article 103 of the UN Charter also applies to authorisations.[1925] The most convincing argument defending this position is

1921 Leiæ and Paulus (n. 1219) 2113.

1922 Robert Kolb, 'Does Article 103 of the Charter of the United Nations Apply Only to Decisions or Also to Authorizations Adopted by the Security Council' (2004) 64 Zeitschrift für ausländisches öffentliches Recht und Völkerrecht 21, 21.

1923 Rudolf Bernhardt, 'Chapter XVI. Miscellaneous Provisions, Article 103' in Bruno Simma and others (eds), *The Charter of the United Nations: a Commentary*, vol. 2 (2nd edn., Oxford University Press 2002) 1296; Jean Combacau, *Le Pouvoir de Sanction de l'ONU: Étude Théorique de La Coercition Non Militaire* (Pedone 1974) 284; Richard H Lauwaars, 'The Interrelationship between United Nations Law and the Law of Other International Organizations International Law' (1984) 82 Michigan Law Review 1604, 1607, as also referred to by Kolb, 'Does Article 103 of the Charter of the United Nations Apply Only to Decisions or Also to Authorizations Adopted by the Security Council' (n. 1922) 24–25; and Leiæ and Paulus (n. 1219) 2125.

1924 Bernhardt (n. 1923) 1296; Combacau (n. 1923) 284; Lauwaars (n. 1923) 1607, as also referred to by Kolb, 'Does Article 103 of the Charter of the United Nations Apply Only to Decisions or Also to Authorizations Adopted by the Security Council' (n. 1922) 24–25; and Leiæ and Paulus (n. 1219) 2125.

1925 For sources supporting the position that Art. 103 of the UN Charter also applies to authorisations, see ILC, 'Fragmentation of International Law: Difficulties Arising from the Diversification and Expansion of International Law, Report of the Study Group of the International Law Commission, Finalized by Martti Koskenniemi' (n. 616) 168–169, para. 331. Leiæ and Paulus (n. 1219) 2122–2123; Kolb, 'Does Article 103 of the Charter of the United Nations Apply Only to Decisions or Also to Authorizations Adopted by the Security

if States would deploy an operation upon the authorisation of the UN Security Council and this authorisation would not be considered as falling within the scope of Article 103 of the UN Charter, States would always run the risk of violating conflicting obligations under other international agreements.[1926] This could seriously impact the effectiveness of the international system of collective security since States might be less inclined to contribute resources and personnel to the UN Security Council to enable implementing resolutions.[1927] This view was also shared by the former UK House of Lords in its *Al-Jedda* judgment, in which the Law Lords unanimously held that in the interest of the effectiveness of the UN system, authorisations fall within the scope of Article 103 of the UN Charter.[1928]

Second, the scope of 'obligations under other international agreements' remains disputed, especially whether this only concerns treaties between UN Member States or also other obligations (e.g. under customary international law). The ordinary meaning of 'international agreements', as interpreted in the context, does not comprise customary international law.[1929] From the *travaux préparatoires,* it also becomes clear that the drafters consciously referred to 'international agreements' instead of 'international obligations' in the broader sense. Initially, Article 103 of the UN Charter did include a reference to 'any other international obligations', but this gave rise to quite some dispute among the drafters.[1930] Hence, in a subsequent stage of the drafting process, the provision

---

Council' (n. 1922) 25–27; Krisch (n. 588) 1262 and 1340; Marko Milanović, 'Norm Conflict in International Law: Whither Human Rights?' (2009) 20 Duke Journal of Comparative and International Law 69, 78; Sarooshi (n. 1221) 150–151; Larsen (n. 1350) 320. See also Michel Virally, *L'organisation Mondiale* (Colin 1972) 188; John Dugard, 'The Legal Effect of United Nations Resolutions on Apartheid' (1966) 83 South African Law Journal 44, 58–59; Vera Gowlland-Debbas, 'The Limits of Unilateral Enforcement of Community Objectives in the Framework of UN Peace Maintenance' (2000) 11 The European Journal of International Law 361, 371, as also referred to by Kolb, 'Does Article 103 of the Charter of the United Nations Apply Only to Decisions or Also to Authorizations Adopted by the Security Council' (n. 1922) 27. A further question that is not addressed in this study is whether Article 103 of the UN Charter is applicable only to authorisations made under Chapter VII of the UN Charter or also to authorisations with another legal basis. In the context of UN (mandated) peace operations, the UN Security Council consistently invokes Chapter VII when authorising a UN (mandated) peace operation to use all necessary means to protect civilians.

1926 Leiæ and Paulus (n. 1219) 2123.

1927 *Ibid.*

1928 *R (on the application of Al-Jedda) v. Secretary of State for Defence, Appeal judgment* (n. 1281), see paras 32–39 (Lord Bingham); paras 115–117 (Lord Rodger); para. 135 (Lord Carswell); para. 152 (Lord Brown), as referred to by Leiæ and Paulus (n. 1219) 2126, fn. 98. For an in-depth analysis of the *Al-Jedda* case before the House of Lords, see Sari, 'The Al-Jedda Case Before the House of Lords' (n. 1220). See, however, also below as regards the views of the ECtHR.

1929 Liivoja (n. 1220) 602.

1930 See e.g. UNIO, 'Documents of the United Nations Conference on International Organizations, San Francisco, 1945' (1945) XIII (Commission IV: Judicial Organization) 662–663 (doc. 899 (English) IV/2/40, 10 June 1945) and 706–707 (doc. 933 (English) IV/2/42 (2), 12 June 1945); UNIO, 'Documents of the United Nations Conference on International Organizations,

was changed to 'their obligations under any other international agreement', as this reflected the highest degree of consensus available.[1931] The subsequent application of Article 103 of the UN Charter also provides little support for the position that customary international law falls under the scope.[1932] Nevertheless, several academics continue to support a broad interpretation of Article 103 of the UN Charter covering both international agreements between States and other sources, such as customary international law.[1933] This view, which is often based on the constitutional nature of the UN Charter, must be refuted.[1934] Article 103 of the UN Charter never intended to affect customary HRL obligations.[1935] If an operation with a PoC mandate is only bound by customary norms of IHL or HRL, Article 103 of the UN Charter cannot be invoked to justify the use of force beyond the limits of HRL and IHL. That said, as discussed above, to exercise its enforcement powers under Chapter VII, the UN Security Council has the power to set aside generally binding legal rules (see also Articles 1 and 24 of the

San Francisco, 1945' (1945) XVIII (Documents of the Coordination Committee, including Documents of the Advisory Committee of Jurists, Part 2) 342 (doc. 296 (English) CO/102 (2), 14 June 1945); UNIO, 'Documents of the United Nations Conference on International Organizations, San Francisco, 1945' (1945) XVII (Documents of the Coordination Committee, including Documents of the Advisory Committee of Jurists, Part 1) 112–113 (doc. 314 (English) CO/122 (2), 14 June 1945); UNIO, 'Documents of the United Nations Conference on International Organizations, San Francisco, 1945' (1945) XV (Coordination Committee, The Charter, Lists) 209 (doc. 1159 (English) CO/181, 23 June 1945).

1931 UNIO, 'Documents of the United Nations Conference on International Organizations, San Francisco, 1945' (n. 1930) 104 (doc. 1153 (English) IV/12 (1), 22 June 1945); UNIO, 'Documents of the United Nations Conference on International Organizations, San Francisco, 1945' (n. 1930) 261, para. 3(b) (doc. 1192 (English) CO/185, 25 June 1945); UNIO, 'Documents of the United Nations Conference on International Organizations, San Francisco, 1945' (1945) I (General) 631 (doc. 1210 (English) P/20, 27 June 1945); UNIO, 'Documents of the United Nations Conference on International Organizations, San Francisco, 1945' (1945) XIX (Documents du Comité de Coordination comprenant les documents du Comité Consultatif de Jurists) 376 (doc. 441 (English) CO/205, 13 September 1945).

1932 For a detailed analysis of the subsequent practice, judicial opinions, and doctrine, see Liivoja (n. 1220) 605–612.

1933 Bernhardt (n. 1923) 1298–1299; Bardo Fassbender, 'The United Nations Charter As Constitution of the International Community' (1998) 36 Columbia Journal of Transnational Law 529, 586; Kleffner (n. 1374) 61. See also ILC, 'Fragmentation of International Law: Difficulties Arising from the Diversification and Expansion of International Law, Report of the Study Group of the International Law Commission, Finalized by Martti Koskenniemi' (n. 616) 176, para. 345. Zemanek also seems to support this approach when taking into account the purpose of Art. 103 of the UN Charter. Nevertheless, he recognises that this interpretation 'rests on shaky ground,' see Karl Zemanek, *The Legal Foundations of the International System: General Course on Public International Law* (Nijhoff 1998) 232.

1934 A number of academics also refute such position, see e.g. Derek W Bowett, 'The Impact of Security Council Decisions on Dispute Settlement Procedures' (1994) 5 The European Journal of International Law 89, 92; Liivoja (n. 1220) 602–612; McLaughlin (n. 38) 401; Orakhelashvili, 'The Acts of the Security Council: Meaning and Standards of Review' (n. 888) 149–150; Watson (n. 1222) 25.

1935 See also White, 'Security Council Mandates and the Use of Lethal Force by Peacekeepers: What Place for the Laws of War?' (n. 31) 110.

UN Charter).[1936] Pursuant to Article 25 of the UN Charter, the UN Member States agree to accept and carry out the decisions of the UN Security Council in accordance with the UN Charter.[1937]

Third, it is still disputed when exactly a 'conflict' occurs between the obligations under the UN Charter and obligations under other international agreements. In general, one must presume that the UN Security Council has no intention of nullifying or suspending applicable international law, including, but not limited to, HRL and IHL, if this is not explicit (or at least implicit) in the text of the relevant resolution.[1938] Article 1(3) of the UN Charter prescribes 'promoting and encouraging respect for human rights and for fundamental freedoms' as one of the purposes of the UN Security Council.[1939] In his concurring opinion in the *Sayadi and Vinck* case, Sir Nigel Rodley, a Committee member of the UN HRC, held that the wording used in Article 1(3) of the UN Charter 'strongly suggests that the [...] interpretation criterion [to determine whether there is a conflict] is that there should be a presumption that the Security Council did not intend that actions taken pursuant to its resolutions should violate human rights.'[1940] The ECtHR similarly confirmed the presumption that the UN Security Council does not intend to impose any obligation on Member States to breach fundamental principles of HRL in its ruling in the case of *Al-Jedda v. the United Kingdom*. Hereafter, the ECtHR added a high threshold for the rebuttal of this presumption:[1941]

1936 Art. 1 and 24 of the UN Charter are discussed in Part I, Section 4.1.1.2(A).

1937 Art. 25 of the UN Charter is also discussed in Part II, Section 3.3.2.

1938 Leiæ and Paulus (n. 1219) 2127. On the general presumption against normative conflict in international law, see ILC, 'Fragmentation of International Law: Difficulties Arising from the Diversification and Expansion of International Law, Report of the Study Group of the International Law Commission, Finalized by Martti Koskenniemi' (n. 616) paras 37–43; Joost Pauwelyn, *Conflict of Norms in Public International Law: How WTO Law Relates to Other Rules of International Law* (Cambridge University Press 2003) 240–244.

1939 See also Art. 55(c) of the UN Charter which sets forth that the UN '[w]ith a view to the creation of conditions of stability and well-being which are necessary for peaceful and friendly relations among nations based on respect for the principle of equal rights and self-determination of peoples [...] shall promote [...] universal respect for, and observance of human rights and fundamental freedoms for all without distinction as to race, sex, language, or religion.'

1940 *Sayadi and Vinck v. Belgium, Concurring opinion by Committee member Sir Nigel Rodley* (2008) UN HRC UN Doc. CCPR/C/94/D/1472/2006, 3216 Oxford Reports on International Human Rights Law, Individual opinion of Committee member Sir Nigel Rodley (concurring), para.5. Wood strongly disagrees with this presumption arguing that '[i]t ignores the fact that, by definition, the Council is acting in an emergency situation, where there is a threat to the peace, breach of the peace, or an act of aggression' and that 'depending what it takes to rebut it, this first presumption could deprive Art. 103, a cornerstone of the Charter, of virtually all practical effect in this context,' see Wood (n. 875) 18–20.

1941 Emphasis added. *Case of Al-Jedda v. the United Kingdom, Judgment* (n. 886) para. 102. See also *Case of Al-Dulimi and Montana Management Inc v. Switzerland, Judgment* (2016) ECtHR (Grand Chamber) App. No. 5809/08 para. 140; *Case of Nada v. Switzerland, Judgment* (n. 1081) para. 171. On systemic harmonisation in the context of case law of the ECtHR, see Linos-Alexander Sicilianos, 'The European Court of Human Rights Facing the Security

> In the light of the United Nations' important role in promoting and encouraging respect for human rights, it is to be expected that *clear* and *explicit* language would be used were the Security Council to intend States to take particular measures which would conflict with their obligations under international human rights law.

The key question now is whether armed forces are allowed to use force that exceeds the limits of HRL and IHL based on Article 103 of the UN Charter when being provided with a UNSC mandate to use 'all necessary means' to achieve a number of objectives. At one end of the spectrum, Aughey and Sari argue that, at least with respect to States acting pursuant to a Chapter VII mandate, practice shows that the UN Security Council uses this formula to authorise the use of lethal force beyond what is acceptable under HRL, often without using more explicit language to qualify or displace HRL obligations.[1942] Hence, they hold that the formula 'all necessary measures' must be understood to satisfy the ECtHR's requirement for 'explicit language'.[1943] At the other end of the spectrum, Milanović contends that vague and open language such as 'all necessary means or measures' should never trump clear and detailed provisions of HRL treaties.[1944] He also advocates for the creation of a 'rebuttable interpretative presumption supported by a clear statement rule' since the use of such a presumption may constitute a useful method for avoiding conflicts of norms.[1945]

If one accepts that the UN Security Council may authorise conduct that violates obligations under HRL and IHL, it is defensible to require assurance that this is indeed the intention of the UN Security Council. Yet, demanding that the UN Security Council *details* the extent to which it considers it 'necessary' to depart from certain HRL or IHL obligations is simply unrealistic.[1946] The UN Security Council will never do so. Moreover, given that it is the operational and tactical leadership as opposed to the political and military strategic leadership which has a clear overview of what is necessary and what is not to successfully carry out the mandate, it is even defendable that the UN Security Council limits itself to more general resolutions. What is feasible is to allow those actors responsible for implementing UNSC mandates to determine which forcible means are to be used with reference to the objectives set forth in the relevant UNSC resolution. If the UN Security Council grants a mandate to pursue certain objectives, there is no 'conflict' between this mandate and a State's international obligations unless those objectives cannot be achieved in

Council: Towards Systemic Harmonization' (2017) 66 International and Comparative Law Quarterly 783.

1942 Aughey and Sari (n. 888) 79.

1943 *Ibid.*

1944 Milanović, 'Norm Conflict in International Law: Whither Human Rights?' (n. 1925) 97.

1945 *Ibid.* 98.

1946 Larsen (n. 1350) 352.

conformity with a State's obligation under international agreements.[1947] In most occasions (and definitely concerning UN peace operations), one must still assume that the UN Security Council intends to authorise actions which can be carried out without violating HRL or, if applicable, IHL. If, however, there are too many contraindications and all other conflict avoidance techniques have failed, the scope of the conflict between the norms is to be 'minimized through interpretation'[1948] of the conflicting norms so that the right can be respected to the greatest extent possible.[1949] This means that even if a UNSC resolution overrides certain obligations under international agreements and activates Article 103 of the UN Charter, it still does not relieve a State of all aspects of the obligations in question.

While the UN Security Council has a certain degree of discretion to overrule or authorise acts contrary to the rules of HRL or IHL, there are limits to the possible impact the UNSC mandate may have on whether force can be used in specific instances. A UNSC mandate may never trump peremptory norms, such as the right not to be arbitrarily deprived of one's life and the fundamental principles of IHL.[1950] However, over the years, the UN Security Council and Secretariat have adopted increasingly strong language to encourage the proactive implementation of mission mandates. It is not always clear how this relates to the applicable legal regimes that regulate the use of force in UN peace operations.

For example, in discussing the IHL principle of distinction, it was already brought up that a statement by a UN Senior Legal Advisor that a person who is not a legitimate target under IHL may become an authorised military target of a UN peace operation[1951] is highly problematic if UN peace forces are commanded to use lethal force against certain persons, in *disregard* for the *jus cogens* principle of distinction between combatants and civilians and the *jus cogens* right not to be arbitrarily deprived of one's life.[1952] A UNSC mandate can never be invoked to justify using lethal force in the conduct of hostilities in violation of a peremptory norm of IHL.[1953] Likewise, a UNSC mandate can never be used to justify using lethal force outside the conduct of hostilities that violates a peremptory norm of HRL.[1954]

1947 Kleffner (n. 1374) 61.

1948 See analysis of the *Al-Jedda* judgment before the former UK House of Lords in this regard, Milanović, 'Norm Conflict in International Law: Whither Human Rights?' (n. 1925) 83.

1949 In this respect, the present author largely follows the approach taken in the *Al-Jedda* case before the former UK House of Lords. See also Larsen (n. 1350) 346 and 349; Leiæ and Paulus (n. 1219) 2120.

1950 See Part III, Sections 2.1.2.2 and 2.2.3.2.

1951 Wills, 'Use of Deadly Force by Peacekeepers Operating Outside of Armed Conflict Situations: What Laws Apply?' (n. 18) 691.

1952 For sources defending the claim that the right to life is a *jus cogens* norm, see Part III, Section 2.1.2.2, fn. 1397, as regards the peremptory nature of the fundamental principles of IHL, see Part III, Section 2.2.3.2.

1953 See also Part III, Sections 2.1.4.1 and 2.1.4.2.

1954 See also Part III, Section 2.2.1.3.

3.3.2.2. Limits to the possible impact: case study on reconciling threats to civilians, imminence, and the right to life in the context of UN peace operations

Around 2014, there was a notable change in the PoC language used in UNSC mandates. A large number of UNSC resolutions dropped 'imminence' from the authorisation to use all necessary means to protect civilians under threat of physical violence. For instance, early mandates of UNMISS authorised UN peace forces to 'protect civilians against the imminent threat of violence,'[1955] but current iterations of its mandate define PoC in relation to generic threats, with no further mention of imminence.[1956] In total, approximately half of all PoC mandates granted to UN peace operations between 1999 and 2021 refer to '*imminent* threat' of physical violence, while the other half have dropped the 'imminence' qualifier and refer to 'threats' only.[1957] At the same time, the UN Secretariat has redefined imminence by downplaying the temporality of threats in its PoC policies since at least 2015.[1958] Both these trends tie in with increasingly robust peacekeeping mandates that seek not only to maintain peace but also to restore state authority and ensure the well-being of civilians.

In Part I of this study, it has been discussed that the practice of instructing UN peace operations to use all necessary means to protect civilians has not necessarily delivered consistent results on the ground.[1959] Over the years, the UN and non-governmental organisations have documented repeated failures to protect civilians. For instance, according to the UN's internal oversight body OIOS, peace forces rarely use force to protect civilians in practice, to the detriment of the populations that need such protection.[1960] Partly in response

---

[1955] 'UNSC Res. 1996' (n. 135) para. 3(b)(v). See 'UNSC Res. 2109' (n. 135) para. 4. (UNSC Resolution 2057 refers to UNSC Resolution 1996 and thus also to the requirement that the threat is 'imminent': 'UNSC Res. 2057' (n. 135) para. 1).

[1956] See 'UNSC Res. 2155' (n. 135) para. 4(a)(i); 'UNSC Res. 2187' (n. 135) para. 4(a)(i); 'UNSC Res. 2223' (n. 19) para. 4(a)(i); 'UNSC Res. 2241' (n. 135) 4(a)(i); 'UNSC Res. 2252' (n. 135) para. 8(a)(i); 'UNSC Res. 2304' (n. 135) para. 10(c); 'UNSC Res. 2327' (n. 19) para. 7(a)(i); 'UNSC Res. 2406' (n. 19) para. 7(a)(i); 'UNSC Res. 2459' (n. 135) para. 7(a)(i); 'UNSC Res. 2514' (n. 135) para. 8(a)(i); 'UNSC Res. 2567' (n. 135) para. 3(a)(i). (UNSC Resolutions 2302, 2326, and 2392 refer to preceding UNSC resolutions and thus also to the requirement that there is a simple 'threat': 'UNSC Res. 2302' (n. 1016) para. 1; 'UNSC Res. 2326' (n. 1016) para. 1; 'UNSC Res. 2392' (n. 1016) para. 1).

[1957] For a detailed overview of the changing language in PoC mandates and in particular the evolutions regarding the terms 'in danger', 'under threat of attack', or 'under threat or imminent threat' of 'physical violence', see Part II, Section 3.2.4.

[1958] The detailed analysis of the UN Secretariat's documentation (see Part II, Section 3.2.4.2) has shown that the meaning of 'imminent' is ambiguous and increasingly disconnected from temporal proximity.

[1959] See Part I, Section 3.1.4. See also United Nations Peacekeeping Law Reform Project, School of Law, University of Essex (n. 485) para. 127.

[1960] For a more detailed discussion of the evaluation of UN peace operations with regard to the use of force to protect civilians, see Part I, Section 3.1.4.

to these criticisms, the UN has searched for ways to encourage peace forces to intervene on behalf of civilians, including by using armed force. One such initiative was to revise the threshold for the use of force for civilian protection goals.

This trend towards robust PoC is often applauded, but the legal parameters for the use of force continue to develop under the radar and are rarely scrutinised. Against the backdrop of the UN's changing approach to 'imminence', complex questions arise concerning the legal parameters governing the use of force for PoC. For example, if the PoC mandate foresees an authorisation to use all necessary means to protect civilians against the threat of physical violence (and thus not 'imminent threat of physical violence'), does this imply that UN peace forces may use lethal force to protect such civilians against remote threats? And if the PoC mandate does include the 'imminence' requirement, how should such a mandate be interpreted and implemented?

In the wake of the changing PoC language, this case study examines the legal relevance of such differences and ambiguities in PoC language, the extent to which such language is compatible with the right to life (and, in particular, its temporal conditions for lawful deprivations of the right to life), and the extent to which this changing PoC language may have an impact on the use of force on the ground.

A. Scrutinising PoC language through the lens of the right to life

Differences in PoC vocabulary in UNSC mandates do not present a problem *per se* for the legal rules governing the use of force by UN peace forces. When the UN Security Council authorises a mission to use 'all necessary means' to protect civilians against a 'threat' or 'imminent threat' of physical violence, the scope of action is not limited to lethal options affecting the right to life. A wide range of measures can be taken to protect civilians against both imminent and non-imminent threats, including guarding a hospital by simply being present, using a water cannon to quell a riot or disperse an angry mob, or using a series of barricades and physical obstructions to prevent vehicles from reaching a crowd. To be sure, such measures may also include using explosives to dismantle an armed group's roadblock that prevents the passage of essential food to a village or stopping a deadly attack on a group of women by eliminating the attackers with a firearm. The point is that while measures to protect civilians may be (potentially) lethal in nature and thus covered by the right to life, UN peace forces may also enforce PoC mandates through a range of forcible measures that do not implicate the right to life at all.

Accordingly, it is not *per se* legally problematic if the UN Security Council includes the qualifier 'imminent' to designate threats in a PoC mandate, nor is it necessarily problematic if the imminence requirement is omitted from the UNSC mandate. A wide-range of less-lethal protection measures may be pursued in furtherance of such mandates. However, from a legal perspective, the core question remains under what conditions peace forces may resort to lethal force. It is problematic if the UN suggests that such mandates provide sufficient legal authority to use lethal force, in *disregard* for the right to life and specifically the imminence requirements imposed by HRL. Lethal force can never be justified by simply arguing that the mandate authorises the use of 'all necessary means' to protect civilians without any further inquiry into whether specific uses of force meet the requirements to deprive someone of their life in accordance with the human right to life.

The (un)lawfulness of specific uses of force depends not only on the legal basis, as enshrined in the UNSC mandates but also on the applicable legal norms. When a UNSC mandate is implemented and translated into the ROE, these ROE may not, at least in principle, be more permissible than what the law applicable to the operation allows.[1961] In the PoC context, this implies that if the UN Security Council provides a mission with a mandate to use all necessary means to protect civilians against the (imminent) threat of physical violence, the mission-specific ROE may not simply provide rules on the use of force to protect civilians but must also reflect either IHL or HRL standards.

It is far from clear that this is currently the case. The above-mentioned Rule 1.8 of the 2002 UN Sample ROE provides that force up to and including lethal force may be used to defend a civilian in need of protection from a hostile act or intent where the competent local authorities are unable to provide immediate assistance.[1962] Outside the conduct of hostilities, when Rule 1.8 is translated into a mission-specific ROE, it should be interpreted primarily through the lens of HRL. Consequently, if intentional lethal force were to be used to protect civilians in a situation with no clear nexus to an armed conflict, such force must be absolutely necessary and proportionate ('strictly unavoidable') to defend civilians against imminent attacks that may result in loss of life, which in turn means a matter of a split second, or at most a few seconds, before fatality strikes, and not just temporally ill-defined 'imminent' threats or a 'hostile intent' established based on prior attacks. Furthermore, depending on the terminology used in the PoC mandate, potentially lethal force can also be used against a person posing a continuing threat to life which may materialise at any time.[1963]

However, this seems not necessarily consistent with the UN's interpretation. By comparing the UN policy (as discussed in Part I, Section 3.1.3) and the changing language in PoC mandates and, in particular, the evolutions regarding the terms 'in danger', 'under threat of attack', or 'under threat or imminent threat' of 'physical violence' (as discussed in Part II, Section 3.2.4) against the

[1961] Unless the UN Security Council authorised lawful derogation thereof, see Part III, Sections 2.1.4.1, 2.1.4.2, and 2.2.1.3.

[1962] UN DPKO (n. 102) Attachment 1, 2.

[1963] See also Part III, Section 3.1.1.3.

legal parameters of lawful deprivation of the right to life (as discussed in Part III, Section 3.1.1), it emerges that the UN's translation of legal norms into practical use of force guidelines for peace forces raises two concerns. On the one hand, the UN conception of the notions of 'imminence' and 'hostile intent' remains ambiguous; on the other, UN policy does not distinguish between potentially lethal force and intentional lethal force.

The 2017 UN Guidelines on the Use of Force by Military Components in UN Peacekeeping Operations, the most recent authoritative restatement of use of force rules for UN peace forces has set forth the following:[1964]

> The use of force in peacekeeping operations must comply with international laws, including applicable international humanitarian law and human rights norms, principles and standards. At all times, the use of force must be consistent with the principles of gradation, necessity, proportionality, legality, distinction, precaution, humanity and accountability. Any force used must be limited in its intensity and duration to what is necessary to achieve the authorized objective and, commensurate with the threat.

Accordingly, the UN effectively invokes the HRL principles of necessity and proportionality. Yet, its interpretation and application of these principles are not entirely consistent with human rights-based jurisprudence and guidance. The 2015 UN Policy on PoC in UN Peacekeeping, the 2017 UN Guidelines on the Use of Force by Military Components in UN Peacekeeping Operations, the 2019 UN Policy on PoC in UN Peacekeeping, and the 2020 UN Handbook on PoC in UN Peacekeeping fail to clearly articulate whether – and if so, how – 'imminent' a threat must be in order for lethal force to be used.[1965] For example, the 2019 UN Policy on PoC in UN Peacekeeping suggests that force, up to and including lethal force, can be used in response to 'threats of physical violence against civilians', which *need not* be imminent in nature *unless* the specific UNSC mandate requires it.[1966] Does this imply that when a PoC mandate does not include the imminence requirement, intentional lethal force can be used

1964 UN DPKO and UN DFS, '2017 UN Guidelines on the Use of Force by Military Components in UN Peacekeeping Operations' (n. 17) para. 8.

1965 See UN DPKO and UN DFS, '2015 UN Policy on PoC in UN Peacekeeping' (n. 16); UN DPO, '2019 UN Policy on PoC in UN Peacekeeping' (n. 35); UN DPKO and UN DFS, '2017 UN Guidelines on the Use of Force by Military Components in UN Peacekeeping Operations' (n. 17); UN DPO, '2020 UN Handbook on PoC in UN Peacekeeping' (n. 35) (as discussed in detail in Section 2.2).

1966 Indeed, in its 2019 UN Policy on PoC in UN Peacekeeping, the UN DPO clarified that an authorisation to use all necessary means to protect civilians under threat of physical violence implies that force (even to a degree of lethal force) can be used to that end. '[T]hreats of physical violence against civilians' include 'all hostile acts or situations which are likely to lead to death or serious bodily injury of civilians.' It added that such a threat does not need to be imminent unless the specific UNSC mandate requires it. See UN DPO, '2019 UN Policy on PoC in UN Peacekeeping' (n. 35) paras 16–18 and 23.

even if there is no imminent (in the sense of a matter of seconds or even split seconds) threat to life? And if the PoC mandate does include the imminence qualifier, must imminence be understood in accordance with HRL or does the UN DPO still adhere to the 2015 UN Policy on PoC in UN Peacekeeping's broad, non-temporal definition of the term? It is concerning that, in the 2015 UN Policy on PoC in UN Peacekeeping, the former UN DPKO and DFS first indicated that 'imminent' does not imply that violence will necessarily take place or that violence is guaranteed to take place in the immediate or near future, but that it is sufficient that the mission can reasonably assume that a potential perpetrator shows, among other indications, a hostile intent,[1967] while subsequently defining 'hostile intent' as '[t]he threat of an impending use of force,' without explaining what 'impending' means.[1968] This definition was then reproduced by the 2017 UN Guidelines on the Use of Force by Military Components in UN Peacekeeping Operations, which remains the main policy document on these issues.[1969]

These terminological imprecisions and contradictions suggest that the UN has reservations about the temporal aspects of peace forces' authority to use force. While the UN has long sought ways to encourage peace forces to take proactive and preventive action to protect civilians under threat,[1970] it is doubtful whether such inducements can be squared with the legal regime that protects the life of potential targets. One interpretation of the UN's policy framework is that the HRL requirement of 'grave threat' to life for potentially lethal force in pursuit of certain legitimate aims, as outlined in the UNSC mandate, is respected (for instance, it can be argued that the 2019 UN Policy on PoC in UN Peacekeeping's understanding of 'threats of physical violence' as 'situations which are *likely* to lead to death or serious bodily injury of civilians' fulfils this legal condition).[1971] A more problematic interpretation of the UN's policies is that, by not distinguishing between the use of potentially lethal force and intentional lethal force and dissociating 'imminence' from questions of temporal proximity, the UN seeks to implicitly authorise actions, up to and including intentional lethal force, to protect civilians even if the threat is not temporally imminent in the 'seconds' sense. The second interpretation runs

---

1967 UN DPKO and UN DFS, '2015 UN Policy on PoC in UN Peacekeeping' (n. 16) para. 47. According to the 2015 UN Policy on PoC in UN Peacekeeping, it suffices that the mission can reasonably assume that a potential perpetrator 'displays a hostile intent, capacity, historical record and opportunity to inflict physical violence.' UN DPKO and UN DFS, '2015 UN Implementing Guidelines for Military Components of UN Peacekeeping Missions on PoC' (n. 103) 25.

1968 UN DPKO and UN DFS, '2015 UN Policy on PoC in UN Peacekeeping' (n. 16) 19.

1969 UN DPKO and UN DFS, '2017 UN Guidelines on the Use of Force by Military Components in UN Peacekeeping Operations' (n. 17) 19.

1970 See also UN DPO, '2020 UN Handbook on PoC in UN Peacekeeping' (n. 35) 8 (discussion of the meaning of '[i]mminent threats').

1971 Emphasis added. UN DPO, '2019 UN Policy on PoC in UN Peacekeeping' (n. 35) para. 23.

counter to the right not to be arbitrarily deprived of one's life and thus violates the underlying *jus cogens* norm.[1972]

B. Reconciling law with practice in UN peace operations

Several observations from practice can clarify the law governing the use of force by UN peace forces under UNSC-authorised PoC mandates. To this end, two scenarios are distinguished: Scenario 1 involves a temporally imminent threat to life or serious injury followed by potentially lethal force or a temporally imminent threat to life followed by intentional lethal force; Scenario 2 involves a temporally removed yet grave threat to life followed by potentially lethal force. It must be remembered that any legal analysis of concrete uses of force is heavily fact-dependent, and the scenarios below serve educational purposes rather than to pass judgment on similar situations in UN theatres of operations.

i. Scenario 1: imminent threat

Regardless of whether a PoC mandate requires threats of physical violence against civilians to be 'imminent' or, alternatively, refers to 'threats' with no further mention of imminence, this study submits that UN peace forces may always use *potentially* lethal force to protect civilians if a temporally proximate threat to life or serious injury exists. For instance, if a UN patrol around a refugee camp encounters an armed group member or a civilian who is threatening another civilian with arms, UN peace forces may resort to *potentially* lethal force to address this threat (provided that all HRL principles are met). Such use of force can be construed as the defence of others in conformity with HRL.

Where the use of potentially lethal force would not be sufficient to avert the threat and would unduly risk death, UN peace forces may use *intentional* lethal force to protect civilians but only from narrowly and temporally restricted threats to life (i.e. an imminent threat of serious injury would no longer be sufficient). Under HRL, the legality of such lethal force will again *not* depend on whether the mission's mandate mentions or omits an imminence requirement or how the UN defines this term. As a matter of law, the threat to civilians must be such that it is, at most, a matter of seconds or even split seconds before fatality strikes. Imminence, understood as a matter of seconds in the human rights system, is a requirement flowing from a *jus cogens* norm, and the UN Security Council cannot set this condition aside – even less so the UN Secretariat through its interpretive guidance, for instance on PoC – by re-defining or omitting

[1972] On the limits to derogation, see Part III, Sections 2.1.4.1 and 2.1.4.2. For sources substantiating the position that the right to life is a peremptory norm, see Part III, Section 2.1.2.2, fn. 1397. On the legal parameters for intentional lethal force, see Part III, Section 3.1.1.3(B).

'imminence'. It must be emphasised that the absence of the word 'imminence' in UNSC mandates cannot be read to somehow 'empower' (grant additional authority to) UN peace forces to address temporally unrestricted threats through intentional lethal force. Chapter VII authority is not a blank cheque to redefine or re-interpret the conditions of a *jus cogens* norm like the right to life, nor is it a 'get out of jail free' card that absolves the UN from the duty to justify why killing alleged hostile actors was necessary and proportionate, even if lethal force was used for the laudable goal of protecting civilians.

This position has concrete operational implications for troops in the field. Under IHL, lethal force may always be used against legitimate targets, subject to that body of law's legal conditions for targeting. For instance, it is assumed that MONUSCO's Intervention Brigade is a party to an armed conflict with the ADF armed group and, hence, the Intervention Brigade may, to fulfil its PoC mandate, intentionally target and kill members of the ADF subject to IHL conditions, especially the principle of distinction.[1973] However, outside of situations governed by IHL, the authority of UN peace forces to kill will be significantly more constrained. In practice, resorting to intentional lethal force will only be permissible if people are a split second away from death, as in the case of killing a sniper in the chest who is about to shoot another peacekeeper patrolling the streets or killing a suspected suicide bomber who is about to detonate a bomb in a crowded IDPs camp likely killing dozens of civilians. Likewise, outside of situations governed by IHL, UN peace forces may never act on a 'shoot to kill' policy except in such narrowly defined temporal (and often also geographical) circumstances.[1974] The most important practical consequence for UN peace operations is that, outside of situations governed by IHL, operations intended to *pre-empt* threats to civilians based on the capability and *past* behaviour of targets, in particular with 'shoot to kill' policies, would always raise legal doubts as to whether intentional lethal force is used in violation of HRL.

To take the example of MONUSCO, it is uncontroversial that UN troops currently operating in Kasai province – where no armed conflict existed as of at least 2019[1975] – cannot ground their authority to protect civilians, as set out in MONUSCO's ROE, on IHL targeting norms and principles. For intentional lethal force against (the remnants of) the Kamuina Nsapu armed group or Congolese army troops in Kasai to ever constitute a proportionate response,

1973 See Geneva Academy Rule of Law (n. 495).

1974 On shoot to kill, see sources referred to in Part III, Section 2.1.2.2, fn. 1399.

1975 See Geneva Academy Rule of Law (n. 495) ('In early 2019, the swearing in of Félix Tshisekedi as new president was seen as a victory for the rebels inasmuch as they consider him a "son of the Kasai". Consequently, a number of rebel fighters decided to lay down their arms and, according to the information at our disposal, no relevant episodes of violence have taken place between the Kamuina Nsapu and the FARDC. Therefore, it seems possible to conclude that the conflict is now over. Nevertheless, since the causes that led to the outbreak of the conflict have not been addressed, the situation could deteriorate again').

UN troops operating in this province must be *responding* to physical violence where the immediacy of the threat to civilian lives is a matter of seconds, rather than *pre-empting* future and hypothetical threats that may – but may not – materialise. Likewise, in peacekeeping environments like the CAR, Mali, and South Sudan, where MINUSCA, MINUSMA, and UNMISS operate in the context of an armed conflict they are not part of themselves, it logically follows that the use of both potentially lethal and intentional lethal force by UN peace forces against members of armed groups or state security forces may not be rationalised by simply invoking a PoC mandate but rather must comply with the strict conditions of HRL. In this regard, MINUSCA's overtly offensive PoC operations, undertaken by its Portuguese contingent, in particular, must raise questions about the legality of killings by UN peace forces in the CAR.[1976]

At the same time, separating reactive from proactive operations raises additional questions for the legality of potentially – as opposed to intentional – lethal force in MINUSCA and other missions. To illustrate: in 2017, MINUSCA invoked its PoC mandate to justify a strike by one of its attack helicopters, resulting in at least one death, against an armed group that had ignored its warnings to not cross a red line around Bambari, a specially designated 'city without armed groups' under the mission's PoC mandate.[1977] Despite MINUSCA's reliance on PoC as a rationale for targeting the armed group's convoy, the mere crossing of a red line several kilometres outside Bambari sits uneasily with the HRL threshold of a temporally proximate threat to civilians inside the city of Bambari. If the helicopters received authorisation from MINUSCA commanders to neutralise the convoy, the killing would be, as explained above, *prima facie* illegal under HRL. Contrary to MINUSCA's press statements, the legality of such operations does not depend only on what the mission mandate says or does not say.[1978] To be sure, this study acknowledges that when operating in a conduct of hostilities paradigm governed by IHL, UN peace forces have considerable discretion to use lethal force even in the absence of imminent – however one defines this term – threats to civilians. However, absent concrete indications that IHL applies and a nexus to the armed conflict exists, deprivations of life in a peacekeeping context should be analysed primarily through the more restrictive lens of HRL. Unless MINUSCA was

---

1976 UN DPO, 'Portuguese Blue Helmets Awarded UN Medals for Impactful Peacekeeping' (*UN Peacekeeping*, 27 February 2020), https://peacekeeping.un.org/en/portuguese-blue-helmets-awarded-un-medals-impactful-peacekeeping, accessed 13 June 2022; X, 'President Congratulates Portuguese Commandos in Bambari' (*The Portugal News*, 9 March 2017), www.theportugalnews.com/news/president-congratulates-portuguese-commandos-in-bambari/41303, accessed 13 June 2022.

1977 Monteiro, 'La MINUSCA Intervient Contre Des Éléments Lourdement Armés Au Nord de Bambari' (n. 24); Monteiro, 'Mise En Garde de La MINUSCA à La Coalition Du FPRC à Propos Des Déplacés de Ippy' (n. 24).

1978 For a detailed analysis, see Labuda, 'The UN Goes to War in the Central African Republic: What Are the Limits of Peacekeeping?' (n. 497).

responding to physical violence where the immediacy of the threat to civilian lives is a matter of seconds, the use of intentional lethal force was not permitted in this situation. In the absence of a temporally proximate threat to civilians, MINUSCA's strike on the convoy could perhaps theoretically be justified as a use of potentially lethal force if the mission had concrete information about a threat to civilians inside the city (see *further below*). Yet, firing a helicopter gun, given its extremely high rate of fire bursts, at a vehicle is unlikely to ever amount to anything but intentional lethal force.

ii. Scenario 2: grave threat

Factual situations that fall outside of imminence *qua* temporally proximate threats to civilians are more legally complex and create more interpretive challenges. If, for example, UN peace forces on patrol encounter an armed group that has attacked a village but, at the point of contact, is retreating from the village and poses no immediate threat to any specific civilians, there is little doubt that *intentional* lethal force is impermissible (for reasons previously explained). Unless the mission is already a party to a pre-existing conflict with the armed group and IHL applies to the UN's targeting decisions, intentional lethal force would not be a legal response under HRL, under both the necessity and proportionality prongs discussed above.[1979]

To comply with HRL proportionality in such factual scenarios, the UN may, however, use graduated force for PoC aims, which includes lethal force but only as a last resort. This study submits that, in such factual scenarios, the wording of PoC mandates, and specifically the concept of 'imminence', may play a role in delineating the UN's authority to take action.[1980] Although intentional lethal force will never be permissible in such cases, UN peace forces may lawfully resort to *potentially* lethal force under the following conditions. If the UN Security Council authorises a UN peace operation to 'use all necessary means to protect civilians against the threat of physical violence' – without requiring the threat to be 'imminent' – UN peace forces may use *potentially* lethal force to protect civilians on the condition that there is at least a 'grave threat to life', which some human rights instruments define as an ongoing threat to life that can materialise at any time. This interpretation flows from the fact that when the UN Security Council adopts a PoC mandate, protecting civilians against more temporally-removed threats is a legitimate aim that may, subject to the facts of each case, justify *potentially* lethal force. To take the examples above, UN peace forces could be justified in firing on a retreating armed group if the UN has concrete indications that the group is likely to return to the same village and

1979 See Part III, Sections 3.1.1.2 and 3.1.1.3.
1980 On the meaning of 'imminent', see Part II, Section 3.2.4.2.

inflict violence on civilians. However, absent such information, UN peace forces should limit their intervention to less-lethal force.

By the same token, when the UN Security Council adopts mandates that cover only imminent threats to civilians, UN peace forces may not resort to potentially lethal force absent threats to civilians understood as a matter of seconds. Indeed, when interpreted in good faith, taking into account the ordinary meaning to be given to this term when read in the context of the resolution as a whole, 'imminent' must be understood as 'impending' and 'a matter of seconds', an interpretation that is consistent with the meaning given to this term in the HRL context.[1981]

In this case, UN peace forces are not authorised to use any type of lethal force to confront a retreating armed group and must instead resort to other forms of coercion based on a graduated force procedure, beginning with their 'authoritative presence' before turning to less-lethal measures such as tear gas, stun grenades, smoke grenades, or soft kinetic projectiles.[1982] In other words, UN peace forces in a few ongoing missions, for instance, in Abyei or Lebanon, enjoy less authority to protect civilians from threats in scenarios that do not rise to the level of a temporally imminent threat to the lives of civilians under their protection. Conversely, peace forces in the UN's large operations, notably in the DRC, the CAR, Mali, and South Sudan, are – subject to the factual circumstances – authorised to respond to a wider range of threats to civilians.

4. OBLIGATION TO (USE FORCE TO) PROTECT CIVILIANS AGAINST THE THREAT OF PHYSICAL VIOLENCE UNDER HRL AND IHL

When UN (mandated) peace operations are deployed in the territory of a State, the question arises whether missions are obligated to take positive action for the protection of civilians. In Part II, Section 3.3.2, this study already dealt extensively with whether a PoC mandate, in itself, can give rise to an obligation to take all necessary measures for the protection of civilians. This Section analyses whether legal obligations to protect civilians can also be found in HRL and IHL.

The norms most relevant to the protection of civilians against treats posed by others under HRL and IHL are the obligation to protect individuals' human rights, and, in particular, the right to life, and the obligation to ensure respect

1981 See also the discussion in Part II, Section 3.4.1 on the possible influence of HRL on the interpretation of UNSC resolutions that contain a PoC mandate.

1982 UN DPKO and UN DFS, '2017 UN Guidelines on the Use of Force by Military Components in UN Peacekeeping Operations' (n. 17) para. 12(b).

for IHL.[1983] Obligations also arise under the Genocide Convention[1984] and the laws of occupation,[1985] and while this provides an interesting debate, a discussion of these obligations falls outside the scope of this book. As this study primarily focuses on the use of force for PoC, it first analyses the obligation of UN (mandated) peace forces 'to protect' the human right to life. This analysis is followed by a study of their obligation 'to ensure respect' for IHL.

4.1. OBLIGATION 'TO PROTECT' THE HUMAN RIGHT TO LIFE

As already set forth in Part III, Section 2.1.2.1, it is common to use the tripartite classification 'to respect, protect, and fulfil' to distinguish between three sets of HRL obligations. While the obligation to respect entails a negative obligation not to impede or restrict the enjoyment of human rights, the obligation to protect and the obligation to fulfil both imply a positive obligation, the former entailing the obligation to protect individuals and groups from human rights violations by third parties, and the latter to take measures to grant, facilitate, and promote human rights by adopting appropriate legislative, administrative, budgetary, judicial, and other measures to ensure their full implementation.[1986]

The obligation of States not to impede or restrict the enjoyment of human rights is, in principle, relatively straightforward, but the obligation to protect individuals from third-party violations and to take measures to grant, facilitate, and promote human rights is less obvious. In the landmark case *Velásquez-Rodríguez v. Honduras*, the IACtHR held for the very first time that a State can be

1983 See also Gill and others (n. 26) 176–177.

1984 Art. 1 of the Genocide Convention sets forth a positive obligation to prevent genocide: 'The Contracting Parties confirm that genocide, whether committed in time of peace or in time of war, is a crime under international law which they undertake to prevent and to punish.' In the *Genocide* case, the ICJ clarified that this obligation 'is one of conduct and not one of result, in the sense that a State cannot be under an obligation to succeed, whatever the circumstances, in preventing the commission of genocide.' Rather, States Parties to the Genocide Convention are obliged to use all means reasonably available to them to prevent genocide to the greatest extent possible. A State is not liable merely because the desired result has not been achieved. Rather, liability arises if the State has manifestly failed to take all measures within its power to prevent genocide, which might have helped to prevent it. In this regard, the ICJ has also invoked to the notion of 'due diligence', which requires an assessment *in concreto*. As for the applicable standard of due diligence, the ICJ considered various parameters, including the capacity to influence effectively the action of persons likely to commit or already committing genocide (*Case Concerning Application of the Convention on the Prevention and Punishment of the Crime of Genocide (Bosnia and Herzegovina v. Yugoslavia (Serbia and Montenegro)), Judgment* (n. 1352) para. 430). See also further Sheeran and Kent (n. 50) 57–58; Murray and others (n. 1694) para. 11.19–11.24.

1985 The law relating to military occupation is laid down in the 1907 Hague Regulations and further elaborated in the Geneva Convention IV and the Additional Protocol I. For a detailed analysis, see Wills, *Protecting Civilians: The Obligations of Peacekeepers* (n. 1667) 171–245.

1986 Kleffner (n. 1374) para. 31; Larsen (n. 1350) 125–126.

responsible for violations by private persons because of 'the lack of due diligence' to prevent the violation or to respond to it as required by the ICCPR.[1987] In this regard,[1988]

> What is decisive is whether a violation of the rights recognized by the [ICCPR] [...] has occurred with the support or the acquiescence of the government, or whether the State has allowed the act to take place without taking measures to prevent it or to punish those responsible. Thus, the [...] [IACtHR]'s task is to determine whether the violation is the result of a State's failure to fulfill its duty to respect and guarantee those rights, as required by Article 1 (1) of the [ICCPR] [...].

To this end, the IACtHR considered that the State has a legal obligation to 'take reasonable steps to prevent human rights violations' and to use the means available to seriously investigate violations committed within its jurisdiction, to identify the individuals responsible, to punish those individuals as appropriate, and to ensure adequate compensation for the victim(s).[1989] According to the IACtHR, this duty to 'take reasonable steps to prevent human rights violations' includes the following:[1990]

> [A]ll those means of a legal, political, administrative and cultural nature that promote the protection of human rights and ensure that any violations are considered and treated as illegal acts, which, as such, may lead to the punishment of those responsible and the obligation to indemnify the victims for damages.

In subsequent case law, the IACtHR has confirmed that the sole requirement to attribute to a State its omission to prevent the violations by private parties of rights recognised in the ICCPR is to demonstrate that the State authorities have 'supported or tolerated' those violations.[1991] In the case of *The Pueblo Bello Massacre v. Columbia*, the IACtHR added that States must have been aware of a situation of 'real and imminent danger for a specific individual or group of individuals' and that, even if the State was aware of such situation, the obligation is still subject to a requirement of reasonableness.[1992]

In its General Comment No. 31 on the Nature of the General Legal Obligation Imposed on States Parties to the ICCPR, the UN HRC has equally underlined

---

1987 *Case of Velásquez-Rodríguez v. Honduras, Judgment* (1988) IACtHR Series C No. 4 para. 172.

1988 *Ibid.* paras 173–174.

1989 *Ibid.* para. 174.

1990 *Ibid.* para. 175.

1991 See e.g. *Case of the 'White Van' (Paniagua-Morales et al.) v. Guatemala, Judgment (Preliminary Objections)* (1998) IACtHR Series C No. 23 para. 91; *Ríofrío Massacre v. Colombia* (n. 1695) para. 48.

1992 *Case of the Pueblo Bello Massacre v. Colombia, Judgment* (2006) IACtHR Series C No. 140 para. 123. For a reference to the need for the existence of a 'real and immediate danger,' see also *Case of Valle Jaramillo et al. v. Colombia, Judgment* (2008) IACtHR Series C No. 190 para. 90.

the duty of the State to take positive measures to prevent human rights violations by non-state parties:[1993]

> The article 2, paragraph 1, obligations [under the ICCPR] are binding on States and do not, as such, have direct horizontal effect as a matter of international law. [...] However the positive obligations on States Parties to ensure [...] rights [under the ICCPR] will only be fully discharged if individuals are protected by the State, not just against violations of [...] rights [protected under the ICCPR] by its agents, but also against acts committed by private persons or entities that would impair the enjoyment of [...] rights [under the ICCPR] in so far as they are amenable to application between private persons or entities. There may be circumstances in which a failure to ensure [...] rights [under the ICCPR] as required by article 2 would give rise to violations by States Parties of those rights, as a result of States Parties' permitting or failing to take appropriate measures or to exercise due diligence to prevent, punish, investigate or redress the harm caused by such acts by private persons or entities.

Other courts and international and regional human rights mechanisms have also adopted some form of due diligence test.[1994] For example, in the case of *Social and Economic Rights Action Center and the Center for Economic and Social Rights v. Nigeria*, the AComHPR referred to the case of *Velásquez-Rodríguez v. Honduras* to substantiate its holding that '[g]overnments have a duty to protect their citizens, not only through appropriate legislation and effective enforcement but also by protecting them from damaging acts that may be perpetrated by private parties [...]. This duty calls for positive action on part of governments in fulfilling their obligation under human rights instruments.'[1995] Also in its General Comment No. 3 on the Right to Life, the AComHPR has recognised that States have to exercise 'due diligence' in ensuring respect for the right to life:[1996]

> A State can be held responsible for killings by non-State actors if it approves, supports or acquiesces in those acts or if it fails to exercise due diligence to prevent such killings or to ensure proper investigation and accountability.

In the case of *L.C.B. v. the United Kingdom* (a case that concerned the alleged exposure to radiation), the ECtHR has equally recognised that the right to life entails positive obligations for Member States. In particular, the ECtHR

1993 UN HRC, 'General Comment No. 31 [80] on the Nature of the General Legal Obligation Imposed on States Parties to the ICCPR' (n. 81) para. 8.

1994 For further case law, see below. See also ECOSOC, Commission on Human Rights, 'Civil and Political Rights, Including the Questions of Disappearances and Summary Executions, Report of the Special Rapporteur, Philip Alston, on Extrajudicial, Summary or Arbitrary Executions, Sixty-First Session, Item 11(b) of the Provisional Agenda' (2005) UN Doc. E/CN.4/2005/7 paras 65–76, and, in particular, para. 74.

1995 *Social and Economic Rights Action Center & the Center for Economic and Social Rights v. Nigeria* (2002) AComHPR Communication No. 155/96, para. 57.

1996 AComHPR (n. 83) para. 9.

considered that 'the first sentence of Article 2 §1 [of the ECHR] enjoins the State not only to refrain from the intentional and unlawful taking of life, but also to take *appropriate steps* to safeguard the lives of those within its jurisdiction' and, further, that it is the ECtHR's task 'to determine whether, given the circumstances of the case, the State did all that could have been required of it to prevent the applicant's life from being avoidably put at risk.'[1997] In the case of *Osman v. the United Kingdom* (a case in which the ECtHR had to rule, *inter alia*, on the alleged failure of authorities to protect the right to life of two individuals from a threat posed by another individual), the ECtHR added that the State's obligation in this regard 'extends beyond its primary duty to secure the right to life by putting in place effective criminal provisions' and extends to an obligation on the authorities 'to take preventive operational measures' in certain well-defined circumstances for the protection of an individual whose life is threatened by the criminal acts of another individual.[1998]

In doing so, however, the ECtHR has expressly held that the positive obligation to protect life is not unlimited. Having regard to the difficulties of policing in modern societies, the unpredictability of human behaviour, and the operational choices to be made in terms of priorities and resources, the ECtHR recognises that such an obligation must be interpreted as not imposing on the authorities an 'impossible or disproportionate burden.'[1999] Therefore, the ECtHR considers that not every alleged danger to life can create a treaty obligation for the authorities to take operational measures to prevent that danger from manifesting itself.[2000] For a positive obligation to protect the right to life to arise, it must be established that 'the authorities knew or ought to have known at the time' that there was 'a real and immediate risk' to the life of an identified person or persons as a result of the criminal acts of a third party and that they failed to take measures within their powers which, if considered reasonable, could have been expected to prevent that risk from materialising.[2001] According to the

[1997] Emphasis added. *Case of LCB v. the United Kingdom, Judgment* (1998) ECtHR App. No. 14/1997/798/1001 para. 36.

[1998] *Case of Osman v. the United Kingdom, Judgment* (1998) ECtHR (Grand Chamber) App. No. 87/1997/871/1083 para. 115, as reiterated in *Case of Paul and Audrey Edwards v. the United Kingdom, Judgment* (2002) ECtHR App. No. 46477/99 para. 54; *Case of Branko Tomašić and Others v. Croatia, Judgment* (2009) ECtHR App. No. 46598/06 para. 50.

[1999] *Case of Osman v. the United Kingdom, Judgment* (n. 1998) 116. as reiterated in *Case of Paul and Audrey Edwards v. the United Kingdom, Judgment* (n. 1998) para. 55; *Case of Branko Tomašić and Others v. Croatia, Judgment* (n. 1998) para. 50. See also *Case of Choreftakis and Choreftaki v. Greece, Judgment* (2012) ECtHR App. No. 46846/08 para. 46.

[2000] *Case of Osman v. the United Kingdom, Judgment* (n. 1998) para. 116, as reiterated in *Case of Paul and Audrey Edwards v. the United Kingdom, Judgment* (n. 1998) para. 55; *Case of Branko Tomašić and Others v. Croatia, Judgment* (n. 1998) para. 50. See also *Case of Choreftakis and Choreftaki v. Greece, Judgment* (n. 1999) para. 46.

[2001] *Case of Osman v. the United Kingdom, Judgment* (n. 1998) para. 116, as reiterated in *Case of Paul and Audrey Edwards v. the United Kingdom, Judgment* (n. 1998) 55; *Case of Branko Tomašić and Others v. Croatia, Judgment* (n. 1998) para. 51; *Case of Choreftakis and Choreftaki v. Greece, Judgment* (n. 1999) para. 47.

ECtHR, that question can be answered only in light of all the circumstances of the particular case.[2002]

Now the next question that arises is whether such positive obligations also arise extraterritorially and, in particular, concerning the right to life. In other words, must a State, when in an extraterritorial situation, act positively to guarantee to the individuals that come under its jurisdiction the full range of HRL obligations, or must it only protect certain rights, such as the right to life, to some extent?[2003] And what about international and regional organisations that carry out a PoC mandate, are they under the positive obligation to protect and fulfil the human right to life when conducting an operation?

To recapitulate, HRL obligations that apply to a UN (mandated) peace operation conducted on the territory of a third State may be derived primarily from the obligation to which the international or regional organisation undertaking the operation, the State undertaking or taking part in the operation, and the State on whose territory the operation takes place (the host State) are bound.[2004] Hence, first and foremost, States' extraterritorial HRL obligations are important in the context of both UN peace operations and UN-mandated peace operations. Second, while international and regional organisations do not have their own territory or nationals, the recognition that States' HRL obligations apply extraterritorially may also apply, by analogy, to international and regional organisations.[2005] Notably, to the extent that regional or international organisations exercise functions in a manner that can be assimilated to the exercise of jurisdiction by States, they are also considered to be exercising jurisdiction.[2006] Needless to say, the question of extraterritorial obligations does not arise in relation to the obligation to respect the law of the host State.

Whether States or regional or international organisations have certain HRL obligations towards individuals when conducting a UN (mandated) peace operation in the territory of a State depends on the model of extraterritorial application used. As discussed above, there are three main models of extraterritorial application that find varying degrees of support in the case law of courts and human rights mechanisms and in legal doctrine, including the spatial model, the personal model, and the functional model.[2007] Because these models, and especially the personal and functional model, can lead to outcomes that are politically or practically extreme or unfeasible, several authors have sought ways to limit the scope of positive obligations. The positive obligation to take action to protect and fulfil human rights only applies extraterritorially when there is

2002 *Case of Osman v. the United Kingdom, Judgment* (n. 1998) para. 116.
2003 Lubell (n. 1517) 227–228.
2004 As discussed above, see Part III, Section 2.1.1.
2005 Maus (n. 1354) 151; Nauta (n. 1366) 139; Zwanenburg, 'UN Peace Operations, International Humanitarian Law and International Human Rights Law' (n. 37) 96–97.
2006 Kleffner (n. 1374) para. 33.
2007 See Part III, Section 2.1.3.

some type of control, ranging from 'control over the effects said to constitute a violation, subject to a foreseeable victim being foreseeably affected by the act,'[2008] the existence of 'a direct and immediate link between the extraterritorial conduct of a state and the alleged violation of an individual's rights,'[2009] or the fact that a State has 'factual control in respect of facts and events that allegedly constitute a *violation* of a human right,'[2010] that the individual 'is directly dependent on the power exercised by the agents,'[2011] or that the State 'has the power to (intentionally, knowingly, or negligently) affect one or several of his/her human rights.'[2012]

This study does not take a position on which of the three models of extraterritorial applicability should be used to determine extraterritorial jurisdiction and which control test should be applied to limit the scope of obligations. What matters on the ground is which model will be applied in the particular case, but this is only ascertained when the court or the human rights mechanism renders an *ex post* ruling on the possible violation of human rights.

Hence, with the three possible models of extraterritorial applicability in mind, a *prudent* approach to the protection of civilian lives in the context of UN (mandated) peace operations with a PoC mandate would be as follows: (i) adhere to the negative obligation 'to respect', in their actions, the right to life of all persons present in the territory of the State(s) where they are deployed; (ii) adhere to the positive obligation 'to protect' the right to life of those whose rights the missions control by taking appropriate and feasible measures to prevent violations of the right to life by non-state actors; and (iii) adhere to the positive obligation 'to fulfil' the right to life, *inter alia*, by conducting effective investigations when individuals have been killed in situations as described under (i) or (ii).

The negative obligation on missions to respect, in their actions, the right to life would mean that if UN (mandated) peace forces use lethal force against individuals, whether in the form of an incidental shooting during a patrol, a planned killing, or outright artillery shelling and aerial bombardment, the person against whom lethal force is used should not be arbitrarily deprived of their right to life.[2013] The positive obligation on missions to protect civilians would involve, *inter alia*, taking reasonable operational measures to prevent the arbitrary killing by non-state parties of civilians whose rights they control.[2014]

2008 Hampson (n. 1518) 570.

2009 Lawson, 'Life after Banković: On the Extraterritorial Application of the European Convention on Human Rights' (n. 1517) 120.

2010 Scheinin (n. 1505) 76. See also Dannenbaum (n. 1520) 158 et seq.

2011 Lubell (n. 1517) 230–231.

2012 Roxstrom, Gibney and Einarsen (n. 1516) 74.

2013 On the right to life and the permissible grounds for deprivation of life, see Part III, Sections 2.2.3.2 and 3.1.1.

2014 Murray and others (n. 1694) 263. See also Nigel D White, 'In Search of Due Diligence Obligations in UN Peacekeeping Operations' 23 Journal of International Peacekeeping 203, 203–225.

For example, if the mission is aware of a real and immediate risk to a person or a group of persons, the UN (mandated) peace operation would be considered to be obligated to take appropriate and feasible measures to prevent the violation of the right to life of those persons or that group of persons.[2015] This without imposing an impossible or disproportionate burden on the duty bearers. Accordingly, they must do so only to the extent of their capacities and within their area of deployment.[2016] The positive obligation on missions to fulfil the right to life implies, for example, that they must conduct a serious investigation into possible violations of the right to life, whether by a member of the UN (mandated) peace force or by a private actor.

In 2011, a UN Report on Human Rights in United Nations Peace Operations and Political Missions confirmed that '[a]ll UN peace operations have a responsibility to ensure that human rights are promoted, respected and protected through and within their operations in the field.'[2017] In early 2013, the UN adopted the UN Human Rights Due Diligence Policy, which lays out measures to be taken by all UN entities to ensure that any support they provide to non-UN troops conforms to the purposes and principles of the UN Charter and their responsibility to respect, promote, and encourage respect for IHL, HRL, and international refugee law.[2018] While this policy accepts the UN's due diligence obligations relative to non-UN forces, White argues that, by accepting the applicability of IHL, HRL, and international refugee law to the UN, 'it also opens the door to more general positive obligations to take measures to prevent and respond to violations by third parties.' After all, the policy sets forth that:[2019]

> Adherence to the human rights due diligence policy is important to maintain the legitimacy, credibility and public image of the United Nations and to ensure compliance with the Charter and with the Organization's obligations under international law.

These policy documents support the position that UN peace forces have certain positive HRL obligations towards the civilian population present on the territory of the host State. However, other scholars are encouraged to conduct additional research on the extent to which both UN peace forces and UN-mandated peace

2015 See also Murray and others (n. 1694) 263; and White, 'In Search of Due Diligence Obligations in UN Peacekeeping Operations' (n. 2014) 220–222 in this regard.

2016 Collinge (n. 1703) 94.

2017 UN OHCHR, UN DPKO, UN DPA, and UN DFS, 'Human Rights in United Nations Peace Operations and Political Missions' (2011) Ref 201120 para. 35.

2018 UNGA and UNSC, 'Human Rights Due Diligence Policy on United Nations Support to Non-United Nations Security Forces, Annex to the Identical Letters Dated 25 February 2013 from the Secretary-General Addressed to the President of the General Assembly and to the President of the Security Council, Sixty-Seventh Session of the General Assembly, Item 69 of the Provisional Agenda; Sixty-Eighth Year of the Security Council' (2013) UN Doc. A/67/775 and S/2013/110 para. 1.

2019 *Ibid.* para. 3.

forces are obliged to protect the right to life when deployed on the territory of a third State and, in particular, on the extent to which missions must exercise 'control' over the rights of individuals creating a positive obligation to protect these rights, as well as on the scope of 'appropriate and feasible measures.'

4.2. OBLIGATION 'TO ENSURE RESPECT' FOR IHL

As discussed in Part III, Section 2.2.3.1, pursuant to Common Article 1 of the Geneva Conventions I–IV and the general principles of IHL, both States and international and regional organisations are under the obligation 'to respect and to ensure respect' for IHL.[2020] This obligation is two-folded. On the one hand, it calls on States and regional and international organisations to respect IHL, which implies that they are obliged to do everything in their power to ensure that the rules in question are respected by their organs and by all others under their jurisdiction.[2021] On the other hand, it calls on States and regional and international organisations to ensure respect for IHL, which means that they must do everything in their power to ensure that the rules are respected.

The meaning of Common Article 1 of the Geneva Conventions I–IV is not established.[2022] Indeed, the nature of these obligations, especially the obligation to ensure respect, has been much disputed.[2023] It is doubtful that the drafters of Common Article 1 intended the provision to comprise obligations beyond compliance by a State's own armed forces and civilian personnel;[2024] this does not mean, however, that today Common Article 1 cannot carry with it a so-called

2020 While the ICJ first confirmed that the obligation 'to respect' and 'to ensure respect' derives not only from Common Art. 1 of Geneva Conventions I–IV but also from general principles of IHL, the ICTY then added that this obligation extends not only to States but also to other international entities, including the UN (see also Part III, Section 2.2.3.1) (References to relevant case law: *Case Concerning Military and Paramilitary Activities in and against Nicaragua (Nicaragua v. United States of America), Judgment (Merits)* (n. 615) para. 220; *Prosecutor v. Tadić, Decision on the defense motion for interlocutory appeal on jurisdiction* (n. 1567) para. 93).

2021 Boisson de Chazournes and Condorellui (n. 1662) 69.

2022 Dale Stephens, 'Military Partners and the Obligation to "Ensure Respect" for IHL' (*Articles of War*, 18 November 2021), https://lieber.westpoint.edu/military-partners-obligation-ensure-respect/, accessed 13 October 2022.

2023 See e.g. Boisson de Chazournes and Condorellui (n. 1662); ICRC, *2016 ICRC Commentary on Geneva Convention I* (n. 86); Frits Kalshoven, 'The Undertaking to Respect and Ensure Respect in All Circumstances: From Tiny Seed to Ripening Fruit' (1999) 2 Yearbook of International Humanitarian Law 3; Michael N Schmitt and Sean Watts, 'Common Article 1 and the Duty to "Ensure Respect"' (2020) 96 International Law Studies 673; Wills, *Protecting Civilians: The Obligations of Peacekeepers* (n. 1667) 100–106; Marten Zwanenburg, 'The "External Element" of the Obligation to Ensure Respect for the Geneva Conventions: A Matter of Treaty Interpretation' (2021) 97 International Law Studies 621.

2024 Wills, 'International Responsibility for Ensuring the Protection of Civilians' (n. 1253) 244.

'external dimension.'[2025] Indeed, quite a few voices argue that Common Article 1 refers not only to a State's own troops and civilian personnel but also to acts committed by other States, organised armed groups, and even members of the civilian population.[2026]

A detailed study of the scope of Common Article 1 of the Geneva Conventions I–IV is outside the ambit of this study. This study only proposes a *prudent* approach based on the ICRC's far-reaching interpretation of Common Article 1 that can be maintained during the conduct of UN (mandated) peace operations.[2027] To that end, when States and international and regional organisations conduct UN (mandated) peace operations, they must not only observe a general duty of due diligence to prevent and suppress violations of IHL by members of the armed forces and other persons or groups whose conduct can be attributed to the State or international or regional organisation in question, but they should also observe a general duty of due diligence to prevent and suppress violations of IHL by private individuals over whom the State or the international or regional organisation exercises power, authority, or control, including persons in occupied territory; and other parties to an armed conflict, including both State and non-state parties, irrespective of whether the State or international or regional organisation concerned is neutral, an ally, or an enemy.[2028]

First, States and international and regional organisations are under the negative obligation to refrain from violating IHL, as well as under the positive obligation to ensure respect for IHL by the armed forces and other individuals or groups whose conduct may be attributed to the States or to international and regional organisations in question. In the context of UN (mandated) peace operations, the duty to respect IHL requires the UN (mandated) peace forces to comply, for example, with the principles of distinction, proportionality, and precautions in attack, among others, when using lethal force to protect civilians.[2029] There is also the obligation to take all feasible precautions to protect the civilian population and civilian objects under their control against

---

2025 Zwanenburg, 'The "External Element" of the Obligation to Ensure Respect for the Geneva Conventions: A Matter of Treaty Interpretation' (n. 2023).

2026 Robin Geiß, 'Common Article 1 of the Geneva Conventions: Scope and Content of the Obligation to "Ensure Respect" – "Narrow but Deep" or "Wide and Shallow"?' in Heike Krieger (ed), *Inducing Compliance with International Humanitarian Law* (1st edn, Cambridge University Press 2015) 428; Oona A Hathaway and others, 'Ensuring Responsibility: Common Article 1 and State Responsibility for Non-State Actors' (2017) 95 Texas Law Review 539. For opposing views, see e.g. Kalshoven (n. 2023); Schmitt and Watts (n. 2023).

2027 ICRC, *2016 ICRC Commentary on Geneva Convention I* (n. 86) 36–67; ICRC, *2017 ICRC Commentary on Geneva Convention II* (n. 86) 43–75; ICRC, *2021 ICRC Commentary on Geneva Convention III* (n. 86) 47–80.

2028 ICRC, *2016 ICRC Commentary on Geneva Convention I* (n. 86) paras 143–183; ICRC, *2017 ICRC Commentary on Geneva Convention II* (n. 86) paras 165–205; ICRC, *2021 ICRC Commentary on Geneva Convention III* (n. 86) paras 176–216.

2029 As discussed above, see Part III, Section 3.2.

the effects of attacks.[2030] The duty to ensure respect for IHL obliges States and regional and international organisations to take appropriate measures, i.e. all measures necessary, to prevent violations of IHL. In principle, there is a certain freedom in choosing the measures to ensure compliance with IHL as long as they are sufficient to achieve the desired result.[2031] Such measures may include the proper teaching of IHL within the armed forces and the adequate curtailment of violations (for example, by tracing, prosecuting, or extraditing alleged perpetrators of serious violations of the Geneva Conventions I–IV).[2032]

Second, it is a prudent approach to consider that States and international and regional organisations are under the positive obligation to take all necessary measures to ensure respect for IHL by all populations over which they have authority.[2033] This obligation is also an obligation of means, the content of which depends on the specific circumstances, such as the foreseeability of the violations and the knowledge thereof on the part of the State or the international and regional organisation, the seriousness of the violation, the means that are reasonably available to them, and the level of influence that they exert on private persons in question.[2034] Measures may include the dissemination of IHL to the civilian population and suppressing violations by, for example, tracing, prosecuting, or extraditing alleged perpetrators of serious violations.[2035] In addition, States and international and regional organisations are also obliged to take the necessary measures to protect specific persons and objects, including from acts committed by private persons. For example, Article 15 of Geneva Convention I and Article 18 of Geneva Convention II explicitly stipulate the duty to protect the shipwrecked, wounded, and sick from pillage and ill-treatment. These Articles, together with Article 34 of Additional Protocol I, establish the duty to prevent the despoiling of the dead. Article 13(2) of Geneva Convention III provides the duty to protect POWs at all times, particularly 'against acts of violence or intimidation and against insults and public curiosity.'[2036]

2030 As discussed above, see Part III, Section 3.2.4.2.

2031 ICRC, *2016 ICRC Commentary on Geneva Convention I* (n. 86) para. 146; ICRC, *2017 ICRC Commentary on Geneva Convention II* (n. 86) para. 168; ICRC, *2021 ICRC Commentary on Geneva Convention III* (n. 86) para. 179.

2032 ICRC, *2016 ICRC Commentary on Geneva Convention I* (n. 86) para. 146; ICRC, *2017 ICRC Commentary on Geneva Convention II* (n. 86) para. 168; ICRC, *2021 ICRC Commentary on Geneva Convention III* (n. 86) para. 179.

2033 ICRC, *2016 ICRC Commentary on Geneva Convention I* (n. 86) para. 150; ICRC, *2017 ICRC Commentary on Geneva Convention II* (n. 86) para. 172; ICRC, *2021 ICRC Commentary on Geneva Convention III* (n. 86) para. 183.

2034 See also ICRC, *2016 ICRC Commentary on Geneva Convention I* (n. 86) para. 150; ICRC, *2017 ICRC Commentary on Geneva Convention II* (n. 86) para. 172; ICRC, *2021 ICRC Commentary on Geneva Convention III* (n. 86) para. 183.

2035 ICRC, *2016 ICRC Commentary on Geneva Convention I* (n. 86) para. 151; ICRC, *2017 ICRC Commentary on Geneva Convention II* (n. 86) para. 173; ICRC, *2021 ICRC Commentary on Geneva Convention III* (n. 86) para. 184.

2036 ICRC, *2016 ICRC Commentary on Geneva Convention I* (n. 86) para. 152; ICRC, *2017 ICRC Commentary on Geneva Convention II* (n. 86) para. 174; ICRC, *2021 ICRC Commentary on Geneva Convention III* (n. 86) para. 185.

Third, it is best to assume that States and international and regional organisations are obliged to ensure that others who are parties to a conflict, both State and non-state parties, respect IHL, irrespective of whether the State or international or regional organisation concerned is neutral, an ally, or an enemy.[2037] This duty to ensure respect by others includes both a negative and a positive obligation.[2038] According to the negative obligation, States and international and regional organisations must not encourage, assist, or aid violations of IHL by parties to a conflict.[2039] This means, for example, that States must refrain from transferring arms if there is an assumption, based on facts or knowledge of past patterns, that those arms will be used to violate the Geneva Conventions I–IV.[2040] According to the positive obligation, States and international and regional organisations must do everything reasonably within their power to prevent and end violations of IHL.[2041] This obligation is not confined to the cessation of ongoing violations but also encompasses the

---

2037 See e.g. UN, 'Resolution XXIII on Human Rights in Armed Conflicts, Adopted on the Report of the Second Committee' (1968) Final Act of the International Conference on Human Rights, 23 April–13 May 1968, Teheran, UN Doc. A/CONF.32/41 preamble ('"Noting" that States parties to the Red Cross Geneva Conventions sometimes fail to appreciate their responsibility to take steps to ensure the respect of these humanitarian rules in all circumstances by other States, even if they are not themselves directly involved in an armed conflict'); 'UNGA Res. 2851 (XXVI), Report of the Special Committee to Investigate Israeli Practices Affecting the Human Rights of the Population of the Occupied Territories' (1971) UN Doc. A/RES/2851 (1971) preamble and para. 9. For relevant case law from the ICJ on this point, see *Case Concerning Military and Paramilitary Activities in and against Nicaragua (Nicaragua v. United States of America), Judgment (Merits)* (n. 615) para. 220; *Legal Consequences of the Construction of a Wall in the Occupied Palestinian Territory (Request for advisory opinion), Order of 19 December 2003, Written statement of the League of Arab States* (2004) paras 158–159; *Case Concerning Armed Activities on the Territory of the Congo (Democratic Republic of the Congo v. Uganda), Judgment* (n. 616) paras 211 and 345, as also referred to by ICRC, *2016 ICRC Commentary on Geneva Convention I* (n. 86) para. 156 (for more references, see further para. 156); see also ICRC, *2017 ICRC Commentary on Geneva Convention II* (n. 86) para. 178; ICRC, *2021 ICRC Commentary on Geneva Convention III* (n. 86) para. 189. For an analysis of the customary nature of this rule, see Henckaerts and Doswald-Beck (n. 91) Rule 144, pp. 509–513 (as quoted above, see Part III, Section 2.2.3.1, fn. 1663).

2038 ICRC, *2016 ICRC Commentary on Geneva Convention I* (n. 86) para. 154; ICRC, *2017 ICRC Commentary on Geneva Convention II* (n. 86) para. 175; ICRC, *2021 ICRC Commentary on Geneva Convention III* (n. 86) para. 186.

2039 See also ICRC, *2016 ICRC Commentary on Geneva Convention I* (n. 86) para. 158; ICRC, *2017 ICRC Commentary on Geneva Convention II* (n. 86) para. 180; ICRC, *2021 ICRC Commentary on Geneva Convention III* (n. 86) para. 191. In the Nicaragua case, the ICJ held that '[t]he United States is [...] under an obligation not to encourage persons or groups engaged in the conflict in Nicaragua to act in violation of the provisions of Article 3 common to the four 1949 Geneva Conventions' (*Case Concerning Military and Paramilitary Activities in and against Nicaragua (Nicaragua v. United States of America), Judgment (Merits)* (n. 615) para. 220).

2040 ICRC, *2016 ICRC Commentary on Geneva Convention I* (n. 86) para. 162; ICRC, *2017 ICRC Commentary on Geneva Convention II* (n. 86) para. 184; ICRC, *2021 ICRC Commentary on Geneva Convention III* (n. 86) para. 195.

2041 ICRC, *2016 ICRC Commentary on Geneva Convention I* (n. 86) para. 164; ICRC, *2017 ICRC Commentary on Geneva Convention II* (n. 86) para. 186; ICRC, *2021 ICRC Commentary on Geneva Convention III* (n. 86) para. 197.

obligation to prevent violations where there is a foreseeable risk that they will occur and to prevent further violations that have already taken place.[2042] This obligation to ensure respect by others must be carried out with due diligence, implying that they must do everything in their power to end the violations, even if they ultimately fail to do so.[2043] As mentioned earlier, the content of the obligation depends on the specific circumstances, including the foreseeability of the violations and the knowledge thereof on the part of the State or the international or regional organisation, the seriousness of the violation, the means that are reasonably available to them, and the level of influence that they exert on the private persons in question. Concrete measures may include the provision of legal assistance to the parties to the conflict and/or support for assistance provided by others, including instruction or training; the adoption of lawful countermeasures such as trade embargoes; or direct intervention in the event of violations, for example, in the event of an imminent unlawful attack on civilians by a coalition partner.[2044] Unlawful attacks against civilians include attacks that violate the rules and principles of IHL, including most importantly, those concerning the general protection of civilians: the principle of distinction, the principle of proportionality, the principles of precautions in attack and precautions against the effects of attacks, and the prohibition of superfluous injury and unnecessary suffering. Any direct intervention must be consistent with the relevant legal regime, be it IHL and/or HRL.

While States and international and regional organisations should not be required to do the impossible to stop and prevent every violation of IHL, wherever it occurs, it is a prudent approach to assume that they are obliged to respond to breaches of IHL and to do all that can be reasonably expected of them to stop or prevent violations of IHL by others.[2045] According to Wills, under IHL, UN peace forces are obliged to protect people in 'their immediate care, insofar as they are capable of doing so; and to take reasonable precautions, where feasible, to prevent attacks where these are clearly foreseeable.'[2046] However, as this matter is still highly controversial and the proposal set out in this study is only a suggestion for a prudent approach, further research into the obligation to ensure respect for IHL when conducting a UN (mandated) peace operation is warranted.

2042 ICRC, *2016 ICRC Commentary on Geneva Convention I* (n. 86) para. 164; ICRC, *2017 ICRC Commentary on Geneva Convention II* (n. 86) para. 186; ICRC, *2021 ICRC Commentary on Geneva Convention III* (n. 86) para. 197.

2043 ICRC, *2016 ICRC Commentary on Geneva Convention I* (n. 86) para. 165; ICRC, *2017 ICRC Commentary on Geneva Convention II* (n. 86) para. 187; ICRC, *2021 ICRC Commentary on Geneva Convention III* (n. 86) para. 198.

2044 ICRC, *2016 ICRC Commentary on Geneva Convention I* (n. 86) para. 181; ICRC, *2017 ICRC Commentary on Geneva Convention II* (n. 86) para. 203; ICRC, *2021 ICRC Commentary on Geneva Convention III* (n. 86) para. 214.

2045 See also Geiß (n. 2026) 441.

2046 Wills, 'International Responsibility for Ensuring the Protection of Civilians' (n. 1253) 266–267.

5. SUMMARY OF PART III

Part III sought to scrutinise the legal regimes governing the use of force to protect civilians by UN (mandated) peace forces carrying out PoC mandates, with a specific focus on HRL and IHL and explore the possible impact of the PoC mandate on whether or not force can be used by UN (mandated) peace forces on the ground. In doing so, Part III addressed the following questions: How do the legal regimes, including HRL and IHL, govern the use of force to protect civilians by UN (mandated) peace forces carrying out a PoC mandate? To that end, do – and if so, how and when – HRL and IHL apply *de jure* to UN (mandated) peace operations carrying out a PoC mandate? Under what circumstances and in what manner may UN (mandated) peace forces use force (up to and including lethal force) in carrying out a PoC mandate when the operation in which they are participating is a party to an armed conflict? And how do the rules change when the operation in question is not a party to the armed conflict? Further, may a PoC mandate somehow regulate the use of force by UN (mandated) peace forces on the ground (a matter primarily governed by legal regimes), and, more specifically, can it influence whether or not force can be used in specific cases and, if so, how? And finally, are UN (mandated) peace forces ever legally required under HRL or IHL to protect civilians (by force) against the threat of physical violence?

HRL as a legal regime for the use of force

HRL applies *de jure* to all UN (mandated) peace operations, whether undertaken in peacetime or in the context of armed conflict. However, this does not prevent States or international or regional organisations from derogating from certain rights in times of public emergency. Furthermore, pursuant to Chapter VII and Article 103 of the UN Charter, the UN Security Council may authorise conduct which does not comply with HRL obligations of States or international and regional organisations. In doing so, States and international and regional organisations can never set aside peremptory norms.

Depending on the status of an operation, peace forces carrying out the operation must abide by the HRL obligations deriving from the international obligations of the following actors: (i) the international or regional organisation undertaking the operation; (ii) the State undertaking or taking part in the operation; and (iii) the State on whose territory the operation takes place.[2047] The obligations are primarily based on HRL treaties or customary HRL. Which set(s) of HRL obligations appl(ies)(y) *in general* as a matter of law may be different from one operation to the other. What is relevant is how the operation

[2047] Gill and others (n. 26) 77–79; White, 'Security Council Mandates and the Use of Lethal Force by Peacekeepers: What Place for the Laws of War?' (n. 31) 105–106.

in question relates to the State and/or the organisation (e.g. is the operation a subsidiary organ of the organisation in question or is it in some other way part of the organisation and, therefore, bound by the international obligations that bind the organisation?).

Which HRL obligations apply *de jure* to a *specific* situation must be decided on a case-by-case basis and solely depends on the factual circumstances. One of the determinants of *de jure* applicability of HRL obligations is the exercise of 'jurisdiction'. Whether States or international or regional organisations are considered to exercise 'jurisdiction' when they operate in the territory of a third State depends on the model of extraterritorial application of HRL used. Indeed, while 'jurisdiction' is first and foremost indicative of States having HRL obligations in their own territory, the scope of HRL has been broadened by advancing the concept of 'extraterritorial jurisdiction'. Applied to this study, 'extraterritorial jurisdiction' implies that the HRL obligations of a TCC under whose authority an operation is conducted may apply extraterritorially to acts committed within its jurisdiction and, to the extent that a regional or international organisation exercises functions in a manner that can be assimilated to the exercise of jurisdiction by a State, it is also deemed to exercise jurisdiction.[2048] Since members of UN (mandated) peace forces usually have a dual legal status and role, which HRL obligations apply *de jure* in a *specific* situation on the ground, depends on the capacity in which a member of a UN (mandated) peace force has acted and thus under whose jurisdiction the individual fell – the TCC or the international or regional organisation. To that end, one must seek a link between the conduct of a physical person and a holder of international obligations.[2049] While still under debate, this link is often drawn by invoking the agency paradigm of attribution.

Three models of extraterritorial applicability emerge from the jurisprudence of courts and human rights mechanisms: the spatial model (power over a territory), the personal model (power over an individual), and the functional model (power over the rights of an individual). The personal model and the functional model, par excellence, can lead to outcomes that are excessive or unfeasible from a political and/or practical point of view. This explains in part why there is great reluctance to accept the applicability of HRL to UN (mandated) peace operations: there is a major concern that a broad set of human rights (ranging from civil and political to economic, social, and cultural rights) will be enforced in *extraterritorial* emergencies without adaptation and in an unrealistic manner.[2050] In the context of UN (mandated) peace operations using force to protect civilians, there is indeed a risk that accepting that the right to life

2048 Kleffner (n. 1374) para. 33.

2049 Zwanenburg, 'International Organisations vs. Troop Contributing Countries: Which Should Be Considered as the Party to an Armed Conflict during Peace Operations?' (n. 1349) 26.

2050 Sheeran, 'Human Rights and Derogation in Peacekeeping' (n. 29) 232.

– being the most relevant rule of HRL in the context of the use of force – applies, creates an obligation not only to respect that right but perhaps also to protect and fulfil it.

A distinction can be made between negative and positive obligations to limit the scope of applicability in extraterritorial situations, whereby negative obligations not to infringe on the rights of an individual without adequate justification apply regardless of whether States or regional or international organisations have actual control over a territory, but positive obligations to take measures to protect and promote human rights only apply where there is some form of control over the individual or the individual's rights. What form of control States or international or regional organisations should exercise is the subject of ongoing debate. With the three possible models of extraterritorial applicability in mind, a prudent approach to the protection of civilian lives in the context of UN (mandated) peace operations with a PoC mandate is as follows: (i) adhere to the negative obligation 'to respect', in their actions, the right to life of all persons present in the territory of the State(s) where they are deployed; (ii) adhere to the positive obligation 'to protect' the right to life of those whose rights the missions control by taking appropriate and feasible measures to prevent violations of the right to life by non-state actors; and (iii) adhere to the positive obligation 'to fulfil' the right to life, *inter alia*, by conducting effective investigations when individuals have been killed in situations as described under (i) or (ii). As this only reflects a prudent approach, the question of the positive obligation to protect the right to life when conducting a UN (mandated) peace operation certainly merits further research.

To respect the right to life, when using lethal force, UN (mandated) peace forces must comply with the principles of legality, necessity, proportionality, precautions, and accountability. These five core principles can be derived from the major HRL treaties, the jurisprudence of human rights courts, guidance from international human rights mechanisms, and other persuasive authority. Likewise, when UN (mandated) peace forces resort to less-lethal force to accomplish tasks, purposes, and objectives defined in a mandate, such force must equally comply with these five principles.

Pursuant to the principle of legality, the right to life must be protected by law. The legal basis for the use of force by UN (mandated) peace forces may be found in national law, but may also be included in the mission's mandate, enshrined in the relevant UNSC resolutions, and then further elaborated in mission-specific ROE. Under the principle of necessity, lethal force must always be a last resort to be used only when less drastic means are unavailable or manifestly unreasonable. A graduated response involves, for example, as appropriate, verbal warning, show of force, less-than-lethal force, and only then lethal force. If force is unavoidable, the amount of force should not exceed what is objectively necessary to respond to the threat, and force should be used only as long as necessary to accomplish the legitimate aim. There should always be as little damage and injury as possible.

The principle of proportionality requires that, even if the use of lethal force appears to be necessary, the nature and degree of force used must be commensurate to the seriousness of the threat and the legitimate aim to be achieved. Under the principle of proportionality, a distinction must be made between the use of potentially lethal force and the intentional lethal use of force, as well as between the various legitimate aims that may be pursued by these types of force. While potentially lethal force can be used in self-defence or defence of others if one or more persons are under 'imminent threat of death or serious injury' ('imminent' means a matter of seconds or even a split second before fatality strikes;[2051] 'serious injury' refers to 'a life threatening or life changing injury')[2052] or to pursue 'other legitimate aims' (as authorised by the UN Security Council) upon the condition that there is a 'grave threat to life' ('grave threat to life' refers to a continuing threat to life which may materialise at any time),[2053] intentional lethal force is permissible only 'to protect life from imminent threat'.

In accordance with the principle of precautions, personnel contributed to an operation must be adequately trained and equipped, and operations must be carefully planned, organised, and controlled to prevent or at least minimise the use of force. Lastly, an appropriate accountability system must be in place for any use of force that does not comply with the above-mentioned principles.

The right to life is contained in a number of international and regional treaties, including Article 6(1) of the ICCPR, Article 4(1) of the ACHR, Article 4 of the ACHPR, and Article 2 of the ECHR. In addition, the right to life has the status of customary international law and thus also imposes obligations on international law subjects who are not parties to the HRL treaties that contain a provision on the right to life. Furthermore, the right to life, or more specifically, the right not to be arbitrarily deprived of one's life, also has a peremptory status which makes it impossible to derogate from (although, unlike its customary law status, this is not generally recognised).

IHL as a legal regime for the use of force

If force is used in a situation which has a clear nexus to an ongoing armed conflict, that use of force is not only governed by HRL but also by IHL. For example, for any use of lethal force with a clear nexus to an armed conflict, the

2051 UN HRC, 'Report of the Special Rapporteur on Extrajudicial, Summary or Arbitrary Executions, Christof Heyns' (n. 109) para. 59; UN OHCHR (n. 1691) 43.

2052 Amnesty International (n. 1717) 23.

2053 UN HRC, 'Report of the Special Rapporteur on Extrajudicial, Summary or Arbitrary Executions, Christof Heyns' (n. 109) para. 33 (discussion of international law standards) and para. 60 (discussion of domestic standards).

rules of IHL must be used to assess if such use of force constitutes an 'arbitrary' deprivation of the right to life. While it is no longer contested that IHL can apply to UN (mandated) peace operations, when it applies is still contested. The central issue is whether the 'standard' test used to determine whether IHL applies – the conditions for which are set out in IHL itself and established by practice[2054] – can also be used for UN (mandated) peace operations, or whether a different test should be considered. Whereas for an IAC to exist, there must, in principle, be recourse to armed force between two or more entities with an international legal personality (including States and international or regional organisations), a NIAC is considered to exist when there is protracted armed violence between governmental authorities and armed groups possessing a certain level of organisation or between such groups within a State.

There are no good reasons why a test other than the 'standard' one should be used to determine whether UN (mandated) peace operations are involved in an IAC or a NIAC and, therefore, IHL applies to the operation when the requisite conditions for the application of this body of law are met. While derogation from the law based on Chapter VII powers and under Article 103 of the UN Charter is possible, as for HRL, unless it concerns peremptory norms (such as the fundamental principles of IHL), the UN Security Council can never alter the applicability of IHL. Hence, the rules and principles of IHL apply by conventional or customary law to all UN (mandated) peace operations as soon as the conditions for applying this legal instrument are met, regardless of whether the operation was established or authorised by the UN Security Council.

In such cases, UN (mandated) peace forces can be bound by IHL obligations primarily arising from: (i) customary IHL to which the international or regional organisation conducting the operation is bound; and (ii) IHL treaties to which the State undertaking or taking part in an operation are a party and/or customary IHL by which that State is bound.[2055] Which set(s) of IHL obligations appl(ies)(y) is contingent upon who is considered a party to the armed conflict. Unfortunately, there is no consensus in legal doctrine on how to determine who is a party to the armed conflict. Indeed, just as for the applicability of HRL obligations in individual cases where it is difficult to determine whether the individual force is acting in the capacity of member of a UN (mandated) peace operation or as an agent for the State, for the applicability of IHL obligations it is equally difficult to determine who exactly is a party to an armed conflict and consequently whose IHL obligations apply. One (admittedly contested by some) method of drawing this connection is the agency paradigm of attribution.

Under Common Article 1 of the Geneva Conventions I–IV and the general principles of IHL, both States and international and regional organisations are obliged 'to respect and to ensure respect' for IHL. The nature of these obligations,

---

2054 Gill and others (n. 26) 93.

2055 Gill, 'Characterization and Legal Basis for Peace Operations' (n. 589) 160.

particularly the obligation 'to ensure respect', has been much debated. To that end, the present study has suggested the following prudent approach. When States and international and regional organisations conduct UN (mandated) peace operations, they should be considered to be under a general duty of due diligence to prevent and suppress violations of IHL by the following actors: (i) the members of the armed forces and other persons or groups whose conduct can be attributed to the State or international or regional organisation in question, (ii) private individuals over whom the State or the international or regional organisation exercises power, authority, or control, including persons in occupied territory; and (iii) other parties to an armed conflict, including both State and non-state parties, regardless of whether the State or international or regional organisation concerned is neutral, an ally, or an enemy. As with the issue of whether there is a positive obligation under HRL to protect the right to life in the conduct of a UN (mandated) peace operation, this is only a tentative proposal for a prudent approach, so the issue of the positive obligation to ensure respect for IHL in the conduct of a UN (mandated) peace operation certainly merits further research.

If a UN (mandated) peace operation has become a party to the conflict, all members of the peace forces carrying out the operation can be targeted at all times by virtue of their membership of an organised armed force and hence no longer enjoy the protection afforded to civilians. Once IHL ceases to apply, the members of UN (mandated) peace forces once again enjoy the protection afforded to civilians unless they take a direct part in hostilities. In principle, IHL ceases to apply to UN (mandated) peace operations when they are no longer a party to an armed conflict. When a UN (mandated) peace operation has been involved in an IAC, the conflict may be considered ended when the armed confrontation between the UN (mandated) peace forces and the State(s) fighting them has ended to the extent that the situation can reasonably be construed as a general cessation of military operations.[2056] In the case of a NIAC, IHL continues to apply until actual and lasting peace has been attained.[2057]

As to the applicability *ratione loci*, in the case of an IAC, IHL applies to the territory of the belligerent States, comprising all occupied territories, as well as to any territory other than the territory of the belligerent States, such as the high seas (including the airspace above them and the sea bed), to the extent that actual hostilities occur. In the case of a NIAC, IHL applies to the entire territory of the State concerned. Thus, as also widely recognised in the jurisprudence of international courts and tribunals, the geographical scope of IHL in both IACs and NIACs is not limited to the actual battlefield or its surroundings but extends to the entire territory of the parties to the conflict. That said, where some rules

---

2056 Ferraro, 'The Applicability and Application of International Humanitarian Law to Multinational Forces' (n. 676) 601.

2057 Gill and others (n. 26) 103.

have relevance to the entire territory, whether or not there is fighting, other rules are, in practice, primarily relevant in the areas where fighting is actually taking place.

At the heart of IHL are a number of principles set out in the major IHL treaties (including the 1907 Hague Convention IV and its Regulations, the Geneva Conventions I–IV, and the Additional Protocols I–II) that also form part of customary IHL and constitute peremptory norms. As such, IHL rests primarily on the need for a balance between the foundational principles of humanity and military necessity. From the foundational principles of military necessity and humanity stem a number of fundamental IHL principles, including the principles of distinction, proportionality, precautions in attack and against the effects of attacks, and the prohibition of superfluous injury and unnecessary suffering.

Death, injury, and damage are virtually inseparable from warfare. The principle of military necessity recognises this necessity but does limit the use of force to that which is necessary to achieve a military objective and prohibits the use of excessive force to achieve this objective. The principle of military necessity is weighed against the principle of humanity. Under this principle, belligerent parties have a duty to respect and protect people (both combatants and non-combatants) and their property and, as such, treat them humanely. The balance between the two principles underlies every IHL standard, whether based on customary law or a treaty, so neither principle taken in isolation justifies a departure from its provisions unless the law expressly provides otherwise.[2058]

The imperative to maintain at all times a balance between military necessity and humanity is reflected in the general principle of distinction. This principle requires that a distinction be made at all times between civilians and combatants and between civilian objects and military objectives. No direct attacks can be carried out against civilians (unless and so long as they are direct participants in hostilities) nor against civilian objects (unless and so long as they are military objectives). Pursuant to the principle of distinction, indiscriminate attacks (i.e. attacks that are such that military objectives and civilians or civilian objects are indiscriminately targeted) are also prohibited. In contrast, inflicting incidental damage on civilians or civilian objects – as opposed to carrying out direct attacks on them – is usually unavoidable, but limits have also been put in place. If, when planning an attack against a legitimate military target, it becomes clear that there is a risk of incidental damage to civilians or civilian objects, the proportionality of such damage must always be considered. An attack is considered disproportionate if the attack is expected to result in collateral

[2058] Dinstein, 'Military Necessity' (n. 1779) para. 7; Schmitt, 'Military Necessity and Humanity in International Humanitarian Law: Preserving the Delicate Balance Commemorative Pieces' (n. 1765) 801.

damage that is excessive in relation to the concrete and direct military advantage anticipated.

To protect civilians from the effects of hostilities, the principles of precautions in attack and against the effects of an attack impose additional restrictions on the use of force. Under the principle of precautions in attack, the party that undertakes an attack must take all possible precautions to prevent and, in any case, minimise incidental deaths, injuries, and damage to civilians and civilian objects. Under the principle of precautions against the effects of attacks, the party being attacked is required to take all necessary precautions to protect the civilian population and civilian objects under its control from the effects of attacks carried out by the opponent. Last but not least, under the principle of the prohibition of superfluous injury and unnecessary suffering, combatants also enjoy additional protection, as the prohibition bans or restricts means and methods of warfare considered to cause needless suffering or injury to combatants.

Relationship between HRL and IHL and the UNSC mandate

While legal bases and legal regimes, at least in theory, exercise fundamentally different functions, the UNSC mandate may come into the playing field of HRL and IHL in two ways.

First, a UNSC mandate may indirectly impose additional limits on the use of force in specific instances (an area that is principally governed by the legal regimes). A mandate is translated into detailed guidelines for the use of force, particularly ROE, and thus affects whether or not UN (mandated) peace forces may use force in specific situations. In doing so, it may impose stricter limits on the use of force than HRL or IHL. Any use of force beyond such limits constitutes a violation of the ROE and/or relevant orders and directives but not necessarily a violation of the applicable legal regime(s). In other words, there is no 'normative spill-over' effect[2059] of the mandate on the legal regimes. Rules and principles of HRL or IHL are not to be interpreted differently simply because the forces operate under a UNSC mandate. While this is relatively straightforward in some situations, it is not so in other situations where UN (mandated) peace forces are involved. To illustrate this point, a case study was presented on the concept of 'military advantage' in the context of UN-mandated peace operations with a PoC mandate. When interpreting the concept of 'military advantage' in such situations, there are quite a few votes in favour of using the mandate to help determine what is legal under IHL. However, such an approach runs counter to the distinction between international law on the use of force and IHL, as well as the equal application of IHL to all belligerents. IHL should not be interpreted

[2059] Terminology used by Lieblich in Lieblich, 'On the Continuous and Concurrent Application of Ad Bellum and In Bello Proportionality' (n. 1894) 73–75.

in light of the mandate. The IHL concept of 'military advantage' considers only whether an attack contributes to the defeat of the adversary and hence not whether it contributes to PoC (i.e. the strategic objective of a UN-mandated peace operation with a PoC mandate).

Second, a UNSC mandate may overrule or authorise acts contrary to the rules of HRL or IHL by virtue of Chapter VII and Article 103 of the UN Charter, as long as the rules are not peremptory. Indeed, there are limits to the possible impact a UNSC can have on whether force can be used in specific instances. A UNSC mandate can never trump rules of *jus cogens*, such as the right not to be arbitrarily deprived of one's life or the fundamental principles of IHL. This tends to run counter to the practice of the UN Security Council and Secretariat of using increasingly strong language to encourage proactive implementation of mission mandates, as exemplified in a second case study. In particular, while PoC mandates previously included an authorisation to protect civilians under *imminent* threat, the word 'imminent' is now increasingly dropped, or, if still present, the UN Secretariat seeks to detach the word's meaning from questions of temporality. While such changes and ambiguities in PoC and use of force vocabularies do not necessarily entail the (il)legality of use of force by UN peace forces, this study suggests that the UN must take greater care to ensure that lethal force is not used with disregard for the right to life. To that end, by interpreting PoC mandates in light of general principles of public international law and HRL, as well as distinguishing between potentially and intentional lethal force, it is suggested how the UN practice of protecting civilians can be reconciled with binding law.

CONCLUDING CHAPTER[2060]

This book has sought to answer the question of what the legal parameters are for the use of force in UN (mandated) peace operations tasked by the UN Security Council to protect civilians.

Following a series of humanitarian crises and dramatic failures of the international community to prevent mass atrocities from occurring, in 1999, the UN Security Council began adopting mandates in which it explicitly authorised UN (mandated) peace operations to 'use all necessary means to protect civilians against the (imminent) threat of physical violence' (by using exactly these terms or by using similar terms). Over the years, adopting PoC mandates has proven to be a ubiquitous tool eagerly used by the UN Security Council when implementing initiatives to maintain or restore international peace and security – seeking to draw particular attention to the protection of civilians. However, practice shows that many questions remain about the legality of using force within such operations. At its roots is a deep gap between international legal scholarship on the one hand and military doctrine and practice on the other. Academics are concerned with the strict legal rules as set forth by customary and conventional law, as well as general principles of law. Practitioners are concerned with the mission-specific PoC mandates and the strategic, operational, and tactical instruments that implement such a mandate.

Respect for the law is crucial, but so is a proper understanding of the daily challenges those in practice face. Practitioners must 'get the job done' and hence protect civilians to the largest extent possible without sacrificing too much on their part. Yet, in the process, relevant legal questions are often side-lined or analysed in cursory terms. For instance, the use of force in specific situations is mechanically justified by referring to the PoC mandate itself, the UN Security Council's powers under Chapter VII of the UN Charter, or the mission-specific ROE or by arguing that such use of force is in self-defence or 'defence of the mandate' and hence permissible. Understanding how the international legal framework factors into the different phases of an operation (ranging from

[2060] This Concluding Chapter is partly based on the following publications: Bourgeois, 'Failure to Protect Civilians in the Context of UN Peace Operations: A Question of Accountability?' (n. 1); Bourgeois, '"All Necessary Means" to Protect Civilians: The Interpretation and Implementation of UN Security Council Mandates Authorising the Protection of Civilians' (n. 1); Bourgeois and Labuda (n. 1); Bourgeois and Perrin (n. 1).

the planning and deployment of an operation to the final evaluation of its performance) is instrumental in ensuring that the appropriate legal parameters for the use of force are considered. Indeed a fundamental understanding of the distinct roles played by the legal bases for an operation (Chapter VII mandates and host State consents) and legal regimes (in particular IHL and HRL) and how they interact is crucial to regulating the operation in conformity with the law and determining when, why, and how force can and should be applied in the context of the operation.

While there are a host of academic analyses on the legal aspects of the use of force in the context of UN (mandated) peace operations, little attention has been paid to how the international legal framework applies in the specific context of PoC by UN (mandated) peace operations and the relationship between the functions of a legal basis for an operation and the applicable legal regimes. To conduct valuable academic research on legal issues pertinent to practice – that is, research that can, in turn, promote compliance with the law – it is essential to understand how the international legal framework permeates practice and to be fully aware of the challenges in the context of UN (mandated) peace operations with a PoC mandate.

With this book, the author seeks to contribute to the academic analysis of the legal parameters for the use of force in UN (mandated) peace operations tasked by the UN Security Council to protect civilians by shedding light on those aspects that have remained underexposed in legal scholarship yet without turning a blind eye to the practice. To fully understand how legal bases and legal regimes interact and influence each other, the author looked into the UN Security Council's practice of adopting PoC mandates. Specifically, how such PoC mandates are implemented in practice, which military planning processes are initiated, which command and control structures are put into place, what strategic, operational, and tactical tools emerge from the mandate, and what role HRL and IHL are assigned in this process.

With this approach, the author seeks to close the gap between international legal scholarship on the one hand and military doctrine and practice on the other. The result is a thorough analysis of the international legal framework on the use of force for protection purposes in the context of UN (mandated) peace operations tasked by the UN Security Council to protect civilians. This analysis is not only to describe how the legal bases and legal regimes regulate the use of force but also to evaluate the relationship between the mission-specific legal bases (in particular, the UNSC mandate) and the legal regimes (with a particular focus on HRL and IHL).

There should be no exclusive reliance on policy- and mission-specific non-legal instruments, broad notions of self-defence, or Chapter VII powers to legally justify the use of force to protect civilians

In practice, there is a tendency to resort to mission mandates based on Chapter VII powers, whereby a UNSC authorisation to take 'all necessary means' is seen as a blank cheque for offensive force to protect civilians. Such approaches are further endorsed by policy documents on the use of force and PoC that advocate a proactive implementation of such mandates while providing little clarity on the legal parameters of the use of force. References are also often made to broad notions of self-defence that cut across the distinction between the legal basis and the different legal regimes applicable to the use of force. For example, in the context of UN peace operations, broad notions of self-defence stemming from a power under Chapter VII to enforce peacekeeping mandates or from peace forces' 'inherent' right to self-defence, based on Article 51 of the UN Charter and customary international law, are often emphasised as independent legal foundations for the use of force by UN peace forces. With respect to the latter, such a horizontal conceptualisation of *jus ad bellum* self-defence – as a norm that gives not only the UN as an organisation a strategic right to defend itself but also a personal tactical right for individual peacekeepers to defend themselves and others, including civilians – has subsequently been adopted in the UN's ROE and has further elaboration there.

While the power to use force in self-defence, defence of others or defence of the mandate may be part of the standard set of rules for the conduct of UN (mandated) peace operations, and while PoC mandates under Chapter VII of the UN Charter indeed provide for legal authority to use force, any use of force to this end must be in accordance with the applicable legal regime(s). As such, there should no longer be exclusive recourse to policy- and mission-specific non-legal instruments, broad notions of self-defence, or Chapter VII powers as a cursory attempt to legally justify the use of force to protect civilians. Of course, this does not prevent the PoC mandate from impacting the use of force, yet the dynamics with other legal instruments must not be forgotten or trivialised. To properly understand these dynamics, a sound understanding of the respective roles of legal bases and legal regimes in regulating the use of force for protection is needed.

There must be a better understanding of the respective roles of the legal bases and the legal regimes in regulating the use of force for protective purposes

Legal questions pertaining to the use of force can be situated at different levels. For one thing, there are questions of whether force can be used on a State's territory, and if so, how much. On the other hand, there are questions concerning the circumstances under which and in what manner armed forces may use force against a particular objective or a particular person. It is the legal bases that principally regulate the *resort* to armed force on the territory of a State as well as the *overall* levels of force used to conduct the operation, while it is the applicable legal regimes that primarily regulate *specific instances* of the use of force by armed forces on the ground. However, this is not to say that the legal bases and the legal regimes each regulate the use of force in their own distinct way and, therefore, must be kept strictly separate. While from a theoretical point of view, the legal bases strictly distinguish themselves from the legal regimes, in practice, the legal bases and the legal regimes somehow seem to intersect when regulating the use of force for protective purposes. Before reiterating the key points in this regard, it is first essential to recapitulate which rules can serve as a legal basis for the establishment, deployment, and functioning of UN (mandated) peace operations and which rules may govern the conduct of the UN (mandated) peace operations.

It is essential to have an understanding of which rules may provide a legal basis for UN (mandated) peace operations

Any (physical) intervention in a State requires a legal basis in international law. The rules providing such a legal basis are, first and foremost, found in the UN Charter and the rules of customary international law relating to the use of force and the maintenance and restoration of international peace and security. Pursuant to Article 2(4) of the UN Charter, States are, for example, prohibited from using or threatening to use force in their international relations unless they are exercising their right to individual or collective self-defence or when the UN Security Council has authorised such use of force under Chapter VII of the UN Charter. In case the State on whose territory force is being used has given its consent, the operation does not constitute a violation of the general prohibition of the use of force. As such, consent is a constituent part of the primary rule of the prohibition of the use of force – a rule that must be understood as a prohibition of the non-consensual use of force only.

Besides a general legal basis in international law, every peace operation requires a mission-specific external mandate which can be issued by a competent international organisation (in principle, the UN Security Council under Chapter VII of the UN Charter) or by a host State's government inviting or consenting to a peace operation conducted on its territory. Such a mission-specific external mandate is a source of legal authority to deploy a mission in the territory of a State and to use force on that State's territory.

The external legal basis for the emplacement and functioning of a mission within the territory of a given State is not to be confused with the internal legal basis for establishing a mission.[2061] While a (physical) intervention in a State requires a legal basis in international law, international and regional organisations or arrangements carrying out the operation also need the competence to set up that operation as they only have those powers granted to them by their Member States. And although it is not necessarily a requirement at the international level, at the national level, too, there are often rules that determine which national authority may take the initiative to deploy national troops on the territory of another State. Hence, the legal basis for establishing a mission can be found in the internal laws of the State, organisation, or arrangement that undertakes the operation.

Besides a general legal basis in the internal laws, the operation in question also needs a mission-specific internal mandate. While for UN peace operations, the UNSC resolution provides for the internal and the external mandate simultaneously, UN-mandated peace operations conducted by an organisation or arrangement require a separate internal mandate issued by the competent body of that organisation or arrangement.[2062] Moreover, when a State undertakes a peace operation upon a PoC mandate, national laws may equally require a competent body of the State to issue some 'national authorisation', be it political, legal, or both.[2063]

It is essential to have an understanding of which rules may regulate the conduct of UN (mandated) peace operations

Once deployed, UN (mandated) peace forces must abide by the rules that regulate their conduct, especially their use of force to protect civilians.

First, as mentioned, the right to use force 'in self-defence', 'in defence of others', or 'in defence of the mandate' may govern the conduct of UN (mandated) peace operations, but only to the extent such conduct is also in accordance with the rules and principles of the legal regimes applicable in the given case, such as HRL, IHL, and national law. Different instruments may indeed serve as a legal source for the use of force in self-defence, defence of others, and defence of the mandate, including not only international law (as a general principle of law and/or as a permissive ground to deprive someone of their human right to life), but also national (criminal) law. Moreover, explicit authorisations by the UN Security Council under Chapter VII, or, in the case of UN peace operations, the implied or inherent powers of such operations to use force, which they may invoke in their capacity as subsidiary organs of the UN, may also serve as a legal source. However, any such use of force must always comply with

2061 In the Leuven Manual, this distinction between 'internal' and 'external' mandate is made (see Gill and others (n. 26) 34–35).

2062 *Ibid.* 35.

2063 Gill, Léveillée and Fleck (n. 609) 118.

the most restrictive rules and principles of the legal regimes applicable to the circumstances.

Hence, the second set of rules regulating the conduct of UN (mandated) peace operations consists of certain bodies of international law (including HRL, IHL, international law relative to the status of forces, the international law of the sea, international air law, international environmental law, and international refugee law, among others) and national law (including the laws of the host States and the sending States involved).

Third, other relevant rules and practices, despite not always being sources of law *per se*, are highly relevant to the conduct of UN (mandated) peace operations. These include mission-specific agreements and arrangements (such as SOFAs or TCC MOUs), mission-specific documents (such as CONOPS, ROE, or OPLANs), and doctrinal and general documents on PoC and the use of force (such as guidelines, policies, and principles on PoC and the use of force issued by the UN, the AU, NATO, or the EU).

A PoC mandate serves as a mission-specific legal basis underlying a UN (mandated) peace operation deployed to protect civilians and requires an interpretation that is legally sound

Every peace operation requires a mission-specific external mandate issued by a competent international organisation or by a host State's government inviting or consenting to a peace operation conducted on its territory. Such a mandate is a source of legal authority to deploy a mission in the territory of a State and to use force on that State's territory. UN (mandated) peace operations underlying this study have always been conducted based on a mandate from the UN Security Council, whether or not complemented by the host State's consent – this is where the PoC mandate comes in. PoC mandates issued by the UN Security Council are mandates whereby UN (mandated) peace operations can be undertaken to 'protect civilians under (imminent) threat of physical violence'. Often, PoC mandates also stipulate that during such UN (mandated) peace operations, 'all necessary means' can be taken to this end, yet 'without prejudice to the responsibility of the host government' and only 'within their capabilities' and 'areas of deployment' (in such or similar terms).

To unravel the precise meaning of these terms, they must be interpreted in good faith, considering the ordinary meaning given to them when they are read in the context of the resolution as a whole and in light of its object and purpose. Account should also be taken of the relevant circumstances of the adoption of these UNSC resolutions, the subsequent practice of the UN Security Council and other relevant practices of UN organs and subsidiary organs, and any relevant rules of international law (to the extent that they are consistent with the UN Security Council's intent).

As such, the term 'protection' has a broad meaning and refers to the acts or risks against which protection is sought as well as to the various strategies and methods by which civilians can be protected from the act or risk. The term 'civilian' is usually understood by analogy with the term 'civilians' in IHL. It refers to everyone who is not a member of the armed forces, a member of an organised armed group engaged in continuous combat duties, or a civilian who directly participates in hostilities. 'Threat of physical violence' likely means a threat of force that may cause death or serious bodily harm to civilians, including sexual violence. 'Imminent' must be understood as 'impending' and 'a matter of seconds' unless clear indications emerge that the UN Security Council has a genuine intention to depart from this ordinary meaning and, consequently, from the meaning given to it in the HRL context. The authorisation to take 'all necessary means, measures, steps, or action' provides those responsible for implementing the mandate with the authority to decide at their discretion which means are needed to prevent, deter, pre-empt, or respond to (imminent) threats of physical violence against civilians (without this being a blank cheque, see below). The terms 'within its capabilities' and 'areas of deployment' are used as caveats and emphasise that units within a mission can only be expected to protect civilians within the area for which they are operationally responsible, but even then, are given the discretion to prioritise threats that could potentially have greater consequences for civilians or a more destabilising effect, and to allocate resources accordingly. They should also have the discretion to assess whether they are adequately equipped to carry out certain actions. References to 'the (primary) responsibility of the host State's government or authorities' for the protection of civilians are also used as caveats to stress that while UN (mandated) peace operations are deployed to support the host State's government and/or authorities in protecting the population, the host State retains primary responsibility.

A PoC mandate is never a blank cheque to use any amount of force, but neither is it necessarily a mere authorisation with no expectations attached

The proposed interpretation for the standardised PoC language leaves sufficient leeway for those actors responsible for the implementation of a mandate to determine at their discretion which means are, for example, 'needed' to ensure PoC or what falls 'within the mission's capabilities' and 'areas of deployment'. However, this interpretation does not necessarily mean that a PoC mandate can be regarded as a blank cheque to use any amount of force or a mere authorisation without expectations attached. On the contrary, there is an upper limit to what UN (mandated) peace operations may lawfully do to protect civilians and an emerging lower limit for what UN (mandated) peace operations must lawfully do to protect civilians.

As for the upper limit, first, any use of force must strictly comply with peremptory norms. Second, the overall levels of force used when carrying out a UNSC mandate must be necessary and proportionate to obtain the general objective(s) set out in the mandate. The principle of necessity requires the mandate to be strictly implemented, and only those objectives authorised, such as PoC, can be pursued. Where force has been used to implement the mandate, the overall levels of force expended should not exceed what was necessary to achieve the general objectives. Similarly, the means used to implement the mandate must be rational and reasonable to protect civilians without unduly affecting the rights of those protected under international law. Third, specific instances of the use of force need to comply with HRL, IHL (if applicable), and relevant national laws of the host State and the TCC(s).

Besides an upper limit, this study has also detected an emerging lower limit for what UN (mandated) peace operations must lawfully do to protect civilians. In this regard, this study is convinced that a revised terminology in several PoC mandates indicates the emergence of an obligation of conduct upon States, the UN itself, its organs (e.g. the UN Security Council and the UN Secretariat) and subsidiary organs (e.g. the UN peace operations), and international and regional organisations other than the UN that decide to undertake a PoC mandate. Indeed, there might be an obligation to make the best efforts, within the operation's capabilities and areas of deployment, to pre-empt, prevent, deter, or respond to attacks or (imminent) threats of physical violence against civilians. This obligation is a responsibility that concerns everyone involved in the interpretation and implementation of PoC mandates.

The applicability de jure *of HRL and IHL to UN (mandated) peace operations cannot be refused when the requisite conditions for the application of the relevant body of law are met*

The applicability *de jure* of HRL and IHL to UN (mandated) peace operations is not always recognised in practice, and often, there is disagreement about when and how much force may be used under each legal regime. The UN Security Council undeniably has wide powers, including the power to override certain norms, but what it cannot do is change the applicability of HRL or IHL. All UN (mandated) peace operations must be conducted in accordance with HRL that applies *de jure* at all times, regardless of whether such operations are undertaken in peacetime or in the context of armed conflict. Depending on the status of an operation, peace forces conducting the operation must comply with the HRL obligations arising from the international obligations of the following actors: (i) the international or regional organisation undertaking the operation; (ii) the State undertaking or taking part in the operation; and (iii) the State on whose territory the operation takes place. The obligations are primarily based on HRL treaties or customary HRL.

If force is used in a situation unmistakably related to an ongoing armed conflict (i.e. there is a clear nexus between the use of force and the armed conflict), such use of force is not only governed by HRL but also by IHL. Indeed, under conventional or customary law, the rules and principles of IHL apply to all UN (mandated) peace operations when the conditions for applying this legal regime are met, regardless of whether the operation was established or authorised by the UN Security Council. This ruling implies that IHL applies equally to all belligerents as soon as an IAC or a NIAC begins, which is a factual inquiry. Depending on who is considered a party to the conflict, UN (mandated) peace forces can be bound by IHL obligations arising from the international obligations of the following actors: (i) the international or regional organisation conducting the operation; and (ii) the State undertaking or taking part in the operation. The obligations are primarily based on IHL treaties or customary IHL.

The use of (lethal) force to protect civilians that has no clear nexus to an armed conflict is governed by five main HRL principles

When UN (mandated) peace forces are deployed in the field with a PoC mandate, a wide range of forcible and non-forcible measures can be taken to protect civilians. Forcible measures to protect civilians may be (potentially) lethal and thus covered by the right to life, yet UN (mandated) peace forces may also enforce PoC mandates through a range of less-lethal measures that do not implicate the right to life at all. The use of lethal force is legal as long as someone is not arbitrarily deprived of their life. The right not to be arbitrarily deprived of one's life has a peremptory status which makes it impossible to derogate from (although, unlike its customary law status, such peremptory status is not generally recognised). Arbitrary deprivation of the right to life depends on the situation in which lethal force is used. If the use of lethal force has a clear nexus to an armed conflict, it is the rules of IHL that should be applied to establish whether a person has been arbitrarily deprived of their right to life. In case no clear link can be established to an armed conflict, the legality of using lethal force must be assessed against the strict rules for taking a person's life under HRL.

Five main HRL basic principles govern the recourse to force that endangers life outside the conduct of hostilities: legality, necessity, proportionality, precautions, and accountability. When less-lethal force is used in the context of UN (mandated) peace operations, such use of force is equally guided by these five principles, as well as any additional legal rules and principles (for instance, the right not to be subjected to inhumane or degrading treatment or the rules concerning the protection of private property) that apply in the circumstances.

By virtue of the principle of legality, the right to life must be protected by law. The legal basis for the use of force by UN (mandated) peace forces may be found in national law, but can also be found in the mission's mandate, anchored in the relevant UNSC resolutions, and then detailed in mission-specific ROE. Pursuant to the principle of necessity, (lethal) force can only be used when necessary for a legitimate aim, e.g. PoC, as determined by the UN Security Council. Force is only necessary when it is the last resort since less drastic means are unavailable or obviously unreasonable to protect the civilians concerned. A graduated response includes, for example, a verbal warning, a show of force, less-lethal force, and, as a last resort, lethal force. If force is inevitable, the amount of force must not surpass the minimum necessary in the circumstances, and force should be used only as long as necessary to achieve the legitimate aim. Damage and injury should always be minimised.

The principle of proportionality requires that the nature and degree of (lethal) force used are commensurate to the seriousness of the threat and the legitimate aim to be achieved. In this regard, the use of potentially lethal force must be distinguished from the intentional lethal use of force, as well as the different legitimate aims that these types of force may pursue. Intentional lethal force is allowed only 'to protect life from imminent threat' ('imminent' meaning a matter of seconds or even a fraction of a second before death occurs)[2064] and only when potentially lethal force would not suffice. Potentially lethal force may be used in self-defence or defence of others if one or more persons are under 'imminent threat of death' or when there is an 'imminent threat of serious injury' ('serious injury' refers to 'life threatening or life changing injury')[2065] or to pursue 'other legitimate aims' (as authorised by the UN Security Council) provided there is a 'grave threat to life' ('grave threat to life' refers to a continuing threat to life that may occur at any time).[2066]

In line with the principle of precautions, personnel taking part in an operation must be adequately trained and equipped and operations must be carefully planned, organised, and controlled so as to prevent or at least minimise the use of force. And last but not least, there should be an appropriate accountability system for any use of force that does not comply with the above principles.

[2064] UN HRC, 'Report of the Special Rapporteur on Extrajudicial, Summary or Arbitrary Executions, Christof Heyns' (n. 109) para. 59; UN OHCHR (n. 1691) 43.

[2065] Amnesty International (n. 1717) 23.

[2066] UN HRC, 'Report of the Special Rapporteur on Extrajudicial, Summary or Arbitrary Executions, Christof Heyns' (n. 109) para. 33 (discussion of international law standards) and para. 60 (discussion of domestic standards).

The use of (lethal) force to protect civilians that has a clear nexus to an armed conflict is governed by the relevant IHL rules and principles

If there is a nexus with an armed conflict, the legality of the force used must be determined according to the rules of IHL. A number of principles set out in the major IHL treaties (including the 1907 Hague Convention IV and its Regulations, the Geneva Conventions I–IV, and the Additional Protocols I–II) constitute the bedrock of the law as it applies to the conduct of hostilities. IHL first rests on a delicate balancing act of two foundational principles – humanity and military necessity. From the principles of military necessity and humanity emerge several fundamental IHL principles, including distinction, proportionality, precautions in attack and against the effects of attacks, and the prohibition of superfluous injury and unnecessary suffering. These principles are also part of customary IHL and can even be considered peremptory norms.

Pursuant to the principle of distinction, UN (mandated) peace forces must distinguish at all times between civilians and combatants and between civilian objects and military objectives. They cannot carry out direct attacks against civilians (unless and so long as they are direct participants in hostilities) nor against civilian objects (unless and so long as they are military objectives). Moreover, UN (mandated) peace forces are prohibited from conducting indiscriminate attacks (i.e. attacks where military objectives and civilians or civilian objects are indiscriminately targeted).

It is not inevitable that UN (mandated) peace forces cause incidental damage to civilians or civilian objects, even when executing a PoC mandate. However, when planning an attack against a legitimate military target, it becomes clear that there is a risk of such incidental damage to civilians or civilian objects, UN (mandated) peace forces must consider the proportionality of such damage. An attack is considered disproportionate if the attack is expected to result in collateral damage that is excessive in relation to the concrete and direct military advantage anticipated.

The principles of precautions in attack and against the effects of attacks impose additional restrictions on the use of force by UN (mandated) peace forces. Under the principle of precautions in attack, UN (mandated) peace forces, when conducting an attack, must take all possible precautions to prevent and minimise incidental deaths, injuries, and damage to civilians and civilian objects. In addition, under the principle of precautions against the effects of attacks, UN (mandated) peace forces are obliged to take all necessary precautions to protect the civilian population and civilian objects under its control from the consequences of attacks carried out by the adversary. Last but not least, under the principle of the prohibition of superfluous injury and unnecessary suffering, UN (mandated) peace forces are prohibited from using certain means and methods of warfare deemed to cause unnecessary suffering or injury to combatants.

The understanding of the relationship between the legal bases and the legal regimes is of paramount importance to the regulation of the use of force for protective purposes

Both the mandate and the relevant legal regimes play a crucial role in regulating the use of force for protective purposes. However, in principle, the mandate is concerned with the use of force at the strategic level, whereas HRL and IHL are concerned with the use of force ordered by military leadership at the operational and tactical levels and conducted by soldiers at the tactical level. In other words, the former addresses the strategic leadership adopting a mandate and supervising the overall implementation of that mandate, while the latter addresses the soldier whose finger is on the trigger or the commander who must choose whether to authorise a certain action. Hence, legal bases and legal regimes exercise, at least in theory, fundamentally different functions. When observing their respective roles in practice, it becomes clear, however, that HRL and IHL may influence the interpretation, implementation, and evaluation of PoC mandates and that, in turn, PoC mandates may have an impact on the use of force on the ground (an area predominantly regulated by the applicable legal regimes).

First, HRL and IHL may influence the interpretation, implementation, and evaluation of PoC mandates. When interpreting terms used in PoC mandates, the meaning given to those terms in HRL or IHL may be considered. Indeed, the ordinary meaning of a term, read in the context of the resolution as a whole and in light of its object and purpose, may reflect the meaning given to it in the context of HRL or IHL. The ordinary meaning of the term 'civilian' is, for example, congruent with the understanding of the term in IHL, and, in particular, civilians are those persons who are not combatants. Once adopted, PoC mandates are translated into military strategic, operational, and tactical instruments, and, as such, they regulate the use of force ordered or used at different levels of the chain of command. The meaning of a term conveyed at the strategic level in a manner consistent with HRL or IHL may equally carry over to the other levels. For instance, different documents may refer to the target group to be protected, i.e. civilians, understanding the term as under IHL. However, one should be well aware of the confusion this can also cause. For example, on the one hand, troops may be expected to apply an IHL analysis when assessing whether someone is a civilian who needs to be protected, and on the other hand, when assessing whether they may use lethal force to protect that same civilian, they should look at HRL. The interpretation may lead to confusion among troops and may eventually result in more force being used outside the conduct of hostilities than legally allowed under HRL. In addition to exerting an influence on interpretation and implementation, HRL or IHL, specifically violations thereof, may affect the evaluation of the implementation of a PoC mandate. The political and military strategic leadership evaluates whether an operation is conducted in accordance with the PoC mandate and is consequently responsible for the overall conduct of an operation. Violations of HRL or IHL may well affect whether the overall levels of force used in implementing the mandate are necessary and proportionate. However, this does not mean that such violations of HRL or IHL automatically constitute violations of the PoC mandate.

Second, a PoC mandate may indirectly impose additional limits on the use of force by UN (mandated) peace forces on the ground. As mentioned earlier, PoC mandates, once adopted, are transposed into military strategic, operational, and tactical instruments and, as such, govern the use of force ordered or used at different levels of the chain of command. A mandate is translated into mission-specific ROE and, as such, affects whether or not UN (mandated) peace forces may use force in specific situations. The mandate may leave less room for the use of force than is normally possible under HRL or IHL. For example, it may determine that the strategic objective of the operation is to protect civilians and that only measures to that end can be taken. Any use of force beyond these limits violates the ROE and/or relevant orders and directives but is not necessarily a violation of the applicable legal regime(s). In other words, the mandate has no 'normative spill-over' effect[2067] on the legal regimes. Rules and principles of HRL or IHL should not be interpreted differently simply because the forces are operating under a UNSC mandate. For example, the principle of proportionality under IHL must not be interpreted as such that all collateral damage is excessive in relation to the concrete and direct military advantage expected when the operation has the mandate to protect civilians. Besides introducing more restrictive rules, the mandate can also go beyond what is legally allowed under HRL or IHL. As such, a UNSC mandate may overrule or authorise acts contrary to the rules of HRL or IHL by virtue of Chapter VII and Article 103 of the UN Charter to the extent that the rules are not peremptory. Indeed, there are limits to the possible impact a UNSC mandate can have on whether force can be used in specific instances. A UNSC mandate can never trump rules of *jus cogens*, such as the right not to be arbitrarily deprived of one's life or the fundamental principles of IHL. Hence, even though the UN Security Council and the UN Secretariat have adopted ever stronger language to encourage proactive implementation of mission mandates in recent years, the substance and limits of imminence, as defined in HRL, remain central to a proper legal interpretation of when and how

2067 Terminology used by Lieblich in Lieblich, 'On the Continuous and Concurrent Application of Ad Bellum and In Bello Proportionality' (n. 1894) 73–75.

UN peace forces may lawfully protect civilians with lethal force outside the conduct of hostilities. It follows that UN (mandated) peace forces can always use potentially lethal force in self-defence or defence of others if a temporally proximate threat to life or serious injury exists, regardless of whether a PoC mandate requires threats of physical violence against civilians to be 'imminent' or, alternatively, refers to 'threats' with no further mention of imminence. UN (mandated) peace forces may also resort to potentially lethal force to pursue other legitimate aims, as authorised by the UN Security Council, upon the condition that there is a grave threat to life unless the mandate specifically requires threats to be 'imminent', which is to be interpreted in good faith as only temporally proximate threats. Where the use of potentially lethal force would fail to avert the threat and pose an unnecessary risk of death, intentional lethal force may be used to protect civilians but only against narrowly defined and temporally limited threats to life. The use of intentionally lethal force likewise does not depend on whether the mission's mandate mentions or omits an imminence requirement or how the term 'imminent' is interpreted.

It is essential to justify compliance of any use of force by (UN) mandated peace forces with the applicable legal regime

The need to justify compliance with the conditions set forth by the applicable legal regimes applies to all UN (mandated) peace operations when using force. The legality of using force for protective purposes in the context of UN (mandated) peace operations never depends on the mandate only; it must also comply with the applicable legal regimes. Going forward, those conducting PoC mandates must do more to justify the legality of their operations in response to PoC threats. While the practice of mechanically invoking PoC mandates, Chapter VII of the UN Charter, and broad notions of self-defence is understandable from a public relations perspective, it is not enough to justify the use of force in specific instances from a legal perspective. For example, when using lethal force for protective purposes, without further explanation as to why such use of force complies with IHL or the HRL requirements against arbitrary deprivations of life, such use of lethal force is *prima facie* unlawful. Whether killing a person was ever justified does not only depend on the PoC language used in the mandate (does the PoC mandate require a threat to be 'imminent' or not?) but also on which legal regime applies and what the specific nature was of the threat to civilians.

Effective protection of civilians is possible under HRL

HRL applicability does not mean that civilians cannot be protected effectively. While it is true that any use of force must follow graduated force procedures,

UN (mandated) peace forces have broad discretion to use various means that, even if less lethal, can be particularly effective in protecting civilians. Moreover, interventions that begin as a mere show of force or consist of less-lethal forcible measures can easily escalate in response to threatening behaviour from hostile actors. For instance, if in attempting to resist an order to leave, to disarm, or to surrender – a hostile actor resorts to force, which in turn endangers the lives of members of UN (mandated) peace forces or people under their protection, UN (mandated) peace forces are authorised to resort to lethal force to protect their own lives or the lives of people under their protection. In that sense, defending others (civilians) from threats can also transform into a case of legally permissible personal self-defence.

To illustrate: the UN Security Council may provide a UN-mandated peace operation with a mandate to protect civilians, promote, and protect human rights, and support humanitarian assistance. Suppose an FC has been informed that insurgents have surrounded a village of 1,200 residents and intercepted all relief supplies. While the members of a UN-mandated peace force taking part in the operation are on their way to evacuate the village, they are confronted by the insurgents who are blocking the road leading to the village. In this scenario, the insurgents do not directly threaten the members of the UN-mandated peace force, nor do they pose an imminent threat to the lives of citizens from the village in question. While potentially lethal force could be used if such a threat qualifies as a grave threat to life (upon the condition that the mandate authorises the use of all necessary means to protect civilians against the threat of physical violence), the forces can also always undertake a number of other actions to enable the evacuation of the villagers. For example, they could employ less-lethal options such as tear gas, baton rounds, or pellets, intercept and arrest individuals intentionally threatening the swift accomplishment of the mission, or try to circumvent the road blockade. However, if the situation escalates to a need to protect life against an imminent threat, the members of the UN-mandated peace force are authorised to use intentional lethal force to respond to this threat.

Whether there is an authority and/or duty to 'put themselves in harm's way' as opposed to a 'duty to retreat' under HRL in PoC scenarios warrants further research

When UN (mandated) peace forces deploy proactively to avert loosely defined threats to civilians, it is not always clear whether PoC mandates serve as a direct or indirect justification for lethal force. For instance, when the UN sends out a patrol in response to a general warning of potential violence and a hostile actor ends up being killed during the operation, the legality of such a killing will depend on the facts and not an abstract concept of PoC or an unspecified threat to civilians. Two questions can be distinguished here: was the lethal force used to avert a direct threat to a civilian? Or did the use of graduated force to address a more temporally removed threat escalate to the point where the soldier had to use lethal force in personal self-defence or defence of others? If it is the former, intentional lethal force is unlikely to ever be lawful, absent a strict temporal nexus between the threat and the use of force. In contrast, the potentially lethal force resulting in casualties may meet the HRL threshold of proportionality and/or necessity, but its legality ultimately depends on the mandate and precise dimensions of the threat's imminence or gravity. If it is the latter, further questions under HRL arise, for instance, about the duty not to provoke and the duty to retreat to avoid loss of life, which are not easily transposable to conflict environments in which peace forces operate.[2068] Accordingly, other scholars are encouraged to pursue further research into the UN (mandated) peace force's authority and/or duty to 'put themselves in harm's way' as opposed to a 'duty to retreat' in PoC scenarios to refine further the legality of using force in the context of UN (mandated) peace operations.

Whether there is an obligation to protect civilians from the threat of physical violence requires further investigation

When UN (mandated) peace operations are deployed in the territory of a State, the question arises whether missions are obligated to take positive action for the protection of civilians. A number of legal bases can be identified that may give rise to an obligation to protect civilians:

First, as mentioned earlier, this study has identified an emerging lower limit for what UN (mandated) peace operations must lawfully do to protect civilians when being provided with a PoC mandate. Indeed, depending on the terminology used in the PoC mandate, there might be an obligation to make the best efforts, within the operation's capabilities and areas of deployment, to pre-empt, prevent, deter, or respond to attacks or (imminent) threats of physical violence against civilians. Developments in UN practice should be further monitored to see whether or not this emerging trend continues.

Second, while the extent HRL obligations must be respected, protected, and fulfilled when acting on the territory of another State remains disputed, a prudent approach to the protection of civilian lives under HRL would be to adhere to the positive obligation to protect and fulfil the right to life of those

[2068] On the duty not to provoke a self-defence situation and a duty to retreat in the context of national law enforcement, see e.g. Hessbruegge (n. 647) 146–150. Whether these duties also apply to the military-operational context was included, e.g., in a questionnaire addressed to national governments in preparation for the General Report of the International Society of Military Law and the Law of War for its 19th Congress (see Gill and others (n. 648) 40–42). Due to lack of input, no concrete answers were given.

whose rights the missions control. These obligations include taking appropriate and feasible measures to prevent violations of the right to life by non-state actors and adhering to the positive obligation to fulfil the right to life, *inter alia*, by conducting effective investigations when individuals have been killed. Adhering to the positive obligation to protect the right to life would involve, *inter alia*, taking reasonable operational measures to prevent the arbitrary killing by non-state parties of civilians whose rights they control. For example, suppose a group of civilians face a real and immediate risk of being killed by approaching rebels, and UN-mandated peace forces deployed in the area are aware of this imminent threat; they must be considered to be under the obligation to take appropriate and feasible measures to prevent those civilians from being killed, without placing an impossible or disproportionate burden on them. Further research should be conducted on the extent to which missions should exercise 'control' over the rights of individuals creating a positive obligation to protect these rights, as well as on the scope of 'appropriate and feasible measures'.

Third, under Common Article 1 of the Geneva Conventions I–IV and the general principles of IHL, both States and international and regional organisations are obliged to respect and to ensure respect for IHL. While the nature of these obligations, particularly the obligation to ensure respect, has been much debated, the present study has suggested following a prudent approach. When States and international and regional organisations conduct UN (mandated) peace operations, they should consider being under a general duty of due diligence to prevent and suppress violations of IHL by the following actors: (i) members of the armed forces and other persons or groups whose conduct can be attributed to the State or international or regional organisation in question, (ii) private individuals over whom the State or the international or regional organisation exercises power, authority, or control, including persons in occupied territory; and (iii) other parties to an armed conflict, including both State and non-state parties, regardless of whether the State or international or regional organisation concerned is neutral, an ally, or an enemy. However, as this matter is still highly controversial and the proposal above is only a suggestion for a prudent approach, further research into the obligation to ensure respect for IHL when conducting a UN (mandated) peace operation is warranted.

BIBLIOGRAPHY

1. TREATIES AND STATUTES

African Charter on Human Peoples' Rights (adopted 27 June 1981, entered into force 21 October 1986) 1520 UNTS 217 (ACHPR)

Agreement on the Status of the North Atlantic Treaty Organization, National Representatives and International Staff (adopted 20 September 1951, entered into force 18 May 1954) 200 UNTS 3 (1951 Ottawa Agreement)

American Convention on Human Rights: 'Pact of San José, Costa Rica' (adopted 22 November 1969, entered into force 18 July 1978) 1144 UNTS 123 (ACHR)

Charter of Fundamental Rights of the European Union (adopted 7 December 2000, entered into force 1 December 2009) OJ C 364/1 (EU Charter of Fundamental Rights)

Charter of the United Nations (adopted on 26 June 1945, entered into force on 24 October 1945) 1 UNTS XVI (UN Charter)

Consolidated Version of the Treaty on European Union (26 October 2012) OJ C 326/13 (TEU)

Constitutive Act of the African Union (adopted 11 July 2000, entered into force 26 May 2001) 2158 UNTS 3 (AU Constitutive Act)

Convention against Torture and Other Cruel, Inhuman or Degrading Treatment or Punishment (adopted 10 December 1984, entered into force 26 June 1987) 1465 UNTS 85 (CAT)

Convention for the Amelioration of the Condition of the Wounded and Sick in Armed Forces in the Field (adopted 12 August 1949, entered into force 21 October 1950) 75 UNTS 31 (Geneva Convention I)

Convention for the Amelioration of the Condition of Wounded, Sick and Shipwrecked Members of Armed Forces at Sea (adopted 12 August 1949, entered into force 21 October 1950) 75 UNTS 85 (Geneva Convention II)

Convention for the Protection of Human Rights and Fundamental Freedoms, as Amended (adopted 4 November 1950, entered into force 3 September 1953) 213 UNTS 221 (ECHR)

Convention with Respect to the Laws and Customs of War and Land and Its Annex: Regulations concerning the Laws and Customs of War on Land (adopted 29 July 1899, entered into force 4 September 1900) 187 CTS 429 (1899 Hague Convention II and the 1899 Hague Regulations)

Convention Respecting the Laws and Customs of War on Land and its Annex: Regulations Concerning the Laws and Customs of War on Land (adopted 18 October 1907, entered into force 26 January 1910) 187 CTS 227 (1907 Hague Convention IV and the 1907 Hague Regulations)

Convention on the Prevention and Punishment of the Crime of Genocide (adopted 9 December 1948, entered into force 12 January 1951) 78 UNTS 277 (Genocide Convention)

Convention on the Privileges and Immunities of the United Nations (adopted 17 September 1946, entered into force 13 February 1946) 1 UNTS 15 and 90 UNTS 327 (corrigendum) (UN Privileges and Immunities Convention)

Convention on the Rights of the Child (adopted 20 November 1989, entered into force 2 September 1990) 1577 UNTS 3 (CRC)

Convention Relating to the Status of Refugees (adopted 28 July 1951, entered into force 22 April 1954) 189 UNTS 137 (Refugee Convention)

Convention Relative to the Protection of Civilian Persons in Time of War (adopted 12 August 1949, entered into force 21 October 1950) 75 UNTS 287 (Geneva Convention IV)

Convention Relative to the Treatment of Prisoners of War (adopted 12 August 1949, entered into force 21 October 1950) 75 UNTS 135 (Geneva Convention III)

Declaration Renouncing the Use, in Time of War, of Explosive Projectiles Under 400 Grammes Weight (adopted 29 November 1868, entered into force 11 December 1868) 138 CTS 297 (1868 St. Petersburg Declaration)

General Convention on the Privileges and Immunities of the Organization of African Unity (adopted 25 October 1965, entered into force 25 October 1965) 1000 UNTS 393 (AU General Convention)

International Covenant on Civil and Political Rights (adopted 16 December 1966, entered into force 23 March 1976) 999 UNTS 171 (ICCPR)

International Covenant on Economic, Social and Cultural Rights (adopted 16 December 1966, entered into force 3 January 1976) 993 UNTS 3 (ICESC)

North Atlantic Treaty (adopted 4 April 1949, entered into force 24 August 1949) 34 UNTS 243 (North Atlantic Treaty)

Protocol Additional to the Geneva Conventions of 12 August 1949, and Relating to the Protection of Victims of International Armed Conflicts (adopted 8 June 1977, entered into force 7 December 1978) 1125 UNTS 3 (Additional Protocol I)

Protocol Additional to the Geneva Conventions of 12 August 1949, and Relating to the Protection of Victims of Non-international Armed Conflicts (adopted 8 June 1977, entered into force 7 December 1978) 1125 UNTS 609 (Additional Protocol II)

Protocol No. 11 to the Convention for the Protection of Human Rights and Fundamental Freedoms, Restructuring the Control Machinery Established Thereby (adopted 11 May 1994, entered into force 1 November 1998) 2061 UNTS 7 (Protocol No. 11 to the ECHR)

Protocol on Prohibitions or Restrictions on the Use of Mines, Booby-Traps and Other Devices as amended on 3 May 1996 annexed to the Convention on Prohibitions or Restrictions on the Use of Certain Conventional Weapons which may be deemed to be Excessively Injurious or to have Indiscriminate Effects (adopted 3 May 1996, entered into force 3 December 1998) 2048 UNTS 93 (Mines Protocol to the Conventional Weapons Convention)

Protocol on the Status of International Military Headquarters set up pursuant to the North Atlantic Treaty (adopted 28 August 1952, entered into force 10 April 1954) 200 UNTS 340 (1952 Paris Protocol)

Protocol Relating to the Establishment of the Peace and Security Council of the African Union (adopted 9 July 2002, entered into force 26 December 2003) (AU PSC Protocol)

Statute of the International Court of Justice, Annexed to the UN Charter (adopted 26 June 1945, entered into force 24 October 1945) USTS 993 (ICJ Statute)

The Treaty of Economic, Social and Cultural Collaboration and Collective Self-Defence (adopted 17 March 1948, entered into force 25 August 1948), www.nato.int/cps/en/natohq/official_texts_17072.htm., accessed 17 February 2022 (1948 Treaty of Brussels)

Treaty of Amsterdam Amending the Treaty on European Union, the Treaties Establishing the European Communities and Certain Related Acts (adopted 2 October 1997, entered into force 1 May 1999) OJ C 340/1 (1997 Treaty of Amsterdam)

Treaty of Lisbon amending the Treaty on European Union and the Treaty establishing the European Community) (adopted 13 December 2007, entered into force 1 December 2009) 2702 UNTS 3 (2007 Treaty of Lisbon)

Vienna Convention on the Law of Treaties (adopted 23 May 1969, entered into force on 27 January 1980) 1155 UNTS 331 (VCLT)

2. DOMESTIC LAW

Belgian Criminal Code of 8 June 1867

French Constitution of 4 October 1958 (as revised on 23 July 2008)

3. INTERNATIONAL CASE LAW

3.1. INTERNATIONAL AND REGIONAL BODIES

3.1.1. AComHPR

Constitutional Rights Project, Civil Liberties Organisation and Media Rights Agenda v. Nigeria (1999) AComHPR Communication Nos. 140/94, 141/94, 145/95

Democratic Republic of the Congo v. Burundi, Rwanda and Uganda (2003) AComHPR 33rd Ordinary Session, Communication No. 227/99

Media Rights Agenda and Others v. Nigeria (1998) AComHPR Communication Nos. 105/93, 128/94, 130/94, 152/96

Noah Kazingachire, John Chitsenga, Elias Chemvura and Batanai Hadzisi (represented by Zimbabwe Human Rights NGO Forum v. Zimbabwe (2013) AComHPR Communication No. 295/04

Social and Economic Rights Action Center & the Center for Economic and Social Rights v. Nigeria (2002) AComHPR Communication No. 155/96

3.1.2. *ECJ*

Yassin Abdullah Kadi v. Council of the European Union and Commission of the European Communities, Judgment (2005) ECJ Case T-315/01, ECR II-3649

3.1.3. *EComHR*

Stewart v. the United Kingdom, Decision as to the admissibility (1984) EComHR App. No. 10044/82
X v. The Federal Republic of Germany, Decision as to the admissibility (1965) EComHR App. No. 1611/62, 8 Yearbook of the European Convention on Human Rights 158

3.1.4. *ECtHR*

Case of Ahmet Özkan and Others v. Turkey, Judgment (2004) ECtHR App. No. 21689/93
Case of Al-Dulimi and Montana Management Inc v. Switzerland, Judgment (2016) ECtHR (Grand Chamber) App. No. 5809/08
Case of Al-Jedda v. the United Kingdom, Judgment (2011) ECtHR (Grand Chamber) App. No. 27021/08
Case of Al-Skeini and Others v. the United Kingdom, Judgment (2011) ECtHR (Grand Chamber) App. No. 55721/07
Case of Andreou v. Turkey, Judgment (2009) ECtHR App. No. 45653/99
Case of Andronicou and Constantinou v. Cyprus, Judgment (1997) ECtHR App. No. 27021/08
Case of Banković and Others v. Belgium and 16 Other Contracting States, Decision as to the admissibility (2001) ECtHR (Grand Chamber) App. No. 52207/99
Case of Behrami and Behrami v. France and Saramati v. France, Germany and Norway, Decision as to the admissibility (2007) ECtHR (Grand Chamber) App. Nos. 71412/01 and 78166/01
Case of Benzer and Others v. the United Kingdom, Judgment (2013) ECtHR App. No. 23502/06
Case of Branko Tomašić and Others v. Croatia, Judgment (2009) ECtHR App. No. 46598/06
Case of Carter v. Russia, Judgment (Merits) (2021) ECtHR (Grand Chamber) App. No. 20914/07
Case of Choreftakis and Choreftaki v. Greece, Judgment (2012) ECtHR App. No. 46846/08
Case of Cyprus v. Turkey, Judgment (2001) ECtHR (Grand Chamber) App. No. 25781/94
Case of Ergi v. Turkey, Judgment (1998) ECtHR App. No. 66/1997/850/1057
Case of Finogenov and Others v. Russia, Judgment (2011) ECtHR App. Nos. 18299/03 and 27311/03
Case of Georgia v. Russia (II), Judgment (Merits) (2021) ECtHR (Grand Chamber) App. No. 38263/08
Case of Giuliani and Gaggio v. Italy, Judgment (2011) ECtHR (Grand Chamber) App. No. 23458/02
Case of Güleç v. Turkey, Judgment (1998) ECtHR App. No. 54/1997/838/1044
Case of Hassan v. the United Kingdom, Judgment (2014) ECtHR (Grand Chamber) App. No. 29750/09

Case of Huohvanainen v. Finland, Judgment (2007) ECtHR App. No. 57389/00
Case of Isayeva v. Russia, Judgment (2005) ECtHR App. No. 57950/00
Case of Isayeva, Yusupova and Bazayeva v. Russia, Judgment (2005) ECtHR App. Nos. 57947/00, 57948/00, and 57949/00
Case of Issa and Others v. Turkey, Judgment (2004) ECtHR App. No. 31821/96
Case of Jaloud v. the Netherlands, Judgment (2014) ECtHR (Grand Chamber) App. No. 47708/08
Case of Juozaitienė and Bikulčius v. Lithuania, Judgment (2008) ECtHR App. Nos. 70659/01 and 74371/01
Case of Kakoulli v. Turkey, Judgment (2005) ECtHR App. No. 38595/97
Case of Karandja v. Bulgaria, Judgment (2010) ECtHR App. No. 69180/01
Case of Kelly and Others v. the United Kingdom, Judgment (2001) ECtHR App. No. 18984/91
Case of Khatsiyeva and Others v. Russia, Judgment (2008) ECtHR App. No. 5108/02
Case of LCB v. the United Kingdom, Judgment (1998) ECtHR App. No. 14/1997/798/1001
Case of Loizidou v. Turkey, Judgment (1996) ECtHR (Grand Chamber) App. No. 15318/89
Case of Loizidou v. Turkey, Judgment (Preliminary Objections) (1995) ECtHR (Grand Chamber) App. No. 15318/89
Case of Makaratzis v. Greece, Judgment (2004) ECtHR (Grand Chamber) App. No. 50385/99
Case of McCann and Others v. the United Kingdom, Judgment (1995) ECtHR (Grand Chamber) App. No. 18984/91
Case of Nachova and Others v. Bulgaria, Judgment (2005) ECtHR (Grand Chamber) App. Nos. 43577/98 and 43579/98
Case of Nada v. Switzerland, Judgment (2012) ECtHR (Grand Chamber) App. No. 10593/08
Case of Öcalan v. Turkey, Judgment (2004) ECtHR (Grand Chamber) App. No. 46221/99
Case of Osman v. the United Kingdom, Judgment (1998) ECtHR (Grand Chamber) App. No. 87/1997/871/1083
Case of Pad and Others v. Turkey, Decision as to admissibility (2007) ECtHR App. No. 60167/00
Case of Paul and Audrey Edwards v. the United Kingdom, Judgment (2002) ECtHR App. No. 46477/99
Case of Putintseva v. Russia, Judgment (2012) ECtHR App. No. 33498/04
Case of Ramsahai and Others v. the Netherlands, Judgment (2007) ECtHR (Grand Chamber) App. No. 52391/99
Case of Solomou and Others v. Turkey, Judgment (2008) ECtHR App. No. 36832/97
Case of Tagayeva and Others v. Russia, Judgment (2017) ECtHR App. No.26562/07
Case of Vasil Sashov Petrov v. Bulgaria, Judgment (2011) ECtHR App. No. 30054/96
Case of Wasilewska v. Russia, Judgment (2010) ECtHR App. Nos. 28975/04 and 33406/04

3.1.5. IAComHR

Alonso Eugénio da Silva v. Brazil (2000) IAComHR Report No. 9/00, Case 11.598
Armando Alejandre Jr and Others v. Cuba (1999) IAComHR Report No. 86/99, Case 11.589, OEA/Ser.L/V/II.106 Doc. 3 rev. at 586 (1999)

Coard et al. v. United States (1999) IAComHR Report No. 109/99, Case 10.951
Franklin Guillermo Aisalla Molina v. Ecuador (2010) IAComHR Report No. 112/10, Case IP-02, OEA/Ser.L/V/II.140 Doc. 10 (2010)
Jean Carlos Abella v. Argentina (1997) IAComHR Report No. 55/97, Case 11.137, OEA/Ser.L/V/II.98 Doc. 10 at 271 (1997)
José Isabel Salas and Others v. United States, Merits (2018) IAComHR Report No. 121/18, Case 10.573
Marcos Aurelio de Oliveira v. Brazil (2000) IAComHR Report No. 10/00, Case 11.599, OEA/Ser.L/V/II.106 Doc. 3 rev. at 413 (1999)
Petition Victor Saldaño v. Argentina (1999) IAComHR Report No. 38/99
Precautionary Measures in Guantanamo Bay, Cuba (2002) IAComHR 41 ILM 532 (2002)
Ríofrío Massacre v. Colombia, Judgment (2001) IAComHR Report No. 62/01, Case 11.654, OEA/Ser.L/V/II.111 Doc. 20 rev. at 758 (2000)
Victims of the Tugboat '13 de Marzo' v. Cuba (1996) IAComHR Report No. 47/96, Case 11.436, OEA/Ser.L/V/II.95 Doc. 7 rev. at 127 (1997)

3.1.6. IACtHR

Advisory Opinion OC-23/17 of November 15, 2017 Requested by the Republic of Colombia: The Environment and Human Rights (2017) IACtHR OC-23/17
Case of Barrios Family v. Venezuela, Judgment (2011) IACtHR Series C No. 237
Case of Montero-Aranguren et al. (Detention Center of Catia) v. Venezuela, Judgment (2006) IACtHR Series C No. 150
Case of Nadege Sorzema et al. v. Dominican Republic, Judgment (2012) IACtHR Series C No. 166
Case of the Landaeta Mejías Brothers et al. v. Venezuela, Judgment (2014) IACtHR Series C No. 281
Case of the Pueblo Bello Massacre v. Colombia, Judgment (2006) IACtHR Series C No. 140
Case of the 'White Van' (Paniagua-Morales et al.) v. Guatemala, Judgment (Preliminary Objections) (1998) IACtHR Series C No. 23
Case of Valle Jaramillo et al. v. Colombia, Judgment (2008) IACtHR Series C No. 190
Case of Velásquez-Rodríguez v. Honduras, Judgment (1988) IACtHR Series C No. 4
Case of Zambrano Vélez et al. v. Ecuador, Judgment (2007) IACtHR Series C No. 166

3.1.7. ICC

The Prosecutor v. Abdallah Banda Abakaer Nourain and Saleh Mohammed Jerbo Jamus, Corrigendum of the 'decision on the confirmation of charges', Public redacted version (2011) ICC ICC-02/05-03/09
The Prosecutor v. Bahar Idriss Abu Garda, Decision on the confirmation of charges (2010) ICC ICC-02/05-02/09
The Prosecutor v. Thomas Lubanga Dyilo, Judgment (2012) ICC ICC-01/04-01/06

3.1.8. ICJ

Accordance with International Law of the Unilateral Declaration of Independence in Respect of Kosovo, Advisory opinion (2010) ICJ Rep 403

Application of the International Convention on the Elimination of All Forms of Racial Discrimination (Georgia v. Russian Federation), Request for the Indication of Provisional Measures, Order (2008) ICJ Rep 353

Case Concerning Application of the Convention on the Prevention and Punishment of the Crime of Genocide (Bosnia and Herzegovina v. Yugoslavia (Serbia and Montenegro)), Judgment (2007) ICJ Rep 43

Case Concerning Armed Activities on the Territory of the Congo (Democratic Republic of the Congo v. Uganda), Judgment (2005) ICJ Rep 168

Case Concerning Military and Paramilitary Activities in and against Nicaragua (Nicaragua v. United States of America), Judgment (Merits) (1986) ICJ Rep 14

Case Concerning Oil Platforms (Islamic Republic of Iran v. United States of America), Judgment (Merits) (2003) ICJ Rep 161

Certain Expenses of the United Nations (Article 17, paragraph 2, of the Charter), Advisory opinion (1962) ICJ Rep 151

Corfu Channel (United Kingdom of Great Britain and Northern Ireland v. Albania), Judgment (Merits) (1949) ICJ Rep 4

Interpretation of the Agreement of 25 March 1951 between the WHO and Egypt, Advisory opinion (1980) 1980 Rep 73

Legal Consequences for States of the Continued Presence of South Africa in Namibia (South West Africa) notwithstanding Security Council Resolution 276 (1970), Advisory opinion (1971) ICJ Rep 16

Legal Consequences of the Construction of a Wall in the Occupied Palestinian Territory, Advisory opinion (2004) ICJ Rep 136

Legality of the Threat or Use of Nuclear Weapons, Advisory opinion (1996) ICJ Rep 226

Reparation for Injuries Suffered in the Service of the United Nations, Advisory opinion (1949) ICJ Rep 174

3.1.8.1. Separate opinions and statements in the context of ICJ judgments

Case Concerning Application of the Convention on the Prevention and Punishment of the Crime of Genocide (Bosnia and Herzegovina v. Yugoslavia (Serbia and Montenegro)), Order, Separate opinion of Judge Sir Lauterpacht (1993) ICJ Rep 407

Case Concerning Military and Paramilitary Activities in and against Nicaragua (Nicaragua v. United States of America), Judgment (Merits), Separate opinion of Judge Singh (1986) ICJ Rep 151

Legal Consequences of the Construction of a Wall in the Occupied Palestinian Territory, Advisory opinion, Separate opinion of Judge Elaraby (2004) ICJ Rep 246

Legal Consequences of the Construction of a Wall in the Occupied Palestinian Territory (Request for advisory opinion), Order of 19 December 2003, Written statement of the League of Arab States (2004) ICJ 3

3.1.9. ICTR

Prosecutor v. Georges Anderson Nderubumwe Rutaganda, Judgment (1999) ICTR ICTR-96-3-T

Prosecutor v. Jean-Paul Akayesu, Judgment (1998) ICTR ICTR-96-4-T

3.1.10. ICTY

Prosecutor v. Ante Gotovina, Ivan Čermak, and Mladen Markač, Trial chamber judgment (2011) ICTY IT-06–90-T
Prosecutor v. Fatmir Limaj, Haradin Bala, and Isak Musliu, Trial chamber judgment (2005) ICTY IT-03–66-T
Prosecutor v. Furundìja, Trial chamber judgment (1998) ICTY IT-95–17/1-T
Prosecutor v. Galić, Trial chamber judgment (2003) ICTY IT-98–29-T
Prosecutor v. Kunarac, Kovac, and Vokovic, Appeals chamber judgment (2002) ICTY IT-96–23 and IT-96–23/1-A
Prosecutor v. Kupreškić et al., Trial chamber judgment (2000) ICTY IT-95–16-T
Prosecutor v. Ljube Boškoski and Johan Tarčulovski, Trial chamber judgment (2008) ICTY IT-04–82-T
Prosecutor v. Radovan Karadžić, Trial chamber judgment (2016) ICTY IT-95–5/18-T
Prosecutor v. Ramush Haradinaj, Idriz Balaj, and Lahi Brahimaj, Trial chamber judgment (2008) ICTY IT-04–84-T
Prosecutor v. Tadić, Appeals chamber judgment (1999) ICTY IT-94–1-A
Prosecutor v. Tadić, Decision on the defense motion for interlocutory appeal on jurisdiction (1995) ICTY IT-94–1-A
Prosecutor v. Tadić, Trial chamber judgment (1997) ICTY IT-94–1-T

3.1.11. SCSL

The Prosecutor v. Alex Tamba Brima, Brima Bazzy Kamara and Santigie Borbor Kanu (the AFRC Accused), Judgment (2007) SCSL Case No. SCSL-04–16-T
The Prosecutor v. Issa Hassan Sesay, Morris Kallon and Augustine Gbao, Judgment (2009) SCSL Case No. SCSL-04–15-T

3.1.12. UN HRC

AS, DI, OI and GD v. Italy (2020) UN HRC Communication No. 3042/2017, UN Doc. CCPR/C/130/D/3042/2017
AS, DI, OI and GD v. Malta (2020) UN HRC Communication No. 3043/2017, UN Doc. CCPR/C/128/D/3043/2017
Delia Saldias de Lopez v. Uruguay (1981) UN HRC Communication No. 52/1979, UN Doc. CCPR/C/OP/1 at 88 (1984)
Husband of Maria Fanny Suarez de Guerrero v. Colombia, Decision as to the admissibility (1981) UN HRC Communication No. R.11/45, UN Doc. Supp. No. 40 (A/37/40) at 137 (1982)
Lilian Celiberti de Casariego v. Uruguay (1981) UN HRC Communication No. 56/1979, UN Doc. CCPR/C/OP/1 at 92 (1984)
Sayadi and Vinck v. Belgium, Concurring opinion by Committee member Sir Nigel Rodley (2008) UN HRC UN Doc. CCPR/C/94/D/1472/2006, 3216 Oxford Reports on International Human Rights Law

3.2. NATIONAL COURTS

Arancibia Clavel, Enrique Lautaro s/ Homicidio Calificado y Asociación Ilícita y Otros, Judgment (2004) Supreme Court of Argentina Case No. 259
Constitutional Case No. C-223/95 (1995) Constitutional Court of Colombia Case No. C-223/95
Constitutional Case No. C-291/07 (2007) Constitutional Court of Colombia Case No. C-291/07
Her Majesty the Queen v. Private DJ Brocklebank (1996) Court Martial Appeal Court of Canada Court File No. CMAC-383, 5, Part 3, 1995–1997 Court Martial Appeal Rep
In Re 'Agent Orange Product Liability Litigation', Judgment (2005) District Court of the United States, Easter District of New York MDL No. 381, No. 04-CV-400
Mehida Mustafić-Mujić and Others v. the Netherlands, Judgment (2011) Dutch Court of Appeal ECLI:NL:GHSGR:2011:BR0132
Ministère Public et Centre Pour L'égalité des Chances et la Lutte Contre le Racisme c C. et B. (1997) Belgian Military Court, 14(5580) Journal des Tribunaux 286
R (on the application of Al-Jedda) v. Secretary of State for Defence, Appeal judgment (2007) United Kingdom House of Lords 58, 832 Oxford Reports on International Law in Domestic Courts

4. INTERNATIONAL PRACTICE

4.1. AU

AU, 'Draft Guidelines for the Protection of Civilians in African Union Peace Support Operations' (2012), www.peaceau.org/uploads/draft-au-poc-guidelines-english.pdf, accessed 22 October 2022
—, 'PAPS – Mandate and Core Functions' (16 June 2021), www.peaceau.org/en/page/77-paps-mandate-and-core-functions, accessed 11 April 2022
—, 'Peace Support Operations' (AU, Date unknown), https://au.int/en/directorates/peace-support-operations, accessed 11 April 2022
—, 'Rules of Engagement for AFISMA Military Component' (2013)
—, 'The Peace & Security Council' (AU, Date unknown), https://au.int/en/psc, accessed 11 April 2022
—, 'The Peace Support Operations Division (PSOD)' (Date unknown), www.peaceau.org/uploads/02-au-psod-brochure-23sep16.pdf, accessed 7 April 2022
—, Solemn Declaration on a Common African Defence and Security Policy' (2004), www.peaceau.org/uploads/declaration-cadsp-en.pdf, accessed 22 October 2022
AU PSC, 'AU PSC Communiqué DCCLXXV' (2018) AU Doc. PSC/PR/Comm.(DCCLXXV)
—, 'AU PSC Communiqué LXIX' (2007) AU Doc. PSC/PR/Comm. (LXIX)
—, 'AU PSC Communiqué XIII' (2004) AU Doc. PSC/PR/Comm. (XIII)
—, 'AU PSC Communiqué XLVII' (2006) AU Doc. PSC/PR/Comm.1(XLVII)
—, 'AU PSC Communiqué XVII' (2004) AU Doc. PSC/PR/Comm. (XVII)

—, 'Report of the Chairperson of the Commission on the Situation in Somalia' (2013) AU Doc. PSC/PR/2.(CCCLXXIX)

—, 'The 326th Meeting of the Peace and Security Council of the African Union Was Held on 26 June 2012' (*AU*, 18 February 2013), www.peaceau.org/en/article/the-326th-meeting-of-the-peace-and-security-council-of-the-african-union-was-held-on-26-june-2012, accessed 21 April 2022

AU Assembly, 'Aide Mémoire for the Consideration of Issues Pertaining to the Protection of Civilians in Africa' (2013)

4.2. EU

Council of the EU, 'Council Common Position 2003/319/CFSP of 8 May 2003 Concerning European Union Support for the Implementation of the Lusaka Ceasefire Agreement and the Peace Process in the Democratic Republic of Congo (DRC) and Repealing Common Position 2002/203/CFSP' (2003) OJ L 115

—, 'Council Decision 2003/432/CFSP of 12 June 2003 on the Launching of the European Union Military Operation in the Democratic Republic of Congo' (2003) OJ L 147

—, 'Council Decision 2006/412/CFSP of 12 June 2006 on the Launching of the European Union Military Operation in Support of the United Nations Organisation Mission in the Democratic Republic of the Congo (MONUC) during the Election Process' (2006) OJ L 163

—, 'Council Decision 2008/101/CFSP of 28 January 2008 on the Launching of the European Union Military Operation in the Republic of Chad and in the Central African Republic (Operation EUFOR Tchad/RCA)' (2008) OJ L 34

—, 'Council Decision 2014/183/CFSP of 1 April 2014 on the Launch of a European Union Military Operation in the Central African Republic (EUFOR RCA)' (2014) OJ L 100/12

—, 'Council Decision 2014/73/CFSP of 10 February 2014 on a European Union Military Operation in the Central African Republic (EUFOR RCA)' (2014) OJ L 40/59

—, 'Council Decision 2014/775/CFSP of 7 November 2014 Extending Decision 2014/73/CFSP on a European Union Military Operation in the Central African Republic (EUFOR RCA)' (2014) OJ L 325/17

—, 'Council Joint Action 2003/423/CFSP of 5 June 2003 on the European Union Military Operation in the Democratic Republic of Congo' (2003) OJ L 143

—, 'Council Joint Action 2005/557/CFSP of 18 July 2005 on the European Union Civilian-Military Supporting Action to the African Union Mission in the Darfur Region of Sudan' (2005) OJ L 188

—, 'Council Joint Action 2007/147/CFSP of 27 February 2007 Repealing Joint Action 2006/319/CFSP on the European Union Military Operation in Support of the United Nations Organisation Mission in the Democratic Republic of the Congo (MONUC) during the Election Process' (2007) OJ L 64

—, 'Council Joint Action 2007/677/CFSP of 15 October 2007 on the European Union Military Operation in the Republic of Chad and in the Central African Republic' (2007) OJ L 279

—, 'Council Joint Action 2008/110/CFSP of 12 February 2008 Amending and Extending the Mandate of the European Union Special Representative for Sudan' (2008) OJ L 143
—, 'Council Joint Action 2009/795/CFSP of 19 October 2009 Repealing Joint Action 2007/677/CFSP on the European Union Military Operation in the Republic of Chad and in the Central African Republic' (2008) OJ L 283
—, 'Draft Guidelines on Protection of Civilians in EU-Led Crisis Management Operations' (2003) EU Doc. 14805/03
—, 'Draft Revised Guidelines on the Protection of Civilians in CSDP Missions and Operations' (2010) EU Doc. 15091/10
—, 'European Security Strategy: A Secure Europe in a Better World' (2003) EU Doc. 15895/03
EEAS, 'EU Concept for Military Command and Control – Rev 8' (2019) EU Doc. EEAS 02246/8/14 REV 8
—, 'Missions and Operations' (*EEAS*, 2001), www.eeas.europa.eu/eeas/missions-and-operations_en, accessed 8 October 2022
—, 'The Shaping of a Common Security and Defence Policy' (*EEAS*, 6 August 2021), www.eeas.europa.eu/eeas/shaping-common-security-and-defence-policy_en, accessed 8 October 2022
EUMC, 'EU Concept for EU-Led Military Operations and Missions' (2014) EU Doc. EEAS 00990/6/14 REV 6
—, 'Concept on Protection of Civilians (PoC) in EU-Led Military Operations' (2015) EU Doc. EEAS 00351/6/14 REV 6
—, 'EU Concept for the Use of Force in EU-Led Military Operations' (2015) EU Doc. 17168/2/09 REV 2 EXT 2
EU, 'Shared Vision, Common Action: A Stronger Europe. A Global Strategy for the European Union's Foreign And Security Policy' (2016)

4.3. NATO

De Vidts B, 'Aspects Related to the Legal Status of the North Atlantic Treaty Organization', Speaking notes, 22 November 2004, NATO doc. CJ(2004)0910
EAPC, 'NATO/EAPC Policy for the Implementation of UNSCR 1325 on Women, Peace and Security and Related Resolutions' (2011) NATO Doc. PO(2014)0253
—, 'NATO/EAPC Policy on Implementing UNSCR 1325 on Women, Peace and Security' (2014) NATO Doc. NATO/EAPC(C)D(2007)022
—, 'Revised NATO/EAPC Policy for the Implementation of UNSCR 1325 on Women, Peace and Security and Related Resolutions' (2014) NATO Doc. PO(2014)0253
—, 'NATO/EAPC Women, Peace and Security Policy and Action Plan 2018' (2018), www.nato.int/nato_static_fl2014/assets/pdf/pdf_2018_09/180920-WPS-Action-Plan-2018.pdf, accessed 18 February 2021
Joint Analysis Lessons Learned Centre, 'Protection of Civilians, How ISAF Reduced Civilian Casualties' (NATO 2015)
NAC, 'NATO Brussels Summit Communiqué: Issued by the Heads of State and Government Participating in the Meeting of the North Atlantic Council in

Brussels on 14 June 2021', www.nato.int/cps/en/natohq/news_185000.htm, accessed 12 April 2022
—, 'NATO Brussels Summit Declaration: Issued by the Heads of State and Government Participating in the Meeting of the North Atlantic Council in Brussels on 11–12 July 2018', www.nato.int/cps/en/natohq/official_texts_156624.htm#77, accessed 18 February 2021
—, 'NATO Chicago Summit Declaration: Issued by the Heads of State and Government Participating in the Meeting of the North Atlantic Council in Chicago on 20 May 2012', www.nato.int/cps/en/natolive/official_texts_87593.htm#unscr1612, accessed 18 February 2021
—, 'NATO Policy for the Protection of Civilians Endorsed by the Heads of State and Government Participating in the Meeting of the North Atlantic Council in Warsaw 8–9 July 2016' (*NATO*, 9 July 2016), www.nato.int/cps/en/natohq/official_texts_133945.htm, accessed 21 September 2021
—, 'NATO Warsaw Summit Declaration: Issued by the Heads of State and Government Participating in the Meeting of the North Atlantic Council in Warsaw on 8–9 July 2016', www.nato.int/cps/en/natohq/official_texts_133169.htm#civilians, accessed 18 February 2021
—, 'North Atlantic Council Statement on Libya' (*NATO*, 21 October 2011), www.nato.int/cps/en/natohq/news_79800.htm?selectedLocale=en, accessed 14 April 2022
—, 'The Alliance's New Strategic Concept, Agreed by the Heads of State and Government Participating in the Meeting of the North Atlantic Council' (1991), www.nato.int/cps/en/natohq/official_texts_23847.htm, accessed 23 March 2022
NAMC, 'MC 362/1, NATO Rules of Engagement ("NATO Unclassified")' (2003)
—, 'NATO Military Guidelines on the Prevention of, and Response to, Conflict-Related Sexual and Gender-Based Violence' (2015) NATO Doc. MCM-0009–2015
NATO, '"Strategic Airlift Capability (SAC) – Initiative Adoption of the NAMO Charter", Note by the Secretary-General' (*NATO*, 20 June 2007), www.nato.int/cps/en/natohq/official_texts_56625.htm, accessed 11 July 2022
—, 'Allied Joint Doctrine for Peace Support Operations' (NATO Military Agency for Standarization (MAS) 2001) NATO Doc. AJP-3.4.1
—, 'Allied Joint Doctrine for the Military Contribution to Peace Support' (NATO Standardization Office (NSO) 2014) NATO Doc. AJP-3.4.1, Edn. A, Version 1
—, 'Allied Joint Doctrine for the Military Contribution to Stabilization and Reconstruction' (2015) NATO Doc. AJP-3.4.5, Edn. A, Version 1
—, 'Crisis Management' (*NATO*, 8 October 2020), www.nato.int/cps/en/natolive/topics_49192.htm, accessed 19 February 2021
—, 'Human Security' (*NATO*, 11 March 2022), www.nato.int/cps/en/natohq/topics_181779.htm, accessed 21 April 2022
—, 'ISAF's Mission in Afghanistan (2001–2014) (Archived)' (*NATO*, 19 August 2021), www.nato.int/cps/en/natolive/topics_69366.htm, accessed 21 April 2022
—, 'Military Committee' (*NATO*, 25 August 2021), www.nato.int/cps/en/natohq/topics_49633.htm, accessed 11 April 2022
—, 'Military Organisation and Structures' (*NATO*, 20 May 2021), www.nato.int/cps/en/natohq/topics_49608.htm, accessed 11 April 2022
—, 'NATO Military Command Structure' (*NATO SHAPE*), https://shape.nato.int/military_command_structure, accessed 27 April 2020

—, 'NATO Military Guidelines on Children and Armed Conflict' (2012)
—, 'NATO Policy for the Protection of Children in Armed Conflict – the Way Forward' (2015)
—, 'NATO Policy for the Protection of Civilians Endorsed by the Heads of State and Government Participating in the Meeting of the North Atlantic Council in Warsaw 8–9 July 2016' (NATO, 9 July 2016), www.nato.int/cps/en/natohq/official_texts_133945.htm, accessed 21 September 2021
—, 'NATO Secretary General Statement on NAC Decision to Extend Libya Mission' (*NATO*, 21 September 2011), www.nato.int/cps/en/natohq/news_78355.htm, accessed 14 April 2022
—, 'North Atlantic Council' (*NATO*, 11 October 2017), www.nato.int/cps/en/natolive/topics_49763.htm, accessed 7 April 2022
—, 'Questions and Answers at the Press Conference by NATO Secretary-General Anders Fogh Rasmussen on the Second Day of the Meeting of NATO Foreign Affairs Ministers, Berlin', www.nato.int/cps/en/natolive/opinions_72785.htm, accessed 26 February 2019
—, 'Resolute Support Mission in Afghanistan (2015–2021) (Archived)' (*NATO*, 8 April 2022), www.nato.int/cps/en/natohq/topics_113694.htm, accessed 21 April 2022
—, 'The NATO Command Structure' (2018) Factsheet, www.nato.int/nato_static_fl2014/assets/pdf/pdf_2018_02/1802-Factsheet-NATO-Command-Structure_en.pdf, accessed 11 April 2022
—, *NATO Legal Deskbook* (2nd edn., NATO 2010)
—, *Protection of Civilians ACO Handbook* (NATO 2021)

4.4. UN

4.4.1. ECOSOC

ECOSOC, Commission on Human Rights, 'Civil and Political Rights, Including the Questions of Disappearances and Summary Executions, Report of the Special Rapporteur, Philip Alston, on Extrajudicial, Summary or Arbitrary Executions, Sixty-First Session, Item 11(b) of the Provisional Agenda' (2005) UN Doc. E/CN.4/2005/7
—, 'Civil and Political Rights, Including the Questions of Disappearances and Summary Executions, Report of the Special Rapporteur, Philip Alston, on Extrajudicial, Summary or Arbitrary Executions, Sixty-Second Session, Item 11(b) of the Provisional Agenda' (2006) UN Doc. E/CN.4/2006/53
—, 'Report of the Economic and Social Council on the Protection of Human Rights in Chile, Thirty-Seventh Session, Agenda Item 12' (1982) UN Doc. A/37/564
—, 'The New International Economic Order and the Promotion of Human Rights, Report on the Right to Food as a Human Rights Submitted by Mr. Asbjørn Eide, Special Rapporteur to the UN Sub-Commission on Prevention of Discrimination and Protection of Minorities' (1987) UN Doc. E/CN.4/Sub.2/1987/23

4.4.2. *ILC*

ILC, 'Addendum – Eighth Report on State Responsibility by Mr. Roberto Ago, Special Rapporteur – the Internationally Wrongful Act of the State, Source of International Responsibility (Part 1)' (1980) UN Doc. A/CN.4/318/Add.5–7

—, 'Analytical Guide to the Work of the International Law Commission on the Responsibility of International Organisations' (ILC), https://legal.un.org/ilc/guide/9_11.shtml, accessed 16 July 2022.

—, 'Articles on the Responsibility of States for Internationally Wrongful Acts with Commentaries' (2001) Yearbook of the International Law Commission vol. 2, part two

—, 'Draft Articles on the Responsibility of International Organizations with Commentaries' (2011) Yearbook of the International Law Commission vol. 2, part two

—, 'Fourth Report on Peremptory Norms of General International Law (Jus Cogens) by Dire Tladi, Special Rapporteur' (2019) UN Doc. A/CN.4/727

—, 'Fragmentation of International Law: Difficulties Arising from the Diversification and Expansion of International Law, Report of the Study Group of the ILC, Finalized by Martti Koskenniemi' (2006) UN Doc. A/CN.4/L.682

—, 'Peremptory Norms of General International Law (Jus Cogens): Text of the Draft Conclusions and Draft Annex Provisionally Adopted by the Drafting Committee on First Reading, Seventy-First Session, Geneva (29 April–7 June and 8 July–9 August 2019)' (2019) UN Doc. A/CN.4/L.936

—, 'Report of the International Law Commission on the Work of Its Fifty-Eight Session (1 May–9 June and 3 July–11 August 2006), UN General Assembly Official Records, Sixty-First Session, Supplement No. 10' (2006) UN Doc A/61/10

—, 'Report of the International Law Commission on the Work of Its Seventy-First Session (29 April–7 June and 8 July–9 August 2019), UN General Assembly Records, Seventy-First Session, Supplement No. 10' UN Doc. A/74/10

—, 'Report of the International Law Commission on the Work of Its Fifty-Third Session (23 April–1 June and 2 July–10 August 2001)' (2001) UN Doc. A/56/10, Yearbook of the International Law Commission 2001, vol. 2, part two, UN Doc. A/CN.4/SER.A/2001/Add.1 (part 2)

—, 'Reports of the International Law Commission on the Second Part of Its Seventeenth Session and on Its Eighteenth Session' (1996) UN Doc. A/6309/Rev.1, Yearbook of the International Law Commission, vol. 2, Documents of the Second Part of the Seventeenth Session and of the Eighteenth Session including the reports of the Commission to the General Assembly, UN Doc. A/CN.4/SER.A/1966/Add.1

—, 'Second Report on State Responsibility by Mr. James Crawford, Special Rapporteur' (1999) UN Doc. A/CN.4/498 and Add.1–4

—, 'State Responsibility (Agenda Item 2): Comments and Observations Received by Governments, 5 March, 30 April, 4 May, 20 July 1998' (1988) UN Doc. A/CN.4/488 and Add. 1–3, Yearbook of the International Law Commission vol. 2, part one

4.4.3. *UN DPO (and its predecessors UN DPKO and DFS)*

UN DPO, 'Policy on the Protection of Civilians in United Nations Peacekeeping' (2019) Ref. 2019.17

—, 'Portuguese Blue Helmets Awarded UN Medals for Impactful Peacekeeping' (*UN Peacekeeping*, 27 February 2020)
—, 'Republic of the Congo – ONUC: Mandate' (*UN Peacekeeping*, 2001), https://peacekeeping.un.org/en/mission/past/onucM.htm, accessed 16 April 2021
—, 'The Protection of Civilians in United Nations Peacekeeping: Handbook' (2020)
UN DPKO and UN DFS, 'A New Partnership Agenda: Charting a New Horizon for UN Peacekeeping' (2009)
—, 'An Overview of United Nations Peacekeeping Operations – Lesson 1.5 on Security Council Mandates in Practice' (2017) CPTM Version, http://repository.un.org/bitstream/handle/11176/400652/Lesson%201.5%20Security%20Council%20%20Mandates%20in%20Practice.pdf?sequence=5&isAllowed=y, accessed 8 April 2022
—, 'DPKO/DFS Policy on the Protection of Civilians in United Nations Peacekeeping' (2015) Ref. 2015.07
—, 'Draft DPKO/DFS Operational Concept on the Protection of Civilians in United Nations Peacekeeping Operations' (2010), www.peacekeeping.org.uk/wp-content/uploads/2013/02/100129-DPKO-DFS-POC-Operational-Concept.pdf, accessed 27 February 2018
—, 'Guidelines for the Development of Rules of Engagement (ROE) for United Nations Peacekeeping Operations' (2002) UN Doc. MD/FGS/0220.0001
—, 'Guidelines: Use of Force by Military Components in United Nations Peacekeeping Operations' (2017) Ref. 2016.24
—, 'Policy on Authority, Command and Control in United Nations Peacekeeping Operations' (2019) Ref. 2019.23
—, 'Protection of Civilians: Implementing Guidelines for Military Components of United Nations Peacekeeping Missions' (2015) Ref. 2015.02
—, 'United Nations Peacekeeping Operations: Principles and Guidelines (Capstone Doctrine)' (UN 2008)
—, 'United Nations Comprehensive Protection of Civilians Training Materials for United Nations Peacekeeping Operations. Military Version' (2017) CPOC V3.0

4.4.4. *UN General Assembly*

4.4.4.1. Resolutions

'UNGA Res. 217 A(III), Universal Declaration of Human Rights' (1948) UNGA Res. 217 A(III)
'UNGA Res. 1000' (1956) UN Doc. A/RES/1000 (1956)
'UNGA Res. 2851 (XXVI), Report of the Special Committee to Investigate Israeli Practices Affecting the Human Rights of the Population of the Occupied Territories' (1971) UN Doc. A/RES/2851 (1971)
'UNGA Res. 60/1, 2005 World Summit Outcome' (2005) UN Doc. A/RES/60/1
'UNGA Res. 64/259 adopted by the General Assembly on 29 March 2010: Towards an accountability system in the United Nations Secretariat' (2010) UN Doc. A/RES/64/259

4.4.4.2. C34

UNGA, 'Report of the Special Committee on Peacekeeping Operations, 2009 Substantive Session (23 February–20 March 2009), Sixty-Third Session, Supplement No. 19' UN Doc. A/63/19

—, 'Report of the Special Committee on Peacekeeping Operations, 2010 Substantive Session (22 February–19 March 2010), Sixty-Fourth Session, Supplement No. 19' UN Doc. A/64/19

—, 'Report of the Special Committee on Peacekeeping Operations, 2011 Substantive Session (New York, 22 February–18 March and 9 May 2011), Sixty-Fifth Session, Supplement No. 19' UN Doc. A/65/19

—, 'Report of the Special Committee on Peacekeeping Operations, 2012 Substantive Session (New York, 21 February–16 March and 11 September 2012), Sixty-Sixth Session, Supplement No. 19' UN Doc. A/66/19

—, 'Report of the Special Committee on Peacekeeping Operations, 2014 Substantive Session (New York, 24 February–21 March 2014), Sixty-Eight Session, Supplement No. 19' UN Doc. A/68/19

—, 'Report of the Special Committee on Peacekeeping Operations, 2015 Substantive Session (New York, 17 February–13 March 2015), Sixty-Ninth Session, Supplement No. 19' UN Doc. A/69/19

—, 'Report of the Special Committee on Peacekeeping Operations, 2016 Substantive Session (New York, 16 February–11 March 2016), Seventieth Session, Supplement No. 19' UN Doc. A/70/19

—, 'Report of the Special Committee on Peacekeeping Operations, 2017 Substantive Session (New York, 21 February–17 March 2017), Seventy-First Session, Supplement No. 19' UN Doc. A/71/19

—, 'Report of the Special Committee on Peacekeeping Operations, 2018 Substantive Session (New York, 12 February–9 March 2018), Seventy-Third Session, Supplement No. 19' UN Doc. A/72/19

—, 'Report of the Special Committee on Peacekeeping Operations, 2020 Substantive Session (New York, 17 February–12 March 2020), Seventy-Fourth Session, Supplement No. 19' UN Doc. A/74/19

—, 'Report of the Special Committee on Peacekeeping Operations, 2021 Substantive Session (New York, 15 February–12 March 2021), Seventy-Fifth Session, Supplement No. 19' UN Doc. A/75/19

4.4.4.3. Other

UNGA, 'Interim Report of the Special Rapporteur, Philip Alston, on Extrajudicial, Summary or Arbitrary Executions' (2006) UN Doc. A/61/311

—, 'Model Status-of-Forces Agreement for Peace-Keeping Operations' (1990) UN Doc. A/45/594

—, 'Question Considered by the Security Council at Its 749th and 750th Meetings Held on 30 October 1956, Second and Final Report of the Secretary-General on the Plan for an Emergency International United Nations Force Requested in the Resolution Adopted by the General Assembly on 4 November 1956' (1956) UN Doc. A/3302

—, 'Report of the Special Rapporteur on Extrajudicial, Summary or Arbitrary Executions, Christof Heyns' (2011) UN Doc. A/66/330
—, 'Report of the Special Rapporteur on Extrajudicial, Summary or Arbitrary Executions, Christophe Heyns' (2013) UN Doc. A/68/382
—, 'Revised Draft Model Memorandum of Understanding between the United Nations and (Participating State) Contributing Resources to (the United Nations Peacekeeping Operation), 3 October 2006, Sixty-First Session, Agenda Item 33' UN Doc. A/61/494

4.4.5. (Former) UNIO

UNIO, 'Documents of the United Nations Conference on International Organizations, San Francisco, 1945' (1945) XIII (Commission IV: Judicial Organization)
—, 'Documents of the United Nations Conference on International Organizations, San Francisco, 1945' (1945) XVIII (Documents of the Coordination Committee, including Documents of the Advisory Committee of Jurists, Part 2)
—, 'Documents of the United Nations Conference on International Organizations, San Francisco, 1945' (1945) XVII (Documents of the Coordination Committee, including Documents of the Advisory Committee of Jurists, Part 1)
—, 'Documents of the United Nations Conference on International Organizations, San Francisco, 1945' (1945) XV (Coordination Committee, The Charter, Lists)
—, 'Documents of the United Nations Conference on International Organizations, San Francisco, 1945' (1945) I (General)
—, 'Documents of the United Nations Conference on International Organizations, San Francisco, 1945' (1945) XIX (Documents du Comité de Coordination comprenant les documents du Comité Consultatif de Jurists)

4.4.6. UN OHCHR

UN OHCHR, *Guidance on Less-Lethal Weapons in Law Enforcement* (UN 2020)
—, 'Opening Statement by Ms. Navi Pillay United Nations High Commissioner for Human Rights at the Human Rights Council 24th Session' (2013), https://newsarchive.ohchr.org/EN/NewsEvents/Pages/DisplayNews.aspx?NewsID=13687&LangID=E, accessed 15 March 2021

4.4.7. UN OLA

UN OLA, 'The Right of Self-Defence of United Nations Peacekeeping Forces and the Exercise of This Right – Article 51 of the Charter of the United Nations' (1993) United Nations Juridical Yearbook 371
—, 'Note to the Under-Secretary-General of the Department of Peacekeeping Operations, United Nations' (2003) United Nations Juridical Yearbook 538

4.4.8. UN Secretary-General

UNSG, 'Action for Peacekeeping: Declaration of Shared Commitments on UN Peacekeeping Operations, Shared by the UN Secretary-General with the UN

Member States on 16 August 2018; Endorsed by 152 UN Member States and 4 Supporting Organisations' (2018), https://peacekeeping.un.org/sites/default/files/a4p-declaration-en.pdf, accessed 9 March 2020
—, 'Eight Report of the Secretary-General on the United Nations Observer Mission in Sierra Leone' (1999) UN Doc. S/1999/1003
—, 'First Report of the Secretary-General on the United Nations Mission in Sierra Leone' (1999) UN Doc. S/1999/ 1223
—, 'In Larger Freedom: Towards Development, Security and Human Rights for All, Report of the Secretary-General, Integrated and Coordinated Implementation of and Follow-up to the Outcomes of the Major United Nations Conferences and Summits in the Economic, Social and Related Fields, Follow-up to the Outcome of the Millennium Summit, Fifty-Ninth Session, Agenda Items 45 and 55' (2005) UN Doc. A/59/2005
—, 'Ninth Report of the Secretary-General on the United Nations Mission in Sierra Leone' (2001) UN Doc. S/2001/ 228
—, 'Note by the Secretary-General' (1964) UN Doc. S/5653
—, 'Protection of Civilians in Armed Conflict, Report of the Secretary-General' (2020) UN Doc. S/2020/366
—, 'Protection of Civilians in Armed Conflict, Report of the Secretary-General' (2018) UN Doc. S/2018/462
—, 'Protection of Civilians in Armed Conflict, Report of the Secretary-General' (2019) UN Doc. S/2019/373
—, 'Report of the Secretary-General on Implementing the Responsibility to Protect' (2009) UN Doc. A/63/677
—, 'Report of the Secretary-General on the Implementation of Security Council Resolution 340 (1973)' (1973) UN Doc. S/11052/Rev. 1
—, 'Report of the Secretary-General on the Protection of Civilians in Armed Conflict' (2002) UN Doc. S/2002/1300
—, 'Report of the Secretary-General on the Protection of Civilians in Armed Conflict' (2005) UN Doc. S/2005/740
—, 'Report of the Secretary-General on the Protection of Civilians in Armed Conflict' (2009) UN Doc. S/2009/277
—, 'Report of the Secretary-General on the Protection of Civilians in Armed Conflict' (2016) UN Doc. S/2016/447
—, 'Report of the Secretary-General on the Withdrawal of the Emergency Force' (1967) UN Doc. A/6730 and Add. 1–3 and A/6730/Add.3/Corr.1
—, 'Report of the Secretary-General Pursuant to General Assembly Resolution 53/35: The Fall of Srebrenica' (1999) UN Doc. A/54/549
—, 'Report of the Secretary-General to the Security Council on Haiti' (2004) UN Doc. S/2004/300
—, 'Report of the Secretary-General to the Security Council on Liberia' (2003) UN Doc. S/2003/875
—, 'Report of the Secretary-General to the Security Council on the Protection of Civilians in Armed Conflict' (1999) UN Doc. S/1999/957
—, 'Report of the Secretary-General to the Security Council on the Protection of Civilians in Armed Conflict' (2004) UN Doc. S/2004/431

—, 'Report of the Secretary-General to the Security Council on the United Nations Stabilization Mission in Haiti' (2013) UN Doc. S/2013/493
—, 'Secretary-General Presents His Annual Report to General Assembly' (1999) UN Doc. SG/SM/7136 and GA/9596, www.un.org/press/en/1999/19990920.sgsm7136.html, accessed 11 February 2021
—, 'Secretary-General's Bulletin on the Observance by United Nations Forces of International Humanitarian Law' (1999) UN Doc. ST/SGB/1999/13
—, 'Secretary-General's Year-End Press Conference' (14 December 2011), www.un.org/sg/en/content/sg/statement/2011-12-14/secretary-generals-year-end-press-conference, accessed 26 February 2019
—, 'Summary Study of the Experience Derived from the Establishment and Operation of the Force: Report of the Secretary-General, Thirteenth Session, Annexes, Agenda Item 65' (1958) UN Doc A/3943
—, 'Supplement to an Agenda for Peace: Position Paper of the Secretary-General on the Occasion of the Fiftieth Anniversary of the United Nations, General Assembly: Fiftieth Session, Report of the Secretary-General on the Work of the Organization, Security Council: Fiftieth Year' (1995) UN Doc. A/50/60 and S/1995/1
—, 'The Causes of Conflict and the Promotion of Durable Peace and Sustainable Development in Africa, Report of the Secretary-General, General Assembly: Fifty-Second Session, Agenda Item 10; Security Council: Fifty-Third Year' (1998) UN Doc. A/52/871 and S/1998/318

4.4.9. UN Security Council

4.4.9.1. Resolutions

'UNSC Res. 143' (1960) UN Doc. S/4387 (1960)
'UNSC Res. 161' (1961) UN Doc. S/RES/161 (1961)
'UNSC Res. 467' (1980) UN Doc. S/RES/467 (1980)
'UNSC Res. 678' (1990) UN Doc. S/RES/678 (1990)
'UNSC Res. 733' (1992) UN Doc. S/RES/733 (1992)
'UNSC Res. 751' (1992) UN Doc. S/RES/751 (1992)
'UNSC Res. 767' (1992) UN Doc. S/RES/767 (1992)
'UNSC Res. 775' (1992) UN Doc. S/RES/775 (1992)
'UNSC Res. 794' (1992) UN Doc. S/RES/794 (1992)
'UNSC Res. 836' (1993) UN Doc. S/RES/836 (1993)
'UNSC Res. 837' (1993) UN Doc. S/RES/837 (1993)
'UNSC Res. 912' (1994) UN Doc. S/RES/912 (1994)
'UNSC Res. 918' (1994) UN Doc. S/RES/918 (1994)
'UNSC Res. 925' (1994) UN Doc. S/RES/925 (1994)
'UNSC Res. 929' (1994) UN Doc. S/RES/929 (1994)
'UNSC Res. 940' (1994) UN Doc. S/RES/940 (1994)
'UNSC Res. 981' (1995) UN Doc. S/RES/981 (1995)
'UNSC Res. 1031' (1995) UN Doc. S/RES/1031 (1995)
'UNSC Res. 1159' (1998) UN Doc. S/RES/1159 (1998)
'UNSC Res. 1244' (1999) UN Doc. S/RES/1244 (1999)

'UNSC Res. 1265' (1999) UN Doc. S/RES/1265 (1999)
'UNSC Res. 1270' (1999) UN Doc. S/RES/1270 (1999)
'UNSC Res. 1272' (1999) UN Doc. S/RES/1272 (1999)
'UNSC Res. 1289' (2000) UN Doc. S/RES/1289 (2000)
'UNSC Res. 1291' (2000) UN Doc. S/RES/1291 (2000)
'UNSC Res. 1296' (2000) UN Doc. S/RES/1296 (2000)
'UNSC Res. 1313' (2000) UN Doc. S/RES/1313 (2000)
'UNSC Res. 1325' (2000) UN Doc. S/RES/1325 (2000)
'UNSC Res. 1378' (2001) UN Doc. S/RES/1378 (2001)
'UNSC Res. 1389' (2002) UN Doc. S/RES/1389 (2002)
'UNSC Res. 1417' (2002) UN Doc. S/RES/1417 (2002)
'UNSC Res. 1464' (2003) UN Doc. S/RES/1464 (2003)
'UNSC Res. 1484' (2003) UN Doc. S/RES/1484 (2003)
'UNSC Res. 1493' (2003) UN Doc. S/RES/1493 (2003)
'UNSC Res. 1509' (2003) UN Doc. S/RES/1509 (2003)
'UNSC Res. 1528' (2004) UN Doc. S/RES/1528 (2004)
'UNSC Res. 1542' (2004) UN Doc. S/RES/1542 (2004)
'UNSC Res. 1545' (2004) UN Doc. S/RES/1545 (2004)
'UNSC Res. 1551' (2004) UN Doc. S/RES/1551 (2004)
'UNSC Res. 1556' (2004) UN Doc. S/RES/1556 (2004)
'UNSC Res. 1561' (2004) UN Doc. S/RES/1561 (2004)
'UNSC Res. 1564' (2004) UN Doc. S/RES/1564 (2004)
'UNSC Res. 1565' (2004) UN Doc. S/RES/1565 (2004)
'UNSC Res. 1575' (2004) UN Doc. S/RES/1575 (2004)
'UNSC Res. 1590' (2005) UN Doc. S/RES/1590 (2005)
'UNSC Res. 1592' (2005) UN Doc. S/RES/1592 (2005)
'UNSC Res. 1594' (2005) UN Doc. S/RES/1594 (2005)
'UNSC Res. 1600' (2005) UN Doc. S/RES/1600 (2005)
'UNSC Res. 1603' (2005) UN Doc. S/RES/1603 (2005)
'UNSC Res. 1609' (2005) UN Doc. S/RES/1609 (2005)
'UNSC Res. 1612' (2015) UN Doc. S/RES/1612 (2005)
'UNSC Res. 1626' (2005) UN Doc. S/RES/1626 (2005)
'UNSC Res. 1649' (2005) UN Doc. S/RES/1649 (2005)
'UNSC Res. 1652' (2006) UN Doc. S/RES/1652 (2006)
'UNSC Res. 1667' (2006) UN Doc. S/RES/1667 (2006)
'UNSC Res. 1671' (2006) UN Doc. S/RES/1671 (2006)
'UNSC Res. 1674' (2006) UN Doc. S/RES/1674 (2006)
'UNSC Res. 1701' (2006) UN Doc. S/RES/1701 (2006)
'UNSC Res. 1706' (2006) UN Doc. S/RES/1706 (2006)
'UNSC Res. 1712' (2006) UN Doc. S/RES/1712 (2006)
'UNSC Res. 1726' (2006) UN Doc. S/RES/1726 (2006)
'UNSC Res. 1739' (2007) UN Doc. S/RES/1739 (2007)
'UNSC Res. 1744' (2007) UN Doc. S/RES/1744 (2007)
'UNSC Res. 1750' (2007) UN Doc. S/RES/1750 (2007)
'UNSC Res. 1756' (2007) UN Doc. S/RES/1756 (2007)
'UNSC Res. 1763' (2007) UN Doc. S/RES/1763 (2007)

'UNSC Res. 1765' (2007) UN Doc. S/RES/1765 (2007)
'UNSC Res. 1769' (2007) UN Doc. S/RES/1769 (2007)
'UNSC Res. 1773' (2007) UN Doc. S/RES/1773 (2007)
'UNSC Res. 1777' (2007) UN Doc. S/RES/1777 (2007)
'UNSC Res. 1778' (2007) UN Doc. S/RES/1778 (2007)
'UNSC Res. 1794' (2007) UN Doc. S/RES/1794 (2007)
'UNSC Res. 1795' (2008) UN Doc. S/RES/1795 (2008)
'UNSC Res. 1820' (2008) UN Doc. S/RES/1820 (2008)
'UNSC Res. 1826' (2008) UN Doc. S/RES/1826 (2008)
'UNSC Res. 1836' (2008) UN Doc. S/RES/1836 (2008)
'UNSC Res. 1856' (2008) UN Doc. S/RES/1856 (2008)
'UNSC Res. 1861' (2009) UN Doc. S/RES/1861 (2009)
'UNSC Res. 1865' (2009) UN Doc. S/RES/1865 (2009)
'UNSC Res. 1870' (2009) UN Doc. S/RES/1870 (2009)
'UNSC Res. 1880' (2009) UN Doc. S/RES/1880 (2009)
'UNSC Res. 1881' (2009) UN Doc. S/RES/1881 (2009)
'UNSC Res. 1884' (2009) UN Doc. S/RES/1884 (2009)
'UNSC Res. 1885' (2009) UN Doc. S/RES/1885 (2009)
'UNSC Res. 1888' (2009) UN Doc. S/RES/1888 (2009)
'UNSC Res. 1889' (2009) UN Doc. S/RES/1889 (2009)
'UNSC Res. 1894' (2009) UN Doc. S/RES/1894 (2009)
'UNSC Res. 1906' (2009) UN Doc. S/RES/1906 (2009)
'UNSC Res. 1911' (2010) UN Doc. S/RES/1911 (2010)
'UNSC Res. 1919' (2010) UN Doc. S/RES/1919 (2010)
'UNSC Res. 1923' (2010) UN Doc. S/RES/1923 (2010)
'UNSC Res. 1924' (2010) UN Doc. S/RES/1924 (2010)
'UNSC Res. 1925' (2010) UN Doc. S/RES/1925 (2010)
'UNSC Res. 1933' (2010) UN Doc. S/RES/1933 (2010)
'UNSC Res. 1935' (2010) UN Doc. S/RES/1935 (2010)
'UNSC Res. 1937' (2010) UN Doc. S/RES/1937 (2010)
'UNSC Res. 1938' (2010) UN Doc. S/RES/1938 (2010)
'UNSC Res. 1944' (2010) UN Doc. S/RES/1944 (2010)
'UNSC Res. 1960' (2010) UN Doc. S/RES/1960 (2010)
'UNSC Res. 1962' (2010) UN Doc. S/RES/1962 (2010)
'UNSC Res. 1973' (2011) UN Doc. S/RES/1973 (2011)
'UNSC Res. 1981' (2011) UN Doc. S/RES/1981 (2011)
'UNSC Res. 1990' (2011) UN Doc. S/RES/1990 (2011)
'UNSC Res. 1991' (2011) UN Doc. S/RES/1991 (2011)
'UNSC Res. 1996' (2011) UN Doc. S/RES/1996 (2011)
'UNSC Res. 2000' (2011) UN Doc. S/RES/2000 (2011)
'UNSC Res. 2003' (2011) UN Doc. S/RES/2003 (2011)
'UNSC Res. 2004' (2011) UN Doc. S/RES/2004 (2011)
'UNSC Res. 2008' (2011) UN Doc. S/RES/2008 (2011)
'UNSC Res. 2012' (2011) UN Doc. S/RES/2012 (2011)
'UNSC Res. 2053' (2012) UN Doc. S/RES/2053 (2012)
'UNSC Res. 2057' (2012) UN Doc. S/RES/2057 (2012)

'UNSC Res. 2062' (2012) UN Doc. S/RES/2062 (2012)
'UNSC Res. 2063' (2012) UN Doc. S/RES/2063 (2012)
'UNSC Res. 2064' (2012) UN Doc. S/RES/2064 (2012)
'UNSC Res. 2066' (2012) UN Doc. S/RES/2066 (2012)
'UNSC Res. 2070' (2012) UN Doc. S/RES/2070 (2012)
'UNSC Res. 2085' (2012) UN Doc. S/RES/2085 (2012)
'UNSC Res. 2086' (2013) UN Doc. S/RES/2086 (2013)
'UNSC Res. 2093' (2013) UN Doc. S/RES/2093 (2013)
'UNSC Res. 2098' (2013) UN Doc. S/RES/2098 (2013)
'UNSC Res. 2100' (2013) UN Doc. S/RES/2100 (2013)
'UNSC Res. 2104' (2013) UN Doc. S/RES/2104 (2013)
'UNSC Res. 2106' (2013) UN Doc. S/RES/2106 (2013)
'UNSC Res. 2109' (2013) UN Doc. S/RES/2109 (2013)
'UNSC Res. 2112' (2013) UN Doc. S/RES/2112 (2013)
'UNSC Res. 2113' (2013) UN Doc. S/RES/2113 (2013)
'UNSC Res. 2116' (2013) UN Doc. S/RES/2116 (2013)
'UNSC Res. 2119' (2013) UN Doc. S/RES/2119 (2013)
'UNSC Res. 2122' (2013) UN Doc. S/RES/2122 (2013)
'UNSC Res. 2126' (2013) UN Doc. S/RES/2126 (2013)
'UNSC Res. 2127' (2013) UN Doc. S/RES/2127 (2013)
'UNSC Res. 2134' (2014) UN Doc. S/RES/2134 (2014)
'UNSC Res. 2147' (2014) UN Doc. S/RES/2147 (2014)
'UNSC Res. 2149' (2014) UN Doc. S/RES/2149 (2014)
'UNSC Res. 2155' (2014) UN Doc. S/RES/2155 (2014)
'UNSC Res. 2156' (2014) UN Doc. S/RES/2156 (2014)
'UNSC Res. 2162' (2014) UN Doc. S/RES/2162 (2014)
'UNSC Res. 2164' (2014) UN Doc. S/RES/2164 (2014)
'UNSC Res. 2167' (2014) UN Doc. S/RES/2167 (2014)
'UNSC Res. 2172' (2014) UN Doc. S/RES/2172 (2014)
'UNSC Res. 2173' (2014) UN Doc. S/RES/2173 (2014)
'UNSC Res. 2176' (2015) UN Doc. S/RES/2176 (2014)
'UNSC Res. 2179' (2014) UN Doc. S/RES/2179 (2014)
'UNSC Res. 2180' (2014) UN Doc. S/RES/2180 (2014)
'UNSC Res. 2187' (2014) UN Doc. S/RES/2187 (2014)
'UNSC Res. 2190' (2014) UN Doc. S/RES/2190 (2014)
'UNSC Res. 2205' (2015) UN Doc. S/RES/2205 (2015)
'UNSC Res. 2211' (2015) UN Doc. S/RES/2211 (2015)
'UNSC Res. 2217' (2015) UN Doc. S/RES/2217 (2015)
'UNSC Res. 2223' (2015) UN Doc. S/RES/2223 (2015)
'UNSC Res. 2226' (2015) UN Doc. S/RES/2226 (2015)
'UNSC Res. 2227' (2015) UN Doc. S/RES/2227 (2015)
'UNSC Res. 2228' (2015) UN Doc. S/RES/2228 (2015)
'UNSC Res. 2230' (2015) UN Doc. S/RES/2230 (2015)
'UNSC Res. 2236' (2015) UN Doc. S/RES/2236 (2015)
'UNSC Res. 2239' (2015) UN Doc. S/RES/2239 (2015)
'UNSC Res. 2241' (2015) UN Doc. S/RES/2241 (2015)

'UNSC Res. 2242' (2015) UN Doc. S/RES/2242 (2015)
'UNSC Res. 2243' (2015) UN Doc. S/RES/2243 (2015)
'UNSC Res. 2251' (2015) UN Doc. S/RES/2251 (2015)
'UNSC Res. 2252' (2015) UN Doc. S/RES/2252 (2015)
'UNSC Res. 2277' (2016) UN Doc. S/RES/2277 (2016)
'UNSC Res. 2281' (2016) UN Doc. S/RES/2281 (2016)
'UNSC Res. 2284' (2016) UN Doc. S/RES/2284 (2016)
'UNSC Res. 2287' (2016) UN Doc. S/RES/2287 (2016)
'UNSC Res. 2295' (2016) UN Doc. S/RES/2295 (2016)
'UNSC Res. 2296' (2016) UN Doc. S/RES/2296 (2016)
'UNSC Res. 2301' (2016) UN Doc. S/RES/2301 (2016)
'UNSC Res. 2302' (2016) UN Doc. S/RES/2302 (2016)
'UNSC Res. 2304' (2016) UN Doc. S/RES/2304 (2016)
'UNSC Res. 2305' (2016) UN Doc. S/RES/2305 (2016)
'UNSC Res. 2308' (2016) UN Doc. S/RES/2308 (2016)
'UNSC Res. 2313' (2016) UN Doc. S/RES/2313 (2016)
'UNSC Res. 2318' (2016) UN Doc. S/RES/2318 (2016)
'UNSC Res. 2326' (2016) UN Doc. S/RES/2326 (2016)
'UNSC Res. 2327' (2016) UN Doc. S/RES/2327 (2016)
'UNSC Res. 2333' (2016) UN Doc. S/RES/2333 (2016)
'UNSC Res. 2348' (2017) UN Doc. S/RES/2348 (2017)
'UNSC Res. 2350' (2017) UN Doc. S/RES/2350 (2017)
'UNSC Res. 2352' (2017) UN Doc. S/RES/2352 (2017)
'UNSC Res. 2363' (2017) UN Doc. S/RES/2363 (2017)
'UNSC Res. 2364' (2017) UN Doc. S/RES/2364 (2017)
'UNSC Res. 2373' (2017) UN Doc. S/RES/2373 (2017)
'UNSC Res. 2386' (2017) UN Doc. S/RES/2386 (2017)
'UNSC Res. 2387' (2017) UN Doc. S/RES/2387 (2017)
'UNSC Res. 2392' (2017) UN Doc. S/RES/2392 (2017)
'UNSC Res. 2406' (2018) UN Doc. S/RES/2406 (2017)
'UNSC Res. 2409' (2018) UN Doc. S/RES/2409 (2018)
'UNSC Res. 2410' (2018) UN Doc. S/RES/2410 (2018)
'UNSC Res. 2416' (2018) UN Doc. S/RES/2416 (2018)
'UNSC Res. 2423' (2018) UN Doc. S/RES/2423 (2018)
'UNSC Res. 2425' (2018) UN Doc. S/RES/2425 (2018)
'UNSC Res. 2429' (2018) UN Doc. S/RES/2429 (2018)
'UNSC Res. 2433' (2018) UN Doc. S/RES/2433 (2018)
'UNSC Res. 2436' (2018) UN Doc. S/RES/2436 (2018)
'UNSC Res. 2445' (2018) UN Doc. S/RES/2445 (2018)
'UNSC Res. 2446' (2018) UN Doc. S/RES/2446 (2018)
'UNSC Res. 2447' (2018) UN Doc. S/RES/2447 (2018)
'UNSC Res. 2448' (2018) UN Doc. S/RES/2448 (2018)
'UNSC Res. 2459' (2019) UN Doc. S/RES/2459 (2019)
'UNSC Res. 2463' (2019) UN Doc. S/RES/2463 (2019)
'UNSC Res. 2465' (2019) UN Doc. S/RES/2465 (2019)
'UNSC Res. 2466' (2019) UN Doc. S/RES/2466 (2019)

'UNSC Res. 2467' (2019) UN Doc. S/RES/2467 (2019)
'UNSC Res. 2469' (2019) UN Doc. S/RES/2469 (2019)
'UNSC Res. 2479' (2019) UN Doc. S/RES/2479 (2019)
'UNSC Res. 2480' (2019) UN Doc. S/RES/2480 (2019)
'UNSC Res. 2485' (2019) UN Doc. S/RES/2485 (2019)
'UNSC Res. 2493' (2019) UN Doc. S/RES/2493 (2019)
'UNSC Res. 2495' (2019) UN Doc. S/RES/2495 (2019)
'UNSC Res. 2497' (2019) UN Doc. S/RES/2497 (2019)
'UNSC Res. 2499' (2019) UN Doc. S/RES/2499 (2019)
'UNSC Res. 2502' (2019) UN Doc. S/RES/2502 (2019)
'UNSC Res. 2514' (2020) UN Doc. S/RES/2514 (2020)
'UNSC Res. 2525' (2020) UN Doc. S/RES/2525 (2020)
'UNSC Res. 2531' (2020) UN Doc. S/RES/2531 (2020)
'UNSC Res. 2539' (2020) UN Doc. S/RES/2539 (2020)
'UNSC Res. 2550' (2020) UN Doc. S/RES/2550 (2020)
'UNSC Res. 2552' (2020) UN Doc. S/RES/2552 (2020)
'UNSC Res. 2556' (2020) UN Doc. S/RES/2556 (2020)
'UNSC Res. 2559' (2020) UN Doc. S/RES/2559 (2020)
'UNSC Res. 2567' (2021) UN Doc. S/RES/2567 (2021)
'UNSC Res. 2575' (2021) UN Doc. S/RES/2575 (2021)
'UNSC Res. 2584' (2021) UN Doc. S/RES/2584 (2021)
'UNSC Res. 2591' (2021) UN Doc. S/RES/2591 (2021)
'UNSC Res. 2605' (2021) UN Doc. S/RES/2605 (2021)
'UNSC Res. 2609' (2021) UN Doc. S/RES/2609 (2021)
'UNSC Res. 2612' (2021) UN Doc. S/RES/2612 (2021)

4.4.9.2. Verbatim records

UNSC, '3968th Meeting (on Promoting Peace and Security: Humanitarian Activities Relevant to the Security Council)' (1999) UN Doc. S/PV.3968

—, '3977th Meeting (on the Protection of Civilians in Armed Conflict)' (1999) UN Doc. S/PV.3977

—, '3978th Meeting (on the Protection of Civilians in Armed Conflict)' (1999) UN Doc. S/PV.3978

—, '3980th Meeting (on the Protection of Civilians in Armed Conflict)' (1999) UN Doc. S/PV.3980

—, '3980th Meeting (on the Protection of Civilians in Armed Conflict) (Resumption 1)' (1999) UN Doc. S/PV.3980 (Resumption 1)

—, '4054th Meeting (at Which UNSC Res 1270 (1999) Was Adopted)' (1999) UN Doc. S/PV.4054

—, '4918th Meeting (at Which UNSC Res. 1528 (2004) Was Adopted)' (2004) UN Doc. S/PV.4918

—, '4919th Meeting (at Which UNSC Res. 1529 (2004) Was Adopted)' (2004) UN Doc. S/PV.4919

—, '5213th Meeting (at Which UNSC Res. 1609 (2005) Was Adopted)' (2005) UN Doc. S/PV.5213

—, '5511th Meeting (at Which UNSC Res. 1701 (2006) Was Adopted)' (2006) UN Doc. S/PV.5511 + Corr.1
—, '5617th Meeting (at Which UNSC Res. 1739 (2007) Was Adopted)' (2007) UN Doc. S/PV.5617
—, '6055th Meeting (at Which UNSC Res. 1856 (2008) Was Adopted)' (2008) UN Doc. S/PV.6055
—, '6064th Meeting (at Which UNSC Res. 1861 (2009) Was Adopted)' (2009) UN Doc. S/PV.6064
—, '6253rd Meeting (at Which UNSC Res. 1906 (2009) Was Adopted)' (2009) UN Doc. S/PV.6253
—, '6330th Meeting (at Which UNSC Res. 1927 (2010) Was Adopted)' (2010) UN Doc. S/PV.6330
—, '6399th Meeting (at Which UNSC Res. 1944 (2010) Was Adopted)' (2010) UN Doc. S/PV. 6399
—, '6498th Meeting (at Which UNSC Res. 1973 (2011) Was Adopted)' (2011) UN Doc. S/PV.6498
—, '6528th Meeting (on the Situation in Libya)' (2011) UN Doc. S/PV.6528
—, '6531st Meeting (on the Protection of Civilians in Armed Conflict)' (2011) UN Doc. S/PV.6531
—, '6800th Meeting (at Which UNSC Res. 2057 (2012) Was Adopted)' (2012) UN Doc. S/PV.6800
—, '6817th Meeting (at Which UNSC Res. 2062 (2012) Was Adopted)' (2012) UN Doc. S/PV.6817
—, '6898th Meeting (at Which UNSC Res. 2085 (2012) Was Adopted)' (2012) UN Doc. S/PV.6898
—, '6943rd Meeting (at Which UNSC Res. 2098 (2013) Was Adopted)' (2013) UN Doc. S/PV.6943
—, '6998th Meeting (at Which UNSC Res. 2109 (2013) Was Adopted)' (2013) UN Doc. S/PV.6998
—, '7040th Meeting (at Which UNSC Res. 2119 (2013) Was Adopted)' (2013) UN Doc. S/PV.7040
—, '7072nd Meeting (at Which UNSC Res. 2127 (2013) Was Adopted)' (2013) UN Doc. S/PV.7072
—, '7109th Meeting (on the Protection of Civilians in Armed Conflict)' (2014) UN Doc. S/PV.7109
—, '7153rd Meeting (at Which UNSC Res. 2149 (2014) Was Adopted)' (2014) UN Doc. S/PV.7153
—, '7182nd Meeting (at Which UNSC Res. 2155 (2014) Was Adopted)' (2014) UN Doc. S/PV.7182
—, '7210th Meeting (at Which UNSC Res. 2164 (2014) Was Adopted)' (2014) UN Doc. S/PV.7210
—, '7250th Meeting (at Which UNSC Res. 2173 (2014) Was Adopted)' (2014) UN Doc. S/PV.7250
—, '7277th Meeting (at Which UNSC Res. 2180 (2014) Was Adopted)' (2014) UN Doc. S/PV.7277
—, '7322nd Meeting (at Which UNSC Res. 2187 (2014) Was Adopted)' (2014) UN Doc. S/PV.7322

—, '7434th Meeting (at Which UNSC Res. 2217 (2015) Was Adopted)' (2015) UN Doc. S/PV.7434
—, '7471st Meeting (at Which UNSC Res. 2226 (2015) Was Adopted)' (2015) UN Doc. S/PV.7471
—, '7659th Meeting (at Which UNSC Res. 2277 (2016) Was Adopted)' (2016) UN Doc. S/PV.7659
—, '7681st Meeting (at Which UNSC Res. 2284 92016) Was Adopted)' (2016) UN Doc. S/PV.7681
—, '7727th Meeting (at Which UNSC Res. 2295 (2016) Was Adopted)' (2016) UN Doc. S/PV.7727
—, '7840th Meeting (at Which UNSC Res. 2327 (2016) Was Adopted)' (2016) UN Doc. S/PV.7840
—, '7851st Meeting (at Which UNSC Res. 2333 (2016) Was Adopted)' (2016) UN Doc. S/PV.7851
—, '7910th Meeting (at Which UNSC Res. 2348 (2017) Was Adopted)' (2017) UN Doc. S/PV.7910
—, '7989th Meeting (at Which UNSC Res. 2363 (2017) Was Adopted)' (2017) UN Doc. S/PV.7989
—, '8037th Meeting (at Which UNSC Res. 2373 (2017) Was Adopted)' (2017) UN Doc. S/PV.8037
—, '8102nd Meeting (at Which UNSC Res. 2387 (2017) Was Adopted)' (2017) UN Doc. S/PV.8102
—, '8204th Meeting (at Which UNSC Res. 2406 (2018) Was Adopted)' (2018) UN Doc. S/PV.8204
—, '8216th Meeting (at Which UNSC Res. 2409 (2018) Was Adopted)' (2018) UN Doc. S/PV.8216
—, '8298th Meeting (at Which UNSC Res. 2423 (2018) Was Adopted)' (2018) UN Doc. S/PV.2423
—, '8422nd Meeting (at Which UNSC Res. 2448 (2018) Was Adopted)' (2018) UN Doc. S/PV.8422
—, '8568th Meeting (at Which UNSC Res. 2480 (2019) Was Adopted)' (2019) UN Doc. S/PV.8568
—, '8692nd Meeting (at Which UNSC Res. 2502 (2019) Was Adopted)' (2019) UN Doc. S/PV.8692
—, '8932nd Meeting (at Which UNSC Res. 2609 (2021) Was Adopted)' (2021) UN Doc. S/PV.8932

4.4.9.3. Other

UNSC, 'Aide-Memoire on the Protection of Civilians in Armed Conflict, Annexed to the Statement by the President of the Security Council' (2002) UN Doc. S/PRST/2002/6
—, 'Aide-Memoire on the Protection of Civilians in Armed Conflict, Annexed to the Statement by the President of the Security Council' (2009) UN Doc. S/PRST/2009/1
—, 'Aide-Memoire on the Protection of Civilians in Armed Conflict, Annexed to the Statement by the President of the Security Council' (2018) UN Doc. S/PRST/2018/18

—, 'Cable Dated 12 July 1960 from the President of the Republic of The Congo and Supreme Commander of the National Army and the Prime Minister of National Defence Addressed to Secretary-General of the United Nations' (1960) UN Doc. S/4382
—, 'Statement by the President of the Security Council' (1999) UN Doc. S/PRST/1999/6

4.4.10. UN HRC

4.4.10.1. Resolutions

'UN HRC Res. 22/10' (2013) UN Doc. A/HRC/RES/22/10

4.4.10.2. Other

UN HRC, 'Concluding Observations of the Human Rights Committee: Belgium' (1998) UN Doc. CCPR/C/79/Add.99
—, 'General Comment No. 31 [80] on The Nature of the General Legal Obligation Imposed on States Parties to the Covenant, Adopted on 29 March 2004' (2004) UN Doc. CCPR/C/21/Rev.1/Add. 13
—, 'General Comment No. 36 (2018) on Article 6 of the International Covenant on Civil and Political Rights, on the Right to Life' (2018) UN Doc. CCPR/C/GC/36, Advanced Unedited version
—, 'General Comment No. 36 (2019) on Article 6 of the International Covenant on Civil and Political Rights, on the Right to Life' (2019) UN Doc. CCPR/C/GC/36
—, 'Report of the International Commission of Inquiry on Libya' (2012) UN Doc. A/HRC/19/68
—, 'Report of the International Fact-Finding Mission to Investigate Violations of International Law, Including International Humanitarian and Human Rights Law, Resulting from the Israeli Attacks on the Flotilla of Ships Carrying Humanitarian Assistance' (2010) UN Doc. A/HRC/15/21
—, 'Report of the Special Rapporteur on Extrajudicial, Summary or Arbitrary Executions, Philip Alston' (2010) UN Doc. A/HRC/14/24/Add.6
—, 'Report of the Special Rapporteur on Extrajudicial, Summary or Arbitrary Executions, Christof Heyns' (2014) UN Doc. A/HRC/26/36
—, 'Report of the Special Rapporteur on the Promotion and Protection of Human Rights and Fundamental Freedoms While Countering Terrorism on the Human Rights Challenge of States of Emergency in the Context of Countering Terrorism' (2018) UN Doc. A/HRC/37/52

4.4.11. UN OCHA

UN OCHA, 'Building a Culture of Protection: 20 Years of Security Council Engagement on the Protection of Civilians' (2019) Occasional Policy Paper

4.4.12. *Review reports of UN peace operations*

HIPPO, 'Report of the High-Level Independent Panel on Peace Operations on Uniting Our Strengths for Peace: Politics, Partnership and People' (2015) A/70/95 and S/2015/446

Holt V and Taylor G, Protecting Civilians in the Context of UN Peacekeeping Operations Successes, Setbacks and Remaining Challenges, Independent Study Jointly Commissioned by the United Nations Department of Peacekeeping Operations and the United Nations Office for the Coordination of Humanitarian Affairs (UN 2009)

OIOS, 'Evaluation of the Implementation and Results of Protection of Civilians Mandates in United Nations Peacekeeping Operations, Sixty-Eighth Session, Item 142 of the Provisional Agenda' (2014) UN Doc. A/68/787

OIOS, Inspection and Evaluation Division, 'Evaluation of the Effectiveness of United Nations Peacekeeping Operations in Deterring and Confronting Armed Elements in the Democratic Republic of Congo, Mali and the Central African Republic' (2017) IED-17.013

—, 'Triennial Review of Implementation of Recommendations Contained in the OIOS Evaluation Report on the Implementation and Results of Protection of Civilians Mandates in United Nations Peacekeeping Operations' (2017) IED-17–010

Panel on United Nations Peace Operations, 'Report of the Panel on United Nations Peace Operations (Brahimi Report), Fifty-Fifth Session of the General Assembly, Item 87 of the Provisional Agenda; Fifty-Fifth Year of the Security Council' (2000) UN Doc. A/55/305-S/2000/809

'Executive Summary of the Independent Special Investigation into the Violence in Juba in 2016 and the Response by the United Nations Mission in South Sudan. Annex to the Letter Dated 1 November 2016 from the Secretary-General Addressed to the President of the Security Council' (2016) UN Doc. S/2016/924

'Report of the Independent Inquiry into the Actions of the United Nations during the 1994 Genocide in Rwanda' (1999) UN Doc. S/1999/1257

4.4.13. *Review reports of UN-mandated peace operations*

Committee Established to Review the NATO Bombing Campaign Against the Federal Republic of Yugoslavia, 'Final Report to the Prosecutor' (2000), www.icty.org/en/press/final-report-prosecutor-committee-established-review-nato-bombing-campaign-against-federal, accessed 3 January 2018

Lieutenant General (Retired) Carlos Alberto dos Santos Cruz, 'Improving Security of United Nations Peacekeepers: We Need to Change the Way We Are Doing Business' (2017), https://peacekeeping.un.org/sites/default/files/improving_security_of_united_nations_peacekeepers_report.pdf, accessed 11 September 2018

4.4.14. *Letters sent to the UN*

'Letter Dated 29 February 2004 from the Permanent Representative of Haiti to the United Nations Addressed to the President of the Security Council and Annex to the Letter Dated 29 February 2004 from the Permanent Representative of Haiti to the United Nations Addressed to the President of the Security Council' (2004) UN Doc. S/2004/163

'Letter Dated 9 November 2011 from the Permanent Representative of Brazil to the United Nations Addressed to the Secretary-General, General Assembly: Sixty-Sixth Session, Agenda Items 14 and 117; Security Council: Sixty-Sixth Year' (2011) UN Doc. A/66/551 and S/2011/701

'Letter Dated 21 January 2014 from Catherine Ashton, the High Representative for Foreign Affairs and Security Policy of the European Union and Vice-President of the European Commission, as Annexed to the Letter Dated 25 February 2014 from the Secretary-General Addressed to the President of the Security Council' (2014) UN Doc. S/2014/45

4.4.15 Other

Inter-Agency Standing Committee, 'IASC Policy on the Protection of Internally Displaced Persons' (1999)

—, 'IASC Policy on Protection in Humanitarian Action' (2016)

Monteiro V, 'La MINUSCA Intervient Contre Des Éléments Lourdement Armés Au Nord de Bambari' (*MINUSCA*, 26 February 2017), https://minusca.unmissions.org/la-minusca-intervient-contre-des-éléments-lourdement-armés-au-nord-de-bambari, accessed 13 June 2022

—, 'Mise En Garde de La MINUSCA à La Coalition Du FPRC à Propos Des Déplacés de Ippy' (*MINUSCA*, 27 February 2017), https://minusca.unmissions.org/mise-en-garde-de-la-minusca-à-la-coalition-du-fprc-à-propos-des-déplacés-de-ippy, accessed 13 June 2022

UN, 'Basic Principles on the Use of Force and Firearms' (adopted by the Eighth United Nations Congress on the Prevention of Crime and the Treatment of Offenders, Havana, Cuba, 27 August to 7 September 1990), www.ohchr.org/en/professionalinterest/pages/useofforceandfirearms.aspx, accessed 22 November 2018

—, 'Resolution XXIII on Human Rights in Armed Conflicts, Adopted on the Report of the Second Committee' (1968) Final Act of the International Conference on Human Rights, 23 April–13 May 1968, Teheran, UN Doc. A/CONF.32/41

UNGA and UNSC, 'Human Rights Due Diligence Policy on United Nations Support to Non-United Nations Security Forces, Annex to the Identical Letters Dated 25 February 2013 from the Secretary-General Addressed to the President of the General Assembly and to the President of the Security Council, Sixty-Seventh Session of the General Assembly, Item 69 of the Provisional Agenda; Sixty-Eighth Year of the Security Council' (2013) UN Doc. A/67/775 and S/2013/110

UNHRC, 'Report of the Detailed Findings of the Commission of Inquiry on Human Rights in the Democratic People's Republic of Korea' (2014) UN Doc. A/HRC/25/CRP.1

UN OHCHR, UN DPKO, UN DPA, and UN DFS, 'Human Rights in United Nations Peace Operations and Political Missions' (2011) Ref 201120

UNSG and the UNSC, 'Identical Letters Dated 21 August 2000 from the Secretary-General to the President of the General Assembly and the President of the Security Council, Fifty-Fifth Session of the General Assembly, Item 87 of the Provisional Agenda; Fifty-Fifth Year of the Security Council' (2000) A/55/305-S/2000/809

4.5. OTHER INTERNATIONAL PRACTICE

AComHPR, 'General Comment No. 3 on the African Charter on Human and Peoples' Rights: The Right to Life (Article 4), Adopted during the 57th Ordinary Session of the African Commission on Human and Peoples' Rights Held from 4 to 18 November 2015 in Banjul, The Gambia' (2015)

WEU Council of Ministers, 'Petersberg Declaration' (1992)

'General Framework Agreement for Peace in Bosnia and Herzegovina' (1995) UN Doc. A/50/790-S/1995/999

'Letter to the UN Secretary-General António Guterres Concerning the Kigali Principles' (2018), www.google.com/url?sa=t&rct=j&q=&esrc=s&source=web&cd=1&ved=2ahUKEwjO0P7Lh_HcAhVH2qQKHZU8BHoQFjAAegQIARAC&url=https%3A%2F%2Fwww.permanentrepresentations.nl%2Fbinaries%2Fnlatio%2Fdocuments%2Fpublications%2F2018%2F7%2F31%2Fletter-to-the-sg-concerning-kigali-principles%2F2018-07-30%2BKigali%2BPrinciples%2BLetter.pdf&usg=AOvVaw2OaLHi2cXrr0PCWifSIFaB, accessed 15 August 2018

'Peace Agreement between the Government of Liberia, the Liberians United for Reconciliation and Democracy, the Movement for Democracy in Liberia and the Political Parties, Annex to the Letter Dated 27 August 2003 from the Permanent Representative of Ghana to the United Nations Addressed to the President of the Security Council' (2003) UN Doc. S/2003/850

'The Kigali Principles on the Protection of Civilians. High-Level International Conference on the Protection of Civilians, 28–29 May 2015, Kigali'

5. STATE PRACTICE

Australia, 'The Manual of the Law of Armed Conflict' (Australian Defence Headquarters 2006) Publication 06.4

Austria, 'Submission from Austria on the Draft General Comment on Article 6 of the International Covenant on Civil and Political Rights – Right to Life' (Undated), www.ohchr.org/en/hrbodies/ccpr/pages/gc36-article6righttolife.aspx, accessed 25 November 2021

Canada, 'Submission from Canada on the Draft General Comment on Article 6 of the International Covenant on Civil and Political Rights – Right to Life' (Undated), www.ohchr.org/en/hrbodies/ccpr/pages/gc36-article6righttolife.aspx, accessed 25 November 2021

France, Assemblée Nationale, ' XIIIe Législature, Compte Rendu N° 36, Commission de La Défense Nationale et Des Forces Armées, Mardi 26 Août 2008'

—, 'Submission from France on the Draft General Comment on Article 6 of the International Covenant on Civil and Political Rights – Right to Life' (Undated), www.ohchr.org/en/hrbodies/ccpr/pages/gc36-article6righttolife.aspx, accessed 25 November 2021

Germany, 'Submission from Germany on the Draft General Comment on Article 6 of the International Covenant on Civil and Political Rights – Right to Life' (2017), www.ohchr.org/en/hrbodies/ccpr/pages/gc36-article6righttolife.aspx, accessed 25 November 2021

New Zealand, 'Manual of Armed Forces Law' (New Zealand Defence Force 2017) DM 69 (2nd edn.), vol. 4

Norway, 'Redegjørelse Av Statsministeren Om Situasjonen i Libya Og Norges Deltakelse i Den Internasjonale Koalisjonsstyrken' (2011) Sak nr. 1 (10:02:13), www.stortinget.no/no/Saker-og-publikasjoner/Publikasjoner/Referater/Stortinget/2010-2011/1103 29/1/, accessed 10 August 2022

—, 'Submission from Norway on the Draft General Comment on Article 6 of the International Covenant on Civil and Political Rights – Right to Life' (Undated), www.ohchr.org/en/hrbodies/ccpr/pages/gc36-article6righttolife.aspx, accessed 25 November 2021

the Netherlands, 'Submission from the Netherlands on the Draft General Comment on Article 6 of the International Covenant on Civil and Political Rights – Right to Life' (Undated), www.ohchr.org/en/hrbodies/ccpr/pages/gc36-article6righttolife.aspx, accessed 25 November 2021

the United Kingdom, Ministry of Defence and Fallon TRtHonSM, 'Government to Protect Armed Forces from Persistent Legal Claims in Future Overseas Operations' (*Gov.uk*, 4 October 2016), www.gov.uk/government/news/government-to-protect-armed-forces-from-persistent-legal-claims-in-future-overseas-operations, accessed 17 February 2022

the United States, 'Instructions for the Government of Armies of the United States in the Field' (1863), https://ihl-databases.icrc.org/applic/ihl/ihl.nsf/ART/110-20014?OpenDocument, accessed 17 August 2022

—, 'Submission from the United States of America on the Draft General Comment on Article 6 of the International Covenant on Civil and Political Rights – Right to Life' (2017), www.ohchr.org/en/hrbodies/ccpr/pages/gc36-article6righttolife.aspx, accessed 25 November 2021

the United States, Joint Chiefs of Staff, Chairman of the Joint Chiefs of Staff, 'Standing Rules of Engagement/Standing Rules for the Use of Force for US Forces' (2005) Document CJCSI 3121.01B

6. DOCTRINE

6.1. BLOG POSTS

Akande D, 'What Does UN Security Council Resolution 1973 Permit?' (*EJIL: Talk!*, 23 March 2011), www.ejiltalk.org/what-does-un-security-council-resolution-1973-permit/, accessed 10 July 2018

Boddens Hosang JFR and Gill TD, 'Soldier Self-Defense Symposium: Netherlands Views on Self-Defence for Military Personnel' (*Opinio Juris*, 29 April 2019), https://opiniojuris.org/2019/04/29/soldier-self-defense-symposium-netherlands-views-on-self-defence-for-military-personnel%EF%BB%BF/, accessed 17 May 2019

Bourgeois H, 'Failure to Protect Civilians in the Context of UN Peace Operations: A Question of Accountability?' (*EJIL: Talk!*, 5 September 2018), www.ejiltalk.org/failure-to-protect-civilians-in-the-context-of-un-peace-operations-a-question-of-accountability/, accessed 5 September 2018

Gaggioli G, 'Soldier Self-Defense Symposium: Self-Defense in Armed Conflicts–The Babel Tower Phenomenon' (*Opinio Juris*, 3 May 2019), http://opiniojuris.org/2019/05/03/soldier-self-defense-symposium-self-defense-in-armed-conflicts-the-babel-tower-phenomenon/, accessed 17 May 2019

Heyns C and Probert T, 'Securing the Right to Life: A Cornerstone of the Human Rights System' (*EJIL: Talk!*, 11 May 2016), www.ejiltalk.org/securing-the-right-to-life-a-cornerstone-of-the-human-rights-system/, accessed 9 September 2019

Labuda PI, 'The UN Goes to War in the Central African Republic: What Are the Limits of Peacekeeping?' (*Just Security*, 23 March 2017), www.justsecurity.org/39151/war-central-african-republic-limits-peacekeeping/, accessed 20 April 2022

Milanović M, 'Georgia v. Russia No. 2: The European Court's Resurrection of Bankovic in the Contexts of Chaos' (*EJIL: Talk!*, 25 January 2021), www.ejiltalk.org/georgia-v-russia-no-2-the-european-courts-resurrection-of-bankovic-in-the-contexts-of-chaos/, accessed 22 November 2021

—, 'Drowning Migrants, the Human Rights Committee, and Extraterritorial Human Rights Obligations' (*EJIL: Talk!*, 16 March 2021), www.ejiltalk.org/drowning-migrants-the-human-rights-committee-and-extraterritorial-human-rights-obligations/, accessed 22 November 2021

Oswald B, 'Soldier Self-Defense Symposium: The Evolution of the UN Doctrine of Self-Defence in UN Peacekeeping' (*Opinio Juris*, 1 May 2019), http://opiniojuris.org/2019/05/01/soldier-self-defense-symposium-the-evolution-of-the-un-doctrine-of-self-defence-in-un-peacekeeping/, accessed 17 May 2019

Oxford Research Group, 'Peacekeeping and Civilian Protection: An Interview with Conor Foley' (20 August 2018), www.oxfordresearchgroup.org.uk/blog/peacekeeping-and-civilian-protection-an-interview-with-conor-foley, accessed 9 June 2022

Stephens D, 'Military Partners and the Obligation to "Ensure Respect" for IHL' (*Articles of War*, 18 November 2021), https://lieber.westpoint.edu/military-partners-obligation-ensure-respect/, accessed 13 October 2022

Wels W, 'The Many Meanings of Protection of Civilians: A Truth Universally Acknowledged?' (*IPI Global Observatory*, 10 October 2019), https://theglobalobservatory.org/2019/10/the-many-meanings-of-protection-of-civilians-truth-universally-acknowledged/, accessed 6 March 2020

Wills S, 'The Law Applicable to Peacekeepers Deployed in Situations Where There Is No Armed Conflict' (*EJIL: Talk!*, 10 April 2013), www.ejiltalk.org/the-law-applicable-to-peacekeepers-deployed-in-situations-where-there-is-no-armed-conflict/, accessed 5 December 2017

6.2. BOOK CHAPTERS

Abass A, 'African Union Operations' in André Nollkaemper and Ilias Plakokefalos (eds), *The Practice of Shared Responsibility in International Law* (Cambridge University Press 2017)

Akande D, 'Classification of Armed Conflicts: Relevant Legal Concepts' in Elizabeth Wilmshurst (ed), *International Law and the Classification of Conflicts* (1st edn., Oxford University Press ; The Royal Institute of International Affairs (Chatham House) 2012)

Anderson M, Becknell K and Taliano J, 'History of Humanitarian Emergencies' in David Townes (ed), *Health in Humanitarian Emergencies* (1st edn., Cambridge University Press 2018)

Bernhardt R, 'Chapter XVI. Miscellaneous Provisions, Article 103' in Bruno Simma and others (eds), *The Charter of the United Nations: a Commentary*, vol. 2 (2nd edn., Oxford University Press 2002)

Biscop S, 'Analysing the EU Global Strategy on Foreign and Security Policy' in Jochen Rehrl (ed), *Handbook on CSDP: the Common Security and Defence Policy of the European Union*, vol. 1 (4th edn., Directorate of Security Policy of the Federal Ministry of Defence and Sports of the Republic of Austria 2021)

Blokker N, 'Outsourcing the Use of Force: Towards More Security Council Control of Authorized Operations?' in Marc Weller, Alexia Solomou and Jake William Rylatt (eds), *The Oxford Handbook of the Use of Force in International Law* (1st edn., Oxford University Press 2015)

Blyth F and Cammaert PC, 'Using Force to Protect Civilians in United Nations Peacekeeping Operations' in Haidi Willmot and others (eds), *Protection of Civilians* (1st edn., Oxford University Press 2016)

Boddens Hosang JFR, 'An Operational Perspective' in Robert Geiß and Heike Krieger (eds), *The 'Legal Pluriverse' Surrounding Multinational Military Operations* (Oxford University Press 2019)

Bothe M, 'Peacekeeping' in Bruno Simma and others (eds), *The Charter of the United Nations: a Commentary*, vol. 1 (3rd edn., Oxford University Press 2012)

Breakey H, 'The Protection of Civilians in Armed Conflict: Four Concepts' in Angus Francis, Vesselin Popovski and CJG Sampford (eds), *Norms of Protection: Responsibility to Protect, Protection of Civilians and Their Interaction* (United Nations University Press 2012)

Bring O, 'The Hammarskjöld Approach to International Law' in Henning Melber and Maxi Schoeman (eds), *The United Nations and Regional Challenges in Africa – 50 Years after Dag Hammarskjöld* (The Dag Hammarskjöld Centre 2011)

Burger JA, 'Headquarters IFOR/SFOR' in Dieter Fleck (ed), *The Handbook of the Law of Visiting Forces* (1st edn., Oxford University Press 2001)

Cammaert PC and Klappe BF, 'Authority, Command, and Control in United Nations-Led Peace Operations' in Terry D Gill and Dieter Fleck (eds), *The Handbook of the International Law of Military Operations* (2nd edn., Oxford University Press 2015)

Cathcart B, 'Command and Control in Military Operations' in Terry D Gill and Dieter Fleck (eds), *The Handbook of the International Law of Military Operations* (2nd edn., Oxford University Press 2015)

Chenwi L and Bulto TS, 'Extraterritoriality in the African Regional Human Rights System from a Comparative Perspective' in Lilian Chenwi and Takele Soboka Bulto (eds), *Extraterritorial Human Rights Obligations From an African Perspective* (Intersentia 2018)

Christakis T, 'Les "Circonstances Excluant l'Illicéité": une Illusion Optique?' in Jean JA Salmon (ed), *Droit du Pouvoir, Pouvoir du Droit: Mélanges Offerts à Jean Salmon* (Bruylant 2007)

Clapham A, 'Protection of Civilians under International Human Rights Law' in Haidi Willmot and others (eds), *Protection of Civilians* (1st edn., Oxford University Press 2016)

Combacau J, 'Obligations de Rêsultat et Obligations de Comportement. Quelques Questions et Pas de Réponses' in Paul Reuter (ed), *Mélanges offerts à Paul Reuter: Le Droit International, Unité et Diversité* (Pedone 1981)

Corten O, 'Necessity' in Marc Weller, Alexia Solomou and Jake William Rylatt (eds), *The Oxford Handbook of the Use of Force in International Law* (1st edn., Oxford University Press 2015)

Crawford E, 'Who Is a Civilian? Membership of Opposition Groups and Direct Participation in Hostilities' in Mark Lattimer and Philippe Sands (eds), *The Grey Zone: Civilian Protection between Human Rights and the Laws of War* (Hart Publishing 2018)

David E, 'Primary and Secondary Rules' in James Crawford and others (eds), *The Law of International Responsibility* (Oxford University Press 2010)

De Cock C, 'Operation Unified Protector and the Protection of Civilians in Libya' in Michael N Schmitt and Louise Arimatsu (eds), *Yearbook of International Humanitarian Law*, vol. 14 (TMC Asser Press 2012)

Dinstein Y, 'The Principle of Proportionality' in Kjetil Mujezinovic Larsen, Camilla Guldahl Cooper and Gro Nystuen (eds), *Searching for a 'Principle of Humanity' in International Humanitarian Law* (Cambridge University Press 2013)

Dobinson I and Johns F, 'Legal Research as Qualitative Research' in Michael McConville and Wing Hong Chui (eds), *Research Methods for Law* (2nd edn., Edinburgh University Press 2017)

Fleck D, 'The Law Applicable to Peace Operations' in Andrew Clapham and Paola Gaeta (eds), *The Oxford Handbook of International Law in Armed Conflict* (Oxford University Press 2014)

Foley C, 'Defining Protection of Civilians in the Context of Armed Conflict' in Dan Kuwali and Frans Viljoen (eds), *By All Means Necessary: Protecting Civilians and Preventing Mass Atrocities in Africa* (Pretoria University Law Press 2017)

Fox GH, 'Intervention by Invitation' in Marc Weller, Alexia Solomou and Jake William Rylatt (eds), *The Oxford Handbook of the Use of Force in International Law* (1st edn., Oxford University Press 2016)

Frowein JA, 'Unilateral Interpretation of Security Council Resolutions. A Threat to Collective Security?' in Volkmar Götz, Peter Selmer and Rüdiger Wolfrum (eds), *Liber Amicorum Günther Jaenicke – Zum 85. Geburtstag* (Springer 1998)

Gaggioli G, 'The Use of Force in Armed Conflicts Conduct of Hostilities, Law Enforcement, and Self-Defense' in Winston S Williams and Christopher M Ford (eds), *Complex Battlespaces: the Law of Armed Conflict and the Dynamics of Modern Warfare*, vol. 1 (Oxford University Press 2019)

Geiß R, 'Common Article 1 of the Geneva Conventions: Scope and Content of the Obligation to "Ensure Respect" – "Narrow but Deep" or "Wide and Shallow"?' in Heike Krieger (ed), *Inducing Compliance with International Humanitarian Law* (1st edn, Cambridge University Press 2015)

Gill TD, 'Legal Aspects of the Transfer of Authority in UN Peace Operations' in Ige F Dekker and Ellen Hey (eds), *Netherlands Yearbook of International Law 2011*, vol. 42 (TMC Asser Press 2011)

—, 'Characterization and Legal Basis for Peace Operations' in Terry D Gill and Dieter Fleck (eds), *The Handbook of the International Law of Military Operations* (2nd edn., Oxford University Press 2015)

—, 'Legal Characterization and Basis for Enforcement Operations and Peace Enforcement Operations Under the Charter' in Terry D Gill and Dieter Fleck (eds), *The Handbook of the International Law of Military Operations* (2nd edn., Oxford University Press 2015)

—, 'Military Intervention with the Consent or at the Invitation of a Government' in Terry D Gill and Dieter Fleck (eds), *The Handbook of the International Law of Military Operations* (2nd edn., Oxford University Press 2015)

Gill TD and Fleck D, 'Concept and Sources of the International Law of Military Operations' in Terry D Gill and Dieter Fleck (eds), *The Handbook of the International Law of Military Operations* (2nd edn., Oxford University Press 2015)

Gormley PW, 'The Right to Life and the Rule of Non-Derogability: Peremptory Norms of Jus Cogens' in Bertrand G Ramcharan (ed), *The Right to Life in International Law* (Martinus Nijhoff Publishers 1985)

Greenwood C, 'Self-Defence and the Conduct of International Armed Conflict' in Shabtai Rosenne, Yoram Dinstein and Mala Tabory (eds), *International Law at a Time of Perplexity: Essays in Honour of Shabtai Rosenne* (Martinus Nijhoff Publishers 1989)

—, 'Historical Development and Legal Basis' in Dieter Fleck and Michael Bothe (eds), *The Handbook of International Humanitarian Law* (2nd edn., Oxford University Press 2008)

Hall S, 'Researching International Law' in Michael McConville and Wing Hong Chui (eds), *Research Methods for Law* (2nd edn., Edinburgh University Press 2017)

Heliskosi J, 'Responsibility and Liability for CSDP Operations' in Steven Blockmans and Panos Koutrakos (eds), *Research Handbook on the EU's Common Foreign and Security Policy* (Edward Elgar Publishing 2018)

Khalil MA, 'Legal Aspects of the Use of Force by United Nations Peacekeepers for the Protection of Civilians' in Haidi Willmot and others (eds), *Protection of Civilians* (1st edn., Oxford University Press 2016)

Kioko B and Wambugu L, 'The African Union and the Protection of Civilians' in Haidi Willmot and others (eds), *Protection of Civilians* (1st edn., Oxford University Press 2016)

Kjeksrud S and others, 'Protecting Civilians: Comparing Organizational Approaches' in Haidi Willmot and others (eds), *Protection of Civilians* (1st edn., Oxford University Press 2016)

Klappe BF, 'International Peace Operations' in Dieter Fleck (ed), *The Handbook of International Humanitarian Law* (3rd edn., Oxford University Press 2013)

Kleffner JK, 'Human Rights and International Humanitarian Law: General Issues' in Terry D Gill and Dieter Fleck (eds), *The Handbook of the International Law of Military Operations* (2nd edn., Oxford University Press 2015)

Kolb R, 'La Nécessité Militaire Dans Le Droit Des Conflits Armés: Essai de Clarification Conceptuelle' in Pendone (ed), *La Nécessité en Droit International* (Société Française Pour le Droit International 2007)

Koutroulis V, 'Jus Ad/Contra Bellum' in Raphael van Steenberghe (ed), *Le Droit International Humanitaire: Un Régime Spécial de Droit International?* (Bruylant 2013)

Krisch N, 'Chapter VII. Action with Respect to Threats to the Peace, Breaches of the Peace, and Acts of Aggression' in Bruno Simma and others (eds), *The Charter of the United Nations: a Commentary*, vol. 2 (3rd edn., Oxford University Press 2012)

Larsen KM (eds), 'Multinational Peace Operations Forces Involved in Armed Conflict: Who Are the Parties?', *Searching for a 'Principle of Humanity' in International Humanitarian Law* (Cambridge University Press 2012)

Lawson R, 'Life after Banković: On the Extraterritorial Application of the European Convention on Human Rights' in Fons Coomans and Menno T Kamminga (eds), *Extraterritorial Application of Human Rights Treaties* (Intersentia 2004)

—, 'Really Out of Sight? Issues of Jurisdiction and Control in Situations of Armed Conflict under the ECHR' in Antoine Buyse (ed), *Margins of Conflict: The ECHR and Transitions to and from Armed Conflict* (1st edn, Intersentia 2010)

Leiæ JR and Paulus A, 'Chapter XVI. Miscellaneous Provisions, Article 103' in Bruno Simma and others (eds), *The Charter of the United Nations: a Commentary*, vol. 2 (3rd. edn., Oxford University Press 2012)

Lie JHS and de Carvalho B, 'Chapter 3: Conceptual Unclarity and Competition: The Protection of Civilians and the Responsibility to Protect' in Benjamin de Carvalho, Ole Jacob Sending and Jan Egeland (eds), *The Protection of Civilians in UN Peacekeeping: Concept, Implementation and Practice* (1st edn., Nomos 2013)

Lieblich E, 'On the Continuous and Concurrent Application of Ad Bellum and In Bello Proportionality' in Claus Kreß and Robert Lawless (eds), *Necessity and Proportionality in International Peace and Security Law* (Oxford University Press 2020)

Liivoja R, 'Protecting Warfighters from Superfluous Injury and Unnecessary Suffering' in Matt Killingsworth and Tim McCormack (eds), *Who Do the Laws of War Protect? Civility, Barbarity and the Evolution of International Humanitarian Law* (Cambridge University Press Forthcoming), https://papers.ssrn.com/sol3/papers.cfm?abstract_id=3738501, accessed 23 August 2022

Lindstrom G, 'History and Development of the CSDP' in Jochen Rehrl (ed), *Handbook on CSDP: the Common Security and Defence Policy of the European Union*, vol. 1 (4th edn., Directorate of Security Policy of the Federal Ministry of Defence and Sports of the Republic of Austria 2021)

Mamiya R, 'A History and Conceptual Development of the Protection of Civilians' in Haidi Willmot and others (eds), *Protection of Civilians* (1st edn., Oxford University Press 2016)

Mbow MD and Souaré IK, 'Protecting Civilians in Mali and Central African Republic' in Jide Martyns Okeke and Paul D Williams (eds), *Protecting Civilians in African*

Union Support Operations: Key Cases and Lessons Learned (African Centre for the Constructive Resolution of Disputes 2016)

Megy SJ, 'The Protection of Civilians in African Regional and Sub-Regional Peace Operations' in David Curran and others (eds), *Perspectives on Peacekeeping and Atrocity Prevention* (Springer 2015)

Melzer N and Gaggioli G, 'Conceptual Distinction and Overlaps Between Law Enforcement and the Conduct of Hostilities' in Terry D Gill and Dieter Fleck (eds), *The Handbook of the International Law of Military Operations* (2nd edn., Oxford University Press 2015)

Milanović M and Hadzi-Vidanovic V, 'A Taxonomy of Armed Conflict' in Nigel D White and Christian Henderson (eds), *Research Handbook on International Conflict and Security Law: Jus Ad Bellum, Jus In Bello And Jus Post Bellum* (Edward Elgar 2013)

Murphy R and Wills S, 'United Nations Peacekeeping Operations' in André Nollkaemper and Ilias Plakokefalos (eds), *The Practice of Shared Responsibility in International Law* (Cambridge University Press 2017)

Myjer EPJ and White ND, 'Peace Operations Conducted by Regional Organizations and Arrangements' in Terry D Gill and Dieter Fleck (eds), *The Handbook of the International Law of Military Operations* (2nd edn., Oxford University Press 2015)

Naert F, 'European Union Common Security and Defence Policy Operations' in André Nollkaemper and Ilias Plakokefalos (eds), *The Practice of Shared Responsibility in International Law* (Cambridge University Press 2017)

Newton M, 'The Legal Interoperability of the Laws of Armed Conflict' in Robert Geiß and Heike Krieger (eds), *The 'Legal Pluriverse' Surrounding Multinational Military Operations* (Oxford University Press 2019)

Novi C, 'EU-UN Cooperation in Multifunctional Peace Operations in Africa' in Giovanni Cellamare and Ivan Ingravallo (eds), *Peace Maintenance in Africa: Open Legal Issues* (1st edn., Springer International Publishing 2018)

Oberleitner G, 'Humanitarian Law as a Source of Human Rights Law' in Dinah Shelton (ed), *The Oxford Handbook of International Human Rights Law* (Oxford University Press 2013)

O'Connell ME, 'Historical Development and Legal Basis' in Dieter Fleck (ed), *The Handbook of International Humanitarian Law* (3rd edn., Oxford University Press 2013)

Okeke JM and Williams PD, 'Introduction: African Union Peace Support Operations and Civilian Protection' in Jide Martyns Okeke and Paul D Williams (eds), *Protecting Civilians in African Union Support Operations: Key Cases and Lessons Learned* (African Centre for the Constructive Resolution of Disputes 2016)

Okimoto K, 'The Relationship Between Jus Ad Bellum and Jus in Bello' in Marc Weller, Alexia Solomou and Jake William Rylatt (eds), *The Oxford Handbook of the Use of Force in International Law* (1st edn., Oxford University Press 2015)

Okumu W and Jaye T, 'Introduction' in Benjamin de Carvalho and others (eds), *Peacekeeping in Africa: The Evolving roles of the African Union and Regional Mechanisms* (Norwegian Institute of International Affairs 2010)

Orakhelashvili A, 'The Acts of the Security Council: Meaning and Standards of Review' in Armin von Bogdandy and Rüdiger Wolfrum (eds), *Max Planck Yearbook of United Nations Law*, vol. 11 (Koninklijke Brill 2007)

Pellet A, '688 (1991): Iraq' in Mélanie Albaret and others (eds), *Les Grandes Résolutions du Conseil de Sécurité des Nations Unies* (Dalloz 2012)

Peters A, 'Ch. V The Security Council, Functions and Powers. Article 25' in Bruno Simma and others (eds), *The Charter of the United Nations: a Commentary*, vol. 1 (3rd edn., Oxford University Press 2012)

Prescott JM, 'Tactical Implementation of Rules of Engagement in a Multinational Force Reality' in Geoffrey S Corn, Rachel E VanLandingham and Shane R Reeves (eds), *U.S. Military Operations: Law, Policy, and Practice* (Oxford University Press 2015)

Ruys T, 'International Law on the Use of Force' in Jan Wouters, Philip de Man and Nele Verlinden (eds), *Armed Conflicts and the Law* (Intersentia 2016)

Rynning S, 'As NATO Looks East, Will It Stumble in the South? The Case of Protection of Civilians Policy' in Roberto Belloni, Paul R Viotti and Vincent Della Sala (eds), *Fear and Uncertainty in Europe: the Return to Realism?* (Palgrave Macmillan 2019)

Sarooshi D, 'The Security Council's Authorization of Regional Arrangements to Use Force: The Case of NATO' in Alan V Lowe and others (eds), *The United Nations Security Council and War: the Evolution of Thought and Practice Since 1945* (Oxford University Press 2008)

Sassòli M, 'Ius Ad Bellum and Ius in Bello – The Separation between the Legality of the Use of Force and Humanitarian Rules to Be Respected in Warfare: Crucial or Outdated?' in Michael N Schmitt and Jelena Pejic (eds), *International Law and Armed Conflict: Exploring the Faultlines. Essays in Honour of Yoram Dinstein* (Koninklijke Brill 2007)

Schabas WA, 'The Right to Life' in Andrew Clapham and Paola Gaeta (eds), *The Oxford Handbook of International Law in Armed Conflict*, vol. 1 (Oxford University Press 2014)

Scheinin M, 'Extraterritorial Effect of the International Covenant on Civil and Political Rights' in Fons Coomans and Menno T Kamminga (eds), *Extraterritorial Application of Human Rights Treaties* (Intersentia 2004)

Sheeran S, 'The Use of Force in United Nations Peacekeeping Operations' in Marc Weller, Alexia Solomou and Jake William Rylatt (eds), *The Oxford Handbook of the Use of Force in International Law* (1st edn., Oxford University Press 2015)

—, 'Human Rights and Derogation in Peacekeeping' in Evan J Criddle (ed), *Human Rights in Emergencies* (2016)

Sheeran S and Kent C, 'Protection of Civilians, Responsibility to Protect, and Humanitarian Intervention: Conceptual and Normative Interactions' in Haidi Willmot and others (eds), *Protection of Civilians* (1st edn., Oxford University Press 2016)

Slim H, 'Civilians, Distinctions, and the Compassionate View of War' in Haidi Willmot and others (eds), *Protection of Civilians* (1st edn., Oxford University Press 2016)

Stöckl W, 'Chapter XV. The Secretariat, Article 101' in Bruno Simma and others (eds), *The Charter of the United Nations: a Commentary*, vol. 2 (3rd. edn., Oxford University Press 2012)

Tladi D, 'Interpretation of Protection of Civilians Mandates in United Nations Security Resolutions' in Dan Kuwali and Frans Viljoen (eds), *By All Means Necessary: Protecting Civilians and Preventing Mass Atrocities in Africa* (Pretoria University Law Press 2017)

Tsagourias N, 'EU Peacekeeping Operations: Legal and Theoretical Issues' in Martin Trybus and Nigel White (eds), *European Security Law* (Oxford University Press 2007)
—, 'Self-Defence, Protection of Humanitarian Values, and the Doctrine of Impartiality and Neutrality in Enforcement Mandates' in Marc Weller, Alexia Solomou and Jake William Rylatt (eds), *The Oxford Handbook of the Use of Force in International Law* (1st edn., Oxford University Press 2015)
Watkin K, 'A North American Perspective: The Overlap of the Laws of Armed Conflict and International Human Rights Law' in Robert Geiß and Heike Krieger (eds), *The 'Legal Pluriverse' Surrounding Multinational Military Operations* (Oxford University Press 2019)
Weisman H, 'The United Nations and International Peacekeeping: A Comparative Analysis' in United Nations Institute for Training and Research (ed), *The United Nations and the Maintenance of International Peace and Security* (Martinus Nijhoff Publishers 1987)
White ND, 'Peacekeeping and International Law' in Joachim Alexander Koops and others (eds), *The Oxford Handbook of United Nations Peacekeeping Operations* (1st edn, Oxford University Press 2015)
White ND, 'Security Council Mandates and the Use of Lethal Force by Peacekeepers: What Place for the Laws of War?' in Caroline Harvey, James Summers and Nigel D White (eds), *Contemporary challenges to the laws of war: essays in honour of Professor Peter Rowe* (Cambridge University Press 2014)
—, 'The Use of Weapons in Peace Operations' in Stuart Casey-Maslen (ed), *Weapons Under International Human Rights Law* (Cambridge University Press 2014)
Williamson JA, 'Protection of Civilians under International Humanitarian Law' in Haidi Willmot and others (eds), *Protection of Civilians* (1st edn., Oxford University Press 2016)
Willmot H, 'The Evolution of the UN Collective Security System' in Haidi Willmot and others (eds), *Protection of Civilians* (1st edn., Oxford University Press 2016)
—, 'Introduction' in Haidi Willmot and others (eds), *Protection of Civilians* (1st edn., Oxford University Press 2016)
Willmot H and Mamiya R, 'Mandated to Protect: Security Council Practice on the Protection of Civilians' in Marc Weller, Alexia Solomou and Jake William Rylatt (eds), *The Oxford Handbook of the Use of Force in International Law* (1st edn., Oxford University Press 2015)
Wills S, 'International Responsibility for Ensuring the Protection of Civilians' in Haidi Willmot and others (eds), *Protection of Civilians* (1st edn., Oxford University Press 2016)
Wolfrum R, 'Ch. I Purposes and Principles, Article 1' in Bruno Simma and others (eds), *The Charter of the United Nations: a Commentary*, vol. 1 (3rd edn., Oxford University Press 2012)
Wouters J and De Man P, 'Legal Instruments for the Prevention of Armed Conflicts' in Jan Wouters, Philip de Man and Nele Verlinden (eds), *Armed Conflicts and the Law* (Intersentia 2016)
Zwanenburg M, 'North Atlantic Treaty Organization-Led Operations' in André Nollkaemper and Ilias Plakokefalos (eds), *The Practice of Shared Responsibility in International Law* (Cambridge University Press 2017)

—, 'Double Trouble: The "Cumulative Approach" and the "Support-Based Approach" in the Relationship Between Non-State Armed Groups' in Terry D Gill and others (eds), *Yearbook of International Humanitarian Law*, vol. 22 (TMC Asser Press 2019)
—, 'UN Peace Operations, International Humanitarian Law and International Human Rights Law' in Robert Kolb, Gloria Gaggioli and Pavle Kilibarda (eds), *Research Handbook on Human Rights and Humanitarian Law: Further Reflections and Perspectives* (Edward Elgar Publishing 2022)
Zyberi G and Andersson A, 'A European Perspective on the International Human Rights and Humanitarian Law Relationship in the Context of Multinational Military Operations' in Robert Geiß and Heike Krieger (eds), *The 'Legal Pluriverse' Surrounding Multinational Military Operations* (Oxford University Press 2019)

6.3. BOOKS

Académie de droit international humanitaire et de droits humains à Genève, *Use of Force in Law Enforcement and the Right to Life: The Role of the Human Rights Council* (Geneva Academy of International Humanitarian Law and Human Rights 2016)
Aust A, *Handbook of International Law* (2nd edn., Cambridge University Press 2010)
Bellamy AJ, Williams PD and Griffin S, *Understanding Peacekeeping* (2nd edn., Polity 2010)
Boddens Hosang JFR, *Rules of Engagement and the International Law of Military Operations* (1st edn, Oxford University Press 2020)
Bowett DW, *United Nations Forces: A Legal Study of United Nations Practice* (Stevens 1964)
Brownlie I, *International Law and the Use of Force by States* (Oxford University Press 1963)
Cameron L and Chetail V, *Privatizing War: Private Military and Security Companies under Public International Law* (Cambridge University Press 2013)
Casey-Maslen S and Heyns C, *The Right to Life under International Law: An Interpretative Manual* (Cambridge University Press 2021)
Cassese A (ed), *United Nations Peace-Keeping: Legal Essays* (Sijthoff & Noordhoff (International Publishers) 1978)
Clapham A and Gaeta P (eds), *The Oxford Handbook of International Law in Armed Conflict* (Oxford University Press 2014)
Cohen A and Zlotogorski D, *Proportionality in International Humanitarian Law: Consequences, Precautions, and Procedures* (Oxford University Press 2020)
Cole A and others (eds), *Sanremo Handbook on Rules of Engagement* (International Institute of Humanitarian Law 2009)
Combacau J, *Le Pouvoir de Sanction de l'ONU: Étude Théorique de La Coercition Non Militaire* (Pedone 1974)
Corten O, *The Law against War: The Prohibition on the Use of Force in Contemporary International Law*, vol. 4 (Hart Publishing 2010)
Crawford J (ed), *The International Law Commission's Articles on State Responsibility: Introduction, Text, and Commentaries* (Cambridge University Press 2002)

—, Brownlie's Principles of Public International Law (9th edn., Oxford University Press 2019)

de Carvalho B, Sending OJ and Egeland J (eds), *The Protection of Civilians in UN Peacekeeping: Concept, Implementation and Practice* (1st edn., Nomos 2013)

de Wet E, *The Chapter VII Powers of the United Nations Security Council* (Hart Publishing 2004)

de Wet E and Kleffner J (eds), *Convergence and Conflicts of Human Rights and International Humanitarian Law in Military Operations* (Pretoria University Law Press 2014)

Dinstein Y, *The Conduct of Hostilities under the Law of International Armed Conflict* (3rd edn., Cambridge University Press 2016)

—, *War, Aggression and Self-Defence* (6th edn., University Printing House 2017)

Dixon M, *Textbook on International Law* (7th edn., Oxford University Press 2013)

Dörr O and Schmalenbach K (eds), *Vienna Convention on the Law of Treaties: A Commentary* (Springer 2012)

Findlay T, *The Use of Force in UN Peace Operations* (SIPRI ; Oxford University Press 2002)

Fleck D and Bothe M (eds), *The Handbook of International Humanitarian Law* (3rd edn., Oxford University Press 2013)

Foley C, *UN Peacekeeping Operations and the Protection of Civilians: Saving Succeeding Generations* (Cambridge University Press 2017)

Forsythe DP, *The Humanitarians: The International Committee of the Red Cross* (1st edn., Cambridge University Press 2005)

Freedman R, Lemay-Hébert N and Wills S, *The Law and Practice of Peacekeeping: Foregrounding Human Rights* (Cambridge University Press 2021)

Gardam JG, *Necessity, Proportionality, and the Use of Force by States* (Cambridge University Press 2004)

Gardiner RK, *Treaty Interpretation* (2nd edn., Oxford University Press 2015)

Geiß R and Krieger H (eds), *The 'legal Pluriverse' Surrounding Multinational Military Operations* (1st edn., Oxford University Press 2020)

Gill TD (eds), *Leuven Manual on the International Law Applicable to Peace Operations* (Cambridge University Press 2017)

Gill TD and Fleck D (eds), *The Handbook of the International Law of Military Operations* (2nd edn., Oxford University Press 2015)

Gray CD, *International Law and the Use of Force* (4th edn., Oxford University Press 2018)

Guldahl Cooper C, *NATO Rules of Engagement: On ROE, Self-Defence and the Use of Force during Armed Conflict* (Brill 2020)

Hannikainen L, *Peremptory Norms (Jus Cogens) in International Law: Historical Development, Criteria, Present Status* (Finnish Lawyers' Pub Co 1988)

Harvard School of Public Health (ed), *Commentary to the HPCR Manual on International Law Applicable to Air and Missile Warfare, Elaborated by the Drafting Committee of the Group of Experts under the Supervision of Professor Yoram Dinstein* (Cambridge University Press 2013)

Henckaerts J-M and Doswald-Beck L, *ICRC Study on Customary International Humanitarian Law. Volume I: Rules* (Cambridge University Press 2005)

Henderson C, *The Use of Force and International Law* (Cambridge University Press 2018)

Henderson I, 'Civilian Intelligence Agencies and the Use of Armed Drones', *Yearbook of International Humanitarian Law*, vol. 13 (TMC Asser Press 2011)

Hessbruegge JA, *Human Rights and Personal Self-Defense in International Law* (1 edn, Oxford University Press 2017)

Holt VK and Berkman TC, *The Impossible Mandate? Military Preparedness, the Responsibility to Protect and Modern Peace Operations* (Stimson Center 2006)

International Committee of the Red Cross, Commentary on the First Geneva Convention: Convention (I) for the Amelioration of the Condition of the Wounded and Sick in Armed Forces in the Field (1st edn, Cambridge University Press 2016)

— (ed), Commentary on the Second Geneva Convention: Convention (II) for the Amelioration of the Condition of Wounded, Sick, and Shipwrecked Members of Armed Forces at Sea (Cambridge University Press 2017)

— (ed), Commentary on the Third Geneva Convention: Convention (III) Relative to the Treatment of Prisoners of War (Cambridge University Press 2021)

Jachec-Neale A, *The Concept of Military Objectives in International Law and Targeting Practice* (First issued in paperback, Routledge 2016)

Kelsen H, *Principles of International Law* (2nd edn., Holt, Rinehart and Winston 1966)

Kolb R, *Interprétation et Création du Droit International: Esquisses d'une Herméneutique Juridique Moderne pour le Droit International Public* (Bruylant 2006)

—, *International Law on the Maintenance of Peace: Jus Contra Bellum* (Edward Elgar Publishing 2018)

Koops JA and others (eds), *The Oxford Handbook of United Nations Peacekeeping Operations* (1st edn, Oxford University Press 2015)

Lamont C, *International Law in the Transition to Peace: Protecting Civilians under Jus Post Bellum* (Routledge 2021)

Larsen KM, *The Human Rights Treaty Obligations of Peacekeepers* (Cambridge University Press 2014)

Leverick F, *Killing in Self-defence* (Oxford University Press 2006)

Lowe V, *International Law* (Oxford University Press 2007)

Lubell N, *Extraterritorial Use of Force against Non-State Actors* (Oxford University Press 2010)

Maus S, *United Nations Peace Operations and Human Rights: Normativity and Compliance* (Brill 2020)

Melzer N, *Targeted Killing in International Law* (Oxford University Press 2008)

—, *International Humanitarian Law. A Comprehensive Introduction* (ICRC 2019)

Meyrowitz H, *Le Principe de l'égalité Des Belligérants Devant Le Droit de La Guerre* (Pedone 1970)

Milanović M, *Extraterritorial Application of Human Rights Treaties: Law, Principles and Policy* (Oxford University Press 2011)

—, 'Extraterritorial Derogations from Human Rights Treaties in Armed Conflict' in Nehal Bhuta (ed), *The Frontiers of Human Rights* (Oxford University Press 2016)

Murphy R, *UN Peacekeeping in Lebanon, Somalia and Kosovo Operational and Legal Issues in Practice* (Cambridge University Press 2007)

Murray D and others (eds), *Practitioners' Guide to Human Rights Law in Armed Conflict* (Oxford University Press ; Royal Institute of International Affairs (Chatham House) 2016)

Nasu H, *International Law on Peacekeeping: A Study of Article 40 of the UN Charter* (Martinus Nijhoff Publishers 2009)
Nauta DRD, *The International Responsibility of NATO and Its Personnel during Military Operations*, vol. 58 (Brill 2018)
O'Connell ME, Tams CJ and Tladi D, *Self-Defence against Non-State Actors*, vol. 1 (Cambridge University Press 2019)
Okimoto K, *The Distinction and Relationship between Jus Ad Bellum and Jus in Bello*, vol. 33 (Hart 2011)
Orakhelashvili A, *Collective Security* (Oxford University Press 2011)
Park I, *The Right to Life in Armed Conflict*, vol. 1 (Oxford University Press 2018)
Pauwelyn J, *Conflict of Norms in Public International Law: How WTO Law Relates to Other Rules of International Law* (Cambridge University Press 2003)
Pictet (ed), *Commentary IV Geneva Convention Relative to the Protection of Civilian Persons in Time of War* (ICRC 1958)
Rodley N and Pollard M, *The Treatment of Prisoners under International Law* (Oxford University Press 2011)
Rowe PJ, *The Impact of Human Rights Law on Armed Forces* (Cambridge University Press 2006)
Sandoz Y, Swinarski C and Zimmermann B (eds), *Commentary on the Additional Protocols of 8 June 1977 to the Geneva Conventions of 12 August 1949* (ICRC ; Martinus Nijhoff Publishers 1987)
Sarooshi D, *The United Nations and the Development of Collective Security: The Delegation by the UN Security Council of Its Chapter VII Powers* (Repr, Oxford University Press 1999)
Sassòli M, Bouvier A and Quintin A, *Un Droit Dans La Guerre*, vol. 1 (2nd edn., ICRC)
Schabas WA, *The European Convention on Human Rights: A Commentary* (1st edn., Oxford University Press 2015)
Schmidt J, *The European Union and the Use of Force* (Koninklijke Brill NV 2021)
Schmitt MN, *Essays on Law and War at the Fault Lines* (T M C Asser Press 2012)
Schwarzenberger G, *International Law as Applied by International Courts and Tribunals*, vol. 2 (Stevens 1968)
Simma B (eds), *The Charter of the United Nations: A Commentary* (3rd edn., Oxford University Press 2012)
Sloan J, *The Militarisation of Peacekeeping in the Twenty First Century* (Hart Publishing 2011)
Sphere Project (ed), *The Sphere Handbook: Humanitarian Charter and Minimum Standards in Humanitarian Response* (4th edn., Sphere Association 2018)
Sur S, *L'interprétation En Droit International Public* (Librairie Générale de Droit et de Jurisprudence 1974)
Thakur RC and Schnabel A (eds), *United Nations Peacekeeping Operations: Ad Hoc Missions, Permanent Engagement* (United Nations University Press 2001)
Tomuschat C, Lagrange E and Oeter S (eds), *The Right to Life* (Martinus Nijhoff Publishers 2010)
Van Engeland A, *Civilian or Combatant?: A Challenge for the 21st Century* (Oxford University Press 2011)
Verdirame G, *The UN and Human Rights: Who Guards the Guardians?* (Cambridge University Press 2011)

Verhelst A and Trifunovska S, *North Atlantic Treaty Organization (NATO)* (2nd edn., Kluwer Law International 2020)
Virally M, *L'organisation Mondiale* (Colin 1972)
Wallace S, *The Application of the European Convention on Human Rights to Military Operations* (Cambridge University Press 2019)
Watkin K, *Fighting at the Legal Boundaries: Controlling the Use of Force in Contemporary Conflict* (Oxford University Press 2016)
Weatherall T, *Jus Cogens: International Law and Social Contract* (Cambridge University Press 2015)
White ND, *Keeping the Peace: The United Nations and the Maintenance of International Peace and Security* (2nd edn., Manchester University Press 1997)
Willmot H (eds), *Protection of Civilians* (1st edn., Oxford University Press 2016)
Wills S, Protecting Civilians: *The Obligations of Peacekeepers* (Oxford University Press 2009)
Zamir N, *Classification of Conflicts in International Humanitarian Law: The Legal Impact of Foreign Intervention in Civil Wars* (Edward Elgar Publishing 2017)
Zemanek K, *The Legal Foundations of the International System: General Course on Public International Law* (Nijhoff 1998)

6.4. DICTIONARY ENTRIES

'Action, n.', www.oed.com, accessed 28 August 2018
'Area, n.', www.oed.com, accessed 18 May 2022
'Capability, n.', www.oed.com, accessed 18 May 2022
'Civilian, n.', www.oed.com, accessed 9 September 2020
'Imminent, Adj.', www.oed.com, accessed 25 February 2021
'Means, n.', www.oed.com, accessed 28 August 2018
'Measure, n.', www.oed.com, accessed 28 August 2018
'Necessary, Adj. and n.', www.oed.com, accessed 28 August 2018
'Physical, Adj.', www.oed.com, accessed 20 May 2020
'Pro-', www.etymonline.com/word/pro-?ref=etymonline_crossreference, accessed 15 September 2020
'Protection, n.', www.etymonline.com/search?q=protection, accessed 15 September 2020
'—', www.oed.com, accessed 9 September 2020
'Self-Defence, n.', www.dictionary.law.com, accessed 4 March 2022
'(S)Teg-', www.etymonline.com/word/*(s)teg-?ref=etymonline_crossreference, accessed 15 September 2020
'Step, n., Fig.', www.oed.com, accessed 9 May 2022
'Threat, n.', www.oed.com, accessed 25 February 2021
'Violence, n.', www.oed.com, accessed 20 May 2020

6.5. DISSERTATIONS

Lieblich E, 'Intervention in Civil Wars: Intervention and Consent' (DPhil thesis, Columbia University 2012)

Naert F, 'International Law Aspects of the EU's Security and Defence Policy, with a Particular Focus on the Law of Armed Conflict and Human Rights' (DPhil thesis, KU Leuven 2008)

Traoré SB, 'L'Interprétation Des Résolutions Du Conseil de Sécurité Des Nations Unies' (DPhil thesis, University of Neuchatel 2018)

Verlinden N, '"Are We at War"? State Support to Parties in Armed Conflict: Consequences under Jus in Bello, Jus Ad Bellum and Neutrality Law' (DPhil thesis, KU Leuven 2019)

Voetelink JED, '"Status of Forces": Strafrechtsmacht over Militairen Vanuit Internationaalrechtelijk & Militair-Operationeelrechtelijk Perspectief' (DPhil thesis, University of Amsterdam 2012)

Wiesener C, 'The Application and Interplay of Humanitarian Law and Human Rights Law in Peace Operations, with a Particular Focus on the Use of Force' (DPhil thesis, European University Institute 2015)

6.6. ENCYCLOPAEDIA ARTICLES

Besson S, 'Sovereignty', *Max Planck Encyclopedia of Public International law* (Oxford Public International Law 2011)

Bothe M, 'Peacekeeping Forces', *Max Planck Encyclopedia of Public International law* (Oxford Public International Law 2016)

Crawford E, 'Proportionality', *Max Planck Encyclopedia of Public International law* (Oxford Public International Law 2011)

Dinstein Y, 'Military Necessity', *Max Planck Encyclopedia of Public International law* (Oxford Public International Law 2015)

—, 'Warfare, Methods and Means', *Max Planck Encyclopedia of Public International law* (Oxford Public International Law 2015)

Dörr O, 'Prohibition of the Use of Force', *Max Planck Encyclopedia of Public International law* (Oxford Public International Law 2015)

Frowein JA, 'Ius Cogens', *Max Planck Encyclopedia of Public International law* (Oxford Public International Law 2013)

Heintschel von Heinegg W, 'Asymmetric Warfare', *Max Planck Encyclopedia of Public International law* (Oxford Public International Law 2010)

—, 'Proportionality and Collateral Damage', *Max Planck Encyclopedia of Public International law* (Oxford Public International Law 2015)

Labuda PI, 'Peacekeeping and Peace Enforcement', *Max Planck Encyclopedia of Public International law* (Oxford Public International Law 2015)

Lowe AV, 'Humanitarian Intervention', *Max Planck Encyclopedia of Public International law* (Oxford Public International Law 2011)

Sassòli M, 'Military Objectives', *Max Planck Encyclopedia of Public International law* (Oxford Public International Law 2015)

6.7. JOURNAL ARTICLES

Aughey S and Sari A, 'Targeting and Detention in Non-International Armed Conflict: Serdar Mohammed and the Limits of Human Rights Convergence' (2015) 91 International Law Studies 60

Bakircioglu O, 'The Right to Self-Defence in National and International Law: The Role of the Imminence Requirement' (2009) 19 Indiana International and Comparative Law Review 1

Bannelier K and Christakis T, 'Under the UN Security Council's Watchful Eyes: Military Intervention by Invitation in the Malian Conflict' (2013) 26 Leiden Journal of International Law 855

Bannelier-Christakis K, 'Military Interventions against ISIL in Iraq, Syria and Libya, and the Legal Basis of Consent' (2016) 29 Leiden Journal of International Law 743

Bellamy AJ and Hunt CT, 'Twenty-First Century UN Peace Operations: Protection, Force and the Changing Security Environment' 91 International Affairs 1277

Bellamy AJ and Williams PD, 'The New Politics of Protection? Côte d'Ivoire, Libya and the Responsibility to Protect' (2011) 87 International Affairs 825

Bilder RB, 'Kosovo and the New Interventionism: Promise or Peril' (1999) 9 Journal of Transnational Law and Policy 153

Boisson de Chazournes L and Condorellui L, 'Common Article 1 of the Geneva Conventions Revisited: Protecting Collective Interests' (2000) 82 International Review of the Red Cross 67

Bothe M, 'The Protection of the Civilian Population and NATO Bombing on Yugoslavia: Comments on a Report to the Prosecutor of the ICTY' (2001) 12 The European Journal of International Law 531

Bourgeois H, '"All Necessary Means" to Protect Civilians: The Interpretation and Implementation of UN Security Council Mandates Authorising the Protection of Civilians' (2020) 24 Journal of International Peacekeeping 53

Bourgeois H and Labuda PI, 'When May UN Peacekeepers Use Lethal Force to Protect Civilians? Reconciling Threats to Civilians, Imminence, and the Right to Life' (2022) Journal of Conflict and Security Law 1

Bourgeois H and Perrin J-E, 'The Use of Force for Mission Accomplishment: A Pitfall in Contemporary Operations?' (2018) 57 Military Law and Law of War Review 59

Bowett DW, 'The Impact of Security Council Decisions on Dispute Settlement Procedures' (1994) 5 The European Journal of International Law 89

Bring O, 'International Humanitarian Law after Kosovo: Is Lex Lata Sufficient' (2002) 71 Nordic Journal of International Law 39

Bugnion F, 'Guerre Juste, Guerre d'agression et Droit International Humanitaire' (2002) 84 Revue internationale de la Croix-Rouge 523

Byrne M, 'Consent and the Use of Force: An Examination of "Intervention by Invitation" as a Basis for US Drone Strikes in Pakistan, Somalia and Yemen' (2016) 3 Journal on the Use of Force and International Law 97

Christakis T and Mollard-Bannelier K, 'Volenti Non Fit Injuria? Les Effets du Consentement à l'Intervention Militaire' (2004) 50 Annuaire français de droit international 102

Collinge D, 'The Missing Link' (2019) 23 Journal of International Peacekeeping 82

Cooper CG, 'Rules of Engagement Demystified: A Study of the History, Development and Use of ROEs' (2014) 53 Military Law and Law of War Review 189
Corten O and Koutroulis V, 'The Illegality of Military Support to Rebels in the Libyan War: Aspects of Jus Contra Bellum and Jus in Bello' (2013) 18 Journal of Conflict and Security Law 59
Couzigou I, 'The United Nations Security Council Sanctions and International Human Rights' (2016) 10 Vienna Journal on International Constitutional Law 277
Cox KE, 'Beyond Self-Defense: United Nations Peacekeeping Operations & the Use of Force' (1998) 27 Denver Journal of International Law and Policy 239
David E and Engdahl O, 'Debate: How Does the Involvement of a Multinational Peacekeeping Force Affect the Classification of a Situation?' (2013) 95 International Review of the Red Cross 659
de Serpa Soares M, '75 Years of International Law-Making at the United Nations' (2020) 23 Max Planck Yearbook of United Nations Law 1
Dembinski M and Schott B, 'Converging Around Global Norms? Protection of Civilians in African Union and European Union Peacekeeping in Africa' (2013) 6 African Security 276
Diehl PF, Druckman D and Wall J, 'International Peacekeeping and Conflict Resolution: A Taxonomic Analysis with Implications' (1998) 42 The Journal of Conflict Resolution 33
Doswald-Beck L, 'The Right to Life in Armed Conflict: Does International Humanitarian Law Provide All the Answers?' (2006) 88 International Review of the Red Cross 881
Droege C, 'The Interplay between International Humanitarian Law and International Human Rights Law in Situations of Armed Conflict Special Issue: Parallel Applicability of International Humanitarian Law and International Human Rights Law' (2007) 40 Israel Law Review 310
Dugard J, 'The Legal Effect of United Nations Resolutions on Apartheid' (1966) 83 South African Law Journal 44
Fassbender B, 'The United Nations Charter As Constitution of the International Community' (1998) 36 Columbia Journal of Transnational Law 529
Ferraro T, 'Determining the Beginning and End of an Occupation under International Humanitarian Law' (2012) 94 International Review of the Red Cross 133
—, 'The Applicability and Application of International Humanitarian Law to Multinational Forces' (2013) 95 International Review of the Red Cross 561
—, 'The ICRC's Legal Position on the Notion of Armed Conflict Involving Foreign Intervention and on Determining the IHL Applicable to This Type of Conflict' (2015) 97 International Review of the Red Cross 1227
Fleck D, 'The Legal Status of Personnel Involved in United Nations Peace Operations' (2013) 95 International Review of the Red Cross 613
Foley C, 'The Human Rights Obligations of UN Peacekeepers' (2017) 22 Revista Relações Internacionais no Mundo Atual 1
Freudenschuss H, 'Between Unilateralism and Collective Security: Authorizations of the Use of Force by the UN Security Council' (1994) 5 The European Journal of International Law 492

Gaggioli G, 'Review Essay: Human Rights and Personal Self-Defense in International Law by Jan Arno Hessbruegge' (2017) 18 Melbourne Journal of International Law 460

Gardam JG, 'Legal Restraints on Security Council Military Enforcement Action' (1996) 17 Michigan Journal of International Law 285

Gaudreau J, 'The Reservations to the Protocols Additional to the Geneva Conventions for the Protection of War Victims' (2003) 849 International Review of the Red Cross 143

Gill TD, 'Legal and Some Political Limitations on the Power of the UN Security Council to Exercise Its Enforcement Powers under Chapter VII of the Charter' (1995) 26 Netherlands Yearbook of International Law 33

—, 'Some Thoughts on the ICRC Support Based Approach' Zoom-in 59 Question of International Law 45

Gill TD, Léveillée JAM and Fleck D, 'The Rule of Law in Peace Operations, XVIIth Congress of the International Society for Military Law and the Law of War, Scheveningen, 16–19 May 2006' (2006) 17 Recueils de la Société Internationale de Droit Penal Militaire et de Droit de la Guerre 49

Glick RD, 'Lip Service to the Laws of War: Humanitarian Law and United Nations Armed Forces' (1995) 17 Michigan Journal of International Law 53

Gourgourinis A, 'General/Particular International Law and Primary/Secondary Rules: Unitary Terminology of a Fragmented System' (2011) 22 European Journal of International Law 993

Gowlland-Debbas V, 'The Limits of Unilateral Enforcement of Community Objectives in the Framework of UN Peace Maintenance' (2000) 11 The European Journal of International Law 361

Gray CD, 'Host-State Consent and United Nations Peacekeeping in Yugoslavia' (1996) 7 Duke Journal of Comparative and International Law 241

Green JA, 'Questioning the Peremptory Status of the Prohibition of the Use of Force' (2011) 32 Michigan Journal of International Law 215

Green JA and Waters CPM, 'Military Targeting in the Context of Self-Defence Actions' (2015) 84 Nordic Journal of International Law 3

Greenwood C, 'New World Order or Old? The Invasion of Kuwait and the Rule of Law' (1992) 55 The Modern Law Review 153

Hajjami N, 'Que Signifie l'expression "Prendre Toutes Les Mesures Nécessaires" Dans La Pratique Du Conseil de Sécurité Des Nations Unies?' (2013) 1 Revue Belge de Droit International 232

Hampson FJ, 'The Relationship between International Humanitarian Law and Human Rights Law from the Perspective of a Human Rights Treaty Body' (2008) 90 International Review of the Red Cross 549

Hathaway OA and others, 'Ensuring Responsibility: Common Article 1 and State Responsibility for Non-State Actors' (2017) 95 Texas Law Review 539

Helmersen ST, 'The Prohibition of the Use of Force as Jus Cogens: Explaining Apparent Derogations' (2014) 61 Netherlands International Law Review 167

Henderson C, 'International Measures for the Protection of Civilians in Libya and Cote d'Ivoire Current Developments: Public International Law' (2011) 60 International and Comparative Law Quarterly 767

Herdegen MJ, 'The Constitutionalization of the UN Security System' (1994) 27 Vanderbilt Journal of Transnational Law 135

Hill-Cawthorne L, 'The Role of Necessity in International Humanitarian and Human Rights Law' (2014) 47 Israel Law Review 225

Hoffman MH, 'Peace-Enforcement Actions and Humanitarian Law: Emerging Rules for "Interventional Armed Conflict"' (2000) 82 International Review of the Red Cross 193

Howe B, Kondoch B and Spijkers O, 'Normative and Legal Challenges to UN Peacekeeping Operations' (2015) 19 Journal of International Peacekeeping 1

Hunt CT, 'All Necessary Means to What Ends? The Unintended Consequences of the "Robust Turn" in UN Peace Operations' (2017) 24 International Peacekeeping 108

Hunt CT and Zimmerman S, 'Twenty Years of the Protection of Civilians in UN Peace Operations' (2020) Journal of International Peacekeeping 1

Kalshoven F, 'The Undertaking to Respect and Ensure Respect in All Circumstances: From Tiny Seed to Ripening Fruit' (1999) 2 Yearbook of International Humanitarian Law 3

Kenkel KM, 'Five Generations of Peace Operations: From the "Thin Blue Line" to "Painting a Country Blue"' (2013) 56 Revista Brasileira de Política Internacional 122

Kioko B, 'The Right of Intervention under the African Union's Constitutive Act: From Non-Interference to Non-Intervention' (2003) 85 International Review of the Red Cross 807

Kirgis FL, 'Security Council Resolution on Multinational Interim Force in Haiti' (2004) 8 American Society of International Law Insights, www.asil.org/insights/volume/8/issue/4/security-council-resolution-multinational-interim-force-haiti, accessed 26 February 2019

Klein E, 'Establishing a Hierarchy of Human Rights: Ideal Solution or Fallacy' (2008) 41 Israel Law Review 477

Kolb R, 'The Relationship between International Humanitarian Law and Human Rights Law: A Brief History of the 1948 Universal Declaration of Human Rights and the 1949 Geneva Conventions' (1998) 38 International Review of the Red Cross 409

—, 'Does Article 103 of the Charter of the United Nations Apply Only to Decisions or Also to Authorizations Adopted by the Security Council' (2004) 64 Zeitschrift für ausländisches öffentliches Recht und Völkerrecht 21

Kondoch B, 'The United Nations Administration of East Timor' (2001) 6 Journal of Conflict and Security Law 245

Koutroulis V, 'And Yet It Exists: In Defence of the "Equality of Belligerents" Principle' (2013) 26 Leiden Journal of International Law 449

Kriendler J, 'NATO Crisis Management: Cooperation with PfP Partners and Other International Organizations' (2004) 3 Connections 59

Kritsiotis D, 'The Tremors of Tadić' (2010) 43 Israel Law Review 262

Labuda PI, 'UN Peacekeeping as Intervention by Invitation: Host State Consent and the Use of Force in Security Council-Mandated Stabilisation Operations' (2020) 7 Journal on the Use of Force and International Law 317

—, 'UN Peacekeeping as Intervention by Invitation: Host State Consent and the Use of Force in Security Council-Mandated Stabilisation Operations' (2020) 7 Journal on the Use of Force and International Law 317

Lamaire M and others, 'Report of the Second Silent Leges Inter Arma International Conference Held in Bruges from 19 to 21 September 2018' (2018) 57 Military Law and Law of War Review 189
Lauwaars RH, 'The Interrelationship between United Nations Law and the Law of Other International Organizations International Law' (1984) 82 Michigan Law Review 1604
Lehmann JM, 'All Necessary Means to Protect Civilians: What the Intervention in Libya Says about the Relationship between the Jus in Bello and the Jus Ad Bellum' (2012) 17 Journal of Conflict and Security Law 117
Levin A, 'Peacekeeper Fatalities and Force Commitments to UN Operations' (2021) 38 Conflict Management and Peace Science 292
Levine DH, 'Peacekeeper Impartiality: Standards, Processes, and Operations' (2011) 15 Journal of International Peacekeeping 422
Lieblich E, 'Intervention and Consent: Consensual Forcible Interventions in Internal Armed Conflicts as International Agreements' (2011) 29 Boston University International Law Journal 337
Liivoja R, 'The Scope of the Supremacy Clause of the United Nations Charter' (2008) 57 International and Comparative Law Quarterly 583
Liivoja R and Chircop L, 'Are Enhanced Warfighters Weapons, Means, or Methods of Warfare?' 94 International Law Studies Series 161
Linderfalk U, 'State Responsibility and the Primary-Secondary Rules Terminology – The Role of Language for an Understanding of the International Legal System' (2009) 78 Nordic Journal of International Law 53
Lubell N, 'Human Rights Obligations in Military Occupation' (2012) 94 International Review of the Red Cross 317
Mathias S, 'UN Peacekeeping Today: Legal Challenges and Uncertainties' (2017) 18 Melbourne Journal of International Law 138
McLaughlin R, 'The Legal Regime Applicable to Use of Lethal Force When Operating under a United Nations Security Council Chapter VII Mandate Authorising All Necessary Means' (2007) 12 Journal of Conflict and Security Law 389
Mégret F and Hoffmann F, 'The UN as a Human Rights Violator? Some Reflections on the United Nations Changing Human Rights Responsibilities' (2003) 25 Human Rights Quarterly 314
Menon A, 'Power, Institutions and the CSDP: The Promise of Institutionalist Theory' (2011) 49 Journal of Common Market Studies 83
Meyrowitz H, 'The Principle of Superfluous Injury or Unnecessary Suffering: From the Declaration of St. Petersburg of 1868 to Additional Protocol 1 of 1977' (1994) 299 International Review of the Red Cross 98
Milanović M, 'Norm Conflict in International Law: Whither Human Rights?' (2009) 20 Duke Journal of Comparative and International Law 69
Murphy R, 'UN Peacekeeping in the Democratic Republic of the Congo and the Protection of Civilians' (2016) 21 Journal of Conflict and Security Law 209
Naert F, 'Observance of International Humanitarian Law by Forces under the Command of the European Union' (2013) 95 ICRC 637
Nascimento DS, 'The Inclusion of Human Rights in Humanitarian Assistance: The Difficult but Necessary Way between Theory and Practice' (2004) 1 Yearbook on Humanitarian Action and Human Rights 41

Okimoto K, 'Protection of Civilians in International Humanitarian Law and by the Use of Force under Chapter VII of the Charter of the United Nations' (2008) 4 Asia-Pacific Yearbook of International Humanitarian Law 1

Olson PM, 'A NATO Perspective on Applicability and Application of IHL to Multinational Forces' (2013) 95 International Review of the Red Cross 653

Orakhelashvili A, 'The Legal Basis of the United Nations Peace-Keeping Operations' (2002) 43 Virginia Journal of International Law 485

—, 'Overlap and Convergence: The Interaction between Jus Ad Bellum and Jus in Bello' (2007) 12 Journal of Conflict and Security Law 157

—, 'The Impact of Peremptory Norms on the Interpretation and Application of United Nations Security Council Resolutions' (2015) 16 The European Journal of International Law 59

Pacholska M, '(Il)Legality of Killing Peacekeepers: The Crime of Attacking Peacekeepers in the Jurisprudence of International Criminal Tribunals' (2015) 13 Journal of International Criminal Justice 43

Paddeu FI, 'Military Assistance on Request and General Reasons against Force: Consent as a Defence to the Prohibition of Force' (2020) 7 Journal on the Use of Force and International Law 227

Papastavridis E, 'Interpretation of Security Council Resolutions under Chapter VII in the Aftermath of the Iraqi Crisis' (2007) 56 The International and Comparative Law Quarterly 83

Parker K, 'Jus Cogens: Compelling the Law of Human Rights' (1989) 12 Hastings International and Comparative Law Review 411

Paust J, 'The Right to Life in Human Rights Law and the Law of War' (2014) 65 Saskatchewan Law Review 411

Pejic J, 'The Protective Scope of Common Article 3: More than Meets the Eye' (2011) 93 International Review of the Red Cross 189

Roberts A, 'The Equal Application of the Laws of War: A Principle under Pressure' (2008) 90 International Review of the Red Cross 931

Ronzitti N, 'The Expanding Law of Self-Defence' (2006) 11 Journal of Conflict and Security Law 343

Ronzitti N, 'NATO's Intervention in Libya: A Genuine Action to Protect a Civilian Population in Mortal Danger or an Intervention Aimed at Regime Change' (2011) 21 The Italian Yearbook of International Law 3

Roth BR, 'Governmental Illegitimacy Revisited: "Pro-Democratic" Armed Intervention in the Post-Bipolar World' (1993) 3 Transnational Law and Contemporary Problems 481

Roxstrom E, Gibney M and Einarsen T, 'The NATO Bombing Case (Bankovic et al v. Belgium et al.) and the Limits of Western Human Rights Protection' (2005) 23 Boston University International Law Journal 55

Ryngaert C, 'Clarifying the Extraterritorial Application of the European Convention on Human Rights' (2012) 28 Utrecht Journal of International and European Law 57

Rynning S, 'Rethinking NATO Policy on the Protection of Civilians' (2017) 47 The US Army War College Quarterly: Parameters 39

Sari A, 'Jurisdiction and International Responsibility in Peace Support Operations: The Behrami and Saramati Cases' (2008) 8 Human Rights Law Review 151

—, 'Status of Forces and Status of Mission Agreements under the ESDP: The EU's Evolving Practice' (2008) 19 European Journal of International Law 67
—, 'The Al-Jedda Case Before the House of Lords' (2009) 13 Journal of International Peacekeeping 181
—, 'UN Peacekeeping Operations and Article 7 ARIO: The Missing Link' (2012) 9 International Organizations Law Review 77
Schabas WA, 'Lex Specialis – Belt and Suspenders – The Parallel Operation of Human Rights Law and the Law of Armed Conflict, and the Conundrum of Jus Ad Bellum Special Issue: Parallel Applicability of International Humanitarian Law and International Human Rights Law' (2007) 40 Israel Law Review 592
Schmitt MN, 'Military Necessity and Humanity in International Humanitarian Law: Preserving the Delicate Balance Commemorative Pieces' (2009) 50 Virginia Journal of International Law 795
—, 'Charting the Legal Geography of Non- International Armed Conflict' (2014) 90 International Law Studies 1
Schmitt MN and Watts S, 'Common Article 1 and the Duty to "Ensure Respect"' (2020) 96 International Law Studies 673
Segal DR, 'Five Phases of United Nations Peacekeeping: An Evolutionary Typology' (1995) 23 Journal of Political and Military Sociology 65
Sheeran S, 'A Constitutional Moment: United Nations Peacekeeping in the Democratic Republic of Congo' (2011) 8 International Organizations Law Review 55
Shesterinina A and Job BL, 'Particularized Protection: UNSC Mandates and the Protection of Civilians in Armed Conflict' (2016) 23 International Peacekeeping 240
Shraga D, 'The Secretary-General's Bulletin on the Observance by United Nations Forces of International Humanitarian Law: A Decade Later' (2009) 39 Israel Yearbook on Human Rights 357
Sicilianos L-A, 'The European Court of Human Rights Facing the Security Council: Towards Systemic Harmonization' (2017) 66 International and Comparative Law Quarterly 783
Simma B, 'NATO, the UN and the Use of Force: Legal Aspects' (1999) 10 European Journal of International Law 1
Sloan J, 'UN Peacekeeping under Kofi Annan: Recourse to Force' (2008) 12 Journal of International Peacekeeping 51
Sloane RD, 'The Cost of Conflation: Preserving the Dualism of Jus Ad Bellum and Jus in Bello in the Contemporary Law of War' (2009) 34 Yale Journal of International Law 47
Somer J, 'Jungle Justice: Passing Sentence on the Equality of Belligerents in Non-International Armed Conflict' (2007) 89 International Review of the Red Cross 655
Toublanc A, 'L'article 103 et La Valeur Juridique de La Charte Des Nations Unies' (2004) 108 Revue générale de droit international public 439
Tsagourias N, 'Consent, Neutrality/Impartiality and the Use of Force in Peacekeeping: Their Constitutional Dimension' (2006) 11 Journal of Conflict and Security Law 465
Uhlmann EMK, 'State Community Interests, Jus Cogens and Protection of the Global Environment: Developing Criteria for Peremptory Norms' (1998) 11 Georgetown International Environmental Law Review 101

Ulfstein G and Christiansen HF, 'The Legality of the NATO Bombing in Libya' (2013) 62 International and Comparative Law Quarterly 159

van Steenberghe R, 'Proportionality under Jus Ad Bellum and Jus in Bello: Clarifying Their Relationship' (2012) 45 Israel Law Review 107

van Steenberghe R and Lesaffre P, 'The ICRC's "Support-Based Approach": A Suitable but Incomplete Theory. In: Question of International Law' (2019) Zoom-in 59 Question of International Law 5

Visser L, 'May the Force Be with You: The Legal Classification of Intervention by Invitation' (2019) 66 Netherlands International Law Review 21

Vité S, 'Typology of Armed Conflicts in International Humanitarian Law: Legal Concepts and Actual Situations' (2009) 91 International Review of the Red Cross 69

Watson GR, 'Constitutionalism, Judicial Review, and the World Court' (1993) 34 Harvard International Law Journal 1

White ND, 'In Search of Due Diligence Obligations in UN Peacekeeping Operations' 23 Journal of International Peacekeeping 203

Willmot H and Sheeran S, 'The Protection of Civilians Mandate in UN Peacekeeping Operations: Reconciling Protection Concepts and Practices' (2013) 95 International Review of the Red Cross 517

—, 'The Protection of Civilians Mandate in UN Peacekeeping Operations: Reconciling Protection Concepts and Practices' (2013) 95 International Review of the Red Cross 517

Wills S, 'Use of Deadly Force by Peacekeepers Operating Outside of Armed Conflict Situations: What Laws Apply?' (2018) 40 Human Rights Quarterly 663

Wippman D, 'Military Intervention, Regional Organizations, and Host-State Consent' (1996) 7 Duke Journal of Comparative and International Law 209

Wood MC, 'The Interpretation of Security Council Resolutions' (1998) 2 Max Planck Yearbook of United Nations Law 73

—, 'The Interpretation of Security Council Resolutions, Revisited' (2017) 20 Max Planck Yearbook of United Nations Law 3

Wright Q, 'The Outlawry of War and the Law of War' (1953) 47 The American Journal of International Law 365

Zwanenburg M, 'International Humanitarian Law Interoperability in Multinational Operations' (2013) 95 International Review of the Red Cross 681

—, 'The "External Element" of the Obligation to Ensure Respect for the Geneva Conventions: A Matter of Treaty Interpretation' (2021) 97 International Law Studies 621

6.8. MEDIA ARTICLES

Buncombe A, 'Civilians Caught in Crossfire during Port-Au-Prince Raids' *The Independent* (2 February 2007), www.independent.co.uk/news/world/americas/civilians-caught-in-crossfire-during-portauprince-raids-434723.html, accessed 20 April 2022

Walker S, 'Kazakhstan President Says He Gave Order to "Open Fire with Lethal Force"' *The Guardian* (7 January 2022), www.theguardian.com/world/2022/jan/07/kazakhstan-protests-thousands-detained-as-president-says-order-mostly-restored, accessed 4 April 2022

X, 'Le Regain de Violences à Bangui Fait Au Moins 18 Morts, Dont Un Casque Bleu' *Le Monde Afrique* (11 April 2018), www.lemonde.fr/afrique/article/2018/04/11/regain-de-violences-a-bangui-ou-un-casque-bleu-a-ete-tue_5283837_3212.html, accessed 20 April 2022

X, 'Libya: Nato Defends Operation during Russia Talks' *BBC News* (4 July 2011), www.bbc.com/news/world-europe-14010305, accessed 26 February 2019

X, 'President Congratulates Portuguese Commandos in Bambari' (*The Portugal News*, 9 March 2017), www.theportugalnews.com/news/president-congratulates-portuguese-commandos-in-bambari/41303, accessed 13 June 2022

6.9. PAPERS

Maj. Lutz JA, 'Operation Unified Protector: Air Campaign' (Canadian Forces College 2015) JCSP 42 – PCEMI 42

Metcalfe V, 'Protecting Civilians? The Interaction between International Military and Humanitarian Actors' (Humanitarian Policy Group 2012) HPG Working Paper

Paust J, 'The UN Is Bound by Human Rights: Understanding the Full Reach of Human Rights, Remedies, and Nonimmunity' (Social Science Research Network 2010) SSRN Scholarly Paper ID 1710744, https://papers.ssrn.com/abstract=1710744, accessed 5 December 2017

United Nations Peacekeeping Law Reform Project, School of Law, University of Essex, 'UN Peacekeeping and The Model Status of Forces Agreement: Background Paper Prepared for the Experts' Workshop Hosted by the New Zealand High Commission in London, 26 August 2010' (2010)

Sassòli M, 'Legitimate Targets of Attacks under International Humanitarian Law', Background Paper prepared for the Informal High-Level Expert Meeting on the Reaffirmation and Development of International Humanitarian Law, 27–29 January 2003, Cambridge (Program on Humanitarian Policy and Conflict Research at Harvard University)

6.10. PRESENTATIONS

Bourgeois H, 'The Relationship between the International Law on the Use of Force and International Humanitarian Law in the Context of Protection of Civilians Mandates' (Specialist Course International Order and Justice, Seminar with Professor Georg Nolte, Ghent University, Ghent, Belgium, 19 March 2018)

—, 'The Relationship between the International Law on the Use of Force and International Humanitarian Law in the Context of Protection of Civilians Mandates' (7th PhD Day, International Humanitarian and Criminal Law Platform, TMC Asser Instituut, The Hague, the Netherlands, 25 May 2018)

6.11. PROCEEDINGS

Arimatsu L, 'Beginning of IHL Application: Overview and Challenges', *Proceedings of the 13th Bruges Colloquium on Scope of Application of International Humanitarian Law, 18–19 October 2012, Bruges, vol. 43, 71* (2013)

Bartolini G, 'Air Targeting in Operation Unified Protector in Libya. Jus Ad Bellum and IHL Issues: An External Perspective' in Stanislas Horvat and Marco Benatar (eds), *Proceedings of the 19th Congress of the International Society for Military Law and the Law of War on Legal Interoperability and Ensuring Observance of the Law Applicable in Multinational Deployments, 1–4 May 2012, Quebec, 231* (2013)

Bivens W and others, 'Report of the Committee on the Study of the Legal Problems of the United Nations: Should the Laws of War Apply to United Nations Enforcement Action?', *Proceedings of the American Society of International Law at Its Annual Meeting (1921–1969), 24–26 April 1952, Washington, DC, vol. 46, 216* (Cambridge University Press)

Bothe M, 'The Responsibility to Protect and International Humanitarian Law' in Gian Luca Beruto (ed), *Proceedings of the 31st Roundtable on Current Problems of International Humanitarian Law: International Humanitarian Law Human Rights and Peace Operations, Hosted by the International Institute of Humanitarian Law, 4–6 September 2008, San Remo, 224* (2008)

Bouvier A, 'Assessing the Relationship Between Jus in Bello and Jus Ad Bellum: An "Orthodox" View', *Proceedings of the American Society of International Law, 29 March–1 April 2006, Washington DC, vol. 100, 109* (2006)

Ferraro T, 'The Geographical Reach of IHL: The Law and Current Challenges', *Proceedings of the 13th Bruges Colloquium on Scope of Application of International Humanitarian Law, 18–19 October 2012, Bruges, vol. 43, 105* (2013)

Gill TD and others, 'General Report for the 19th Congress of the International Society for Military Law and the Law of War' in Stanislas Horvat and Marco Benatar (eds), *Proceedings of the 19th Congress of the International Society for Military Law and the Law of War on Legal Interoperability and Ensuring Observance of the Law Applicable in Multinational Deployments, 1–4 May 2012, Quebec, 231* (2013)

Khalil MA, 'Peace Forces at War: Implications Under International Humanitarian Law, Remarks by Mona Khalil', *Proceedings of the American Society of International Law at Its Annual Meeting, 7–12 April 2014, Washington, DC, vol. 108, 152* (Cambridge University Press 2014)

—, 'Voices from the Field: Challenges Confronting UN Field Legal Advisers, Introductory Remarks by Mona Ali Khalil', *Proceedings of the Annual Meeting of the American Society of International Law, 8–11 April 2015, Washington, DC, vol. 109, 97* (Cambridge University Press 2015)

—, 'Robust Peacekeeping - Not Aggressive Peacekeeping', *Proceedings of the Annual Meeting of the American Society of International Law, 4–7 April 2018, Washington, DC, vol. 112, 114* (Cambridge University Press 2018)

Kjelgaard L, 'The Importance of Law in the Theatre' in Edoardo Greppi (ed), *Proceedings of the 37th Round Table on Current Issues of International Humanitarian Law: Conduct of Hostilities: the Practice, the Law and the Future, Hosted by the International Institute of Humanitarian Law, 4–6 September 2014, San Remo* (2015)

Koutroulis V, 'International Organisations Involved in Armed Conflict: The Material and Geographical Scope of Application of IHL', *Proceedings of the 12th Bruges Colloquium on International Organisations' Involvement in Peace Operations: Applicable Legal Framework and the Issue of Responsibility, 20–21 October 2011, Bruges, vol. 42, 29* (2012)

Kolb R, 'La Nécessité Militaire Dans Le Droit Des Conflits Armés: Essai de Clarification Conceptuelle', *Proceedings of the 40th Colloquium of the Société Française pour le Droit International on La nécessité en Droit International, 8–10 June 2006, Grenoble* (Pendone 2007)

Milanović M, 'End of IHL Application', *Proceedings of the 13th Bruges Colloquium on Scope of Application of International Humanitarian Law, 18–19 October 2012, Bruges, vol. 43, 83* (2013)

Zwanenburg M, 'International Organisations vs. Troop Contributing Countries: Which Should Be Considered as the Party to an Armed Conflict during Peace Operations?', *Proceedings of the 12th Bruges Colloquium on International Organisations' Involvement in Peace Operations: Applicable Legal Framework and the Issue of Responsibility, 20–21 October 2011, Bruges, vol. 42, 23* (2012)

—, 'Peace Forces at War: Implications Under International Humanitarian Law, Remarks by Marten Zwanenburg', *Proceedings of the American Society of International Law at Its Annual Meeting, 7–12 April 2014, Washington, DC, vol. 108, 151* (Cambridge University Press 2014)

6.12. REPORTS

Amnesty International, 'Use of Force: Guidelines for Implementation of the UN Basic Principles on the Use of Force and Firearms by Law Enforcement Officials' (Amnesty International 2015)

Briggs C, 'Non-Refoulement in the Context of Internal Displacement: The Case of IDPs in South Sudan's Protection of Civilians Sites' (Norwegian Refugee Council 2017)

Center for Civilians in Conflict, 'Civilian Harm Tracking: Analysis of ISAF Efforts in Afghanistan' (Center for Civilians in Conflict 2014)

de Langlois MGM and Capstack A, 'The Role of the Military in the EU's External Action' (Institut de Recherche Stratégique de l'École Militaire 2014) Laboratoire de l'IRSEM No. 23

Gaggioli G, 'The Use of Force in Armed Conflict: Interplay between the Conduct of Hostilities and Law Enforcement Paradigms, ICRC Outcome Report' (ICRC 2013)

Haider H, 'International Legal Frameworks for Humanitarian Action: Topic Guide' (Governance and Social Development Resource Centre, University of Birmingham 2013)

Human Rights Watch, 'Killings in Kiwanja: The UN's Inability to Protect Civilians' (Human Rights Watch 2008)

ICISS, 'The Responsibility to Protect' (International Development Research Centre 2001)

ICRC, 'Report on the Work of the Conference of Government Experts on the Reaffirmation and Development of International Humanitarian Law Applicable in Armed Conflicts, 24 May–12 June 1971, Geneva' (ICRC 1971) ICRC Doc. 345.21/28

—, 'Strengthening Protection in War: A Search for Professional Standards' (ICRC 2001)
—, 'How Is the Term "Armed Conflict" Defined in International Humanitarian Law?' (ICRC 2008) Opinion Paper
—, 'Report on International Humanitarian Law and the Challenges of Contemporary Armed Conflicts, Report for the 32nd International Conference of the Red Cross and Red Crescent, 8–10 December 2015, Geneva' (2015) ICRC Doc. 32IC/15/11
—, 'Report on International Humanitarian Law and the Challenges of Contemporary Armed Conflicts, Recommitting to Protection in Armed Conflicts on the 70th Anniversary of the Geneva Conventions' (2019) ICRC Doc. 4427
International Law Association, 'Committee on Formation of Customary (General) International Law, Final Report, Statement of Principles Applicable to the Formation of General Customary International Law' (International Law Association 2000) London Conference
—, 'Final Report on the Meaning of Armed Conflict in International Law' (2010) The Hague Conference
—, 'Report of the Committee on the Use of Force' (International Law Association 2018) Sydney Conference
International Refugee Rights Initiative, 'From Non-Interference to Non Indifference: The African Union and the Responsibility to Protect' (International Refugee Rights Initiative 2017)
Koops JA and Patz C, 'UN, EU, and NATO Approaches to the Protection of Civilians: Policies, Implementation, and Comparative Advantages' (International Peace Institute 2022)
Melzer N, 'ICRC Interpretative Guidance on the Notion of Direct Participation in Hostilities under International Humanitarian Law' (ICRC 2009)
Sebastián S and Gorur A, 'UN Peacekeeping & Host-State Consent. How Missions Navigate Relationships with Governments' (Stimson Center 2018)
Sheeran S and Case S, 'The Intervention Brigade: Legal Issues for the UN in the Democratic Republic of the Congo' (International Peace Institute 2014)
University Centre for International Humanitarian Law Geneva, 'Targeting Military Objectives, Report of an Expert Meeting Organized by the University Centre for International Humanitarian Law Geneva and Convened at the Centre de Conférences de Varembé in Geneva, Switzerland, 12 May 2005' (2005)

6.13. OTHER

Center for Civilians in Conflict, 'NATO's Time Drawing to a Close, But Protection Work Unfinished' (2011), https://civiliansinconflict.org/press-releases/natos-time-drawing-close-protection-work-unfinished/, accessed 14 April 2022
Institut de Droit International, 'Résolution sur le Principe de Non-Intervention dans les Guerres Civiles' (1975) Wiesbaden Session, 8th Commission, Sub-Group D
—, 'Résolution sur l'Autorisation du Recours à la Force par les Nations Unies' (2011) Rhodes Session, 10th Commission, Sub-Group D

ICRC, 'Practice Relating to Rule 1. The Principle of Distinction between Civilians and Combatants' (*IHL Database*, [date unknown]), https://ihl-databases.icrc.org/customary-ihl/eng/docs/v1_rul_rule1, accessed 22 August 2022

—, 'Treaties, States Parties and Commentaries: Protocol Additional to the Geneva Conventions of 12 August 1949, and Relating to the Protection of Victims of International Armed Conflicts (Protocol I), 8 June 1977' (*ICRC*), https://ihl-databases.icrc.org/applic/ihl/ihl.nsf/States.xsp?xp_viewStates=XPages_NORMStatesParties&xp_treatySelected=470#divArticle90, accessed 24 August 2022

Geneva Academy Rule of Law, 'Non-International Armed Conflicts in Democratic Republic of Congo' (*Geneva Academy Rule of Law*, 22 April 2021), www.rulac.org/browse/conflicts/non-international-armed-conflict-in-democratic-republic-of-congo#collapse4accord, accessed 20 April 2022

Security Council Report, 'In Hindsight: The Informal Expert Group on the Protection of Civilians' (*Security Council Report*, August 2016), www.securitycouncilreport.org/monthly-forecast/2016-08/in_hindsight_the_informal_expert_group_on_the_protection_of_civilians.php, accessed 11 February 2021

—, 'Cross-Cutting Report 2008 No. 2: Protection of Civilians' (2008), www.securitycouncilreport.org/research-reports/lookup_c_glkwlemtisg_b_7566867.php, accessed 25 February 2019

White ND, 'Security Council Mandates and the Use of Lethal Force by Peacekeepers', Summary of a lecture given to the Australian Centre for Military & Security Law, Australian National University, 2 February 2013, http://eprints.nottingham.ac.uk/1956/1/White_for_ANU%5B2%5D.pdf, accessed 24 August 2018

www.ingramcontent.com/pod-product-compliance
Ingram Content Group UK Ltd.
Pitfield, Milton Keynes, MK11 3LW, UK
UKHW051933150926
8656IPUK00005B/34